RUDOLF STEINER ~ A BIOGRAPHY

Rudolf Steiner

RUDOLF STEINER

≈

a biography

Christoph Lindenberg

SteinerBooks | 2012

2012
SteinerBooks
An imprint of Anthroposophic Press, Inc.
610 Main Street, Great Barrington, MA 01230

Copyright © 2012 by SteinerBooks. This volume is a translation of *Rudolf Steiner—eine Biographie*, 2 vols., Verlag Freies Geistesleben, Stuttgart (1997). All rights reserved. No part of this publication may be reproduced, stored in a retrieval system, or transmitted in any form or by any means, electronic, mechanical, photocopying, recording, or otherwise without the prior written permission of the publisher.

Translated from the German text by Jon McAlice

Design by William Jens Jensen.

≈

Library of Congress Cataloging-in-Publication Data

Lindenberg, Christoph.
 [Rudolf Steiner. English]
 Rudolf Steiner : a biography / Christoph Lindenberg ; [translated from the German text by Jon McAlice].
   p. cm.
 Includes bibliographical references (p. 781).
 ISBN 978-1-62148-015-0 (hardcover) — ISBN 978-1-62148-027-3 (ebook)
 1. Steiner, Rudolf, 1861-1925. 2. Anthroposophists—Biography.
 I. Title.
 BP595.S895L55513 2012
 299'.935092—dc23
 [B]
                                                          2012031634

CONTENTS

	Foreword	vii
	Introduction	xi
1.	The Stranger	1
2.	Learning	13
3.	Student in Vienna	22
4.	The Lonely Wanderer	38
5.	Goethe: A Source of Hope	56
6.	In Need of Special Care	66
7.	Theory of Knowledge	75
8.	Social Life in Vienna	84
9.	The Editor: An Excursion into Politics	93
10.	Aesthetics	100
11.	First Journeys	105
12.	Friedrich Eckstein, Theosophy, and Rosa Mayreder	109
13.	Spirit and Nature: The Foundation of a Spiritual Philosophy	116
14.	Weimar: At the Goethe-Schiller Archive	125
15.	Lonely in the Company of Many Friends	132
	Images, Part One	140
16.	The Philosophy of Freedom	150
17.	For and against Nietzsche	175
18.	A New World Opens Up	189
19.	The Maelstrom of Berlin	200
20.	Time of Trial	208
21.	Three Attempts at the Turn of the Century	220
22.	The Way into the Theosophical Society	230
23.	The Theosophical Society	247
24.	Establishing the German Section of the Theosophical Society	263
25.	Attempts to Fructify the Art of Living	285
26.	The Three Paths	295
27.	The Munich Congress: A Conference in a Rosicrucian Temple	305

28.	Breadth and Depth	314
29.	The Illumination of the Christian Mysteries	324
30.	The Mystery Plays	342
31.	Separation from the Theosophical Society	355
32.	Surrounded by Artists: 1907–1918	373
33.	Building	387
	Images, Part Two	408
34.	Wartime in Dornach	422
35.	The Destiny of Central Europe	430
36.	The Idea of the Threefold Human Organism	444
37.	The Threefold Social Movement during the War	465
38.	Preparations for the Postwar Period	478
39.	Struggle for the Threefold Commonwealth	488
40.	The Independent Waldorf School	506
41.	Commercial Ventures	530
42.	The Need to Communicate Impulses for Cultural Renewal	546
43.	A Broader Understanding of Healing	560
44.	Establishing The Christian Community	568
45.	Possibilities—Realities	580
46.	The Goetheanum Fire	602
47.	Stuttgart 1923	609
48.	Spring 1923: The Struggle to Rebuild	623
49.	Summer 1923: England	632
	Images, Part Three	640
50.	Autumn 1923: The Way to Decision	654
51.	The Christmas Conference of 1923	666
52.	Foundations	683
53.	Spring 1924	694
54.	The Final Intensification: Summer 1924	711
55.	Sickbed and Death	737
	Epilogue	761
	The Collected Works of Rudolf Steiner	765
	Bibliography	781

FOREWORD

*"I do not want to be revered!
I want to be understood."*
—Rudolf Steiner, 1915

This biography should contribute to the present understanding of Rudolf Steiner. Anyone who follows the life of Rudolf Steiner will get the impression that, after a certain point, his constant attempt was to awaken, using numerous methods, an active, working understanding for Anthroposophy. Steiner used creative imagination to treat particular themes and tasks, ever anew, and in many forms. If we look at the variations of these presentations, we can see in them the intentions that guided his life. A biography that shows Steiner's intentions and efforts in the context of the times and life circumstances will not only relate what happened, but also why, and thus lead to understanding.

Therefore, it is not merely a matter of relating facts in the course of his life here, but also, and most important, comprehending Steiner's work within the context of his life. His work shall not—as is the case with many modern biographies—disappear behind the life story. The meaning and development of various life motifs will be shown within the work. At the same time, however, I have abstained from any highly elevated esoteric interpretation, which for me would lapse into making ungrounded assertions, as was common within theosophical circles at the beginning of the twentieth century. Indeed, I wished to describe what we can observe in our thinking when we think through Steiner's assertions.

Of course, a biographer must pick and choose from an abundance of material, showing what was characteristic and symptomatic. One must present the symptoms that provide a view of the essential, which cannot be arbitrary. Precisely in the case of Rudolf Steiner, it is easy for biographers to notice what appears important to them. For Steiner, it was never about offering isolated suggestions (for instance in medicine, social life, or pedagogy). Rather, it was always a matter of taking a foundational approach, of taking up the practice out of a comprehensive and heightened knowledge. From this perspective, we can see Steiner's work as the sum of the metamorphoses of intention, expressed in his *Intuitive Thinking as a Spiritual Path: A Philosophy of Freedom**: to understand and to act from knowledge.

It seemed that in our perplexing times, in which every opinion claims equal validity, it is first and foremost necessary to follow the foundational themes as they changed, and to present these themes very clearly, regardless of how complex they may be. With this, however, such a biography can follow only certain lines or threads. I must openly admit that it was not possible for me to take into account in the same way all of the available material—the nearly 400 volumes** in Rudolf Steiner's Collected Works and the documents belonging to them, as well as the many memoirs. It was especially painful for me that an exhaustive description of Rudolf Steiner's efforts in poetry, painting, and architecture was beyond the scope of this biography. I have the impression that only individual monographs dedicated to showing each art in practice would do justice to these themes.

Out of similar considerations, I was unable to include the whole complex of the workers' lectures, the cosmology, the scientific courses on light and warmth, and much more. Yet I think that this biography, into which readers can insert their own particular study and insights in the proper places, will meet some measure of the need for an overview of Rudolf Steiner's life and work.

This biography is the result of spending forty years collecting what has been handed down and scattered in many places while, at the same time, deepening myself ever again in the areas of the theory of knowledge, philosophy, knowledge of the human being, Christology, the view of history, Steiner's social thinking, and many other questions. Each time, where possible, I gave priority to the authentic source—that is, to Rudolf Steiner's written work.

My book *Chronik* (chronicling the significant events in Rudolf Steiner's life) was published in 1988 and, along with published and unpublished

---

* *Philosophie der Freiheit* [Philosophy of Freedom] was the original title. It is now also available as *Intuitive Thinking as a Spiritual Path: A Philosophy of Freedom*, SteinerBooks. In this biography the title will be given as *Intuitive Thinking as a Spiritual Path,* or at times simply as *Intuitive Thinking.*

** This number results from also including the documentations of the Blackboard Drawings, the artistic work, and so on.

studies, arose from the preparatory work for this biography. With the *Chronik*, I tried to present the facts of Rudolf Steiner's life and let them speak to the reader. The intention behind my other works, and above all this biography, is to make visible the spiritual actuality. My way of working (with few exceptions) was to examine very little other biographical presentations on Steiner's life. I do owe thanks to Emil Bock's foundational studies, however. Guenther Wachsmuth's book, *Rudolf Steiner's Life and Work*, in which a great deal of material is collected, seemed to me more of a resource than a biography. On the whole, my presentation finds its orientation almost exclusively from the work of Rudolf Steiner, as well as from existing records. This book was not written out of examinations of other Steiner biographies or interpretations of Steiner.

I strove not to bias the questions that naturally arise out of Steiner's life toward one or the other side, but to make Steiner's thoughts, processes, and manner of behavior understandable. Of course, I brought to expression all the critical points of Steiner's life that I knew of. The love of truth demands this. But with these critical points, I also tried to understand Steiner's thinking and behavior. I abstained from extensive psychological interpretations, but I attempted to show how these critical points can be understood from Steiner's whole life, his bearing, or his character. The way I understand the task of the biographer and the writer of history is not to judge but to understand and to describe spiritually. This does not mean that the writer abstains from every judgment; but where a judgment is expressed, the reader should be able to see that it is the writer's judgment, and not confuse it with the facts.

When I place this biography before the reader, I do not do so lightly. I do not claim any authority from the fact that I occupied myself with Steiner's life for forty years, because one can indeed spend forty years stuck in bias and misunderstandings. I draw the courage to publish this work, not from my studies of the intellectual and historical environs in which Steiner's life took place, but quite simply from the fact Rudolf Steiner always expressed himself clearly and understandably in all the essential points. It is, therefore, necessary only to read exactly and to duplicate inwardly what is being spoken of, in order to conceive of Steiner appropriately. I believe one does Rudolf Steiner a grave injustice by acting as if Steiner cannot ultimately be understood, believing that we must limit ourselves to presentiment and belief.

I wish to apologize to the reader who is dismayed by the size of this book. I have kept it as short as possible and eliminated much from my previous drafts. Beyond this, the chapters are arranged to be clear. For example, the chapter on Steiner's *Philosophy of Freedom* presents the development of the idea of freedom (or spiritual activity) from 1882 on. The chapter on the threefold nature of the human being attempts to outline the history of research into this idea from the beginning onward. In this sense, the orientation of many of the chapters is thematic. The chapters are arranged chronologically only with the beginning of events in 1922.

I have tried not to repeat my earlier presentations. A full biography is subject to different rules than a specialized study is. Therefore, for some specific questions, I allow myself to refer to my earlier works.

Finally, I have the pleasant duty to thank all who have helped me with this work. First, there are those I already named in my *Chronik* and whose work provided the foundation for this biography, as well as those who allowed me to examine documents. Also my gratitude goes to all of the people who gave of their time and effort to reading through the text and offering suggestions, which helped me in many ways. And not forgotten are all of the people with whom I could have conversations and thereby have many questions explained. Above all, however, I thank my friend, Götz Deimann, who constantly encouraged and supported this work.

Christoph Lindenberg
Zarten, February 1997

INTRODUCTION

When Rudolf Steiner began to write his *Autobiography* in December 1923, he turned to memories of the events and experiences that determined or distinguished his path of development. Thus, his presentation was limited mainly to describing the questions that moved him inwardly, the thoughts he formed, and those who inspired him. Nevertheless, he did not focus on the outer obstacles and difficulties that accompanied his inner development. Nor did he complain about the lack of spiritual stimulation from his parents. He barely mentioned the poverty that lasted through his childhood and until he was forty-five years of age. Steiner simply passed over the miserable honorarium for his literary work and did not write at all about the financial crisis connected with the publishing of the *Magazine for Literature*. Readers of his *Autobiography* will not find any description of the outer conflicts, the bitterness, and the dashed hopes with which Steiner had to wrestle. He could easily have made his autobiography into a story of going from poverty to a lack of recognition and then to success, but it was nothing like that.

Nor was it Rudolf Steiner's intention to portray his times in his autobiography—Vienna in the 1880s, life at the Weimar court, or theater life in Berlin at the turn of the century. He could easily have woven in witty anecdotes or a bit of color concerning the cultural history. It would have been quite easy for him to write a humorous chapter about the Theosophical Society. Many comments in his lectures hint that there was a great deal of material about the Theosophical Society for a storyteller, and Steiner could tell stories. All of these things were mentioned only inasmuch as they played a role in Steiner's path of development or distinguished the milieu in which he lived.

In *Autobiography,* Rudolf Steiner says, "I do not wish to relate private matters in this account of my life, except when they are connected in some way with my spiritual development" (28, p. 192).* And a little further on it says even more clearly, "As for the rest, a person's private life does not

---

* Where page number are given, quotations are from a current English edition.

belong to the public. It is of no concern to them" (28, p. 192). His relationships with his mother and siblings apparently fall into this area of private life; he was totally silent concerning them. For all that, the relationship was extremely harmonious. Just as soon as Rudolf Steiner could, he began to support his mother and siblings, and even during the last days of his life, he was concerned about the care of his siblings. Yet nothing is said about them in his autobiography. Steiner remained silent in this way about many other facts and circumstances, or mentioned them only in passing. He also wrote only briefly about his marriage to Anna Eunike and was completely silent about their separation.

The reader of Steiner's *Autobiography* must guess at the difficulties of his collaboration with Otto Erich Hartleben in publishing the *Magazine for Literature*. The yearlong suffering under the pedantic nature of his superior, Bernhard Suphan, at the Goethe Archive was condensed into this sentence: "I cannot deny that I often felt disturbed by what Suphan did—the way he handled the management of the archives and his supervision of the editing of Goethe's works—and I never made any secret of this" (28, p. 107). He was just as brief in mentioning Elisabeth Förster-Nietzsche's intrigues, to which he fell victim. In the end, he said he was grateful to Mrs. Förster-Nietzsche for bringing him into Nietzsche's sickroom—an unforgettable experience for Steiner. In this sense, he always turned his memory to what furthered him in whatever he encountered, even when circumstances brought an obstacle or disadvantage. Thus, a great deal that fills other biographies is missing in Steiner's autobiography.

There is also not much in *Autobiography* about Steiner's inner struggles and experiences. This is connected with the fact that Rudolf Steiner initially published his autobiography in installments in the weekly publication, *Das Goetheanum*. These installments were intended to be excerpts of a future book. In a lecture, Rudolf Steiner commented, "I could relate only the outer aspects of these things in *Das Goetheanum,* and the articles will be published as a book with annotations in which also the inner aspect will be taken into account" (238). How Rudolf Steiner would have described these inner aspects of his development can best be gathered from indications given in the chapters he wrote in 1924/25 from the stillness of his sickbed. On the whole, however, what would fully clarify the inner struggles and problems are often lacking. Steiner's autobiography follows his life up to 1907. One misses two elements: first the intended

Introduction

continuation beyond 1907, and second, the description of specific inner aspects of the life story.

Although Steiner's autobiography is incomplete, and although much of his intended expansion of details are missing, one must acknowledge *Autobiography* as the foundational source for every Steiner biography. Everyone who wishes to study Steiner's life seriously must read his *Autobiography*. It would also be senseless merely to paraphrase what was given there for the content of this book; the reader would be better served by the original. The autobiography covers especially Steiner's development during his childhood and youth, and this is known for the most part only through his descriptions. For this reason, this biography will summarize Steiner's childhood and youth in broad strokes and supplement it only somewhat from other, mostly unknown sources.

Biographers who want to describe Steiner's life are faced with several tasks and difficulties. They do not have to hold back the way Steiner did concerning his struggles, sufferings, and deprivations. They have every reason to portray the life of the subject—as far as the witnesses allow it—the way it was most likely lived, from the perspective of the experiences of that time. Steiner's letters from 1881 to 1925 provide some insight that makes it possible to give a fairly reliable description of his personal experiences. The biographer can also attempt to search for hints of the hidden biography of Steiner in his lectures and in the few existing records, but here one must be very careful and can only formulate questions from much of it. In our time of voyeurism when people would be very interested in Rudolf Steiner's private relationships, what is said about them must be what is important and what can be seen as well-founded, otherwise people could suspect that something is being covered up. But one should not overestimate the significance of Rudolf Steiner's private life that in itself is not very informative.

What is essential in this biography may be found in his development and work. An abundance of evidence exists for all to see, and it must only be *seen*. The task of this biography will be largely to make Rudolf Steiner's path visible on hand of what his contemporaries had to say. The statements of his contemporaries come from letters and early essays, in the first editions of many of his works, and later from lectures and records. These are in many respects quite informative, because they add to Steiner's later self-interpretation. For example, through the eyewitness accounts, Steiner's sudden change when he was thirty-six years old—he merely mentions this in his *Autobiography*—became quite vivid. This seems to me to be legitimate, because Rudolf Steiner's condensed interpretation of his development is explained by the eyewitnesses in such a way that makes it much clearer for the reader. In this biography I quite consciously avoid making any esoteric speculations and dispense with such speculations by other authors. I do this, not because it would not be fascinating, but because respect for Rudolf Steiner on the one hand and for the reader on the other demands that this be left up to the efforts of the reader. Just as soon as esoteric insights are translated into popular concepts and ideas and then fixed in writing, they open a door for innumerable misunderstandings, because others then interpret them all too easily in their own sense and connect them with ideas that are not accurate.

Above all, esoteric connections are so alive and flexible that it is not good to express them once and for all with finality and to formulate them in such a way that they are simply accepted. For this reason, I stick with Goethe who commented in his maxims and reflections, "The esoteric causes harm only when it tries to become exoteric." Rudolf Steiner gave a very helpful commentary concerning this maxim. He said, "A concept is esoteric, when it is considered in connection with the manifestations out of which it was attained. It is exoteric when it is separated out as an abstraction and is considered on its own" (1e). In this sense the ideas and concepts shall remain esoteric; they are not formulated abstractly in themselves. It is my intention with this biography to let the spiritual, soul, and outer facts speak for themselves, *leaving the interpretation of those facts to the reader.*

Finally, I must point out two peculiarities of Rudolf Steiner's *Autobiography*. He did not always present the events in the correct chronological order. He had brought out the first volume of Goethe's Natural Scientific Writings (they were published initially in five volumes) *before* he worked as a teacher and private tutor in the home of Ladislau Specht. In *Autobiography*, however, the description of his work on Goethe comes after the narrative on entering the Specht home. In other places, namely in lectures, Steiner tended to give dates that were too early for events, even dates that could be ascertained exactly.* In this presentation the dates are reported without further comment.

---

* Steiner mentioned twice the day of the founding of the Austrian Social Democratic Party that took place near Neudörfl in 1874 (330 & 354). The second time he mentioned it, he said, "At that time I was eight, ten or eleven years old." But he was already thirteen years old. Concerning his first Kant readings, he said in his autobiographical lecture of February 4, 1913, that at that time he was "between

Introduction

Second, the reader should take into account that from 1916 on Rudolf Steiner was vehemently attacked. Among other things, people uncovered his early writings and essays, compared the first edition of *Intuitive Thinking* with the second edition and decided Steiner had completely changed his mind. In *Autobiography*, as in other connections too, Steiner stressed the inner continuity of his spiritual development. He does this—change and transformation are after all not a disgrace—because in his understanding, the continuity is more important than the change. Therefore, one meets in many paragraphs of the autobiography the defence against certain interpretations of his development. Had these many attacks that spoke of a break with his earlier works or a change of mind not happened, Steiner could have more freely presented the steps of his own development, transformations or trials in *Autobiography*.

The last chapter of Rudolf Steiner's *Autobiography* begins:

> It will be difficult to separate what follows as an account of my life from the history of the anthroposophic movement. Nevertheless, I do not want to bring any more than is necessary of the society's history into this description. (28, p. 237)

Rudolf Steiner was not able to write this last part of his autobiography. However, there are enough of Steiner's own records in existence, in order to be able to write more than just an outer description of his further path. Of course, the biographer has the difficult task, in the first place, of not writing a history of the Anthroposophical Society or of Steiner's work within the anthroposophic movement, but first and foremost, to describe Steiner's life and experience, and where possible, his further development. For this reason, the reader will not find a detailed presentation on the financial initiatives, The Coming Day (*Der Kommende Tag*) or Futurum, Inc., or the history of building the first Goetheanum. One will find only what Rudolf Steiner did or experienced in connection with these, as far as the source can yield the information. One could doubt whether this is even possible, but it must be attempted. We can hope that in the future other

---

fourteen and fifteen years old." The Reclam edition, which Steiner always mentioned using, of Kant's *Critique of Pure Reason* came out in spring 1877. Steiner got it in May 1877, at the earliest. Thus he was sixteen years old. Further, Steiner mentions that his first visit with Nietzche in Naumberg took place on May 26, 1894, at the latest. However, there is a record in Rudolf Steiner's handwriting that shows the first vist was on January 22, 1896.

authors will come along who can bring more comprehensive and unforeseen viewpoints to such a presentation. But a beginning had to be made. That is the purpose of this book.

Certainly, I do not intend to repeat here the many details and dates already contained in my book *Rudolf Steiner—eine Chronik* [Rudolf Steiner: A Chronicle]. When this chronicle is issued again, it will be expanded a great deal to include new information that has come out since its first publication in 1988.

RUDOLF STEINER

a biography

Chapter 1

THE STRANGER

Born a stranger in a strange land, Rudolf Steiner grew up as a stranger both at home and in his surroundings. This experience colored both his childhood and his youth. Homelessness—the core experience of modern humanity—sculpted his destiny. With the exception of the ten years he spent in Neudörfl and the seven spent in Weimar, Rudolf Steiner spent his life traveling. His domiciles (Kraljevec, Mödling, Pottschach, Neudörfl, Oberlaa, Brunn, Vienna, Weimar, Berlin, Stuttgart, and finally, Dornach) were but stops along the way. Never did he own his own house. From 1904, when he began to lecture widely, his wandering intensified. The lecture tours took him first through Germany, then Switzerland, Austria, Scandinavia, England, Italy, Hungary, France, and Holland. In some years, he was on the road more than at home.

This signature of homelessness first became apparent when Rudolf Steiner's parents decided to leave their home in order to marry. The Lower Austrian Waldviertel, the home of Steiner's parents and forefathers, was an idyllic region of gently rolling hills and deep forests, at that time still untouched by industrialization. Life there was still imbued with the gentle, traditional friendliness that can be heard in the local dialects, which differ significantly from the Viennese. His parents' inner connection to this wooded landscape north of the Danube remained strong throughout their lives. When his father finally retired from the railroad after forty years of service, the family returned to the little village of Horn.

Johann Steiner grew up in Geras, close to the border of what is today the Czech Republic. He served in the monastery there and was educated by the monks. Through them, he received a scholarship to attend the local high school. His father's introduction to the idea of higher education had a decisive effect on Rudolf Steiner's life. Because of the impression made on him by his short time at school, Johann Steiner decided that his son should have a complete education. Johann left the high school and went on to become a forester and hunter in the service of an Austrian duke who kept a small estate near the village of Horn. Here Johann Steiner met Franziska Blie. Their friendship blossomed and they decided to marry. This was more easily said than done for, as the story goes, Count Hoyos kept only unmarried men in his service. Johann had to give up his position and find new work. Courageously, he decided to leave behind everything he was accustomed to, and applied for work on the new southern Austrian railroad. The railroad hired him as a telegrapher, and sent the young man of thirty-one to a station in what is now Slovenia, between Maribor and Ljublyana. He began in the summer of 1860. In January 1861, shortly before Rudolf Steiner's birth, he was transferred to a small town on what is now the northern border of Croatia. Kraljevec lay on the newly opened route between Pettau in southern Austria, and Nagykanizsa in Hungary.

It is not difficult to imagine how Franziska Steiner felt when she arrived in Kraljevec in the bitter January cold to join her husband. She was in her eighth month of pregnancy. Their cottage was poor, extremely simple, dark with low ceilings. The only furnishings were the oven that heated the living space, a bed, a table, chairs, and perhaps an armoire or chest. Water had to be carried in from the well. In the evening, a petroleum lamp brought meager light. The neighbors spoke only Croatian. Her husband worked three-day shifts. He returned home exhausted, stayed a day, and then returned to the railroad. All her relatives lived far away. Franziska Steiner must have been terribly isolated and lonely. The only relief was perhaps the fact that the cold broke in February that year, and spring returned early to the fertile plain between the Mur and the Drau.

It was here, according to an undated autobiographical sketch from the early 1920s, that Rudolf Steiner was born on February 25, 1861, and was christened two days later. Official documents give the later date, February 27, 1861, as Steiner's birth date. This is also the day on which Steiner's birthday was celebrated, even in the most intimate circles, as letters between Marie Steiner and Rudolf Steiner attest. Steiner himself mentioned his place of birth only briefly: "I was born in a Slavic region, which was completely foreign to the cultural milieu and traditions from which my forefathers came" (158). This remark has been interpreted as meaning that Steiner felt it was significant that he had been born in a Slavic region. The newborn did not, however, come into contact with the Slav nature of his surroundings. Croatian was not the language spoken at his cradle. The fact that he was born far from the homeland of his parents was the symbolic expression of his life's task to free what would emerge as Anthroposophy from all special interests (158). As both the context and other remarks show, the emphasis lies primarily in the expression "completely foreign." A later remark of Rudolf Steiner's underscores this: "It was for me to a certain extent, I'd like to say, symptomatic, that I grew up in an environment in which the most important things had nothing to do with me" (185).

In another connection Steiner emphasized that it was "coincidental" that he was born in Kraljevec and added, "I don't come from Hungary, I come from Lower Austria. My roots are in Lower Austria. I come from an old German family. I was born in Hungary only because my father worked for the southern Austrian railroad... and he was stationed on the Hungarian line in Kraljevec where I happened to have been born and to have spent the first year and a half of my life" (176).

Toward the end of her life, Leopoldine Steiner, Rudolf's younger sister, related what she had heard from her mother concerning the birth.

> At his birth, Rudolf Steiner was so poorly handled by the midwife that he lost a lot of blood. It was only as the blood seeped through the bandages that we noticed it. Because of this bleeding, Rudolf was always a sickly child. He was eight before he could begin school in Neudörfl.

Whether or not Rudolf Steiner's weak constitution as a child was due to the midwife's laxity is a matter of dispute. In any case, he was not a strong, healthy child.

Marie Steiner, who lived with Steiner from 1902 until his death and could observe him closely, experienced nothing of this weakness; but she did recognize his Lower Austrian peasant roots.

> A fine, slender, and resilient physique; lithe, tough, and bold; with gem-like lines of the facial characteristics... combines here with amiable sincerity and inner fire, and metamorphoses in the human intellect to such manifestations such as Robert Hamerling, Fercher von Steinwand, and Rudolf Steiner. All three came from the same mountainous region and have a certain similarity in common. There is no better instrument capable of adapting to great tasks than this physical nature is. (Marie Steiner, *Schriften I* [Writings])

A characteristic of Rudolf Steiner's early childhood is the fact that he grew up protected from the influences of the surrounding world. There were no relatives, no grandmother or aunts to look after him. His family had no friends in Kraljevec. Little "Rudl" was taken care of exclusively by his mother. All we know about these early days was that the child cried, long and loud, and that the mother would carry him around the house to quiet him. Perhaps she spoke to him at those times, murmuring calming phrases in her Austrian dialect. The time in Kraljevec was not long, however. After a year and a half, his father was transferred to Mödling by Vienna; and then in the beginning of 1863, he went to Pottschach as stationmaster.

Pottschach lies in the valley of the Schwarza, protected by mountains to the south, west, and north (Wechsel, Semmering, Raxalp, and Schneeberg). Looking back on his childhood, Steiner remembered best the evocative, pastoral landscape in which Pottschach stood; the characteristic mountains and the idyllic valley with its meadows, hedgerows, streams, and woods.

> At any hour of the day, what the boy would see were, on the one side, the Austrian mountains, often radiant in the sunlight and often covered with snow. On the other side was a landscape filled with plant life and other blessings of nature to be enjoyed and savored. This valley, at the foot of the Schneeberg and of the Sonnwendstein, is perhaps one of the most beautiful parts of Austria. (B 83/84)

The magnificence and beauty of this pre-alpine landscape had a positive effect on the boy's healthy development. "I believe that it was significant for my life that I spent my childhood in such an environment" (28).

The Steiner family could have settled down in Pottschach. They soon formed a friendship with the miller, whose mill stood close to the railroad station. The minister of the neighboring village of St. Valentin stopped by to chat almost daily, telling stories and enjoying greatly the laughter they brought. The bookkeeper of the local manor was a frequent visitor. All in all, the railroad station was the center of the local life. The schoolteacher, the mayor, and the minister turned up at the station to watch the trains and to chat. It was also here that Rudolf Steiner's sister and brother were born: Leopoldine in 1864 (who was known as Poldi in the family); and in 1866, Gustav, a child who was deaf and mute from birth.

Into this still pristine and untouched natural landscape came, with the railroad and the spinning factory, the first harbingers of the industrial, technical world. The young Steiner lived between two worlds: The natural landscape was the refreshing, vital background of his life; the technical world gave rise to many questions. What actually was happening behind the closed doors of the spinning factory? How can a railroad car go up in flames? How does the telegraph work? Where do the trains come from and where are they going? "[My]...interest was drawn strongly toward the mechanical quality in that existence, and I realize that this interest always tended to obscure the deep bond of sympathy that my young heart felt with that charming and majestic natural world into which the train (always subject to the mechanical) disappeared in the distance" (28).

The finances of the family were always dire, in Pottschach as well as later. The stationmaster's salary barely sufficed to cover the most necessary expenses. Meals were simple, especially in winter when there was nothing to be had from the garden. But poverty dampened neither the calm dignity of the father, nor the son's sense of justice and love of freedom. He refused to greet his father's employers, the train officials who would come to Pottschach for holidays, with any show of servility, or to speak with them. Usually he managed to avoid these unpleasant encounters by disappearing. Two episodes illustrate the approach his father took in protecting his children. Rudolf Steiner was to be given a whipping in the village school for something he had not done. He related the situation at home with such clarity that his father withdrew him from school and taught him at home. Had this happened a year later, it would not have been possible for Steiner to be homeschooled, because Austria introduced mandatory schooling. Some years later a similar incident took place in Neudörfl. As an acolyte, Rudolf Steiner had to serve for communion. He wrote:

> A number of acolytes, myself included, arrived late for communion. All of us were to be given a whipping at school for our tardiness. I had a deep antipathy for such punishment and knew how to avoid it. Up until then I had never been whipped. My father, however, was so enraged by the thought that "his son" should be given a whipping that he said, "Now it is over with church services. You are not going back." (B 49/50)

Just as important as his father's liberal approach to education was the unsentimental atmosphere at home. Free of the baggage of higher education and tradition, here the focus of interest was on the practical matters of life. His father thought of himself in these years as a "free spirit"; a skeptic. He was never seen at church. "The climate was not conducive to developing fanciful tendencies. The interests of the people I met were for the railroad and the spinning factory. The minister from St. Valentin was a rather dry fellow, with a tendency to be cynical and ironic. He could also play the fool" (B 49/50). "In the course of my boyhood, I never encountered anyone who was superstitious, although I think that this was not planned. In fact, I never heard anyone speak of things relating to the superstitious with anything but strong antipathy." There "was never a mood of religious devotion," not even by the priests. "In fact, certain shadow sides of the Catholic clergy became apparent to me" (262). This picture of a fairly modern, pragmatic family is important to keep in mind. That Steiner had been christened in a Catholic church was due simply to the fact that the Catholic Church was at that time responsible for registering births and deaths. That he had been an acolyte was simply an accepted part of country life at that time.

During the family's last year in Pottschach, an episode occurred that marked the beginning of a new phase in the life of the seven-year-old Steiner. He gave two different accounts of this episode. This is the published version:

> The following experience made a deep impression on the boy. My mother's sister died quite tragically. The place where she lived was quite a distance from our village. My parents had received no notice of her death. I sat in the waiting room of the train station and saw a vision of what had happened. I tried to tell my parents. They replied, "Don't be a silly boy." Some days later, I saw my father become pensive after receiving a letter. Later, in my absence he spoke with my mother, who cried for days thereafter. I heard the details of my aunt's death only years later. (B 49/50)

In the second account, from a lecture of Steiner's, he told how the aunt, whom he had never met, had committed suicide and had appeared before him pleading for help for her life in the spiritual world. He then continued, "The boy had no one in the family with whom he could speak about this experience. Even then, he would have been met with derision for his silly superstitions if he had tried to tell anyone the story"(B 83/84, S.6). Rudolf Steiner found himself totally alone with this experience, which troubled him, and which he would have liked to be able to share with someone. This repeated itself later. As an acolyte, he experienced the communion service as a form of mediation between the sensory and the suprasensory worlds.

> From the very beginning, this was not a mere form to me, but was a profound inner experience. And this was even more so since it made me a stranger in my own home. Nevertheless, my home environment did not diminish the spiritual richness I received through the ritual. I lived in my environment without participating in it. I saw it, but I actually thought, contemplated, and sensed continually in relation to that other world. (28)

From these early experiences, Rudolf Steiner learned silence. Already at seven, he realized that it was not possible to speak with most people about inner questions or spiritual experiences.

Another aspect of these experiences, however, was decisive for Steiner's path. He relates that "beginning with these episodes, a life within the soul began for the boy. Here those worlds revealed themselves, out of which not only the outer trees and mountains spoke to the human soul, but also what lives behind them. And the boy began to live to a certain extent with the spirits of nature, which are especially present in such landscapes, with the creative beings behind the things, in the same way as he let the outer world affect him" (B 83/84). Hence this experience stands, perhaps even sparking it, at the beginning of a childhood clairvoyance that awakens as "a life within the soul." In it, the world of nature spirits first reveals itself, which appeared to him to be especially present in their elementary nature in the landscape around Pottschach. Shortly after, the family moved to Neudörfl, where the powerful spirituality of the mountains was perceptible only from afar, awakening memories from the distance. Instead, the spirit of a different landscape was now present; that of the transition to the low Hungarian plains. Steiner doesn't speak of this change in his *Autobiography*, but he does mention the long walks through the surrounding forests. In the second of his four mystery plays, there is a fairy tale about a forest spring, which is perhaps reminiscent of this landscape and the walks between Neudörfl and Sauerbrunnen, or by Maria's Fountain.

Rudolf Steiner hints briefly about the nature of his inner life at this time. "I had two notions, both of which were rather vague, but that already played a large part in my inner life before I was eight. I differentiated between the things and beings 'that one saw' and those 'that one did not see'" (28). One could imagine that these experiences were more than simply a delight for the young Steiner. In itself, the encounter with his aunt, who had committed suicide, was an encounter with darkness. More than anything, however, what was missing for Rudolf Steiner in the face of these experiences was a sense of orientation and support. He had no one with whom he could speak of his experiences. For a long time, they lived on in him as a burden, a question with no answer.

A solution to the riddle first began to appear shortly after the family moved to Neudörfl and Rudolf Steiner began going to the local school. The lessons in this small one-room school were not especially fulfilling. "One could only brood dully and let one's hand do the copying almost mechanically" (28, p. 8). But in addition to the general lessons, Rudolf Steiner received "extra lessons" from the teacher's aide, a man named Heinrich Gangl, at the monthly cost of an Austrian gulden. In Gangl's study, the young Steiner came across a geometry book.

> Since I was on very good terms with the teacher, I was allowed to borrow the book to study privately. I plunged into it with enthusiasm, and for weeks my soul was completely filled with the congruence, the similarity of triangles, quadrilaterals and polygons. I racked my brains over the question of where parallel lines actually intersect; the theorem of Pythagoras fascinated me.
>
> I derived a deep feeling of contentment from the fact that one could live with the soul in building forms that are seen wholly inwardly, independent of the outer senses. I found consolation for my mood caused by so many unanswered questions. The ability to grasp something purely through the spirit brought me an inner joy. I realize that I first knew happiness through geometry. (28, p. 9)

In working with geometry, Rudolf Steiner found that it was possible through inner activity to bring into being a form of knowledge that was independent of the sensory world. "In regard to geometry, I could say that one may know something that the soul experiences solely through its own power. I found in this feeling the justification for speaking of the spiritual world I experienced, just as I spoke of the physical" (28, p. 9). Experiencing the spiritual world and the revelations of the spirituality in nature evoked questions for Steiner: What am I experiencing? How can I gauge these experiences? How must I think about myself, since I seem to be alone with these experiences? These questions must have grown increasingly insistent, since there was no one with whom he could speak of them. They troubled him. In working with geometry, he found comfort in the face of the anxiety "caused by so many unanswered questions" (28, p. 9). Here he found a sense of self-formed inner certainty. Here he found something through which he could hold his own in the face of his experiences of the spirituality of nature, because of its absolute clarity. The self-polished crystal of geometric thinking was something he could hold up to the manifold spirits in nature. Here we find one of the points of departure for what would later become Anthroposophy. Rudolf Steiner summarized this experience:

> I told myself: the objects and processes that the senses perceive exist in space. Just as this space is outside the human being, there exists within the human being an inner space, which is the stage upon which spiritual beings and occurrences can be perceived. In thinking, I could not see the sort of images that one forms of the perceived objects, but rather revelations of a spiritual world one comes to experience within this soul space. Geometry seemed to me to be a form of knowledge, which, although formed through human consciousness, still had a significance that was independent of the human being. As a child this was of course not clear to me, but I felt that one must carry knowledge of the spiritual world within oneself as one carried geometry. (28)

The ten-year-old Rudolf Steiner came to experience something for which most people have only a vague feeling, if any at all. Immanuel Kant knew that all our knowledge begins with experience, yet cannot be defined by the experience alone. He reached this understanding on a long path of philosophical contemplation. For Rudolf Steiner it was clear at the beginning of his reflections that within this inner space of soul glowed an independent world of thought whose source did not lie in the world that could be perceived by the senses. It was clear to him that the sensory world is essentially a riddle veiled in darkness that needs illumination from another source if it is to be solved. This fundamental experience stayed with Steiner throughout his life, and came to expression in his earliest philosophical writings. He wrote in 1882, "One must let the concept retain its elemental nature, a form of existence that is constructed solely upon itself; and find it again simply in another form in the sense object" (B 63). It is in this sense that Steiner described time and again the substantive, self-supporting character of thinking and the world of thought. First, however, the young Steiner faced the challenge of orienting himself not only in the world of thought, but also in his earthly environs.

The railroad station in Neudörfl lay on the east side of the hamlet, separated from the rest of the village by the church and the graveyard. He had no friends in the village. In the church, however, he did share the previously mentioned duties of acolyte and choir boy with the other boys of the town. This did not continue for long, but he enjoyed it, because he treasured and experienced intensely the majesty of the Latin language and the sacraments. Here he also was able to spend time in the proximity of the village priest, Franz Maraz. "He was by far the most significant personality I met before my tenth or eleventh year" (28, p. 11). Maraz was a "Magyar, from head to foot. A cleric to the point. He could preach the solid earth out from under chairs in the small church there" (B 49/50).

It was this priest who first introduced Rudolf Steiner to the modern view of the world. One day he appeared in the schoolhouse, gathered those pupils around him who he thought would understand, and unfolded one of his own drawings, with which he began to explain the Copernican model of the heavens.

> He spoke in a particularly vivid way about the Earth's revolution around the Sun; its rotation and inclination on its axis; and about summer and winter and the climatic zones of Earth. I was completely absorbed, and spent days making copies of his drawings; later I had another special lesson from the parson concerning Sun and Moon eclipses, and after that all my desire for knowledge turned to this subject. (28, p. 12)

It is symptomatic that the first educational experience that affected the young Steiner from outside was the mechanistic view of the Earth and the heavens. Here he encountered the same clear, sober type of thinking that gave birth to modern physics and to a great extent defines modern thought. He learned from the most notable authority in the village how to think about elementary natural phenomena. It was not to be long before he encountered this way of thinking in other forms as well.

The move to Neudörfl had torn Steiner's family out of the social context that had begun to emerge in Pottschach. On the east side of Neudörfl, the Steiners lived by themselves. The handicapped Gustav brought the family worries and concerns that bound them more closely together, but that also led to a certain isolation. They had contact only with the poorest of the village, whose shacks were also on the east side of town. "Every year, along with the small cottagers, I participated in gathering grapes, and once in a village wedding" (28, p. 11). Among the other boys, Steiner was viewed as a "'stranger' in the village" (28, p. 10). They included him neither in their games nor in the yearly sport of seeing who could harvest the most nuts. His isolation grew when he began attending school in Vienna. Except for the holidays, he was away from the village the greater part of the day. Neither did close friendships develop with his schoolmates in Vienna. One classmate, Albert Pliwa, recalled:

> During all seven years [of school], Rudolf Steiner was never once here in Vienna in the evening. He never went walking with us on the "Glacis" or through the city. He didn't really count as a classmate. He was never mentioned as a part of all the devilry and pranks we did, got caught doing, and were punished for. The situation turned him into a loner, so that after school he would sit in the railway car reading until the train left to take him home. (Picht)

Enjoyment and relaxation came from long, lonesome hikes through the forest to Sauerbrunnen, where he would fill a clay pot with spring water to carry home. In summer, he picked the wild strawberries that grew there. "Another pleasure one could derive in the proper season from those walks was to return richly laden with the gifts of nature. One could find blackberries, raspberries, and strawberries in the woods. After a couple of hours of berry-picking, it was very satisfying to bring home a delicious contribution to the family's evening meal, which otherwise consisted of a piece of bread and butter or bread and cheese" (28, pp. 6–7).

Living in Neudörfl gave Rudolf Steiner an especially clear sense of the socio-political situation at that time. Neudörfl lay in "Transleithania," the Hungarian part of the double monarchy, east of the Leitha; Vienna, on the other hand, was in the Austrian part. On his trip to school and back each day, Steiner crossed the river marking the boundary between the two parts of the kingdom. This was the period of "Maygarization." In the village school, children learned stories of the Hungarian heroes. The first known drawing from Rudolf Steiner's hand is of the Hungarian Duke Széchenyi (1792–1860). Neudörfl's official name was Laitha Szent Miklos (St. Nikolaus on the Leitha); Sauerbrunnen was named Savanyukut. His father was constantly worried that he might be transferred elsewhere and would have to learn Hungarian. In a childlike way, Steiner, too, experienced the tension of life on the border. "One day Steiner got out of the train in Sauerbrunnen and refused petulantly to give the stationmaster his ticket. Nothing at the station said Sauerbrunnen; the Hungarian 'Savanyukut' didn't mean anything to him. Finally the stationmaster drew back his arm to box Steiner's ears. Steiner ducked, calling him a 'Hun'" (Pliwa, in Picht).

Rudolf Steiner's childhood passed in a rural setting, in a relatively untouched natural environment. Both the magnificence and the gentle magic of this landscape made an impression on the boy. The modern industrial world made itself known through the railroad, the telegraph, and the spinning factory. These gave rise to a multitude of thoughts. It seems especially important that his childhood was relatively free of outside cultural influences. At home, a sober, pragmatic atmosphere reigned. The language that surrounded him was the soft, evocative dialect of the Forest Quarter, a traditional dialect free of modernization. Their life was simple, as humble as one can imagine. There was nothing to give the boy affectations or an exaggerated sense of his own importance; he was neither a snob nor a bigot. Much of what he encountered was strange or curious to him. This destiny, to remain in many ways a stranger in a strange land, held him back from becoming one with his surroundings, and from simply taking the incursion of modern civilization for granted.

The boy was thus shielded from much of what caught the attention of his contemporaries in Vienna. His inner life evolved out of his own individual experiences and questions. His thoughts were developed independently. Although his father certainly took time to explain the workings of the station's telegraph, geometry was something he mastered on his own. The Copernican model was brought to him by the village priest, but here too it was his own thirst for knowledge that led him to question further and to develop independently the inner imagery. Steiner thus crafted an inner world out of his own activity to a much greater degree than is usual among children. The price of this independence was loneliness.

Chapter 2

LEARNING

Learning was a determining factor in Rudolf Steiner's destiny. Through learning he moved beyond the limitations of village life and found a connection with the wider world. And at least in the first half of his life, his ability to learn determined his career. Even from the middle of his life, at a time when Steiner had long been a teacher, he continued to be a learner. Gunther Wachsmuth tells that even as Steiner's life drew to an end and he was unable to leave his sickbed, he perused weekly the new books that came on the market, chose the ones that seemed to him most important, and studied them.

Steiner's father seems to have laid great value on education, although he was able to accompany his son only on the first stages of his learning path. Both parents must be praised for the unequivocal manner in which they supported their son's education. It was his father who made it possible for Steiner to attend high school and college; his mother made sure that he had the necessary quiet at home to study. This was a huge financial burden on the family. Although Steiner's grades were high enough that he did not have to pay school fees, and he soon earned part of his expenses by tutoring other students after school, his parents' efforts were extraordinary, especially given the social milieu from which they came. Following his final exams, Steiner's father was able to arrange a scholarship for him to attend the Technical College in Vienna. Rudolf Steiner did not forget this. In a letter to his parents and siblings from 1892, he wrote: "I can assure you that my duty to you is deeply impressed upon my soul, and that I will strive as best I can to fulfill it" (39). He remained faithful to this vow throughout his life. Especially following the death of his father, he took on the financial support of his mother as well his brother and sister. One of his last letters, written just five days before he died, concerned the care of his sister, who had gone almost completely blind.

Steiner began attending the secondary school (a technically oriented secondary school) in Wiener-Neustadt in 1872. His interest was not awakened by the lessons during the first two years. He had trouble keeping up. Often bored, he tried to hide in the back of the room, secretly reading fairy tales. Caught by the teacher, he was thereafter tested daily for attention. Some of the subjects were poorly taught. "We had two Carmelite monks, one who taught us French, the other English. The one who taught us English...could barely speak an English word, not to mention sentences. In natural science, we had a man who truly knew nothing of God and the world." In religion lessons, the student merely learned the text, well-written as it was, by heart (185).

The language arts were difficult for Steiner from the beginning. He writes of his own performance: "The only thing that gave him trouble were the languages, even German. Until he was fourteen or fifteen years old, this boy made the most ridiculous mistakes in German in his schoolwork." Elisabeth Vreede relates a story about his difficulties with the foreign languages. Steiner had "no feeling whatsoever" for language. He read her a piece from an English newspaper "with an accent that was so incredibly silly" (Vreede).

Attending school was not easy. It took effort and was draining. In winter, the train tracks were often blocked with snow. Steiner would have to walk the three miles, his heavy sack of books thrown over his shoulder. At times, no train ran in the evening. Steiner arrived home as a "snowman." Sometimes his sister Leopoldine walked to meet him, so he wouldn't be alone with his fear of the Gypsies. He would arrive home fairly exhausted and still have his homework ahead of him. Years later, he wrote to Anna Eunike about this time of his life: "I've told you...at times about the difficult years I had from eleven to seventeen. They provided rich opportunity to strengthen my constitution" (39, compare also B 83/84, S.10). It is true that Steiner was, in comparison to his more robust classmates, a physically weak young man. Getting to school every day was a challenge.

For the twelve-year-old, the discovery of an article by the school director, Heinrich Schramm, was more important than the lessons themselves. The article appeared in the yearbook and was entitled, "The Force of Gravity as an Effect of Movement." The schoolboy couldn't understand much of the article, because "it began immediately with higher mathematical formulas" (28). But it brought to his attention a book that Schramm had written, *The Movement of Matter as the Basis for all Natural Phenomena*

(Vienna, 1872). The young Steiner saved what little money came his way, until he had enough to buy the book. He studied it on his own, and slowly taught himself enough to be able to understand both the article and the contents of the book. This project took him several years in all. It was the boy's introduction to modern science, albeit in a rather one-sided form. Steiner summarized Schramm's teachings as follows:

> The headmaster's idea was that it is an unjustified "mystical" hypothesis that "forces" go out from matter into the distance. He tried to explain the "attraction" between heavenly bodies and between molecules and atoms without such "forces." He said that between any two bodies are many smaller bodies, all in motion. The smaller bodies, moving back and forth, impinge upon the larger ones, and these larger bodies are impinged upon everywhere, even on those sides turned away from one another. These impingements are more numerous than those in the space between the two bodies. Hence, they approach one another. Consequently, he did not consider "attraction" a special force but merely an "effect of motion." On the first page in the book, I found two assertions: 1) Space and motion within it have existed for a long time; 2) Space and time are continuously homogeneous magnitudes; matter, on the other hand, consists of separate small particles (or atoms). (28, p. 16)

Steiner encountered the materialistic view of the world initially in the form of mechanical atomism: the world is nothing other than matter and movement. He recognized very quickly the relationship between this approach and that of Copernicus. "I began to see a connection between that article and what I had learned from the priest about the structure of the universe" (28, p. 16). At the same time he became aware of how representative individuals thought about the world. He didn't feel moved to adopt this kind of thinking, but he did feel that it was important for him to understand it. He began to collect books on mathematics and physics that would help him come to an understanding. "I repeatedly began reading the article and the book; each time it went a little better" (28, p. 16).

Rudolf Steiner first encountered the materialistic worldview through radical atomism, in which the world is held to be made of solid atoms and their movements. The significance of this for his spiritual development should not be underestimated. He soon came to realize that there was no connection between this mental picture of the world and what he experienced within. Sooner or later he had to reach the conclusion that the postulated worldview could not lead to an explanation of the experienced world. To begin with, however, Steiner did not strive to argue against this approach, but simply to understand it. In this regard, he became acquainted with the purely ideal nature of mathematics.

Steiner's study of mathematics received special support from the teacher who took over mathematics in the third year of the secondary school, "He was a person I could emulate. He taught arithmetic, geometry and physics and his lessons were extraordinarily ordered and lucid. He built everything up from the very foundation and with such clarity that to follow him was tremendously beneficial for one's thinking" (28, p. 16). The teacher's name was Laurenz Jelinek. He was a mathematician, with no interest for either botany or zoology, and was both Steiner's class teacher and also his math and physics teacher for the rest of secondary school. Interestingly, Steiner remarked, following his description of Jelinek: "What he taught gradually helped me toward a better understanding of the enigma presented to me by the headmaster's writings" (28, p. 17). Somewhat later, Rudolf Steiner came to a close relationship with another teacher, Georg Kosak, who taught geometric drawing and descriptive geometry. He was an excellent though somewhat one-sided draftsman. Based on his drawings, he had developed the idea that the curve of constant quotient is a circle. Since he had done no analytical geometry, he viewed himself as the discoverer of this relationship. From the description of his lessons, it seems clear that his approach was the seed of the main lesson books used in Waldorf schools.

> The way this teacher presented geometry to us and taught us how to use our rulers and compasses was eminently practical. It may be said that this boy fell in love with geometry through the guidance of his teacher and with geometrical drawing. The clear, practical approach to geometry was enhanced by the teacher's relation to the textbooks as a sort of decoration. Everything he brought us, he dictated to the students and drew on the blackboard. We constructed the drawings in our own notebooks, needing to know nothing beyond what we had developed for ourselves in these notebooks. It was a good way to work in an active manner with the teacher. In other subjects, however, we received excellent guidance in sleeping through the lessons. (B 83/84)

Rudolf Steiner received clarity and a sense of security in his self-evident view of the spiritual world through the study of mathematics and geometry. On the other hand was the world of nature. These two worlds appeared separate and distinct. "I was convinced that one could come to terms with the spiritual world through the soul as long as thinking assumes a form capable of grasping the true nature of physical phenomena. These feelings accompanied me during my third and fourth years at the secondary school. Everything I learned I mobilized in order to come closer to this goal" (28, p. 17). This extraordinary state of consciousness (which distinguished sharply between the mathematical world grasped in thinking and the experience of the suprasensory on the one hand, and sense experience on the other hand; and thus grasped the independent existence of the spiritual) provided the background for Steiner's later epistemological writings. It was reflected as well in the fact that Rudolf Steiner did not grow naturally into his environment, but remained "a stranger" to it.

The boy's unique character went unnoticed in Rudolf Steiner's immediate surroundings. He appeared to be an especially gifted, eager student who also didn't shy away from practical work. He helped turn the garden, planted and harvested potatoes; he did the family's shopping, fixed his own shoes, and learned to bind his books. He practiced stenography zealously. One of his schoolmates related that "Rudolf Steiner was a passionate stenographer. He stenographed all the lectures, practicing to be able to follow any lecturer. He did get to the point where he could follow each and every lecturer" (Pliwa, in Picht).

It comes as no surprise that Rudolf Steiner's teachers at the secondary school were more than happy to send him students who needed extra help. He had students from his own class as well as from the lower classes. "I owe very much to this tutoring. Because I had to pass on to others what I had absorbed from a lesson, I had to wake up, as it were, to the subject. I can describe it only by saying that I received knowledge given to me at school as if in a dream" (28, p. 20). These sentences not only shed light on the psychology of learning; they also illumine an image used often by Steiner: that of awakening. He used this image to describe an intensification of one's own activity; in this context, meaning the step from a more passive appropriation to an active assimilation of knowledge. Through tutoring, he began also to acquire an understanding for learning challenges and problems, thus gaining an initial insight into applied psychology. Tutoring allowed Rudolf Steiner "to contribute at least a little toward my tuition, which my parents provided from their meager income" (28, p. 20). A small part of the money was left for other things.

The only shops in Wiener-Neustadt that drew Rudolf Steiner's interest were the bookstores, with their displays that were small at that time. He often stopped to study the books there. Seldom did he enter these treasure troves, as he had too little money to buy books. But every so often, he managed to save enough money to purchase something. Among the first books he bought were the series that Heinrich Borchert Lübsen had written to teach oneself mathematics. "This is how I learned analytical geometry, and trigonometry, as well as differential and integral calculus, long before I was taught those subjects at school. This enabled me to return to my study of the books on the general motion of matter as the fundamental cause of all physical phenomena" (28, p. 19). He also acquired Rotteck's *World History*, and books by Tacitus and Johannes von Müller. This independent study sharpened Steiner's sense for the questionable nature of the school's history lessons. "But I worked to enrich the lessons at school with what I gained from other sources" (28, p. 20).

One day, probably in May or June, 1877, Rudolf Steiner discovered the newly published Reclam edition of Immanuel Kant's *Critique of Pure Reason*. The sixteen-year-old Steiner had as yet no notion of Kant's place in the history of philosophy. The title alone must have fascinated him. "In my boyish way, I strove to understand to what degree human reason is capable of true understanding of the nature of things" (28, p. 17). Steiner began to save his pennies in order to buy the book.

Rudolf Steiner didn't have much spare time as he began his study of Kant. Since the history professor lectured only from the textbook, however, one didn't have to pay attention in class. Rudolf Steiner carefully disassembled Kant's book and stapled the sections into his history textbook and, while the teacher read from the rostrum, used the lesson to attempt to read Kant. The question with which Steiner initially turned to Kant did not address spiritual experience, which was for him "a part of human ideation." He strove much more to clarify the relation between religion and reason, as at that time he was intensely interested in religious teachings, dogma and symbolism, church history, and descriptions of the rituals. "On the other side, the question concerning the scope of the human power of thought occupied me constantly" (28, p. 18).

How can human thought, which lives in a purely ideal, sense-free environment, come to know nature? What is the connection between spirit and the world that appears to the senses? This question, which had already occupied the fourteen-year-old Steiner, reappeared in a new and clearer form. "I felt that thinking could be developed into a power that truly includes the things and processes of the world. 'Subject matter' that remains beyond thinking, as something merely 'reflected upon,' was an unbearable idea to me. I told myself again and again that what is in the thing must enter one's thoughts" (28, p. 17). During the summer holidays, Rudolf Steiner took long walks and pondered this question. Now and then, he would sit down and open Kant's *Critique*. He read some pages twenty times through, and still the study of Kant's writing did not help him answer his question. "My attitude toward Kant was very uncritical at the time, but I got no further through him" (28, p. 19). Steiner's additional philosophical studies during his school years, examining the works of Herbartian Gustav Lindner, did just as little to help him resolve the problem.

Equally unhelpful were the German lessons given by Dr. Joseph Mayer. Although other students recall his "wonderful presentations," Steiner picked up on the fact that he was influenced by the philosophy of Johann Friedrich Herbart, and alluded to Herbart's philosophical thoughts in the essays he wrote for class. This was something the teacher did not appreciate. The titles of the assignments, especially the essays that Mayer gave, show clearly what spirit prevailed in his lessons. The topic of one exam essay was "Civil Patriotism Is the Strongest Buttress of the Government (illustrated with historical examples)." Two years before their final exams, the students were asked to write about the adage "Not everything that glitters is gold."

Rudolf Steiner found guidance in this field in quite different circumstances. In school, literature was taught in a cursory manner using excerpts from German poets and authors. In addition to Goethe and Schiller, the students were introduced to the work of Klopstock, Wieland, Geibel, Grillparzer, Platen, Eichendorff, and others. These lessons did not mean much to Steiner. He had, however, an acquaintance, the railroad doctor Carl Hickel, who had known the family from Pottschach. He had spoken to Steiner about German poets and literature even before he began attending the secondary school. When Steiner was in the fifth or sixth year, Hickel invited Steiner to visit him. They spoke again of literature; Steiner borrowed a copy of Lessing's *Minna from Barnhelm* and was invited to return and talk about it. "He repeatedly loaned me books in this way to read, and he allowed me to go and see him occasionally. Each time I had to tell him my impressions of what I had read. Thus he actually became my teacher in poetry" (28). The memory of this lovable, generous doctor stayed with Steiner. In 1892, he sent him a copy of his doctoral dissertation. Hickel wrote back, thanked him warmly and wrote, "You thank me for what little I was able to do for you. What more could I have done, if I had known of the ideals toward which you strove" (B 49/50).

The lessons of the chemistry teacher Hugo von Gilm were challenging and at the same time liberating. "He taught almost exclusively through experiments. He said little and let the phenomena speak.... There was something about his gaze that drew one's attention. One felt that the man looked so intensely at nature that in his gaze he retained a complete picture of what he observed" (28). Having to continually follow the complicated experiments, observing the processes and the multitude of facts, did not come easily to Rudolf Steiner. At that time, his thinking strove for unification. Hugo von Gilm, however, pointed him to the colorful world of observation.

In his last year of school, Rudolf Steiner met a history teacher who appeared to the students as a true personality. Outside of school, Albert Löger was a strong voice for the progressive liberal party. Although he did not bring his personal views to expression in class, his presentations of modern history were colorful and lively, thanks to his personal involvement in the historical processes of the time. Based on his study of the historical writings of Karl von Rotteck, Steiner recognized the significance of Löger's spirited classes. "I must consider it very significant that I could take in modern history precisely in this way" (28). Steiner's connection to Löger continued even after he graduated. When Löger was taken to task for his membership in an Old Catholic congregation that refused to accept the 1870 dogma of papal infallibility, Steiner publicly defended his former teacher in a newspaper article, in which he wrote glowingly of Löger's influence as a teacher.

On July 5, 1879, Rudolf Steiner passed his final exams (*Matura*) "with commendation." In physics, he had to explain the newly invented telephone. In the six science and math subjects and in history, he received a grade of "excellent." Only in German and freehand drawing did he have to make do with "satisfactory." Whether the low grade in German was because of Steiner's ongoing feud with the teacher or his often excessively long essays is not known. At *Valet*, the ceremonial farewell dinner for the exam students, Joseph Mayer, the German teacher, said to Steiner, "Yes, you were a most powerful wordsmith. It was with something like fear that I received your work" (B 83/84).

Looking back over Rudolf Steiner's education up till the *Matura*, what becomes apparent is how it differs from that of other well-known Austrian contemporaries. He was born of a family that had little education. At home, attention was paid neither to literature, nor to art and religion. There was no library at home; concerts were out of the question. What he learned at the village school and later at the secondary school was far removed from a classical education. On the whole, he had very little exposure throughout his youth to music, which was so important for many of his contemporaries. What impressed itself upon him from the outside were, on the one hand, the technical world of the railroad and, on the other, the natural world of Lower Austria and Burgenland. At the secondary school, mathematics, geometry, physics, and chemistry were very well taught; German and the language arts were mediocre. Without question, the technical and scientific were the areas in which Steiner attained the most positive dialogue with his surroundings. He had to search for and create his own access to literature, history, and religion. The German literature that he received from Carl Hickel and what he otherwise found, he read with enthusiasm and completely unsystematically. *Faust* and other works remained unknown to him. His introduction to history came about through independent study of the works of older historians. He more than likely read books on religion with the questions that arose out of his own spiritual experiences.

More important than the nature of the outer stimulation and guidance is the fact that Rudolf Steiner taught himself, through independent study, much (if not most) of what he learned. It began with the geometry book of the village school teacher, and led through the study of the school director's work to the independent study of trigonometry and differential and integral calculus. In literature and history, Steiner sought his own way through independent study. His early study of Kant (Steiner read other works in addition to the *Critique*) was not so uncommon at that time. For example, Ernst Mach is reported to have read the *Prolegomena* at fifteen. It is important, however, that Steiner lived with a very specific question. "I worked to form a judgment concerning the relationship of human thinking and the workings of nature" (28). He found no answer to this question in Kant. As he had no one with whom he could speak of this, he acquired knowledge independently and formed his own thoughts and questions. It was with these questions that he left school in the summer of 1879.

CHAPTER 3

STUDENT IN VIENNA

Rudolf Steiner came to Vienna for the first time in the summer of 1879, at the end of July or beginning of August. The train from Inzerdorf, where his father had been transferred, brought him to Vienna's South Station. From here, his path took him into the inner city, across the Ring, where at that time the Parliament, the City Hall, and the Votivkirche were approaching completion. The decorative nature of the different nostalgic architectural styles appeared to the eighteen-year-old Steiner to be foreign and curious. He didn't notice the buildings by Semper, Hansen, or Ferstel on his first walk through the city. These buildings, however, give the city its special feeling. Later Steiner went to lectures by Joseph Bayers at the Technical College. Bayers explained Vienna with the sentence "Ornamentation is a form of external technique." This was an odd summary of what was a complete mixture of various styles. The subjugation of form by technical considerations was for Steiner the depressing signature of the artistic materialism that would color his surroundings for the next eleven years (286).

Steiner's goal on that first visit to Vienna was to visit the used book stores in the inner city. Under his arm he carried a pile of his old schoolbooks, which he had meticulously rebound and for which he did, in fact, receive a "pretty sum" that was immediately used to buy philosophy books. The best finds were two books by Johann Gottlieb Fichte, *Science of Knowledge* and *The Determination of Man*. Because Steiner didn't know much about philosophy at that point he also bought, in addition to some of Kant's earlier works, books by Traugott Krug and Karl Leonhard, as well as a history of philosophy by C. A. Thilo, a disciple of Herbart. He returned home that evening, by train to Inzerdorf and by foot from there to Oberlaa, where the family lived, well laden with books. Until his courses began at the Technical College of Vienna on October 1, he had opportunity to immerse himself completely in his philosophical studies. "And I experienced intensely the contrast in thinking between Fichte and Herbart" (28). The content of these studies will be addressed later. What is important biographically, is that the student did not begin a new series of courses with any specific preparation, but had a few weeks to work through and clarify his own thoughts. First he focused on Fichte, who helped him think through and give form to his own spiritual idealism. He found that Fichte had articulated the idea of freedom and independent activity that had so moved him, and in which human dignity has its foundation. Fichte also directed his attention to the *Vocation of the Scholar* and to the cultural tasks of the German people. Personal and historical perspectives opened for him that enabled him to come to an understanding of his time and of modern science, and that, at the same time, fortified him against some of the intellectual futility of his time.

Finding the time to independently bring form and clarity into his thoughts was a necessity, for Steiner was about to enter a spiritually, politically and economically confusing environment, a spiritual space of hopelessness. Thanks to his father's political interests, he may well have had some notion of the political storm that had broken in the summer of 1879. Since 1861, the German liberals had attempted to push Austria toward political modernization. Following the collapse of the Austrian stock market in 1873, which led to a longer period of economic recession, the liberals lost support and finally, in the federal election of 1879, were badly beaten, a defeat from which they were never to recover. Based on the election results, on August 12, 1879, Emperor Franz-Joseph appointed his friend Count Eduard Taffe as Prime Minister. The formation of the Taffe Cabinet ushered in the transition from a German liberal government to one that found its support in a coalition of Poles, conservative Czechs, and German-Catholic conservatives. This coalition formed an "iron ring" around German liberalism.

From his *Autobiography*, we are aware that during his time as a student Steiner followed political life more closely than many of his classmates. He did so by observing it at its source, from the galleries of the houses of parliament. From there he followed the debates in both the Austrian Chamber of Deputies and the Upper House. He was primarily interested in the individual speakers, some of whom made a deep impression on him. In 1924, he could still give a lively description of some of the speakers. The politics of the time were, however, confusing and incommensurable. "I had no real insights into the public affairs of Austria that stirred me inwardly. I merely *observed* the extremely complicated situation" (28).

His observations did lead him to draw certain conclusions. In 1910, Rudolf Steiner remembered:

> The form of liberalism that blossomed for a short time following the defeat at Koniggratz, which some powerful figures had hoped would save the government from total bureaucratic chaos, had lost public support. It no longer could set the tone in the governance of the kingdom, partially due to its own weakness, partially due to the fact that there had been too little time for the achievement of the liberal goals.
> We young people had no great expectations that any good would come of it. (31)

Less hope was placed in Taffe's government, which had raised the practice of bumbling along on well-trodden paths to a high art and acted on the cynical principle of keeping all the various ethnic groups in a state of well-tempered dissatisfaction.

The political gaze of the student body turned to look over the border at Germany. Some Austrian students even went as far as to demand the annexation of Austria by the Berlin government, a demand that found no echo there. The majority of the German students in Vienna called themselves "German nationals," which should not be seen in connection with the German National Folk Party during the Weimar Republic. This was rather a diffuse, idealistic movement of students and petit-bourgeois who no longer felt at home in the multinational state. Steiner also felt himself to be a part of this movement, which had caught the imagination of the students following the collapse of liberalism.

> With even more enthusiasm we joined the emerging German national movement. The leaders of this movement did not concern themselves with what used to be called the "idea of the Austrian state." They viewed this as abstract and inimical to reality. An Austrian state that took no interest in the multitude of ethnic cultures of which it was comprised, but merely strove to maintain a sort of creeping progress with a compromised democracy that bowed to all possible inherited prejudices and rights, seemed to the younger of these leaders an impossibility. Young German students believed that they could view the future with greater hope if they were able to emphasize their own ethnicity, to immerse themselves in their national culture, and to nurture a connection to the development of spiritual

life in Germany. It was with such ideals that young German students lived in the '80s. (31)

Rudolf Steiner entered the movement with unusual engagement. He became a member of "The German Reading Room of the Technical College." This was a political student association in which Steiner was initially elected as the librarian and later, for one semester, chairman. "After I had been chairman for six months, everyone voted against me. By then they had discovered that I did not agree as fully with any one party as its members wished" (28).

Two of Steiner's writings from these years give insight into his political thinking. Both are from 1884, roughly three years after his work in The German Reading Room. In the first he turns his attention to the strivings of the European peoples "to find a form of government in which the moral dignity and freedom of each individual can come to full expression."

> Government has to ensure that individual happiness is not solely dependent on coincidence or willfulness. Within the rationally constructed whole it must be able to guarantee the well-being of the individual to such an extent that the individual is able to develop himself in freedom, both physically and spiritually. Government cannot make people free; only education can achieve this. Government does, however, have to ensure that each individual can find the soil in which his freedom can grow and blossom. (30)

Rudolf Steiner always remained true to this in its original form, the still very general, basic idea that places individual freedom at the center. While he knew at the same time that the state could not make people free, he believed public life should strive to overcome coincidence and willfulness. His later recommendations for the threefold social order would show the ways in which reason can come to practical expression and create the foundation upon which productive freedom can flourish.

Steiner was especially interested in the fate of the individual. At the time he wrote that it was most important for a viable fellowship of nations that individuals are able to bring their full capacities into the fellowship. "What is important is that one's position within a group is such that one can bring the full force of one's individuality to bear. This is possible only when a political organism is such that each person can find the spot upon which to apply leverage. Whether one finds this spot or not must not be left to coincidence" (2). These words no doubt reflect Steiner's own painful experiences. He felt his own development continued to be a question of chance. Unnoticed and unrecognized, he was left to forge his own path. There was no one to guide gifted young people to a place where they could best bring their individual capacities to bear.

It is interesting that, in 1884, Steiner was of the opinion that the "first truly viable seed" of such a state in which "reason ruled" could be seen in Germany. He welcomed the fact "that in Germany the man responsible for giving direction to the government was deeply permeated by the mission of the state" to create for its citizens the foundation of freedom. By 1898, this initially positive assessment of German social politics had given way to quite a different tone. Steiner wrote of "the socialist allures of King Bismark" and emphasized that Bismark owed his political success to the fact that "at no point was he even a few years ahead of his time" (31).

This second piece is unfortunately fragmentary. It is taken from a letter to an unnamed friend and deals with the situation in Austria:

> For Germans in Austria there are only two possible parties. Either he is in the minority and must unfold the flag of national culture in order to impress the Slavs and the Magyars. Or he is in the majority with his hand on the rudder. Then, in true democratic spirit, he must raise the flag of autonomy and self-determination of the various peoples and work toward the sort of future state that is most conducive to culture: the closed trading state free of both "money" and "stock markets." (38)

This passage is extremely interesting not only in that it gives insight into Steiner's political thinking, but, more importantly, because it alludes to concrete ideas about the form of the social organism. Steiner recognized that the fundamental problem in the social structure lay with the uncontrolled dominance of wealth that was not in the service of production or trade, but able to willfully steer national economy in a one-sided manner. He viewed the speculative interests of the stock market as an obstacle to a sound regulation of economic forces. Such interests focused economic development on increasing profits rather than on better meeting the needs and rights of human beings. Steiner's lack of confidence in political liberalism was rooted in the effects of the economic policy connected to the crash of the Austrian stock market in 1873. Political liberalism in Austria was primarily economic liberalism supporting a purely market economy. The idea of a "closed trading state" points to Fichte's idea that the government would guarantee the ability of individuals to sustain themselves by their own efforts through a form of planned economy. The unpredictable ups and downs of the market would be evened out by the wisdom of the state. Steiner would later cease to support this idea. In 1919, he showed the connection between the "closed trading state" and the work of Lenin and Trotsky (89), and sketched out the problems connected with this idea. However, the core idea of a society founded on human dignity rather than competition and conquest continued to concern Steiner.

The idea that the state should oversee and regulate the national economy allowed Steiner to conceptualize the possibility of confronting economic liberalism and articulate his desire for a just society. For others, the social injustice of those "money and market" years became one of the triggers of a new wave of anti-Semitism that swept through Vienna under the leadership of Georg von Schönerer. It was easy to inflame public feeling with allusions to the Jewish banking institutions. Within a decade, anti-Semitism became the dominant political force in Vienna. Within the idealistic circles in which Steiner moved, the danger connected to this development, which was but a symptom of a deeper social disease, was not clearly recognized. "They didn't realize that things had moved in a direction in which only a much rougher approach than their own would become dominant. Even the success of Georg von Schönerer, who replaced the ideal of German nationalism with the racist specter of anti-Semitism, did not bring us to change our ways" (31).

Steiner received his college education in the years leading up to the collapse of the double monarchy. In 1879, the weak reform efforts of the Austrian liberals came to an end. These were perhaps ineffective, yet still idealistic. Taffe's political wheeling and dealing followed, with no goal but to continue to prop up political relationships that were no longer truly viable. The rapid rise of anti-Semitism in Vienna in 1883 was one of the results of this lack of political direction. For the petit-bourgeois, the racist anti-Semitism of the late nineteenth century took the form of a new scientific ideology. The upper classes did not initially notice the new tone that had crept into politics. They didn't take the populist anti-Semitism seriously. In hindsight, Steiner remarked, "The idealists in Austria at that time had the rug pulled out from under their feet" (31).

Political idealism came to an end in other countries at this time in different ways: 1884 is the year given for the emergence of conscious imperialism. In Germany, the terms *power politics* and *real politics* were met with enthusiasm. In general, social Darwinism, the struggle for existence among the nations and races, gained ever-wider popularity.

Rudolf Steiner began studying at the Technical College with an eye on becoming a secondary school teacher there. He found himself drawn to mathematics, in addition to which he signed up for courses in natural history and chemistry. Neither in his *Autobiography* nor in other documentary sources does Steiner tell us much about his formal studies. There are two things he does mention, however.

The first has to do with the problem of space. The then accepted concept of space as stretching in all directions into infinite emptiness gave him great difficulty. Through his studies of synthetic geometry, he had come to a sense of the conceptual structure of space, recognizing that the infinitely distant point to the right was identical with what lay to the left. "After the lecture during which this had first appeared inwardly to me, I walked away feeling as if a great load had fallen from me. I felt liberated. Again geometry brought me happiness as it had done in my childhood" (28). Steiner does not appear to have ever gone into more detail concerning this experience. The significance of the moment lay in the realization that through synthetic geometry it was possible to understand space as having a conceptual structure, not simply being "empty."

The other aspect that Steiner mentions has to do with his physics professor, Edmund Reitlinger. He worked in the physics lab on spectral analysis under Reitlinger and attended two of his lecture series concerning the history of physics. This genetic introduction to the problems and methods of physics, which Reitlinger was able to present in a very imaginative manner, made a deep impression on Steiner. Through them, he encountered not only the key concepts of thought in physics, but also the practically forgotten alternatives to this approach. Later, in connection with the publication of Goethe's history of the theory of color, he would study the history of science intensively. In 1882, he was struck by the universal approach taken by the then deathly ill Reitlinger, who presented the development of research in physics while at the same time opening a wide range of cultural historical perspectives. Steiner passed the semester exam given by Reitlinger on July 1, 1882, and received from him a number of letters of recommendation through which Steiner received some new tutoring students. Reitlinger died two months later, on September 3, 1882.

Steiner's course attendance record shows that he had quite a rigorous schedule of studies. In addition to mathematics, physics and chemistry, he took botany, zoology, mineralogy, and geology, as well as international law. Since he was receiving a scholarship of 300 gulden annually, he was required to take regular exams to prove that he was doing well in his studies. In these exams he received ten "excellents," three "very goods" and six "goods." The exams took a good deal of preparation. From July 1 to July 22, 1881, Steiner had to stand for four different exams. He wrote to a friend: "Exams have to be taken and the last two"—in mathematics and mathematical physics—"have taken me longer than I expected. I can assure you that the whole thing is but a form of spiritual dressage, learning a whole series of fiddly, fussy formulas at one time" (38). To another friend in a letter written on the same day, he wrote:

> The sciences are full of fussiness and pedantry that push away a healthy mind.... The worst thing about it is that the social situation is such that one is forced to acquire what is merely ornament, as well as what is true; also one's sense of duty brings one to it, for how can one form a judgment about something one has not experienced. If one wishes to say that something stinks, he must first have smelled it. (38)

One year later Steiner wrote to his old history teacher, Alfred Löger: "Hopefully I will soon have put the gray mediocrity of the Technical College behind me. But first comes the sorry excuse for an exam on the heaps of mathematical wisdom piled high in the library. When I think about the amount of mindless repetition, I mean the written work, I am horrified. But I must do it, will do it, am doing it" (38). These meager contemporary sources show, as does Steiner's relative silence about his formal studies, that he approached his studies conscientiously, but dutifully, without much enthusiasm. With the exception of the moments mentioned above, Steiner found no joy in his studies. Thus it is not at all surprising that he strove to break out of the pedantic rut of college studies in as many ways as possible.

The first available possibility was to audit courses at the university. Steiner's *Autobiography* gives the impression that he especially admired Franz Brentano and Robert Zimmermann. This is not the case. We can begin with Zimmermann. In letters dated 1881, there are two passages that point to Steiner's negative appraisal of Zimmermann's work. In writing about his planned *Intuitive Thinking as a Spiritual Path*, he says "that it will not resemble Zimmermann's work" (38). Another passage reads: "What would Lessing say about Zimmermann's aesthetic or what would Schiller or Hegel say about 'Force and Matter' if they became aware that books with such content existed in German?" (38). The harsh critique of Zimmermann's work apparent here surfaces again in 1913 when Steiner recalled the impression that Zimmermann had made upon him as a student. Steiner had already studied Herbartian philosophy before encountering Zimmermann, who was viewed as one of the predominant Herbart scholars of his time. Steiner went to his lectures with high expectations. "That was a real disappointment. My regard for Herbartian philosophy was dampened by hearing Robert Zimmermann, who was a brilliant man, but an absolutely incomprehensible speaker."

His appraisal of Franz Brentano was similar. Steiner periodically attended his lectures on moral philosophy but was not impressed. In 1913, he noted that Brentano's lectures "did not make a strong impression on the young man" (ibid.). In fact Steiner was very critical of Brentano as a student, although he did study his work more closely around 1908. In 1900, he characterized him as an "intellectually brilliant pretender" (30). Still, he never ceased to have interest for Brentano's work and later would honor him both with a long obituary and an essay entitled "The Philosopher's Hands."

Steiner had great distaste for Erich Schmidt, a disciple of Scherer, who lectured on German literature. He held, however, the historian Ottokar Lorenz in high esteem. Not only Steiner but the entire student body was impressed by his liberal, critical spirit and his ability to be self-critical as well. He did not, however, have a lasting influence on Steiner's development.

If one disregards the few outstanding exceptions, it is easy to understand that Steiner sometimes expressed a general negativity about his time as a student. "Those were things that didn't have anything to do with me. Nowhere could one experience anything that was connected to the evolutionary impulses of the time" (185). He missed having the opportunity of encountering the central questions of the time—for instance, the problem of freedom or fundamental questions concerning modern science and the scientific method. What he found was, for the most part, merely an intellectual obedience that passed down knowledge and methods that were long past their flowering. He described "the academic scholarship of all the faculties" as "antediluvian" (185). The questions that occupied him found no answers in college; they were not even discussed. The outcome was that Steiner followed his own path of independent study in addition to his formal studies, focusing on light and sound, space and time.

It would seem that this judgment would need to be reversed when we take into consideration that it was at the Technical College that Steiner met Karl Julius Schröer, his true academic teacher and paternal friend. His significance in Steiner's life cannot be overestimated. The first mention of this encounter is resonant with the providential nature of the meeting. In January 1881, Steiner wrote to a friend: "Thanks to God and my good fortune, I have become acquainted with a man here in Vienna who—after Goethe, of course—is the greatest *Faust* scholar imaginable, a man who I hold in high esteem as a teacher, a scholar, a poet, a human being. His name is Karl Julius Schröer." (38). It is true that Schröer taught at the Technical College, and that Steiner met him there. The fact, however, that Schröer was teaching at the college was an "objective misunderstanding." Schröer was not a representative of recognized science; he was not viewed as belonging to the local guild of philologists. Emil Kuh, Hebbels biographer, had torn apart Schröer's 1875 book, *The Poetry of the Nineteenth Century in its Most Important Pieces*, in a review that labeled it "an off-the-cuff history of poetry." Erich Schmidt thought Schröer was addle-brained, and for the technicians and natural scientists at the college, he must have been an exotic figure.

Schröer, who was born in 1825, was fifty-four when he first met the eighteen-year-old Steiner. For part of his studies, he had been in Germany and picked up lingering traces of German idealism. He had made a name for himself as a scholar with his studies of the dialects of the German communities in the lands along the Danube. His true love, however, was reserved for Goethe. What drew Steiner to Schröer was the enthusiasm and warmth with which the latter embraced things. But although Steiner found the earnestness and the mood of soul that he experienced in Schröer's company comforting, Schröer couldn't help him find answers to his own questions, since he could find no inner connection to them. "I listened to all Schröer's thoughts with the greatest possible spiritual sympathy. Yet even in his company, I found myself in the position of having to develop independently the thoughts of my intimate spiritual striving" (28).

In one respect, Schröer left a deep imprint on the views of his student. In his opinion, "a time of the flowering of poetry" had come to an end with Goethe. Schröer lived inwardly as a citizen of Goethe's epoch in a time long past. Everything that had followed Goethe's work he viewed as the fall from once great heights. Through his lectures and discussions, Schröer led Steiner on a journey into this world. He saw, through Schröer's eyes, the sublime glory of the German classical period and viewed the present as a period of decline. In 1881, the twenty-year-old Steiner wrote: "It is now clear to me that not every period of time is equally rich with fundamental ideas. Often centuries are needed to spin such seminal thoughts out in all possible directions. These are the times of the epigones, as is the time we live in now" (38). Steiner returned repeatedly to this appraisal over a number of years. In an early essay from 1884 is the passage: "The heights of culture, upon which the Germans once stood, appear today to belong to the past. We young people look with sad longing back on those better days. It appears that the only task left for us is to be the gravediggers and the erectors of monuments for those great spirits who ushered in that magnificent period" (30).

The view of one's own time as a period of decline is a two-edged sword. On the one hand, it lends a certain stability—one can hold on to what has proven its worth in the past and is not inclined to embrace the new simply because it is new and modern. Steiner discovered in the ideas and work of Goethe's period, and in the language of German idealism, a deep resonance and a confirmation of his own inner striving. From this perspective, Steiner's assessment of his time provided him with some self-protective inner distance to what was going on around him, a stance he maintained until at least 1890. His time offered him nothing that he felt he could build on; he picked up the threads of Fichte's and Goethe's work.

On the other hand, such a distancing brings with it the danger that one turns away from one's surroundings, does not notice them and thus isolates oneself from one's own time and space. This did in fact happen to Steiner. An article from 1890 gives his verdict concerning modernism: "In our opinion, modernism is nothing other than the idiotic prattle of an immature populace that lacks entirely the goal of becoming mature" (29). Maintaining distance from his own time while concurrently seeking and finding guidance in Goethe's world was for a while an existential necessity. It wasn't until 1897 that he would shift direction and plunge completely into the world of modern literature, now with a very conscious, independent relationship to his world and its artistic strivings.

Through Schröer, who had for many years followed the tracks of the German communities that had settled in areas where the Hungarian and Slavic languages predominated and empathized strongly with their destinies, Steiner had also begun to ponder the question of the mission of German culture. He and Schröer saw Germany as an intersection of European development (30). Significant discoveries were being made in England and France, giving birth to a whole new slate of questions. One of these had to do with evolution. German thinkers approached this as a moral and philosophical problem. For them the most important aspect was not the factual proof of the origin and evolution of species, but rather the impact this would have on humanity's sense of its own identity. In England and France, human rights were being postulated. German thinkers strove to substantiate the idea of freedom and give it living meaning, while German statesmen addressed the challenge of realizing these rights in social and economic relationships. In relation to the culturally less-developed peoples to the east arose the task, especially for the German communities in Austria, of *"spreading the seeds of Western culture throughout the East"* (20). It was in this sense that Steiner and Schröer viewed the mission of the multitude of Germans—the Siebenburgen Sachsens, the Banat Schwabs, even the Volga Germans—who settled in the East: "Perhaps it is not the most insignificant part of the communal cultural work that these peoples carry on" (30). Such thoughts about the mission of German culture were not uncommon. In the 1860s, a number of liberals took the position that it was not in any way the task of Germans to assume political power over the other peoples of the Danube; their task was to bring European education and culture to the peoples of the East.

In addition to his lectures, Schröer offered practical courses in "verbal discourse and composition." During these exercises, Rudolf Steiner became acquainted with a number of the other students. Schröer let students choose the topics they wished to present, and through these choices the students were able to catch a glimpse of the questions that moved one another. This resulted in debates and conversations that quickly led to friendships. Most of the students who found their way to Schröer came from reduced circumstances and following graduation from the secondary school were unable to go on to the university. For the most part they had landed by mistake at the Technical College and had little interest in either technology or the natural sciences. The first of the friendships that Steiner describes in his *Autobiography* was with Emil Schönaich, who was a Wagner enthusiast; the next two, Rudolf Ronsperger and Moritz Zitter, both viewed themselves as poets; the fourth, Josef Köck, was a dour fellow, a dreamer. They all felt as though life had in some way been unkind to them. "Their efforts were crippled by a contemporary spirit, of which they wanted to have no part" (31). Steiner saw how these and other students, overcome by a feeling of resignation, turned to the popular trends of pessimism and materialism. Steiner fought against these tendencies in letters, in "words of real thunder" in discussions, and in endless conversations. As a comforter, an adviser, a confessor, Steiner, who was known as the "prior"—a nickname derived from *a priori*—did what he could to help keep up his colleagues' spirits. But the darkness of the time with its lack of perspective was at times stronger than he. His friend Ronsperger committed suicide, and Schönaich's life ended tragically. In a letter from 1890, Köck wrote: "You remember well how we once set out with such proud plans. But you had strong legs and courage; I remained behind. You climbed higher, ever higher. And now you are standing in the light. Oh, tell us what you see up there, describe to us the beauty of the world that is hidden from us—perhaps it will give us new courage..." (B 55). The only one of these friends who was relatively successful later in life was Moritz Zitter.

In 1900, looking back on his years as a student, Steiner saw the lives of his friends as being symptomatic of the general outlook in Austria and its development, symbolizing a political approach that robbed the masses of any hope of a meaningful existence and ushered in the decline of the Danube empire. The political show and the mood of deterioration were mirrored in the destinies of individual people.

> One politician called the present lives of Austrian Germans a graveyard, wherein lay buried a magnitude of hopes. An outsider would have a hard time imagining the reasons that have determined the destinies of Germans in the Danube countries and the alpine countries over the course of the last decades. But for someone like me, who spent the first thirty years of his life in Austria and who studied in Vienna in the 1880s, there is nothing in the development of Austria that cannot be understood. It could be seen in the destinies of individual people, which are nothing other than a repetition on a small scale of the course of evolution. (31)

In a brilliant essay, "Hoffmannsthal and his Time," Herman Broch attempted to characterize late nineteenth-century Vienna. He described the city as the "center of the European moral vacuum, in which emptiness was hidden by ornamentation and nothing was taken very seriously. A giddy hedonism had its heyday on a stage set with museum pieces, a 'joyful apocalypse.'" In contrast to Germany, where this period gave birth to a workers' frenzy, in Austria it led to what is known as the *Backhendlzeit*, a time of decoration and ornamentation. Although this description is fairly accurate when applied to some circles of the bourgeoisie, it masks the social misery of the lower classes and the hopelessness of those who strove to better their circumstances. The apocalypse was in no way joyful for them, and there were certainly no chickens in their pots. Behind the expensive ornaments and magnificent pageantry was a slowly spreading rot and the rise of the poisonous climate of the specifically Viennese form of anti-Semitism. Rudolf Steiner's attention was drawn to those who were not taken up by these tendencies and who found it hard to breath in this atmosphere. He summed up: "Only a few pulled themselves together to find satisfaction in life far from the public sphere in Austria; many, in unpleasant resignation, are addicted to a dull life of the philistine; more than a few have suffered a completely shipwrecked life" (31).

Steiner wrote little in his *Autobiography* about the bleak nature of the time during his years as a student or about the financial difficulties that forced him to earn money through private tutoring. He no doubt viewed these as being merely adverse outer circumstances against which also stood positive opportunities. He certainly grasped at the opportunity to study the books that interested him—but that he could not afford—in the college library or in the court library. He quickly caught up with the studies not offered at the Technical College. Even his early letters give evidence that he was quite well read in both philosophy and general literature. The time spent, however, with others and in personal conversations seems to have been most important, especially as he had had almost no friends during his younger years. "I had a great thirst for social life" (28). Steiner was introduced to ever-new social circles, primarily thanks to his friendship with Moritz Zitter. "He loved introducing me to everyone he knew" (ibid.). This modest social life was a boon after the loneliness of Neudörfl, even though it did not offer that much stimulation. In his *Autobiography*, Steiner compared Vienna and Weimar in this regard and wrote of the "narrowness, in which I was forced to live in Vienna" (28). In the small city of Weimar, Steiner found a wider connection to the "big world" and had more personally significant encounters. In Vienna, at least until 1884, Steiner spent most of his time in the society of other relatively poor students; their social life was limited to long walks through the streets of the city and cups of coffee in small cafés. He hardly mentions this ambiance, nor does he speak of Prater and excursions to the then still quite rural Grinzing. Only the time spent with other individuals had lasting significance, only the conversations.

At the end of the nineteenth century, Vienna was a city of music. Brahms, Bruckner, Hugo Wolf and Strauss lived there; the concerts, operas and operettas were public affairs, reviewed and critiqued by the music critic Eduard Hanslick. Hanslick favored Brahms above all others. He was an outspoken detractor of the work of Richard Wagner, who was not only favored by Anton Bruckner but by many of Steiner's acquaintances. One, who Steiner speaks of later, was Friedrich Eckstein, who walked to Bayreuth in 1882 to hear the first, private performance of *Parsifal*. Many of the "searching souls" of that time saw in Wagner's pageantry the harbinger of the new culture for which they longed.

Steiner, who never played an instrument, loved music. The "world of tone" appeared to him, as did pure thinking, to "reveal an essential aspect of reality" (28). He listened with enthusiasm to what he called pure music. Most of his college friends were Wagner enthusiasts. They celebrated the "strength of expression" and weighty significance of his music, things that Steiner found distasteful. He often went to concerts and to the opera with Emil Schönaich. "We always had differing opinions. The "expressive music" that sent him into ecstasy made my limbs feel like they were filled with lead; he was bored stiff listening to music that simply wanted to be music" (28). A performance of *Tristan* was for Steiner "deadly boring" (28).

Their difference of opinion concerning Wagner led to endless debates. Steiner spoke of Wagnerian "barbarianism" and spoke out against Wagner in the strongest terms, while his friend defended Wagner and spoke of him as the discoverer of true music. It is known that during this period of his life, Steiner was most enthusiastic about the work of Beethoven. But beyond that, we know little about his musical experience. What was his relationship to the music critic Hanslick, whom he later mentions a number of times? Did he listen to Mozart? Did he belong to the circle of friends of Johannes Brahms? We know that he was present for a performance of Bruckner's Fourth Symphony, but we don't know how he experienced this work. The only thing we know for sure is that, during his time in Vienna, music played an existential role in his life.

In 1896, he formulated in a brief, concise passage his thoughts about music. Goethe had written, "The dignity of art is perhaps most apparent in music as there is nothing substantial to be formed. It is purely form and content and ennobles everything that is expressed." Steiner commented on this thought:

> In reality, music has no archetypes. The musician creates form and content from within. Thus among all the arts, music is the least likely to be in danger of being seen in terms of what is placed in the world rather than in terms of how the artist works. For this reason, music is best suited to rise above the mundane and lead toward the deeper aspects of life, while letting the seriousness of reality be forgotten. (1-e)

CHAPTER 4

THE LONELY WANDERER

In his *Autobiography*, Steiner interrupts the descriptions of his friendships with a number of comments that cast a stark light on his inner life. On the one hand, the time he spent with his friends was significant and essential to him. On the other hand, he found himself confronted with epistemological questions that were just as important. He found himself living "a double life in his soul." Although his friends were interested in the questions that moved him, they had little to contribute. "I remained rather alone in the experience of these enigmas.... Thus my inner life was divided: I followed one path as a lonely wanderer, the other as a lively participant with others whom I held in affection" (28). This lonely striving toward knowledge, although imbedded as it was in Steiner's outer life, had its own laws and consequences. We can therefore follow the path of the lonely wanderer without worrying too much about the outer circumstances of Steiner's life.

Even as a schoolboy Steiner had struggled with two key questions. One concerned the nature of spiritual experience, the other the boundaries of human thinking. How does thinking find its way into the reality of what appears before us? Upon returning to Oberlaa from his first visit to Vienna, he began immediately to read Fichte's *Science of Knowledge*. It is remarkable that without knowing anything about Fichte's work or his place in the evolution of philosophy, the eighteen-year-old Steiner managed to find this work. How could he have known that Fichte would provide him with the challenge that he sought?

Steiner wrote, "I had reached a point in my study of Kant where I could formulate an idea (though immature) of how Fichte wanted to take a step beyond Kant" (28). Fichte had striven to substantiate the causal factors of human consciousness upon which Kant had developed his epistemology. This historical aspect of Fichte's work did not especially interest Steiner. He wanted to form a "stringent conceptual picture" of the life of the spirit in the soul. In Fichte he read, "The 'I' is that whose being (becoming) is—only in that it places itself in beingness—an absolute subject. It is, as it places itself; as it places itself, so it is; and the 'I' is firstly, solely and necessarily for the 'I.' Whatever does not exist for and of itself is no 'I'" (*Science of Knowledge*). As Steiner re-created the process leading to this and further conceptual stations, he was brought into an inner activity that helped clarify the nature of the self. It was decisive that Steiner not only rethought Fichte's ideas, but rather took them up actively. They led him initially to the conclusion that he summarized in 1924: "When the 'I' is active and engaged in observing its own activity, one has in an unmediated manner a spiritual presence in one's consciousness" (28).

In order to gain greater clarity concerning these thoughts, Steiner began to write them down. Luckily we still have this manuscript. It consists of ten pages, containing an introduction, the first chapter and the beginning of the second chapter. The goal of the introduction is to show that all types of knowledge throughout history have been brought forth by people, that it is individuals who are the bearers and creators of knowledge and that knowledge does not simply arise out of experience. "For we cannot determine through experience the cognitive value of this experience." He comes to the conclusion: "The source of certainty and thus also the science of knowing is in the cognizing individual." As the conclusions drawn by various individuals are sometimes contradictory or simply fragmentary steps in a larger developmental stream, it is necessary to undertake a fundamental study of human knowledge and its genesis. This is the task of epistemology. It "does not need to concern itself with the what of knowledge, but only with the how" (B30). In order to grasp the how of knowing, Steiner turns his attention to the true core of human identity, the "I." "We can see that in the rich multitude of experience, the core of the knowing individual, the 'I,' provides a stable center from which we will proceed." The fragmentary second chapter bore the title "The Theory of the Person or the 'I.'" This "I" was defined as the center of identity around which all the various actions of the person revolved and stood in relation to. It remains throughout time both qualitatively and numerically identical with its self. However, if one attempts to examine it explicitly, the following results: "The 'I' is the focal point of the full spectrum of experience and insight; to grasp this focal point is impossible, as it slips away whenever we try to find it" (B30). In other words:

The individual knows itself to be fully identical with itself, and the full range of individual experience focuses itself in one point; the "I" itself, however, cannot become the object of observation, since it is in essence not the objective center of the conscious experience with which it identifies itself. The latter is the psychological "I" that can become the object of reflection.

In this early epistemological fragment, even if it is quite influenced by Fichte, we find the germinal indications of a theme that will later be central in Steiner's work: the question of observation. In *Intuitive Thinking as a Spiritual Path*, he applies the concept to contrast the observed experience of thinking with the reflective activity of thinking about thinking. Here, he is more concerned with the question as to how the "I" can become an experience than with the construction of a concept of the "I."

Steiner's initial conclusion that the "I" cannot be observed is, even in this early fragment, not the final word. In the next paragraph, he goes on to describe how the "I" may be grasped: "The pure 'I' has no *is-ness* nor is it something in the strict sense of the word. The totality of its recognizable being is only given through its activity; we cannot know what it is, but we can grasp what it does" (B30). Steiner's concept of the "I" differs from that of Fichte, who also understood the "I" to be pure activity and saw this activity as taking on a certain stability, of settling into existence. For Steiner this concept was too narrow. The active "I" can be different in different activities. It modifies itself in relation to various activities and yet, in all its difference, remains identical to itself.

In this chain of thought, the eighteen-year-old Steiner demonstrates a transformation of Fichte's ideas in a manner that is absolutely characteristic for Steiner. He clearly supports Fichte's philosophical approach, but at the same time feels that the idea of the "I" settling into existence is a cul-de-sac. First, a cognitive philosophy is not concerned with producing a form of existence and, second, the concept of settling is much too rigid. Steiner conceives the "I" as something eminently fluid. He cannot, therefore, think it to be limited unto itself, but rather quite open to the world. With this conceptualization of the "I" as a continuously opening activity, Steiner laid the foundation for an understanding of the human self that would be a keystone in his anthroposophic work.

In his *Autobiography*, Steiner describes how he sought to find a way to an understanding of nature from out of this active core of beingness:

> Beginning with the "I"-being, I wanted to penetrate the creative processes in nature. Spirit and nature manifested before my soul in full contrast. I experienced a world of spiritual beings, and to me it was a matter of direct perception that the "I"—which is itself spirit—lives in a realm of spirit. But I could not reconcile physical nature with my experience of the physical world. (28)

In the above-mentioned fragment from 1879, this problem surfaces in the question of how "something completely foreign can enter the activity of the 'I'" (B30). This question would be relatively easy to answer if it applied simply to the recognition of the different parts of nature and their logical relationships, such as the leaves of the plant or the plant as a living being. One must, however, keep in mind Steiner's statement in his *Autobiography* that what he strove for was to truly grasp the objects and processes of nature in thinking, and that he wrote: "'Subject matter' that remains beyond the grasp of thinking, as something merely 'reflected upon,' was an unbearable idea to me" (28). The challenge was thus not merely to think about the lily or iron, but to grasp the very beingness of the object in thinking, to think the lily or iron. He wanted to understand how thinking made its way, unmediated, into the essence of the object. The fragmentary exploration ends, however, before Steiner begins to answer the question as to how something foreign can enter the activity of the "I."

Since the relationship between what is directly experienced and the inner activity of thinking remained a riddle, Steiner focused on deepening his understanding of the nature of the human "I." This led him from Fichte to the work of Schelling, especially his *Philosophical Letters Concerning Dogma and Criticism* (1795). The oldest surviving letter we have of Rudolf Steiner, dated 1881, speaks of his study of Schelling:

> In the night from January 10 to January 11, I didn't sleep a wink. I had struggled with various philosophical problems until after midnight and finally crawled into bed. Last year I had been striving to prove or disprove Schelling's statement: "Within each of us exists a secret, miraculous capacity to step out of the course of time into the naked reality of our true selves and there, immutable, to view what is eternal within us." I believed and still think that I have discovered this capacity within myself—I have been inclined to suspect it for quite a while; the full spectrum of philosophical idealism now stands revealed in quite a different form; what is a sleepless night when compared to such a discovery! (38)

Schelling expanded on this experience, "which can be brought forth only in freedom," as follows: "This intellectual experience appears when we cease to view ourselves as an object, when, within the inner chamber of the self, the observing self is identical to the self observed" (Schelling).

This passage is best understood when we proceed from the statement "The full spectrum of philosophical idealism now stands revealed in quite a different form." This remark indicates that Steiner is not speaking of an isolated experience. The new insight opened an organ of understanding that transformed his earlier concepts. The ideas of the German Idealists did not remain mere abstract thought constructions, brought forth by the "I" in the re-creation of another's thinking. They appeared to be born out of the inner substance of the "I" and belonged to the very essence of the "I" itself; this essence woven of the powers of freedom and love—not empty concepts but creative forces. There was an awareness that human activity and the organization of the human form both find their meaning in these qualities. This experience is first articulated in philosophical idealism, which strove to structure the world of thought in such a way that it corresponded to the forces of freedom and love. In doing so, it freed the entire world of thought from the rigidity of dogmatism and from the non-committal nature of criticism and brought it into a space of fluidity within which the "I" could move freely and creatively.

Following this shift in his understanding of the world of the human spirit, the question of the relationship to the natural world grew in significance for Rudolf Steiner. In pondering this, he came up with the idea of "writing a so-called peasant philosophy" (327), which would be inspired by the thoughts and sayings that had developed out of the peasant's daily contact with nature. Perhaps he also hoped to find in the peasants' way of thinking a balance to the scientific approach he was immersed in. In a letter, Steiner wrote: "I spoke of studying the philosophy of the peasants. This may have seemed strange to you, but I can assure you that not everything the peasant thinks is the product of sermons and whatnot; the people of the land have their own theories, their own unique sense of ethics and even aesthetics, some of which are quite interesting" (38).

Thus, in the summer of 1881, Steiner made a number of excursions to Munchendorf to study the life and work of the local schoolmaster, Johannes Wurth. From there he went on to Trumau to visit Felix Koguzki, an herb collector with whom he had become acquainted on the train to

Vienna. Koguzki was not there the first time Steiner visited Trumau on August 21; he did find him at home, however, when he returned the following Friday, August 26. Rudolf Steiner writes of this visit: "Above the entrance stood the words *"In Gottes segen is alles gelegen"* (God's blessing is in everything). I visited the cottage only once as a youth. A man lived there, who was outwardly rather unremarkable. When one entered his cottage, one saw that it was full of medicinal herbs.... One day each week, he would pack these into a satchel" (192) and take them to Vienna to sell. Steiner met the herb collector on the train when he was taking his herbs to market. The man's austere countenance and his deep, sober gaze caught the student's attention. It took Steiner awhile until he began to understand the older man's spiritual dialect. We don't know exactly how strong their friendship became that summer. In a letter written the day he met Felix Koguzki in Trumau, Steiner makes no mention of the visit: "I have just returned from Münchendorf after having walked from there to Trumau and back, about an hour each way.... On the way I became better acquainted with the lower Austrian people and have grown quite fond of them. They meet one with a remarkable attentiveness and quickly become quite trusting" (38).

Steiner does tell of accompanying the herbalist a number of times on his lonely treks. Koguzki tried "to explain each plant out of its essence, out of its esoteric background" (B83/84). Koguzki led him to the places where the rare plants grew and spoke to him about their properties. A poetic echo of this, not one that should necessarily be taken as an actual account, is to be found in the *Paralipomena* to Steiner's *Four Mystery Plays*. There the "lily" tells the "man with the lamp" what the "human" had told her about his travels with him:

> He told me about the walks on which he accompanied you, on which you collected herbs and roots for the apothecaries. And he told me how you had led him to a hidden place, where rare forms of plants were growing on a hard stone ledge, barely covered with earth, how there thunder and lightning raged, but in a manner that people would otherwise not know, and how, from a distant cave, the elements revealed their mysteries. (44)

The world of the elements revealed itself in thunder and lightning to the one standing upon the rock.

In his *Autobiography*, Rudolf Steiner summed up his thoughts:

> He gave the impression that he was simply the mouthpiece for spirituality from the hidden worlds seeking a voice. With him, one could look deeply into the secrets of nature. He carried on his back a bundle of healing herbs; in his heart, however, he carried the results of what he had gained from nature's spirit while gathering them.... From our first meeting I had a deep affinity with him. Gradually it seemed as though I were in the company of a soul from antiquity—one untouched by civilization, science, and modern views—who brought me natural knowledge of ancient times. (28, p. 29)

For Rudolf Steiner's spiritual striving to find a way into the creative essence of nature from a point centered in the human "I," the encounter with Felix Koguzki was not only a spiritual wink of fate but rather a spiritual revelation of the elemental world taking place with "thunder and lightning." Still, Steiner could take in the wisdom of the herbalist directly. He had to recreate the spirit language of nature, which spoke to him through Koguzki, through the activity of his own "I." Felix Koguzki, however, was significant for Steiner in yet another manner.

In an autobiographical lecture from February 4, 1913, Steiner speaks of the herbalist as "the harbinger of another personality," a theme we find again in what he wrote for Édouard Schuré in 1907: "I did not meet the M. [Master] at first, but rather his envoy, who was initiated into the hidden powers of the plants and their connection to the cosmos and to human nature. He was completely at home with the nature spirits and spoke about them with a certain dry lack of enthusiasm that called forth enthusiasm in his listener." The herbalist, the herb collector, prepared, either knowingly or not, the meeting with the true esoteric teacher who Steiner, using a theosophical term, calls the Master.

This encounter was made possible by a double path of preparation. Through his philosophical studies, Rudolf Steiner had acquired a fully conscious understanding of the eternal nature of the human "I." This led him to the meeting with Felix Koguzki. Koguzki was then able to illuminate for him the secrets of nature. Had he not been ready to hear what the herbalist could speak of, the latter would have remained silent, for he was bound by the law of the "old man with the lamp" from Goethe's "Fairy Tale": "You know that I am not allowed to illuminate the darkness."

Rudolf Steiner was reticent concerning the meeting with his spiritual teacher, barely touching on it a number of times. In his book *Mystics after*

Modernism, we find a description of the meeting between such a spiritual teacher and a student. There he writes of the teacher, the "Friend of God from the Oberland."

> No one knew when he had been born or when he died, nor what he had done outwardly in life. The fact that the writer had striven to keep these details of his outer life an eternal secret belongs to the manner in which he had chosen to work. It is not the "I" of a given personality born at a certain time that would speak to us, but rather the being of the "I," which is the cornerstone upon which "the uniqueness of the individual" evolves. (7)

One must think of Rudolf Steiner's teacher in a similar manner. He never mentioned the teacher's given name and said only that in his outer life he was as "unremarkable" as was Felix Koguzki. We know neither his name, his position, nor where he lived.

In 1907, Steiner spoke to Édouard Schuré about his meeting with the "Master," a conversation that Schuré later put into writing. This account must be taken with a grain of salt and has limited usefulness as a biographical source. It contains a number of mistakes and reflects both Schuré's sense of poetic license as well as his tendency to pathos. Two passages, however, are presented here because they seem to have captured something of the essential nature of this meeting. After Schuré had described Steiner's "almost feminine perceptiveness," he wrote about the Master: "It was a masculine spirit with the character of a ruler. He saw only the species as a whole; the individual had for him little meaning. He was unsparing both of himself and others. His will could be likened to a cannon ball, which, once it is fired, continues irrevocably toward its target, destroying everything in its path" (B 42). If one strips away the fierce rhetoric, one can imagine a personality whose actions are decisively guided by a sense of historical responsibility, without regard for the small matters in life. The second indication of the meeting that one finds by Schuré is that Steiner's training was brief: "Quickly he led him through the different levels of inner discipline to a state of conscious clairvoyance, rooted in conceptual integrity. Within a few months, in dialogue with his teacher, the student had become acquainted with the incomparable depth and beauty of esoteric understanding" (B 42).

In his own brief account, Rudolf Steiner emphasized that since his own spiritual experience allowed him to move independently in the spiritual world, his teacher focused on "the regular, systematic aspects of which one must be aware in the spiritual world. This personality used the work of Fichte to develop ways of seeing in which the seed of *An Outline of Esoteric Science*, which the boy wrote when he became a man, may be found. Much of what later evolved into *An Outline of Esoteric Science* was explored at that time in relation to Fichte's thought." In addition, the teaching focused on the proper orientation in the spiritual world: "The peculiar currents that flow through the esoteric world, which one can only recognize when one envisions an upward and downward double flow, appeared at that time in their full vitality" for his soul (B 83/83).

In the handwritten notes made in preparation for the lecture from which the passage above has been taken, Steiner speaks of "the double stream of time" and "the double stream of becoming." The notes close with a remark that, at that time, he had not yet discovered the second part of Goethe's *Faust*. Letters from the summer of 1882 speak of reading this part of *Faust*; the period that Steiner spent with Felix Koguzki probably ended in early spring of 1881, and the winter of 1881/82 seems to be the time of his work with the esoteric teacher. In February 1882, Steiner turned twenty-one years old.

The terse indications made by Steiner have been subjected to a number of interpretations. While making no claims to being conclusive, the following thoughts attempt to give an idea of how this period can be understood. We must proceed from the assumption that Steiner did participate in a path of esoteric learning. Although Fichte's thoughts provided a point of departure, the focus was not on philosophical exploration, but rather on the spiritual insights that can arise from the development of a philosophical chain of thought. Rudolf Steiner spoke of "regular, systematic things," which serve to orient one in the spiritual world. One part of this systematic inner structure was certainly the differentiation between the stages of evolution—old Saturn, old Sun, old Moon, and Earth are states in the developmental process described in *Outline of Esoteric Science* and can be found reflected in the human being and in nature as the physical body, etheric body, astral body and the "I." In the teaching of Spiritual Science the focus is of course not on the words or terms and concepts, but on the facts, perceptions and experiences to which the words point. The stages of evolution point toward the stages of aging; through this the concept of time becomes concrete. A person who is not schooled in spiritual teaching has a mental image of time that reflects the face of a clock or some other *spatial representation of time*. A first step is taken toward an understanding of time when, in the encounter with the spatial appearance of an object, one becomes aware of its age and arrives at a qualitative perception. A true understanding of time, however, arises only then when one recognizes its "double stream." This is the "recognition that there is a retrogressive stream of evolution, which interferes with the progressive stream" (262). Rudolf Steiner called these two streams involution and evolution and said: "Evolution is the expansion of the spirit into the outward appearance of substance. Involution is the contraction of the spirit within the soul nature. No evolution is possible without a corresponding involution. No involution is possible without corresponding evolution" (B 67/68).

Each evolutionary process has a double nature: a "coming into manifestation" and a "moving into the depths of inwardness." When manifest, the spirit is hidden; when hidden, the spirit is revealed. Evolution remains a riddle without an understanding of this double stream. Most important, one must be able to differentiate between these two simultaneous streams in oneself. The stream of thinking cognition is always retrogressive: it begins in the present and strives toward an understanding of the causes and conditions of what has come into being. At the same time, one longs to grasp what is in the process of becoming. One tends to think about the future by extrapolating from the present and thus all too often projections are the mere representation of a naïve causal construction. One forms a mental image of one stream of development, forgetting that this is but a reflection of a thought process.

True understanding becomes possible when esotericists observe these processes within themselves and come to the experience. The human being must become the key to understanding. One example in which this double relationship between involution and evolution becomes apparent is in the processes of speaking and listening. In speaking, something becomes manifest; in listening, it is taken up within. Speaking is the expansion and manifestation of the spirit; in listening, understanding and contemplating, it gains new life within.

The conscious inner experience of this double stream is what Steiner refers to in *How To Know Higher Worlds* as the "spiritual power of perception." In the first publication of this text in the magazine *Lucifer-Gnosis*, this power of perception was termed *Kundalini fire* (No. 24). Steiner once noted that the term *Kundalini fire* espresses a double stream, "initially warmth and light." He continued, "Until the Kundalini fire has been ignited, one can only feel one's way among the objects and beings of the higher worlds, the way one feels one's way in the night among the objects of the physical world. Once it is there, one illuminates the objects oneself" (B 51/52). In the passage mentioned from *Lucifer-Gnosis*, he further remarks: "How this Kundalini fire is ignited within the heart can be approached as an only esoteric teaching. Nothing is said about it publicly."

The two core qualities of light and warmth appear at important junctures in Rudolf Steiner's work. In the meditation, which raises Johannes into the spiritual heights in Steiner's first mystery play, Benediktus, the hierophant, speaks the following words:

> Light's weaving essence radiates
> through far-flung spaces
> to fill the world with life.
> Love's blessing pours its warmth
> through time's long ages
> to call forth revelation of all worlds.
> And messengers of spirit join
> light's weaving essence
> with revelation of the soul.
> And when with both the human being
> can join his own true self,
> he is alive in spirit heights.

And the divine light, the Christ-Sun, is called on in the last verse of the Foundation Stone meditation for the General Anthroposophical Society.

> Light Divine
> Christ-Sun!
> Warm thou
> Our hearts
> Enlighten thou
> Our heads,
> That good may become
> What we
> From our hearts would find
> What we
> From our heads would direct
> In conscious willing.

The warmth that leads to action and the light of understanding are brought into a relationship in which the clear light does not bring coldness to the warmth, nor does the fire of enthusiasm cloud the light.

Even if this approach to understanding the initiation by the Master was not valid—it was in any case a path of transformation, which awakened within the spiritual student a new, higher quality of life. Rudolf Steiner's teacher led him to a conscious practice of associating with spiritual forces and showed him how to understand these forces. There were no "theories" in the forefront of this learning process; it focused on spiritual techniques, the categorical elements that enabled one to orient oneself in the world of spiritual experience. Even with this new foundation of experience, Rudolf Steiner had to continue upon his spiritual-conceptual path independently. But having reached a new state of knowing, he could approach his questions differently.

In his *Autobiography*, if I am not mistaken, Steiner described this shift in consciousness in a more general manner. This becomes apparent if we understand that what is described does not merely reflect a shift in thought content, but rather the outcome of an existential spiritual transformation; that the forms of consciousness arise out of creative capacities of soul and spiritual dispositions. This is how Steiner speaks of it:

> Schiller spoke of the state of consciousness needed to experience the world's *beauty*. Is it not possible to think of a state of a consciousness, which can bear witness to what is true within the essence of something? If so, one cannot, in Kantian style, simply observe what is initially apparent in human consciousness and whether or not this is capable of grasping the true nature of things. One must first explore the state of consciousness through which one enters into such a relationship with the world, so that the latter reveals to one her true nature.
>
> And I realized that such a state of consciousness is achieved to some extent when we not only entertain thoughts that portray external things and events, but when we have thoughts that we experience as the *thoughts themselves*. This life in thoughts revealed itself to me as something completely different from the life of thought in ordinary existence and that of the usual scientific research. By increasingly penetrating the experience of thoughts, one discovers that spiritual reality comes to meet us within this life in thought. One follows the soul's path into the spirit. But the spiritual reality one meets upon this inner soul path one finds again in the inner being of nature. (28, pp. 34–35)

Thus, Steiner comes to an experience of himself as being independent both in the encounter with thought and with the natural world, and able to illuminate both thought and nature with an inner light. In this process thought becomes more concrete, nature more transparent and spiritual. One can recognize in this experience of thought, which is touched by the presence of the spiritual, an especially significant stage of involution.

Luckily, one document has been preserved in which this discovery is reflected. It was found in 1938 in the papers of Friedrich Theodor Vischer. It is an article, "The Single Possible Criticism of Atomistic Concepts," which Steiner had sent to Vischer on June 20, 1882. In the letter accompanying the article, Steiner emphasized, "What I develop in the article is not mere dialectic, but rather my own inner experience" (38). The article argues against the view that concepts and ideas are but abstractions of the sensory world. Steiner calls for an examination of the concepts and ideas themselves. "One must let the concept retain its own primordial nature, its own unique, innate form of existence and rediscover it in a new form in the objects of the sensory world." The concepts must first be experienced, an experience that Steiner had known even before his encounter with his spiritual teacher. It was obvious to him that this was an experience unknown to most of his contemporaries; they saw concepts as "representations of sense-perceptible objects" (38). He could now stand in freedom in the face of concepts and ideas, and in this relationship he discovered that the sensory world is but another form of revelation of the spirit. From within, through an intentionally heightened contemplative thinking, one grasps the formative power of the idea; the same formative power is encountered without, in nature's processes.

One is dealing with two forms of experience, both of which are important: In inner contemplation the driving forces reveal themselves in their lawfulness; in the sensory world one can observe their activity. The objective nature of the idea in the sensory world leads the observer to ever-new questions, through which one's inner activity can be tested. As Steiner wrote in the above-mentioned article: "Only when one acknowledges that perception offers one concepts and ideas—but in quite a different form from that pure thinking that is free of all empirical content and in which this form is most significant—can one conceive that one must take the path of experience" (B 63). There are then two forms of experience for a human being: the inner experience of the idea (involution) and the outer experience through the senses (evolution). For the human being, both of these forms are important. Everything depends on overcoming whichever form arises initially. In relation to nature, this occurs when, with warm interest, one follows the processes through which one comes into being, and in doing so immerses oneself step by step in the natural stream of time and the lawfulness of one's becoming. Through the light of the idea, which is always both result and goal, however, one follows in memory, and thus retrospectively, how things have become as they are. In this relationship between perception and idea, one finds the imprint of the double stream of becoming. One can see the downward stream of thinking in the process of transforming the idea into an imagination; the upward stream of warmth in the intensification of experience to the point at which thinking is able to illuminate its depths.

In his *Autobiography*, Rudolf Steiner closes the passage in which he writes of his struggle to achieve a state of consciousness that "mediates the true nature of the object" with a description of the state of consciousness for which thought becomes visible and nature becomes transparent.

> A spiritual perception was disclosed to me not through vague mystical feeling, but through spiritual activity that is fully comparable in clarity to mathematical thinking. I approached a state of consciousness that allowed me to justify my perception of the world of spirit, even to the forum of scientific thinking. I was in my twenty-second year when I had these experiences. (28, p. 35)

The twenty-one-year-old had found a point of departure to answer the question awakened by his study of Fichte: How can the "I" find the path to nature? Initially it became spiritually, pictorially clear to him that in addition to the ego activity of thinking, there is the no-less-important ego activity of perception. The "I" is both a thinking and a perceiving being. As Steiner admits in his *Autobiography*, it would still be many years before this insight would become a living experience. To begin with, however, as of 1882 he turned his attention to the natural sciences and set out on the path of scientific research.

He met in his studies the two concepts of light and sound, both of which were interpreted as vibrations. Steiner disagreed with this theory. The conscious exploration of perception revealed an essential difference between the two. In listening, we perceive tones and sounds directly, and we abstract from the droning, humming and singing, from the whistling and squeaking, the consolidating, nominalistic concept *sound*, which includes all the immediate sense impressions of hearing. On the other hand, we see lit and radiant objects; we see colors, shades of gray and darkness. We do not see light. The word *light* does not indicate a sum of perceptions. Light itself is invisible; thanks to the light we are able to see a tree or a candle. Light makes objects and colors visible. Thus the word light does not indicate a direct sense perception, but rather what makes visual perception possible. The light itself is not perceived. "Thus, for me, light was in fact an extrasensory reality *within the sensory world*" (28, p. 47).

> I told myself: Colors do not, as Newton believed, come from light; colors appear when light encounters obstacles to its own free development. It seemed to me that this could be seen directly from the experiments. This proved to me that *light* does not belong to actual physical entities. It presents itself as a stage between reality that is tangible to the senses and reality that is spiritually perceptible. (28, P. 48)

Light can thus become for thinking a bridge between the sensory and the extrasensory. It selflessly, without announcing its own presence, makes other things visible, allows them to reveal themselves in a manner similar to that of thinking, which forgets itself when it contemplates things and elucidates their relationships. That thinking has access to the things of the world, and that it can contemplate them in peace from afar, is due to light among other things.

For a student of the history of philosophy, this will call to mind the metaphorical allusions to light present in the works of Parmenides, Plato, and Plotinus, a theme that was further developed in the Middle Ages, continued until the Age of Reason and is even present in the work of Fichte and Hegel. Justifiably so. One must, however, be aware of the differences. Steiner's point of departure does not lie in a metaphorical interpretation of light. He is not interested in the simile Knowledge = Light. He is more interested in the question of a scientific conceptualization of light. His answer is that light is present in its beingness, whereas sound is a collective term used for a variety of phenomena. The scientific onset differentiates Steiner's conceptualization from the metaphorical approach found, for instance, by St. Augustine.

After Steiner had developed his thoughts on light and brought them to an initial conclusion, he discovered a second bridge between the sensory and the extrasensory. "Thus I arrived at the *sensory/suprasensory form*

Goethe speaks of, which to true observation—whether physical or spiritual—places itself between the object of the senses and what is perceived spiritually" (28, P. 48).

Form, or the *Gestalt*, does come into appearance in the sensory world and, thus, belongs to the sensory world to the extent that it is spatial and temporal: spatially, the *Gestalt* is a multi-membered totality; temporally, it is a continuous series of developmental stages. This spatial/temporal totality, the intricate tapestry of the parts and the developmental path, can only be grasped conceptually. The deciding factor is the observer's certainty that a linden tree is in fact a totality and that the parts can only be seen as integral parts of the whole; the whole not merely as the sum of the parts. Continued observation leads to the recognition of the relationship between the single member and the whole and the understanding that it is in fact one part of a larger organism. Thus the spatial/temporal manifestation is simultaneously a conceptual or sensory/suprasensory form.

Whereas light is an elementary phenomenon, which, in the encounter with other things, calls forth multi-colored impressions, the *Gestalt* does not only appear in a tapestry of manifold parts formed through a developmental process, there are also manifold species; one constantly glimpses the *Gestalt* in new forms. Thus it mediates between the concrete sense-perceptible being and the concrete individual spirit. Precisely in this realm is it possible to follow the polar processes of evolution within the sensory world and involution into the spiritual. One sees and experiences how *Gestalt* appears and evolves outwardly; in contemplative thinking one strives to understand the hidden laws of each type.

Steiner developed this line of thought alone. "At the time, I found no one with whom I could speak of these things." Looking around, Steiner's gaze fell upon Goethe. He stumbled on an essay entitled "Blissful Encounter," in which Goethe writes of his conversation with Schiller concerning the archetypal plant. "I found relief from the feeling that I was living in spiritual isolation only when I read and reread the conversation between Goethe and Schiller as they left a meeting of the society for Scientific Research in Jena" (28). It is well-known that in this conversation they were in disagreement whether the archetypal plant was, as Schiller thought, an idea, or, in Goethe's opinion, an experience. Just a year after first reading about this conversation, Steiner commented on it in a footnote to his edition of Goethe's work. "When Schiller contemplated what Goethe had described, it was clear to him that what was being spoken of was an idea." Schiller proceeded from the assumption that ideas and reality were polar opposites, "and in this sense the plant that Goethe had described did not lie within the reaches of the experiential." Goethe, however, had arrived at his idea of "the archetypal plant through a series of observations" (1-a). In this manner, the fundamental contradiction between idea and reality is overcome. The ideas are not simply experiences; they can be found through the experience of observational thinking.

What moved Steiner was the fact that an idea not only can be thought but also can be found through an experiential process. He became aware of Goethe's natural scientific writings and began to study them in detail. A number of "shorter expositions" came out of this study, which Steiner showed his teacher, Karl Julius Schröer. These writings were not yet "developed out of Goethe's way of understanding," but rather out of the concrete question at hand. Steiner merely noted in the conclusion that "Goethe's research will be given proper credit among scientists only when it becomes possible to consider nature from this perspective" (28).

During this period, Rudolf Steiner experienced something else that moved him deeply. In one of his many notebooks, there is an outline of a lecture that he gave on May 10, 1914, in Kassel: "My vision of thirty years ago. Its result in the Fr. Schles. press. It was the awkward expression of what slept in the background of my soul" (B49/50). Unfortunately, the articles that Steiner wrote for the Independent Schlesian Press in Toppau have been lost. We only know that they were written in the first half of 1882 from the letters of his friend Emil Schönaich. In the lecture on May 10, Steiner recalls the circumstances behind one of these articles. In doing so he speaks of himself in the third person:

> I know a person who, when he was twenty-three or twenty-four, had a sort of vision. He published this in a rather awkward manner. The vision was such that he placed the individualities who had made important contributions to German spiritual development during the end of the eighteenth and the beginning of the nineteenth century somewhat awkwardly in a kind of landscape. He didn't quite know why he had designed this landscape, or what Goethe had done, what Lessing, Schiller and Herder had done, except what they had all done having left this world and having entered into the world that a human being enters after passing through the gates of death. It was thus a vision of the life of these geniuses in the spiritual world. He had a

vision of what they are doing now. As a spiritual researcher, one has to ask oneself: What is the significance of such a vision? What does such a vision represent? Such a vision is an intense permeation of the human soul from out of the spiritual world. Certain influences from the spiritual world overcome the soul; they enter it and become something like a terrible dream that expresses itself in feelings and impressions that one then visualizes in a vision like this. Influences out of the spiritual world affect the soul.... The one having the vision feels, although this feeling doesn't rise to consciousness, that he is standing upon the earth and is observed from the spirits that have been sent to serve the evolution of humanity. This can become muddy; it then mixes in with the vision, which he then awkwardly clothes in words: how Lessing, like a general of the spiritual world, marches forward with Goethe, Schiller and Herder behind him, leading and guiding those who follow, those living upon the earth. (B49/50)

In trying to fathom what Steiner related, the first thing that comes to attention is the notebook entry: "It was the awkward expression of what slept in the background of my soul." The "vision" that affected the soul from out of the spiritual world is like an impulse that took hold of the sleeping, willing human. He felt himself to be seen by the spiritual world. He experienced it as his task to work in a way that was meaningful to those beings, who observed him from out of the spirit. This impulse permeated his soul and found resonance in Rudolf Steiner's conscience. He felt himself to be responsible to the spiritual powers. Out of the not completely conscious connection to the individualities now in the spiritual world, courage and esprit to take up his task grew in him.

This task came to him as though from without following his initiation by his spiritual teacher, following the filling of his soul from the spiritual world, following his first independent thoughts concerning knowledge of the natural world.

CHAPTER 5

GOETHE: A SOURCE OF HOPE

During the summer of 1882, when Rudolf Steiner was contemplating how to independently research and describe a natural scientific question, Karl Julius Schröer had an idea that was to have a decisive affect on the course of Steiner's life. On June 4, Schröer wrote to Joseph Kürschner and suggested that he entrust an upperclassman, Steiner, with the task of editing and publishing Goethe's natural scientific writings. Kürschner was at that time the editor-in-chief of Speman Publishing and in the process of producing a monumental edition entitled *German National Literature*. Schröer was also involved in this undertaking. Kürschner answered on June 21, saying that he was interested. Steiner knew nothing about this exchange. Through the month of July, he took his regular semester exams and in August he wrote to Albert Löger, his former teacher, about the approaching final year of his studies. It was only in September, when Schröer returned to Vienna after a long journey, that he spoke to Steiner about his plans.

Everything fell into place quickly. On September 28, Steiner wrote to Kürschner to say that he was willing to take on the project. Then, only five months later, he notified him that the work on the first volume was finished. Steiner must have plunged into the work with fiery enthusiasm immediately after speaking with Schröer. At the same time he made another decision. He gave up his plans to become a teacher and put a de facto end to his studies at the Technical University. A year later, he formally resigned his place at the university. In taking over the publication of Goethe's work, Rudolf Steiner embarked on a literary career with all its risks and challenges.

The publication of the first volume of Goethe's scientific writings is in many ways a remarkable feat. The body of literature that needed to be worked through was enormous. In addition to his work on morphology and geology, Steiner had to work his way through a large part of Goethe's letters, his journals and notebooks, as well as the corresponding writings of Goethe's contemporaries. In addition, there were a large number of technical questions that needed to be clarified.

Steiner had two helpers. Salomon Kalischer had produced a solid edition of Goethe's scientific writings in 1877. Even today, many Goethe commentators, often without realizing it, work with Goethe quotes discovered by Kalischer. Thanks to his work, Steiner knew the writings and where they had been found. A comparison of Steiner's work with that of Kalischer shows, however, that Steiner's contribution is independent of Kalischer's work. The second source of help was Karl Julius Schröer, who knew all of the previously published work well and certainly pointed Steiner in the right direction. In addition, he worked through the entire manuscript and the proofs with Steiner. It was under Schröer's guidance that the introduction took on its final form with precise footnotes and citations. The introductions to the later volumes lacked this philological polish both in the footnotes and in the presentation of the historical development of *Goethe's Theory of Color* as well as science in general. In other words, Schröer, who had recommended Steiner, made sure that the work was done well. The revision of the manuscript must have taken a number of months. Steiner gave Schröer the draft at the end of February 1883; a letter from May 11, 1883, indicates that the work had been completed. Not including Schröer's foreword, the first volume was completed in just nine months. For the majority of Goethe's manuscripts, Steiner used Kalischer's edition. His piece on the intermaxillary bone was the only exception. This Steiner compared with a previously unexamined handwritten manuscript and cited the diverging passages. Neither the philological precision nor the extensive notes are what set Steiner's work in this volume apart. The most important contribution is his interpretation of Goethe's scientific approach. It is in this that we can recognize the completely independent achievement of the then twenty-one-year-old student.

In the foreword, Karl Julius Schröer outlines Steiner's accomplishment, thus making him known to his literary contemporaries.

> Beginning with the scientific studies, I watched him being drawn to Goethe's personality. He dedicated himself to the study of the manuscripts with devoted enthusiasm. He recognized that they could only be adequately interpreted in the context of Goethe's entire being. He saw that the key to Goethe's way of thinking was to be found in the spiritual life of his time. Although not counted among the

philosophers, Goethe was certainly stimulated by the philosophical stream of his day and his own work affected the course of its development. The editor, here too working out of immediate sources, did not fail to strive for clarity in the historical context. (1-a)

Goethe's significance within science is still questioned today. The physicist Carl Friedrich von Weizsäcker remarked in the afterword to volume 13 of the Hamburg edition of Goethe's work that, poetically, Goethe was a star that "would accompany us on each and every travel." In addressing the actual content of the book, *Goethe's Theory of Color,* the star turns into a will-o'-the-wisp, and Weizsäcker writes, "How can such a magnificent, universal spirit make such a mistake? I know only one answer: because he wanted to." The perfidy of this statement is typical. Writers like to express their respect for the great poet; his poems are often quoted. His discovery of the *ossa incisiva* is acknowledged, but his polemic against Newton is not to be forgiven. Whoever speaks out against the father of modern physics must be in error—yes, must want to be in error. The result is that Goethe, although praised as a poet, as a scientist is seen as merely a lover of nature, someone who observed plants and tapped on rocks—in short, a dilettante and Renaissance man. Although the multitude of theoretical problems and questionable practical results in the technical and chemical industries seem to cry out for an in-depth, critical assessment of modern scientific praxis, this is not the case.

It is refreshing then when a scientist refuses to bow before Olympia and refrains from noncommittal poetry. This took place just as Rudolf Steiner was beginning his work on Goethe. On October 15, 1882, Emil du Bois-Reymond, an "officer in the spiritual bodyguard of the Hohenzollern family," as this doctoral candidate in physiology termed his Berlin university, held a talk titled "Goethe and No End." Even *Faust* had displeased him. He thought that "Faust, instead of going to the royal court, printing paper money and then traveling into the fourth dimension to seek out the mothers, would have been better off to have married Gretchen, legitimized his child and invented the electrical generator and the vacuum pump." Du Bois-Reymond primarily attacked Goethe's scientific work. He conceded that Goethe had made a couple of discoveries, but scientifically one would have been just as far without them. In general, Goethe, together with natural philosophical idealism, had damaged German science. His elemental phenomena were illusions; he had misjudged the value of experimentation, and his theory of color was the "stillborn game of an autodidactic dilettante." These are honest words, and even Steiner acknowledged that du Bois-Reymond was "perfectly correct given his point of view." "Any polemic against him that was based on the same premises would be unjustified.... That others come to different results based on similar premises is a matter of inconsequence" (1-a).

In addition to the rejection of Goethe as a scientist, which rarely appeared as openly as by du Bois-Reymond, was the attempt at the end of the nineteenth century to connect his work to that of Darwin. In *General Morphology* and in his *Natural History of Creation*, Ernst Haeckel presented Goethe as the father of the theory of heredity. Haeckel viewed Goethe's idea of the "type" as the actual beginning of the hereditary process; it evolved and diversified through selection, mutation and adaptation. There was opposition to this interpretation. Others asserted that the "type" was merely an abstraction, an idea that had no reality. When Salomon Kalischer published Goethe's writings in 1877, he included an extensive introduction in which he supported Haeckel's position. He wrote that "alone, Goethe's well-known realism and the eminently objective character of his thinking leave no doubt that a purely ideal notion of the 'type'" would not satisfy him. Kalischer came to the conclusion that Goethe's archetypal animal was nothing other than Haeckel's archetypal cell or Cytode. Kalischer was more than willing to accept Goethe as a natural scientist. He saw him as "the creator of ideas that form the secure footings of today's science" (ibid.). Goethe was different than the "professional scientists" who made their way through abstraction from the specific to the general, because of his highly trained intuitive capacity. At the same time, it was clear to Kalischer that Goethe erred "when pure observation cannot lead to certain conclusions, but rather experimentation is needed...in the realm of physics" (ibid., S. LVIII).

These remarks illustrate the difficult field that Steiner entered with his interpretation of Goethe's work. His striving was twofold. First, he wanted to prove that Goethe's epistemological approach was justified in scientific research. To do so, he had to show that Goethe was systematic in his experimental approach, that he strove to bring the totality of the phenomena to appearance and that the conditions under which specific observations were made possible were drawn from the nature of the phenomena itself. In connection with this, he also had to show that Goethe had developed a new approach to understanding the organic, a method of research and observation that had grown out of the nature of the organism. His second challenge was to give a true interpretation of Goethe's work. He wrote that "the attempt will be made to explain Goethe out of his own work" (30). He did not attempt to measure Goethe's accomplishments using premises derived from other approaches. Rather he tried to explain "Goethe's way of seeing purely from the point of view of Goethe's own nature, from the totality of his spirit, without applying the prejudices of any other positive point of view" (1-a). In other words, Goethe's approach to research should be justified based on a factual, historically accurate presentation of his scientific work.

Rudolf Steiner began the edition of Goethe's scientific writings with his work on morphology. These could be linked with the contemporary discussion; the prejudice against Goethe in this field had not yet become rigid and the amount of observable material was so large that Steiner could hope to awaken interest and understanding for the work. In the historical introduction, Steiner used a multitude of examples to show that Goethe always proceeded from what could be experienced, that he observed concrete facts and processes, how he increased the number of specific observations, comparing and ordering them, and how, after discarding what proved to be coincidental, he arrived at what he understood to be an idea. "The method that Goethe applied remains based on pure experience even when he raises himself to the level of the idea" (1-b). Steiner supports this assertion by presenting the historical development of Goethe's botanical studies, using passages from the *Italian Journey* as well from letters. Goethe's anatomical and osteological studies were equally suited to show the reader how, through an increasingly exact descriptive approach, Goethe came to an idea. In this manner, Steiner was able to show that Goethe was an eminently experiential scientist, that he never began with a hypothesis or a preconceived idea but let himself be taught by nature itself, and that he strove only to express what nature would say. An idea was for Goethe the result of an experiential path.

The morphological studies are studies of form, of the *Gestalt*. *Gestalt* is what evolves and is passed from one generation to the next; it is the signature of the living organism. It is thus the central question in any attempt to understand life. The "type" comes manifest in the *Gestalt*. Steiner's first task in his interpretation of Goethe's work was to accurately define the meaning in which Goethe used the term "type." He was faced with two contradictory interpretations. One viewed the "type" as an abstraction, simply the sum total of various characteristics; the other, the Darwinian view, saw it as an actual archetypal form that had evolved through selection and adaptation. Abstraction or thing? This erroneous either-or was much discussed in the early 1880s. Steiner showed that with the term "type," Goethe had indicated the presence of a creative idea in the experienced world, in the living organism, and had described the way in which this active, generative idea manifested. In doing so he pointed out emphatically the difference in the causal relationships found in organic and inorganic phenomena.

> In inorganic phenomena, the causal relationships between the single parts or moments of a process stand in the foreground, each part reciprocally conditioned by the others. This is not so in organic phenomena. Here it is not the parts of an organism that determine one another, but rather the whole (the idea) that determines each and every part in accordance with its nature. We can follow Goethe in calling this self-determining whole an entelechy. Entelechy is thus the force that calls itself into existence from within itself. Once manifest, it has sensory existence, continuing however to unfold in the manner determined by the entelechy. (1-a)

In fact, each living organism appears before us as a totality; we understand each of its parts out of a recognition of the whole. It appears always in the process of development, and we recognize it at its different formative stages. It is imbedded in a greater context. The idea of the "type" in the living organism is the unvoiced precondition of Darwin's theory: the striving, adapting, changing, evolving being. Only a true being, the living "type," has the capacity to bring about the changes that Darwin described.

After identifying Goethe's "type" as the living principle that gives the organism its specific form from within, he goes on to explore the concrete formative expression of the "type" based on its two integral gestures of expansion and contraction. "In the whole life of the plant, three expansions alternate with three contractions. Everything that enters as differentiation in the plant's formative forces—which are identical in their essential nature—stems from this alternating expansion and contraction" (WL88). Steiner describes the forces of concentration in the seed, the bud, the stamen and pistil, and those of expansion in the leaves, blossoms and fruit.

He then shows how these are the "types'" response to specific environmental pressures—the life of the seed within the earth, the life of the bud in below-freezing temperatures. This threefold process takes hold also of the physical substances that are part of the plant's metabolism. In the earth, in the realm of the roots, the plant is dependent on the surrounding, inorganic environment. "Each subsequent organ thus receives a nourishment prepared for it, as it were, by the preceding organ. Nature progresses from seed to fruit through a series of stages in such a way that what follows appears as the result of what precedes. And Goethe calls this progressing *a progressing upon a spiritual ladder*" (WL88).

It is important to recognize that Steiner did not merely interpret Goethe's idea of the archetype from a general philosophical standpoint. He took his interpretation into specific questions of plant physiology. That Steiner's approach was correct is evident in his ability to follow the thread into the details. Steiner concludes with the following summary:

> The ideas presented here are the elements inherent in the being of the archetypal plant—inherent in a way that conforms, in fact, only to this archetypal plant itself, and not as these elements manifest in any given plant where they no longer conform to their original state but rather to external conditions. (WL88)

A description of the animal organization follows the exploration of the archetypal plant. We want to take a closer look at this description. In the differentiation of inorganic nature, vegetative life and animal existence, we find fundamental elements of Steiner's later anthroposophic work in an especially clear conceptual framework. The relationships described here in 1882 appear in 1904 as those of the physical, etheric and astral organizations. The plant is a general expression of life in the characterized alternation of expansion and contraction, formation and refinement of substance. "In the case of the plant, the whole plant is in every organ, but the life principle exists nowhere as a particular center; the identity of the organs lies in their being formed according to the same laws" (WL88). In the popular vernacular, the plant as a whole is thus the expression of the "leaf." The life of the plant is completely dependent on the environment. The archetype of the animal appears in quite a different relationship to its sense-perceptible manifestation. The animal organism is differentiated into functionally different systems of organs. The archetype makes use of the various organs. "In the case of the animal, every organ appears as coming from that center; the center shapes all organs in accordance with its own nature" (WL88). But this center is to be found, in a certain sense, above the organs. The individual organs are not metamorphoses of the center, but rather merely determined by it. In different animal species certain systems of organs stand in the foreground: in one species, certain sense organs; in another, the metabolic system; in yet another, the organs of movement are more highly developed. At the same time, the animal, although it must also adapt to its specific ecology, has a higher degree of independence from the environment than does the plant.

Finally, it was important for Steiner to clarify the manner in which the "type" is recognized. If this were to take place only within the boundaries of intellectual concepts, one would arrive at the view that the "type" is merely the interaction of a series of factors, the product of a series of causal relationships. This view, which is quite common still today, does not reflect reality, even though many such interrelationships can be identified. Initially, the type comes to consciousness in unmediated beholding. Goethe recounts in his "History of My Botanical Studies" that he began with direct observation of the plant kingdom. "I followed all the forms, as they presented themselves to me, through their changing shapes." He came through active observation of the *Gestalt* to the idea "that observation could be enlivened in a still higher manner," that present "beneath the sense-perceptible form [was] a suprasensory archetypal plant...and thus at the end of my journey, in Sicily, the genetic identity of all parts of the plant became for me self-evident" (1-a). Thus it was that Goethe became convinced that he beheld the idea, the "type." Steiner commented on this experience of the "type."

> It is characteristic of the ideal form of the "type" of the organism, in fact, that it consists of spatial and temporal elements. For this reason, it also appeared to Goethe as a sensible-suprasensory form. It contains spatial-temporal forms as ideal perception (intuitive). (WL88)

The roots of this view, which can grasp the suprasensory in the sensible, lay for Goethe in his understanding of Spinoza, who spoke of *scientia intuitive*. Intuitive knowing grasps the eternal in things. "Nature hides God! But not from everyone," noted Goethe. In his essay "On the Power to Judge in Beholding," he describes the path upon which he came to this manner of knowing. He made himself, "by observing the never-ending creativity of nature, worthy to become a spiritual participant in her productions" (1-a). Those who observe the plants and animals normally focus their attention on the sense-perceptible details of, for instance, the plant, and the gentle presence of the whole is usually not brought to consciousness. Only through conscious awareness and active, co-creative thinking, which intentionally calls the complete impression to mind and in wakeful beholding recreates the formative tendencies, is the presence of the wholeness in the sense-perceptible brought to light. What can be grasped conceptually and what is sense-perceptible "are not identical, but the concept no longer appears outside of the living unity as a natural law, but rather within it as a principle. What we call the 'type' permeates the organism—not sense-perceptible but fundamental" (1-c). Productive, intuitive comprehension penetrates sense perception and grasps the ideal quality that is active in it.

Rudolf Steiner's interest in intuitive comprehension—which was postulated by Spinoza, denied by Kant, and practiced by Goethe—is easy to understand. In Goethe's work, he found a bridge to the suprasensory that was rooted in the reality of the phenomenon. Goethe's path toward understanding nature was for Steiner the first step toward higher knowledge in the context of his later anthroposophic work. Goethe was welcomed as a fellow traveler in his loneliness. It seems, though, that already here, in his earliest Goethe interpretation, Steiner takes a step beyond what Goethe so gently points toward. He speaks of a way of knowing,

> that can apprehend not merely what is sense-perceptible, but also what is purely ideal, by itself, separated from the sensory world. Now one can call a concept that is not taken from the sensory world by abstraction, but rather has a content flowing out of itself and only out of itself, an *intuitive concept* and knowledge of this concept an intuitive one. What follows from this is clear: *An organism can be apprehended only in an intuitive concept*. Goethe shows, through what he does, that it is granted to the human being to know in this way. (WL88)

Goethe always emphasized the connection between the power to judge in beholding and through sense experience. Steiner points toward the "purely ideal, by itself" that can be apprehended, "separated from the sensory world," because he was permeated by the view that intuitive conceptualization, which holds true in the sensory world, has its source in the suprasensory.

It took until September 15, 1883, for the complete text of the first volume of Goethe's scientific writings to be sent to Kürschner. In March 1884, when Joseph Kürschner had edited Steiner's work and sent it to the printer, he wrote to Steiner: "I have truly taken it to heart to help your masterful work find full acknowledgement. Today, I am pleased to continue your work and regret only that Goethe did not write six volumes of scientific writings instead of only three" (38). Further recognition was soon to follow. Influential academics gave the work good reviews, such as the Viennese geologist Eduard Suess, who congratulated Schröer on his student. One could read in the *Literarischen Zentralblatt für Deutschland* that the edition of Goethe's scientific work promised to be "one of the most valuable contributions to the collection" of German literature, and the Munich Daily regarded "Steiner's presentation as the most significant in this field" (38). The philosopher Eduard von Hartmann, to whom Steiner sent a copy of his work, honored him with an extensive critical review. It looked as though Steiner had made his breakthrough in the academic world. Was the road to a scientific career now open?

Rudolf Steiner, who knew the value of what he had accomplished, no doubt anticipated that it would not merely be noticed and praised by a handful of professors, but that this exceptional achievement would open the door to an academic career. Weren't Schelling and Nietzsche made professors as young men?

Chapter 6

IN NEED OF SPECIAL CARE

It took Rudolf Steiner only a few months to finish the first volume of Goethe's work, and it was printed within a year. In 1897, thirteen years later, after constant insistence by the fully resigned Kürschner, the final volumes were ready. We often find this fluctuation between periods of highly productive activity and times of holding back in Rudolf Steiner's biography. The structure of the first Goetheanum was finished between October 1913 and July 1914, but then World War I began and slowed the building process dramatically. When the building burned on New Year's Eve 1922/23, it had still not been finished. In 1902, Rudolf Steiner envisioned developing spiritual-scientific work in Germany based on an understanding of reincarnation and karma. His efforts were met with little understanding. After a further ten years of preparatory work, he made another attempt in 1912. Once again his approach found no echo. Only in the last years of his life did he put all his energy into realizing his original intentions.

These periods of restraint were of immense significance in Rudolf Steiner's spiritual development. Until 1897, the slowing of his professional development was connected with his work on Goethe. Looking back, he acknowledged the meaning of this apparent delay for his spiritual development.

> Because my destiny brought me the Goethe task as part of my life, this development was slowed considerably. Otherwise I would have pursued my spiritual experiences and described them exactly as they presented themselves to me. My consciousness would have widened into the spiritual world more rapidly, but I would have felt no need to work hard at penetrating my inner being.... While I worked to interpret Goethe, he was always beside me in spirit, admonishing and continually reminding me that one who rushes too quickly along the spiritual path may attain a circumscribed experience of spirit but leaves behind the fullness of life, poor in the substance of reality. (28, pp. 90–91)

The time in Vienna from 1884 until 1890 is especially colored by this gesture of restraint, as the acclamation that Steiner received for his initial Goethe publication had no impact on his daily life. His scientific success did not open the door to an academic career. He ended up taking a position as a private tutor. During this period, he addressed himself not only to his tasks as a teacher, but had time to continue his Goethe studies, do extensive philosophical research, explore questions of aesthetics, edit the *German Weekly* for six months, and still be able to cultivate a rich social life. He became acquainted with the Catholic theologians from the University of Vienna, with the theosophists who gathered around Marie Lang and Friedrich Eckstein, and with a number of Austrian poets. He was a regular at the Café Griensteidl, where he spent time with the poets of "young Vienna" and became acquainted with Viktor Adler and Engelbert Pernerstorfer, the leaders of the Austrian Social Democrats. In short, the time of restraint widened the horizon of his practical experience and knowledge of the world. But let us return to 1884!

By the summer of 1884, Rudolf Steiner, who had withdrawn from the Technical College in the fall of 1883 without taking his final exams, had no vocational perspectives or income. Karl Julius Schröer, who was also an outsider, could not do much for him, but he recommended him to the local Minister of Education, who found him a position with the family of Ladislaus Specht, who ran a cotton import business. On June 16, 1884, Pauline Specht asked Steiner if he would be willing to take on the position of private tutor for her sons. It wasn't the sort of position that Steiner necessarily had hoped for, but he had given private lessons for the last eight years. In the beginning of July he must have written a despairing letter to his friend Emil Schönaich, who, alarmed by the tone of Steiner's letter, replied by the next mail: "Your letter from yesterday distressed me greatly...each word told me that you are deeply troubled.... My only friend, what has happened to you? I have never known you to complain." Unfortunately, this "sad, disheartening" (B51/52) letter disappeared. We can only assume that Steiner felt bitter about having to give up his freedom, seeing his hopes disappear, and having to assume a very regular job as a private tutor. On top of this, the family did not live in Vienna at that time, but in Vöslau, some twenty miles south of the city. They moved into Vienna in the autumn of 1885. Later, Steiner once mentioned his "Vöslauer period" (38). The practical consequence was that, for over a year, Steiner was away from Vienna, splitting his time between Vöslau and Brunn, where he lived in a tiny room in his parents' house. The Vöslauer period was a watershed in Steiner's life. His life as a student came to an end, as did his ability to spend his time as he chose. When Steiner returned to Vienna in 1885, he began a completely different life, which took him away from the society of struggling students, and, depending on how one looks at it, placed him in "better circles."

Steiner was fortunate to have found the Specht family. The atmosphere at home was intellectually stimulating, music was cultivated, and there was great literary interest. Ladislaus and Pauline were generous, open and tolerant, and well-to-do although not wealthy. During the Vöslauer period, there were "small differences." Steiner, who had been used to living a very free life as a student, now found himself in a fairly structured situation. But within the course of a year, things had fallen into place and Steiner had become a welcome addition to the family. Although he certainly didn't earn much money working for the family, he didn't have to worry about his daily expenses, he was relatively free, and he could occasionally afford to buy a new book. Through Ladislaus Specht, he learned about the expansion of international trade. He found Specht's negotiations between cotton dealers in America and India and the Austrian textile manufacturers extremely interesting. He studied "the samples of American and Indian cotton that were piled in the office" (203). Attached to each sample was a strip of paper with exact specifications, and he learned how to read the coded dispatches with the offers for different amounts of the various types of cotton.

Although Ladislaus Specht played an important role in Steiner's life, Pauline Specht came to play an even more important one. She concerned herself with the education of her children. "She was talented and very enthusiastic about music. When the boys were still young, she taught part of their music lessons herself." She cared about her son's development. "One found in her a wonderful expression of motherly love" (28). She viewed psychological or moral development as being "related to a healthy or unhealthy physical constitution. In other words, her medical view of the human being was instinctive and was, consequently, somewhat naturalistic" (28). Her medical thinking had a significant background. Pauline Specht had been friends since her youth with the famous Viennese doctor Josef Breuer (1842 to 1925) (28). Breuer was one of the leading figures at the Viennese School of Medicine. He had studied under Rokitansky, Skoda and Oppoholzer, all of whom had been influential in the development of the Viennese school, and had gone on to make significant contributions in the field of physiology with research into the autonomic regulation of respiration and into the function of the cochlea *(Bogengänge)*. During the 1880s, Breuer's work focused on hysteria and depression, and he explored the possibility of alleviating the effects of these psychic disturbances through the use of hypnotism. Today he is best known on account of his connection to Sigmund Freud, who, based on Breuer's subtly interpreted discoveries, went on to develop psychoanalysis. Breuer visited the Spechts from time to time, and Steiner had the opportunity to listen to his conversations with Pauline Specht. Here he learned of the questions that most concerned the doctor: the problem of drug addiction and its accompanying illnesses, mechanisms of suppression, and extraordinary states of consciousness. Such questions interested Steiner immensely and he continued to ponder them throughout the years in Weimar and in his later anthroposophic work (compare 30; 178; 253). In this manner he became acquainted with themes in contemporary research—for instance, Wilhelm von Brücke's work on the physiology of the brain. In any case, as late as 1924 he spoke of "the Viennese School of Medicine, with which I actually grew up" (316). To some extent, he had Pauline Specht to thank for this connection to what was at that time the leading school of medicine in the world.

The encounter with the school of medicine opened for Steiner new horizons. As though through an ocular, he was able to study the social effects of a scientific way of thinking driven to the extreme. Pure natural science celebrated its triumph in Viennese medicine. Research was focused primarily on diagnosing illnesses. One of the leading anatomists of the Viennese school, Carl von Rokitanski (1804 to 1878), performed more than 85,000 autopsies and made pathological anatomy a diagnostic discipline. The enthusiasm for diagnoses displaced the interest in therapy. There was a general notion that one should not intervene in the natural course of an illness. This position, represented most strongly by Joseph Dietl, was called "therapeutic nihilism," a philosophy that was to be found not only among the doctors but also among many Viennese thinkers. "Otto Weininger, Richard Wahle, Karl Kraus and Ludwig Wittgenstein were convinced that it was not possible to heal social ills, nor the degradation of language. Bertha von Suttner, Rosa Mayreder, Josef Popper-Lynkeus, Theodor Herzl and Otto Nuerath were vehement opponents of this view" (Johnston).

Joseph Breuer also did not support this view. Steiner indicated, however, in his *Autobiography* that Pauline Specht was inclined to think this way and that the conversations between her and Breuer allowed him to become acquainted with this approach and follow the discussions concerning it.

Pauline and Ladislaus Specht learned to appreciate Steiner over time and showed a remarkable willingness to tolerate his wishes and idiosyncrasies. In a letter, written shortly after Steiner's move to Weimar in 1890, he wrote, "You always gave me everything I most needed: concern for my welfare and friendly acceptance. Your generous nature enabled you to overlook unpleasantness caused by my intermittent moodiness and dissatisfaction. I value that greatly and will always do so. I also owe you gratitude for your helpfulness, something that the inexperienced bookworm often needed" (39). Pauline Specht took care of Steiner during a long illness in the beginning of 1887. During his convalescence, Steiner wrote to a friend: "I have been given much more than I deserved and I owe my returning health not to my own efforts but to this extraordinarily dear human being. The woman of this house is one of the best women I have ever met" (38).

There was, however, one moment of deep dissent between Ladislaus Specht and Rudolf Steiner. Steiner had commented on Judaism in a review of Robert Hammerling's epic novel *Homunkulus*. In the review, Steiner describes "racial conflict" as the most disgusting form of social strife and takes a strong stance against all forms of anti-Semitism. At the same time, he wrote:

> We can't overlook the fact that today Judaism still appears as a closed block and as such has often intervened in the development of modern society in ways that have been less than supportive for the ideals of Western culture. Judaism as such has come to an end. It has no real place in contemporary ethnicity, and the fact that it has been able to sustain its existence is a mistake of history, the effects of which will make themselves known. It is not the form of the Jewish religion alone, but more importantly the spirit of Judaism, the Jewish way of thinking, that is meant here. (35)

The Spechts were Jewish and when Ladislaus read the article, Steiner wrote:

> He turned to me, filled with pain, and said, "What you have written here cannot be interpreted as friendly. But the thing that really troubles me is that it was your close relationship with us and our friends that provided you with the experiences that allowed you to

> write about Jews in this way." He was wrong, however. My article was based solely on a survey of cultural history; there was nothing personal in my judgments. But he was unable to see this. His response to my explanation was, "No, according to this article, the man who is teaching my children is no friend of the Jews." Nothing could convince him otherwise. (28)

Ladislaus Specht was sovereign enough to overlook this faux pas, and the relationship between the two men remained warm and friendly despite their differences.

Steiner's actual work in the family was to take care of the four boys—Richard, Otto, Arthur and Ernst Specht. The parents worried most about Otto. Steiner wrote of him: "When I came into the family, he had barely acquired the rudiments of reading, writing and arithmetic. He was considered so abnormal in his physical and mental development that the family doubted that he could be educated at all. His thinking was slow and sluggish, and even slight mental exertion caused a headache, lowered vitality, pallor, as well as alarming emotional behavior" (28). Steiner felt that an appropriate form of education could awaken the sleeping capacities of the boy. It was agreed that Otto, as much as was possible, would be cared for and taught by him. First he had to win the child's trust. "After a short time, I succeeded in gaining the boy's love." In the beginning, Steiner could only hold the boy's attention for short periods of time. Longer lessons and any intensive learning had negative effects on his health. Steiner had to use the short time as conscientiously as possible. The preparation of lessons took many hours and each step had to be considered carefully "in order to take the greatest advantage of the boy's intellectual capacities in the shortest possible time and with the least strain on his mental and physical forces" (28).

In the course of the first two years, Steiner was able to help the boy overcome his learning weaknesses. Otto was able to follow the lessons at the *Gymnasium*. His health problems also improved markedly. His constitutional weaknesses retreated into the background. This educational challenge was for Steiner a study of psychology and physiology. He had to learn to measure the effects of his teaching as they expressed themselves in the boy's condition. He soon learned to differentiate the different kinds of exertion called forth by the various subjects and to balance them against each other. Through fine movements of the limbs he learned to offset the one-sided exercise of the intellect. Looking back he noted, "I am grateful that destiny brought me such a circumstance in life. I gained an understanding of human nature in a living, practical way that otherwise would have been barely possible" (28). As their tutor, it was understood that Steiner would help the boys with their homework, take them on walks in the park, go to concerts with the older boys, and watch over their play. With them he learned to play, something he had missed as a child, especially during the summer holidays when he accompanied the family to Unterach on Attersee.

Richard Specht, the oldest of the four sons, wrote down his memories of those days shortly after Steiner's death. Although this account contains a number of inaccuracies and exaggerations, it does capture the way that the highly gifted young man experienced the time.

> He looked exactly as he did later with the somewhat pale, slightly wrinkled face of an ascetic and brown eyes behind clear eyeglasses. He was tall, with long black hair and a long neck with a prominent Adam's apple. The long mantel that he wore gave him a somewhat spiritual appearance in which there was also a hint of a philosopher and a taste of sanctimonious pedantry.

Specht went on to mention the "strange mix of scholarly earnestness and boyish playfulness" and the remarkable strength of will with which Steiner addressed his work.

> Physically he was so weak that he would fall to the ground when one of us boys out of love or exuberance would jump up and throw our arms around his neck. Spiritually, however, he had enormous energy. I often observed him sitting late at night at his desk, struggling with sleep, a struggle he often lost. But he never gave up, he never let me talk him into going to bed. Rather he would find help in strong black coffee or with the mechanical copying of a completely uninteresting page of grammar—anything to keep him awake. At that time, he wanted to take his doctorate, a path that was closed to him because of his studies at the Technical College, and learned Latin like a young student at the *Gymnasium*. At the same time, with his left hand, he took care of all the other studies that were necessary to reach his goal. His was promoted in a relatively short time. (*New Viennese Journal*, April 26, 1925)

Once Rudolf Steiner had become accustomed to the challenge of tutoring and teaching Otto Specht, he again found time for his own work and studies, which had been placed on the backburner in the first two years of work for the family. These two years had, however, helped him become more firmly rooted in the daily tasks of life and had helped him to widen his interests. In the summer of 1886, he began to study intensely the work of the philosopher Eduard von Hartmann. He was fascinated by this thinker, who had allowed himself the amusement of disproving his own philosophy from the standpoint of Darwinism. This anonymous work met not only with the resounding approval of the Darwinists, but, more than anything else, proved that the writer was at least as clever as they were. The most rabid Darwinists were more than surprised when the second edition, which they greeted with the call "Let the writer name himself, he is one of ours," named the writer as Eduard von Hartmann.

The fundamental ideas in von Hartmann's philosophy were repugnant to Steiner. He rejected his pessimism and dualism categorically. Nonetheless, that did not stop him from reading and learning from von Hartmann's work on the history of culture, politics and education. "I found in this pessimist the kind of sound understanding of life that I had failed to find in many optimists. I experienced something I needed particularly in relation to Eduard von Hartmann: the ability to appreciate what I had to oppose." And Steiner went on to relate, "I spent many late nights in Attersee when my boys could be left on their own, and I had admired the starry sky from my balcony, studying *Phenomenology of Moral Consciousness* and *The Religious Consciousness of Humanity in its Gradual Development*. As I read those works, I gained more and more certainty of my own epistemological views."

> Hartmann's observations about the moral sphere appealed to me, because he allows his views on the "beyond" to retreat completely, remaining with only what can be observed. I wanted knowledge to be attained not by pondering about what exists "behind" phenomena, but by entering phenomena themselves to the extent that they reveal their spiritual nature. (28)

For Steiner, Eduard von Hartmann was a symptomatic figure in the spiritual life of the then present. Hartmann had mastered contemporary science; his questions were focused on deeper things. Thus, in the winter of 1886/87, Steiner wrote in the introduction to the second volume of Goethe's scientific writings:

The philosophy of this thinker is of immense historical significance. His further writings, which take the basic ideas further in many directions... are a mirror of the total spiritual content of our time. Hartmann's work is admirably profound and shows a remarkable mastery of the various branches of science. He stands today at the top of the tower of scholarship. One does not have to be his disciple, and for this one will grant him absolute recognition. (1-b)

In addition to Eduard von Hartmann, Steiner was at that time taken by the work of Johannes Volkelt. His opinion of Volkelt was similar to his views on Hartmann, for here, too, he was in disagreement with the basic ideas. He did, however, respect Volkelt's boldness and independence, with which he took a courageous and clear stand against the political and moral decay of the time, a stand that kept him from receiving a professorship although he was Austrian. Volkelt's book about the psychology of dreams was one of the books that made a deep impression on Steiner and stimulated him. No less interesting were Volkelt's analyses of unmediated experience. Steiner quoted Volkelt's *Experience and Thinking* repeatedly in his book *Goethe's Theory of Knowledge*, written in 1886. Additionally, in his time with the Specht's, Steiner studied books by Richard Wahle, Johannes Rehmke and other contemporary philosophers. But his primary work was on Goethe's scientific writings, a task he took up again in 1886.

CHAPTER 7

THEORY OF KNOWLEDGE

On December 1, 1884, Rudolf Steiner wrote to Joseph Kürschner requesting that he ask Spemann, the publisher of *German National Literature*, to publish a "6-8 signature brochure" with the title "A Theory of Knowledge based on Goethe and Schiller's Worldview and on German Idealism." He was willing to forego any honorarium if Spemann would be willing to publish the book. Kürschner took up Steiner's request and replied affirmatively on December 6. On December 18, Steiner notified them that the manuscript was finished and included an foreword. It wasn't, however, until May 9, 1886, a year and a half later, that Kürschner received the manuscript that was immediately published under the title *Goethe's Theory of Knowledge*.

It is highly improbable that the manuscript that Steiner submitted for publication in May 1886 was the same one that had been copied in 1884. It is more likely that Steiner was unsatisfied with the original version, let it rest for several months, and then rewrote it. In any case, he changed the title and this change indicates that Schiller's work and German idealism played a more significant role in the original. We can also imagine that the scope of the original plan: an epistemology of Goethe, Schiller and the German idealists was too broad. The highly refined, systematic approach of the finally published version indicates that it was the result of intense revision. In his *Autobiography*, Steiner wrote, "The booklet was completed in 1886" (28).

To understand the unique nature of this book, we must keep in mind that in Rudolf Steiner's life, periods in which he was occupied with Goethe's work alternated with those in which he focused more on his own work. After the intensive work on Goethe's morphological writings, a time of breathing in followed a period of breathing out during which Steiner worked to articulate his own thoughts. He wrote about this pendulum movement of his soul: "While I was looking for the proper conceptual form to express Goethe's stance in relation to natural science, I also had to make headway in conceptualizing my own spiritual experiences as I contemplated natural processes. As a result, I was pushed continually from Goethe toward presenting my own worldview and then back again, so that I could better interpret his thoughts through my own" (28).

By writing *Goethe's Theory of Knowledge,* Steiner wanted most to bring his own spiritual experiences of knowing into conceptual form. The difficulty that such an undertaking presents is easily underestimated as there are only a very few individuals who understand the problem of trying to give spiritual experience conceptual form. Goethe's approach to knowing was helpful to Steiner in this regard. In the morphological writings, Steiner found a spiritual experience of true understanding and he succeeded in articulating the principles of this path of understanding nature. Now he strove to articulate in an accessible form the general principles of the process of coming to knowledge. Ever since his encounter with the unknown "Master," he had been privy to specific experiences in the field of knowledge. He now wanted to place these insights into a conceptual whole and thus outline an epistemology that would embrace all knowledge. In his attempts to formulate his thoughts on the subject, it became clear to him that his own thoughts coincided with Goethe's epistemological approach. In 1923, he wrote in the introduction to the second edition of *Goethe's Theory of Knowledge*: "It became clear to me in the course of my research into Goethe's work that my thoughts led to a view of the nature of knowledge that was present throughout Goethe's work and in his relation to the world. I discovered that my point of view brought me to an epistemology, upon which Goethe's worldview is based" (2).

Before Steiner began to write about Goethe's way of understanding the world, he had developed his own ideas about knowledge. Only later did he discover that the path of knowledge that Goethe practiced was alive in his epistemological understanding. *Goethe's Theory of Knowledge* was thus more of an exploration of Steiner's own thoughts than it was an interpretation of Goethe's understanding. This was clear to Steiner during his work on the book. He wrote an explanatory letter to Friedrich Theodor Vischer, to whom he sent a copy of this, his own first philosophical writing:

> Although it does follow on Goethe's work, I can quite openly say that my primary objective was to contribute to epistemological thought, not to further research into Goethe's thought. It wasn't the positive

approach in Goethe's work that was most important for me, but rather the way he viewed the world. Goethe's and Schiller's scientific writings present for me a middle, for which one must find the beginning and the end. The beginning: by presenting the principles upon which this way of seeing the world rests; the end: by exploring the consequences that this way of seeing has for our lives and our relationship to the world. (38)

Thus *Goethe's Theory of Knowledge*, even as it relates to Goethe, is the first philosophical justification of Steiner's own understanding. Readers quickly realized this. Robert Hamerling, a now forgotten Austrian poet and philosopher, wrote to Steiner: "I almost wish that you had left the reference to Goethe out of the title. What you have offered is much more than an explanation of Goethe's relation to nature. In fact, in my opinion, this is not as clearly characterized in your book as it would need to be for a wide circle of readers" (Goetheanum, 1930). Naturally, there were also critics. The question was posed, whether it was at all justified to write of a Goethean view. Gideon Spicker, who had worked on Lessing's worldview and was highly respected by Steiner, wrote that he was "not wholly" in agreement with Steiner's approach and went on:

> I am of the opinion that Goethe was not yet inoculated with the contemporary disease of epistemology, that because of his intuitive, pantheistic point of departure, he would have no understanding for it. This is implicit in a number of his own comments and in the way in which he approaches nature and life. Despite this, your work is very clear, fluid and persuasive. (38)

It was clear to Steiner that Goethe's approach was far removed from a theoretical epistemology. Through Spicker he encountered the objection that one should not try to follow Goethe's way of thinking back to its source; this was unworthy of Goethe. Further, Spicker held epistemological argumentation to be but a foolish fad. Spicker raised the call to stop the "eternal knife sharpening" and focus concretely on the practice of knowing.

Steiner could have given a historical, philological presentation of Goethe's approach. He could have described the experiential method from a number of different points of view and shown how the practical, active Goethe constantly found orientation in experience, how in his travels he constantly collected new experiences, how carefully he experimented—Goethe's work provided a wealth of sources for such an approach. It would also have been easy, based on the essay "The Experiment as Mediator Between Object and Subject," to show that Goethe was conscious of his method. Neither would it have taken much to distill his fundamental principles from his essays concerning questions of knowledge and from his maxims and reflections. This approach would have had immeasurable advantages. It would have been possible, taking for instance Goethe's color theory, to present his epistemological practice, his concept of experience, and the relationship between thinking and experience, and to place the idea of the type within a philological context. Beyond that, Steiner would have produced a work that could not be passed over by academics concerned with researching Goethe.

It is characteristic for Steiner that he did not take this path. He wasn't interested in presenting historical truths, neither did he want to present in detail how Goethe thought; that would have resulted in a merely historical tome, a spiritual portrait of a long-dead hero. For Steiner the historical dimension was not what was important. Not only because to do so would involve working through and clarifying Goethe's sometimes questionable positivist approach, but primarily because Steiner wanted to explore the essential questions of the process of knowing. To do so, he didn't rely on historical indications, but rather cut straight to the chase and wrestled with fundamental principles. He remained true to this approach throughout his life. Much later, he refused to argue the truth of the anthroposophic approach to medicine based on the efficacy of the medicines. "We have to have the courage to find such an approach to be untruthful" (260). The twenty-five-year-old Steiner did not want to enter the arena of contemporary philosophy through the back door of historical philology, but rather through the front door with a work that addressed the fundamental questions.

There are a number of very frank, biographical confessions in the book. In the passage concerning the process of knowing, for instance, stands:

> Living in these two worlds, that of the senses and that of thoughts—with one pressing in from below and the other shining down from above—human beings become masters of knowledge and thus unite the two into an undivided whole. From one perspective, the outer form calls to us, from the other, the inner being calls, and we must unite the two. (2, p. 56)

The biographer sees through these words into Steiner's state of consciousness in the 1880s. The reality of the spiritual world, revealing itself in thought forms, filled his soul. He is certain that the essence of things reveal themselves through the spiritual world and that thinking is the organ through which the human being unites himself with this higher world. It is no less characteristic that he says of the sensory world that it presses upon him from below. For the human being, the sensory world is at first foreign. The "sense appearances" must be "overcome" (2) for one to approach the essential core of the object. "All sense impression dissolves finally into ideal content" (2). Thus, knowing appears as a victory over the world that presses upon one from below.

Even more important is another passage of the book. Popular idealism is always in danger of mere Platonism or Hegelianism. The idea comes to be viewed as ruling the universe, surpassing man and nature. Besides the world of ideas, nothing is real. Reason rules the individual, the eternal sun of objectivity scorches the world. If one does not read the *Theory* completely and carefully, one can come to the conclusion that Steiner, too, was an advocate of this type of objective idealism, in that he described thinking as the organ through which one grasps the world of ideas.

> An indefinite number of beings endowed with minds may be confronted by a single thought content. The mind thus perceives the thought content of the world like an organ of comprehension. There is only a single thought content of the world. Human consciousness does not constitute the ability to produce thoughts and store them up, as is generally believed, but rather the ability to perceive thoughts (*ideas*). (2, p. 56)

This view appears to point toward a world of thought that is complete unto itself, working in lonely grandeur above the world we know.

This is a misunderstanding that Steiner addresses in two ways. The world of ideas is not in Steiner's view a grand, untouchable absolute. It does not live in a world beyond and does not subjugate the human being.

> The world-foundation has poured itself completely into the world. It did not remain outside of the world in order to control it externally; it has not withheld itself from the world, but impels everything internally. Its highest form of appearance in the reality of ordinary life is thought and, with it, the human personality. If, therefore, the ground of the world has goals, they are identical with the goals that the

human spirit sets for itself in life. We are not acting according to the purposes of the guiding power of the world when we search out one of the commandments of this power; rather, when we act according to our own individual insights, the guiding power of the world manifests in them. This guiding power does not live somewhere outside of humanity as will; rather, it has entirely renounced its own will so that everything depends on human will. (2, p. 91)

This passage is an invitation to contemplate its meaning more deeply. In the final analysis, it appears to be the expression of a philosophy based on the life of Christ that has left the Old Testamentary world of commandments behind. By emptying itself completely into the world, the spiritual essence of the universe has entrusted itself to humanity and placed itself at its disposal. It no longer appears as the divine judge holding sway over his servants. There is an echo of the Gospel of St. John that says, "I no longer call you servants, for the servant does not know what the master does; I call you friends, because everything that I have learned from my father I have shared with you" (John 15:15).

The emptying of the cosmic essence, the Christianization of thinking, which had at this time not yet been so identified, has yet another aspect that becomes apparent in the act of knowing. The fact that the spiritual essence of the cosmos is present in the human personality through thinking can be understood in two ways. Firstly, that the wisdom of the cosmos is present, unchanged and unified, or, secondly, that it speaks a new language in that it has become one with humanity. What does it mean that one actively produces opinions and ideas? What meaning does the creative activity of producing thoughts have? Is this but a mere reproduction of the spiritual lawfulness of the cosmos, patterns of a predetermined world of ideation?

There is an answer to this question in *Goethe's Theory of Knowledge*, which leads to the view that knowledge achieves a new, human visage. In Chapter 14, "Cognition and the Ultimate Ground of Things," is the following passage:

> The essential nature of a thing thus comes to light only in relation to the human being. the essential being of each thing appears only for human beings. This forms the basis for relativism as a worldview; a trend of thought which assumes that we see all things in the light that the human being lends to them. This view also bears the name

anthropomorphism, which has many representatives. Most of these, however, believe that this peculiarity of our cognition alienates us from objectivity as it is, in and of itself. We perceive everything, so they believe, through the spectacles of subjectivity. Our worldview shows us the exact opposite. If we want to reach the essential nature of things, we must view them through these spectacles. The world is not merely known to us as it appears, but rather appears as it is, though only to contemplative thinking. The form of reality that the human being in this way delineates through scientific knowledge is ultimately its true form. (2, pp. 60–61)

Steiner expanded on this idea in his book *Goethe's Worldview* and in other publications, coming to the conclusion that personal human experience alone is the key to a spiritual understanding of the cosmos. After 1900, he began to show that the human being as an organ of cosmic understanding can consciously school himself to be able through his thinking, experience and perception to manifest the essence of things. In 1886, *Goethe's Theory of Knowledge* bore witness to the belief in anthropomorphism, in which Steiner had already recognized the dangers of Hegelianism—the view that the human being is subjugated to the world of ideas—and tried to steer around.

One finds wonderful passages, mostly brief and to the point—for instance, concerning intellect and reason in Chapter 12—that without fanfare resolve central philosophical questions. To these belong the passage in which Steiner disproves Kant's grounds for considering mathematical laws to be synthetic *a priori* judgments. This is a passage that can be overseen due to its simplicity; for a logically thinking reader, it is a powerful proof. Even more magnificent are the thoughts concerning the knowledge of nature, which climax in the articulation of a "rational organic understanding" (2) and, in passing, indicate the shortcomings of Darwin's theory with the remark: *"Darwin's theory presupposes the type"* (2, p. 75).

Steiner had the greatest difficulty in developing the concept of *pure experience*. This is due primarily to the nature of the subject: Pure experience can only be characterized by what it is not. It cannot be grasped in a conceptual, language-based description. Further, the concept *pure experience* is an abstract concept, coined for philosophical discourse, one that possibly cannot be realistically interpreted. "Pure experience is the form of reality in which this appears when we encounter it in a fully selfless manner" (2). A related concept appears later in similar form, that of "pure perception." Steiner acknowledges in his *Autobiography* that it was fairly late in his life that he began to grasp the unique nature of the sensory world (28). One feels compelled to ask whether what Steiner described in his early philosophical writings as *pure experience* or *pure perception* would have been approached differently later in life.

In one passage of the book, the trials of the young philosopher condemned to be a private tutor appear. The remarks are to be found in the chapter "Psychological Knowing Activity." It is focused on the individual in society. A human being does not only belong to himself. He is also part of a group of people and as such has been formed by this belonging. What is the destiny of the individual in the midst of his society? It was at a time in which the choice of vocation was no longer determined by family and tradition as it had been just two generations earlier. Thus the path of an individual's life had become more open. Steiner writes about the life path of an individual in society:

> Human beings are not just self-contained, but also belong to a society. The activities and achievements of both the oneself and one's folk-group are made manifest in the individual. The individual mission of each human being also fulfills the mission of that person's larger community. The important thing is that the position of each person within the community allows the power of that individual to develop its full effectiveness. This is not possible unless the social group is the kind in which each human being can find an appropriate place to work, and finding such a place must not be left to chance. (2, p. 88)

In these words we can recognize, in addition to the general call for societal form based on human insight and reason, Steiner's now objective complaint: He had not found the place to set his lever. It is the cry of an individual who had been placed at the mercy of chance and because of the fact that his father had sent him to the Technical College was not able to enroll in an Austrian university to study philosophy and embark on an academic career.

In the winter of 1886/87, Steiner wrote the introduction to the second volume of *Goethe's Scientific Works*. This introduction contains de facto a revision of *Goethe's Theory of Knowledge*. The form is somewhat different, though. The problem of "art and science" with which *Goethe's Theory of Knowledge* ended is at the beginning of the introduction—where many thoughts are explained differently, connections to other worldviews are presented, and some themes are more extensively covered—while the central content is predominantly the same. Philologists would have noticed with discontent that the historical development of Goethe's epistemology was missing, as were footnotes. The first volume, done under the guidance of Schröer, contained both. In this second piece, Steiner appears on his own, sovereign; he even speaks of "my philosophy" (1-b).

Although we don't have the space to go into this second version of Steiner's epistemology at length, it is important to mention the foreword. Here Steiner finds a completely new tone of voice. The pathos of a philosophy of freedom is present. Steiner speaks quite personally:

> It raises the value of the human being, which is constantly being cruelly destroyed, for he must continually work to create. In our actions lies our happiness, in what we bring into being ourselves. The gift of happiness is like the revelation of truth. It is only worthy of the human being that he seek the truth himself and not be led by either experience nor revelation. (1-b)
>
> Thinking becomes one with cosmic existence in that it makes ideas its own; what works without enters into the spirit of the human being: he becomes one with objective reality in its highest potential. Becoming aware of the existence of the idea in reality is the true communion of the human being. (1-b)

This last sentence—"Becoming aware of the existence of the idea in reality is the true communion of the human being"—was later often quoted by interpreters of Steiner to prove that his approach was fundamentally religious. It is true that the word *communion* does indicate a religious context; one thinks of communion in the church. When viewed, however, in the context of the previously quoted passage in which the gift of happiness as well as any guidance of the individual through revelation is rejected, it is clear that communion is understood in the same way. Human joy lies in action, in our creativity, in the self-discovered truth. The religion that moved the young Steiner was of a Faustian nature, of the individual who strives to experience what holds the universe "in its most inward nature" together and does so through his own forces.

Thus Rudolf Steiner began the introduction to the second volume of *Goethe's Scientific Writings* with a series of quite personal trumpet blasts, which frankly were not noticed at the time and certainly did not find an echo.

Chapter 8

SOCIAL LIFE IN VIENNA

Starting in the winter of 1885/86, the Specht family's house became the setting of a spring council for Steiner's excursions into Viennese society. There was a small circle of friends who were Steiner's age. Walter Fehr belonged to this circle, as did his sisters Johanna and Radegunde, Josef Köck and others. He had a special relationship to the Fehr family. It started with his friendship with Walter Fehr, who Steiner admired for his loyal, open nature and steadfast opinions. Walter Fehr introduced Steiner to his family. The father seemed to be a highly educated eccentric. Steiner never saw him, although he lived in the room adjoining the parlor where Steiner would visit with the Fehr siblings. Through their stories and by perusing the father's library, Steiner began to gain a sense of his character. When he died, the siblings asked him to speak at their father's funeral; they had clearly seen that their young friend was as though called to this task. His words moved his friends deeply, and they were of the opinion that Steiner had been able to paint a true picture of their father.

Steiner discussed literary questions with Walter and other friends, and together they gathered for parties where the drinks flowed freely. During this time a deep friendship grew between Steiner and Walter's youngest sister, Rademunde. "We loved each other, and both of us knew this; neither of us, however, could overcome our shyness in order to say that we loved each other. Consequently, our love lived in between our spoken words, but never in them" (28). The impoverished circumstances in which both of them lived made further plans impossible, and Steiner was only able in letters to reveal to the "most treasured maiden" his affection and tell her that nothing would destroy his feelings for her (38). The hopes, which stirred in Gundi, as she was called, evaporated slowly after Rudolf Steiner left Vienna for Weimar. She died at age thirty-five in Vienna in 1903. Steiner's first mystery play, *The Portal of Initiation*, contains what is perhaps a remembrance of this relationship in the passage where Johannes Thomasius recalls his young love, who, after he left her, died in despair.

These purely personal friendships could only have taken up a small part of Steiner's free time as his lust for society, the urge to learn to know people, led him into the most diverse circles. In February or March of 1886, he visited his teacher Karl Julius Schröer. Schröer had just become acquainted with the poetry of the then twenty-one-year-old Marie Eugenie delle Grazie (1864–1931). He was especially fascinated by her epic poem "Hermann" and the play *Saul*. He shared his excitement with Steiner, adding that Robert Zimmermann had remarked that delle Grazie was the only true genius that he had met in his life. Steiner devoured the young poet's work. Soon he had written a feuilleton about it that his friend Emil Schönaich printed in the Independent Schlesian Press. Uncritically and with complete naiveté, Steiner celebrated the "genial poet."

> We have here an enormous figure. Delle Grazie is as original as only a writer can be who is formed out of the undying source of the German being. She is as strongly rooted in the characteristic as is only possible for the German spirit with its loving immersion in the human heart and soul. She speaks with such bitterness of Roman decadence, a bitterness that can only spring from the noble thoughts of an educated German who, from her moral stand, has no mercy for adulteration and corruption, only contempt. (32)

Toward the end of the thorough laudation, one finds the beautiful statement: "A person that is able to produce such flowers has nothing to fear" (32). In brief, Steiner was also spellbound.

This feuilleton became Steiner's ticket to the regular salon that delle Grazie held at the house of her fatherly friend Laurenz Müllner in Vienna. Müllner was then a professor of Christian philosophy on the theological faculty at the University of Vienna. He had studied Thomas Aquinas, Schelling, Darwin and natural science. His most respected teacher was Karl Werner, who had written a comprehensive biography of Thomas von Aquinas. Müllner was a connoisseur of literature and art; the salons were a colorful mixture of people: Catholic theologians, philosophers, poets, musicians, sculptors and publishers. Schröer, however, stayed away after his second or third visit. He found the pessimistic, naturalistic undertone of delle Grazie's epic *Robespierre*, from which she read, extremely displeasing.

Rudolf Steiner's response was completely different. Although her pessimism and her dark naturalism went against his grain, he found the consequence with which she depicted the terrible grand. In the summer of 1886, he wrote an "open letter to the author of 'Hermann,'" in which he compared her pessimism with the idealism of creative freedom. From that point on he was a welcome guest in delle Grazie's circle.

A new world opened up for him here. In Laurenz Müllner, Vincenz Knauer and Adolph Stöhr, he met philosophically trained thinkers; among the professors of the theological faculty—especially the Cistercian father and Old Testament scholar Wilhelm Neumann—he encountered a rich, comprehensive education; he met the authors Emilie Mataja and Fritz Lemmermayer, neither of whom were outstanding writers, but neither were they run-of-the-mill people. It was a new social milieu that opened up for Steiner. He found people to talk to who had something to say. Even the topics of conversation were new. Contrary to popular belief, the main topic of this circle was not Catholic theology but rather modern literature. When someone began to tell about Dostoyevsky's Raskolnikov, it was as though a bolt of lightning had struck. "A new world was there, a world—yes it was though one had found himself suddenly transported to another planet" (258). Leopold von Sacher-Masoch was seen as "a brilliant writer, starkly truthful in his presentations of devastating human weaknesses thriving in the swamp of modern life" (28). The discussions also touched on Darwinism, Haeckel's work, and now and again on the work of Bartholomaus Carneri, a person who delle Grazie revered. At times, when most of the visitors had left, delle Grazie would read new passages from the manuscript of her epic poem *Robespierre*. In regular iambic pentameter and with a nobility of language, she presented images of the terror of the French Revolution.

Steiner relates, "She read from her poems and spoke in the spirit of her worldview with assured emphasis, and she illuminated life with those ideas. It was not the illumination of the Sun—indeed, it was always somber moonlight with threatening, overcast skies. But in that dusky gloom, flames arose from human hopes, carrying high the passions and illusions that consume humanity. Yet all this was humanly touching, always enthralling, and the bitterness was softened by the noble magic of a truly inspired personality" (28). "There was something almost magical about these Saturday gatherings. After dark, the red shade of the ceiling lamp spread a festive light over everyone" (28). Fritz Lemmermayer's recollections add to the picture: "Decades later I can still see the picturesque scene in all its details: the young blond poet, robed in fine, brightly colored silk, tall and slender in the red salon, standing next to a plaster cast of an Apollo von Belvedere, reading with solemn pathos" (Lemmermayer).

Steiner characterized delle Grazie's house as "a place where pessimism revealed itself with a direct and living strength" and as "an abode of anti-Goetheanism." And he added, "Nevertheless, for me every visit to this home (where I knew I was welcome) was immensely fruitful; I truly benefited from the cultural atmosphere" (28). Why? To begin with, Steiner found a circle of equals with whom to enter discourse, not a group of students most of whom he was many steps beyond intellectually. He also must have had a very invigorating experience of how these discourses widened his own horizons. While his paternal friend Schröer remained inwardly fixated on Goethe and lived with his focus on the good, the noble and the beautiful in the past, here other worlds came into play. Although much that took place in the Müllner/delle Grazie home was not truly modern, it was all stimulating. Third, and perhaps most importantly, Steiner truly respected and revered delle Grazie. By 1900, he had dedicated five essays to her, one of which was more than twenty pages long. In an essay written in 1893, he compared her favorably with Goethe, about whom he wrote, "He did not become the Messiah of the new epoch. Instead he brought us the most beautiful and the ripest fulfillment of a now dead period." Concerning delle Grazie, he wrote:

> I have not found the signature of truly modern striving, which dawned with Byron, so clearly brought to expression by any contemporary writer as by the Austrian poet Marie delle Grazie. This opinion is not based on her early poems—"The Gypsies," "Hermann," *Saul*—but on those that have appeared recently in various magazines. These poems reflect starkly the modern worldview through a deep, passionate soul with clear vision and enormous artistic ability. Delle Grazie brings to expression in her poems what a sensitive, proud character must suffer in the face of this worldview. (32)

What Steiner treasured was delle Grazie's honesty, her inner consequence. She surrendered herself completely to the modern, materialistic view. Materialism became for her a personal experience. Thus she voiced with certainty that in the face of this view of nature, the traditional views were but "soap bubbles and empty forms" that dissolved into nothingness.

Solemnly she celebrated the emptiness of human existence. As though in counterpoint, Steiner formulated the fundamental impulse of his philosophy of freedom in his *open letter*:

> What would remain of divine freedom if nature were to treat us as children, leading us, caring for us, protecting us? No, she has to deny us everything so that when we find joy, it is born out of the innermost of our independent selves! Nature should destroy what we build daily, that we might each day rediscover the joy of creation! We wish to thank nature for nothing, and ourselves for everything! (30)

The encounter with delle Grazie and her circle and the experience of the inner consequences of the modern view of nature, which came to expression as well in the clever, sarcastic, often biting remarks of Laurenz Müllner about philosophical and artistic questions in delle Grazie's poetry, led Steiner to a new sense of his own self. In Schröer, he had found someone with whom he was in complete harmony; with delle Grazie, he became much more conscious of his own views. Here he was not spiritually at home, as with Schröer, but rather a stranger in a strange land, where one becomes much more aware of one's difference.

Steiner's early remarks concerning delle Grazie should be seen in light of this experience. In meeting delle Grazie, he experienced a biographical challenge. He recognized that in "the substance of her ideas was the antithesis of everything that I understood the world to be" (28). He came to see her worldview as being at odds with his view of life. This fascinated him. His assessment was not based on the outer agreement or disagreement of her ideas with his. Even later, this was something that barely interested him. He looked at the honesty and consistency of a person's thoughts and feelings. The fact that he did not seem to notice the conventional, artificial quality of her poetry, that he did not recognize that they had no strength, were not born out of experience, may be a reflection of the positivity with which he approached those who held contradictory views, or it may reflect the general acclaim for delle Grazie at that time. That he enjoyed giving praise and recognition is a sympathetic quality present throughout Steiner's life. Especially those who were close to him received generous praise. For example, in reviews he praised the verse of his friend Ludwig Jacobowski. It was only toward the end of his life, in writing his *Autobiography*, that he admits that these poems "were not completely original." Similarly, regarding Schuré, his praise for his work was generous; only later, in looking back, did he note that Schuré had only been able to connect weakly to the ancient mysteries. But with delle Grazie, Steiner never changed his tone, although she, especially after 1912, turned her back on her youthful pessimism and returned to the religious beliefs of her childhood. She was actually also guilty of what Steiner had accused Goethe: "His later years were in poor accord with his youth. Nowhere do we find the fulfillment of what he held as promise" (32).

Other scholars have noted that it was in delle Grazie's house that Steiner no doubt encountered the philosophical ideas of medieval philosophy, especially the world of thought of Thomas Aquinas. There is no doubt that delle Grazie had the greatest reverence for Carl Werner, an Aquinian scholar and theological historian. She often spoke of this simple, childlike professor who approached his work in a selfless, precise manner. Although Werner was never present at delle Grazie's during the time Steiner visited the house, his spiritual presence was tangible. However, whether or not the work of Thomas von Aquinas was discussed during those Saturday afternoon gatherings must remain an open question. Steiner never mentioned it, and even in 1891 he was of the opinion that he did not understand medieval philosophy well enough. In a letter from November 19, 1891, he writes, "I am studying the philosophy of the Middle Ages, an area in which my knowledge is full of holes" (39). Aquinas' presence at these gatherings may have been similar to that of Werner's: he was present in the background of some of the speakers thoughts, without ever coming explicitly into the foreground.

We can assume that the conversations that developed between Steiner and the Catholic professor of theology Wilhelm Neumann on their walks to and from delle Grazie's cottage often revolved around religious questions. These conversations must have been quite amusing.

> The conversations that we had that were important for me were those related to Christianity. He spoke at one point about the immaculate conception. I tried to prove to him that there was an innate inconsistency in this dogma, since it applied to both Mary and her mother, Saint Anna, one would just have to keep on going. Now Neumann was not one of those theologians who had had a narrow sense of theology. He was a freethinking theologian, and he added, "No we certainly can't do that; by and by we would arrive at David and then things would get terribly complicated." (B 83/84 & 342)

In another conversation, Steiner developed his thoughts on the nature of Christ and how he appears in Earth evolution, and he relates how Neumann found himself trapped by Catholic dogma and unable to agree with Steiner's ideas. In a third meeting, Steiner began to speak about reincarnation, a topic that Neumann had no inclination to explore (28). In none of these recollections is there any indication that Aquinian philosophy was ever explicitly addressed in the circle around delle Grazie, nor was it suited for such discussions. It seems more likely that Pope Leo XIII's questionably decreed neo-Thomism, general questions of dogma, and developments within the Catholic church were themes of discussion. But even these topics were probably not the primary focus of the conversations. According to Steiner, Neumann spoke to him explicitly about Aquinas only once. On November 9, 1888, after Steiner had given a lecture on Goethe's aesthetics, Neumann approached him and said, "The seeds for this lecture, they were already present with Thomas from Aquinas!" (74). This remark, which pointed him in the direction of Thomas' work, lived on in Steiner for quite awhile; whether or not it sparked a study of scholasticism at that time is an open question.

In late autumn, Fritz Lemmermayer introduced Rudolf Steiner to the circle of "German" writers living in Vienna. This group formed, in a certain sense, a counterweight to those writers grouped around Hermann Bahr, whose work would soon become known as the "Viennese modern." In addition to Lemmermayer, members of the former group included Hermann Hango, Franz Gristel and Josef Kitir, who soon brought Fercher von Steinwand into their circle. The latter made a strong impression on Steiner. When he published von Steinwand's poems "Chorus of Archetypal Impulses" and "Chorus of Archetypal Dreams" in the *German Weekly*, Steiner wrote to Radegunde Fehr, "That is a true original. He has a fundamental striving that has worked its way with elemental force to the surface" (38). The idea of reincarnation took on clear form for Steiner when observing von Steinwand. In contemplating what he encountered, he saw something that had its source in a time far past. Looking back on what he experienced, an intuition came to him that pointed to an individuality in an earlier incarnation. In his *Autobiography*, he wrote the following about this experience: "I view it as one of the important events in my youth that I was privileged to know Fercher von Steinwand" (28).

Fritz Lemmermayer, who was clearly a mercurial talent, also brought Rudolf Steiner to the house of a Protestant minister, Alfred Formey. Formey was married to a retired singer who took care of the guests with "enchanting grace." Among the guests were Christine Hebbels, Friedrich Hebbels, the actress Irma Wilborn, the poet Friedrich Schlögel, the composer Alfred Stross and other prominent figures from Vienna's cultural life. Lemmermayer described these gatherings: Christine Hebbel and Irma Wilborn recited poetry, Friedrich Schlögel gave readings from his satirical sketches of Viennese life, Stross played his own compositions, Mrs. Formey sang arias and *Lieder*, Lemmermayer contributed a novella and Rudolf Steiner held now and again extemporaneous lectures. Irma Wilborn transformed the serious, earnest discourse into a firework of wit and humor and laughter until the "chairs clattered."

The circles in which Steiner moved in Vienna in those days, and where he felt quite at home belonged without exception to an older cultural tradition. With few exceptions—Eugenie delle Grazie and Fritz Lemmermayer—his acquaintances were of the generation born before 1850. Christine Hebbel was born in 1817; Schlögl, 1821; Schröer, 1825; Vinzenz Knauer and Fercher von Steinwand, 1828; Wilhelm Neumann, 1837; Alfred Formey, 1844; and Ludwig Müllner, 1848. These individuals provided Steiner with a window looking out onto aspects of Austrian cultural life that belonged to the past. They shared in one way or another an idealistic striving. Without doubt, the earnestness of this striving was for Steiner the decisive criteria of genuine spiritual work. It was this earnestness, which is not put on for its effect and does not follow fashion's whims, that characterized the people with whom Steiner spent his time, discussing, arguing and laughing "until the chairs clattered."

He was thus in a certain opposition to the then-fashionable culture of the arts section, which later became so well known. In an essay from this period, he wrote polemically about "the clever, superficial, imitation French posturing brought out by gentleman such as Ludwig Speidel, Eduard Hanslick, Hugo Wittmann or even Oppenheim and Spizer, in which they would seem to be speaking about significant topics, but in fact merely entertaining their readers with shallow wit and empty phrases" (30). With such remarks, Steiner placed himself in conflict with the leading Viennese journalists and the newspapers in which their work was being published. Not only the elegant arts sections, no, but the fundamental stance of these papers, which supported economic liberalism, seemed to him to have a corruptive influence (30). He was very skeptical of those who took to the barricades for "progress"; his respect was given to what he experienced as upright and healthy.

For instance, he celebrated Robert Hamerling and Ludwig Anzengruber as the "two greatest voices" of Austria, and was outraged when these two independent figures, neither of whom belonged to any of the recognized schools or styles, went unrecognized in their homeland. The superficiality of Viennese public culture was responsible for this.

> In addition we must take into account the mendacity of the local press, which knows no shame when it sets out to paint a skewed picture of one of our contemporaries, someone who was either unwilling to do their bidding or whose work went against the flow. We watched this happen a few months ago with Hamerling, now with Anzengruber. The reports from the Viennese press about the former show an absolute lack of knowledge about his life and his work and deliberately misrepresented him both personally and professionally. What they have done with Anzengruber is the same. There is no indication of a calling to express honorably who he is as a person nor his significance for his people and for German literature. (32)

This appraisal contradicts historical opinion, which judged the *New Independent Press* to be an example of liberal journalism and viewed publication in the feuilleton section to be an indication of the writer's national literary status. In fact, the newspaper did have a strong team of correspondents abroad and was thus able to report international news. Steiner, however, disagreed with the newspaper's national, political and cultural position. A decade later, Karl Kraus took up the battle with the Viennese press in his own way and quoted Karl Liebeknecht in his own magazine, the "Torch."

> There is no malice that the press does not publish as something meaningful, no crime that it is not prepared to turn into a magnanimous deed; there is no crook upon whose head they are not prepared to place the laurel wreath of fame or the oak leaves of citizenship, as long as it serves their own ends. (Fackel 54)

Using the sharpness of his pen, Kraus took up the battle against the "New Independent Press," against literary and aesthetic opportunism, against genuine backdrops with fake actors, and against the flirt with the arrogant "decadence" trend.

Chapter 9

THE EDITOR: AN EXCURSION INTO POLITICS

On January 1, 1888, Rudolf Steiner unofficially, precipitously, and with no preparation took over the position of editor for the *German Weekly*. There is no record as to how this happened or any indication of what Steiner may have hoped for with this move. In any case, he added this responsibility to his palette, which at the time also included collaboration on a dictionary being published by Joseph Kürschner.

The *German Weekly* called itself a "voice for the national interests of the German people." It had been started five years earlier by a free-thinking, well-respected historian, Heinrich Friedjung. Steiner began by writing weekly summaries, the chronicles of an attentive, interested contemporary. In April, Steiner's review of Hamerling's "Homunculus" appeared; toward the end of May, he began to write lead articles on political topics; and then, just as he was beginning to really get the hang of it, publication ceased due to the publisher's inability to settle with Friedjung on a price. It was a sudden cessation, a cessation that caused Steiner no end of trouble, even landing him in court.

The eight political articles that Steiner wrote between May and July are, however, quite interesting. They don't only give us a sense of the political ideas of the twenty-seven-year-old Steiner, they also shed light on a number of things that were to come later. The first and the last of these articles addressed the question of parliamentary representation for the Germans living in Austria. The political situation at the time was such that under Taaffe's administration the German voice—and with it that of the actual liberal contingency—was being silenced. Taaffe attempted to ally himself more strongly with the Czechs and the Poles who, together with the clerics, gained increasing influence in the Austrian administration. Positions and jobs were handed out accordingly. Political representation of the Germans had, however, splintered into small, even tiny groups centered around individual delegates.

At the beginning of his first article, Steiner recalls the political life that had developed during the time in which the Germans held the leadership in the government. They had been led by "an abstract ideal of a nation, which was based on the liberal model. The actual situation was never taken into consideration. They thought that it was possible to make the *Volksgeist* follow the idea, and didn't realize that the central idea of a nation's government must arise out of the *Volkgeist*" (31). Nobly forgetting themselves, they also "overlooked the cultural mission of the German peoples in Austria" as well as the historical reality. In Steiner's observations, we can see a philosophy of history through which his thoughts concerning the process of culture come to expression.

> If the peoples of Austria wish to enter competition with the Germans, they first have to catch up with the evolutionary process that these have already gone through. They will have to take on German culture through the German language, just as the Romans acquired Greek culture through the Greek language and the German acquired Roman culture through Latin. The evolution of cultures, working out of the past with historical necessity, should provide a point of view with which to address, for example, the battle around the creation of Slavic schools. (31)

In other words, the Slavs should not focus primarily on maintaining their national traditions, but more importantly work to acquire German culture. This idea recurs in the second article, where it is spoken out with a certain vehemence:

> The Slavs will have to live for a long time before they begin to understand the tasks borne by the German people. It is an incredible display of cultural enmity to constantly attack the ethnic group from whom one receives spiritual light, without whom European education would remain a book with seven seals. (31)

It is worth noting that in the second article Steiner descends from the heights of general principles and makes some practical demands. "A German convention, called by true representatives of German culture, should articulate the coming tasks of the Germans and proclaim them to all the world" (31). The German "associations should acquire a unified form of organization; they must be aware of one another. Then their demonstrations, wherever they are needed, have the right impact" (31). In short,

Steiner calls for all true German thinking people to join forces. In unification is strength. He warns, "Only an opposition that never thinks to take the reins in their hands can allow itself the luxury of forming factions" (31). In politics, the challenge is not to protect individual character and personal views, it is to gain control of government.

A second important topic addressed by Steiner in 1888 concerned the politics of education. The Austrian minister of education at that time, Paul Gautsch von Frankenthurn, who would later become president, was being celebrated as a "man of action" and a successful educational reformer. In Steiner's opinion, his reforms consisted solely of bureaucratic gains, which, through detailed curricula and a flood of rules and directives laying out what each teacher should present in each lesson, served to regulate the entire life of the school. Teacher training became "a form of methodological drill" (31). This all seemed to Steiner to be completely ridiculous. Keeping in mind that humans learn best through the interaction with other humans and that education is a personal, highly individual process, he could see it making sense to support individual teachers—and perhaps in better working and living conditions than teachers had in general—rather than working to perfect curricula. Thus, he was decidedly against Gautsch's reforms. "Such an approach makes the development of individuality impossible, and yet education is totally dependent on the cultivation of the individuality of the future teachers. They will have the best effect on education if they are given space to develop freely" (31). Steiner went so far as to point out the dangers of a normative approach to teaching methods in training teachers. To underline his point, he risked using the earlier minister of education, Count Leo Thun, as an example. A modern historian, William M. Johnston, summed up Thun's work accurately:

> This devoted Catholic did away with the confessional prejudices of Metternich's time and introduced humanistic and scientific approaches both in secondary and university education. Using Leibniz's view that religion and science could not contradict one another as his point of departure, Thun took the risk of teaching students to think independently, thus helping to bring about a rebirth in Austrian scholarship. (Johnston)

In 1888, Thun was still seen by many as an extreme cleric. Regardless of this, Steiner wrote:

There was a time in Austria in which the education of strongly individualistic teachers was seen as the task of the universities. Although the focus at that time was primarily on higher education, it brought about an upward trend that has no comparison in the history of Austrian education. Strangely enough, this period lies in the tenure of the cleric Thun. We can all remember which spirit found its way at that time into education, and how Thun, disregarding his own personal opinion as well as his clerical position, took on the challenge to raise wherever he could the level of higher education by cultivating individuality. (31)

These remarks are significant for a number of different reasons. Mentioning Thun was courageous and contradicted the general prejudice. Steiner was reprimanded for it; even Schröer expressed his disapproval. It is characteristic of Steiner that he acknowledged excellence without any confessional blindness, recognizing it even where the general consensus said it could not be present. But more than anything, these thoughts contain the seed to an accurate interpretation of the idea of the "free spiritual life" articulated by Steiner in 1919. Free spiritual life is dependent on the presence of individualities. Individuality is not a product of nature. It must be nurtured and supported. This does not happen through the idolization of personality, but rather in that the individuality grows into the general stream of spiritual life.

> Future teachers should know the goals of the cultural development of their people, the direction that this development takes. A study of history and aesthetics should form the center of such understanding. They should be introduced to the spiritual development of humanity, a spiritual development on which they too shall work. (31)

Here Steiner sketches out the way in which individuality can be nurtured by ensuring its participation in a comprehensive spiritual life. In the middle point stands the individual's growing understanding of the evolution of humanity and the development of an artistic sensibility. Once an awareness for humanity is awakened, a study of the sciences can follow.

A third topic, which Steiner addressed in his articles for the *German Weekly,* was clericalism. These articles were triggered by the activities of Catholic political groups that, together with the conservatives and the Slav nationalists, formed the backbone of Taaffe's government. Steiner was not inclined to underestimate his opponents. He writes that Taaffe is, in a conventional sense, an unimportant politician (31), and he reminded his readers just how "sharp the weapons are that the Jesuits still wield against modern science" (31). It was also clear to him that Catholicism was deeply rooted in a large percentage of the Austrian people, and that it was difficult to express liberal views in a folksy manner.

Politicians with German sympathies were weighing the possibility of collaboration with German clerics. Steiner energetically took a position against such a collaboration.

> The enmity that the Slav people have for German culture falls together with the enmity that the Roman Catholic church has for modern culture, which is primarily carried by Germans. Only those who never venture onto the stage of history can allow themselves the illusion that a reconciliation is possible between German character, German culture and the Roman Catholic church. (31)

Steiner, who saw the battles against the dogma of infallibility as clearly as centuries of German protests against Rome, made a historical case for the impossibility of a coalition with the clerics. "It is not possible to join forces with such a party as long as we do not wish to lose ourselves, as long as we do not wish to give up what we alone are justified to bear: our name as Germans" (31). This example indicates that Steiner did not base his political ideas on pragmatic considerations, but on a cultural-political or spiritual point of view.

What especially concerned Steiner was the change in Catholic strategy that took place at that time. From 1846 until his death, Pope Pius IX had taken a stand against anything modern. With the dogma of Mary's virgin birth from her mother Anna (1854), the *Syllabus errorum* (1864), and the dogma of infallibility (1870), he had met the *Zeitgeist* head on. His successor, Pope Leo XIII, had taken a different approach. In 1891, he revised Catholic social understanding with the encyclical *Rerum novarum*, and in *Aeterna Patris* he called for a reconciliation of religion and science based on the work of Thomas von Aquinas. In June 1888, Leo XIII published an encyclical, *Libertas praestantissimum*, in which he described the meaning and limitations of human freedom. Steiner took this to a spring council to address the pope's intentions. Leo had already earlier recommended the study of the modern sciences "on the one hand to interpret them in as much as it is possible in a Catholic sense, and, on the other hand, to be better able to refute them from the point of view of the Catholic church....

He was not unhappy to see Darwin's and similar theories taught in the theological seminaries and illuminated from the Catholic point of view.... For Catholism, this new strategy is quite advantageous, for modern culture, however, not at all" (31). The new matter-of-fact tone of Catholic propaganda appeared more than anything to Steiner to be dangerous because, for example, the Catholic teaching of the necessity of authoritative structures seemed to justify the misuse of human freedom in economic liberalism.

Steiner's statements concerning Catholicism and clericalism were born of his understanding of the principle of human freedom. He believed that citizens were able to deal reasonably with their own issues and rejected the church's prerogative of guardianship. His ideal was "a reasonably ordered system..., within which each individual can move completely freely. In this system each will fulfill his task without being limited, opposed or exploited by another; he will be restricted in his freedom neither by authority, as in the Catholic view, nor by egotism, as in the modern pseudo-liberal approach" (31). This ideal sprung from an understanding of history that recognizes evolution in the path of humanity, and in this case Steiner had an unambiguous standard. "The barometer of progress in the evolution of humanity is the way freedom is seen and how this view is realized in practice" (31).

An article covering the speech made by Wilhelm II at his coronation shows to what extent these articles are children of the time and how unfortunate some of Steiner's statements are. He credits the German emperor with deep insight into the historical demands of the time, selflessness, lack of partisanship and other welcome traits. Not a single critical word. The speech itself was praised: "Our thanks to the new ruler that he understood to speak such balsamic words to his people" (31). It wasn't long before Steiner had to revise his assessment of the emperor. In 1918, he described him as a German braggart who spoke without thinking (185a).

His six-month tenure as an editor forced Steiner to pay much closer attention to public life than he would have on his own. This job was one of those moments of holding back, which helped in the development of his multi-faceted interests. According to various witnesses, it is clear that from this time on Steiner paid close attention to political developments. Later, in the concept of the threefold nature of the social organism, the insights that he gained were brought to practical expression. In his lectures, one finds mention of the observations he had made since this period.

Although his editorial tasks were time consuming and, at times, a burden, they were also stimulating in that they brought him into contact with many people. The daily visit to the Café Griensteidl was an integral part of the journalist's life. It was a place where important politicians were likely to meet, usually between 2:00 and 4:00 p.m. It was here that Steiner met Victor Adler, the then controversial leader of the Austrian Social Democrats. "That slender, unassuming man concealed an energetic will. As we spoke over a cup of coffee, I always sensed that what he had to say was unimportant, commonplace, but that the way he spoke revealed an unbending will" (28). Steiner also met Engelbert Pernerstorfer in the same cafe, in whose journal, *German Word*, he was later able to publish a number of articles. Here he was introduced to the writings of Marx and Engels and other socio-economic writers, and for the first time had grounds to study them. In the years after 1898, when Steiner was teaching at the Workers' Educational School in Berlin, he learned to know the full spectrum of Marxist theory. But in the beginning what he knew was that the questions that were raised in the discussions were enormously complex and could not be solved simply theoretically. Social questions concerned him repeatedly. He approached them from the point of view of the individual, the point of view of *Intuitive Thinking as a Spiritual Path*.

Chapter 10

AESTHETICS

After Rudolf Steiner had been freed of the editorial work and after the court case involving the newspaper had been resolved, he finished, in an "extraordinary rush," a number of articles for the Pierer encyclopedia and returned to his studies of aesthetics, which he had begun the previous fall. Eduard von Hartmann had sent him, in 1887, his book *The History of Aesthetics* and then, at Christmas, surprised him with a copy of his *Philosophy of Beauty*. The topic probably had interested Steiner since he had sat in on Robert Zimmermann's lectures on aesthetics. In any case, he knew Friedrich Theodor Vischer's work and had touched on the question of artistic creativity in the last chapter of *Goethe's Theory of Knowledge*. On November 9, 1888, he gave a lecture at a meeting of the Viennese Goethe Society entitled "Goethe as the Father of a New Aesthetic," in which he summarized his early ideas concerning art. This is the first of his lectures to be documented. It marks the beginning of his extensive lecturing, which ended with his last address on September 28, 1924.

This lecture is important biographically for Steiner for a number of reasons. Following the lecture, the Cistercian father Professor Neumann came up to Steiner and made a remark "that could not be otherwise interpreted as that this man in this moment had complete understanding for an individual in the present and, at the same time, for his relationship to an earlier incarnation. And what he said about the connection between these two incarnations was absolutely right, not wrong" (240). As Steiner later recounted to Rittelmeyer, it was thus that he was made aware of his own earlier incarnation.

This indicates that we can gain a significant degree of insight into Rudolf Steiner through the main ideas of this lecture. In fact, the central thesis of this lecture—that all artistic creativity originates in reality, then transforms it in such a way that it appears ideal—is a central principle in Steiner's life. He lived in the act of taking up the challenges that life presented to him. This is especially apparent in his social action. It finds its direction in those individuals who were at hand. Again and again, he picked up on the questions that other people posed to him. He reached out to the other; whether theosophist or Berlin worker is irrelevant. He tried to challenge and bring people together in such a way that their reality began to take on a spiritual light and manifest its ideal character. He helped many of his students grow beyond themselves by trusting them and giving them a chance to work.

Steiner, however, did not simply answer people's questions or take up tasks that others brought to him. He naturally also created new things and unexpected possibilities for which no one could have asked directly. Take, for example, the creation of eurythmy. He developed this new artistic form, which he had envisioned as early as 1908, beginning in 1912, after a mother came to him with the question of a possible training for her daughter. Eurythmy became thus an unexpected answer to an existential question. At the same time, it brought hidden laws of human speech to expression, which until then had slept unrecognized in the spiritual organism of human movement.

More than anything, this lecture is the documentation of Steiner's active interest in art and his striving for forms of artistic expression. This is something that is difficult to overemphasize; it pulses throughout Steiner's work. One finds this deep love of art and artistic activity—as well as of artists and his ongoing interest in aesthetics—alive up to the final days of his life. During the three years following this lecture, Steiner developed first a conceptual framework within which to approach the question. He began to write a book on aesthetics, from which only the draft of a chapter concerning comics remains (the draft of a chapter concerning naturalism seems to have been lost). From letters written to the Specht family, it is apparent that he had spent time studying tragedy. In 1889/90, he shared his thoughts on aesthetics verbally with Richard and Pauline Specht.

At the same time he published a series of theater reviews in one of the Viennese newspapers. These were the cause of heated discussions at the Café Griensteidl, where Steiner met Herman Bahr, who, at that time, presented himself as the prophet of naturalism. Friedrich Eckstein recounted these encounters:

> [It] was very enjoyable for us to listen when the two of them locked horns and let go with a firework of sharp invectives against one

another. "Rudolf Steiner is unable to follow my ideas," explained Bahr at one point, "because he has become completely rusted by his outlived, totally primitive notions." "Not at all!" rejoined Steiner, "There is nothing easier for me to understand than Hermann Bahr. I just have to think back to the time when I had not yet learned anything at all!" (Eckstein)

The intensive exploration of artistic questions led to his wrestling with thought forms during his time in Weimar and revealed itself anew in Berlin, now visible for everyone and guided by fully new criteria.

In the November 9, 1888, lecture, Steiner focused on presenting Goethe's artistic work and his aesthetic principles. Goethe's contemporary, Merck, had said to him, "Your striving, your undeviating direction, is to give reality a poetic form; the others strive to realize the so-called poetic, the imaginative, and that results in nothing but dumbness." Goethe, who "repeated these words and often found them significant," remarked, "If one understands the enormous difference between these two approaches, takes hold of it and applies it, one gains insight into a thousand other things" (HA). To illustrate this, Goethe speaks about inanities that "arise out of a concept."

Steiner took these thoughts philosophically and attempted to show how an artist begins with what is real in the sensory world, through his imagination grasps what is significant, and then brings what is hidden to expression.

> The content of what is beautiful, the material foundation of beauty, is thus always real, an unmediated actuality, and the form of its manifestation is *ideal*. We see that the opposite of what the German school of aesthetics claims holds true; this school has simply turned things upside down. Beauty is not the divine in an earthly garb. The artist does not bring the divine to earth by letting it flow into the sensory world, but rather in that he lifts the sensory world into the realm of the divine. (30)

Steiner formulates this idea slightly differently in one of his notebooks from this time.

> The artist *transforms* what is individual into something with a general character; he turns what is coincidental into a form of necessity, what is earthly into something divine. It is not the task of an artist to give an idea sense-perceptible form, but to enable reality to come to expression in the light of the ideal. The *what* is drawn from the real

world; it is not important. The *how* belongs to the creative powers of the genius and *this is what matters*. (B 6)

As accurate as the characterization of Goethe's artistic approach was in this lecture, Steiner's critique of the aesthetic approach of German idealism, namely Hegel's approach, was highly controversial. Hegel had stated in his lecture on aesthetics that "there also exists what is true in and of itself. Because it has outwardly immediate existence for consciousness and the concept remains in unity with its outer manifestation, the idea is not only true, but beautiful. The beautiful is determined through this as the outer appearance of the idea" (Hegel's Works).

Steiner took this chain of thought, which was in need of interpretation and was based on many references in Hegel's earlier work, and reduced it to the formula "Beauty is the sense-perceptible form of the idea." He added that Hegel also concedes "that what is important in art is the expressed idea" (30). If one reads further, it is clear that Hegel did not mean this. For example, he says, "An idealistic beginning in art and poetry is always suspect, because the artist has the superabundance of life and not of abstract generality out of which to draw, because unlike the thought in philosophy, in art the actual outer form yields the element of production. The artist must therefore be at home in this element" (Hegel). There is no question that Hegel is difficult to understand in this passage; even more modern interpreters have understood him as Steiner did.

What is new in Steiner's *Goethe as the Father of a New Aesthetic* is most apparent in comparison to his earlier work. In *Goethe's Theory of Knowledge*, he had developed the idea that the human being can raise himself in spirit to the source in which all possible forms of creation live. Out of the contemplation of this source flow both art and science.

> Now science and art are the objects into which the human being impresses what this contemplation offers him. In science, this occurs only in the form of the idea, which means in a directly spiritual medium; in art, it occurs in an object that is sense-perceptibly or spiritually *perceivable*. In science, nature manifests itself in a purely ideal way as "what encompasses everything individual"; in art, an object of the outer world appears as *depicting* what encompasses everything individual. That infinite element, which science seeks within the finite and seeks to present in the idea, is what art impresses into some medium taken from the real world. (2)

Later in the same passage, Steiner writes, "In a work of art, everything depends upon the degree to which the artist has implanted the idea into his medium" (2). Steiner takes a similar approach in the second volume of *Goethe's Scientific Writings*: Art "interprets the secrets of the world, as does science in a different way. This is the view that Goethe held of art. Art was for him *one* revelation of the archetypal laws of the universe; science was for him the *other*" (1-a).

The step that Steiner took in this November 9 lecture becomes clear when one compares his earlier understanding with the new one. The earlier understanding, based on Hegel, saw beauty as the incarnation of an idea; the idea is impressed into the medium. This can be thought in a number of different ways. The idea can live in the genius and come to expression in his work. Alternately, the idea can be recognized and brought to expression in a medium. In each case, the idea is what determines the form that the medium takes. The new understanding sees what is individual and sense-perceptible being raised and allowed to flower. Reality is transformed. It is not a preconceived notion that guides this transformation, but rather the force of creative imagination. This brings to expression what does not yet exist but what is present as potential. Thus a work of art reveals what is secretly already there and striving toward expression, something that appears as an idea does. It is not a matter of incarnating ideas, but of transubstantiating the world. Art does not merely bring a pre-existing idea to expression; it creates something new, something that did not exist before.

Art is thus no longer the handmaiden of the idea or of science; what she brings forth is not right, but freely created. Goethe called what comes to expression "secret laws of nature": "Beauty is a manifestation of secret laws of nature, which would have otherwise remained forever hidden." These laws are not those that one discovers on other paths—for instance, scientific research—but rather such laws as can be experienced and brought to expression by a creative genius. One can easily recognize this in music, which has an innate lawfulness and yet creates a fully new world that doesn't exist outside of music. It was in this sense that Steiner began in 1912 to develop eurythmy, a completely new art form that strove to bring to expression hidden laws of language and music.

Chapter 11

FIRST JOURNEYS

Up until he was twenty-nine, Rudolf Steiner, who beginning in 1905 was constantly on the move, often traveling thousands of miles each year, had almost never traveled. He was familiar only with the area around Vienna, the only exceptions being the two or three short trips with the Specht family to their house on Lake Attersee. That changed in 1889. In that year, Steiner took three trips that were significant for him. "Such experiences enabled me to cultivate my awareness of external phenomena and circumstances, which was not easy for me" (28).

Steiner, who had taken on his own education, was a diligent, engaged traveler. Years later, when writing his *Autobiography*, he remembered the impression that the monument to Franz Deak made on him when he visited Budapest for the first time in the summer of 1889. He wrote to Otto Specht in July from Weimar, "Almost in every square stands a noble monument, each of them full of grand memories.... Grander than all is the double Goethe-Schiller monument. It is a magnificent creation, as is the monument to Herder" (38). Monuments and buildings caught his eye, not merely the ancient classics, but especially the contemporary works (30). Later, he would take advantage of his trip to London for the theosophical congress to visit numerous museums. "I tried to see as much as possible of the science and art collections. Those collections evoked many ideas in me concerning natural and human evolution" (28). From Paris, he wrote of visiting the Louvre, "I walk from picture to picture with my book in my hand. But I have still only seen a small part of it" (39). He absorbed many things in the course of his travels, and not only museums, concerts and theater. In Paris, he wandered through the neighborhoods described by Zola, the places of the French Revolution fascinated him, as did the traffic, the landscapes, the booksellers, and the peculiarities of the people. The shopping centers, on the other hand, interested him as little as the military parades or the culinary delights.

A short trip over the Alps to Graz on July 15 followed his trip to Budapest. Here he, together with Peter Rosegger and the sculptor Hans Brandstetter, attended the funeral of Robert Hamerling in the little cemetery at St. Leonard's (154). After this, from the end of July until the middle of August, Steiner took his first longer trip to Germany. Already in 1886, he had been invited to work on the Weimar edition of Goethe's works, at that time to oversee the publication of *Goethe's Theory of Color*. This original plan didn't work out; now Steiner was being asked to edit the morphological writings. For the first time, this work gave him cause to travel to Weimar. The weeks he spent there were a grand celebration. For the first time, the Goethe student entered Goethe's house. Reverentially he crossed the threshold, entered the little study, and sat silently in the simple bedroom where Goethe had passed away. Weimar had not yet become a museum. Horse-drawn carriages clattered over the paving stones in the alleys, peasant life was still present in the city, and there were still some people living there who had seen Goethe.

In the archives, he held Goethe's own writings in his hands and contemplated his handwriting. He discovered just how much of Goethe's work still lay unread in bundles and boxes. With tense interest he searched for things that he thought must be there and, in fact, discovered an essay in the form that he had imagined it would take. It was soon clear to him that the treasures lying in the archives would make an important contribution to an understanding of Goethe the scientist. Steiner and the director of the archives, Bernhard Suphan, drew up a plan and signed a contract.

He was also personally met with an unexpectedly warm welcome. Bernhard Suphan was enthused by his knowledgeable, enthusiastic coworker. Julius Wahle took the newcomer under his wing. After work, they went to Tiefurt and Belvedere. They visited Goethe's garden house, walked up the Ettersberg, even went out to Eisenach to visit the Wartburg. Steiner felt the historical atmosphere of these places. There was still a hint of the different historical streams that had flowed through the Wartburg in the air. He experienced the battle of the minstrels, Saint Elizabeth, Martin Luther and the students of 1817 as still present. In a letter from Weimar to Richard Specht, he wrote,

> It is a remarkable feeling to be standing on the ground that carried the great German masters. I do not only mean that in regard to Weimar. For I must tell you that there have been few moments in my life

as when I stepped into Luther's study in the Wartburg yesterday. It was as though I sensed the spirit that had poured itself like an enlivening sap into the stream of German evolution during the last centuries in its immediate presence. There are no doubt few places in Germany that affect one so strongly as the Wartburg, which contains so many historical memories. (38)

He wrote to Friedrich Lemmermayer about the sensations awakened by his experience of Weimar:

It was as though a breath of fresh air swept through the part of my soul in which Goethe's and Schiller's thoughts live. The double monument made an overwhelming impression on me. Goethe's visage bears witness in every point to the magnificence of his spirit; I could not help but be in awe of the artist.... The atmosphere surrounding the spiritual-cultural life here is totally different from in our Austria. It all bears the stamp of self-possessed people with clear, unified goals. (38)

From Weimar, Steiner traveled to Berlin, where he introduced himself to Herman Grimm, one of the publishers of the Goethe edition, and visited the revered Eduard von Hartmann to discuss epistemological questions. At that time, Steiner viewed Hartmann as the definitive representative of contemporary thought. The thinker, who was suffering from a knee injury, received him reclining on a sofa. Quite a long discussion ensued concerning the nature of consciousness and of a mental image. Hartmann stated his views with a sharp clarity and cast a critical light on opposing views. "He spoke about philosophy, about the highest truths like an officer—without enthusiasm, indifferent and with a certain roughness" (235). It was an incisive moment for Steiner to realize just how far removed his own thinking and striving was from contemporary philosophy. It chilled him, and he wrote that as "I sat in the train and continued my journey, I thought about that visit, which had nevertheless been so valuable to me, and I again felt an inner chill" (28).

He traveled then on to Stuttgart, where he met Professor Kürschner, the publisher of "German National Literature," to speak about the progress of his edition of Goethe's work. Perhaps he took a walk from Alexander Strasse, where Kürschner worked, to Kannonenweg, a few steps away, or even up to the Uhlandshöhe to see the view of the city. Returning to Austria, he stopped in Munich to visit the museums. Fortunately, upon his return, he was able to spend time at Lake Atter, living with the impressions this journey had made on him before entering back into the rush of life in Vienna. He could not have imagined, however, that this journey had taken him to those places in Germany that would play significant roles in his future life: through Weimar, where he was to spend seven years working in the Goethe archive, to Berlin, which would be his official domicile for almost twenty years, on to Stuttgart, which would become in 1919 a center of anthroposophic work, and then to Munich, the place where his mystery plays would be premiered.

A third trip took Steiner during Christmas of 1889 to Hermannstadt in Transylvania. He traveled over the wide Hungarian plains. After missing the connecting train in Budapest, Steiner traveled through Szegedin and arrived in the afternoon in the border town of Mediasch. The next train left at 2:00 a.m. The only other guests in the restaurant with him were playing cards at another table. "Every nationality in Hungary and Transylvania was represented, and they played with a great passion. Explosive outbursts occurred every half hour and gathered like clouds of fighting demons, as it were, above the table, robbing them of all human dignity" (28). He arrived in Hermannstadt the following morning. The world of the Transylvanian Sachsens was like an oasis, where the paternal ways were practiced in the simplest manner and people looked with longing toward Austria and the "empire": "A noble people who held themselves valiantly in the face of the coming catastrophe, which they did not see." On December 29, Steiner gave a lecture there with the title "Women in Light of the Goethean Worldview: A Contribution to the Question of Women's Rights." He characterized the male, who distances himself from nature and the immediacy of sensation and becomes dry, pedantic and unnatural. In comparison, the female harmoniously develops the whole human being, and in overcoming one-sidedness brings the wholeness of humanity to expression. "Thus women appear as the true messengers of God; a man finds in them what he has lost" (B61/62).

The next day, a sleigh ride: wrapped in heavy furs against the bitter cold, through lightly crackling snow south to the Carpathian Mountains that at first appeared as black soaring forested walls and then—as they drew closer—showed themselves as a wild fissured mountain landscape with terrifying cliffs. Sadly, Steiner took leave of his friend Moritz Zitter and his Transylvanian circle of friends and returned to Vienna at the beginning of January 1890.

CHAPTER 12

FRIEDRICH ECKSTEIN, THEOSOPHY, AND ROSA MAYREDER

Friedrich Eckstein and Rudolf Steiner probably met one another at the Café Griensteidl. In his memoirs, Eckstein relates his memories of Steiner in the late 1880s, "Around this time a fully beardless youth appeared in our circle,"—Eckstein, who was born on February 17, 1861, was just a week older than Steiner!—"quite slender, with long dark hair. A sharp pair of glasses gave him a somewhat pointed look, and with his long black mantel, buttoned-up vest, the black Lavalliere and the old-fashioned top hat, he looked like nothing else than a poorly nourished theology student" (Eckstein). Rosa Mayreder, on the other hand, described Eckstein's much more eccentric appearance:

> Even his appearance bore the mark of the unusual; a sort of hairy pilgrim's robe, which showed no sign of white under clothes at the wrists and neck, covered his thin form, and waves of curls formed a frame around his face on which an equally curly beard grew out into twirled moustaches and sideburns. His dark eyes behind the glasses were mild and serene; they seemed to look on past the world rather than into it. (Mayreder)

Eckstein, a devotee of Wagner, a Bayreuth pilgrim and a vegetarian, was not only outwardly a remarkable figure, but as a chemist he was an extremely knowledgeable scientist who had tackled very difficult mathematical problems and had also studied music with Anton Bruckner. More than anything, Eckstein was well-versed in esoteric literature and symbols. In his *Autobiography*, Steiner mentions Eckstein only as being of the conviction that esoteric knowledge should not be made public. He says that he knew "ancient wisdom" very well and added, "When I first knew him, he did not write much, but what he wrote was full of spirit. Yet, at first no one would sense from his writings that he was an intimate who knew of ancient spiritual knowledge. This is active in the background of his spiritual work" (28).

One of Steiner's letters to Eckstein has been preserved. It shows that the encounter with Eckstein was—at least for a time—more significant than the passage in Steiner's *Autobiography* indicates. At the end of November 1890, Steiner wrote to him from Weimar:

> There are two occurrences in my life that I consider to be of such importance that if they had not taken place, I would be a completely different person. Concerning the first, I must be silent; the second is the fact that I have met you. What you are to me, you know better than I do; I do know that I owe you endless gratitude. Your laconic letter, "Reading Jung-Stilling's *Homesickness*," holds the scale with so much dense writing. Such a book shows us the path to "die and become!" Did you know that Jung-Stilling also wrote a "Key to *Homesickness*?" (39)

This letter indicates clearly that Steiner and Eckstein had discretely discussed esoteric questions—for instance, concerning "die and become." Even more, Eckstein, who used "Mighty Eck" as his signature at the time, had been helpful to Steiner in this regard. Unfortunately, Eckstein says little more about his relationship with Steiner than mentioned above. But he does share somewhat more than Steiner did.

> I had met him earlier, often accompanying the well-known Goethe scholar Professor Karl Julius Schröer, and we had discussed the question of symbolism in Goethe's work. He had in the meantime heard that I was acquainted with Madame Blavatsky and the leading members of the Theosophical Society in Madras. Dr. Steiner explained to me that he was very interested in learning more about these things and asked me to initiate him into the esoteric teachings. Thus began my regular meetings with him, which continued for many years and led him finally, after years of wandering and other episodes, to the formulation of his own "anthroposophic" system. (Eckstein)

This recollection needs to be corrected in a number of points, as well as complemented. Friedrich Eckstein had unsuccessfully tried to be introduced to H.P. Blavatsky in Elberfeld in 1886. In the beginning of 1887, he was then able to visit her at her bedside in Ostende, where she lay ill, smoking and cursing. Blavatsky immediately made him president of the Lodge of the Theosophical Society in Vienna and he returned to the city with a wealth of theosophical literature. An encounter between Steiner and Eckstein concerning theosophy was only possible after this point. Steiner relates, however, that his first contact with theosophical circles came about in 1889, following his return from Germany. Eckstein's statement that their meetings continued for years is certainly incorrect. Even if they had begun in the summer of 1887, which seems improbable, they could only have continued for three years. It is more probable that their relationship was limited to the period from September 1889 to September 1890.

Eckstein's statement that he had initiated Steiner into the *Esoteric Teachings* is also problematic. Blavatsky's book was published in London at the end of 1888; Eckstein could only have received it and told Steiner about it early in 1889. But was Blavatsky's work really the topic of their discussions? Steiner himself relates only that at that time he read *Esoteric Buddhism* by A.P. Sinnett and *Light on the Path* by Mabel Collins (B 83/84). In the context in which he tries to show just how early he encountered theosophy, he does not mention the *Secret Doctrine*, although this would be the place to do so. Later remarks by Steiner and a letter from 1902 point to his first receiving the book in the summer of 1902.

Contemporary documents attest to the fact that Eckstein and Steiner did have discussions and correspondence concerning Goethe and his use of symbolism. In Eckstein, Steiner found a scholar of symbolism for whom the symbols were not merely drawings, but rather indications of spiritual realities. It was very important for Steiner that this should be taken seriously—thus his respect for Eckstein. In this light the mention of Jung-Stilling's *Homesickness* takes on a special significance. In his *Autobiography*, Jung-Stilling speaks with a brief clarity about this book:

> The emotional state in which Stilling entered when writing this book, which consisted of four octavo volumes, is indescribable. It was as though his spirit were raised up into the etheric heights; a spirit of peace and quietness flow through him, and he found himself in a state of bliss that words cannot describe. When he began to work, ideas lit up in his soul, which so enlivened him that he was barely able to write quickly enough to keep up with them;…in a state between sleeping and waking he envisioned paradisiacal landscapes of unearthly beauty.… A feeling was connected with these visions to which no earthly enjoyment can be compared. (Jung-Stilling, *Autobiography*)

When and in what connection had Eckstein brought this book to Steiner's attention? Did Eckstein's laconic letter come after Steiner had left for Weimar, in November or December 1890, at which point he was reading Goethe's fairy tale, *The "Fairy Tale" of the Green Snake and the Beautiful Lily*? Was it written as an answer to one of Steiner's personal questions? We don't know the answer to these questions. Strangely enough, Steiner was quite reticent in this regard and mentioned Jung-Stilling only seldom (172).

It is possible that Stilling's book accompanied Steiner during the period in which he studied mysticism, which he describes in his *Autobiography*. He felt a certain sympathy for "the *nature* of inner mystical experience. Mystics wish to unite inwardly with the source of human existence, not merely theorize about it as though it were an external thing" (28). It is quite possible that Steiner had embarked on the path of Christian mysticism during the winter of 1889/90 as a form of inner experiment, just as he would repeatedly immerse himself completely in different conceptual approaches. In a letter from Weimar, he speaks of the mystical element "in which I swam for a time in Vienna in a manner that could almost cause concern" (39). In any case, the excursion into the realm of mysticism showed him clearly that this was not his path. He sought the warmth of inner experience in the immersion in the world of ideas, in which spirit revealed itself. Mere immersion in the world of the soul, in pictures and emotions, however colorful they may be, seemed to him to be misguided, a form of escape from the real questions of the time. "The forces in my soul opposed mysticism with even greater strength as I placed this before my soul's vision" (28).

Friedrich Eckstein also introduced Steiner to the circle around Marie and Edmund Lang. Marie Lang was the soul of this circle. Her beauty and grace alone were alluring; her bearing was permeated with an earnest and deeply-felt mystical-theosophical view of life. Because her mysticism was genuine, she did not only attract people such as the theosophist Franz Hartmann, who had joined Blavatsky's followers six years earlier, and the diplomat Carl zu Leiningen-Billigheim, who would later translate Harrison's *The Transcendent Cosmos*, but also artists and writers who held other views. The composer Hugo Wolf; the architect Julius Mayreder; Rosa Mayreder, who at that time saw herself as a painter; and for a time, Rudolf Steiner, who was especially fond of Marie Lang, all spent time at the Lang's house.

Rosa Mayreder described Marie Lang as "a woman my age"—she was thirty-one years old—"at the summit of her beauty and unique talent. With her glowing imagination, which found meaning in dreams and symbols, [and] her overflowing emotions, which would not let itself be fenced in by reason, one of her friends once characterized her in the following manner: 'She had the intelligence of people at the stage of the creation of mythology.' But she drew me in with her warmth and the directness of her feelings to the point that I was totally at her mercy" (Mayreder). Later, both Marie Lang and Rosa Mayreder became leading figures in the Austrian women's movement, which was very active for the rights of women and of illegitimate children.

Here Steiner also had the opportunity to become acquainted with the beginning of the theosophical movement. He relates that he had "a quite friendly" relationship to Franz Hartmann and other theosophists, but that "the posturing and the mannerisms of these people, the artificiality" repelled him (B 83/84). Marie Lang's manner, however, struck him as being genuine. "Within herself she had a store of mystical knowledge that life's difficult trials had made conscious in a completely elemental way" (28).

In the middle of March 1890, Marie Lang took it upon herself to introduce Rosa Mayreder to Rudolf Steiner. Steiner first became acquainted with her as a painter. Shortly thereafter, it became apparent that she had also written a number of novellas. Steiner persuaded her to let him read them. He shared his impressions with her: "It is a sin for you to disregard your writing talent and continue to paint." For Rosa Mayreder, these words pointed her toward her true vocation, for which she never forgot Steiner. She added to her recollections, "He did not, however, take very good care of my manuscripts. Three of them disappeared forever."

Soon their discussions came to focus on philosophical questions. Steiner found Rosa Mayreder to be not only a highly educated and deliberate person, she also had a burning interest in philosophical questions of existence. "Rosa Mayreder is the person with whom I spoke the most about these forms"—the ideas that make up *Intuitive Thinking as a Spiritual Path*. "She relieved me in part of the loneliness with which I lived at that time" (28).

In the beginning, their relationship was colored by a curious game of hide-and-seek. "Since I thought him to be a dyed-in-the-wool theosophist," Mayreder relates, "I tried to steer clear of conversations that touched on this point. After a while it turned out that he believed the same about me and had also steered clear of any talk concerning theosophy. He had hoped to learn more about this spiritual direction by spending time in our circle, but was, however, much more decidedly inimical to it, as I was. For me, theosophy was a realm in which I did not feel at home, as I did not possess an inner aptitude for the form of knowledge that was needed; he, on the other hand, judged it to be a form of spiritual weakness and warned me to steer clear of it, since it would be dangerous for one's spiritual development. His views concerning personal freedom resonated fully with what I strove for, and he helped me become clear about this in his first philosophical writings" (Mayreder).

In the course of numerous conversations about the problems of materialism, and concerning literature and aesthetics, Rudolf Steiner and Rosa Mayreder became close friends. Just before he moved to Weimar, Steiner visited she and her husband at their summer cottage in Waidhofen. In his *Autobiography*, he recalls "a walk through the wonderful alpine forest, during which Rosa Mayreder and I discussed the true meaning of human freedom" (28).

In their conversations Steiner noticed an inclination by Rosa Mayreder toward naturalistic, materialistic ideas. Given this, it seems possible that an article dated Sept. 23, 1890, and discovered in 1935 in a Viennese archive, was written explicitly by Steiner for her. The article, which bore the title "Atomism and its Rebuttal" presented the contemporary approach to atomic theory as well as the view of human life that arose from it at length, and then went on to refute these theories based on their own results. In any case, we can be reasonably certain that Steiner spoke with Mayreder about these ideas. He also spoke about a series of germinal ideas concerning the interpretation of Goethe's fairy tale, a story he had been introduced to about a year earlier. In his interpretation, the images of this tale reveal the transformations a person goes through along the path to true individuality. To be able to have these thoughts reflected back to him in the mirror of another person's soul helped Steiner develop them further.

On the whole, this last year in Vienna was a very exciting time for Steiner. He encountered the dawn of the "Viennese Modern," he became acquainted with the theosophists, some of whom had known Blavatsky personally, and he had had the opportunity to discuss questions of spirituality with Friedrich Eckstein, someone who was clearly knowledgeable concerning "ancient wisdom." In Marie Lang and Rosa Mayreder, he met two very different, yet important, women who would go on to play significant roles in the women's movement. Quietly, he began to explore Goethe's fairy tale, a theme that would concern him for the rest of his life. In Nietzsche's *Beyond Good and Evil*, he first met the work of a thinker, who appeared to him to be the personification of the riddles of the time and would accompany him through the coming years. He also wrote the introduction to the third volume of *Goethe's Scientific Writings*, a fascinating work with which, in the next chapter, we will round off Steiner's years in Vienna.

CHAPTER 13

SPIRIT AND NATURE: THE FOUNDATION OF A SPIRITUAL PHILOSOPHY

"If one did not have the duty to speak the truth frankly when one believed oneself to have recognized it, the following thoughts would no doubt have remained unwritten" (1-c). Thus begins the introduction to the third volume of *Goethe's Scientific Writings*. It catches one's attention. This sentence indicates that Steiner knew explicitly that his presentation would place him in radical opposition to the prevailing thought of his time, for he shook the fundamental dogmas of then contemporary philosophy. It is not that he developed a specific view of morality or a special theory of nature—that would not have been risky. However, Steiner knew that he was entering into battle with the thought habits that for centuries had been the roots of the Western world. He could foresee that his work would be viewed as "the attempt of a dilettante" who "for all his 'insight' has already been judged and found wanting."

It was already clear to him at that time that modern science, which he attacked, drew its authority from the "magnificent and wondrous achievements" of technology. He was certain that the fascination with technology served as the proof of the truth of modern science. But he didn't hesitate to state that these achievements had "nothing to do with the true longing for an understanding of nature." He offered the thesis: "It is something quite different to observe natural processes in order to place their forces at the service of technology than it is to do so in order to gain a deeper understanding of the being of nature. True science is only present when the spirit seeks to satisfy *its own* needs without any *outer reason*" (1-c).

In light of the problems that have arisen through the technological approach to understanding, it is not difficult to come to the conclusion that this approach is based on controlling and exploiting nature. In view of the consequences of this approach, one can develop a certain distrust of the technological approach to nature and have a feeling that something is not quite right. Usually the consequence of this feeling is the view that technology needs to be made better, and in the long run everything will come back into balance. Seldom does this feeling of distrust extend to modern science itself and its claims of understanding nature. One does come to the conclusion that modern science is perhaps, in fact, not science at all, but merely the theory of the control and exploitation of nature, its measurement and its use. One does not recognize the fact that knowledge and science are something quite different than the examination of nature, with the goal of discovering how it can be made useful—that science doesn't simply have the task of formulating the laws of nature mathematically, but that science can lead, as in Goethe's work, to seeing the *ideas* that are at work in nature. This is what Steiner attempted to articulate in philosophical terminology.

With the introduction to this volume and by laying the theoretical foundation of Goethe's color theory, Steiner crossed a Rubicon. What he had written up till now could be viewed as another interpretation of Goethe's work with a valid place within the genre. In this introduction, however, Steiner challenged mainstream science. This was clear in the form alone. The text lacks what a philologist expects from such an introduction. There is no historical presentation of the development of Goethe's ideas, in which the stages of his thought are explained; and an exploration of the thinkers who may have "influenced" Goethe and his relationship to other scientists is completely missing. Steiner wastes no time, but goes directly to the point.

Instead of a philological excursus, we find a theoretical defense of *Goethe's Theory of Color*, fundamental questions about the nature of science, a rebuttal of materialism, an in-depth exploration of the concepts of time and space, and an outline of the structure of science. To conclude, Newton's theory is placed in an appropriate context. If one wished to interpret this very concentrated text in terms of traditional philosophy, one could view it as the draft of an ontology. Steiner quite consciously does not use this title. He speaks instead of a "system of science."

Steiner's audacity is most apparent when one examines the consequences of his chain of thought. Take the nature of sense experience. In the generally accepted view, a sensation—for instance, a sound—is the product of a specific mechanical process. Sound is caused by vibrations in the air. With good reason, Steiner claims that it is the sound that causes the vibrations. "The space-time process is the *effect* of a sensation in an object present in space and time." In other words, sound affects different media differently, causing them to react in the manner that they are able. Air reacts with vibrations, because this is the reaction of which it is capable. Electricity, which carries sound through a cable or enables its wireless transmission, reacts with corresponding "waves." The audio nerves "carry" sound in a neuron-specific manner. Sound is conserved on a record in a manner that corresponds to the material that the record is made of. But sound is sound. It is neither "vibrations," nor "waves," nor impressions in a record. All of these are but traces of the sound, like footprints left behind in movement, matter or electricity. The fact that these impressions—for instance, the stimulation of the audio nerve—have something to do with sound cannot be directly experienced.; it is instead the logical result of scientific research. The waves and vibrations are, however, actually the tracks and impressions of sounds in other fields of perception.

In actuality, one attempts in vain to find sound in the "vibrations" and the "waves." Popular opinion holds the vibrations, the waves, or the nerve processes to be the only objective reality. Our sense experiences—sound, color, smell, touch, and so on—are held to be merely subjective. One forgets, thereby, that it is through our senses alone that we become aware of the air, or of processes in the nerves. It is possible to see or touch a nerve. Our knowledge of the nerves, the atmosphere and so on rests on direct sense impressions. They form the primary reality, the point of origin of all our research. What science examines is thus not at all the source of our sense impressions. When one asks how the processes in our nerves are connected with our impressions of sound, he is examining the relationship between two different fields of perception. If one asks how movement is connected to sound, he is also examining the relationship between two different fields of perception. Scientific research, therefore, can never go "behind" the sense impressions, for even when researchers view the world through the lens of an electron microscope, they remain dependent upon their capacity to perceive, on sense impressions. The object of science is thus, inasmuch as it involves observation, the sum total of the perceived impressions. The world dissolves completely into *perceptions*. *"The perceived world is consequently nothing other than a sum of metamorphosed perceptions"* (1-c).

The second important topic presented concerned the concept of time. The naïve mind sees time as an infinite expanse, a time-space. Things exist within this time-space. The objective, material things of one's mental pictures have duration in time, which is pictured as a time-space. In addition, one believes that time itself exists in this form of a time-space. The immediate, elementary experience of time is translated into a form of pictured spatiality. One doesn't notice that this mental image of time has nothing to do with the experience everyone has of the present. Time-space is merely a crutch for a way of thinking that is unable to find an appropriate image for our experience of time. Steiner presented another approach: "Time is not a receptacle within which changes take place; it is present neither before nor outside of the things. Time is the sense-perceptible expression of the act of things taking place in an interdependent sequence." Time comes into being through the lawfulness in which a being brings itself step by step to expression. A plant shows itself in a specific sequence of forms of appearance; history develops in a certain sequence of events. Time, as it is experienced by humans, has another qualitative dimension: it is youth and age, morning, autumn, or the time of the Reformation. "Here we can see that time first enters the picture where the essence of something comes to appearance. Time belongs to the world of appearances. It does not have anything to do with the essence itself. This essence can only be grasped as an idea" (1-c).

The simple sense impression teaches us that time has nothing to do with the essence of something. It does not matter when I see green or orange; what is important is what I see. This is even more apparent if we turn our attention to a phenomenon that is usually viewed as being determined by time: velocity, expressed as miles per hour. When we ask ourselves what is actually experienced, we see that elemental velocity, distance, and time are merely numbers through which we attempt to grasp the speed. They are truly abstracted from the phenomenon of velocity itself; they are abstractions. The reality is the velocity itself, which comes in its elemental nature into experience. Thus it is apparent that time is not an independent being. The beingness of something brings time into being. This beingness or essence exists through itself and is not dependent on a pictured time-space to be raised into the world of duration.

If one grasps the concept of time in this manner, there is no necessity to conceive of the essence or being enduring in time as a permanent, fixed material that one imagines behind the manifestations. Thus Steiner arrives at his third significant thesis: "The sense-based picture of the world is the sum of metamorphosing perceptions without any fundamental matter"

(1-c). In this manner, Steiner argued against the metaphysical status of some reality, which was thought to lie behind the sense impressions. He doesn't question what appears to the senses in a phenomenological manner—the earth in the garden, the hammer in the hand, and the moon in the sky. By each of these we are dealing with a sum of sense perceptible facts. We can touch the earth and experience its coolness, smell its odor, experience its weight and see its dark brown color, and then we designate the sum of these impressions: earth. We also know that these impressions undergo changes. When the sun dries out the earth, it becomes lighter in color, can become warmer and lighter in weight, and if one were to send it out into space, without gravity it would lose its weight completely. In this sense, the perceptions undergo constant metamorphosis. Perceptions change under specific conditions and influences. The various aspects of an impression affect each other reciprocally. When the aspects A, B, and C are present and aspect D joins them, the former can change so that we now have A', B', and C'. In this sense, the phenomena condition and influence one another reciprocally; there is no need to hypothesize some form of fundamental matter.

Just as little as time is a receptacle in which things occur is space a box with infinitely distance walls. In his passage concerning the concept of time, Steiner concludes, "Space is an idea" (1-c). And it is a special idea, which allows us to grasp the cosmos as a unity without having to address the inner essence of objects. Objects are placed in relation to one another purely externally. At least one relationship is always present between any two objects: they are either close together or far apart. A similar relationship exists to at least two other objects. If one disregards the concrete objects and focuses on the relationships themselves, one recognizes a relationship between relationships. This relationship of relationships is in itself not absolute, for in an ideally concrete manner it refers to the specific objects that serve as its starting point. If one thinks of these relationships as purely external, one has the concept of space.

In overcoming the conventional notions of space, time, and matter in this manner, Steiner dismisses neither the experienced distances in space nor the experience of time in the present. Neither does he reject individual sense experiences of pressure, weight, sound or color. He pulls the rug out from under the abstract notions of the metaphysical existence of an absolute space, an absolute time and an absolute matter in order to make a methodologically transparent approach to science possible.

The structure of science rests on two pillars: perceptions gained through observation and the concepts that are grasped in thinking. Perceptions give us direct, qualitative impressions. "The qualities, which my sense impressions give me, cannot be transformed into something else through conceptual reflection. Neither can I find any conceptual quality through which I can construct what is present in the sense-perceptible reality if I do not have the perceptions. I cannot give a person who is blind to the color red a mental image of red, even if I describe it to him with all possible conceptual tools. *Sense perceptions thus have something that never fully enters the conceptual, something that must be perceived if it is to be in any way part of our understanding*" (1-c).

Sense perception is something that cannot be grasped conceptually. It is in and of itself and cannot be reduced to something else. It is the point of origin of our knowing that, as perception, cannot be placed in question.

Our thinking can only build relationships *between* individual perceptions. I can ask why a spot of light appears on my wall and discover the relationship that exists between a reflecting surface on my desk and the sunlight shining on my desk, and in the concept of reflection I can find an explanation for the spot of light. In thinking, I find the law of reflection. In thinking, I find the lawfulness that explains to me the relationships between the various sense perceptions. Through thinking and the recognized lawfulness, the connections between the various phenomena become clear. All of these laws stand for their part in an integral relationship. For example, the above-mentioned concept of reflection is related to other concepts such as light, surface, angle of incidence and so on.

"The senses, which are not able to grasp this unified content, get stuck in the multiplicity. They are natural pluralists. Thinking overcomes the multiplicity and, through hard work, finds its way back to the unified cosmic principles" (1-c).

Scientific systems arise out of the relationship between concept and natural law, on the one hand, and sense perception on the other. "If an obviously real essence or manifestation achieves only such an existence that it stands completely outside the concept and is controlled only by the lawfulness in its changes, we call this inorganic. Everything that happens with this essence or phenomena is caused by the influences upon it by another entity or essence" (1). The appearance of inorganic phenomena is thus determined by some external influence. For instance, water's appearance is determined by the temperature, among other things. Everything belonging to the physical world is determined by the relationship between things.

There are, however, sense-perceptible phenomena that appear as a unified whole and are in no way simply the expression of external influences. To understand these phenomena, one must go beyond what is immediately apparent and follow the process through which they developed. This is determined from within and has a specific lawful nature. It is here that "what can be grasped conceptually is revealed as a sense-perceptible whole. The two are not identical, but here the concept does not appear outside the sensed multiplicity as a natural law, but within the same as a principle. What we call the *type* forms the unifying essence of this multiplicity—it permeates it but is no longer sense-perceptible" (1-c).

The concept appears in its conceptual nature within the context of human consciousness. Here the concept itself is perceived; when it becomes a motive, it then gives human action a meaningful direction. The "system of science" comes most clearly to expression in Steiner's summary.

> *Natural law*, *type* and *concept* are the three forms in which the ideal manifests. A natural law is abstract. It stands above the multiplicity experienced by the senses and rules inorganic science. Here, idea and reality are completely separate. The type unifies both in one being. What is spiritual is present in its activity, but it doesn't act as such It is not present in its own nature, but, if it is to be observed, must be beheld within the realm of the senses. This is the case within the realm of the organic. The concept is in a perceptible manner present. In human consciousness, the concept is in and of itself perceptible. Concept and image are one. For this reason, the ideal seeds of existence of the lower forms of nature can also come to expression. (1-c)

In these passages, Rudolf Steiner sketches an outline of his own philosophy of nature at the end of his Viennese period. In doing so, he sums up ten years of thoughtful consideration. He continued to build upon this foundation in his later work. From the point of view of his fully developed anthroposophic work, it is noticeable that he does not yet speak about the later differentiation between the animal and the plant kingdoms, between the astral and the etheric. This is not important to him at this point. The introduction to the first volume of *Goethe's Scientific Writings* shows that essential aspects of this differentiation were clearly present. But in 1890, Steiner was focused on laying the foundation of a spiritual understanding of nature.

It was crucial that this understanding not be trapped in the system of coordinates laid out by the general notions of space, time and matter, but that it could unfold itself as a spiritual whole out of the idea of beingness. This quality of being appears initially in human consciousness as idea, concept and natural law; it appears in the various levels of natural phenomena either as present within them or affecting them from outside. The essence of being lives in the multiplicity experienced by the senses in human consciousness as type and natural law.

In an essay dated Sept. 23, 1890, just a week before he left for Weimar, Steiner addressed once more the question of atomism and its refutation, with the theory that both sense phenomena and the human spirit are brought into existence through the activity of tiny particles. To refute this theory, Steiner utilized a remarkably simple example that one has to consider carefully to recognize its significance:

> Let us imagine that someone posts a telegram to me at point A. When the telegram is delivered, all I have is a piece of paper with letters on it. When I focus my attention on these things and know how to read, I discover much more than merely the paper and the letters. I discover a very specific conceptual content. Is it possible to maintain that I have created the conceptual content in my brain and that the paper and the letters are the only things that are real? Certainly not. For the content that is now in me is also present at point A. This example is in fact the most pertinent example one could choose. For nothing visible was transferred from point A to me. Who would want to assert that the telegraph lines actually carry thoughts from one point to another? (B 63)

One can argue that such a technical process illustrates nothing about the relation between the sensory world and the spiritual world. Such a rebuff does not, however, take the principle illustrated in the example into consideration. The example confronts us with the riddle that the medium, through which thought content is transmitted, quite often has no significance for the content itself. The human spirit is certainly dependent on there being a mediating substrate. But the substrate has only a secondary significance for the spiritual content. Our spirit always turns its attention to what is meaningful; the sense-perceptible substrate is only of significance in that it serves to carry and mediate the meaning. When we look at a painting, it captures our interest because it is a picture of something, and the physical colors—whether they are thickly applied or gently merging oils, for instance—are only of interest inasmuch as they contribute to the meaning of the picture. When one looks a tree, one might notice what kind of a tree it is or whether it is healthy or not and then based on this recognition raise questions concerning the chemical makeup of the soil. It is only within the context of the search for meaning that an examination of the substrate makes sense. In this sense, everything depends on the ideal, conceptual essentiality that focuses our attention and guides our questions.

Chapter 14

WEIMAR: AT THE GOETHE-SCHILLER ARCHIVE

Rudolf Steiner first announced his planned move to Weimar in the spring of 1890, then continued to postpone it. Finally, on Sept. 29 1890, he traveled from Vienna to Weimar and found a neat but rather expensive apartment on the Junkerstrasse. The following morning began with a brisk walk across Wielandplatz and Frauenplan to the archive, which at that time was housed after a fashion on the second floor in the northeast corner of the castle. Bernhard Suphan, the director of the archive, gave him a friendly welcome and said that he hoped to have finally found in Steiner not only help in the work of the archive but also a spiritual support, something he had been looking for since his arrival in the city. Being named a special friend affected Steiner strangely. "I lacked, one could say, the needed faith" (39).

A few days later, he was introduced to the Grand Duchess Sophie, the owner of the archive. Steiner always spoke of this princess of the house of Orange with respect and emphasized that she had the ability to master her task. She took good care of the archive, initiated the construction of a permanent home for the archive over the Ilm, and was the one who had suggested offering Rudolf Steiner a position. The respect that Steiner in turn enjoyed from the grand duke and duchess did not mean, however, that he was well paid. His monthly salary was 180 marks, just marginally higher than a trained worker, and during the initial years he received an extra ten marks for each sheet that was ready to go to print. This bonus was meant no doubt to speed up the process of publication. The original plan had been to publish ten volumes annually.

The first months in the archive were more than satisfactory for the Goethe scholar. No day passed during which Steiner, poring through the papers that had lain untouched for over fifty years, did not discover something new. He could follow the tracks of Goethe's work everywhere. He could discuss things at length with his two colleagues: Julius Wahle, a spirited Viennese who was the same age as Steiner, and Eduard von der Hellen, a quiet, introverted man from Westphalia.

The working conditions in the cramped archive were anything but ideal. Publication had begun before the uncounted papers had been examined, ordered and catalogued. Examining and searching were part of each day's work. Outlines, notes and thoughts jotted down on the backs of envelopes were found in the files that Reimer and Eckermann had put into storage. Drafts were written by his secretaries and coworker, with corrections in Goethe's hand. Much of it was difficult to decipher. Finally, there were the proofs that had to be finished.

The ongoing work was constantly interrupted by high-ranking visitors and foreign scholars, all of whom had to be taken care of. There were questions to be answered, manuscripts to be found, and each visitor counted on having time to chat. Afterward, one had to pick of the threads of one's own work. Difficulties soon arose concerning the guidelines for the work itself. The publishers had originally wanted to include only finished pieces in the edition. This principle did not seem to Steiner to be appropriate for the scientific texts. Outlines, rough conceptual sketches, fragments, and even notes could in Steiner's opinion cast a light on Goethe's scientific approach. He drafted a statement to the publishers, in which he recommended including anything that could give a clearer picture of Goethe's scientific intentions. In the end, the committee accepted most of his recommendations, which did not include the intention of printing everything available. Steiner did not envision publishing a critical historical study in chronological order. He wanted to present a picture of Goethe's scientific work, its methods and results.

In the beginning, Steiner went to work with remarkable zeal. By the end of January he had announced that the first volume of the morphological studies would soon be ready to go to press and, in fact, by early spring the volume was finished and had been printed. This tempo could not have been sustained even under ideal conditions. Although Steiner initially had a good relationship with Suphan and even for a while tutored his sons, in the beginning of March he complained:

> Suphan, the director of the archive, is one of the pettiest of the petty. A truly philistine school master without any larger points of view. Wherever something free, independent and unshackled would develop, his disposition hangs on it like a lead weight. Naturally, he can't help

himself.... But whoever has to work with such a person feels himself to be continually crippled. (39)

As could be expected, the novelty that had lent wings to Steiner's work wore off. Following the first viewing of Goethe's papers, with its wealth of discoveries, something truly new and important seldom turned up. In April 1891, Steiner complained that "the archival work, which deadens the spirit" caused "a spiritual malaise" in him (39). The amount of material that had to be worked through philologically and the guidelines of the edition, which demanded that all possible interpretations be noted, grew into an ominous nightmare. The initially fascinating documents transformed themselves gradually into a dusty heap of files, whose presence made it hard to take a breath. Steiner began to realize that he was going to spend the coming years comparing handwritten manuscripts, initial printings, and later editions, as well as correcting proofs, creating indexes and putting together catalogues of possible linguistic interpretations. In the six volumes that Steiner edited, the indexes and catalogues filled 670 pages of small print. For someone like Steiner, who had an insurmountable antipathy for any form of pedantry and cared little about spelling and punctuation, this fussy philological nitpicking must have been torture. In May, he wrote to Pauline Specht:

> There is something tragic in the fact that all of my earlier writings were connected in some way or another to Goethe.... At the Goethe celebration, a minister from Württemberg introduced himself, who proved to be a true believer of my ideas. He quickly realized the tragedy in the fact that I am still chained to researching Goethe himself. He said that the introduction to the third volume alone shows that I no longer inwardly have anything to do with researching Goethe. Ach! If only my present work were but the sleeping state of the chrysalis out of which I could emerge as a butterfly to fly into the heaven of pure philosophical teaching activity, free of all followers. (39)

And no less pointedly in a letter to Rosa Mayreder, "Thus I find myself all day engaged in work that my 'I,' as it was four or five years ago, would have done with great devotion. In that I do *it* now, *I* do not do it at all." And: "As I said, except for the fact that I want to finally shed my skin, which, as it has for the last two years been organically separate from me, is but an inorganic shell. Otherwise my entire existence is nonsense and a lie; my activity is not my own, but that of a miserable puppet, dancing on threads that I spun years ago and that I no longer want to touch, let alone guide" (39).

The years that Steiner spent in the Goethe archive became, increasingly, years spent far away from Goethe. It is symptomatic that, except for a celebratory address on the occasion of Goethe's birthday, he personally wrote nothing about Goethe that went beyond the duties in the archive. As soon as the door to the archive shut behind him, he turned to other concerns. He wrote his dissertation, he wrote *Intuitive Thinking as a Spiritual Path,* he worked on his book about Nietzsche—all works in which Goethe is barely mentioned. He was interested in theater, studied hypnotism and suggestion as well as modern literature, and battled with the "Society for an Ethical Culture"—without mentioning Goethe in any significant way. Only in the winter of 1896/97, when his work at the archive had come to an end, did he turn back to his own research into Goethe's work and write his final study of Goethe: *Goethe's Worldview.*

There is no question that Steiner, whose interests lay in other areas, was not an exemplary philologist. The manuscripts that he delivered needed—as we know from the files of the archive—repeated corrections. The printer didn't have an easy time with his texts. The Böhlau Publishers wrote to Suphan, "The corrections, when they are returned to us, are usually worse and more difficult than a really bad manuscript. Page 18 is at the moment being corrected for the fifth time by a colleague." In some of the volumes, though not in all of them, Steiner let many mistakes slip through. Texts were not read correctly or not reprinted correctly in the manuscripts. Even in selecting the order of the texts, Steiner took idiosyncratic liberties. In one example, Goethe wrote two essays: "Concerning Geology, Especially in Böhme" and "Excursion to Zinnwalde and Altenberg." When Goethe published these, the latter came directly after the former, as the text is a continuation. The first essay closes with the sentence: "What follows is the little I was able to notice during an excursion from Töplitz to Zinnwald." And then came the description of the excursion. But Steiner placed another essay in between these two, with the title "Problematical," and in the following section is the excursion to Zinnwald. In this sense, Steiner disregarded certain connections. Others he simply did not recognize. In his *Autobiography,* he writes, "I do not deny that 'experts' may consider some details in the Weimar edition erroneous; they are free to correct those" (28). He spoke even more clearly about it in a lecture for members of the

Anthroposophical Society. "He"—meaning himself—"was never especially proud of his actual philological work. He could point out many of his own mistakes and would not want to make light of any of them" (B 83/84).

The work in the Goethe archive and as editor for the Weimar edition was again a retarding element in Rudolf Steiner's biography and served to slow his development markedly. The journey through the desert of linguistic interpretations and manuscripts took time and effort. In this situation, genial originality was of no use. The spirit remained chained to the letters and had to fall into a "chrysalis stage."

In later years, Steiner could find meaning in this wise guidance of destiny. His descriptions of the Weimar period written from historical distance give barely a hint of the bitterness that filled him at the time. As a poorly paid research assistant, he had to produce six volumes of Goethe's scientific writings out of completely unsorted material. What that meant becomes clear when one takes into consideration that a team of researchers working with well-sorted archived materials took twenty-five years to publish the new Leopoldina edition of *Goethe's Scientific Writings*, which consisted of eleven volumes. It is not surprising that after five years of work in Weimar at the end of 1895 Steiner wrote, "I know now that I was betrayed and sold out the moment that I came here. I have to look upon the time spent in Weimar as lost" (39).

Looking back, on the other hand, Steiner would focus his attention on the light-filled aspects of the years in Weimar. Thanks to his position at the archive, he was able to meet Herman Grimm, for whom he had great respect. Grimm spoke with him about his plans and ideas, among others about a history of the imaginative themes of the nation, an idea that fascinated Steiner (36). Similarly, Steiner looked back on a number of meetings that came about through the archive. He came to know the already-aging Heinrich von Treitschke, Gustav von Loeper, Otto Harnack—whose insight into Goethe was full of originality—and others. But in addition to these personal encounters, the work in the archive made something else possible. Rudolf Steiner had promised to edit two additional volumes of *Goethe's Scientific Writings* for the series that was being published by Joseph Kürschner. Besides *Maxims and Reflections*, the work focused on the *History of the Color Theory*. This was a task that could be best done in Weimar, with the necessary libraries close by where it was possible to find the books that Goethe had studied and at times quoted. Rudolf Steiner used this opportunity well, and these two last volumes contain the most comprehensive footnotes. At least here Steiner had the opportunity to show in part how he would approach the publication of Goethe's work.

Kürschner, however, had to wait almost six years for these volumes, which originally should have gone to print in 1891. With a certain lack of consideration, Steiner put Kürschner off, postponed deadlines, and eventually put Kürschner's letters and telegrams aside and turned his attention to other tasks. The manuscripts finally arrived long after Kürschner had given up.

Another potential that Steiner grasped hold of was connected with this work. The research into the history of the theory of color gave him the opportunity to study the history of science in detail as well as other philosophical questions. The table of contents of these last volumes bear witness to the comprehensive nature of Steiner's studies. They cover the development of science from Pythagoras, Empedocles, Democritus, and the classical philosophers and naturalists of antiquity, through Bacon, Paracelsus and the alchemists, to Goethe's contemporaries. In later years, audiences were often surprised by Steiner's knowledge of arcane relationships and otherwise unknown writers; an explanation for this remarkable knowledge is to be found in the research behind the *History of the Theory of Color*.

Readers of these footnotes who are interested in Anthroposophy can also discover methodological indications concerning the work with Anthroposophy, for instance:

> Truths, which belong to a whole system of ideas, can usually be truly understood and valued only when examined in context. One recognizes then their deeper meaning, their esoteric meaning, which they cannot have when seen in isolation. This latter will only be grasped by those who learn to know the entire circle of corresponding views to which the idea belongs. Truths, which are understandable when standing alone, are called exoteric. The superficial tendency to tear esoteric truths out of their context and address them exoterically can lead to the most dangerous errors. (1-d)

If we apply this to the years Steiner spent in Weimar, we can see that the work in the archive was but one aspect of his life and if viewed alone gives a skewed sense of what these years meant. In addition to his archival job, Steiner nurtured individual initiatives, in the center of which was the work on *Intuitive Thinking as a Spiritual Path.* At the same time, he made many new friends. His life was not limited to his work as a scholar and writer. He led an active social life, and the society of friends and conversation with others was like fresh air for him to breath. Still, the work in the archive was always there in the background. A gray wall, but still colossal.

Chapter 15

LONELY IN THE COMPANY OF MANY FRIENDS

The days in Weimar consisted of work, lots of work, and the work in the archive was monotonous and tedious. The conferences of the Goethe Society brought some variation, and the summertime influx of Goethe tourists led to the archivists being overloaded with tours in addition to their regular work. Rudolf Steiner wrote letters in this period, pointing out that there wasn't much to report about his outer life. He mentions that he has almost no holidays and that the raw Weimar climate was taking its toll through colds, and even the loss of his voice. Writing to his parents, he says that he hopes life there will make him more hardy.

In addition to the work in the archive, Steiner took on other tasks. First, he had to write his dissertation and prepare for his orals, and then he began work on *Intuitive Thinking as a Spiritual Path*. In 1895, he published a book on Nietzsche; in 1897, *Goethe's Worldview*. On the side, he oversaw a twelve-volume edition of Schopenhauer's work and an eight-volume selection of the work of Jean Paul. Perhaps to give himself a change of pace, he also wrote essays, reports and book reviews. He took on too much and, as a result, his work was constantly delayed. His publishers sometimes waited for years before receiving the pieces he had promised them. Even the completion of *Intuitive Thinking as a Spiritual Path*, which Steiner very much wanted to see published, was delayed for over a year. Steiner was constantly under pressure; it was only shortly before he moved to Berlin that he was able to wrap up all his various duties.

In light of the amount of work to be done, one must actually picture Steiner leaving his work in the archive only to rush home to his apartment to write and study until midnight. But in his *Autobiography*, he writes of his lively social life. Friendships upon friendships. He and his friends tell stories of long walks—with the author Gabriele Reuter through the streets of Weimar, with Oldens in the parks throughout the city, and with the painters Otto Fröhlich and Joseph Rolletscheck in the countryside.

They tell of long conversations with various friends, the evening debates on the veranda of the Hotel Chemnitius, of parties following the theater or the opera. One could, when reading these recollections, imagine Steiner out with his friends every evening. In reality, most of the conversations, debates, walks and parties took place on the weekends, or perhaps by regular weekly gatherings.

During the week, Steiner spent his evenings and nights alone in his study, at a desk piled high with books and manuscripts, lit by a reading lamp given to him by the Spechts. "I had to come to terms, entirely on my own, with everything related to my spiritual perception. I lived in the spiritual world; not one of all those I knew followed me there. My social interactions involved visits to the world of others. Nevertheless, I loved those excursions.... This was the nature of my 'loneliness' in Weimar, where I led an active social life. But I did not hold it against others that they sentenced me in this way to loneliness" (28).

Weimar was not a university town, where the intellectual life sets the general tone. It was at that time, besides being a royal residence, primarily a city of the arts. The spiritual climate was influenced by the theater, music and the art school. The art school was still strongly under the influence of the artistic impulse developed by the landscape painter Count Leopold Kalckreuth. Kalckreuth, a rigorous impressionist, had broken through the traditional approach to art with his brightly colored mix of realism and impressionism. After he left Weimar in 1890, he became the president of the German Artists Fellowship, the group of artists that embodied the modern liberal approach. In this sense, the painters, with whom Steiner spent time in Weimar, were at that time modern artists. They strove to capture, as did the impressionists, light, color and mood in their paintings. One of the painters who struggled to capture the joys and sorrows of color on canvas was Otto Fröhlich (1869–1940). Steiner, who wrote about him at length in his *Autobiography*, tried to stimulate him to paint subjects that could only be pictured imaginatively—for instance, Nietzsche in the valley of death. That, however, was not Fröhlich's métier. His light-filled landscapes, some of which remain in the collection at the Weimar castle, are quite convincing. Similarly, Steiner suggested to his friend Curt Liebich (1868–1937) that he paint the themes from Goethe's "Fairy Tale." Although Liebich did make the attempt, he too became a landscape artist working primarily with themes of the region he called home, the Black Forest. Steiner himself was at that time an admirer of the art of Arnold Böcklin (1827–1901). In 1882, in Vienna, he had seen four of Böcklin's pictures, which seemed to him to be a living protest against painting from models. At the same time, this inclination shows just how strongly Steiner was drawn to thematically oriented, illustrative pictures. It wasn't until 1902 that another artistic direction began to interest Steiner, when he discovered the work of William Turner in the National Gallery in London and admitted that Turner seemed to him to be "more significant" than Böcklin (39).

Theater life in Weimar was, however, more traditional, and Steiner was able to learn a lot by observing how different artists strove to modernize their work. He was most interested in the very personal formative strivings of the actors and actresses themselves. In his *Autobiography*, he remembers the "fire spirit," Paul Wiecke, who blustered and cursed his way into new roles. An in-depth review of Alwine Wiecke's interpretation of Goethe's Gretchen was found in Steiner's papers. He celebrated her artistry with great respect. She is not mentioned in his *Autobiography*, though, due to Steiner's disapproval of her personal behavior (39). This was connected with his feelings about acting. One passage in his *Autobiography*, in which he speaks of the then very popular youthful hero of the Weimar theater scene, Dagobert Neuffer (1851–1939), gives insight into the expectations he had of actors:

> I became acquainted with Neuffer, an actor, when he was still engaged at the theater in Weimar. What I valued first was his earnest, conscientious approach to his profession. In his judgment of stage art, he allowed nothing amateurish to pass. This was especially satisfying, since people are generally unaware that dramatic art must conform to definite technical rules, just like music, for instance. (28)

The friendship with Neuffer's family lasted for many years. Just how deeply Neuffer understood Steiner is shown by the present he gave him for Christmas: a bust of Hegel, which accompanied Steiner to Berlin and later to Dornach.

The Weimar music scene was still under the influence of Franz Liszt, who had lived there for many years. His influence was still so strong that Steiner referred to the years he spent in Weimar as the Liszt years. Yet it was in the field of music that something new began to emerge. Richard Strauss, the *enfant terrible* of the German music scene, was at that time concert master in Weimar and receiving stormy public acclaim. With his first pieces, he broke through the pleasant plumpness of traditional music. At the reception following the premier of his first opera, *Guntram*, it was Steiner who first spoke up and praised Strauss as the one who had finally brought about something new in Weimar. At 1:30 the next morning, Strauss was finally accompanied home by a candlelight procession. Richard Strauss also was the one who invited Gustav Mahler to Weimar in 1894, to a music festival during which Mahler premiered his first symphony. "One could not forget the way he used the baton, creating music not merely in the flow of forms, but pointing meaningfully between those forms in experience of suprasensory, hidden reality" (28).

Liszt's influence was kept alive in Weimar primarily through the composer and pianist Conrad Ansorge. Ansorge had put poems by Nietzsche to music. Steiner belonged to his circle of friends and was almost always present when these songs were performed for the first time. In them the music combined with the poems and thoughts of Nietzsche, with the question of a true, independent humanity that strove to become melody and tone. Rudolf Steiner was known in this circle as a true Nietzsche scholar; he was drawn into the conversations in which the goal was a better understanding of Nietzsche's thought. Beyond that, the circle was deeply moved by the earnest question, "What will happen as German culture develops, if a place like Weimar fulfills so little of its destined mission?" (28).

Of all the authors then living in Weimar, Steiner was most taken by Gabriele Reuter. In his *Autobiography*, he writes joyfully of his admiration for her, "I must say that some of the most beautiful hours of my life were those I experienced with Gabriele Reuter." (28). She was two years older than Steiner. Born in Alexandria, Egypt, she had a certain distance from German issues. A difficult destiny had taught her to focus on the essentials. She was free of prejudice, happily accompanied Steiner often to Naumberg to the Nietzsche archive, and was part of the small circle of people to whom Fritz Koegel in the summer of 1894 read passages from Nietzsche's yet unpublished *Antichrist*. Usually, however, Gabriele Reuter and Steiner met at Hans and Grete Olden's, in the house on the Altenburg where Liszt's "New Weimar Society" had once gathered. Gabriele Reuter recounts these gatherings in her memoirs:

> Each of us was the lord of the world and the center of his existence, and the sovereign nature of the individual was constantly affirmed using the most grotesque reasons and the riskiest logic. Rudolf Steiner was

a master at stating baroque, exorbitant premises, and then defending them with an astonishing display of logic, knowledge, clever insights and paradoxes. How amusing he was when he became excited, the free-thinker with the narrow monk's head, the high, radiant forehead; how agitated he became when Hans Olden put on his lovely faun's smile and countered with a witty cynicism.... Steiner struggled with hunger and poverty. Often late at night he would accompany me from Olden's home, for we both lived in the western part of the city. He would become serious, and I have to thank this extraordinary spirit with his breadth of knowledge for many ideas and much stimulation in questions of philosophy. He especially taught me to understand Goethe in a completely new light. (Gabriele Reuter)

Among other things, Steiner developed in these conversations the ideas of his *Philosophy of Freedom*, which he was working on at that time. He spoke with her especially about the idea of moral imagination and showed her how the free spirit can only be truly free and creative when it can experience a situation imaginatively and discover a new guiding idea in the imaginative experience. This made sense to Gabriele Reuter and, writing thirty years later, she recalled the conversations and added that by developing his Anthroposophy, Steiner had stimulated the moral imagination of a multitude of people.

For his part, Steiner remembered Gabriele Reuter's inner decisiveness and radical views. She was never loud, never raised her voice, but voiced her sharply accentuated ideas calmly. "I recall one time when we stood on a street corner in the blazing sun for more than an hour and debated issues that roused her. Never for a moment did Gabrielle lose her inner calm when discussing things that would quickly upset others" (28). She seemed to be a truly modern soul, one who brought a strong inner life to expression with a high grade of consciousness.

Hans Olden (1859–1932) was completely different. He was a sharp-witted dramatist and journalist who enjoyed letting his tendency to criticism and cynicism run free. It was impossible for him to keep his sudden flashes of wit to himself. Naturally, much of what he said or wrote was justified, and it was a relief when a mood of overblown sentimentality was popped by his sharp wit like a balloon. It was a gift for Eduard von der Hellen and Rudolf Steiner to be able to speak freely at the Olden's, for day in and day out they suffered under the schoolmasterly thumb of Suphan and under the constraints of the bourgeois sense of morality that held sway in Weimar. It was liberating to find in Olden's company a vent and to be able to speak about things pointedly, which otherwise could not be expressed at all.

The criticism that came to expression was fueled by higher interests and ideals. These remained in the background—no one wanted to fall prey to pathos—and they were of the opinion that the rest of humanity had absolutely no understanding of what was truly human. Olden's critique of the Weimar situation included the grand duchess. In the *Magazine of Literature,* he published an article entitled "From the Seat of Muses and Widows" in which he mentioned an indiscretion. After that, his days in Weimar were numbered. After his departure, Steiner no longer had the desire to speak about the situation there; he realized that there was nothing to be done and became silent.

Franz Ferdinand Heitmüller (1864–1919) was another of Steiner's literary friends. He joined the archive in 1894 to work on the publication of Goethe's letters. But he had an artistic bent and cast his experiences in the archive and in Weimar in the form of novellas. One of his sketches, "New Vineta," which appeared in the *New German Review* and depicted Weimar as a sunken city, as a graveyard, caused some excitement. Steiner's letters from Weimar bear witness that he certainly would have agreed with this interpretation. At the end of 1891, he had written of the "spiritual desert Weimar" in which there was no light, but rather "circumstances...that constantly disgust us." Weimar was for him a place ruled by "misery, pettiness and ignorance" (39).

Through his connection with Eduard von der Hellen, Steiner was introduced to a completely different world. "His dissatisfaction with philology drove him into Weimar's animated political life, which, to him, seemed to open a broader perspective on life" (28). Politics was not one of Steiner's fundamental interests, but, just as his work at the *German Weekly* had forced him to pay more attention to Viennese politics, his friendship with von der Hellen gave him the opportunity to gain insight into German politics. Being Austrian and a foreigner, he remained an observer. Von der Hellen tried to make inroads with a non-Marxist social platform. He clearly had no hope of success in conservative Weimar. Steiner accompanied von der Hellen to political gatherings and through his participation in this absolutely progressive and well-meant program learned to understand how politics worked there.

There are some indications of Steiner's political views to be found in the letters he wrote to friends in Vienna. He wrote to his teacher Schröer, "The reaction that has flooded middle and western Germany is naturally also to be seen in Thuringen. The wind that blows will certainly not support independent research in the coming years" (39). What concerned Steiner was the widespread hypocrisy in Germany, the constantly growing tendency to submissiveness. He was especially worried about the increase in votes for the anti-Semitic party during the Reichstag election in June 1893. He offered the following critique in a letter to Pauline Specht: "On the whole, if one has observed these events from inside the Holy Roman empire, the last election has shown an increase of crudity and ignorance in the masses that I find truly terrifying. The fact that a ridiculous person, who, as a lying genius outdoes Lueger"—a leading Viennese anti-Semite—"by miles, has won two seats in parliament and has a large number of followers, indicates a complete depravity of the public spirit." (39). In light of the monopoly of power held by large agricultural interests and the industrial sector, the positive impressions that Steiner had when first visiting Germany in 1889 were completely erased. He now had begun to know the situation in the empire from within.

It was a woman who made it possible for Steiner to weather these difficult years in Weimar without lasting damage. At some point during the summer of 1892, he moved out of the furnished apartment on the Junkerstrasse and into the ground floor of Anna Eunike's house on the nearby Preller-Strasse. "Anna Eunike, who quickly became a good friend, selflessly provided for all my needs" (28). Ms. Eunike was a widow and, for her part, happy that Steiner was there to help her with the education of her four daughters and son. They soon developed a close and loving relationship. In a letter written from Vienna at Sylvester in 1892, he addresses her as "My dear, good Anna" and hoped "to receive a few lines from my dear" (39). A few years later, when he was working for a time at the Nietzsche archive in Naumburg, he wrote, "I believe that I would not have made it through this last year without your loving care and support" (39). Anna Eunike, who was eight years older than Steiner, must have truly loved and mothered him. This freed Steiner from many cares and allowed him to concentrate on his work. He expressly states that he was able to write his *Philosophy of Freedom* and *Nietzsche, A Fighter for Freedom* in the Eunike home. Steiner in turn not only helped with the children, but also did all the things that she was unable to do as well as dealing with financial and legal questions.

Anna Eunike also enjoyed being part of the life that came into the house through Rudolf Steiner. If they wanted to have a "pleasant" time, Steiner's friends would meet at Anna's house. Franz Ferdinand Heitmüller, August Fresenius, Joseph Rolletscheck, Otto Harnack, and Heinrich Zeller all enjoyed coming here. It was a place where they could be among themselves. Otto Erich Hartleben and Steiner met here to put together the Goethe breviary that Hartleben later published. Steiner was thus obliged to Anna Eunike for a place that he could call home in Weimar and a feeling of having shelter, something made even more important by his poor health during those years. Although Anna Eunike couldn't dispel his spiritual loneliness, she did give him a healthy basis for his existence.

IMAGES, PART ONE

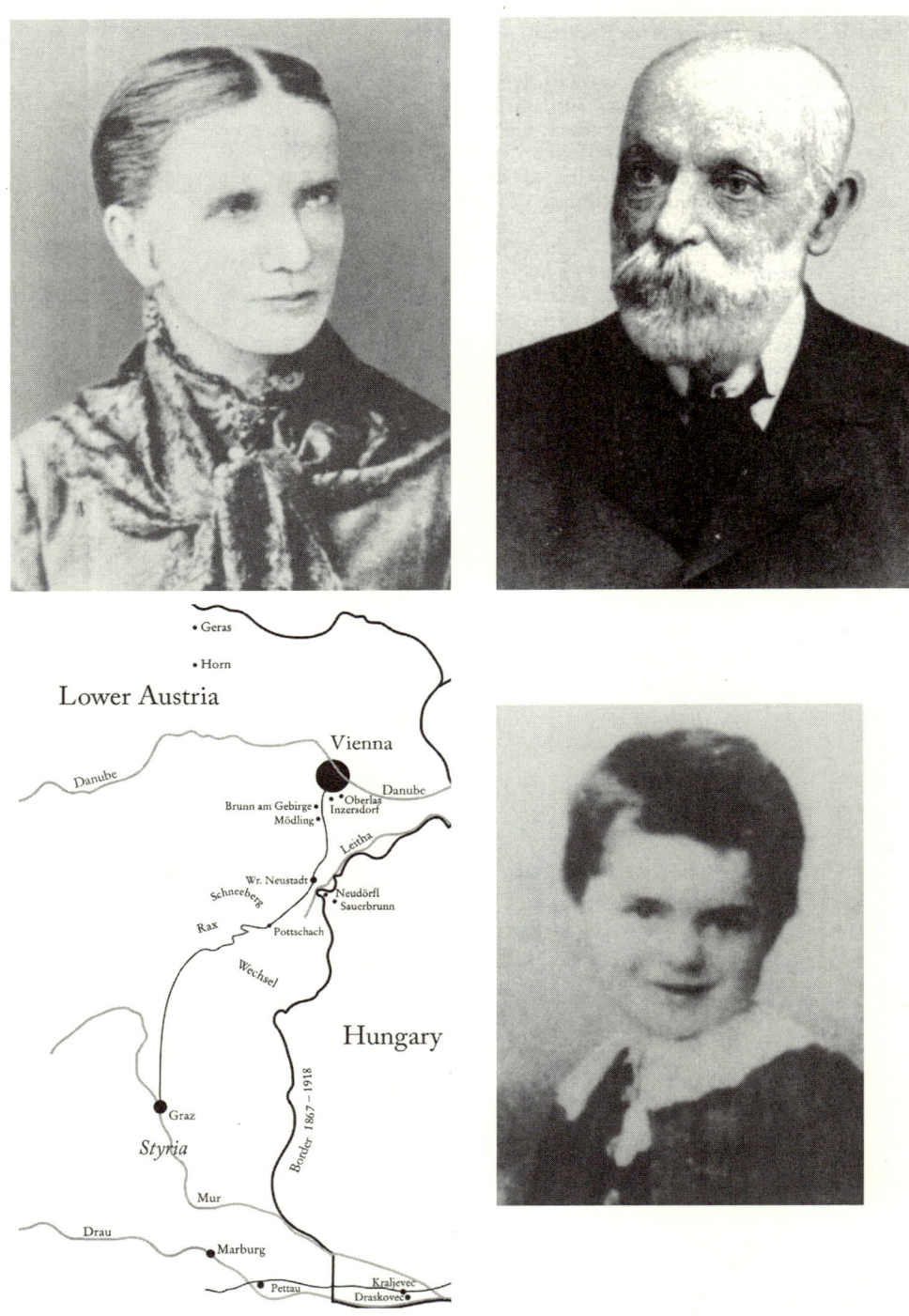

*Above: Rudolf Steiner's parents, Franziska and Johann Steiner;
below: the area where the Steiners lived, and Rudolf Steiner in 1867.*

Above: the town of Neudörfl; Franz Maraz, the local pastor in Neudörfl; below: the school director, Heinrich Schramm; and Laurenz Jelinek, Steiner's beloved mathematics teacher.

*Above: Rudolf Steiner's school class photo of 1876;
below: Edmund Reitlinger (1830– 1882);
Rudolf Steiner, from his class photo of 1879.*

Top: Karl-Julius Schröer, 1880; Moritz Zitter (see p. 34); bottom: Felix Koguzki (1833– 1909), the herb collector; and Rudolf Steiner as a student in 1882.

Above: Friedrich Theodor Vischer (1807–1887; p. 50); Joseph Kürschner (1853–1902), editor of German National Literature *(p. 56); below: Josef Breuer (1842–1925; p. 68) and Pauline Specht (p. 67).*

*Top: Rudolf Steiner, 1889; Otto Specht (p. 72);
bottom: Richard Specht (1870–1932) became a poet and writer;
and the philosopher Eduard von Hartmann (1842–1906; p. 65).*

*Above: Gideon Spicker (1840–1912; p. 77);
Marie Eugenie delle Grazie (1864–1931, p. 85);
below: Laurenz Müllner (1848–1911; p. 85); and
Wilhelm Neumann (1837–1919), Cistercian father and Bible scholar (p. 86).*

*Top: Vienna, 1888;
bottom: Fercher von Steinwand (1828–1902, p. 90);
and Rudolf Steiner (1889).*

Above: Friedrich Eckstein (1840–1912), the great student of ancient wisdom (p. 101); Marie Lang (1858–1934, p. 112); below: Rosa Mayreder (1858–1938; p. 112); and Bernard Suphan (1845–1911), Director of the Goethe Archive (p. 125).

Top: Rudolf Steiner, 1891; Herman Grimm (1828–1901), literary historian (p. 107); bottom: Gabriele Reuter (1859–1941, p. 135); and Hans Olden (1859–1932, p. 136).

CHAPTER 16

THE PHILOSOPHY OF FREEDOM

When Rudolf Steiner moved to Weimar, he hoped to lay the foundation for his further career. He envisioned some form of philosophical teaching position and his letters speak repeatedly of plans to attain a professorial chair or at least become a private docent. Initially, there was talk of a professorship in Jena, later a teaching position in Vienna, which with the help of Laurenz Müllner was to be created especially for him. He had, however, produced no major philosophical work; such a work would give cause for him to be so honored. Such a book would have to be written (39).

In July 1891, when his dissertation had been finished and he was about to receive his degree from Rostock University, Steiner had a visitor in Weimar with whom he was on the best of terms. Ludwig Laistner was the literary advisor of the Cotta Publishers in Stuttgart. He suggested that Steiner write a book about "The Fundamental Problems of Metaphysics." Steiner was excited by the suggestion, not only because he was aching to tackle a major philosophical project, but also because Cotta was an excellent publishing house. In the beginning of October, Steiner visited Stuttgart. The book was once again discussed and probably agreed to. On October 7, having returned to Weimar, "the graveyard of German greatness"(39), he wrote that he hoped to begin his philosophical book in the near future. "That is work that is truly able to carry a person, because it can only be brought to fruition by focusing all of one's spiritual forces. Now I will have the opportunity to bring to expression much of what I have to say and much of what I stand for" (39). The challenge clearly gave Steiner new energy. At the beginning of December, he thought that he would be able to finish the book by Easter. In January, he wrote that his book "was moving forward; the basic arrangement and distribution of the content is finished" (39). But it wasn't until November 1893, with constant pressure from the publishing house, now no longer

Cotta but Emil Felder, that the book was finally published. Its title was *Die Philosophie der Freiheit.**

Developing the Idea of Freedom

Steiner first had the idea of writing a philosophy of freedom somewhere around 1880. In July 1881, he wrote to a friend as though speaking of an already known plan, "I hope to have enough quiet in August to get a large part of my dear philosophy of freedom on paper." He thought then that people would read his philosophical ideas "like an entertaining, educational novel" (38).

The essential idea of this unwritten book lived completely in the world of German idealism. "Only what is absolute is of the highest reality. Everything that is not absolute is but semblance, illusion and error—'mortal opinion,' as Parmenides said. The striving to achieve the absolute, this longing in the human being, is freedom." In light of the absolute, the Godhead, all willful goals set by the "I" disappear.

> If we call this recognition of the highest truths: the communion of the human being with the absolute, we find that the highest form of freedom blossoms in this communion. One finds himself at one point of the universe, and now has a standpoint..., from which one can look out over the world. One forms judgments about it, about oneself, and is satisfied with oneself, the world and with everything. In the highest form of freedom, bliss is made manifest, the highest form of satisfaction. The human being has found his reason to exist and is at peace with everything. (38)

In such words speaks the inner experience that Steiner had when studying Fichte. From the point of view of what later would become *Intuitive Thinking as a Spiritual Path*, it is clear that in this early concept of freedom the individual is in danger of disappearing into the absolute; so seen, individual action could only be an expression of the absolute. The conceptual outline of 1881 gives us a good sense of the long path Steiner took from a purely ideal concept of freedom to an empirical concept of freedom based on soul observations. It also becomes clear that the question of freedom was for Steiner, from the beginning, the fundamental question of human

---

* Published in English under different titles, including *The Philosophy of Freedom; The Philosophy of Spiritual Activity;* and *Intuitive Thinking as a Spiritual Path.*

existence. The entirety of his philosophical striving from 1881 to 1895 focused on the challenge of rightly understanding the concept of freedom.

His second attempt to form this central concept comes in chapter 19 of *Goethe's Theory of Knowledge*. This passage was probably written in the winter of 1886. It is a difficult one to interpret. It is clear that Steiner rejects both moral commandments and external guidance or revelation. "It is not by searching out this or that commandment of the guiding power of the world that he acts in accordance with its intentions but rather through acting in accordance with his own intentions" (2). The question is only as to how this intention arises.

In chapter 13, Steiner compared the human spirit with the eye and the ear and comes to the assertion, "The spirit perceives the thought content of the universe as an organ of perception" (2). The thought content that is perceived or apprehended in this manner is brought to expression through the individual activity. Thus, human activity is also determined by thought content. "When a moral ideal comes about, therefore, it is the inner power lying within the content of this ideal that guides our actions. It is not because the ideal is given us as law that we act in accordance with it, but rather because the ideal, by virtue of its content, is active in us, leads us." And Steiner draws the conclusion, "The stimulus to action does not lie outside of us; it lies *within* us" (2).

A critic could ask, if the inner guiding force of the ideal is not in fact a form of inner coercion, which, while freeing one from external influences, subjugates one to the power of ideas. This question appears to us to be especially justified, because Steiner describes human thinking as an organ of perception that apprehends ideas as the eye or the ear apprehends sense impressions. One could conclude that what appears to be coming from within is but an illusion, and that the individual is in fact guided by cosmic thoughts, which he takes in through his thinking. Remaining within the conceptual framework of *Goethe's Theory of Knowledge*, one would have to respond to this argument by pointing out that thoughts, in their lawful relationships, are brought forth by individuals and that the inner lawfulness of thinking is not experienced as a form of coercion (2). Furthermore, it should perhaps be pointed out that the determination of thoughts is not rigid. Steiner speaks of "ever-fluid thoughts," which are brought into a given form based on the external visual perception. The consequence of this would be that each individual holds on to the thoughts in a specific manner based on one's mental images. This too is not fixed; mental images can be dissolved. Finally and most important, the human aspect of an occurrence or phenomena comes to expression in knowing.

> Thus, the essential nature of a thing comes to light only when the thing is brought into relationship with the human being. For only within the human being does there manifest for each thing its essential being. This establishes relativism as a worldview—that is, the direction in thought that assumes we see all things in the light bestowed upon them by human beings themselves. (2)

This passage opens the possibility that thoughts brought forth by individuals not only must be viewed as cosmic thoughts but could be of human origin. The ideals that determine human action would then be human creations. Steiner does not take this final step in *Goethe's Theory of Knowledge*. Instead, he sketches out a somewhat ambivalent image of the substance of cosmic origin pouring itself fully out into the world in order to guide it from within. This original cosmic substance comes to appearance both in human thinking and in human personality (2). In May 1886, shortly after finishing *Goethe's Theory of Knowledge*, Steiner became acquainted with the then twenty-two-year-old poet Marie Eugenie delle Grazie. In her work, he found himself confronted with the poetic consequences of materialistic nihilism. One of her poems, entitled "Around Midnight," ended with the lines:

> All-conquering and free reigns
> Only the giant death:
> With gleaming sword he mows away
> The glittering lies of existence
> And speaks, in eternity,
> Pointing to dust and decay,
> The only eternal truth:
> It is nothing!

Steiner was deeply moved by the intellectual honesty with which delle Grazie not only conceptualized materialism but emotionally grasped and gave form to its pessimism. The encounter with radical pessimism was for him a spiritual challenge, and he addressed it immediately in *Open Letter—Nature and Our Ideals* with which he honored delle Grazie. In relation to our topic, this open letter is of interest, because Steiner described it as containing the germinal idea of *Intuitive Thinking as a Spiritual Path* in his *Autobiography*. Since it seemed that the seed of *Intuitive Thinking as a Spiritual Path* was to be found in the works mentioned above, this remark from Steiner gives us cause to look more closely at the passage that he quoted in 1924. Is there a new—a different—quality to it?

> Our ideals are no longer so shallow that they are satisfied by the all too frequently superficial and empty external reality. Nevertheless, I cannot believe that it is impossible to rise above the deep pessimism this insight can bring. And I find the means to rise above it when I look into our inner world—that is, when I approach the actual nature of our world of ideas. It is a sphere enclosed and complete in itself; it neither gains nor loses through the transient nature of external phenomena. Are not our ideals, when they are truly living individualities, entities in their own right and independent of the favors or disfavors of external nature? If the lovely rose is shattered by heartless gusts of wind, it has fulfilled its mission nevertheless, because it has delighted hundreds of human eyes. If tomorrow it pleases murderous nature to destroy the whole starry sky, nevertheless for thousands of years people have reverently looked up to the stars, and that is enough. It is not their temporal existence but their inner being that makes things perfect and complete.
>
> Our ideals are a world of their own with a life of their own that gains nothing through the cooperation of a well-disposed nature. What pitiable creatures human beings would be if they were unable to find fulfillment within their own world of ideals but instead needed help from outer nature! Where would our divine freedom exist if external nature nursed and protected us and led us by the hand like helpless children? No, external nature must deny us everything, so that the happiness we achieve is fully the product of our own free self. May nature daily destroy what we have built up, so that daily we may rejoice in creating anew. We wish to owe nature nothing, but ourselves everything!
>
> One might say that such a freedom is merely a dream. While believing ourselves to be independent, we simply obey the iron necessity of natural laws. Our noblest thoughts are merely the result of nature working blindly within us. Oh, we finally admit that a being who has attained self-knowledge cannot be unfree!...We see the web of laws ruling over phenomena, and it gives rise to necessity. But, in our cognition, we have the power to detach those laws from nature, and despite that we are supposed to be involuntary slaves of nature's laws? (28)

When Karl Julius Schröer read these lines, he recognized the new tone and wrote to Steiner that, if he was serious about what he had written, then they had never understood one another. Whoever could write in this manner about nature shows that he could not take Goethe's words "Know thyself and live in peace with the world" seriously enough. In the open letter, an abyss does in fact appear between humans and nature that was not visible in Steiner's earlier work. With a certain rough, youthful enthusiasm, the active, creative human being, who has liberated himself from his origins, is elevated and placed in the center. What becomes apparent here, although still not clearly articulated, is a concept of individualism that Steiner would go on to formulate in the beginning of the 1890s. Characteristic of this later individualism is the renunciation of the security of the individual through a "world foundation" that had poured itself into each person. In a completely non-Goethean manner, human beings turn away from nature and begin to build solely on their own activity.

It is possible to follow this change in Steiner's thinking fairly closely as he developed his views on a Goethean epistemology again in the second volume of *Goethe's Scientific Writings*. This can be read with an eye to the new accent in Steiner's thinking. In doing so, we have to remember both versions deal with the same question—forming Goethe's epistemological practice into a conceptual framework. The core idea is the same in both.

However, when Steiner turns to the idea of freedom, he uses different imagery:

> We do not recognize a universal guide who defines the goals and directions of our actions from outside of us. The universal guide has divested himself of his power and has given everything into the hands of human beings, challenging them to continue working. Human beings find themselves in the world, experience nature, and recognize in it something deeper—conditions, an intention. Their thinking makes it possible for them to understand this intention. It becomes their spiritual possession. They have penetrated the meaning of the world. They act and in doing so set forth this intention. In this sense, the philosophy presented here is the true *philosophy of freedom*. (1-b)

In *Goethe's Theory of Knowledge*, the original spiritual substance of the universe "poured" itself out into the natural world in order to guide it from within. In the later introduction, written in the spring of 1887, the "universal guide" abolished its own special existence. It left behind only its testament, tracks and intentions, which humankind should carry further. "Carrying further"—however problematic this concept may be—is more than merely re-creating. Later in the text, Steiner argues explicitly that "carrying further" cannot be understood as a simple execution of the testament. "Ethical action is the expression of what has taken on meaning in the individual; it is present always in the specific event, never as a general law. There are no general laws determining what a person should do or should not do" (1-b). This is the first mention of action in a specific, non-replicable instance, an idea that plays a decisive role in Steiner's later work: All rules and norms fail in the concrete situation. Carrying the intentions of the universal guide further can thus only be realized through creative individual initiative.

Rudolf Steiner thought through these ideas more carefully during his work on *Intuitive Thinking as a Spiritual Path*. In an altercation with the "Society for Ethical Culture," a movement that had originated in the United States that stood up for moral principles, he articulated his arguments against the propaganda for ethical norms and rules. He pointed out the futility of ethical propaganda. Ethicists overlooked the fact:

> that all general rules and laws prove themselves to be worthless phantoms when a person finds oneself in a living reality. Laws are abstractions; actions, however, always take place under very specific, concrete conditions. When faced with the necessity of action, we must weigh the different possibilities and choose the one that appears to us to be most practical. An individual person always faces a very specific situation and makes a decision based on the nature of the situation.

And:

> Two different people will act differently in the same situation, because they, based on differences of character, experience and education, come to a different understanding of what their task in the situation is. Whoever recognizes that the judgment about the nature of a situation is the significant factor in determining the action can only endorse an individualistic approach to ethics. It is only a clear view of the given situation that can support the formation of an appropriate judgment, not predetermined norms. (31)

Or, in still other words, the ethical impulses and plans that are brought to bear in a given situation are dependent on the way the individual views it; "the judgment about the specific situation is what is important."

No moral imperatives are set within the situation itself. An individual must find these for oneself. The moral bar an individual sets for oneself depends on one's worldview. Seen through Darwinian glasses, a war can be viewed as a productive process of selection, a process that should not be disturbed. For others, however, a war presents a moral challenge; it must be stopped or the victims should be given help. Thus Rudolf Steiner focuses attention on the role that the different worldviews—the different moral paradigms—play. And he places a totally unexpected requirement on what a worldview should achieve.

> A worldview that is able to satisfy us fully must truly remove us from the position we have taken in the cosmos; it must set us into absolute motion. Through it, we must not simply gain insight into what we are. It must help us become something. Naturally, at this point, all those who prefer to stand still will speak up and say, "We want a science of what is, not information about what doesn't exist." Those are the weaklings who do not want to acknowledge that as human beings they have the right to create and that what they create has no less claim on existence than anything else. This is why I have never been able to believe that a human being is but a child of God. This is but a way to say that what we create is only a re-creation. In our weakness, we ask for forgiveness for our creation of ideas and explain that they are not from us but have been willed by the heavenly Father. (39)

The concept of freedom presents itself as the freedom of the individual who takes hold of oneself through self-knowledge, lives out of one's ideals, and comes to one's decisions out of freedom in the specific situation. This freedom unfolds in radical opposition to nature. "May nature daily destroy what we have built up, so that daily we may rejoice in creating anew! We wish to owe nature nothing, but ourselves everything!" This is a concept of freedom that does not view it as a living out of divine intention, because there are no markings in which this intention is to be found. In the concrete situation, which in itself is silent, an individual must bring one's intentions into play creatively and decisively.

"Prelude" to *The Philosophy of Freedom*

In 1892, Rudolf Steiner published an expanded version of his dissertation as the "prelude of a philosophy of freedom" with the title *Truth and Knowledge*. The original title of the dissertation was "The Fundamentals of a Theory of Cognition with Special Reference to Fichte's Scientific Teaching." In contrast to *Goethe's Theory of Knowledge*, which took Goethe's work as its point of departure and in which Steiner did not "analyze the basic elements in the act of cognition," (3) *Truth and Knowledge* strove to lay out a general theory of knowledge. This theory would examine that upon which all the other sciences were based: the act of knowing. "It is thus a philosophical science, fundamental to all other sciences" (3).

Steiner had followed the contemporary epistemological discussion and had been inspired especially by the works of Johannes Volkelt and Johannes Rehmke. As a starting point for his thesis, he chose a concept that had often been in discussion: the postulate of unconditionality. Steiner used this postulate not to question the supposed axioms that served as building blocks for an epistemology, but rather to place the then accepted concept of knowledge itself in question.

In this gesture alone an important element of the philosophy of freedom is apparent. An unconditional examination can, of course, not incorporate preconceived knowledge from any other branch of science, neither can it rest upon an unexamined notion of what knowledge is. The most common view is that the universe is in and of itself finished and that the subject, thought to be separate and isolated, has to find a way to understand it—through representation, abstraction, analysis, or whatever. This notion, as Hegel pointed out in the introduction to *A Phenomenology of the Spirit*, does not belong at the beginning of an epistemology. This must, in that sense, show unconditionally that all familiar concepts are set aside and the question as to the nature of knowing is consciously left open.

The requirement of unconditionality cannot be met by imagining oneself biographically at the onset of knowledge and creating a hypothetical picture of how a baby comes to know. To return to the point at which knowing begins and thus eliminate everything that we have gained through knowledge from our picture of the world would require a form of artificial operation that separates what is given from what is known. "This division between the 'given' and the 'known' will not in fact coincide with any stage of human development; the boundary must be drawn *artificially*. But this can be done at every level of development so long as we draw the dividing line correctly between what confronts us—free of all conceptual definitions—and what cognition subsequently makes of it" (3).

Steiner designates the totality of what we experience as the "given." To create an artificial dividing line that makes it possible to describe the process of cognition, he designates what is at first unknown as "directly given" or as a "finished given." No judgment is made as to the significance of the "given." It can be a sense impression, a dream, a hallucination, a feeling, or something else. In the creation of this artificial dividing line, the validity of any statement concerning the given is erased. Linguistically, this would correspond to a state of being in which there were no declarative sentences. In addition to the "directly given," there is also a given that we bring forth. This does not appear to us in any perceptible form, but rather in the form of ideas and concepts. Concepts and ideas are not perceived; they appear intuitively in us as the conditioning factors of the directly or finished given.

Words like function, system, organism, cause, and so on indicate concepts; love, justice, and self-determination represent ideas. We attempt through concepts to bring relationships into the disconnected, finished given. The act of knowing appears to be an experiment. It does not always work on the first try, but life and the history of science show that we have grown more able to conceive of and recognize the relationships, that errors have been corrected, and that hypotheses have either been rejected or confirmed and then refined. We relate, for instance, the concept organism to a specific given and think, "If this is indeed an organism, it must fulfill certain conditions." These include things like evolution, structural segregation into functional systems, and behavioral relationship to the environment, and we try to examine and understand the various details of what is given in relation to these points of view. This experiment can either succeed or not. The encounter with a specific given can also cause us to modify our concepts or bring other concepts into relationship with it. A given can stimulate us to differentiate between self-initiated movement and a being moved by an external force, where we suppose causality to be in play and to see a chain of events.

The "directly given" is but a disconnected chaos, a conglomeration of things beside one another in space, following one another in time; what we bring forth as a given appears as a context. This connectivity is brought forth through thinking. Thinking of content constantly produces new variations of concepts that illuminate the relationships and lawfulness of what is directly given. When we notice something unknown and the question awakens within us as to its nature, we find ourselves trying out various possible concepts and following up on them. We try to place it in a meaningful context, perhaps without success. In this process it is something in our thinking that can be designated the active "I," which decides whether or not we are satisfied with the explanation.

The details are what first appear when the questioning consciousness turns to examine something; in the act of knowing, the details, which initially appear isolated, are brought into relationship with one another.

> Knowledge therefore is based on the fact that the world content is given to us originally in an incomplete form. It possesses another essential aspect, apart from what is immediately present. This second aspect of the world content that is not originally given is revealed through thinking. Therefore, the content of thinking, which appears to us to be separate, is not a sum of *empty* thought forms, but comprises determinations (or categories). However, in relation to the rest of the world content, these determinations represent the organizing principle. *The world content can be called "reality" only in the form it attains once the two aspects of it just described have been joined through knowledge.* (3)

Knowledge is thus not an arbitrary addition to the universe, but rather the revelatory bringing forth of the thought-content of the universe. The separation of the merely given from the engendered concept, which is necessary for the awakening of consciousness, is overcome in the act of knowing. Thinking activity brings the thought *universe* to expression.

In the last chapter of *Truth and Knowledge*, Steiner summarizes the results of his epistemology and draws consequences for the praxis. "Our discussion has shown that the innermost core of the world comes to expression in our knowledge. The harmony of laws ruling throughout the universe shines forth in human cognition" (3). Since human beings are capable of bringing the laws of the universe to expression, they are also able to bring forth the laws of human action. There are two ways to think of this. Humans could act as creatures of nature do, which would mean that the laws of the universe, which can be understood in different ways, determine human action; these could then subsequently be recognized by the one who has acted or by others. If, however, specific ideas or ideals that we have consciously conceived guide our actions, then we give our actions their lawfulness ourselves. Steiner described this process in the following manner:

> If the "I" has really penetrated its deed with full insight, in conformity with its nature, then it also feels itself to be master. As long as this is not the case, the laws ruling the deed confront us as something foreign. *They* rule *us*; what we do is done under the compulsion they exert over us. If they are transformed from being a foreign entity into a deed completely originating within our own "I," then the compulsion ceases. What compelled us has become our own being. The laws no longer rule *over* us; *in* us they rule over the deed issuing from our "I."... *To recognize the laws of one's deeds means to become conscious of one's own freedom.* Thus the process of knowledge is the process of development toward freedom. (3)

Steiner raises the idea of freedom to a new level. In contrast to his earlier work, humans are no longer free simply because the original spiritual substance has poured itself into their thinking and they are able to set their own goals. In *Truth and Knowledge*, the words *transformation* and *evolution* appear for the first time in connection with the idea of freedom. Therefore, humans transform and evolve themselves. They are not free, per se; rather, they become free in that they learn to understand the laws of their actions, overcome blind compulsion, and become able to determine their actions out of their "I."

Here, Steiner does not primarily address actions that are of necessity connected with our physical existence, but rather the compulsive nature of psychological urges. In a letter to Rosa Mayreder at this time, he writes:

> It is not the dark, undefined, magical motive that can make us capable of free deeds, but only what stands before us in loving form, clear in all its parts. Only then, when I have completely penetrated the content of my spirit, so that nothing remains in the form of a dark emotion or magical power, can I be certain that what I bring to outer expression is truly my deed. It is herein alone that I see true freedom and the full blossoming of human personality. (39)

In other words, humans must also penetrate their ideals and motives with knowledge, gaining clarity concerning the ideals that act as a driving force within them if they want to develop toward freedom. Many noble deeds—for instance, out of loyalty—can arise out of a noble but at the same time un-illuminated urge. Such a deed—regardless of its moral value—cannot be viewed as a free deed. As it is developed in *Truth and Knowledge*, freedom presupposes self-knowledge. Freedom arises in a process of self examination, not merely out of idealism.

Precursors of this concept of freedom can be found both in the *Open Letter* to Marie Eugenie delle Grazie and, in 1887, in the introduction to the second volume of *Goethe's Scientific Writings*, where Steiner writes about the relationship of the individual to history and to society. Each individual belongs to a specific time (cultural epoch) and a specific social context (folk). "I am dependent on the cultural epoch in which I was born; I am a child of my time" (1-b). Influences of the time and of the social context can affect an individual unseen. One can, however, refuse to go with the stream, examine these influences and form judgments concerning them.

> Through one's capacity for knowledge, an individual penetrates into the particular character of one's people; it becomes clear to a person whither fellow citizens are steering one. An individual overcomes this by determination and takes it up into oneself as a picture that has been fully known; it becomes individual within oneself and takes on entirely the personal character that working from inner *freedom* has. (1)

Individuals can place themselves in a similar relationship to the fashions and ideas of their time. Human beings can work their way up to knowledge of the guiding ideas. They can make an effort to understand their time in order not to follow blindly. The concepts used here—*overcoming, raising themselves up, working their way up*—point to a special form of the then generally accepted concept of evolution, which was not only applied to historical and social tendencies, but also to the relationship of the human being to oneself. Thus we have arrived at the point of departure for *Intuitive Thinking as a Spiritual Path,* and Steiner closed what was originally the opening chapter of the book with the passage:

> This book interprets the relationship of science to life not in the sense that human beings must bow down before the idea and dedicate their forces to its service, but rather in the sense that we take possession of the world of ideas to use them for our human goals, which extend beyond those of mere science. We must be able to confront an idea while experiencing it; otherwise, we fall into its bondage. (4, p. 257)

Such a statement shows us how far Steiner came in his contemplations since 1886. In *Goethe's Theory of Knowledge*, he says quite ingenuously, "We do bnott follow ideals because they are given to us as laws, but because the ideal, based on its content, is active within us and leads us" (2). By 1891, it had become clear to Steiner that ideals do not lead us directly. An individual confronts the ideal, thinks it through in all its consequences, makes the content one's own, and reforms it to reflect one's particular human goals. In this manner, Steiner overcomes his earlier naïve idealism.

"I DON'T TEACH, I RECOUNT..."

On May 7, 1902, a fundamental discussion concerning truth and science and their place in a productive view of life was held at the Giordano Bruno Society in Berlin. Rudolf Steiner gave the introductory talk. He sharpened his already provocative thesis by asserting that most productive scientists went beyond the given facts, twisting and reinterpreting them in order that science might progress. Following a lively discussion, he closed the meeting with an indication of what he was trying to get at: "The forum that decides the justified approach must be a forum of individuals, sovereign personalities." Only what is fruitful and supports evolution is true. The creative individual brings something new into being that goes beyond what is simply given. The question is whether what one creates proves fruitful or not. "For this reason the question of whether a worldview is valid or not must be decided in a forum of life, not in a forum of knowledge" (51).

These thoughts give a perspective to *Intuitive Thinking as a Spiritual Path* that must be taken into consideration if one wishes to do justice to the work. It is a "book of life," not a philosophy in the common use of the word, which analyzes the work of earlier thinkers in light of contemporary epistemological problems. In contrast to Kant, whose work picks up on the problems Hume articulated, or Fichte, who strove to take Kant's work a step further, Steiner's work connects only marginally to other existing philosophies. He didn't belong to a "school" of philosophy, which made it difficult for other philosophers to take the book seriously, for it did not address specific philosophical problems but rather these two existential questions: What is the human being's place in the world? Can individuals think of themselves as being, at least in part, free?

In one letter, Steiner called his book "the biography of a soul striving toward freedom" and said that "every line" should be considered "a personal experience." Then, following Montaigne's lead, he added, "I *do not* teach; I recount what I have *experienced* within. I relate it in the manner that I have experienced it" (39). These statements do not make an interpretation of the book any easier, as the reader does not initially notice its biographical, experiential character at all. It seems as though nothing personal at all is mentioned. It seems to focus on theoretical questions, not on the biography of an individual striving for freedom. For a true understanding of the book, it is necessary to find the space in which the questions raised in the book become living, personal questions. To do this, one must reconsider in rich detail the common notions about individual action.

One such notion is that the individual encounters the world as a lonely, isolated being. The extreme position of this approach, based on Kant's work, is that the isolated subject, caught within the boundaries of one's subjectivity, can only have knowledge of one's own mental images. The individual sits alone in the ivory tower of one's subjectivity; what is known of the world is but one's own interpretation of the coded impressions received. "The world is my mental image"—this was the fundamental premise of philosophers at that time, whether they were neo-Kantian or followers of Schopenhauer. Generally, this idea, supported as it was by research into the physiology of the senses, found its way into public consciousness in the notion that "everything is subjective," accompanied by a vague uncertainty.

This thought, however, becomes dramatic if an individual thinks it through intensively: I sit in the tower of my subjectivity and all I have of the world are illusory mental images. For philosophically sensitive people, such a mental image is at once a "personal experience." Today, thanks to the influence of the media, this illusion has become the true representation of the world, although it is not consciously experienced. What was a theory in the nineteenth century has become fact for people today and in this process has also become an existential question. As Niklas Luhmann phrased it, "What we know about our society, what we know about the world we live in, we know through mass media" (Luhmann).

The first question that raises itself is that of the truth and reality of our knowledge. Can I gain a true relationship to the world through thinking, experiencing and knowing? Are my insights valid? How and where do I find the path to reality?

A second common notion of the twentieth century concerns human action. There are many variations on a central theme that says that each human being exists within an unbroken chain of effects and that a human action is caused by some external factor. Depending on one's preference, the primary cause of action is genetic, based on one's education or social milieu, formed in the unconscious depths of one's soul, or has a physiological basis. Freedom is an illusion that arises because we cannot see the threads that move us. A dull, ever-moving cosmic process determines our existence. This notion permeates much of modern social life: There is really nothing that one can do.

Those who popularize such notions do not stop to think that each organism owes its existence to the fact that it can shield itself from external influences and follow its own laws. In addition, it is the signature of human ingenuity to master causality and thus bring about effects that follow one's thoughts. Today, the denial of freedom and responsibility has cast its spell over all of our ideas about social interaction.

Thus, the second question that presupposes a positive answer to the first question is: Can I find within myself a freely created point of departure for self-determined, independent action?

In this sense, *Intuitive Thinking as a Spiritual Path* addresses the deepest existential questions. These questions must, of course, be explored with conceptual clarity or, if one prefers, with scientific precision. But one should not expect that they can be addressed only theoretically, as though in a conceptual laboratory. A true clarification of the questions can only take place in a forum of life. Steiner's work is a truly existential philosophy that finds its affirmation in life and that, in turn, gives direction to the life of the individual.

In regard to action, the questions that arise are: Where shall I place the lever? When is there even a chance to begin to imagine independent action? Both in life and in philosophy, the starting point is the individual biography. There are aspects of human life that we can affect only peripherally—for example, digestion and breathing regulate themselves. Different, but in some ways similar, is our emotional life. Under certain circumstances these aspects seem independent of us. We can try to overcome them, but initially they are simply there. Similarly, we enter a reciprocal relationship with our environment that we cannot completely control. As physical humans, we are "in close contact with purely physical nature" (30). We can recognize other areas or our lives in which this is also true.

When we act out of conscious intent, the situation is completely different. The possibility exists here that our decisions are guided by our own insights. Insights can be consciously attained, expanded upon and tested. Each of us can be aware of gaining insight and how it happens and can continue to ask questions, weigh different possibilities, and finally adopt a certain approach as a motive to act. In this process, we are direct participants in the guidance of our actions. This is where the possibility of freedom arises; this is where we must begin to explore the question as to whether or not we can also manage to free up our heads (4).

How do we make decisions? Why do we not act with instinctive immediacy? Whoever wishes to find clarity concerning these questions is confronted with the problem of human consciousness. In an essay written at the time of the conception of *Intuitive Thinking as a Spiritual Path*, Steiner articulated a completely new analysis of the nature of consciousness.

> Let us look at the content of the world that surrounds us. It is a continuous whole. If we turn our attention to any given point of the world we experience, we find that it connects to other things in all directions. There is nothing isolated, nothing that exists for itself alone. One impression attaches itself to others. We can remove it from our experience only artificially; in actuality, it is connected with the complete reality that surrounds us.... Our constitution is such that we cannot grasp the world as a whole, as one single perception.... We can only turn our attention in one direction and perceive as separate what is in nature joined. Our eyes can only perceive single colors from out of a manifold totality of color; our intellect, single concepts out of a unified structure of ideas. (30)

This separation of the detail from the whole is what determines our consciousness. It is always a focusing of attention. By focusing our attention, we isolate things. We take a detail out of the diffuse totality and differentiate it from everything else. This is consciousness. Consciousness appears as human *activity*, which tears us out of the continuous stream of the universe. It is the great interrupter of the universal stream. In daily life, the unique nature of consciousness shows itself in the fact that we can stop and think about things. At the same time, the urge arises to place what we have isolated back into the unified whole. On the one hand, consciousness appears as a concrete isolated focus, a separation, a differentiation, yet awakens within us a searching and questioning concerning the whole. Thus we experience ourselves in our questioning as *standing across from* the world. "The universe appears to us as two opposite parts: *I* and *World*. We erect this barrier between ourselves and the world as soon as consciousness first dawns in us" (4).

Taking this into consideration, consciousness no longer seems to be an arbitrary human inner space, out of which a path to the world must be found, nor does it appear to be something in which the world is pictured as in a *camera obscura*. Rather, it is something that is always in the world, something that is related to the various aspects of the world, a two-sided activity of differentiating and searching. It is through this two-sided activity that we must find what we have not been given. The separation that arises out of the activity of focusing and differentiating challenges a new unification, which is crafted in clearly experienced steps (comp. 4). A decision is a special instance of this process of unification; it is the spiritually conscious step with which we place ourselves in action in the world.

It is important for the subsequent discussion that the description of consciousness as an activity, as it is sketched out above, be brought to personal experience. Through this experience, one becomes aware of the presence of conscious activity in the world. The spontaneous emergence of questions belongs to this activity, as does the search to find connections between what appears to be separate. An innate knowledge of the unified nature of the whole is present in this questioning. This arises from the fact that one, in actuality, lives within the wholeness and that the differentiation is but the price one pays for consciousness (comp. 4).

In the questioning search for connections, we clearly experience an activity through which we ourselves bring something forth. We hear a sound and ask where it comes from and what made it. The way we experience the sound gives us various conceptual possibilities to weigh. We test them on a recurrence of the sound and, finally, decide in which context to place it. We know that this activity is our own. We call it "thinking." We know that any later corrections to our thoughts are only possible through thinking.

Steiner calls the unique way we become aware of our thoughts "*intuition.*" Intuitions live in us and we in them. We know what we mean when we grasp a concept in thinking. Once we have grasped the concept, we can develop it further for ourselves by bringing it into relationship with other concepts. For instance, we can connect the concept of *energy*, which initially appears to be completely abstract, to output, energy source, the transformation of energy and other concepts and by doing so give the initial intuition a specific context and more clarity. Thinking gives our thoughts and itself meaning, content and definition. It is autonomous and one cannot question its independence, as all questioning is in itself thinking (4). In thinking, we find the place where the possibility of self-determination first arises.

This possibility only becomes a reality when the activity of thinking does not exhaust itself in sifting through different conceptual possibilities for a given perception and thus remaining a rather coincidental activity. It does so when thinking consciousness is also applied to our emerging thoughts and we examine their inner integrity with the same precision with which we examine our interpretation of perceptions. In this way, insights are transformed into a conceptual context that we ourselves have sculpted. In chapter 5 of *Intuitive Thinking as a Spiritual Path*, Steiner uses the image of awakening to describe this awareness of one's own thinking (4).

The biographical point at which an awareness of the autonomy of the act of knowing appears is attained in stages, beginning with a new understanding of consciousness and culminating with the awakening in thinking. We experience that consciousness that separates the world into details, placing us before a world of perceptions that appears chaotic. The things of this world do not tell us what we are to think of them. The relationships between the separate details, which are suppressed by our consciousness, are created through our own activity (4). This activity is in as much a free activity as something we can control. And we know that we can consider the same fact from different points of view. We place the given perception in this or that conceptual context, depending on which one we choose. Knowledge is thus not a mere representation of something complete unto itself, but rather the completion of the incomplete world of perceptions to a meaningful reality. The individual is not dictated to by the facts. The facts receive definition through thinking.

Admittedly, there is a differentiation here that must be recognized. Inasmuch as we are speaking about the conceptualization of natural phenomena or objects, the concept is determined by the object or phenomenon.

> For cognition, the concept of a tree is determined by the percept of a tree. Faced with a specific percept, I can select only a very specific concept out of the general conceptual system. The connection between a concept and a percept is indirectly and objectively determined by thinking about the percept. (4, p. 135)

It is different in the case of our will. The direction of an act of will is gained through an intuition that does not necessarily have to belong to the world of perceptions. The nature of the connection between percept and concept in the natural world is not such that the latter is absolutely determined by the former. If this were so, there would be no possibility of error. Second, thinking is a fluid process that sculpts concepts, gives them new contours, and is able to view something from different perspectives and place it in various relationships. The connection between percept and concept is given in the sense that when we see the ocean, we do not think "oak."

Steiner was quite aware of the consequences of this idea of the autonomy of knowing. He wrote:

> The conceptual content that, in order to have full reality, human beings must connect with a percept through thinking cannot be fixed once and for all, and bequeathed in finished form to humanity. Individuals must gain their concepts through their own individual intuitions. How an individual should think cannot be derived from some generic concept. Each individual must set the standard all alone. (4, p. 228)

These words characterize the freedom of knowing. The thinking of an individual, who is discriminate in the development of his concepts, can be free. Can this also be true of human action?

People are quite different from one another. Some have an inclination to observe things closely and in depth. Those who are more emotionally inclined gain richly differentiated impressions. Some individuals who have developed a rich, flexible world of thoughts are able to see the world through high ideas. In many cases, we are not satisfied in bringing our perceptions into a relationship with but one conceptual context. We relate them to ourselves and to everything connected to them. This is when feelings, which appear to us in the form of perceptions, come into being (4).

In thinking, we strive to craft universal relationships; feeling leads us into our personal being. These poles of our existence interweave in various ways.

Our life is a continual oscillation between our individual existence and living with the universal world process. The farther we rise into the universal nature of thinking, where what is individual continues to interest us only as an example, an instance of a concept, the more we let go of our character as particular entities—as completely specific, separate personalities. The more we descend into the depths of our own life, allowing our feelings to resonate with the experiences of the outer world, the more we separate ourselves from universal being. A true individual will be the person who reaches highest, with his or her feelings, into the region of ideals. There are people for whom even the most universal ideas entering their heads still retain a special coloring that shows them unmistakably connected with their bearer. (4, p. 102)

When, in a given situation, an intuition lights up in such a personality, it fills the individual completely. All one's spiritual and psychological forces are placed in the service of the intuition—for instance, in helping. The observation is guided to search out the reasons for the situation, to look for obstacles, injuries, etc. The individual feels compassion and asks oneself, "What could truly be of help in this situation?" In this moment, one begins to imagine possible helpful actions.

This is when freedom becomes concrete. When we focus our forces of imagination on an external situation, we connect ourselves with the world of the senses. Through these forces, we craft new, independent images of action. If we were to only have ideal intuitions, we would find ourselves to be helpless when facing the world; we could only observe and judge. The forces of imagination show us what we can become. Without question, to act we also need to understand the way things work, but it is through the forces of imagination that the bridge connecting us to the world is created. These forces are children of the cosmos.

In addressing the forces of imagination, Steiner takes up a theme that he first spoke about in the lecture "Goethe as the Father of a New Aesthetic." The creative individual find his point of departure in perceptible reality. He unites himself with the sensory world through the forces of imagination. It is thanks to these forces that he is able to experience the world, to feel what sleeps within it as a tendency or as a problem. Through these experiences, his imagination begins to find the hidden gestures and figures that strive toward expression. Something new, something higher than the readily accessed reality is thus brought into being through the human being. He owes this capacity to the fact that spiritual forces, which are related to the forces of nature, can come to expression within his being. The human spirit does not only come to expression in what we commonly regard as thinking, does not only reveal itself in the form of ideas, but also in the spiritual urges that well forth.

Steiner called the quality of imagination that gives us the capacity to act morally "moral imagination." The articulation of this moral imagination is what is completely new in *Intuitive Thinking as a Spiritual Path*.

> Ethical ideas spring from human moral imagination. Their realization depends on being desired strongly enough to overcome pain and suffering. Ethical ideals are human intuitions, the driving forces that our own spirit harnesses. We want them because their realization is our highest pleasure. We do not need ethics to forbid us to strive for pleasure and then tell us what we should strive for. We shall strive for ethical ideals if our moral imagination is active enough to endow us with intuitions that give our willing the strength to make its way against the obstacles—including the unavoidable pain—lying within our organization. (4, p. 220)

In writing this Steiner was describing a given. He did not assert that everyone should exercise moral imagination. His contribution lies in having discovered a psychological fact, which we can now observe for ourselves. It is perhaps easiest to observe these forces at work when one has fallen in love. We can watch our imagination give birth to ideas whose goal is to bring joy or pleasure to the one with whom we are in love. In the first edition, Steiner called a free act "one with which I am in love." One does it with joy. It is not difficult to recognize that being in love does not necessarily have to mean being in love with a person. One can also be in love with a project or a task.

From a biographical perspective, we see that Steiner first formulated the idea of moral imagination in the middle of his life. Only in his book on Nietzsche did he expand on this idea in a philosophical context. Gabriele Reuter, however, with whom Steiner often spoke about the question of moral imagination as they walked the streets of Weimar, remarks in her memoirs that Steiner later exercised this capacity fully and thus helped many people find meaning in their lives. This is true. One can view Anthroposophy as a significant contribution to the stimulation of moral imagination. For instance, the ideas of karma and reincarnation expand the possibilities of moral imagination beyond the here and now into wider dimensions of time. In addition, Steiner showed through his own work the new creative possibilities that arise when imagination is able to grasp the suprasensory.

A theme for the coming years of Steiner's biography appears in the middle of his life with the idea of moral imagination. Most of the other conceptual pieces of *Intuitive Thinking as a Spiritual Path* can be found in one form or another in his earlier writings, although they do come together in the composition of this book. The discovery of moral imagination as the source of ethical striving, however, opens the door to the future.

Looking Ahead

In a lecture on October 27, 1918, which was published in the series entitled "From Symptom to Reality in Modern History," Steiner sketched the milieu in which *Intuitive Thinking as a Spiritual Path* was written and described how the book was received by his contemporaries. He could have mentioned that the book was given serious reviews, both positive and negative, in fourteen different papers. He is, however, silent about this and only remarks that the positive reviews remained "isolated birds" and added that in the "first period only very few books were sold" (185).

In fact, the book was only well received in a few, small circles. "Basically the time was not conducive to the position expressed in *Intuitive Thinking as a Spiritual Path*." Some interest, concerning the question of ethical individualism, was expressed by the theoretical anarchists around John Henry Mackay.* Mackay had become known for his work as the biographer and publisher of the work of Max Stirner and had written a novel, *The Anarchists*. The approval that Steiner's book found in these circles worked to frighten away the educated middle class.

The book did catch the attention of some individuals among the contemporary modern writers. Among them were the playwright Max Halbe,

---

* In 1893, Rudolf Steiner sent his book to Mackay and wrote in his accompanying letter in connection with Max Stirner's main work, *Der Einzige und sein Eigentum* [The individual and his property]: "In my opinion, the first part of my book forms the philosophical foundation for Stirner's philosophy of life. What I develop in the second half of my *Philosophy of Freedom*, as the ethical consequence of my presuppositions, is, I believe, in complete agreement with what is presented in *Der Einzige und sein Eigentum*." (39)

who mentioned *Intuitive Thinking as a Spiritual Path* at length in his memoirs, and the writer and director Karl Weiser, who dedicated one of his plays to Steiner in gratitude for the book. Bruno Wille, who had also written a *Philosophy of Liberation by Pure Means* and was one of the leaders of the alternative scene in Berlin, also wrote a critically friendly review of Steiner's book.

In the academic world, Steiner was met either with silence or rejection. Eduard von Hartmann, who Steiner so respected, made extensive comments on the edges of the pages and sent the book back to Steiner with a scathing review:

> In this book is neither Hume's phenomenalism—absolute in itself—reconciled with Berkley's phenomenalism based on God, nor is Berkley's imminently subjective phenomenalism reconciled with the transcendental panlogism of Hegel, nor is Hegel's panlogism reconciled with Goethean individualism. Between each of these pairs there stretches an unbridgeable chasm. Above all, it overlooks the fact that phenomenalism leads unavoidable to solipsism, absolute illusionism and agnosticism. And phenomenalism does nothing to prevent this slide into the abyss of non-philosophy, because the danger is not even recognized. (4a)

Steiner responded to von Hartmann's critique both in a number of revisions to the new edition in 1918, as well as in a long letter in 1894. In this letter, he not only tried to answer von Hartmann's objections, which arose from the philosopher's own basic position, but was also critically open about what he had not been able to achieve in writing the book. "I feel that it is one of the gravest weaknesses of the book that I was not able to clarify the question as to the extent that an individual is indeed something universal, the manifold a unity. But this is perhaps the most difficult challenge for a philosophy of immanence." Steiner is referring to the contradiction von Hartmann mentioned between Hegelian panlogic and Goethean individualism, which appears in *Intuitive Thinking as a Spiritual Path* as the tension between universal thought and individual self-determination. One could with theoretical justification pose the question, If an autonomous ethical individual is possible, would he have to respond to those intuitions that arise out of a universal thinking? In the above-mentioned letter, Steiner proposes a possible solution:

> Because of the way an ethical idea appears in the individual, it is here singular, and only in its logical context universal. The difficulty lies, in my opinion, in that our *life* is *individual* while our conceptual reflections tend to be *universal*. Both points of view appear to me to be capable of unification in the higher sense. This can occur when we shed—indeed not in the mystical, but in the logical-ideal way—the individual nature of consciousness and recognize that *in thinking* we are no longer single individuals, but that we merely live a general world-life together. (39)

Eduard von Hartmann did not address this point in his reply to Steiner on June 13, 1897. This is at once regrettable and symptomatic. They came to no true dialogue concerning *Intuitive Thinking as a Spiritual Path*.

The German schools of philosophy were at that time, if not dogmatically Catholic, Neo-Kantian and caught up in the idea that "the world is my mental image" and in quite conventional understandings of morality. They couldn't make heads nor tails of the book.

Thus it was that Steiner's main philosophical work went almost unnoticed for a quarter of a century, until the second edition in 1918. Then it was first taken up by the younger generation of anthroposophists, who had found their way to Steiner's work following World War I. By 1945, 33,000 copies of the book had been printed. After World War II, including the paperback edition, 160,000 copies were printed in German alone. Even if one takes into consideration that not every book that is printed is also read, the size of the editions shows considerable interest in the work. For many people, it became a book that accompanied them through their lives. The actual philosophical discussion concerning the ideas formulated in *Intuitive Thinking as a Spiritual Path* was still to take place.

CHAPTER 17

FOR AND AGAINST NIETZSCHE

Steiner's relationship to Nietzsche can be viewed through a variety of lenses. Philologists will always tend to see Steiner as a poor philological interpreter of Nietzsche. True believers will tend to dismiss his encounter with Nietzsche's spirit as a moment of temptation. Earnest moralists will depict the young Steiner as a "Nietzsche-fool." Although each of these viewpoints is justified for those who hold them, all of them miss the actual significance that Nietzsche had for Steiner. Steiner didn't see him as a philological problem, an object for painstaking interpretation, nor was he a devil or a tempter; he was a fascinating spiritual instance of the end of the nineteenth century, one that Steiner could not avoid. In his *Autobiography*, written in 1924, he repeated the words that he had originally written some thirty years earlier, "I am among those readers of Nietzsche who, once they read a page, know absolutely that they will read every page and listen to every word he has ever spoken" (28).

From the beginning, Steiner's exploration of Nietzsche's thought was a spiritual exploration—a breathing, a taking in and rejecting, an experiencing and a wrestling. The very different remarks and assessments in many books and articles bear witness to this spiritual struggle. The differences in the views Steiner expressed in his writings and lectures seem to be irresolvable. The tracks only begin to reveal meaning when they are seen as traces of an ongoing movement, a biographical path. In any case, it doesn't appear to have been Steiner's intention to offer a purely historical description of Nietzsche's development, nor to merely interpret his work. Steiner took the liberty to start each time with what was important to him and to express what it meant to him.

In Chapter 18 of his *Autobiography*, Steiner wrote for the last time of his relationship to Nietzsche. This passage is worthy of note, because in spite of all his other comments over the years, Steiner reaffirms the positive nature of his relationship to Nietzsche.

I was fascinated by the free-sailing levity of his ideas. And I found that his free floating had caused many ideas to develop in him that were like those I experienced, though attained along a very different path. Because of this kinship, in 1895 I could write..., "As early as 1886, in my book *Goethe's Theory of Knowledge*, the reader will find that I express the same sort of convictions as those expressed by Nietzsche in some of his works." (28)

What Steiner perceived in Nietzsche was a familiar disposition, a disposition that was focused consequently on finding spiritual freedom, one that overcame prejudice and freed up one's ability to see the true spiritual situation of the time. He admired the intellectual honesty of the "fighter against his time," who experienced in his own heart more clearly than others the problems of his time. But Steiner goes even further in his diagnosis of Nietzsche. "It was natural for Nietzsche to bring all that he thought and felt out of the depth of his soul in a purely spiritual way. It was his nature to create a universal image based on spiritual processes experienced in his soul" (28).

In Steiner's view, it was this manner of experiencing the world that, in the encounter with the scientific views of his time, led to the tragic turn of Nietzsche's life—he took scientific positivism to its extreme. The only thing that Nietzsche, with his tendency to personal, spiritual experience, found to take seriously in the world around him was positivism. Nietzsche seemed to Steiner to be someone who, although he shared a quality of spiritual experience, could not find appropriate conceptual content for this inner inclination. "Nietzsche's spirituality had its place in my own spiritual experiences. That experience of spirit could join in Nietzsche's struggle and understand his tragedy; but what does that have to do with Nietzsche's thoughts formed out of positivism!" (28). Steiner was drawn to the nature of Nietzsche's experience, not to his ideas.

Steiner was still living in Vienna, probably around 1889, when he first read *Beyond Good and Evil: Prelude to a Philosophy of the Future*. It made a deep, conflicting impression on him. The style and the audacity of the ideas fascinated him; the way Nietzsche addressed the deepest questions repelled him. It was three years before Steiner began to write about Nietzsche. In an 1892 review of three books about the already silent thinker, who was living just an hour away from Weimar in Naumberg and being cared for by his mother, we find traces of an in-depth study by Steiner of Nietzsche's work.

This review is like walking a tightrope. Nietzsche's thinking "is based on absolutely justifiable philosophical principles" (31). Steiner defends Nietzsche against his critics and interpreters, and some of his thoughts are quoted with a slight distancing on the part of the author, but what is remarkable is Steiner's personal opinion. "I found it to be a matter of honor to in theory follow him everywhere. Sometimes it seemed to me that my brain had broken loose of its moorings, sometimes that the finest threads of the same began to twitch; I believed I could feel their resistance at having to abandon so suddenly the ground they had inherited from the elders." The problems, in which Nietzsche "sometimes totally senselessly" buried himself, devoured him. He became a medical problem. Nietzsche's readers needed "weeks of healthy alpine air and lots of cold baths, not theoretical refutations" to get themselves back in shape (31).

At the end of the article, as diagnosis, is a spiritual encephalograph. "Nietzsche's nerves took on a certain elastic resistance; they sprang back light as feathers when confronted with an object. Nietzsche became increasingly an electrical nerve apparatus. He would bump up against something earthly, give off an electrical spark, bounce back and be thrown onto another hard corner, and so on. His later works came into being in this manner. The unbearable state continued to worsen until he went crazy" (31).

Steiner's most critical remarks at this time were reserved for the growing circle of Nietzsche's followers: the "Nietzsche dandies," the "Nietzsche herd" and the "Nietzsche monkeys" (31). A review of the fourth part of *Zarathustra* was aimed directly at Nietzsche's followers and ended with a sarcastic paraphrasing of Zarathustra's "last sin": *Thus Zarathustra sat up*" (31).

In another book review, Steiner gave a gentle hint of his spiritual connection to Nietzsche, although the pathological nature of Nietzsche's brilliance is still in the foreground.

> The allure of Nietzsche's ideas comes from the abnormal mantle in which they appear. There are things that one notices because of their outward appearance, which one would otherwise have passed by. Nietzsche's ideas impressed me as follows. Their content does not appear to me to be new. I had already formed this within myself, before I became acquainted with him. They seemed to have been twisted, made into caricatures as they passed through Nietzsche's spirit. A chain of thought, which was in and of itself healthy, had to squeeze through a crack in

a cliff, which broke its calm flow. Nietzsche was never a philosophical problem for me, but always a psychological problem. (31)

Following this book review in 1892, Steiner did not discuss Nietzsche again for over a year. He was working at this time on finishing *Intuitive Thinking as a Spiritual Path*, in which Nietzsche is not mentioned. Immediately after finishing this book, Steiner turned to finishing the Schopenhauer edition, for which Cotta Publishing was waiting desperately. It is possible that Nietzsche would have been put aside for longer if Elisabeth Förster-Nietzsche had not appeared at the Goethe-Schiller archive in May 1894. She was planning to open a Nietzsche archive and wanted to see how the Goethe-Schiller archive was organized. She was introduced to the coworkers—Eduard von der Hellen, Julius Wahle, Franz Ferdinand Heitmüller, August Fresenius, and Rudolf Steiner—and extended to them the invitation to visit her in Naumburg.

A small group, including Gabriele Reuter, then traveled to Naumburg on May 26, 1894, to view the "papers of the incomparable man." Gabriele Reuter relates that during the train ride Heitmüller was suddenly overcome with pangs of conscience: What would his deceased father think of the son's visit to the one who had denied God?

They met a friendly welcome at the comfortable, old-fashioned rectory in Naumburg and could wonder at Nietzsche's manuscripts while Ms. Förster-Nietzsche spoke at length, often with tears, about her "much loved brother." Rudolf Steiner recalled, "At the time, she had aroused great sympathy in me because of her multifaceted and charming personality" (28). They were invited to return later that summer, and Fritz Koegel, Nietzsche's publisher at that time, read Nietzsche's *Antichrist* from the manuscript in his warm, lively voice—an unforgettable moment for the visitors. This piece made a deep impression on Steiner, and in December of that year he wrote to Pauline Specht, "One of the most important books that has been written in centuries! Every sentence called forth once again my own feelings. At the moment I can't find the words to describe the degree of satisfaction that this book called forth in me" (39).

Not only were Nietzsche and archival matters spoken about during the visits in Naumburg.

> We spoke about a second edition of Nietzsche's works. I was invited twice to Naumburg. Then they hired Dr. von der Hellen, who was

then the archivist of the Goethe-Schiller archive, and told me that I was too independent to be able to work with the present editor. This did not only embarrass me but also other people who had been following the process. From the very beginning, I had been seen as the one predestined to publish Nietzsche's work. (39)

Just how deeply the outcome angered Steiner is apparent in a letter to Karl Julius Schröer. "You have no doubt heard that Dr. Eduard von der Hellen has left the Goethe archive. He is now publishing Nietzsche with the same inner conviction, namely none, with which until October 1 he had worked on Goethe's papers" (39). Steiner wanted not only to flee the poorly paid work in the Goethe archive; Nietzsche truly interested him more than the "fat minister with his double chin" (188). He had hoped to find more freedom in the Nietzsche archive—and he was probably not completely disinterested in the better salary.

In fact, Steiner was fortunate. Shortly after he had been hired, von der Hellen found himself in conflict with Fritz Koegel, the first editor of Nietzsche's work, and in January 1895 decided to resign from the Nietzsche archive. Elisabeth Förster-Nietzsche informed Steiner immediately. Once again, she invited him repeatedly to Naumburg. Steiner, however, conscious of von der Hellen's fate, was hesitant to follow her wishes.

Steiner finished *Friedrich Nietzsche, Fighter for Freedom* in April 1895. We are in the dark concerning how this book came into being. Steiner relates that Elisabeth Förster-Nietzsche "during the first of my many visits took me into Friedrich Nietzsche's room." The deep impression that Nietzsche made on him inspired him to write the book (28). This is without doubt an error of memory. Steiner, who repeatedly stated that he had seen Nietzsche only once, did so on January 22, 1896. Immediately after this visit, which took place with Nietzsche's mother—not Elisabeth Förster-Nietzsche—he noted his impressions, "January 22, 1896. Just saw Nietzsche..." (Rudolf Steiner Studies, VI). Steiner's book on Nietzsche, which was published in May 1895, was written a year before Steiner met him. Steiner's assertion, made during a lecture (Aug. 8, 1892), that his book was written before *The Antichrist* was published is also not accurate. He quotes *The Antichrist* in the book, but could no doubt not explain to his anthroposophic audience to what extent Nietzsche's piece had moved him, having just laid out how Ahriman, the spirit of darkness, had been included in the work as the "writer." In any case, the two errors point to a problem.

In the foreword, Steiner explicitly thanked Elisabeth Förster-Nietzsche for her friendliness and added, "The following thoughts have their source in the atmosphere that I was gratified to experience during the hours spent in the Nietzsche archive in Naumburg." These excessively friendly words, which, with the exception of the readings of *Ecce Homo* at the end of 1895, do not seem to reflect the reality of the visits, as well as Steiner's mention of Fritz Koegel, "the exemplary editor of Nietzsche's work," give rise to the question whether this book was an attempt on Steiner's part to be chosen as editor of Nietzsche's work, one who had already made a name for himself as a Nietzsche scholar.

It is quite possible that Steiner began the 110-page book in February 1895, after hearing of von der Hellen's resignation, and finished it in the next two and a half months. Viewing the book as Steiner's attempt to identify himself with Nietzsche in the hope of becoming the next editor would make the truly astonishing suppression of all his earlier critiques and his not mentioning anything about Nietzsche's pathology understandable, even if it could not explain it. It is also possible that based on the *Antichrist* and intensive study of Nietzsche's work, Steiner had momentarily overcome his critical stance. Whatever happened, from 1900 on, Steiner once again took a critical position in relation to Nietzsche.

In his book on Nietzsche, Steiner, however, tried to present in as transparent a manner as he could what he experienced as justified in Nietzsche's ideas, most importantly Nietzsche's battle against the tendencies of his time. This is the key to understanding the book. Nietzsche concluded part six of his *Untimely Meditations II: On the Use and Abuse of History for Life* with the words, "And if you look for biographies, then look no longer for those with the refrain "Mr. So-and-So and his time," but for those whose titles should read a "fighter against his time." Steiner picked up on this suggestion of Nietzsche's and showed how he confronted the common opinions, the norms and prejudices, and the popular beliefs and mirrored them back.

The source of Steiner's interpretation of Nietzsche is to be found where Steiner felt himself to be in agreement with him, in the autonomy of the sovereign individual. In *Intuitive Thinking as a Spiritual Path*, Steiner claims complete self-determination and self-realization for the individual, which he believes he recognizes again in Nietzsche's *Superman*. The individual determines his own truth and his own morality, trusts in his own strength. This is in contradiction to the spirit of that time, which played on the urge of the weak to subjugate themselves. This submissiveness thirsted for rules and regulations, for adaptation and commonality. The weaker ones strove to do things the way everyone else did. Those in the faceless herd submitted themselves to common moral values, the public conscience and the superiority of science. They subjugated their judgment to statistics and experiments. But they who submit deny that they are the ones who hear the voice of conscience, who decide how to bring morality into action. They want to think what everyone else is thinking. They want to place themselves in the service of a "higher" idea or truth. Even the leading thinkers do not have the courage to be themselves. They want to be "objective" and only express what pure reason supports. "Such people want to deny their person in order to assert that their expressions are those of a higher spirit" (5). In contrast to this, Zarathustra, or Nietzsche, "wishes to make no prescriptions of what humans should be; he will refer each one only to himself, and will say to each: Depend upon yourself, follow only yourself, put yourself above virtue, wisdom, and knowledge" (5). And in the words of an individualistic *Philosophy of Freedom*, Steiner writes, "Humans themselves are the creators of truth. The 'free spirit' arrives at the awareness of his or her own creation of truth. An individual no longer regards truth as something to which one subordinates oneself but looks upon it as one's own creation" (5).

This understanding of truth and knowledge necessarily leads to a view of life that finds its meaning in the self-realization of the independent spirit.

> Strong individuals seek their life's task in working out their creative *self*. This *self-seeking* differentiates them from weak individuals who, in the *selfless* surrender to what they call "good," seek morality. The weak preach selflessness as the highest virtue, but their selflessness is only the consequence of their lack of creative power. If they had any creative self, they would then have wished to manifest it. Those who are strong love war because they need war to manifest their creation in opposition to those powers hostile to them. (5)

Thus, Steiner interpreted Nietzsche in light of Max Stirner's philosophy and, at the same time, explained his own *Philosophy of Freedom*. The gist of this interpretation becomes clear, however, only if one also takes into consideration where Steiner contradicts Nietzsche. In Steiner's opinion, Nietzsche underestimates the significance of consciousness for human personality. Nietzsche viewed consciousness as the final and most recent stage of organic evolution. It seemed to him to be what was least refined and impotent in animals and in humans. He thought that consciousness should be ruled by healthy, unconscious instincts for as long as possible (*The Joyful Science*, Book I).

Steiner countered, "Indeed, Dionysian individuals are not slaves to tradition or to the 'will beyond,' but are *slaves of their own instincts*." The only human beings who are free are those who can create their own tasks and goals through moral imagination. "Moral imagination is missing in Nietzsche's presentations." Thus for Steiner—who in no way wishes to disavow the significance of the instincts—it is true "that human beings are free only insofar as they can create *within their consciousness* thought motives for theri actions" (5). For human behavior that does not occur in a state of sleep, consciousness is absolutely essential for every human intercommunication, and even for working on the strong instincts. Steiner goes further, explaining the following in looking at successful communication among people. "It is a fact based on experience that these thought motives, which human beings produce out of themselves nevertheless manifest an overall consistency to a certain degree in single individuals" (5). This agreement or consistency among individuals does not come from some prescribed norm or from a moral law, but from experience, as one sees when one looks back later at the behavior of people. From this experience, it follows that "the free person is justified in assuming that harmony in human society enters of its own accord when society consists of sovereign individuals" (5). Indeed, consciousness is imperative for the human being, and freedom can originate only in the free creation of thought motives and in awakening moral imagination. For Steiner, the original nature of human beings is first the freely created thoughts, not animal instincts. "The free individual most certainly adhere to the opinion that would allow the animal instincts to reign in complete freedom and thus do away with all law and order" (5).

Rudolf Steiner therefore pleads for the free spirit and sees the instincts of the human being in the spiritual impulses. So the instinct for education, the desire to ask that we see already in the young child, is no less a basic instinct than the drive to eat. The impulse to educate oneself is clearly a strong drive that motivates the behavior of the human being. It is similar in the realm of morality.

> Moral instincts, for example, are a special level of instinct. Even if one acknowledges only that they are simply higher forms of sensory instinct, nevertheless they do appear in a special form in human

existence. This shows itself in the possibility that individuals can carry out actions that cannot be led back directly to sensory instincts, but only to those impulses that can be defined as higher forms of instinct. Individuals themselves create impulses for their own actions, which are not to be derived from their own sensory impulses but only from conscious thinking. (5)

So Apollo triumphs (unlike with Nietzsche) over Dionysius. Here, a biological, Darwinian–Nietzschean interpretation, which promulgates the worship of the blond brute in the cult of the biologically stronger, is stopped by what Steiner said in another connection: "My ethical individualism was a pure inner experience of the human being" (28). Steiner's individualism, in fact, wants to stress the importance of the strength of the individual. However, this strength should not lead to the war of all against all, but because the strong individual is open to others and to other things, it should bring understanding. The formulations in the Nietzsche book are clearly not meant for children, but rather—as Novalis wrote in a letter to Friedrich Schlegel—for the "members of the master class of the lodge of morality."

Steiner's book met a mixed reception. Elisabeth Förster-Nietzsche was naturally quite taken by it since it was positive about Nietzsche throughout. A large number of both positive and critical reviews appeared. A second edition appeared relatively quickly. Rosa Mayreder voiced perhaps the most accurate assessment of the book in a letter to Rudolf Steiner. Everything in the book, she wrote,

> that is born of your spirit seems to me to be excellent. As long as Rudolf Steiner speaks about Rudolf Steiner, as long as he unpacks Nietzsche to reveal Steiner, I am able to listen with undivided acclamation. But I can only accept the book in the most limited sense as an interpretation of Nietzsche. For me it is almost exclusively an interpretation of Rudolf Steiner with the help of Friedrich Nietzsche. Possibly, this was your intention, but it seems to me it would have been better if a third person had undertaken this. An independent spiritual individuality must of necessity rape another spiritual individuality in its own self-realization. For this reason it is the task of a non-creative individual to translate and interpret. (8/13/1895, Hoffmann)

Fritz Koegel saw the situation in a similar manner. The references to Max Stirner disturbed him, and he felt that Nietzsche had been made prosaic, had been rationalized and simplified. "In spite of this," he wrote in a letter to Josef Hofmiller, "I think that the positive affect this little book will have will outweigh its harm. It disperses many prejudices and misunderstandings and doesn't approach Nietzsche from outside with such twisted perspectives in the way that all the others, with the exception of Peter Gast, have" (Hoffmann).

It was six months after the publication of the book that Steiner finally agreed to Elisabeth Förster-Nietzsche's request and traveled to Naumburg. He stayed there ten days to catalogue Nietzsche's books and put his library in order. During this visit, Steiner became acquainted with her constantly changing moods and her fluctuating views. He soon realized that one had to express oneself very carefully in this house. "One experienced an uncertainty there that soured one's every word. Add to that, that this was taking place where the remaining writings of the greatest thinker of the time were stored, and one's heart grew heavy" (39).

This period, however, also left Steiner with an impression that would accompany him throughout his later life. He visited Nietzsche on his sickbed. Immediately following this visit, he noted:

> January 22, 1896. I just saw Nietzsche. He lay on the sofa like a tired thinker who, lying, continues to contemplate a long held problem. I could not look into his eyes.... O, this magnificent forehead, revealing both the thinker and the artist. Fresh color over his whole face. He spread the peace of wisdom around him. One believed that the whole, vast world of thought dozed behind his forehead. The thought came to me, "He is fully conscious, he sees and hears everything that is happening around him. He simply cannot express himself." An impression of greatness, now removed from the earth, overcame me. (Rudolf Steiner Studies, VI)

Many years later, Steiner's memory of this moment had taken on a spiritually transparent quality. "In inner perception, I saw Nietzsche's soul hovering above his head. It was infinitely beautiful in its spiritual light, freely surrendering to the spirit worlds it had longed for so much but had been unable to find before illness clouded his mind" (28). A comparison of the two depictions shows how such early impressions become oculars for spiritual research. The intensive impression that Steiner had in 1896 only revealed its spiritual significance later.

The Nietzsche archive moved to Weimar on August 1, 1896. Elisabeth Förster-Nietzsche intensified her efforts to talk Steiner into working for her. She asked Steiner to give philosophical lectures for her. This request embarrassed him; he felt that Koegel was being ignored. Before agreeing, he spoke about it with Koegel, who could do nothing other than, nolens volens, agree. Since the move to Weimar, Koegel's relationship to Elisabeth Förster-Nietzsche had become increasingly tense. Finally, when Koegel announced his engagement, it came to a head and Elisabeth Förster-Nietzsche asked Steiner to become the junior editor of the archive. This brought Steiner into a terrible dilemma. He knew the legal situation. She had a contract with Koegel and couldn't hire a junior editor without both his and the publisher's permission. His relationship with Koegel was such that he certainly didn't want to stab him in the back. On the other hand, he would very much have liked to work on the publication of Nietzsche's papers. He wrote to Anna Eunike shortly before Elisabeth Förster-Nietzsche finally offered him the position:

> Koegel and Frau Elisabeth Förster-Nietzsche are drifting ever further apart. She is quite clearly working to put him out in the street. There have been terrible scenes. At the moment, it is also quite clear that she would like me to continue the work on the Nietzsche edition. We should, I mean you and I, think about the possibility. I can tell you how things lie. I think the edition could be finished in three or four months. (39)

Disregarding the fact that Steiner's estimate of the time needed to complete the edition was well off the mark—it would take much longer—he was certainly inclined to accept Frau Förster-Nietzsche's offer. However, when she actually made the offer, in a private conversation, he could only point out to her how inappropriate her actions had been and have her promise not to mention a word concerning their conversation. She did exactly the opposite. This led to a series of dramatic confrontations, first between Koegel and Steiner, then, after Koegel had recognized the situation, between Elisabeth Förster-Nietzsche on the one side and Koegel and Steiner on the other. Koegel summarized the events in a letter. "Frau F. has made it impossible for Rudolf Steiner, whom I hold to be the best alternative, to work here by playing him up against me. Since Steiner is a loyal friend, he has resisted the intrigues that Frau F. has raised against me" (Hoffmann).

In spite of these experiences, negotiations concerning a possible connection between Steiner and the archive continued until 1898. In his last letter to Frau Förster-Nietzsche on August 23, 1898, Rudolf Steiner couched his final refusal in the following words:

> You know best, most respected and esteemed Frau, that I have never pushed to be given this, for me an enticing task, and that I have never done anything, even during the time of the unpleasant occurrences, to force anyone else aside. You may believe me: it is the most difficult thing in life not to be able to fulfill a task to which one feels himself called. But one must know when to resign himself, when one, as in this situation, is completely misunderstood. And your last letter showed me that you misunderstand me deeply.... I see things happening the way they unfortunately must. I have made mistakes that will come back to haunt me. But this is my destiny. I can do nothing to change it. (Rudolf Steiner Studies, VI)

The pendulum swung back. At a lecture in February 1898, Steiner spoke uncritically and positively about Nietzsche. But in an essay published in November 1899, the tone had changed. He described the final phase of Nietzsche's work.

> Nietzsche went to war against idealism. He worshipped healthy nature. He tried to incorporate scientific beliefs into his soul. But he could only take them into a weak, sickly organism. His own personality was not a bearer, not a seed bed for the *Superman*. He could place it before humanity as an ideal, and he could speak of it with enthusiasm, but he experienced how deep the contrast was when he compared it to himself. The dream of the superman is his philosophy; his own soul life, colored as it was with disappointment that his own existence did not measure up to the ideals of the superman, is the source of the mood out of which his lyrical works were born. (33)

After Steiner had begun to overcome what had become a one-sidedly positive view of Nietzsche, and as he ceased to feel duty-bound to uphold the image of the "greatest spirit of our time," it began to become clear to him what had actually taken place in regard to the Nietzsche archive. In February 1900, the publication of Ernst Horneffer's *Nietzsche's Teachings of the Eternal Return and Its Early Publication* caused Steiner to write a number of articles in which he spoke about "in whose hands Nietzsche's papers" were. The first revelations of the situation behind the scenes at the Nietzsche archive did more to hurt Steiner than it did the archive. The readers of the *Journal for Literature* were not happy about the feud that was carried out in its pages. And Steiner was alone with his accusations. Koegel remained silent. Erich Friedrich Podach's expose from 1932 met a similar fate. It was only in 1956, with the publication of the "Philological Review" of Karl Schlecta's Nietzsche edition, that interested scholars began to realize just in whose hands the papers had been.

Before Nietzsche's death, Steiner wrote two articles in which he distanced himself from his one-sided assessment of Nietzsche. In these articles, Steiner applied the ideas of psychopathology, as he understood it, to Nietzsche's life and work. The title of the first article, "The Philosophy of Friedrich Nietzsche as a Psychopathological Problem," indicates that this would not only apply to Nietzsche's bodily illness. The problem is Nietzsche's philosophy, not his body. On the second page we find the sentence, "A characteristic that is to be found throughout Nietzsche's work is his lack of attention to objective reality" (5).

In 1895, Steiner celebrated Nietzsche's question *"why not untruth instead"* as an idea "of insurmountable audacity" (5); in 1900, he sees it as a symptom of the battle against the truth (5). Nietzsche's sledgehammer approach to philosophy becomes "a destructive urge that leads him in his judgment of certain views and beliefs well over the mark of what is acceptable as criticism" (5). And Nietzsche's aphoristic, associative style becomes the expression of "the incoherence of his mental images" (5). Steiner does, at the end of his article, acknowledge that "Nietzsche was a genius, in spite of his illness" (5).

Following this nadir of Steiner's assessment of Nietzsche, the pendulum swung back, and in his later anthroposophic lectures Steiner spoke often about the tragedy and greatness of Nietzsche.

> Nietzsche's life is a terrible tragedy. I don't think anyone can truly understand the nature of human civilization during the last third of the nineteenth century and how it affected the twentieth century who has not experienced such a tragedy as played itself out in Nietzsche's soul, which experienced the path of this civilization so strongly. It is a fact that all the disasters that we now see and experience are caused by what Nietzsche called the dishonesty of modern civilization. (221)

In 1900, Steiner, after breathing Nietzsche in for so many years, had to stop and breathe out deeply. He could even write in an obituary that Nietzsche "stood at a distance to the true life of the present, to the great needs of the time." Thus, one cannot see him as a thinker who was characteristic for his time, and he ended the obituary with the words, "A noteworthy thinker died on August 25, not one of the spirits who will lead into the future" (31). In a different but related manner, Steiner wrote about Nietzsche in the final lines of the second volume of *World and Individual Philosophy* (later, *The Riddles of Philosophy*), "Nietzsche's worldview is one of agnosticism, *personally experienced as an individual experience and as individual destiny.*" In the second edition of this book in 1914, Steiner revised this passage to point to what is justified in Nietzsche's thinking (18).

CHAPTER 18

A NEW WORLD OPENS UP

In 1896, Rudolf Steiner officially ended his work for the Goethe-Schiller archive and his work on the last two volumes of Kürschner's edition of *Goethe's Scientific Writings*. His career as a scholar of Goethe came to an end and he summarized it in the winter of 1896/97 in the book *Goethe's Worldview*. It was also the end of his academic career. He probably gave up his intention to find a university position in 1896 at the latest. His life took on a completely new form.

Steiner relates in his *Autobiography* how, toward the end of his time in Weimar, his soul-life went through a profound transformation. Independently of external influences, it was only in his thirty-sixth year that Steiner awakened to exact observation of the sensory world. Before this, it had been very difficult for him to grasp sense-perceptible details. "I had always found it easy to comprehend the broader scientific relationships that have to be understood in a purely spiritual way. It had taken tremendous effort, however, to observe material objects accurately and, especially, to commit them to memory. This changed completely. A new attentiveness for sensory-perceptible phenomena awakened within me" (28).

For Steiner, it was highly significant that he awakened to the sensory world much later in life than most others do. In the time leading up to this awakening, he was able to develop the ideal experience of the spiritual world much more purely than was usually the case; with the awakening, it was possible for him to grasp the sensory world without it being clouded by personal subjectivity. "This increased precision and more thorough penetration of sensory observation opened a door for me to an entirely new world" (28). "I soon discovered that this way of observing the world, in fact, leads into the spiritual world. By observing the physical world this way, one completely leaves oneself; this in turn enables one to return to the spiritual world with enhanced powers of spiritual observation" (28).

It is clear that the awakening of awareness for the sense-perceptible world is an inner soul process. The soul's ability to experience enters into the world of the senses; the details of the outer world, which have been passed over, are now experienced in their substantiality; their language becomes audible within. Sounds, colors, words, and forms begin to speak a profound language. The fact that the sensing human is also a part of the whole human being, that one participates in the life of the world through the senses, becomes a living experience. The sensory world ceases to be merely something outside of the individual—it reveals itself as a part of human totality. The connection between the ideal world and the sensory world takes on a new quality of experience. The world of the ideas becomes richer; that of the senses, deeper and more profound. Emphasis is laid on the *and* when speaking of idea and perception.

What one experiences when immersed in the world of sense experience is practically impossible to speak about with others, as all language appears to already point toward thoughts. Words usually express concepts. One can actually only say: Look here or look there. Thus, Steiner wrote in his *Autobiography*, "For me this insight was a crystal clear, soul experience. But it was extraordinarily difficult to express it" (28). To begin with, Steiner practiced pure observation. He related, "I once had, for instance, the opportunity to see a play that a theater company performed fifty times in the town I was living, every evening. Each evening I went to the performance and let it work its magic on me, and I discovered that although the fifth viewing was perhaps boring, the fifty-first was not at all" (279). The nuances, in this case the imperfections, became increasingly apparent in the pure experience.

One finds other examples of this striving for exact observations in some of Steiner's articles. He wrote a sketch for a drama magazine entitled "What is Insignificant," in which he described how each seemingly insignificant gesture or mimic either supports or weakens a performance (29). In a study called "About Acting," he tried to show how individual observation, a continuous learning from life, can lead to an individual, not mechanical, performance (29). In "Concerning the Art of Speaking," he attempted to unveil the secrets of the art of recitation (29). These and other writings point to his struggle to bring the unspeakable to the reader's attention and lead into observation. We can also recognize in these writings documents of Steiner's own self-education.

This transformation of soul comes naturally also to expression in *Goethe's Worldview*, the last book Steiner wrote while in Weimar. It is not to be found in a shift in the conceptual approach. Steiner had always given the idea of the perceptible world considerable space. But it was at this time that what had earlier been an idea became "intense soul experience" (28).

Steiner described the new quality of comprehension as one in which the ideal experience of earlier became an experience in which the whole human being participated. "My *Philosophy of Freedom* was born from the experience of ideas that encompassed spiritual reality. The experience involving the whole human being contains the spiritual world in a much more *substantial* way than idea experience" (28).

Fortunately, Steiner made it easy to find this shift in the quality of experience to one in which the whole human is present in *Goethe's Worldview*, as he presented it in a most straightforward manner:

> In the simplest judgment about a thing or event of the outer world, there can be found a human soul experience and an outer perception in inner association with one another. When I say that one body strikes another, I have already brought an inner experience into the outer world. I see a body in motion; it hits another one; this one also comes into motion as a consequence. The content of the perception cannot tell me more than this. I am not satisfied by this, however. For I feel that still more is present in the whole phenomenon than what mere perception gives me. I reach for an inner experience that will enlighten me about the perception. I know that I myself can set a body into motion by applying force, by striking it. I carry this experience over into the phenomenon and say that the one body strikes the other. (6)*

---

*   Precisely, this passage makes Steiner's change of thought clear. This paragraph corresponds to the beginning of today's chapter 3 in *Intuitive Thinking as a Spiritual Path*, where Steiner starts with the example of how a billiard ball transfers its movement to another and goes on to state that, from this observation, one cannot predict the movement of the ball that was struck. He goes on to say: "But the situation is different when I begin to think about the content of my observation. The purpose of my thinking is to form concepts about the process I observe. I connect the concept of an elastic sphere with certain other concepts of mechanics and take into consideration the particular circumstances prevailing in the given case." (4) Steiner lists a series of concepts—sphere, elasticity, movement, impact, velocity, and so on—which are to be brought into connection with each other. Thus, a thought-structure is built. Then in 1897, he says simply, "I reach for an inner experience that explains the perception to me." There is no talk of lengthy contemplation and building of concepts and a connecting together of the concepts.

Human experience is not limited, of course, to such primitive experiences as force and collision. These bodily experiences are "the most superficial and trivial" (6). They belong to the general experience of all humans and are similar for each person. The experiences that individual make when encountering the world vary widely, however. We experience a plant sprouting and blossoming, the tension in the body of a hunting animal, and, more than anything, the manifold differences of our fellow human beings. In addition, everywhere we experience more or less as a whole human being what is taking place within the other person. We must only pay attention to what happens within ourselves when we immerse ourselves by looking, listening, and sharing the experience of another, when we opens ourselves completely to the world that surrounds us. We notice then that the world speaks within us, that the phenomena reveal themselves through us.

Rudolf Steiner also understood Goethe in this sense. He wrote, "To *know* the truth means for [Goethe] *to live in the truth*. And to live in the truth is simply to watch, when looking at each individual thing, what inner experience occurs when one stands in front of this thing" (6). The sense-perceptible brings itself to expression in this manner in the ensouled physical human being, for each of us truly lives immersed in this world. The individual is formed and nourished by the world and is an integral part of the universe, not merely an observer. The human being is a microcosm able to share the experience of the macrocosm to various degrees.

For instance, if an individual listens to another person talk about his or her ideas and reconstructs them within the framework of one's own conceptual capacity, one remains within one's own world. If the individual, however, actively experiences the other with one's complete being and lets his or her voice, with its cadences and melody, work upon oneself, the other is experienced as an embodied, sense-perceptible being, and one feels how the other grasps the body with the forces of his or her soul. What is sense-perceptible becomes the *direct revelation* of the soul-spiritual nature of the other human being. Steiner described this in some of his education lectures:

> When we learn to listen to a child's voice, whether harmonious and pleasant or harsh and discordant, and when we understand that this is related to movements of the lungs and to the blood circulation—movements inwardly vibrating through the whole person right into

the fingers and toes—we know that this speech expresses something imbued with soul qualities. And now something like a "higher being" appears, finding expression in this image that relates speech to the physical processes of circulation and breathing. (310)

Everything that can be perceived with the senses reveals itself as the direct expression of what is actually spiritual. With such knowledge, it is clear what is to be done and where one can help.

As early as 1887, Steiner had spoken about "becoming aware of the idea in reality" as the true communion of human beings. By 1897, this insight has ripened into personal experience and Steiner turns his attention to the historical developments in philosophy that deny the revelation of the spiritual in what is sense-perceptible, that degrade the sense-world to a mere illusion. He sees Plato as the primary exponent of this way of thinking, a way of thinking that is based on a distrust of the sensory world and that continues into the present. In *Goethe's Worldview*, there are extensive passages concerning *Plato's view of the world* and *the consequences of a Platonic worldview*. In these expositions, we meet a fiery Rudolf Steiner, ready for a fight. He takes a strong stand against Platonism and everything that grew out of it. This new, fiery voice is also a symptom of the transformation of soul of which Steiner speaks.

He writes the following about the Platonic view of the world: "The Platonic view tears the picture of the world-whole into two parts, into the mental picture of a seeming world and into a world of ideas to which true eternal reality alone is thought to correspond." Although the world, in fact, reveals itself to the human being as concept and percept, and one gains knowledge of the world on both paths, Plato denies the truth of the sense perceptions, as these are forever changing. They are not "eternal." Thus the question arises as to the relationship between the eternal world of ideas and the world of semblance belonging to the senses.

[Plato] tasked Western thought with a fully superfluous riddle. For centuries, an endless amount of sagacity has been focused on the question: How do the ideas that reveal themselves within the human being relate to the things we perceive in the outer world? Much of the substance of all the Platonic philosophies consists of attempts to resolve this question, which in fact does not exist. Such brooding thinkers overlooked precisely what common sense teaches us every moment—that the language of perception and that of thinking combine to reveal the full reality to us. Instead of turning their attention to the way that nature speaks to human beings, they create artificial concepts about the relationship between the world of ideas and experience. To paralyze the vision of this relationship completely, Platonism was combined with Christianity. This religious belief, with its faith in an afterlife and its denial of the sensory world is simply a popular form of Platonism. (6, 1st ed.)

While the platonic view was most common among the educated classes and soared into rarified heights of abstraction, the clergy and the church popularized denial of the outer world and made certain that the love of sensual pleasures was accompanied by a guilty conscience. The "emotional life of the West has thus been reorganized in the wrong direction. The clergy have seeded in the feeling soul what were for Plato mere thoughts. What is rooted in the emotions is much more difficult to weed out than what rests in reason. For this reason it has not been possible to overcome the unnatural, Christian-platonic view of reality within Western education" (6, 1st ed.).

Aristotle's conception was for Steiner at that time the counter image of an unhealthy Platonism. Aristotle was a true scientist who trusted his observations and studied the manifold details of appearances. He didn't imagine an ideal republic, ruled by philosophers, but asked how the actual Greek polis functioned.

> He saw nature as a unified being, which consisted of ideas as well as of what could be perceived through the senses. Ideas can only have independent existence within the realm of human consciousness. But within this realm of independence they lack reality. Only the soul can separate them from the perceptible things, together with which they form what is real. If Western philosophy had connected itself to a correctly understood Aristotelianism, it would have been protected from the erroneous, winding paths that it instead has followed. (6, 1st ed.)

In this manner, with strong yet simple lines, Steiner sketches a picture of the development of Western thought. He is thoroughly partisan. Finally he comes to speak of the philosopher Immanuel Kant, who, through his careful, ascetic approach to life, manages to steer clear of not only any possible adventure, but also having to look closely at the world, and who spends his entire life in one place, studying the world through books.

A New World Opens Up

In Kant, Platonism brought forth a bad apple. Plato turned away from the world of perception and focused his attention on the world of eternal ideas, because the sensory world did not seem to him to be able to express the essential being of things. Kant, however, denied that ideas can offer insight into the essence of the world if all that remains are the qualities of the eternal and the necessary.... Kant is satisfied when he can but affirm only these qualities of the ideas. They no longer need to express the essential nature of the world. (6, 1st ed.)

In later editions, Steiner revised and softened these passages. They are of biographical interest to us here. The feistiness of these statements give us a hint of what was important for Steiner at that time. First, an appropriate assessment of the value of perception—the entire perceptible world—which expresses itself so clearly to the observing individual. Here he praises Goethe, who "felt himself to be closely entwined with nature. He saw himself as a living part of nature. What came to be within his spirit, he viewed as having been brought about by nature" (6). Steiner points to Goethe as an artist, who lived as a practical, active person in the world and brought it to expression through his work. Second, and this was especially important to Steiner, this world is a unified whole that speaks to us through both idea and perception. Goethean understanding is thus not described as an abstraction, as reflection or logical reasoning. It is not a purely conceptual activity, but rather an active encounter with the world, one in which experience is constantly broadened and deepened. As a gardening botanist, in his travels and his work as a geologist, and through drawing and experimentation, Goethe actively takes the world in. "He had to immerse his spirit in experience in order to come to the ideas. The reciprocity of idea and perception was for him a spiritual breathing," wrote Steiner, and went on to quote Goethe, "The movement of the pendulum reigns over time. The reciprocal movements of idea and experience rule the world of morality and science" (6).

Biographically, Steiner's description of this side of Goethe's work has another aspect. Until now, Steiner had been a scholar. As such, he was without doubt active and productive, but financially dependent—first on scholarships, then as a tutor to the Specht children, and finally as an employee of the Goethe-Schiller archive. Now he experienced the urge to be independent. His time in Weimar came to an end when he decided to become the publisher and editor of the Berlin *Journal for Literature*. This was an entrepreneurial step. He would be on his own. This step is another symptom of his changing relationship to the world.

This new relationship to the world, which expressed itself inwardly as the discovery of the sensory world, is rooted in a deep transformation of his entire being. Steiner summarized the change in his *Autobiography*.

> I could feel a certain aspect of the conceptual element of my inner life receding, replaced by an element of will. This could happen only when volition abstained from all subjective impulsiveness in regard to developing knowledge. The will increased in direct proportion to the decreasing conceptual element. The will also took over spiritual cognition, which had previously been accomplished almost exclusively by the conceptual element. (28)

This new orientation, which transformed Rudolf Steiner's entire being, occurred on a number of levels. In cognition, conceptual insight was no longer primary, even though the challenge of *forming* concepts remained central in his further work, because the knowledge gained had to be articulated in the form of ideas. Forming ideas and insights is however a task for the artistically active will. This will comes to expression in forms of daily meditative practice in which ideas are re-formed in their composition and gesture and re-imagined within their various contexts. In Chapter 22 of his *Autobiography*, in which he describes the transformation of his soul, Steiner also writes extensively for the first time about his inner, meditative work.

Work of this nature proceeds slowly. The will awakens and ripens in an organic manner; a new ring is laid down each year. This quality of will is not one that exhausts itself in sudden outer action. Step by step, it lets a new individual come forth; cognition through the will is self-cognition, self-transformation. Steiner writes about it in his *Autobiography*. "I also thought: The whole world, except for the human being, is a mystery—the actual 'world mystery.' *And human beings themselves are the solution.* Consequently, I could think: The human being, at any moment, can speak of that universal mystery, but they can never say more of the answer than they have learned about themselves as human beings" (28, p. 29).

In practical life, the maturation of the will expresses itself in a different way. Whoever reads Steiner's correspondence with Joseph Kürschner must find Steiner's inability to meet deadlines—and the way he continually tries to satisfy his poor editor with promises that he then does not keep—embarrassing. By 1892, Kürschner is completely resigned and writes to

Steiner, "It is now almost two years since I received the first telegram from you in reply to my letter: 'The manuscript will be there on Saturday.' Since then, eighty-seven weeks have passed and I have received at least four more such telegrams, but I have still not seen a single page from the last volume of Goethe's scientific writings" (39).

During the Weimar period, Steiner appeared to many contemporaries to be an "Austrian loafer" (Hoffmann). Now, in 1897, he wraps up all his commitments by early spring. By doing so, he closes another chapter of his life. Then he makes the decision to take on the *Journal for Literature*, a paper that had to be finished and sent out to the subscribers on a weekly basis. He creates an outer scaffold that can support the training of the will. By 1900 at the latest, in addition to the timely publication of the *Journal*, one sees Steiner meeting all his deadlines and commitments and managing an enormous amount of work.

There is a third aspect. Rudolf Steiner mentions it in his *Autobiography* at the beginning of Chapter 53. "I must conclude this second chapter of my life with the transformation (I have described) in my soul life. My destiny turned in a completely new direction" (28). Steiner wrote that up until about 1896 the work he had done in the Goethe archive and in tutoring the Specht boys had arisen out of "the insights of my own soul." The outer expectations connected to his work were never in conflict with his own inner intentions. After 1897, Steiner turned his attention to a whole new spectrum of challenges. As the editor of the *Journal*, he had to cater to, at least to some extent, the taste and expectations of the subscribers. He also had to fulfill the wishes of the *Free Literary Society* and, beginning in 1899, meet the expectations of the *Workers' Educational School*. Later he would join *Die Kommenden* [The coming ones], the Giordano-Bruno Society, and the "Independent University" founded by members of this society and the theosophists. In each case, in the period following this transformation of soul, Steiner allowed himself to be led by the tasks that came to meet him. This led to a completely different lifestyle; he had to deal directly with the stream of cultural development in which he lived. "This was the state of my soul life, and I found it necessary to introduce an entirely new note into my outer activity. It was no longer possible to retain such a close rapport between the factors that determined my outer destiny and the guidelines that arose inwardly from my experience of the spiritual world" (28).

Steiner illustrated this shift quite clearly. "Thus for the *Review* I had readers whose cultural needs I had to understand. And the membership of the Independent Literary Society expected something very specific—exactly what they had always been offered. In any case, they certainly did not expect the kind of thing I could offer them from my innermost being" (28).

The liberated will took on real earthly tasks. It didn't monomaniacally follow self-envisioned goals. True will does not lose itself in missionary zeal. It listens to the world, it listens to the voice of destiny, and it learns to take hold of the tasks that the world brings to meet it. This quality of will needs a certain flexibility and cannot be trapped in the stubborn rigidity of the brutal idealist. The will that lets itself be led by destiny can unfold its own intentionality, because the tasks are never narrowly defined. This will does, however, always work with the people who are there. It does not complain that there aren't better, more perfect, more insightful colleagues to work with. This would be a waste of time. Led by the idea of moral imagination, it finds meaning in helping to bring forth the hidden fruits in those it encounters. Thus, the "shift of soul" in Rudolf Steiner's thirty-sixth year led to a turning point of destiny.

This shift did not appear suddenly. It began in 1897. Only in the course of the ensuing years did Steiner recognize that the encounters that led to this turning point had a definite meaning. He acknowledged the individuals who brought him closer to his unique task in his *Autobiography*, and wrote in 1924, "I had similar experiences with many of those in that circle, and I realized that *meeting them* was a part of my destiny, or karma (28).

In this manner, Rudolf Steiner brought to this turning point his time in Weimar, during which he had "followed the developments of the time" as an onlooker (185). Now he desired to immerse himself in that stream. Here he began to encounter the obstacles and contradictions of life. The move from the idylls of Weimar to Berlin was symptomatic. Steiner entered into a new world. Only now did the actual dialogue with the world as it was begin. In 1900, Steiner noted that in 1897, as he entered into life in Berlin, he "was no longer young, but still quite inexperienced" (39).

In the negotiations that led up to Steiner becoming editor of the *Review*, his successor, Otto Neumann-Hofer, had requested that Otto Erich Hartleben join Steiner as co-editor. Steiner and Hartleben had been friends for some time. They had met during one of the Goethe celebrations in Weimar and Hartleben had helped Steiner publish a Goethe breviary. By lending his name to the reputable, but financially struggling *Review*, Hartleben, who was at that time part of the literary avant-garde, was to help secure its future success. For Rudolf Steiner personally, the collaboration with Hartleben led to close acquaintance with the circle of young artists and writers living in the German capital and an introduction into the maelstrom of excitement that was present there at that time. This too was a "fact of destiny, or karma" (28).

CHAPTER 19

THE MAELSTROM OF BERLIN

When Rudolf Steiner began his work as editor of the *Review of Literature* at the beginning of July 1897, Berlin was the third largest city in Europe after London and Paris. The population was growing rapidly and was well on its way to reaching two million. The building industry was going wild. The countryside around the city was being eaten up by buildings. Surrounding villages disappeared into the city. Where only ten years earlier there had been meadows, fields and pine forests, there were now six-story tenements. At that time, Berlin was a city of many faces. Its east side was an industrial park with companies of international repute: Siemens, Borsig, AEG, Pintsch, and Schering. The whole city was garrisoned; eighteen regiments were stationed in Berlin. The middle of the city housed both the center of German government and the court of the German Kaiser and his retinue. Berlin was also a city of the press and of publishers: Mosse, Ullstein, and Scherl. And it was a city of learning, housing the first university of the German Federation with professors such as Max Planck, Robert Koch, Wilhelm Dilthey, Georg Simmel, Adolf von Harnack, Heinrich Wölfflin, Emil Fischer, and others.

The different groups and classes lived beside one another for the most part with little connection. It was possible to live in Berlin without ever seeing the Kaiser or knowing of the existence of Max Planck. The different circles were—consciously or unconsciously—fairly exclusive. The different classes did not mix. Rudolf Steiner found himself initially in the circle of writers to which Hartleben, Otto Julius Bierbaum, Paul Scheerbart, Walter Harlan, Franz Ferdinand Heitmüller, and others belonged. This limited his ability to circulate in other groups, which was painful for him. "How dear it would have been if I had been able to visit Eduard von Hartmann more frequently" (28). This segmentation of Berlin society even kept Steiner from contact with the artists of the Berlin secession—who were protégés of the city's upper middle class. He was also a stranger to the young Berlin publishing houses of Cassirer and S. Fischer.

The circle in which Steiner found himself was neither that of official academia and art that was supported by the court nor the circle of artists supported by the upper middle class. He belonged initially to the literary circle around the *Review* and the Independent Literary Society and spent time with the Friedrichhagenians, groups that were interested in themes like Darwinism, socialism, anarchy, and women's suffrage as well as experimental literature and drama. The expression "Green Germany" has a double meaning when applied to the colony of outsiders living on Müggelsee, between the pine forests and the heath. This was not good middle-class society. Steiner's friends met at the "thieves table" in a local pub on the Dorotheenstrasse, the "Old Artists' Hermitage." It was the kind of place that no university professor would be likely to stumble onto.

In retrospect, Steiner noted the difficult, even questionable nature of his presence in this circle.

> Because of my conscious experience of the spiritual world, I inwardly participated fully in all the relationships I entered at the time. I tried to identify myself completely with the readers of the *Review* and the members of the society, so that I could discover through their view how to best articulate the spiritual impulses I intended to convey. (28)

What Steiner means by this is indicated in a letter from 1904 to Anna Steiner, who experienced all these struggles closely.

> I have never been interested in anything but what has to do with the spirit. Even if it appeared otherwise in the years when I first moved to Berlin, it was not so. I truly wanted to understand what the young writers were saying. I should not, however, have let myself become involved in the dirt that accompanied them. This was an honest mistake. And I have had to pay for it with really nasty gossip. (39)

The phase during which Steiner spent most of his time in the company of Hartleben, Bierbaum, and Scheerbart came to an end after about a year and a half.

Steiner expanded his circle of acquaintances when he began to teach at the Workers' College and immersed himself in the activities of this school and in the union circles connected with it. He didn't stand on the sidelines here, either. He accompanied his students on Sunday excursions and spoke at their socials—evening concerts with dancing. He developed an intense connection with the life of the school. This connection removed him even further from "better society." This didn't seem to have bothered Steiner in the least, for he stood completely in the stream of the time. Beginning in 1900, Steiner's activities in Berlin expanded greatly—but more on that later.

The R*eview of Literature* was founded in 1832 and had gone through a number of changes since it first appeared. Even before Rudolf Steiner became editor, it had become the voice of what was then new in literature, without focusing exclusively on "modern" literature. The magazine was published weekly and came out each Saturday. A year's subscription cost sixteen German marks. Although the actual management of the *Review* was the responsibility of the publisher, the editor's job was quite demanding. Every issue of the magazine consisted of twelve narrow-spaced pages, each with two columns. Otto Erich Hartleben was officially the coeditor. Rudolf Steiner recalls that Hartleben often stood on his right to have a say and work with Steiner, but "then for lengthy intervals he wouldn't. He spent long periods of time in Italy" (28). One observer of the situation noted, "Now and again Otto Erich would appear. He was now coeditor with a former Goethe scholar of the *Review of Literature*. 'An excellent publication,' he would say, when one asked about his work, 'concerning whose content, I know absolutely nothing.' All the editorial work he placed on Dr. Steiner's patient shoulders" (Martens).

For the first issue of the *Review* for which he was responsible, Steiner wrote an article in which he examined critically the principles of modern art criticism. He distanced himself clearly from any normative approach to art or aesthetics: There are no eternal laws of art. What Lessing, Carriere, Vischer and Lotze proposed as general aesthetic laws were for him a form of superstition.

> No, just as each work of art is the individual, personal expression of one person, each criticism is also but the totally individual account of the sensations and thoughts that arise in the soul of the observer when he immerses himself in the piece. I can never say whether a poem is objectively good or not, for there are no norms deciding what is good and what is bad. (30)

The concrete individual alone is the source of artistic understanding!

In 1898, when the new literary magazine *Literary Echo* appeared, which addressed in a reactionary way the lack of general norms and a common focus, Steiner responded by writing about his editorial principles: "The editor presents his position with as much force as he can. But he also leaves space for other opinions. He is in fact proud to be able to provide his readers with a "playground for criticism, with tendencies toward all the points of the compass" (32). Steiner had a liberal approach to his task as editor; he gave space to everything that, in his opinion, had quality.

In addition to his editorial responsibilities, Steiner wrote regularly for the *Review* as well as for the *Journal of Dramatic Art*, which he also edited from 1898 to 1899. These articles total about 1200 pages in Steiner's collected works. Most of them—more than half—address topics of literature, theater and drama. The others touch on a wide spectrum of questions: journalism, sociology, psychology, and specific political questions. He did not write about music, concerts or the opera; and general questions concerning the development of science—with the exception of the problem of Darwinism—are also missing. Steiner was writing to an audience that was interested in literary questions.

His literature and theater critiques are remeniscent of a passage from Steiner's *Autobiography*, in which he assesses his understanding of art when he lived in Weimar: "At the time, I had advanced less in my feeling for art than I had in conscious experience of cognition" (28, p. 139). In relation to form and content, he seldom reached his own stated goal of describing art through his own individual experience. In his reviews, he usually focused on the plot and the characters, but paid little attention to the actual artistic form elements of language, presentation, and dramatic structure. Here he often fell into clichés:

> He knows them all, the eternally youthful emotions, the exultation of the blessed and the drunken and the bitter pain of an unhappy heart. And he has soft gentle voices to sing of sweet soul mysteries and lovely fantasies. Neither does he lack the strength to voice the cries of a tortured soul, or one who has lost through heartless fate what he had once enjoyed. (29)

Steiner's judgments concerning art were also not well-grounded. For instance, he celebrated Jacobowski's novel *Loki* as a great visionary work that raised daily existence into the realms of the mythical. In Steiner's defense, Jacobowski was a friend and he didn't want to say anything belittling about his work. But he might have been able to characterize the artificial, Germanized mead that Jacobowski had brewed with somewhat more reserve. Steiner's uncertainty, his lack of an aesthetic sense for literary art, and even a lack of knowledge of the discipline come most strongly to expression in his work "Literature and the Spiritual Life of the Nineteenth Century," which he wrote for a monumental compilation, *The Nineteenth Century in Word and Picture*. There he writes about Hölderlin,

> He dreamed of the ancient world of the Greeks. He sings of this world in his most important lyrical poems. One is tempted to call Hölderlin a romantic spirit, which has remained standing on the first level. The Schlegel brothers also began with an enthusiastic devotion to all things Greek, and later turned to Medieval Christianity. (33)

Should Hölderlin also have turned away the Greeks and embraced the Middle Ages? E. T. A. Hoffmann had no mercy for Steiner's presentation. "Everything was capricious and subjective in his presentation" (33). Concerning Kleist's *Käthchen*, Steiner can only comment that she "followed her husband faithfully, like a good dog" (33). But about Jacobowski's *Loki*, he writes that he "illuminates the depths of the human soul and illustrates the eternal nature of human striving in the struggle of Loki, the destroyer, against the Asen" (33).

What we can glean from these critiques is that Steiner turned toward modern literature with good will, that he studied the work of his friends and acquaintances, and that he explored the work of Maeterlinck, Clara Viebig and John Henry MacKay. He was most enthusiastic about modern theater. He wrote eighty-three drama critiques during his stay in Berlin, only five of which addressed performances of traditional or classic playwrights. The rest were of performances of contemporary works.

Together with Hartleben, Steiner also tried his hand at directing. When living in Vienna, he had learned to respect the now practically unknown dramatist Gunnar Heiberg. In 1890, Steiner had seen his play *King Midas* and held it to be the harbinger of a new day. In Berlin, he staged Heiberg's *Balcony*. The production was a catastrophe. Sarcastic laughter accompanied the entire performance. Steiner recounted, "Everything was drowned in the laughter. We worked for days to prepare a serious piece and only managed to produce a caricature" (29).

Steiner's articles concerning contemporary events were more accurate than his unfortunate love for the theater. This clarity is found, for instance, in the articles he wrote concerning the Dreyfus case. From the beginning, he stood up for Dreyfus' innocence and spoke out against the injustice of his conviction. He wrote at length of Zola's great speech in support of Dreyfus and went into detail about the political machinations that were behind his conviction. From the Dreyfus letters, Steiner constructed a completely accurate picture of the man. "Dreyfus is by nature a stubborn soldier" (31). For their "clever statesmanship," he took to task the German journalists who publicly supported not interfering in France's internal affairs by writing, "Does human compassion stop where the laws of a country do?" (31). In light of the political willfulness, he wrote, "How shall we lead our lives, if our belief in the appropriate development of world events can be shaken in this way on a daily basis? To live, we must have some sense that our insight into the development of humanity will not be transformed daily into dull uncertainty" (31).

A pearl among Steiner's essays concerning world events is his obituary for Bismark. Bismark is accurately portrayed as a genial pragmatic, who does not let himself be led by ideas but seized the opportunities as they presented themselves. "Bismark owes his success to the fact that he was never even a little bit ahead of his time" (31). "Bismark never thought about how the world should be. He viewed such pondering as superfluous, mere idle speculation. He let himself be shown by the events themselves what had to be. His genius lay in acting strongly in the way he was asked to by the events themselves" (31). Bismark went to war three times, wars in which many thousands of people died. This is something that he, as Steiner quotes, had to *reconcile with God*. Thus, the titan finds harmony as the true servant of his heavenly master. "One wonders about the source of such harmony. I recognize in it the effects of religion. To be a ruler like Wilhelm I or a statesman like Bismark, one must be a Christian" (31).

Steiner's critiques of sociological literature were equally successful. In an article entitled "The Social Question," he criticized the simple application of Darwinism to social questions as thinking in fixed patterns. In the article "Freedom and Society," he formulated what he called the fundamental social law.

> Humanity strives in the beginning of cultural conditions to form social associations. First of all, the interests of the individual are sacrificed

to the association; then the further development leads to the freeing of the individual from the interests of the association and to the free development of the needs and strengths of the individual. (31)

This article also contains quite pointed political opinions: "No socialist or communist political form can do justice to the natural inequality of people" (31); and "The worst form of rule is what the Social Democrats are striving to achieve" (31). Steiner's own social ideal, which he described at the time as *individual anarchism*, is expressed clearly in "Freedom and Society" without ever mentioning the word *anarchy*, a word that evokes wild associations.

> Governments and societies, believing to be an end in themselves, must strive to control the individual regardless of whether they do it in a totalitarian manner, constitutionally, or as a republic. If they cease to see themselves as ends, but as means, they no longer need to emphasize the necessity of control. Then things will be arranged in such a manner that the individual can come fully into his own. The ideal will be no authority, no control. (31)

Steiner's portraits of his contemporaries, written either as obituaries or as laudations, can still be read today with enjoyment. Among these are sketches of the founder of modern geology, Charles Lyell; the physiologist Wilhelm Preyer*; the popular voice of materialism, Ludwig Büchner; the French historian Michelet; and the English historian Macaulay. It is astonishing how positively he writes, for instance, of Ludwig Büchner. Steiner sees him as a one-sided yet progressive thinker, a thinker who does not join the reactionaries who, with their finely woven thought tapestries, attempt to rescue the old beliefs. "The finest thoughts of the modern philosophers, who see the origins of the world in a special spiritual being, appear antediluvian when compared with the robust chains of thought of this materialist" (30).

---

* The series of essays Steiner wrote in July and August 1897 (30) on Wilhelm Preyer disproves the view sometimes expressed that Steiner was a "materialist" at that time. In the praise he gave in Preyer's obituary he said, in agreement with Preyer, "Preyer derives what is lifeless out of what is living. To him the universe is a great, all-encompassing organism. This view is only one step away from the further idea of the world as an ensouled, spirit-filled organism. Preyer took this step also." And he went on, "The spirit slumbers originally in the mother, but it is active in this sleep-condition. The spirit forms the matter. The spirit organizes the matter until it takes on such a form that the spirit itself can manifest in the way appropriate to it." (30)

Steiner wrote about the great Indologist Max Müller, "He unlocked for us the Orient, to show us the similarities and differences of the manifold cultures and, in doing so, to come to an understanding of the majestic laws present in all of them" (31).

Rudolf Steiner recalled his work as editor in 1918. He recognized that it hadn't been possible for him actually to launch the *Review*. He crossed swords, for instance, with all of Berlin's art critics on account of the completely negative reviews Max Halbes's *Conqueror* received when he said "what had to be said about their powers of discernment." That "was not the proper approach to launching the *Review*." It wasn't "launched into the world of the modern philistines. However, without question I was…launched, step by step, by the modern philistines" (185). They were stirred up most strongly by Steiner's defense of Dreyfus and Zola. He received a postcard from the Germanist Max Koch saying, "This notifies you that I am canceling my subscription to the *Review* forever. I will not have a magazine in my library that defends Zola, the traitorous Jewish mercenary" (185).

The situation of the *Review* was not made precarious based on the cancellations—there were enough new subscriptions to balance them—but by the bankruptcy of Emil Felber, the paper's publisher. In the summer of 1898, there was a financial crisis. The paper was saved through the help of Moritz Zitter, Steiner's friend from the university. Steiner also found a new publisher, Siegfried Cronbach. In his *Autobiography*, he gives what is a realistic summary of the paper's chances at that time.

> Amid all the turbulence of life in those days, there was a constant concern about the survival of the *Review*. If material means had been at my disposal, the circulation of this weekly paper could have been enlarged despite all my difficulties. But the periodical could not thrive on the very small circulation it had when I took over, since it could pay only minimal fees and provide me with almost none of the bare necessities of life; and nothing could be done to make it known. While I was editor, the *Review* was a constant concern to me. (28)

Chapter 20

TIME OF TRIAL

In his *Autobiography*, Rudolf Steiner speaks of the years before the turn of the century as a time of trial, "a trying time for my soul" (28). This inner drama did not come outwardly to expression, and Steiner's contemporaries in Berlin took no or, at best, little notice of it. The tracks of this journey are to be found in the inner spiritual decisions that come to expression in Steiner's conceptual work.

It is however necessary to say a few words about the outer symptoms that accompanied this inner path. What first becomes apparent is that Steiner's social life changed. The period of intense socializing with Otto Erich Hartleben, Scheerbart, Harlan, and the others in their circle came to an end. A new circle emerged made up of individuals like Ludwig Jacobowski. In contrast to Hartleben, Jacobowski was not only a poet, but also a social activist and teacher. He headed up the *Anti-Semite Resisitance Office*; he published penny pamphlets with the work of German poets for the workers; he collected material that shed light on prehistoric life; and he was the co-editor of a magazine entitled *Society*, a fairly reputable journal at that time. He was one of those people who worked themselves to death. In January 1899, Rudolf Steiner also took on a task in adult education: he became a teacher at the Workers' College in Berlin. At this time, in addition to his editorial work, he also began to write a great deal. The longer pieces—"Literature and Spiritual Life in the Nineteenth Century," "Egoism in Philosophy," his study "Contemporary Lyrical Poetry," and the essay "Haeckel and his Opponents"—all appeared during this year, and he began the manuscript for the first volume of *World and Individual Philosophy in the Nineteenth Century* [Part of this volume was combined with a second volume published in 1901 as *The Riddles of Philosophy* (18)].

This level of productivity was only possible thanks to a change in Steiner's lifestyle. Stories relate that already in Vienna he imbibed a good deal of alcohol when socializing with his friends. In one greeting card from 1888, he wrote, "Tomorrow there will no doubt be a second-degree hangover. We drank and drank until we couldn't drink anymore." Similar stories have been related about Berlin, dramatically so in Hartleben's *Letters to a Girlfriend*, and one observer recalled: "He led a very worldly life. Under the influence of Otto Erich's alcoholic temptations, he spent a lot of time with him in shadier public houses" (Martens).

This all stopped in 1899. From here on out, coffee became his main drink. When he took time to relax, he took long walks with Ludwig Jacobowski. He helped Jacobowski in negotiations with his publishers and comforted him, as he "was a personality whose soul constitution breathed inner tragic" (28). He also took up questions posed by individual students at the Workers' College. Living for others took on a new dimension. Although one cannot say that Rudolf Steiner had not been there for the Specht children, he was present in a new way when it came to Ludwig Jacobowski. According to Maria Stona, he became Jacobowski's "support and guide" (Stern).

Finally, his outer living circumstances also changed. In the beginning of his time in Berlin, Steiner had lived alone in a third floor furnished apartment on Karlsbad Str. 33. This changed when the Eunikes moved to Berlin.

> My outer life took a completely satisfying turn when the Eunike family moved to Berlin and I was able to live with them with the best of care after having experienced for a while the complete misery of living alone. A short while later, my friendship with Frau Eunike was transformed into a civil marriage.... My life with the Eunike family afforded me an undisturbed basis for a life that was extremely eventful, both inwardly and outwardly. (28)

Visitors have described the hospitable house in Friedenau on Kaiserallee 95. Steiner's desk was in the living room by the window. It was covered with books. Pictures and book shelves covered the walls. Anna Steiner and her daughter Wilhelmine attended the guests and did not hesitate to show how much they admired and respected Rudolf Steiner. For Steiner, who was now freed of many of life's small worries, Anna Steiner's care was a gift. He introduced his wife to his various social circles. She accompanied him on excursions undertaken with students from the Workers' College, and now and again she was present at meetings of the *Kommenden*.

Steiner wrote of the inner side of this "time of trials," this "trying time of the soul," in his *Autobiography* and spoke of it in three different ways:

in relation to scientific thinking, in relation to the question of individualism, and finally in relation to Christianity.

It is necessary to interject something here. When Rudolf Steiner characterized this time of trial, he wrote of "Ahrimanic beings." Although it is possible to understand what he means by this out of the context, some explanation might be helpful. In the beginning of 1909, Rudolf Steiner first described how spiritual insight recognizes two polar forces at work in the human being and the world. One of these, which strives to draw the human being away from the earth and the tasks connected with it, he names the "luciferic force"; the other, which strives to fetter human thought to earthly "facts," he names ahrimanic. While the ahrimanic forces place the individual on the solid footing of so-called facts, the luciferic forces liberate him from such bothersome details and lead him into the heights of self-experience. Both of these forces always appear together as powerful polarities for the human being. One could, for instance, characterize a machine as an ahrimanic construction, and the wishes and desires of those who use the machine as luciferic. In his *Autobiography*, Steiner wrote about the dangers of scientific thinking.

> I recognized that in thinking one can go from an understanding of nature to insight into the spiritual world (though this was not true at the time). Consequently, I stressed especially a knowledge of the fundamental structure of nature, which must inevitably lead to knowing spirit. One without direct perception of the spiritual world will experience immersion in a trend of thinking merely as mental activity. But the experience will be essentially different for one who experiences the spiritual world directly. One enters a realm of spiritual beings who are intent on making this trend of thinking singularly dominant. This is a realm where one-sided knowledge results in more than abstract errors. Errors of the human world become in that realm living, spiritual interactions with certain beings. Later on I spoke of *ahrimanic* beings when I wanted to indicate this. The absolute reality of these beings is that the world must be a machine. Their realm is directly adjacent to that of the senses.
>
> Not for a moment did I succumb to influences of that realm in my own realm of ideas—not even unconsciously. I took great care to make sure that all my inquiries were carefully considered. Even more conscious was my inner struggle with those demonic powers who tried to develop natural, scientific knowledge—not through perception of spirit, but in a mechanical and materialistic way of thinking. (28, pp. 187–88)

This aspect of Steiner's struggle can be seen clearly in his writings on Darwinism and Ernst Haeckel. Steiner writes that he "stressed knowledge of the fundamental structure of nature," which must necessarily lead to spiritual knowledge. This emphasis is clearly apparent in his defense of those aspects of Haeckel's thought that were justified. It comes to expression in a number of written works: *Haeckel and his Opponents*, written in 1899; the essays "The Struggle over Haeckel's Riddle of the Universe" and "Bartholomäus Carneri, the Moral Philosopher of Darwinism," both written in September 1900; and finally, the chapter "Darwinism und Philosophy" in the second volume of *World and Individual Philosophy in the Nineteenth Century*. The latter chapter was reprinted practically without revision in Steiner's *The Riddles of Philosophy* in 1914, although the other portions of the book were completely revised and given new foci. The position he took in 1900 in relation to Darwinism and Haeckel was one he still supported in 1914.

Haeckel, following the approach laid out by Darwin, emphasized the natural evolution of the organism and the species. He rejected divine creation of the species and thought of nature as a unified whole. His theories were based on observation, and he was able to show that even the individual development of the human being proceeded according to nature: The human being develops out of a fertilized egg. Haeckel was a man who courageously acknowledged the consequences of the facts and did not, as his opponents chided, speculate as to how the consequences could be avoided. They wanted to rescue both the idea of creation and teleology. Arthur Drews wrote, "Even a piece of art comes to completion through mechanical means if we only consider the outer sequence of steps that lead to its completion and do not consider that each step is led by the artist's conception. Even then, anyone who declared that the piece of art came about through purely mechanical means would justifiably be called a fool." Eduard von Hartmann took a similar position. For him the "struggle for existence" was but a "slave of the idea" (30).

Steiner defended Haeckel against these and other critics who tried to justify the old beliefs through the use of anthropomorphic and simple analogies and were not willing to accept the consequences of scientific thought. He knew that it was not only hopeless but also erroneous to try to explain nature based on anthropomorphic analogies. He wrote, "How does logic or an aesthetic conception originate as a function of the brain? Alone, the disciplines of comparative physiology and neuro-anatomy can explore this question. Their explorations show that rational consciousness does not exist in isolation, only using the human brain to express itself, as a pianist uses a piano, but that our spiritual forces are just as much functions of the form elements of our brain as 'every force is a function of a solid body' (Haeckel, *Anthropogeny*)" (30).

Steiner does not take an adversarial stance in relation to the consequences of scientific thought. It is apparent to him that one cannot deal with what he later calls "ahrimanic beings" by creating castles in the sky to explain the world—romantic fiction in which one can lose oneself. He remains within the boundaries of observation and reason, pointing out, however, that no scientific thinker believes that "organic substance can cast light on what is logically true or false. Spiritual relationships can only be recognized by the spirit" (30). Just as the insights gained through natural science apply to the sense-perceptible world, Spiritual Science gains insight into the nature of the spirit. Based on an unbiased application of natural scientific method, Steiner articulates a factual context that makes the independence and integrity of the spirit evident. Materialism is thus not overcome in that one argues against the factual relationships uncovered by natural science, in this case the relation between thinking and the brain, but in that one calls attention to further aspects of the phenomena: the inner lawfulness of the spirit that reveals itself in thinking and that is evidently independent. Here the ahrimanic beings have no power over one; rather, one places them where they belong.

Steiner followed the dictum of the aging Faust, who articulated his belief before he was overcome by care and lost his vision.

> And what's beyond is barred from human ken;
> Fool, fool is he who blinks at clouds on high
> Inventing his own image in the sky
> Let him look round, feet planted firm on earth:
> This world will not be mute to him of worth.

However, in this world, in the here and now, we are privy not only to sense observations but also to spiritual facts. Steiner emphasized this from the beginning in all his works. By sustaining and cultivating this recognition, he prepared himself for his "time of trials." In *Haeckel and his Opponents*, he again summarized this insight:

Both observation and thinking are sources of our knowledge of things. This is true for all things and processes, not just for the thinking consciousness itself. We could not add anything to it through any explanation that was not already in the observation. It (consciousness) gives us the laws for everything else, and for itself at the same time. When we want to demonstrate the correctness of a law of nature, we do so by differentiating and ordering observations, perceptions, and by drawing conclusions—that is, we build concepts and ideas about the experiences with the help of thinking. Only thinking itself decides about the correctness of thinking. Thus it is thinking that leads us beyond the mere observation in all that occurs in the world, but yet does not lead beyond itself. (30)

Whoever focuses attention on the essential nature of thinking, the inner activity, discovers that it is impossible to explain the content and the lawfulness of *thinking* through any other medium. Thinking explains itself. Whatever role the brain plays in the manifestation of thinking can also only be discovered through thinking. Thus thinking and the spirit that becomes apparent in thinking reveal themselves to be determining factors in the world. Steiner remained true to this insight. "I have to mention that during the time my destiny required me to make such observations I never lost my connection with the spiritual world. It was always there" (258).

The ahrimanic beings are held at bay when the human spirit retains sovereignty over observable facts and does not try to deny or distort them. The recognition of the independent nature of thinking counteracts their attempts to overstep the boundaries, which expresses itself in the mechanistic interpretation of life or society.

The second of the inner aspects of this time of trial has to do with the problem of ethical individualism. In his paper about "Egoism in Philosophy," Steiner clearly states his position by saying that "in the 'I' is to be found the essence of all things" (30). This is a double-edged sword. If one understands the "I" to be the isolated personality, the center of self-will, the danger of titanism or hubris looms. The problem of intercourse, the fact that the "I" is open to the world in which it lives, is disregarded. This danger was readily apparent in the philosophy of Max Stirner, someone with whom Steiner felt himself to be in agreement (39, 30).

This problem is presented in a passage from the first volume of *World and Individual Philosophies in the Nineteenth Century*. Steiner describes Stirner as the proponent of the absolute sovereignty of the individual.

Through radical criticism of the forces that subjugate the "I," by overcoming divine determination of human nature, Stirner liberates the "I." "As though it had been shot from the muzzle of a pistol, he lets the free, sovereign individual appear upon the stage of the evolving conception of the world. He recognizes it through genial intuition" (18). Steiner praises Stirner's "battle to destroy" the illusions upon which humankind had become dependent.

> Stirner, a truly free thinker, shows one how strong the tendency is among people to throw themselves into the arms of some power. Didn't Bruno Bauer, for instance, believe that he could completely liberate man by making him into a thinking being? Doesn't he, in fact, make him once again dependent, this time on *thinking*? A person should not be the slave of religion, justice, government or laws; he shouldn't think specific thoughts, as he might become dependent on these. But he should give himself completely up to thinking, and make himself its slave. (18)

In this non-deterministic view of the "I," which postulates an antithesis between the "I" and thinking, lies the *necessary* danger. It cannot be avoided by inoculating the "I" with "correct" thinking as a form of higher power. Each true individual has to pass through the narrows of self-will and independent thinking and see just what comes out of it.

This experience was not merely a theoretical question for Steiner. It came to him in the form of another person. In 1898/99, he became friends with John Henry MacKay, who championed Stirner's individualism then in Berlin. "I developed a great affection for him" (28). In an open letter to Mackay, he confessed, "It is of great value to me to have you speak of me as a colleague" (39). The warmth of their relationship is further illustrated by the fact that, at Steiner's request, Mackay was a witness at his marriage to Anna Eunike. In his *Autobiography*, Steiner summarized the inner significance of this philosophical and personal encounter:

> Destiny now turned my experience with Mackay and Stirner in such a way that there I also had to delve into a world of thought that became a *spiritual test* for me. My ethical individualism was a pure inner experience of the human being. To make it the basis of a political view could not be further from my intention when I elaborated the concept. But at the time (about 1898) my soul, along with pure ethical individualism, was dragged down into a kind of abyss. From being a

pure human inner experience, it was made external. The esoteric was to be diverted into the exoteric. (28, pp. 191–92)

Only after the turn of the century, continues Steiner, after he had developed his own experience in the manner expressed in his books, *Mystics after Modernism* and *Christianity as Mystical Fact,* did "ethical individualism once more take its proper place after the test" (28).

This has a different tone than Steiner's description of his relationship to natural science and the battle with the ahrimanic beings. He calls this a "testing of the soul," whereas he speaks in relation to what is described above as a "spiritual test." He can say in regard to the ahrimanic temptation, "Not for a moment did I succumb to influences of that realm in my own realm of ideas." (28). The next chapter speaks specifically of endangerment: "My soul, along with pure ethical individualism, was supposed to be dragged down into a kind of abyss." And he added, "My inner experience at the time was an inner churning that brought all my soul forces into waves and waves" (28).

Only "at the beginning of a new century," after an expansion of his spiritual horizon, did "ethical individualism [find] its proper place" (28). At the end of the last century, this inner testing came to expression in "certain statements that appeared to be much too radical" and in the way in which Steiner expressed himself, primarily when he spoke of "social affairs" (28). He seems here to be speaking of the one-sided emphasis on individualism. Examples of this can be found in the open letter to John Henry Mackay in which he writes that the individual needs to validate itself in open competition and declares his opposition to every form of power and authority manifested in the state (39). Thus, the problem is outlined philosophically.

In an esoteric sense, one can recognize a luciferic impulse in the one-sided emphasis of the individual and its unfettered freedom. This luciferic impulse is in a certain sense a necessity in any spiritual development: The seeker must free himself from the fetters of the world and his environment in order to work his way upward in the spiritual world. The spiritual seeker cannot enter the spiritual world as a weak, undefined person. The strength of the spiritual individual, the force of the "I," is completely justified in the realms of the spirit. It becomes something unjustifiable when it manifests itself in other realms—in earthly life or in business (17). On the other hand, only a strong "I" can truly take the world up into itself and let it live on within.

In this connection, Rudolf Steiner spoke of the abyss into which he was being pulled. We would not understand him correctly if we were to view *abyss* as a simple metaphor. Steiner uses this word in various places in its esoteric significance. If we keep this in mind, what follows makes sense.

Friedrich Rittelmeyer recounts intimate conversations with Rudolf Steiner during which the latter speaks of his own biography.

> What impressed me most was how he spoke of the great teachers who crossed his life's path. Extraordinary individuals, completely unknown to the public, were there at the right moment to help him in the decisive periods to recognize and develop his capacities.... I will never forget his face as he told of one of these spiritually gifted individuals: "That was a very important person!" His inner eye seemed to follow him. In his visage was a look of devotion, what one great seeker owes another. He told me later that he was once suddenly rescued by a "master" as he was about to do something that would have "been the death of me." (Rittelmeyer)

From Steiner's own recollections, we know of his encounter with his esoteric teacher that took place when he was twenty-one or twenty-two years old. At this juncture of his life, on the edge of the abyss, he hears the call of his other teacher. Without mentioning that he was speaking autobiographically, Steiner describes the encounter with that individuality known in the spiritual world as Christian Rosenkreutz:

> Being chosen by Christian Rosenkreutz takes place when a person arrives at a decisive moment in his life, at a crisis of destiny. Take for instance the example that a person is about to do something that would bring about his death.... A person follows a dangerous path, perhaps along the edge of an abyss without noticing it. It happens then that when he is perhaps just a few steps from the edge of the abyss that he hears a voice: Stop! and he stops without knowing quite why. It always occurs in such a way that one knows the voice has come out of the spiritual world. (130)

One can sense that by bringing Steiner's statements together and comparing them, the spiritual drama that took place behind the outer events becomes somewhat visible. It would be superfluous at this point to speculate about the details or the exact timing. One should perhaps mention one remark from Emil Bock, whose research into Rudolf Steiner's biography led him to write that in 1899 Rudolf Steiner "completely changed his way of life from one day to the next" (Bock). And perhaps it is good to remember that such a *voice at the abyss* gives one a new sense of higher freedom.

Steiner's meeting with the first of his two esoteric teachers found expression in his paper "The Only Possible Criticism of Atomic Theory." The second meeting also found a spiritual expression, in the essay "Goethe's Secret Revelation," which appeared in the *Review* on August 28, 1899, in commemoration of Goethe's 150th birthday. It was written at about the same time that Steiner took a stand defending Haeckel's work. For nearly a decade, Steiner had lived with the hidden revelations in Goethe's fairy tale. Especially during the end of his time in Vienna and the beginning of his stay in Weimar, he had worked intensively with the story. Later the themes contained in it had—as Steiner relates—"sunk into the depths" of his soul (125). Now they were reawakened.

The interpretation of Goethe's fairy tale that Steiner published in 1899 sheds light on his own inner state. In the fairy tale, Goethe describes the transformation of the human soul through a series of characters. In his imagination he held a picture of the way the various aspects of the soul work together. In the story he introduces nineteen characters, each of whom has a role to play in this process. Some like to view either the youth, the beautiful lily or the old man with the lamp as the central figure in this drama. Steiner writes, however, about the green snake, "She is the most important part of the entire process" (30). The snake transforms the gold that has been shaken out by the will-o'-the-wisps into inner light; as she glides along the earth, her experience ensouls her with wisdom. At the same time, the snake is the one who sacrifices herself to become the bridge that leads to catharsis. The selfless sacrifice of the snake stands in the center of the transformation. Steiner viewed this sacrifice in a very specific way:

> Goethe has brought to expression through the self-sacrifice of the snake what the mystic Jakob Böhme expressed with the words "Death is the root of all life." Whoever is unable to free himself from his own small "I," whoever is unable to develop within himself the higher "I" cannot, in Goethe's view, achieve perfection. The isolated individual must 'die' in order to be reborn in a higher sense.... In "Divan" we can read Goethe's "And as long as this escapes you, this: Die and become! You are but a sorry guest upon a darkened earth." And in one of his "Verses in Prose," we find, "One must sacrifice one's existence,

in order to exist." The snake sacrifices her existence to bridge the two realms, that of sensuality and that of spirituality. (30)

These words reflect the beginning of Steiner's overcoming his earlier one-sided individualism. It is clearly but a beginning. Until around September 1900, Steiner remained enamored of Stirner's concept of individualism. At the same time, we can recognize in the living reality of the sacrifice a Christian motif, something that emerges conceptually for Steiner in 1888. The path that would lead to knowledge of the Christian mysteries was present as a seed in the reality of the sacrificial nature of Goethe's snake. This seed grew in the subsequent years; in 1899, it began to put down roots in Steiner's soul. Writing about this time, during which he outwardly rejected Christianity, he says, "During the period when my statements about Christianity seemed to contradict my later comments, a conscious knowledge of real Christianity began to dawn within me" (28).

Thirteen months after this essay appeared, Rudolf Steiner gave his first anthroposophic lecture on September 29, 1900. It was titled "Goethe's Secret Revelation." Speaking in 1920, just before the opening of the first Goetheanum, he called this lecture the "germ cell" of the anthroposophic movement. "The germ cell was the lecture about Goethe's secret revelation" (Address, September 25, 1920).

When Rudolf Steiner brought the fairy tale to a new imaginative level in his first mystery play, he revealed the source of inspiration from which this mystery flowed by calling what he authored a "Rosicrucian Mystery."

Finally in 1924, in one of his lectures on karma, Rudolf Steiner points out that in the fairy tale's miniatures one has a reflection of the actual, spiritual-cosmic movement that, in its earthly form, became the anthroposophic movement. The fairy tale was in this sense a symbol through which those souls with a destined affinity to Anthroposophy could be reminded of their pre-birth resolutions. For this reason, Steiner spoke repeatedly of the fairy tale in the early years of his spiritual scientific activity.

Steiner writes of the third aspect of this "time of trial" in his *Autobiography*. "That was a trying time for my soul as I looked at Christianity.... These kinds of tests are obstacles, placed in one's path by destiny (or karma), and they must be overcome through spiritual development" (28). What he found in the outer forms of the Christian religion, the tenor of the confessions and theology at that time, was completely foreign to him, and, in resonance with Nietzsche, he rejected it. "The Christianity that I had to find was not in any of the existing confessions" (28). His search for true Christianity led him into "the world where spirit itself speaks of it" (28). He turned his attention to the spiritual origins of Christianity and to the development of their historical forms of expression. The first results of this search are to be found in *Christianity as a Mystical Fact* (1902), in which he focuses on the mysteries of birth, death and resurrection in their various manifestations. In Chapter 29, this question is explored more fully.

The dramatic change that led Rudolf Steiner to change his way of life fundamentally in 1898 to '99 was preceded by a longer period of inner testing. Steiner wrote that this period began "with my departure from Weimar and continued until I began work on *Christianity as a Mystical Fact*" (28). Steiner's time of inner testing extended over a period of five years and went through a series of stages.

In 1899, we see the first stage of this process and can recognize how Rudolf Steiner, having heard the summons of Christian Rosenkreutz, begins to change the nature of his life. He places himself in the service of others. While he does focus primarily on his own intentions, he responds to the questions, needs and spiritual receptivity of others. He becomes a true teacher, initially at the Workers' College. He brings the concept of sacrifice to practical expression.

Chapter 21

THREE ATTEMPTS AT THE TURN OF THE CENTURY

It must have been in December 1898—the financial crisis at the *Review* had not yet been resolved—when the trustees of the social-democratic Workers' College approached Rudolf Steiner and asked if he would be willing to teach history there. Just a few months earlier, Steiner had written about "the social-democratic nonsense of Marx, Engels and Liebknecht" (31) and publicly made known his antipathy for the social-democratic movement. Now he saw "an interesting task" ahead of him, "to teach mature men and women from the working class" (28). Steiner agreed to take on the task if he could teach history in his own way and not have to follow Marxian schematics. The trustees agreed to this condition. For his part, Steiner no doubt welcomed the honorarium offered by the school, however small it might have been. One of his students described Steiner:

> I never again had a teacher like him. He was gaunt, shabbily dressed. He always wore an old coat; his trousers looked like corkscrews, much too short and worn out. At first he sported a van Dyke, then a mustache, then he was clean shaven.... Everyone loved him dearly, and I would have—as would most of the others—gone through fire for him.... He was loving and concerned in a way that I have never again discovered in another person. Funny—I often asked my fiancée whether he was really as poor as he seemed to be. During breaks, he always took a dry roll out of his pocket and ate it with visible enjoyment. But if you think that they left him in peace during the break, you are way off base. The whole group gathered around him and the questions were endless. (B 111)

Johanna Mücke, who later worked with Marie and Rudolf Steiner and was at that time the secretary of the council of the Workers' College, tells of Steiner's first lecture, which had been met with a great deal of anticipation. In the past, the history lectures had been so boring that participation had regularly fizzled away to nothing.

> A slender, dark gentleman stood before us. He had a strong—for us—north German's somewhat-foreign-sounding voice. Everyone listened with the greatest attention. When the lecture ended, one heard the students talking excitedly with one another. One of them, an especially active comrade and a very sharp individual, came up to me and said with some measure of enjoyment, "It wasn't exactly materialistic history, *but it was interesting*!"

The number of students in the course grew.

> What was especially new for us was the way Dr. Steiner engaged his listeners and guided them into a lively encounter with the subject. Before we had always simply listened to the lecture and then gone home more or less satisfied or exhausted. Now a lively discussion broke out, with innumerable questions. All the questions were answered in a generous, heartfelt way; all arguments were listened to, then objectively refuted. Soon the courses were going on past midnight. (Mücke)

Over the years, Steiner gave many courses on a wide variety of topics. He spoke about the history of culture up to the present, the French Revolution, and the history of industrialism in the nineteenth century; about literature, art, and the history of religion; but also about human anatomy and the development of the cosmos. He often gave the address at the Founder's Day celebration, held special lectures on Gerhart Hauptmann, Ferdinand Freiligrath, and Emile Zola, and he spoke about Goethe and Haeckel's *Riddle of the World*. Once he spoke about "Modern Fanatics and Science" and compared the direction taken by the "New Community" of the Hart brothers to the *Wiedertaufer* of the Reformation. On another occasion, he addressed what was for this circle a loaded question, "How is scientific socialism possible?"

In 1900, he initiated courses in public speaking and writing. Here he followed in the footsteps of his teacher Karl Julius Schröer, whose courses in public speaking he had attended in the '20s. The students were challenged to speak about something that was important to them, and Steiner made suggestions to help them improve their style and rhetoric. One participant related that Steiner had taken the manuscript he had handed in and carefully corrected it, wrote notes "in his characteristic scratchy scholar's hand in red ink" on the borders and encouraged him to further production. At the end of a novella that one student had written, he wrote, "Your progress pleases me to no end. The novella is ready for the press. Just keep working diligently. But note: before each new subject, you need a comma. For instance, 'He smiled at her, and she left.' 'She' is a new subject" (Unger-Winkelried).

Often Steiner took his wife and her daughters with him on the Sunday excursions of the workers. They set up camp in the high grass; they played and sang; Polish-Jewish workers performed their traditional dances; and lively discussions sprang up.

> Steiner was there in the middle of it all. We talked, or we asked him questions about books and the theater, about antique and modern literature.... He showed us the flowers growing amidst the grass, the ferns, the insects that swarmed about us.... Once we thought we had found the caterpillar of a peacock butterfly, but he explained to us that it belonged to a privet hawkmoth and went on to describe them to us with all their colors and markings. (Mücke)

Teaching at the Workers' College challenged Steiner to develop a new way of speaking and presentation. He had to adjust himself to his listeners, who, although they were eager to learn, belonged to a milieu that had a specific relationship to language and how things were understood. Today, this has been almost completely eradicated by mass media. Steiner remembers, "The mental outlook of my 'students' was my business. I had to find a completely different way of expressing myself than I had become used to until then. To make myself understood to some degree, I had to find my way into their form of concepts and judgments" (28). In the coming years, Steiner would find himself in this position repeatedly—he had to adopt the language of the theosophists; to speak for the English or the Dutch; and to make himself understood to the *Wandervögel* or students of theology. The extent to which he was willing to find his way into the interests and educational horizons of each audience is noteworthy.

Naturally, in his lectures to the workers, he did not rub them the wrong way. His audience was for the most part marked by labor and life, and they thought, in as much as they were schooled, materialistically. This had to be Steiner's point of departure. He began thus with the facts and relationships that justified such views, then worked his way toward wider horizons. How successful he was in this is shown by the fact that the printer's union invited him to give the address celebrating Gutenberg's jubilee. This lecture is still in print (31). Steiner does a masterful job in describing the transformation of cultural/spiritual life brought about by the introduction of the new medium.

One of the students from that time, Emil Unger-Winkelreid, summed up his opinion of Steiner's work: "If patriotic German academics had taken such a warm interest in the young workers, the last twenty years would have been very different for Germany. Such a multifaceted individual as Steiner was certainly didn't take on the task of teaching because of the meager salary, but because he enjoyed it and the students loved him" (Unger-Winkelreid).

It is interesting that Steiner says much the same thing in his *Autobiography*, without the patriotic undertones.

> I have the impression that if more unbiased individuals had taken an interest in the workers' movement in those days, and if the proletariat had encountered real understanding, that movement would have developed very differently. But the people were left to life in their own class, while the others lived within theirs. (28)

In any case, Steiner recognized "a mission in the work within these circles" (262) and was dismayed when orthodox Marxists began—at the latest in 1903—to agitate against his work. On October 7, 1924, it came to a head in an open discussion during the school's general assembly. Rudolf Steiner presented his case to the assembly. He said that he had the same relationship to his work as he had had five years earlier when he first joined the faculty and that he challenged historical materialism's absolutely validity. The debate led to a heated war of words that ended in a resolution being passed with only seven nays that gave Steiner a vote of confidence and stated that he could continue to teach courses there. But the scheming continued and Steiner felt himself compelled to resign, which he did on January 15, 1905, in the festive address on the occasion of the fourteenth anniversary of the school.

The proletariat looked forward to the new century with anticipation that it would bring the collapse of the old society, yet it was in the realm of science that a revolution took place, although this went unnoticed for the most part. In 1898, Marie Curie discovered the radioactive element radium and described it fully in 1902. On December 14, 1900, Max Planck articulated in a talk to the Physics Society in Berlin the ideas that laid the groundwork for quantum theory. The age of modern physics, which would lead to research into the nature of atomic particles, had begun.

A sense of excitement was present throughout much of the middle and upper middle class. The first Steglitz *Wandervögel*, who would give birth to the youth movement, were already afoot. The women's suffrage movement, which had begun toward the end of the nineteenth century, was growing. Ideas leading toward a change in lifestyle became increasingly popular. The Swedish educator Ellen Key proclaimed the *century of the child* and initiated the educational reform movement. In the arts, impressionism approached its end, and, beginning in 1907, the first experiments in expressionism appeared. In all these different movements, including the peace movement, there was a certain sense that a new age was about to begin. Using a term out of one of the many Indian traditions, Steiner later spoke of this as the end of "Kali-Yuga," the time of darkness.

Rudolf Steiner experienced the turn of the century as a summons to spiritual awakening. "It seemed to me that the turn of the century had to bring a new spiritual light to humankind. It seemed that a climax had been reached in excluding spirit from human thought and activity. A complete change in human evolution seemed an absolute necessity" (28). "From the spiritual world, a new light was ready to break into human evolution through the intellectual accomplishments of the final third of the nineteenth century" (28). In speaking of a new spiritual light, Steiner was not thinking of a sentimental awakening to something new, a diffuse movement to a better life while looking back scornfully at the past. When Julius Hart came out with *The New God* and *The New Community*, proclaiming the advent of a new culture, Steiner responded:

> The nineteenth century witnessed an eminently productive cultural period. Many things came together to make this possible. Julius Hart overreaches himself by saying that we have what is but an Alexandrian century, a century of abstract scholarship behind us. Then he reaches even further and lays out the premises that are to form the foundation of the culture of the next century, of the "new god." (32)

Steiner did not agree with Mephisto's advice, "Be scornful only of reason and science." He didn't want to exchange a handful of sentimentally charged slogans that didn't even deserve to be called abstractions for the fruits of honest research. He found himself searching for individuals who were more honest in their striving than most. Initially, he found such individuals in the Giordano Bruno Society that had been formed in 1900 under the guidance of Bruno Wills.

> The society consisted of individuals who in their style and focus were exemplary for the time, individuals who were truly interested in everything that one could be interested in then. And even in the somewhat abstract manner, which is common still in the present, in the Giordano Bruno Society there was a recognition of the spirit. (258)

The discussions in the society were far-reaching, from Haeckel to Hegel, from the psychology of genius to the theory of inheritance; members of the society were instrumental in the formation of the "Independent University," a school that worked toward socializing science.

On the whole, the leading figures in the Giordano Bruno Society did their best to be open to what Steiner had to bring, although this was not always easy. His ideas were different than those of the other members. For instance, he found the constant talk about a unified worldview or monism painfully abstract and not thought through. According to his own testimony, Steiner put up with the generalizations for a time, then did something provocative. He gave a lecture for this group of well-meaning people in which he presented the carefully crafted system of Thomas Aquinas as an example of consequent, carefully structured monism. "They did not know whether I had gone insane overnight when I gave that lecture. They didn't have the faintest idea of what to do with it. These were the most honest people. There was only one who spoke up to try and smooth things over, the poet Wolfgang Kirchbach" (258). In his opinion, Steiner was only trying to show that the monists were not strong enough to challenge the spiritual might of Catholicism.

In spite of this and other difficulties, one of the most telling descriptions we have of Steiner from that time came from the pen of one of the society's trustees. Hermann Friedmann was a lawyer and scientist, an important thinker who later wrote a paper on morphology and is unknown in Germany primarily because he left the country before World War I. He recalls his fellow trustee Steiner, who even at that time began "to go his own, esoteric path."

> At this point, I will write about Rudolf Steiner. My respect for his personality is not based on specific characteristics but on the relationship that existed between various aspects of his personality. If I say, for

instance, that he played a major role in the discussion, that should not be seen to indicate that he had monopolized it. Others could have done this too, without one having to recognize their greatness. In respect to topics that he had not raised, Steiner was reticent or silent, yet he listened with his whole being, and no one could have accused him of not "participating" in the discussion. I think that he could hear, see, feel and understand the speaking individual. This in and of itself is remarkable. But I truly experienced his greatness in the relationship between this almost mystic listening—the silence of the participating mystic, not the silence of disinterest—the relationship between this wordless listening and the power of his own speaking, how he would twist and turn a topic, the drama of his presentation. There was a dynamic in this relationship, an incredible tension.... Sometimes he spoke only one short sentence: "You are taking the same position that I am, only you do not realize it yet." And one believed him completely, it was not an empty phrase or strategy but rather the expression of the depth with which he had listened to his opponent. (Friedmann)

The members of the society experienced Rudolf Steiner with his earnestness and enthusiasm positively. But they did not understand him. He, however, did not give up easily and remained active in the society until 1905.

The second group in which Steiner was at that time active had formed in 1900 around Ludwig Jacobowski. They called themselves *Die Kommenden* [the Coming Ones] and met every Thursday at the Nollendorf Cinema on the Kiestrasse. The club blossomed under Jacobowski's leadership. The meetings on the second floor of the cinema were a colorful mixture of poets, architects, musicians, journalists, Russian students, and light, blond Scandinavian girls. First there were Jacobowski's friends—Clara Viebig and Anselma Heine—about whom he wrote, "I am positively certain that she drinks moonlight from the lily blossoms." Then in the background there was the quietly listening Johannes Schlaf, known together with Arno Holz as one of the founders of naturalism. There was Peter Hille, wrapped up in an old winter coat, who would pull bits of crumpled paper out of his pocket on which he had scribbled poems and, in part improvising, read them aloud. Else Laske-Schüler often accompanied Steiner. In addition, there were Kathe Kollowitz, Hans Pfitzner, Lulu von Strauss, Ernst von Wolzogen, the ethnologist Leo Frobenius, Hans Oswald, a natural historian, and Samuel Lubinski, who specialized in the history of literature.

Three Attempts at the Turn of the Century

The club was but three months old when word got around and outsiders, curious about these gathering of independent artists and writers, asked to join. The young writer Stefan Zweig came whenever he visited from Vienna. He was most devoted to the elder of the group, the forty-eight-year-old Peter Hille. He wrote, not completely accurately, about Steiner:

> At this time (1902), Rudolf Steiner had not yet found his own path; he was still a searcher and a learner. Sometimes he spoke to us about Goethe's theory of color, giving it a Faustian, Paracelsian character. It was stimulating to listen to him, for he was profoundly knowledgeable about a wide range of topics as compared to us who only knew literature. From his lectures and from some good conversations with him, I always returned home at once enthused and somewhat overwhelmed. (Zweig)

Just nine months after he had founded *Die Kommenden*, Jacobowski died quite suddenly on December 2, 1900. He was only thirty-three. The loss of this close friend affected Steiner deeply. On the first anniversary of his death, Steiner wrote to one of Jacobowski's female friends, "Today I am heavy at heart. It has already been a year since I left the hospital in grief, unable to think straight. The wound has yet to heal" (39). Steiner spoke the eulogy at Jacobowski's grave. He also edited his papers and "inherited" the leadership of the *Kommenden* from him.

In contrast to the Giordano-Bruno Society where the discussion focused on conceptual questions and the philosophy of life, in the meetings of the *Kommenden* it was a question of artistic presentations, readings of new poems and stories. The moderation of the evenings was difficult as there was often naturally a clash of sensibilities. Once, before Jacobowski's death, although he was absent that evening, things had taken a bad turn when the chairman for the evening had insulted Else Laske-Schüler. That led to a series of letters back and forth, and in the end the *Kommenden* reformed themselves. The troublemaker was, however, excluded.

One of the young writers who found his way to the *Kommenden* was Erich Mühsam, a diehard socialist; he thought of himself as a revolutionary poet and liked to play the devil's advocate. In his *Nonpolitical Recollections*, he writes about the period when Steiner had already taken over moderation of the gatherings,

> The place where the spirits met weekly to wrestle for the best place on Parnassus was the Nollendorf Cinema on the Kleiststrasse. Every Friday the *Kommenden* met there, a loosely-knit association of young poets and artists. Ludwig Jacobowski was the founder. When Margarete Beutler introduced me to this circle, he was already dead. Dr. Rudolf Steiner moderated the evenings.... He guided the literary discussion masterfully, provoking sharp polemics, directing the clash of usually quite heterogeneous characters only to finally end the heated debates with a soothing sermon.

That annoyed Mühsam, who had of course taken sides, and he believed that he "heard a false undercurrent" in Steiner's closing remarks (Mühsam).

The exclusive focus on literature could not be sustained. Rudolf Steiner invited various members to hold talks. Eugen Reichel spoke, for instance, a number of times about Gottshed (compare 32), and Wolfgang Kirchbach and others seem to have also spoken. In October 1901, Rudolf Steiner also began to speak. He gave a series of talks on the history of religion entitled "From Buddha to Christ." The following year, he gave a second series of talks, "From Zarathustra to Nietzsche. The History of Human Development in Light of their Beliefs from the ancient Orient to the Present, or Anthroposophy." There is no record of these lectures in the memoirs of those who were present. The lectures simply disappeared into the audience. This is probably not surprising as Steiner's listeners were only willing to let themselves be stimulated by his presentations and to take them up in their literary work. For Steiner, however, it was important to make this attempt to spread his seed as far as possible—among the workers, in the Giordano-Bruno Society, and within the *Kommenden*—for only through these attempts could he begin to recognize destiny. Through these excursions, he posed destiny questions, and destiny answered.

Marie Steiner, at that time still Marie von Sivers, experienced the latter phase of Steiner's activity in the winter of 1902/3. She was already at that time Steiner's closest coworker, and she accompanied him to the evening gatherings of the *Kommenden*. She was the daughter of an aristocratic family who had had a very strict education and she found the atmosphere, in which Steiner moved about as though he were at home, quite unpleasant.

> It was a literary circle in which one could encounter the most modern poetry, the *Kommenden*. One had to ask oneself how in the world did Steiner end up there?... He looked like a prince in disguise among

the ravens.... For the wings of those poets hung heavy—the dust of daily life lay on them, the incessant nervousness of Berlin flickered in their eyes, the unaesthetic surroundings draped a grey cloak about them. This was how they appeared and this was how they read their works. Dolorosa and Maria Magdalena were the favorites. They were strange and oppressive. It was like an artificially-lit hothouse. Men came to the table. I remember best the tired casualness and the inner emptiness. (M.Steiner, Recollections II)

Steiner saw this all with different eyes. Only a few years earlier, he had sat with Hartleben and the others at the "thieves table." Among the *Kommenden*, he was able to perceive many homeless souls and gain a wider perspective on life. What he says about his presence as an observing participant among his acquaintances in Vienna holds true here also: "Naturally this was not a cold, disinterested observing, but one full of warmth and interest; one is not set apart from the others intentionally to make observations intentionally, because one is completely part of things—friendly, warm and polite. One stood among them and learned to know them, not in order to observe them, but because that was the gift life gave (258).

CHAPTER 22

THE WAY INTO THE THEOSOPHICAL SOCIETY

In the late summer of 1900, Rudolf Steiner must have decided fairly quickly to hand responsibility for the *Review* over to others. We don't know the details of this decision. What is certain is that the demanding editorial work did not pay enough to cover Steiner's living expenses. He was always dependent on other sources of income. As is still common today, the "brotherly" cultural life supported the "free" world of economic growth. In his farewell article to the readers of the *Review*, Steiner speaks of the various "sacrifices" he has had to make for the magazine. "I can say that for three years I have brought these sacrifices and taken these struggles upon myself willingly. The support of so many people who I admire has helped me over much of it. However, I do not have the energy to continue in this manner" (29).

When Steiner made the decision to step back from his editorial responsibilities, he does not seem to have known how he was going to earn a living. Only toward the end of September did he apply for a teaching position at the Humboldt Academy. From a letter written to Steiner by Jacobowski, it is clear that his application was submitted too late.

Now something unexpected happened. Following Nietzsche's death on August 25, 1900, Steiner had held three eulogies for him. A Miss Schwieb, who was a member of the theosophical circle around the Duchess Brockdorff, seems to have either heard one of them or have heard about one of them. She recommended Steiner to the Duchess, who invited him to hold his Nietzsche talk again in the Theosophical Library (261). Steiner spoke there on September 22, characterizing Nietzsche as an individual worthy of interest because of the depth with which he experienced the questions of his time. "The transformation from the old to the new, which most people only experience with their heads, was for Nietzsche a very personal, heart-tearing individual experience" (31). This is when the unexpected took place: Steiner's way of speaking gripped the imagination of his listeners so deeply that immediately after the lecture, the Duchess invited him to hold a second lecture the following week.

For his part, Steiner had noticed that some members of the audience appeared to have genuine, concrete spiritual interest. He suggested the title "Goethe's Secret Revelation." Then on September 29, he spoke about the path of the transformation of the soul as it is depicted in the "Fairy Tale." For the first time, he dared to present the soul alchemy of 'die and become' in a spiritually imaginative manner. He recalls, "And in *this* lecture, I spoke of the fairy tale from a purely esoteric perspective. This was an important experience for me. I was able to speak with words created directly from the spiritual world. Circumstance in Berlin had thus far limited me to hints about the spirit, allowing it only to shine through my presentations" (28).

This lecture found in the listeners such a clear resonance that Countess Brockdorff decided to reanimate the theosophical work in Berlin. She asked Steiner to hold a series of lectures. Steiner, who was now free of the pressures of his earlier editorial responsibilities, gladly agreed and suggested German mysticism as the topic. The lectures began on October 6 and grew into a series of more than twenty lectures.

It is important here to note that Steiner did not in any way connect these lectures to the theosophical content developed by Blavatsky, Sinnet or Besant. This was for the most part unknown to him. Neither did he base his presentations on ancient Indian teachings. His presentations in the theosophical circles began with Goethe; in the course of the next years he returned to the subject of Goethe's fairy tale repeatedly. The series of lectures on mysticism that began on October 6, 1900, picked up a second central motif of Western spiritual development. Rudolf Steiner began this series with the words of the Delphic Apollo "Know thou thyself." He then explored the meaning of this phrase through the work of Valentin Weigel, Hegel and Fichte. Thus Steiner, from the very beginnings of his theosophical activities, placed himself in the stream of spiritual development of the West, which is apparent as the individual striving of many different people and expresses itself in manifold ways.

Something else needs to be remarked upon at this juncture. Some people have interpreted the shift to the topic of mysticism as a shift to the content of Christianity. Steiner did explore Central European mysticism from Meister Eckhart to Jakob Böhme, and these mystics were without exception Christian. Mystic Christianity is, however, not the central theme of the lectures or the book that followed. What they focus on is the inner development of the human being and the relation of this inner development to the modern views of the world. This is apparent, for instance, in the following passage concerning Nicholas von Kues:

> Nicholas was "prevented by his priestly cloth" from following without reservations the path that this insight indicated to him. We see him making a good beginning with the advance from "knowing" to "not knowing," but, at the same time, we must note that in the field of "not knowing" he has nothing to impart except the theological teachings offered us by Scholasticism.
>
> It is true that he knows how to develop this theology in an ingenious way. His teachings on providence, Christ, the Creation, the Redemption and the moral life are completely in harmony with Christian dogma. In keeping with his spiritual direction, he might have said: "I am confident that human nature, having immersed itself in every science, can transform from within itself 'knowing' into 'unknowing,' and that, consequently, the highest cognition brings satisfaction." In this case, he would have rejected (which he did not) the traditional ideas of soul, immortality, Redemption, God, Creation, the Trinity, and so on, and would have upheld those that he himself had discovered. (7 and AP 2000)

Nicholas von Kues retreated from the threshold of self-knowledge. He sought "refuge in revelation coming from outside himself." This critique is in keeping with Steiner's description of the path toward the discovery of the inner human core, which he published in a booklet entitled *Individualism in Philosophy* in 1899. In this presentation, Steiner recognizes in the life of Jakob Böhme the stage of development upon which God, who until then had been thought to exist outside of the human being, is discovered within. This was for Steiner a significant step on the path of self-knowledge. Yet, although he has the highest praise for Böhme, he admits with disappointment that what Böhme encounters within "is not the human 'I' but merely the Christian God" (30).

Some years later Rudolf Steiner spoke about the stage of inner development and transformation expressed in the words of St. Paul in Letter to the Galatians, "I live no more as myself, it is Christ that lives within me." At the time Steiner gave the lectures on mysticism, he too was on the way toward this goal, although in silence and refusing to expedite his path by falling back on faith or belief. In the winter of 1900/01, he was struggling with the stages of individual self-knowledge. In accordance with the path described in *Intuitive Thinking as a Spiritual Path*, these stages begin with the contemplation of thinking or, in other words, the development of the forces of intuition. In the lectures about mysticism and in the book that followed, Steiner uses what is for him a new realm of expression. He uses the experiences of the mystics to illustrate the stages of intuitive experience. The teachings of the mystics are not subjected to historical or philological interpretation, but rather used to express spiritual views. Steiner acknowledges this explicitly. "I found a way of expressing the spiritual knowledge I wanted to convey in the views of the mystics, from Master Eckhart to Jakob Böhme" (28, p. 202).The first chapters of *Mystics after Modernism* describe the stages of self-knowledge. The first stage is the conscious experience of intuition; the second stage entails transcending the personal; and the third stage brings one to the creative development of intuitive capacity. The path then leads out into the world. Intuition comes to realization in the sciences and in the recognition of what has been experienced in the perceptible world.

Reflection alone shows us that we have intuitions. Think once about the comprehensive, global tapestry of thoughts connected to the word "tulip." Even a superficial moment of reflection points to the number of concepts this entails; a whole tapestry of connections stands before us. Usually we don't notice that this web of connections is something that we bring forth through thinking. We tend to think of the connections as something factual, although the only perceptible fact we have before us is the tulip bulb. The challenge is to think more strongly and more consciously, thus to awaken to intuition and to discover step by step how the world lives on within us. "If I were a king but knew it not, I would not be a king at all" (7). For the first stage of self-knowledge through which the human spirit takes hold of itself, the following holds true: Consciousness (or awakening) is the spiritual state of being. We are spiritually present only when we know that we are present.

Steiner describes the second stage of self-knowledge in connection with the life of Meister Eckhart. Eckhart strives to experience the God within, to bring to life the divine "spark" within himself. "The Heavenly Father brings forth his only begotten son in himself and in me" (7). God is not to be found outside but rather inside ourselves. But the soul, "which is entangled in the world of the senses and thus in the finite, does not automatically contain the essence of primordial nature; it must first develop this. It must annihilate itself as an individual being. Meister Eckhart has aptly characterized this annihilation as an '*un-becoming*'" (7). Today we might say: When we awaken to our intuitions, we have good reason to examine them, to question them, to clarify them in order that universal meaning can replace subjective opinion.

It is at this stage that the actual development of the spirit begins. When an individual gives himself trustingly to the conceptually experienced universal thought content, what has been actively worked through leads to an ongoing correction of what was initially an amorphous experience, to a widening of the conception and to a pushing back of his own pre-formed organization.

The third stage of self-knowledge appears in the chapter "Friendship with God." Steiner points out the differences between the various stages at the beginning of the chapter when he says:

> If Eckhart seems to be a man who, in the blissful experience of spiritual rebirth, speaks of the qualities and nature of knowledge as of a picture he has succeeded in painting, then the others appear as wanderers to whom this rebirth has shown a new road. They plan to walk this road, but the end of it seems to them to have been removed to an infinite distance. Eckhart describes the splendors of his picture; they characterize the difficulties of the new road. (7)

In such a picture we can find "only a reflection, an image of the universal essence" (7). In anthroposophic terminology, this is the stage of Imagination, the realm of the inner picture in all its various forms. The next stage of self-knowledge leads from the picture to the reality. It is a process of transformation. Initially, in the realm of knowing, "Knowledge of nature is not *enriched* by knowing God; it is *transformed*. A person who knows God does not know something *different* from the one who knows nature; such a person *knows differently*" (7, p. 52). This leads to a new life. "Not only is the worldview of such a one different from that of the person who is merely rational, but that one also lives life differently. This person does not speak of the meaning that life already has by virtue of the forces and laws of the world; rather this individual gives a *new* meaning to life" (7, p. 59).

At this stage, the individual brings forth a new human being. One's new thoughts, one's new way of thinking, is rooted in the soul that transforms it. The concepts and ideas become imbued with a spiritual beingness (7).

The fourth stage of self-knowledge and the difficulties that arise at this stage of the journey are described in relation to the life of Nicholas von Kues. Like Meister Eckhart, Nicholas is a mystic. He is, however, at the same time a scientist and a man of the world with a wealth of experience and knowledge. The question that arises is, "How does outer knowledge relate to inner experience?" In modern thought, sense impressions are the *indicators* for what exists outside ourselves. The redness of a berry indicates that it is ripe. Sense impressions and sense-perceptible things are at this level of relationship mere external facts. It is not innate to the things that, at a lower stage of knowledge, "only appear to be outside of us. Individuals must, through transformation, raise themselves to a higher level, upon which things cease to be merely external" (7). The challenge lies in not seeing the red of the berry merely as an indication of its ripeness, but to immerse ourselves in the red—experience it, feel it, understand it, let it speak to us. Nicholas von Kues struggled with this problem. He knew that the recognition of the sensory "signs" that the world gives us was not true knowledge, and through his own experience he recognized a form of knowledge that originates within, can be developed through outer knowledge and lives then as unknowable certainty in the soul.

> With knowledge, they separate themselves from the whole, thus creating a spiritual world within. Within this world, people confront nature in solitude. They have become richer, but this wealth is a difficult burden, weighing on each individual alone. People must find the way back to nature through their own resources. They must understand that now they themselves must integrate their wealth into the stream of universal effects.... It is here that all the evil demons lie in wait for human beings whose strength can easily fail. Instead of accomplishing that integration themselves, people take refuge in revelations from outside. (7, p. 88)

Nicholas von Kues finds his refuge in the affirmation of his faith.

In Steiner's descriptions, Paracelsus appears as the individual who finds his way to nature. He is not trapped by the cloth; he is independent. Steiner shows us the Paracelsus who chooses to say, "No one who can stand alone should be the servant of another" (7, p. 95). Paracelsus knows that the universe brings itself to expression in the individual who seeks actively to gain understanding, that the micro-cosmos is an organ of the macro-cosmos. He follows the path of extensive experience; he wanders the length and breadth of Europe. Through the enhanced experience, universal knowledge and individual knowledge inter-merge. He creates his own sensually concrete language: When he speaks of sulfur, he speaks of a sensible/super-sensible reality that is active both in nature and the human being as a spiritual-physical process. In connection with Paracelsus, Steiner is able for the first time to develop a concrete image of the sevenfold human being (7). This is possible, because Paracelsus was aware of the higher, creative nature of the human being and could "assign a role to human beings that makes them co-architects in [cosmic] creation" (7). Finally, and most importantly, Paracelsus did not regard the processes of nature and the sense appearances to be outer phenomena. Each of them appears to him in its relation to the whole, which reveals itself within the human being. He "does not begin by reinterpreting them, because those natural processes as they confront us with their sensory reality reveal in their own way the mystery of existence" (7). The step from inner experience into the world has now been taken. Higher knowledge proves itself by understanding the language of nature in direct observation.

In his presentation of the prescient knowledge of Jakob Böhme, Steiner goes a step further. He shows how Böhme struggled to resolve the riddle of the cosmos and that of the nature of evil through imaginative contemplation. Böhme designed a cosmogony in which a cosmic being revealed its sevenfold nature in a series of meaningful images. He did not merely accept what was at the time believed to be factual, but transformed what was given into an inner image, rich with meaning. In the poetry of Angelus Silesius, with whom Steiner concludes his presentations on mysticism, we see the image of the individual who has been reborn at a higher level of existence, the individual who is completely at one with the cosmos.

With these presentations, Steiner did not intend to create an logical analogy in which nature or the cosmos is seen as ensouled, or the spirit, which we know as human spirit, is projected into nature. This is quite clearly shown in relation to Giordano Bruno, who in his work developed quite beautiful, profound thoughts about the universal soul. Although Steiner acknowledges Bruno's courage in expanding his view over the entire cosmos, he says, "He had not really experienced spirit within himself and thus imagined it in terms of the human soul, the only form in which it confronted him" (7).

In the last chapter of *Mystics after Modernism*, Steiner asks how the worldview of someone like Jakob Böhme relates to modern science. His answer is, for someone who knows of his later work, somewhat surprising. And although Steiner revised other parts of the book for later editions, he left this passage untouched. In it, he rejected the traditional approach, which thought to discover the Creation in nature, because he recognized that such ideas were mere academic projections and were not true conceptualizations. Further, he says that only in the human being does one find spirit in sense-perceptible form. "This spirit does not create nature, it evolves out of nature" (7). Thus at the end of the book, Steiner confesses:

> I stand completely upon the ground of this natural science. I am convinced that a view of nature like that of Ernst Haeckel becomes shallow only when people approach it with a world of ideas that is already shallow. When I let the *revelations* of a "natural history of creation" affect me, I feel something higher and more glorious than when I confront the stories of supernatural miracles of the Creed. I know of nothing in "holy" books that reveals anything as sublime as the so-called dry fact that every human fetus rapidly progresses through a succession of all the forms through which its animal ancestors evolved.... Let us fill our minds with the magnificent facts that our senses perceive, and we will have little care for supernatural miracles. If we experience spirit within ourselves, we do not need spirit in external nature.... I do not look for divine spirit in nature, because I believe I perceive the essence of human spirit in myself (7, p. 128)

Here Steiner marks a certain stage of his development. He described in more depth in his *Autobiography*:

> Through imaginative perception, once I had developed the substance of *Concepts of the World and Life in the Nineteenth Century*, I gained insight into the actual evolution of organic life from primordial times to the present. While working on the book, I still saw before my soul's vision the scientific view of evolution as presented by Darwin. To me, however, this simply described the sequence of physical events in nature. Within that sequence, I recognized the activity of spiritual impulses as Goethe visualized them in his ideas of metamorphosis. (28, p. 208)

In regard to the period following the conclusion of his work on this book, he writes, "And I made a particularly important discovery in the spiritual realm soon after I had finished *World and Individual Philosophy*" (28).

Aspects of this "discovery" become apparent if we call to mind Steiner's position as he came to the conclusion of the above-mentioned book. In October 1900, he wrote on the last page, "The *essence* of the things does not come to me through them, I add it to what they reveal to me. I *create* a world of ideas, which I accept as the essence of the things. They receive their essence through me. It is thus impossible to question the essence of existence. In the act of knowing, the ideas show me nothing that lives on in the things. *The world of ideas is my experience.* Cognition, like ethical action, is a further step in universal evolution; it is "a new shoot of what has previously evolved." The human challenge is to continue the path of evolution.

The next step in the continuation of the evolutionary path is what Steiner addresses in *Mystics after Modernism*. It begins with an inner step: the enhancement and transformation of intuition. As this capacity awakens, it initially brings forth insights that are determined purely from within and then develops into a living spiritual activity. At the same time, Steiner addressed the views of Darwin and Haeckel. These, when viewed intuitively in the right light, provide a starting point for something new.

In 1924, Steiner described the path he took in the years following 1900 and recommended it to his listeners.

> Now that you have been touched by the Rosicrucian path of initiation presented here today, you should study the work of Haeckel with all its materialism and let yourselves be permeated by the methods of knowledge presented in *How to Know Higher Worlds*. Take what you can learn from Haeckel's *Anthropogeny*, even if it disgusts you, and take everything that science can teach you and bear it to the gods, and you will find what is described in my book *Outline of Esoteric Science*. (233a)

In *Mystics after Modernism*, we can see how on the one hand Steiner works with the Rosicrucian principles of self-knowledge and self-transformation and on the other hand the study of Haeckel. In the foreword to *Mystics after Modernism*, he mentions that he has "given roughly thirty lectures in the last months" about Haeckel's *The Riddle of the World*. Until September 1901, at which time the foreword was written, he worked intensively with Haeckel's ideas and ardently defended his work. Then, what he had taken in during the course of this study was ever more deeply penetrated by the light of self-knowledge—it was "laid in the hands of the gods." Beginning in 1903, it returned completely transformed.

The stage of inner development that Steiner had achieved in 1901 comes to expression in one passage from the book *Mystics after Modernism*. After writing of the fateful resolution of Nicholas von Kues' struggle with the forces of conceptualization and his return to the refuge of traditional religious belief, he sketches the spiritual state of *standing at the edge of the abyss*.

> In general, there are three paths upon which one can walk once one arrives at the point Nicholas had reached. One is *positive faith*, which comes to us from outside. The second is *despair*, when one stands alone with one's burden and feels all existence shattered within oneself. The third path is the *self-development* of one's deepest faculties. One necessary quality that leads one along this third path is *trust* in the world, and the other is the *courage* to follow that trust no matter where it leads. (7)

Apparently, here Rudolf Steiner describes his own path, something he confirms in an addendum to the new edition of 1923. In 1901, he was committed to beginning with Haeckel's scientific work and developing it further with absolute courage "regardless of where it led" him.

One would like to be able to describe the audience in attendance at Steiner's lectures on German mysticism. Unfortunately, we have little information. The heart of the circle was undoubtedly the Duchess Sophia Brockdorff, who "in her friendly and for many people sympathetic manner was able to keep the theosophical movement afloat in Germany" (261). Toward the end of Steiner's thoughts on Meister Eckhart, a slim blonde woman began to attend the lectures: Marie von Sivers. Steiner mentioned once that "it would be interesting to mention some small details concerning her presence" (254)—which he unfortunately never did. Marie von Sivers, who at that time was in correspondence with Édouard Schuré (she was translating his *Children of Lucifer*), wrote him about the circle around the Duchess. Her letter has unfortunately been lost, but we do have Schuré's answer: "The people who gather around the Duchess seem to be peculiarly interesting and amusing" (Rudolf Steiner Studies, I). In any case, these gatherings were not limited to a group of well-educated aristocratic young ladies but included people from many professions, classes and milieus: women with short hair and men with long hair, theosophists of all colors, Wagnerians, spiritualists, social reformers—Steiner called them "homeless souls." They all, however, had the courage to break away from what was then conventional thought and behavior.

Among some of them there was a quality of listening present that empowered Steiner to continue. Some of them didn't merely want to listen to what he was saying; they strove to bring it to a level of individual experience that would inform their own efforts.

For Steiner, the winter of 1900/01 was a flurry of inner and outer activity. He taught two courses at the Workers' College, appeared regularly at the Giordano-Bruno Society, and to the *Kommenden* he not only gave roughly thirty lectures about Haeckel's *Riddle of the World*, he also spoke about Hebbel, Keller, Freiligrath and other topics. He corrected the proofs of *World and Individual Philosophy of the Nineteenth Century*. At the end of November, his friend Jacobowski was taken to the hospital—presumably with typhus—and died there on December 2. He was deeply shaken and wrote in Jacobowski's obituary, "On December 2 we found ourselves forced to sink into barren nothingness all the proud hopes we had connected with the personality of Ludwig Jacobowski" (32).

The workload of courses and lectures only began to ease up at the beginning of the summer. He went to work on the manuscript of *Mystics after Modernism*. Since 1899, he had lived with his wife and her two daughters in Friedenau and was able to work in relative peace. Only on two or three evenings a week did he venture into the city—to the Workers' College, to the *Kommenden*, and now and again to the Giordano Bruno Society. After he had delivered the book to the publisher and Berlin's cultural summer break had begun, he took a trip to Austria, where he visited Josef Köck in Salzburg, the Specht family near Lake Attersee, Rosa Mayreder and Moritz Zitter in the Vienna area, and his parents and siblings in the town of Horn in the Waldviertel. On the return trip, Steiner spent a number of restful days with Maria Stona (a friend of Jacobowski) at Schloss Strzebowitz, where he corrected the proofs of *Mystics after Modernism*. He then returned to Berlin.

He probably used the month of September to prepare the lectures he was slated to give the coming winter. Some, like the twelve lectures on nineteenth century German spiritual life that were scheduled for late autumn, no doubt came relatively easily to him. But the lectures on "Christianity as a Mystical Fact," which he had agreed to hold in the Theosophical Library, took him into territory that he had to study anew. He worked his way once again through the *History of Idealism* by Otto Willmann, which he much admired and which described the birth of Greek philosophy out of the ancient mysteries; he studied Edmund Pfleiderer's *The Philosophy of Heraclites von Ephesus in the Light of the Mysteries* and, naturally, the original texts themselves: the pre-Socratics and Plato.

The transcripts of the original lectures about "Christianity as a Mystical Fact," which in many details are inaccurate and have never been published, show that Steiner drew from many other contemporary sources. It is also clear that when he began the series, the concept of the 1902 book had not yet taken shape. He felt his way step by step into the topic in the course of the lectures. Only after he had studied and presented the various aspects of the topic did the book, with its clear premises, take on form.

The winter semester began punctually on October 1 with five or six obligations weekly. The lectures in the Theosophical Library began on October 19. Marie von Sivers visited Berlin for two weeks on her way from the Baltic to Italy. Together with Nina Gernet, she was hoping to inaugurate theosophical work in Bologna, an endeavor supported by a number of prominent theosophists. Nina Gernet considered herself to be a theosophical initiate and wondered whether Steiner, who spoke of the mysteries, was aware that such mysteries existed in the present? Why didn't he speak of the contemporary mysteries? She wanted to win his support for the theosophical work that had grown up around Annie Besant.

Marie von Sivers also found time to speak with Steiner and asked him "if it wasn't quite important to call to life a spiritual movement in Europe?" In the course of the conversations, Steiner responded, "Certainly it would be important to bring a spiritual scientific movement into being; I would, however, only be willing to participate if it originates exclusively out of the stream of Western esotericism and works to develop this further" (254). Steiner was thinking of Greek antiquity and Goethe and no doubt the German mystics when he said this. In another version of this conversation, Marie von Sivers asks Rudolf Steiner why he had not joined the Theosophical Society. He responded that there were more significant spiritual impulses than Eastern mysticism. He would give the world the wrong impression if he were to connect his work with a society whose "shibboleth" was "Eastern mysticism" (264).

After Marie von Sivers left Berlin at the end of October, the Duchess Brockdorff also had the idea to win Steiner over to the theosophical work in Germany. In December, the subject of an ongoing collaboration was broached. The conversations must have run a peculiar course. Somehow Steiner neglected to submit a request for membership in the Theosophical Society, then did so under the condition that he would not have to pay any dues. "Then they sent me the certificate, which was unpaid, and I became the Chairman of the German Theosophical Society" (264). "German Theosophical Society" was at that time the name of the Berlin branch led by the Brockdorffs. Steiner's membership certificate was dated January 17, 1902.

At the same time, the Brockdorffs, after having spoken with Steiner, approached Marie von Sivers and asked if she would be willing to help in building up the Theosophical Society in Germany. By the end of January, they notified Steiner that she had agreed and was already looking for an apartment in Berlin; until she had found one, she would continue her work in Italy, then travel to London for the gathering of European theosophists. She arrived in London in May 1902 and became acquainted with the theosophical scene around Annie Besant.

Before we take a closer look at the lectures and the book *Christianity as a Mystical Fact*, a general observation is necessary. This topic led Steiner into new territory. His fields of interest from 1882 until 1900 did not include religious or theological questions. He had only spoken about religious themes parenthetically or in response to a direct question. He regarded confessional Christianity as an otherworldly religion and, as such, rejected it. Later, too, he repeatedly emphasized that his research originated in natural science.

> Whoever peruses the unfortunately long list of my publications will be able to see that religious problems never provided me with a starting point, even though it is quite clear that Anthroposophy must lead toward religious sensibility and religious views. The source of my work was not religious beliefs, the source was the natural scientific worldview to which I was introduced as a young man. Whoever grows up within the framework of natural science has to initially have the greatest respect for what science has achieved in modern times and even greater respect for both the experimental approach, the methods of scientific observation, and the schooling of thinking..., into which modern science can lead one. (B 116)

Thus Steiner emphasized in the foreword to *Christianity as Mystical Fact* that his goal was to explore the evolution of truth and the different worldviews from a scientific point of view (8). This type of research requires a corresponding method. The critique of historical sources, research into literary correspondences, an so on, can merely serve to help the process along. Whoever wishes to research historical-spiritual contexts must first be able to understand them; they must develop within themselves the capacities that enable them to grasp the inner meaning of the traditional texts. Just as a chemist is better able to interpret a paper concerning chemistry than a philologist, someone who has developed an inner sense of the mystical can understand a text that speaks of mystical experience better than someone who simply understands Greek or who has been able to collate similar descriptions.

In 1904, Steiner, who at that point was already able to grasp more than he could in 1902, articulated this in an especially illuminating manner.

> Such a statement should certainly not be used against research into "historical truths." But no one can recognize the historical truth of texts such as the Gospels if one has not personally experienced the mystical meaning that they contain. All analyses and comparisons in this direction are worthless. Not one can be found who "was born in Bethlehem" who has not had a mystical experience of Christ; no one can discern how the "cross on Golgotha" redeems us from evil who has not felt it raised up within. "Purely historical" research can discern about as much about "mystical facts" as one can discover about a great poet in a dissection. (34)

His book *Christianity as a Mystical Fact* is a first attempt to decipher the language of the mysteries, the myths and the Gospels on the basis of mystical experience. The step Steiner takes here beyond what was contained in *Mystics after Modernism* is to immerse himself in the imagery of the traditional texts. The imaginative stories of the myths and the Gospels are looked at as pictures of mystical experience. Such an approach can be considered an intellectual interpretation. For that reason, Steiner tries to show that the actual soul processes through which the mystic passes were more than mere thoughts. These were realities that could only be expressed adequately in images. This is best shown in a passage from the end of the chapter "The Mysteries and Mysteriosophy."

> To comprehend merely the things of the world around, leads only to a denial of God. On the evidence of the senses, God does not exist anymore than he does for the intellect that interprets sensory experience. God lies spellbound in the world. To find God requires a power from

God himself. That power must actually be awakened in the candidate for initiation, it was stated in the ancient teaching.

So began the great cosmic drama in which the initiand's life was engulfed. The drama consisted of nothing less than the deliverance of the spellbound God.

Where is God? Such was the root-question of the soul of the *mystes*. God is not existence; but nature exists. In nature he must be discovered, where he lies in his enchanted grave. The *mystai* understood that "God is love" in a special higher sense. For God has gone to the utmost lengths of love. He has sacrificed himself in infinite love, poured himself out, and dismembered himself into the manifold things of nature. They live, but he is not alive in them; he slumbers in them, but comes alive in human beings who are able to experience the life of God within themselves. But if human beings are to attain this gnosis, they must creatively release it within themselves. Looking into their own being, they find the divine as a hidden creative power, not yet released into existence. Within the soul lies the place where the spellbound God may return to life.

The soul is the mother who can receive the divine seed from nature. If the soul allows herself to be impregnated by nature she will give birth to the divine. Out of the marriage of the soul with nature the divine is born, no longer a "hidden God" but something manifest, alive—palpably alive and moving among humankind. In human beings the spirit has been released from enchantment; yet it is the offspring of the spellbound God. He is not the great God who was, and is, and shall be, yet he may in a certain sense be taken as a revelation of him. The Father remains at rest in the unseen. The Son is born to human beings out of their own souls.

Initiatory knowledge is thus an actual event in the cosmic process. It is the birth of a divine child—a process just as real as any natural process. The great secret of the *mystai* was precisely this, that they creatively release the divine child in themselves. First of all, however, they must be prepared so as to recognize it. The uninitiated know nothing of the Father of this divine child. The Father slumbers under a spell. The child seems to be born of a virgin, the soul giving birth to him without impregnation. Whereas all her other offspring are begotten by the world of the senses, and have a father who can be seen and touched in perceptible existence, the Son of God is uniquely begotten of the eternal, hidden Father himself. (8, pp. 20–21)

It is a fairly straightforward process to give this passage a conceptual interpretation based on Steiner's philosophy. This was not his intent. The inner soul processes should become an imaginative experienced reality; it is less a question of understanding them conceptually than of bringing them to an inner pictorial experience and thus "living" them. They are not one-dimensional thought shadows but manifold realities. This is why Steiner chose various myths to characterize the mystic path—from Prometheus, from Heracles, from the Argonauts and from Odysseus—a variety of images through which the hidden content of the mysteries were depicted. In the Egyptian mysteries, he finds the sweeping images of death and resurrection. What is earthly in the human being is annihilated; one enters the nether world, the world of the dead, and there overcomes death through resurrection.

> The initiate had died to earthly things, and was indeed dead, having died as a lower being and having been in the underworld among the dead—that is, with those who are already united with eternity. After a sojourn in the other world, the initiate had risen again from the dead, but as another, no longer as one belonging to transitory nature. All that is transitory was absorbed into the all-permeating Logos, and the initiate belonged henceforth among those who live forever at the right hand of Osiris. (8, p. 90)

In 1902, Steiner is able to recognize the mystical meaning of Christianity. He interprets Christianity—in the 1902 edition of the book—as the revelation of the mysteries; what had earlier been hidden now took place openly. "The ritual pattern enacted by the Mysteries of the ancient world in the secrecy of their temples was taken up as a historical reality by Christianity" (8). The inner experiences of the mystics in the Mysteries could not of course be simply disseminated freely. But Jesus was able to awaken a belief in the divine. "He wanted to give to everyone the certainty of what in the Mysteries could be beheld as truth. He wanted to let what lived in the Mysteries flow out into the historical development of humanity" (8).

These lectures made it quite clear to Steiner's theosophical audience that he did not build on the then predominantly Buddhist or Hindu oriented theosophy. There was no mention of Blavatsky or Besant. He did not draw from the Bhagavad Gita as a source for his explorations, something that would have been completely non-tendentious. Steiner stood there as the representative of independent mystical knowledge. It was evident that he understood what he was presenting. His excursuses followed a definite method and a number of his listeners realized that someone spoke to them who knew spiritual experience not merely by having heard about it.

On October 2, 1902, Steiner sent a first edition of his new book to Wolfgang Kirchbach, his colleague from the Giordano-Bruno Society, and wrote in the accompanying letter:

> Please don't regard my book *Christianity as Mystical Fact* as more than it is meant to be. I know its shortcomings, explicitly the *historical* ones, quite clearly. The addendum should be taken *very* seriously. I did not want to destroy this impression by referring in certain places to the work of others, namely Strauss. The conceptual mood that I have brought to expression is what I value. I know that what I have attempted is similar to what Fritz Schultze once tried. Today almost nothing of his *positive* statements is seen as valid while the biogenic law—perhaps with some correction—will live on into the future. (39)

Steiner was thus concerned with the principle that would make it possible to interpret possible mystic experiences in the present in the light of historical documents. The hermeneutic concept alone was important to him, which views self-knowledge and the drama of the individual quest for knowledge as the necessary prerequisites for an understanding of the mystical and mythological traditions. In order to not cloud this approach, he did not discuss the seemingly similar work of David Friedrich Strauss. In regard to the primary documents, he was only able to do minimal research, as he was at the time up to his ears in work. Thus, he based much of his presentation on the work of other scholars. He was aware of the fact that this gave his presentations a rather narrow foundation and that the choice of material could be criticized. For this reason, he openly admitted the historical shortcomings. He could do so unconcernedly because his focus was not historical detail but the methodological approach.

CHAPTER 23

THE THEOSOPHICAL SOCIETY

In January 1902, it wasn't only planned that Rudolf Steiner would become the head of the "German Theosophical Society." At least the Brockdorffs had other ideas. A "German section" of the Theosophical Society, which H. P. Blavatsky (or "HPB") and Henry S. Olcott had founded with its center in Adyar (Madras), should be formed. Until now, Steiner had taken a critical stance regarding this theosophical work, which was represented in Germany by Franz Hartmann. He wrote that one heard from this corner "nothing but empty phrases, borrowed from the Eastern texts, completely lacking in substance. The inner experiences are blather" (32). Later he recalled, "When I first lectured in Berlin, I had not read anything by Blavatsky or Besant.... The lectures, and then the book *Mystics after Modernism*, were finished before I had even decided to read anything from either of them" (Lecture, June 5, 1920).

Now Steiner had to decide not only to read Blavatsky and Besant, but also to form for himself a picture of the Theosophical Society—as it was unthinkable that he should base an opinion on what he had learned of the society en passant in Vienna in 1889. The Brockdorffs had a good library. Among others, it contained a book that served Steiner well: *The Transcendental Universe* by C. G. Harrison, published in 1887. Based on this and similar works, Steiner was able to research fairly quickly the history of the Theosophical Society and gain an understanding of Blavatsky's path. The picture that was presented deserves some attention.

According to this understanding, the effects of materialism revealed themselves strongly in the middle of the nineteenth century. The mental images of mechanical materialism formed a sort of armored helmet around humans' heads and threatened to isolate both humankind and the earth from the suprasensory. Due to this situation, certain esoteric circles decided to call a counter movement to life to call attention to the suprasensory. The spiritism movement was thus founded and during the 1840s spread with almost epidemic rapidity. The movement was well-regarded and even attracted a number of famous scholars like Alfred Russel Wallace, who had formulated the theory of inheritance at the same time as Charles Darwin, or, in Germany, Friedrich Zöllner. The supposed messages from the world of those who had died, which came through the medium, were sensational enough. The movement's success was remarkable. But the esotericists were shocked. They had expected something different. It was clear to them that the spiritist messages could in no way have come from the souls of those who had died.

The story goes that leading esotericists gathered in Vienna in 1874 to take counsel as to how the situation might be rectified. Their attention fell on Helena Petrowna Blavatsky. Born in 1831 in Jekaterinoslaw, she was gifted both artistically and in matters of the esoteric. After extensive travels, documented almost solely in legends, she arrived in New York in 1873. In 1874, in Chittenden, Vermont, she encountered spiritism and a man named Colonel Olcott. Olcott was a respected judge and excellent organizer who had, as Blavatsky realized, fallen in love with the spirit manifestations. Blavatsky seemed to be clear about the questionable nature of these manifestations. In May 1875, she wrote in a notebook, "I have been ordered to tell the truth about the manifestations and the mediums. And now my path of suffering will begin. I will make enemies of the spiritists and, in addition, of the Christians and the skeptics." A further entry in her notebook from July 1875 stated that she had been tasked with working with Olcott to form a philosophical-religious society. The Theosophical Society was founded in New York on November 17, 1875, with the intent of countering the success of spiritism with a new teaching about the nature of the suprasensory.

This is not the place to write of Blavatsky's trials and tribulations, the various influences to which she was subjected, or of her work. She published her first major book *Isis Unveiled* in 1877, followed in 1888 by *The Secret Doctrine*. Most important, HPB, as she was called in the Theosophical Society, was to cultivate an earnest interest for spiritual questions and to support spiritually striving individuals in the Esoteric School that she founded.

It is impossible to overlook the value of her efforts, although there are various aspects of her work that deserve criticism. Fearlessly, she took a stand for the reality of the spiritual world. Although she was not always

The Theosophical Society

discerning in her choice of methods, she stood alone with almost no scientific training in the midst of rampant materialism, unable to trust anything but her constantly fluid intuitions and her "Masters." Rudolf Steiner, who for as long as he was a member of the Theosophical Society loyally defended Blavatsky's work against narrow-minded critics, characterized her briefly in his *Autobiography*. The guardians of a tradition that originated in the ancient mystery schools had imparted this knowledge to her.

> She combined what she attained in this way with revelations that arose within herself. She was an individual with peculiar atavistic powers. Spirit worked through her in a dreamlike state of consciousness, just as in ancient times it had acted through leaders of the mysteries—unlike our modern consciousness, which is illumined by the consciousness soul. Thus in "Blavatsky the human being" something recurred that was innate within the mysteries during primordial times. (28, p. 218)

Helena Petrowna Blavatsky was fortunate in 1889 to find in Annie Besant a student who, although not a congenial successor, would become a highly dedicated leader of the Theosophical Society. When Annie Besant met HPB, she already had a life of stormy battles behind her. In her youth, she had been a fanatic Christian, and after an unsuccessful marriage with an Anglican minister, she had become a militant atheist and had marched with the socialist workers. She confronted the mounted police courageously during demonstrations and organized a strike that she carried through successfully until its end. For a number of years she was a member of the *Fabian Society*, a group that supported efforts toward a more just society. For a time she was close friends with George Bernard Shaw. But her first encounter with HPB decided her further path. By the time of the latter's death on May 8, 1891, HPB had found in Annie Besant a gifted although controversial successor.

Alongside Annie Besant there were a number of serious theosophists working in the Theosophical Society, including Mrs. Kennigdale Cook—a.k.a. Mabel Collins—who had written the profound breviary *Light on the Path*, as well as Bertram Keightley, who saw clearly the difference between true and dangerous paths of esoteric development. Thus Rudolf Steiner wrote in his *Autobiography* in 1925, "Only among the English theosophists did I find inner meaning that arose from Blavatsky and this"—from 1902 to 1904—"was still cultivated in the right way by Annie Besant and others. As for myself, I could never have worked as they did, but I found a spiritual center there with which it was possible to unite if one was serious about spreading spiritual knowledge in the deepest sense" (28, pp. 212–13).

Annie Besant was able during the years prior to her meeting with HPB to live out a part of her personal destiny. After turning to theosophy, she became for a number of years a student, a novice, and as such around the turn of the century she followed the critical counsel of her friends at becoming for a time a medium through which significant impulses could work powerfully. Rudolf Steiner noted in his *Autobiography* that her experience of the spirit had a dreamlike quality. "Yet, what she said about the spiritual world did come from that world" (28, p. 221). "I recognized that she had a certain right to speak of the spirit world from her own experience. She certainly had an inner ability to get through to the spiritual world" (28, p. 221).

Concurrently, he realized that certain outer, political aspirations lived in her. At the time, however, that Steiner joined the Theosophical Society, these had receded into the background and would only reappear later in conjunction with the Krishnamurti affair and then again during World War I. Among Annie Besant's prominent colleagues was also Charles Webster Leadbeater, who had written many booklets. In theosophical circles he was seen as an eminent clairvoyant. Bertram Keightley, who was prudent in such things, believed that Leadbeater "in spite of many friendly warnings followed a very risky path of psychic development. Due to the forced development and constant use of the astral and more primitive spiritual senses, this led to an overemphasis of the personal at the cost of true higher self and then to extremely unhealthy events" (Tillet). However, in 1902, the tendencies that emanated from Leadbeater's activities were balanced by the work of other leading theosophists.

It is not without humor that Steiner in 1923 describes the situation in the Theosophical Society. It lived completely in the images with which the lives of venerated, highly developed spiritual masters on higher planes of existence were represented. But in addition to the slightly ridiculous, it also had positive aspects:

> This is something that worked strongly to bind the Theosophical Society into a coherent whole and led to an incredible strong sense of belonging—that each member felt oneself to be a representative of the society as a whole. The society was something that existed in

and of itself. The individuals were there, but the society had its own existence. One can even say that it had its own self-consciousness. It had its own ego. This ego was so strong that even when the absurd activities of leading personalities curiously surfaced, those who had felt a sense of belonging to the Theosophical Society held on with a grip of steel and had something of the feeling: It is treasonous when even in light of the stark errors of the leading personalities we do not hold together. (258)

In the spring of 1902, efforts were being made to bring about the formation of the German branch of the Theosophical Society that had been initiatied by the Brockdorffs. It was a delicate process; at the Brockdorff's recommendation, a man who had not been a member of the society for even a year was to take on the leadership of the German branch. Obviously there were older candidates for this post. First there was Dr. William Hübbe-Schleiden, a former colonial administrator who together with Helena Blavatsky and others had formed the "Theosophical Society of Germany" on July 27, 1884. Although this "Society" had dissolved, Hübbe-Schleiden had continued to publish the theosophical periodical *Sphinx* and thus carry on the theosophical work. Then there was Richard Bresch, who published the theosophical monthly *Vahan* in Leipzig. In Munich lived the author Ludwig Deinhard, who was an older, respected theosophist. There were theosophical groups in a number of German cities: in Hamburg around Bernhard Hubo, in Kassel with Dr. Ludwig Noll, in Düsseldorf led by Bruno Berg, and in Stuttgart around Adolf M. Oppel. In addition, there were theosophical groups following other approaches than Blavatsky's. The "Theosophical Society in Germany" led by Paul Raatz followed the theosophical work of Catherine Tingley. And finally there was the International Theosophical Brotherhood founded in Munich by Blavatsky's former comrade Dr. Franz Hartmann. None of the candidates were especially active, but they all had their reputations and pretensions as well as the potential to create dissension. In many places, people did not want to be disturbed as they waited for the scientific proofs of theosophy being worked out by Dr. Hübbe-Schleiden.

It took all the Brockdorff's skill and Steiner's patience even to lay a possible foundation for the envisioned step. Steiner spoke about the negotiations in 1911.

> Then the German Section was founded amid "hopes and fears, in passionate pain," amid terrible discussions backward and forward—I will spare you that! A person appeared then (he has since left the Society) who was also an agent of destiny—in an esoteric connection there would be much to say about it. It so happened that Mr. Richard Bresch, who was then chairman of the Leipzig group, went to Count Brockdorff one day after talking it over with various persons and said, "If Dr. Steiner is already chairman of the Berlin Lodge, he can also become chairman of the German Section." (264)

Renouncing the post of general secretary was probably not too difficult for the other possible candidates as it came with no salary and no authority. It promised only work and duties. In the end, the founding of the German branch was a minor event. Membership in the new branch was predicted to consist of roughly 100 members.

At the time of his nomination in 1902, Steiner was not at all certain of how things were going to play out. The risks that accompanied this new task were clear to him. He knew that he would be compromised by connecting himself with theosophy, with all the strange things and destinies that belonged to it, and he spoke about this (51). The unproductive discussions of 1902 had shown him with what questionable existences this post would bring him into contact. Finally, he must have weighed the inner risks that were connected with the theosophical work.

He questioned destiny whether it was not possible for this cup to pass him by. His old friend Moritz Zitter had visited Dr. Heinrich Kanner, the publisher of the famous weekly newspaper *Die Zeit*, recommending Steiner as the perfect editor for the feuilleton and arranging for a meeting of the two. At the beginning of June 1902, Kanner was in Berlin and received Rudolf Steiner. Steiner wrote to Zitter on June 10:

> Dr. Kanner was here. But I unfortunately cannot write to you with any hopefulness. He bid me come to his hotel, and then had me come again. He let me talk for hours. What he finally said to me he could just as well have said at the beginning, before listening to me. At the end he said to me I should write down everything I think about how a modern feuilleton should be managed and what I, should I be hired, would do. Naturally, I will do what he asked. It appears to me, however, just to be a way to get rid of me without directly saying "no." Everything he said to me is what he already said to you. It is exactly what you wrote about what he said to you. In the end, I had no idea

what he actually wanted from me. I made all the outer preparations that you ordered me to. I bought the kind of suit you suggested, a stiff hat, gloves. I think that you were right about these. (They completely emptied my wallet.)

I spoke to him of a number of ideas of what destined a person to be the editor of a modern feuilleton, a person who has experience in many different areas. This was a point that he said made sense to him. He didn't mention anything against me except the view that *for me* it would probably be better not to cut myself off from freelance writing to take a job in an office. I replied that I had long hoped for such a position and that it didn't really matter what was better for me. (39)

In spite of all his efforts, Steiner was not asked to take the position. It was as he had thought: Dr. Kanner didn't want him. So, at the end of June, Steiner brought his courses at the Workers' College to a close, wrote the last chapter of *Christianity as Mystical Fact*, and brought the book to the printer. On June 29, he left Berlin. His first stop was in Hannover, where he visited the "elder" of the German theosophists, Hübbe-Schleiden, and ended up meeting not only him but also Ludwig Deinhard, who couldn't pass up the chance to take a look at the designated general secretary of the German branch. The inspection seems to have gone well and Steiner left on the afternoon of June 30 for Vlissingen to catch the steamboat to London.

On the morning of July 1, Steiner arrived in London. Marie von Sivers met him at the Liverpool Street Station. They took a carriage straight through the city to Bayswater, where Bertram Kneightley, Helena Blavatsky's old colleague, met them and welcomed Steiner into his home. Kneightley sent him first to the bathroom. "A pure blessing: in England in such houses, one *must* bathe every morning. So—my first English experience: a bath" (39). He immediately found a good rapport with Kneightley, and their acquaintance became a friendship that would endure many storms. In 1923, Kneightley visited Steiner in Dornach.

Steiner was not "unknown" to Kneightley at the time of their first meeting. The latter had written of Steiner's *Mystic* in the *Theosophical Review*, translated some passages, and recommended it to the readers. In intimate conversations, Kneightley would relate his personal acquaintance with Blavatsky, while Steiner spoke of his experiences with the German theosophists. During one conversation, the then celebrated scholar of Gnosticism, G. R. S. Mead, was present. The conversation touched on Steiner's *Mystic*, and Mead remarked, "The whole of theosophy is contained in your book"

(264). Marie von Sivers and Rudolf Steiner also became acquainted with another of Blavatsky's old inner circle, the Duchess Wachmeister, who had supported HPB since the difficult days in Würzburg after she had fled India in 1885 and had begun to write the *Secret Doctrine*. Steiner was able to gain a sense of the history of this movement through some of its best representatives. This was the spiritual center to which Steiner felt he could honorably connect himself.

As the designated general secretary of the German branch, Steiner of course had an "audience" in Annie Besant. She was fifty-five years old; Steiner, forty-one. She was at the height of her spiritual development. Both sides were positively impressed with one another. Annie Besant, who was very busy, agreed to come to Berlin for the founding of the German branch. Steiner wrote of his first appearance before the gathered theosophists:

> The first time I spoke at the congress of the Theosophical Society in London, 1902, I said that the union of individual sections should be a matter of each section's contribution to the center of what it bears within itself. I sharply stressed that, above all, this was my intention for the German section. I made it clear that *this* section would never work merely according to set dogmas; it would engage in independent spiritual research, and, in meetings with the whole society, seek mutual understanding about the cultivation of genuine spiritual life. (28)

The ten precious days in London were not spent merely penetrating the secrets of the Theosophical Society. In every bit of free time, Steiner visited the museums and natural historical collections in London. He discovered William Turner's landscapes, which fascinated him so that Turner replaced Arnold Böcklin as Steiner's favorite modern artist. The natural historical museums were no less important to Steiner. In them "a number of ideas concerning the evolution of nature and human civilization became clear." "Thus, for me that visit to London was significant and stimulating. I traveled back to Germany with many different and deeply soul-stirring impressions" (28).

The return trip took Steiner first to Brussels, where he visited the Wiertz Museum. Here he found a painting that, although it cannot be numbered among the greatest works of art, seems to have impressed him deeply. After returning to Berlin, he often spoke about this piece and said that the task of contemporary humanity is to insure that the prophecy pictured in this painting does not become reality (51).

> The Museum in Brussels devoted to the work of the fascinating artist Antoine Wiertz (1806–1865) contains a picture entitled *The Things of the Present before the Human Being of the Future*. It depicts a giant, holding for his wife and his child to see certain tiny things—cannons, scepters, emblems of honor, triumphal arches, the banners belonging to different factions, all such as we know today. These important products of our culture seem tiny to the future world's way of thinking, and to a civilization that is an intellectual "giant" in comparison with ours. We need not dwell on the prophetic intention of this picture; but to an observer of the course of intellectual life who stands before it, it conjures up another idea. May not our modern philosophies of life and the world seem equally small to the scrutiny of future thought? (8, p. 172)

The intensity with which Rudolf Steiner speaks of this relatively insignificant painting lets one believe that it brought home to him once again the actual nature of his task. One can have the impression that Steiner recognized the wink of fate in all three of these experiences: the fact that the job of feuilleton editor did not materialize, the deeply soul-stirring experiences of London, and Wiertz's picture. Perhaps he even recognized in these the voice of the "Master" urging him to work courageously for Anthroposophy. In 1905, he wrote about his choosing Anthroposophy and that the "Master" had convinced him to do so. "I can only tell you, if the "Master" had not convinced me of the importance of theosophy for our time, in spite of all its problems, I would have continued after 1901 to merely write philosophical books and to speak of philosophical and literary subjects" (262). Destiny seems to have confirmed what the "Master" wanted to say quite clearly.

As a historian one can venture to say that Steiner's decision to work theosophically—or better, anthroposophically—must have been made between the letter of rejection from Vienna and before he returned to Berlin. Once he returned, he dove into the work of forming a German section of the Theosophical Society.

Before returning to Berlin, Steiner allowed himself a visit to Paris, where he arrived on the evening of July 13 and observed the celebrations of July 14 as an "enormous fair." He made his way once again to the museums, and also to the market halls and the historic places of the French Revolution. On the way from Paris to Berlin, he visited theosophical groups in Cologne, Düsseldorf and Kassel, and perhaps in other places also, to prepare for the coming founding of the German section and to introduce himself to the members of the Theosophical Society.

He didn't arrive in Berlin until July 29. The next day the intensive work leading up to the founding began. Almost daily, new difficulties arose. The arrival of the charter, which had to be prepared by Olcott in India, was delayed; the branches in Leipzig (Richard Bresch) and Hamburg (Bernhard Hubo) caused difficulties; the lodge in Kassel (Ludwig Noll) joined forces with Bresch; and the Stuttgart branch didn't answer any letters. It began to look as though the whole thing was going to fail in the last minute, as seven branches were needed to found a section. Difficulties also arose in trying to create a publication for the section. In whatever free time all these problems left him, Steiner corrected the proofs for *Christianity as Mystical Fact*. At the same time, he was engaged in an intense correspondence with Dr. Hübbe-Schleiden, who hoped to publish a book to coincide with the founding entitled *Serve the Eternal—Why does the Theosophical Society Need Its Members?* Steiner also read the initial proofs of this book and gave Hübbe-Schleiden ongoing suggestions concerning the layout and style of the text.

In these letters one finds many passages that show how Steiner saw the situation at that time. Perhaps the most important one is to be found in a letter dated August 16 in which Steiner shared his views quite openly with Hübbe-Schleiden.

> But dear, revered Doctor: Is not in this case perhaps what is best the enemy of what is good? The best thing would be something completely new, with no connection to what is already there. But I do believe that we can *perhaps* bring about the best solution even within the framework of the Theosophical Society. You are aware, based on our short acquaintance, that I could *never* do anything within the context of the Theosophical Society that would not live up to your intentions. The danger in which I have placed myself I can see clearly. I believe that I *must* place myself in this danger. What could come out of it? What *must* come out of it? Either we will be able to place a new picture that we think appropriate in the frame formed by the German section of the Theosophical Society—then the present personalities will have to decide how they want to relate to us—or we will not be able to do so. *Then* the sum of the present personalities, even if they have managed to form a section, by the very nature of this fact will sink into nothingness. For then they would have renounced for all time a movement footed on German spirituality. And we would be faced with a *tabula rasa*, for which

we would not be responsible, that would open a field for our work. For as long as that is not the case, we are condemned to inactivity. I would prefer to be completely *positive* in my work; the senseless, empty opposition I prefer to leave in the hands of Bresch and Hubo. I will build on the forces that enable me to help "students of the spirit" find their path of development. This alone will have to be the significance of my inauguration. For this reason, I prefer to be *positive* in everything....

What I believe is this: The movement that HPB and Annie Besant inaugurated can progress beyond the two of them.... This is the reason I have articulated the point of view that you also hold. (Correspondence II)

The boldness of this letter speaks for itself. It states clearly that the German section will only provide the frame in which a new, still-to-be-formed picture will be placed. Not less remarkable is the here-stated intent that Steiner will develop theosophy beyond what Blavatsky and Besant had done. Most significantly, Steiner's fundamental approach, which does lie in the propagation of a dogmatic teaching, is clearly articulated. "*I* will build on the forces that enable me to help 'students of the spirit' find their path of development."

This was truly Steiner's intent and he remained true to it. In only one aspect could the goals of this letter not be achieved. Steiner had been fundamentally mistaken in regard to Hübbe-Schleiden. He saw something in him that obviously was not there. He had written to Marie von Sivers on August 20, 1902: "A truly potent quality in the history of spiritual evolution lives in Hübbe-Schleiden" (262). This erroneous assessment of the man appears even stranger as he had revealed to Steiner—as Steiner himself told—his extremely obtuse theories possibly even before Steiner's first visit in Hannover (258). In addition, in 1892 Steiner had sarcastically torn apart one of Hübbe-Schleiden's pieces entitled "Existence as Joy, Pain and Love" by writing, "Zeus in tails with a white scarf—that is the impression that this Indian teaching of evolution draped in modern Darwinism makes" (30). By 1902, Steiner should have known the identity of the author even though it was published anonymously. We are presented with a riddle.

Perhaps the solution lies in the words of the above-mentioned letter. "For that reason I prefer to be positive in *everything*." This resolution to embrace positivity is the key without which one cannot understand Steiner's work in the following years. For a critical observer, there are many instances in Steiner's life that call forth questions. Why was he so willing to embrace the wishes and aspirations that people brought to him? Why did he not speak a clear "No!" or at least set out strict rules? Why did he energetically support initiatives that were questionable to him instead of trying to hinder them? He obviously wanted to be positive in everything and to help the initiatives that arose in any way possible.

On September 17, Marie von Sivers arrived in Berlin. Three days later she took over the management of the soon to be inaugurated German section, and after only another five days Steiner could write with satisfaction, "Miss von Sivers has begun her work. She is truly a great and radiant figure in the present misery. I am happy that she is here. I can count on her in *every* sense" (Correspondence). This passage actually says everything about Marie von Sivers—later, Marie Steiner—that needs to be said. She was born in 1867 in the Polish city of Wlotzlawek, the daughter of a Russian general. She grew up in St. Petersburg, where she received a rigorous training in the most important European languages as well as in the dramatic arts. From 1902 on, she placed herself totally in the service of Rudolf Steiner's work. Her work as the secretary of the German section was executed with precise attention to details, and her language skills made her an ideal colleague for Steiner, who only spoke German. Marie von Sivers shared with him the critical days around September 29 as Rudolf Steiner contemplated not calling a general assembly to formally constitute the section. Then came the final decision to go ahead, and Annie Besant was notified and agreed to come.

On October 8, 1902, in a lecture to the Giordano Bruno Society in the Bürgersaal of the Berlin Town Hall, Rudolf Steiner acknowledged his connection to theosophy: "Monism and Theosophy." He felt that it was important for him to present in this public manner the way in which he would represent theosophy. People should learn through his own words what he was doing and what his plans were. The German section was not to be founded secretly.

Two thoughts stand in the center of this lecture—evolution and self-knowledge. Natural evolution had brought humankind to its present stage of development and the conscious striving for knowledge. Natural scientific understanding was discovering the laws of what is, and what has become. However, the individual could, by directing the activity of conscious understanding upon himself, create his own laws and through his own forces further his development. The enhancement of knowledge through self-knowledge and creative self-development is theosophy.

Just a few days after this, Rudolf Steiner wrote, "Our die have—so to say—fallen. I gave a public lecture in the Giordano-Bruno Society entitled 'Monism and Theosophy.' It was surprisingly successful."

> Wolfgang Kirchback was the moderator that evening and he too was highly interested.... I certainly don't give myself over to illusions, but I think that those who were present left for the most part with the awareness that they were confronted with something that they should not simply let slip by. (Correspondence)

One week later, as was the custom in the Giordano-Bruno Society, Steiner's lecture came up for public discussion. The moderator for the evening, Otto Lehmann-Russbüldt, said by way of introduction that he personally wished the audience had not been merely the 250 or 300 who had been present, but rather "the 2,000 or 3,000 people who represent public cultural life in Germany." At the conclusion of his words he welcomed the theosophical movement "with the type of program that Dr. Steiner articulated" (51). Steiner's assessment of the lecture's effects seems to have been accurate.

These and an assortment of other facts rectify reports and presentations of Steiner's life that have enjoyed a fairly wide dissemination. There is an opinion that Steiner's relationships with other people and to other circles came to an abrupt end with the beginnings of his theosophical activities. It is also related that Steiner's lecture on October 8 was received with "icy bemusement," and that his behavior following the trip to London had changed suddenly; specifically, he had worn a different hat and a different suit. It was mentioned above that the hat and suit had been acquired for his meeting with Dr. Kanner from *Die Zeit* and had nothing to do with theosophy. There is no dearth of documentation for the fact that Steiner continued his activities in all the areas in which he had been working. As previously, he received requests for lectures with which he continued to comply. In 1904, he was still a council member of the Giordano-Bruno Society; he held his last lecture there in 1905. He sent a number of his colleagues on the council the magazine *Luzifer*, which he began to publish in 1903, and as late as December 1905 was thanked for this by Otto Lehmann-Russbüldt. "I want to thank you for the latest issue of *Luzifer*. The 'greater Guardian of the Threshold' awakened an extraordinary interest in me" (B 79/80). In other words, Steiner for his part did not break off any relationships, neither did he cloak himself in an aura of being unapproachable. He was, as one used to say, a "common man."

Following these preparations, the inaugural assembly of the German section of the Theosophical Society took place from October 19 to 21 in Berlin. In the opening address, Steiner sketched out a "picture of the time." The development of natural scientific and religious ways of thinking had come to an end. Natural scientific thought was unable to grasp the inner life of the human being; religious and moral sensibilities had lost the power to say anything about the world. Between these two approaches was an unbridgeable chasm. Only a new development and deepening of the spiritual forces of humanity could lead further. German spiritual-cultural life, by overcoming natural scientific materialism, was being called to an important task.

Mathilde Scholl reported the negotiations concerning the constitution of the section.

> This assembly went from 10:00 in the morning until 6:00 in the evening. Dr. Steiner moderated. Among the representatives of the German lodges there were a number of querulous individuals. They had a difficult time coming to agreement. Only through Dr. Steiner's wise guidance were we able to find a peaceful resolution. He impressed me especially by his tactful, calm, yet confident and firm posture in this somewhat chaotic setting. (Meffert)

A general council was finally selected. This can best be characterized by saying that it did nothing memorable and that it lost six of its members within a few years.

Then, about half of the gathering went to the train station to welcome Annie Besant. Rudolf Steiner, however, excused himself for a time in order to continue the series of lectures he was giving to the *Kommenden* to which he had given the subtitle "Anthroposophy." The next day, Annie Besant ceremoniously handed over the charter of the new section. Rudolf Steiner officially became the general secretary of the German section. That evening, Annie Besant gave a public lecture to roughly 400 people at the hotel Prince Albrecht about "Theosophy, its Meaning and Objects," which Rudolf Steiner then summarized in German. The following day, Annie

Besant left Berlin after having, probably on the last day of her stay, accepted Marie von Sivers and Rudolf Steiner into the Esoteric School (28).

In connection with the formation of the section, Rudolf Steiner had a much more important experience. Initially, he had not planned to develop theosophy as a magnificent set of teachings with a panoramic view of the higher worlds and evolution. His goal was to *help students of the spirit find the path of development.* He was concerned with supporting the development of individual human beings and the attainment of individual insight. Such insight begins as self-knowledge that is not satisfied merely to turn inward but strives to grasp individual destiny as it appears in the challenges presented by the world. Rudolf Steiner had first mentioned this path in his book *Mystics after Modernism*; he called it the third path and wrote that this was his own path. "*Trust* in the world must be one of the guides on this third path. *Courage* to follow this trust wherever it leads must be the other" (7). The path that leads into the world is that of one's own individual destiny as it leads through the tasks and challenges that come to meet one.

In order to describe this path into the world, Rudolf Steiner had planned to speak about "The Study of Karma" or, as he later expressed it, "Practical Karma Exercises" during the inaugural assembly of the German section. Only in 1924, after he had in fact begun to speak about such exercises and observations, did he speak about this initial attempt. Six times—in Prague, Stuttgart, Bern, Breslau, London, and Dornach—he mentioned this failed beginning. In London he said, "The first lecture that I was to give within the context of the German section of the Theosophical Society bore the title 'Practical Karma Exercises.' But the persons who at that time were present at the founding received a terrible shock when they saw this title, and still now I could describe to you the astral waves of anxiety that appeared in these older gentlemen" (240). They suspected that Steiner wanted to obliterate their "decades of work," meetings were arranged, and in the end Steiner could barely say what he had hoped to (239). "Then it was completely impossible to stick to our plan, because there was no chance for it to bear fruit. Thus the theosophical movement in Germany took on a more theoretical bent" (240).

It would have been a straight path from *Intuitive Thinking as a Spiritual Path*, over *Goethe's Worldview* and the *Mystic*, to an understanding of karma. In progressive stages of self-knowledge, the "I" would first have discovered its unfettered spiritual essence; then, step by step, the depths of its own intuitive nature; and then again, in a series of steps, it would have met itself upon the path of its own individual destiny. One would have learned to recognize that what comes to meet us seemingly from without belongs in fact to one's own self. Anthroposophy would have been developed in the manner it had been conceived, consciously as the self- and spiritual experience of each individual. But those individuals who came together in the Theosophical Society and later in the Anthroposophical Society could not take this path; the approach that Steiner initially envisioned had no chance to bear fruit. He faced the necessity of having to alter his plans and to begin his work in a manner that was not of his own making, for "in Germany there was too strong a tendency toward dogma, to a *mere* intellectual grasp of the doctrines" (264).

Thus Rudolf Steiner sacrificed his own, most inner intentions and placed himself in the service of those who were there. He addressed their questions and their deeper needs. Another twenty-one years would pass before he was able to begin the work that reflected his own inner intentions.

CHAPTER 24

ESTABLISHING THE GERMAN SECTION OF THE THEOSOPHICAL SOCIETY

In 1903 and 1904, Rudolf Steiner continued to teach at both the Workers' College and the Free University. These teaching positions provided him with an income that almost covered his living costs. He had to fight at that time, as he wrote in one letter, "for every crumb of bread" (39), and this led him to also take a teaching position at a school for girls. One of his students there remembered him as "the teacher who never scolded." It was in this way, financially completely independent, that Rudolf Steiner began very gently to establish the theosophical work, first in Berlin, and then in Weimar, Düsseldorf and Cologne. The only real help or support he had at this time was Marie von Sivers. She took on all the organizational tasks and much of the correspondence. She probably also suggested in late autumn that he move into a cottage in Schlactensee that had been placed at her disposal. Perhaps she was attempting to alleviate the difficult financial situation. In any case, Steiner moved into the cottage with his wife in the beginning of 1903 and stayed there until October of that year.

The cottage was located idyllically—close to the lake and not far from the forest. It was a place where one could work in peace, but Steiner had to take into account the long daily trip to and from Berlin, where he had courses seven days a week. His collaboration with Marie von Sivers led to a close friendship. She was at that time thirty-six years old. She focused all her artistic energy on the theosophical work. As early as 1903, Steiner wrote her in a letter from Weimar, "You understand me. That gives me strength; it sets my wings free" (262). It seems clear that Steiner had shared his fundamental ideas with her in these first months. He gave her an introduction to Goethe's theory of color in March 1903 using the simplest materials—a candle and transparent colored paper (262 & 291a). From June 30 to July 20, he traveled with her to London for the congress of the European sections. They were treated as special guests this time with accommodations in Esher near London, close to where Annie Besant stayed when she was in London. Annie Besant was in India that summer, but Steiner made the acquaintance of the elderly Colonel Olcott and, as Elisabeth Vreede recalled, spoke with extraordinary force in the assembly of the sections about the spiritual foundations of German culture, with no attempt to gain the sympathy of the audience (Vreede & 34). Together with Marie von Sivers, he once again visited the museums, again viewed Turner's paintings, and took the opportunity to visit "Oxford with its wonderful character and quite remarkable university" (39). Then they returned to Berlin. That summer Marie von Sivers's friend, Maria von Strauch-Spettini, and at times Olga von Sivers visited Schlactensee. The more peaceful weeks of summer in the quiet by the lake gave space for intense spiritual work (Rudolf Steiner Studies, I).

The close collaboration led, however, to difficulties. Anna Steiner was naturally aware of the intensity and depth of the friendship between Rudolf Steiner and Marie von Sivers. The theosophical world was foreign to her, so she could find no inner connection. A certain sense of distrust awoke in her. This had also occurred once earlier. Already in 1897 she had, after being swayed by the Weimar gossip, reproached Steiner soundly: he had been seen wandering the streets with a person of questionable reputation. Steiner wrote her at that time, "No distrust, my dear Anna! Until you have managed to ban this ill-fated distrust from yourself, you will be afraid of every little thing" (39).

The close collaboration between Rudolf Steiner and Marie von Sivers was inconceivable for the then prevalent middle-class mentality and led to all sorts of gossip. Although Steiner repeatedly sought understanding and assured his "dear, good Anna" time and again "that I love you, love you deeply, as always" (39), she was unable to understand either the theosophical work or his friendship with Marie von Sivers, without whom he was unable to do this work. But Steiner was not willing to let himself be locked into a "Philistine cage" (39). He counted on the continued close contact with Marie von Sivers. Anna Steiner drew from this the only consequence that her point of view would allow. In the spring of 1904, she left Rudolf Steiner. They never divorced. Anna Steiner passed away in March 1911. For Rudolf Steiner, who was well aware of what she had done for him, the situation held no solution. He had told her in various ways: "Try to understand that I have a task to fulfill, that I am not being led by personal intentions" (39). He was not able to act differently. But he understood Anna Steiner well. He wrote to Johanna Mücke, his colleague at the Workers' College, "And don't ever forget: my wife, *given her point of view*, was absolutely right" (39).

With these things in the background, the theosophical work in Berlin began. Steiner gave a lecture each Saturday evening in the Berlin branch. These lectures, given to an audience of twenty or thirty people, covered the "whole of theosophy." In addition, Rudolf Steiner led "theosophical conversations" on Tuesday or Saturday evening or afternoons. Only five or six people participated in these. The small number didn't bother Steiner in the least. He worked with the people who came and never complained that they were too few or not as interesting as they might be. The outer conditions were more than humble. In 1923, Steiner related, "For instance, during the first years in Berlin, I held lectures in a room in the back of which one heard the beer mugs clinking. It was a sort of bar that opened onto the street. When this was no longer available, they moved us into a space that was a sort of stable" (258).

It seems possible that Steiner viewed these gatherings as exercises through which he could gain a connection to the way of thinking of the members and those interested in theosophy. He struggled to find forms of expression and means of representation and had to truly gain an understanding of the world in which he was now given to work. For about a year, Steiner felt his way into this world. Then, in the fall of 1903, he began to present theosophy systematically in lectures for members and to work on a book with the title *Theosophy*. Leading up to Christmas, he gave eight lectures concerning the astral world; in January 1904, two lectures concerning Atlantis; then six lectures about the world of the spirit.

He had, however, no intention of only cultivating the theosophical work in small settings. In the spring of 1903, he began to organize public lectures, which then continued from March 1904 regularly each winter through 1918. The venue was almost always the "House of the Architects" on the Wilhelmstrasse. In these lectures, Steiner developed the key gestures of theosophy—and later, Anthroposophy—in connection with events of the time or through the presentation of symptomatic individuals. Over the years, these lectures drew an ever-growing audience. In the beginning, they took place in the small auditorium (Hall C), and later in the large Hall A. In his *Autobiography*, Steiner writes:

> The work within the existing branches of the Theosophical Society—the necessary point of departure—was only a part of our activity. Our primary work consisted of arranging my public lectures to people quite unrelated to the Theosophical Society; they came to the lectures solely because of their content. Thus, the nucleus of what would become the Anthroposophical Society was formed within the Theosophical Society, partly by those who had heard the public lectures and what I said about the spirit world, and also by those who discovered this form of spiritual knowledge through their activity within one or the other trend of theosophy. (28)

There is a modest indication here that the establishment of first the Theosophical Society and then later the Anthroposophical Society was accomplished practically on the strength of his and Marie von Sivers's work. That was in fact the case. When the German section was founded, it had about 130 members; by 1910, due to Steiner's lecturing, the number had grown to 2000, most of whom had found their way to theosophy through Steiner's public lectures. Of the 130 original members, only a small number remained active; most of the prominent personalities from the time of the founding either withdrew during the first few years or ceased to play significant roles.

In order to present theosophy in a manner that would make it palatable for the spiritually seeking modern individual, Rudolf Steiner founded the magazine *Luzifer*. The idea of publishing a monthly magazine had first been broached in September 1902. It took some time, however, before the first issue appeared, as there was too little of everything that was needed: money, subscribers and capable coworkers. The needed start-up capital came together through a series of donations in the spring of 1903. In the middle of June, the first issue appeared with a light blue cover and cinnabar lettering: *Luzifer—A Magazine for Soul Life and Spirit Culture—Theosophy*. With the name *Luzifer*, Steiner consciously expressed a connection with the magazine of the same name that Helena Blavatsky had published at the end of the 1880s (54). In his introductory article he did not, however, mention Blavatsky but formulated that the intent of the magazine was to develop a true science of the spirit that would be able to satisfy the deeper soul needs of humanity.

> The most significant symbol of wisdom, revealed to us through research, is Lucifer, translated as the bearer of the light. All who strive

for knowledge, for wisdom, are children of Lucifer. The Chaldean stargazers, the wise Egyptian priests, the Indian Brahmins: they were all children of Lucifer. Even the very first human was a child of Lucifer as he let the serpent teach him "what is good, what is evil."... What Lucifer brought to them they saw as divine. It was through Lucifer that they had a God. The heart would have to be severed from the head if we wished to make God and Lucifer opponents. (34)

The other contributors to this first issue were Marie von Sivers, who wrote enthusiastically about Annie Besant; Annie Besant, with the transcript of a lecture; Hübbe-Schleiden, who began a series of articles about "The Ideals of Life"; and Ludwig Deinhard, who submitted an article about the dousing rod.

In the subsequent issues of *Luzifer*, one finds a three-part series about "Initiation and the Mysteries," which must come as a surprise to anyone with linguistic sensibility. Suddenly, Rudolf Steiner is speaking a completely new language. Already the first sentence makes one take note: "The place that one enters when the secrets of the world are revealed to him was called by the ancient wise men the 'garden of ripeness.' There is no flower in this garden whose fruit has not ripened, no egg that has not ripened the life burgeoning within it. Yet the path that leads to the 'narrow door' through which the garden is entered is described as being dark and dangerous" (34). Such words do not speak to reason or the cool thinker. Here we find no argumentation—everything is suddenly pictorial, a mood is created. The new breath that stirs in these words seems to be quite different than what we have heard from Steiner in the past. Steiner was conscious of this quality that he now used repeatedly. In a letter to Marie Steiner he wrote, "I gave the lecture in the language of the mystic. This was not a discussion. I wanted to insure that on this evening the mood that the lecture was calculated to bring forth remained" (262).

In the articles mentioned above, one finds passages that appeal to the feeling of truth that exists in each and every soul. "But above the altar upon which the true mystic lays his sacrifice was written in all the times of which we know in letters of flame the highest law: *Nature is the greatest guide to the Divine; and the conscious search of human beings for the sources of wisdom shall follow the tracks of her sleeping will*" (34).

It was in this form of language, in which the higher truths are brought directly to expression, that a year later Rudolf Steiner wrote the book that describes the path of the soul to the spirit, *How To Know Higher Worlds*. It seems obvious that these keen, powerful presentations were meant to reach people directly.

But the next series of articles—"Reincarnation and Karma from the Point of View of Natural Science" and "How Karma Works"—brings again a new quality of language to expression. The ideas of reincarnation and karma are presented in simple, clear thought images—not one-sided philosophical formulations—that show the unprejudiced thoughtful reader how these ideas can connect to modern scientific views. Toward the end of the presentation, the thoughts are borne up by themselves and need only the support of inner observation. These articles are a precursor to another of Steiner's key written works: *Theosophy*.

The articles published in *Luzifer* in 1903 allow us to accompany Steiner as he crafts the new forms of presentation and thought through which he intends to develop his spiritual teaching. At the core of these changes, one can sense a powerful inspiration. Rudolf Steiner placed himself in the stream that resonated with the work of the greatest spiritual teachers of humankind.

Rudolf Steiner described the mood of bustling activity that accompanied the work on the magazine with a touch of humor.

> Then we founded the magazine *Luzifer*. Naturally, we began with only a small number of subscriptions, but the number grew relatively quickly and we never really had a deficit as we only printed the number of copies that could be sold. The distribution was organized so that when an issue had been written and printed it was sent to my apartment in large bundles. [Marie Steiner] and I glued on the mailing wrappers. I addressed them. Then each of us took a wash basket and carried them to the post office. We felt that it worked out quite well. It was my job to write the things, to give the lectures. Frau Doktor managed the entire Anthroposophical Society, only without a secretary at that time. If she had had a secretary, she would have had to do her work too. So we did it all alone and we never did more than one could want, very concretely. We took as many steps forward as the situation allowed. For instance, we never carried laundry baskets that were too big—just almost too big. When the number of subscriptions grew, we made more trips back and forth. (258)

Beginning in January 1904, *Luzifer* merged with the journal *Gnosis* and appeared as *Lucifer-Gnosis*. The pleasing cover of the first seven issues was replaced by a more sensible olive-green and the layout was changed. Steiner started the year with a series of four articles on "The Aura of the Human Being." He began to write clear, concrete descriptions of the suprasensory. A feeling for the suprasensory can only be awakened through the portrayal of spiritual realities. At the same time, from Steiner's pen came remarks concerning contemporary culture, about the theosophical work, book reviews, responses to questions, etc. The journal also contained contributions from other authors about questions of interest to the readers.

In June began the publication of the series called "How to Attain Knowledge of Higher Worlds," and in July came "From the Akashic Record," These portrayals of spiritual content balanced those more focused on the methods of knowing. The articles "From the Akashic Record" appeared, interestingly enough, without the name of the author. The shorter articles contained numerous hints for the interested reader. In August 1903, Steiner expressed his disagreements with the views of C. W. Leadbeater. In November 1904, he called attention to the development of modern physics, which was replacing primitive materialism with an electrodynamic model.

Lucifer-Gnosis was soon awaited excitedly by its readers, who enjoyed often receiving a handwritten greeting from either Rudolf Steiner or Marie von Sivers on the wrapper. Beginning in the spring of 1905, the demands on Rudolf Steiner's time by the Theosophical Society—his travel schedule and the amount of questions and wishes from the members—had increased so much that the publication of the journal began to lag behind schedule. At the same time, there were too few authors who could write articles able to give the readers guidance. In a letter from the beginning of August 1906, Steiner wrote, "The manuscript of issue number 32 of *Luzifer* is finally finished. This time I wrote the whole thing, from the first line to the last" (262).

Since the demands continued to grow, and as it was not Steiner's intent to merely see the pages of the journal filled up with anything, it began to appear more seldom. During this period Elise Wolfram, a not ungifted theosophist in her own right but seemingly somewhat ambitious, came up with, as Steiner relates, "the 'genial' idea that *Luzifer* should be published regularly." She suggested to him that he turn the editorial work and the publishing over to her. Steiner had no choice but to become "rough, rough, rough" and dismiss the suggestion in the sharpest manner possible (262). He took questions concerning publication very seriously. When he founded the weekly *The Goetheanum* with Albert Steffen in 1921, he took time whenever possible to work through each issue in depth with Steffen. When *Die Drei* got caught up in unproductive, meaningless discussions in 1922, he admonished them sharply. When the weekly *Anthroposophy* printed an article from an opponent of Anthroposophy, the editor was let go without notice. In any case, the journal that he had created was to have a certain style and content, not merely become a well-meaning newsletter; *Luzifer* was there to lead its readers along the paths of the spirit. Even more important to Steiner, however, than writing the articles were the individual relationships. The last issue of *Luzifer*, number 35, appeared in May 1908.

We have gotten ahead of ourselves with this quick history of the journal *Luzifer*. Let us return to the year 1903. Throughout this entire year, Steiner's Theosophical work was not only a year of preparation but also one of change and of finding a new orientation. We mustn't forget that Steiner's original intention was "to help 'students of the spirit' find their path of development." The exposition of this path of inner schooling was to have begun with "Practical Karma Exercises." Such an approach would have necessitated working through with individual students the basic categories of a conceptualization of karma and the secrets of how to learn from karma through courageously taking up life's tasks, learning through what comes to meet us.

Now Rudolf Steiner, who took up his tasks with enormous energy and unflagging persistence, found himself confronted with the necessity of taking on an entirely different challenge. In a letter to Mathilde Scholl from May 1, 1903, he wrote, "My next exoteric task is to disseminate the teachings, as much as I can" (264). This new task asked from Steiner something that was not really a part of him. In 1894, he had written to Rosa Mayreder:

> I do not teach; I simply relate what I have lived through inwardly. I relate it the way I experienced it. Everything in my book is meant personally. This applies also to the form of the thoughts. A more professorial nature could expand upon it. Perhaps I could, too, at the right time. At the moment I wanted to depict the biography of a soul that raises itself toward freedom.... Perhaps the time of teaching such things is past. I find interest now in philosophy only in as much as it is individual experience. (39)

Initially, Steiner did not think of himself as a teacher. He thought that the time in which one could teach the things that were important to him was past. But then he had to become a teacher to develop a style of teaching, a way of presenting things didactically. An entire generation of anthroposophists experienced Steiner as "our great teacher."

The new *exoteric* task "to disseminate the teachings, as much as I can" required modification, even transformation on Steiner's part. That needed time and the months that they spent in Schlactensee were, in spite of all the work, a time in which Steiner was somewhat removed from the tumult of Berlin. He could spend time at the lake or in the woods and work on this transformation of the thought forms. The articles "Initiation and the Mysteries" were written in Schlactensee.

This period came to an end in the beginning of October 1903. Rudolf Steiner and his wife moved to an apartment at 17 Motzstrasse. Marie von Sivers moved there at the same time and took her own apartment. Motzstrasse, which was to be a focal point for Steiner's work until 1918, is just west of the old city center between Nollendorf-Platz and Prager-Platz. The apartments were not in the main house, which stood directly on the street, but behind it off a small courtyard. Here Steiner began to draft *Theosophy*, which was finished in the spring of 1904.

This book, written as an introductory and exercise book, casts light on the way in which he solved the problem of having to teach. In the foreword there is a variation on "I don't teach, I merely relate": "The author of this book describes nothing to which he cannot bear witness based on experience—the kind of experience that one can have in these regions. Only what is in this sense self-experience is presented" (comp. 9, 1st ed.).

What is meant becomes apparent in the introduction. The book is not intended to merely impart knowledge. It would lead the reader to a quality of knowing that is transformative. Rudolf Steiner writes that one can fulfill his task as a human being without understanding anything of the mainstream sciences, but "one cannot be 'human' in the highest sense of the word without drawing closer to the essence and destiny of humanness as they are described in 'higher wisdom'" (9, 1st ed.). In a later edition, Steiner revised this to read: "Without drawing closer to the essence and destiny of humanness as they are revealed through suprasensory knowledge" (9). This is a motif that we have already encountered in *Mystics after Modernism*, knowledge that has a formative effect on the spiritual. "If I were a king and knew it not, then I would not be a king" (Meister Eckhardt, *German Sermons*).

There is a clear connection between what a person knows, the knowledge that gives us an orientation, and what we do. Steiner had this connection in mind when, in opposition to the "Society for Ethical Culture," he wrote, "Ethical behavior is always the result of a time's, a people's, or a person's spectrum of knowledge. For this reason great individuals who bring new wisdom to their time also bring a new quality to the way of life. The Messiah of a new truth is always the bringer of a new morality" (31).

The intention of *Theosophy* was not to bring a new truth. It is a book of exercises, a path upon which the individual can find the way to an awakening in the spirit. Already in the chapter "The Nature of the Human Being," the reader finds an evolving chain of thought that leads him upward as in a spiral until he recognizes the nature of his humanness in the body that has formed, the soul in its presence and the spirit in *status nascendi*.

The chapter "Reincarnation of the Spirit and Destiny" was of special interest for Steiner. He reworked it for each subsequent edition. Steiner calls attention to the essential nature of human life and shows how, on the one hand, experience flows from the world into the human being and is preserved in memory and, on the other hand, human existence is impressed upon the world through individual action. Then he shows how what is taken up and learned from the world is transformed into human capacities and how what flows from the human being into the world through action lives on and is transformed. Based on these observations, Steiner goes on to develop the ideas of reincarnation and destiny in a way that can make sense to a serious reader. He writes, for instance:

> In the effects of its actions, the human soul lives on in a second independent life. This gives us grounds for examining how the processes of destiny enter life. Something happens to us, "bumps into us," enters our life as if by chance—or so we tend to think at first. We can become aware, however, that each one of us is the result of many such "chance" occurrences. If at the age of forty I take a good look at myself and refuse to be content with an empty, abstract concept of the "I" as I ponder my soul's essential nature, I may well conclude that I am nothing more and nothing less than what I have become through what has happened to me until now as a matter of destiny. (9, p. 84)

One is led to experience the "I" not only within oneself, but also in everything that works upon us formatively from outside: destiny or karma. If one continues to follow these observations, one comes to experience one's own "I" actively at work in the processes of karma.

The entire book consists of such revelatory observations and, as it unfolds the teachings, gives the reader ways of looking at life as the basis for understanding practical karma-exercises. The composition of the book, the clearly articulated thoughts that allow one to see through them to the realities of which they speak, is remarkable. The book teaches us to *see* what is being spoken of. We shouldn't lose sight of what Steiner wrote about in his *Autobiography* concerning this time in his life.

> For me the period between 1902 and about 1907 or 1908 was when I experienced, with all the powers of soul, the realities and beings that approached me from the spirit world. Specific insights developed from those more general experiences of the spirit world. Many experiences arise when writing a book like *Theosophy*. At every step I endeavored to retain a connection with scientific thinking. This assumes particular forms as a spiritual experience deepens and broadens. (28)

Steiner had written about his comprehensive view of the essential nature of the human being in a purely conceptual form in *Intuitive Thinking as a Spiritual Path*. In the years following the "transformation of soul," this view led through meditative practice to the experience of the "inner spiritual human" who lives "in the spirit, completely emancipated from the physical organism" (28). After 1901, what had been clear to him as an idea and as an inner experience came to meet him in a new form. He experienced "with all the powers of soul, the realities and beings that approached [him] from the spirit world." He experienced the perceptual side of the spirit. Helena Blavatsky, for instance, related such experiences verbatim, just as they appeared to her. Steiner brought them into articulated thought forms, which changed from chapter to chapter as the subject matter changed. This clearly ideated presentation of what are in themselves overwhelming spiritual impressions is Steiner's greatest accomplishment. He did not let himself be overcome by the spiritual realities and beings.

> I do not adopt a style that allows subjective feelings to be detected in the sentences. In writing, I subdue what comes from warmth and deeper feelings to a dry, mathematical style. *This* style alone can be an awakener. For the readers themselves must awaken inner warmth and feeling. They cannot let those feelings simply flow into them from a description while their attentiveness remains passive. (28)

From 1902 to 1904, Steiner was joined by his first real coworkers—coworkers who were able to take on tasks and were not merely tasks themselves. Naturally, here we have to mention Marie von Sivers, an extraordinary personality without whom Rudolf Steiner would not have been able to do the work. In a manner similar to Edith Maryon, who later worked with Steiner on the large sculpture in Dornach, Marie von Sivers placed all her abilities at the service of the shared work. Among other things, she took care of the correspondence, rented venues, had posters printed, and took care of travel planning and accommodations. She knew what was needed and followed up on the details. When she realized that it was impossible for Steiner to cope with the demands and routines of the various publishers, she founded the Philosophisch-Theosophisch publishing house and together with Johanna Mücke ran it as an intermediary between the fruits of Steiner's spiritual work and the wishes of the readers—a sterling example of a business as described later in Steiner's threefold social impulse.

The efforts made by Marie von Sivers and her understanding of what was needed were essential for Steiner to fulfill his task. Already in 1904, he wrote her: "*Together* with you, my dear, I will always have a feeling of certainty" (262). In 1911, when she became seriously ill, he minimized his own work and wrote, when he had to request a postponement of a planned trip to Finland:

> If I am to fulfill the demands mentioned above and the give the theosophists what they deserve, the needs that arise during a longer stay can only be taken care of by Fraulein von Sivers. On shorter trips here in Germany I travel alone. Still it takes a good deal of spiritual strength to not decimate my physical forces during each trip. No one can replace Fraulein von Sivers, even if this fact is not readily apparent for an onlooker. (262)

Mathilde Scholl (1868–1941) stepped into the picture at the founding of the German section in 1902. She was a questioning, striving theosophist who soon recognized Steiner's significance, although at that time she was a follower of Annie Besant, whose book *Esoteric Christianity and the Minor Mysteries* she had translated, a translation that was published in 1903. She became an esoteric student of Rudolf Steiner quite quickly and, in 1905, took the initiative to publish a newsletter for the German section. She had a knack for this sort of work and certainly relieved Marie von Sivers and Rudolf Steiner of a variety of tasks, especially as she worked in complete harmony with Steiner, free of personal ambitions. During the Krishnamurti affair, she backed Steiner energetically and with a sharp pen. Following her initiative, the council of the German section opposed Annie Besant's questionable actions. In 1914, her work for the Anthroposophical Society came to an abrupt end. She turned her attention to private studies and courses in Dornach.

A letter from Steiner to Marie von Sivers from March 1907 indicates that he was at times concerned about Mathilde Scholl. "Scholl is letting herself be magnetized by Weiler. Such things I can *only* acknowledge *after the fact*. If I were to do anything else, it would appear to be against Weiler. From *his* point of view, he is in the right. But that Scholl doesn't realize that she abdicates the position she should have here when she does such things is difficult" (262).

The next collaborator appeared at the general assembly of the section in October 1903. This was Adolf Arenson (1855–1936) from Stuttgart. Arenson had become interested in spiritism and the esoteric and had independently found his way to the idea of reincarnation. He attended the 1903 general assembly as the delegate from the branch in Stuttgart. Upon his return to Stuttgart, he reported about his meeting with Steiner, "This is the one for whom I have been waiting for the past twenty-one years." In 1905, Arenson founded with Carl Unger what would become the most important branch in Stuttgart. In 1906, he became the sub-warden responsible for the work of the Esoteric School in Stuttgart. He took on a variety of tasks for Steiner: he composed all the music for the mystery plays, proofed a majority of Steiner's lecture transcripts for publication by the Philosophisch-Theosophisch publishing house, and with his *Leitfaden durch 50 Vortragszyklen* completed the first indexed guide to Steiner's work.

In February 1904, Carl Unger (1878–1929) traveled to Berlin to the Motzstrasse "to protest loudly about the fact that one never heard anything from the section." He brought his complaint, however, quite moderately to Steiner. Marie von Sivers was called into the meeting and suggested that, since *Theosophy* was almost finished, the time had come to start the lecture tour they had been thinking about. That evening, Unger attended one of Steiner's lectures. "This lecture brought home with one blow the certainty that this was a man to whom I would dedicate my life. My strongest impression was: Before me stands a seer *and a knower*" (Unger, *Schriften*, I).

Dr. Carl Unger had trained as a technical engineer. He was also interested in the methodological, reasoned acquisition of Anthroposophy. Steiner was highly appreciative of the work of this philosophically schooled technician. Soon after meeting Steiner, Unger established a small precision-tool factory near Stuttgart, which he operated in such a way as to have enough time for his spiritual-scientific work. In 1913, he was appointed, along with Marie von Sivers and Michael Bauer, to the three-person executive council of the newly established Anthroposophical Society. In 1914 and 1915, he volunteered his skills at the building site in Dornach. Each week he commuted for three days to Dornach to oversee the accounts.

At the end of March 1904 in Weimar, Michael Bauer and Rudolf Steiner become acquainted. Bauer, who worked as a teacher, was an independent, striving mystic who had adopted his own, very strict path of schooling. On March 25, he traveled to Weimar to attend one of Steiner's lectures. Here, too, the first encounter seems to have been decisive. Before long, Bauer was leading the branch he founded in Nuremberg. He was an esoteric student of Steiner, and, like Arenson in Stuttgart, was responsible for the work of the Esoteric School in Nuremberg. He was appointed to the executive council of the Anthroposophical Society in 1912. He was highly respected both in the section and in the society as a whole, because those who listened to his lectures could experience that he had tapped his own sources and could follow his own path. This was also true in his relationship to Steiner. Although he acknowledged and revered Steiner, Bauer maintained his spiritual independence and did not hesitate to voice his own views.

In the beginning of April 1904, Ita Wegman (1876–1943), who had visited Steiner in 1902 when she came from Holland to make the acquaintance of the German theosophists, discovered him anew. She attended a lecture about Goethe's "Fairy Tale" at the House of the Architects and felt as though Steiner were speaking directly to her. She soon became one of Steiner's esoteric students. At that time she was working as a Swedish massage therapist. In 1905, Steiner recommended that she take the *Arbitur* exam and then study medicine in Zurich. She dropped out of sight in the work of the society for many years until she opened a clinic in 1921 in Arlesheim and became one of Rudolf Steiner's coworkers. More on this later.

Finally, in 1904, Steiner made the acquaintance of Sophie Stinde (1853–1915) and her friend Duchess Kalckreuth (1856–1929), who together led the work in Munich in an exemplary manner, as well as with Günther Wagner (1842–1930), who soon volunteered to be the section's librarian. Thus, in a remarkably short period in 1903/04, many of the people who would be important collaborators in Steiner's work found their way to each other: Arenson, a quiet scholar and musician; Unger, a sharp thinker and engineer; Bauer, a mystic; and Sophie Stinde, a painter. For most of the theosophists, however, Steiner was just one theosophical teacher among others. Many held him to be the most gifted of Annie Besant's students. Others connected him with Franz Hartmann. He was treated pretty much as one would treat anyone. This was easy as Steiner did not make much ado about himself. He was modest and chose to make do on his travels with the simplest accommodations. Naturally, on his travels he sought to visit the members in their own apartments and become acquainted with them in their own milieu. Sophie Stinde related that during Annie Besant's visit in Munich in 1904 she had sent him to the printer with a job and Steiner had gone without question. The queen of the Theosophical Society was without a doubt Annie Besant. Sophie Stinde comfortably wrote to a student who had not been able to hear her: "There is of course no other comparable speaker in the world, but Dr. Steiner and Dr. Hartmann are also good speakers and it would be worthwhile for the students to hear them" (Kleeberg).

In 1904, Steiner was able to begin traveling in order to establish the German section. In 1903, his travels were limited to short trips to Weimar, Cologne, Düsseldorf and London, as he was still teaching in Berlin. In addition he needed to prepare inwardly for the work and wanted to finish the book *Theosophy*. His trips in 1904 also had to be planned between courses, during the Easter and summer holidays, as he was dependent on the teaching for his income. He still managed to make five longer lecture tours. The first one was to Stuttgart, Munich, Zürich, and Lugano, then back to Berlin by way of Stuttgart, Munich and Nuremberg.

His experiences during this first trip were varied. In Stuttgart, where up to this point no theosophists had appeared publicly, he immediately sparked interest. Almost 500 people attended the first public lecture. The members from Stuttgart were exuberant when they saw the full auditorium, and Steiner was able to bring the members—who were somewhat at odds with one another—to the beginnings of a collaboration. The situation in Munich was much more difficult. Other theosophists had spoken publicly there before and had effectively scared away the audience. In addition there were a number of heterogeneous theosophical groups in the city. Steiner had to visit each of them. Steiner held talks and discussions in small circles to lay the foundation for future work. He then traveled—now together with Marie von Sivers—over the Alps to Lugano, to visit the group that had formed there around Günther Wagner. The return trip took them again to Stuttgart, as Steiner thought it would be productive to build immediately on the positive experience of his earlier visit. He spoke in Stuttgart on "Goethe as a Theosophist." He had given a lecture three weeks earlier in Berlin with the same title and had spoken about Goethe's "Fairy Tale." This basic motif of the anthroposophic movement was now sounded in Stuttgart. After leaving Stuttgart, Steiner visited Michael Bauer in Nuremberg. The goal was to deepen his initial encounter with Bauer and to become acquainted with the members in his area.

From March 7 to 14, Rudolf Steiner traveled to London. It was necessary for the further development of the theosophical work to create an esoteric school for those individuals who strove to deepen theosophy through soul-spiritual exercises and to advance to an independent experience of the suprasensory. Since he was working within the context of the Theosophical Society, he connected this work, as everyone expected of him, to the Esoteric School formed by Helena Blavatsky, which was led then by Annie Besant. Steiner met with Besant "to gain her full esoteric authorization for my efforts in this field" (262). On May 10, Annie Besant appointed him to be "the arch-warden of the E.S. in Germany and the Austrian empire, with full authority, as my representative, to call meetings of the school, to organize groups, and to appoint wardens." (264).

It would be interesting to know how Steiner experienced these things. He was silent about it. It is certain that he had been giving Marie von Sivers esoteric guidance before his appointment to "arch-warden" (262). It is also certain that his guidance was fairly independent of what Annie Besant had related to him, although in the first period he gave his students the opening meditation of the Esoteric School ("More radiant than the sun...") that had originated with Helena Blavatsky. He also recommended Mabel Collins's book *Light on the Path* as a text to study and also used other materials from the Esoteric School. But he was not so naïve that he couldn't recognize what was questionable in the Theosophical Society and the Esoteric School. Just four months after his appointment as "arch-warden," he wrote to Marie von Sivers, calling her attention to what lay ahead: "There is, I believe, a crisis looming in the T.S. that will also affect us" (262). Such a statement indicates that Steiner had recognized the problem that was there during his trip to London.

In regard to those who strove for esoteric deepening, there was no call to sow skepticism and doubt right at the beginning of the work. For the students, it was important to set out on the path and to develop a consciousness that one is not alone but striving with others. "Truth experienced in community / Becomes cosmic force in human striving" (40). Hence, Rudolf Steiner took up the practices and myths with a positive gesture. He also worked with the forms of representation that lived in the school with the same positivity, as he felt that they would have a good effect on the development of the students' souls. In regard to the content of the schooling, Steiner followed his own path.

At the time, he was also conscious of being led. In a letter to one member of the Esoteric School, he wrote, "I can only guide to the extent that the sublime Master who leads me can give me guidance. I follow *him* completely consciously in everything that I say to others" (264). One can imagine this "Master" with whom Steiner communicated in purely spiritual manner as a purely spiritual figure. When Friedrich Rittelmeyer asked him "if he saw him sometimes," Steiner answered, "I don't need to" (Rittelmeyer). Rudolf Steiner wrote of the "voice of the Master" (264) and of the admonishments that the Master "clearly let sound" (262). What the Master spoke was decisive. "I have the charge to cultivate the Christian element" (264). And: "The German theosophical movement is of special significance," for the Germans were the harbingers of an emergent culture and, so spoke the Master's voice, "read the great idealists: J. G. Fichte, Jakob Böhme, and especially Angelus Silesius" (262).

This deserves to be taken note of. This Master obviously says something different than the Masters of which Annie Besant spoke. Perhaps one can even say that the spiritual authority to which Steiner turned differed from the other Masters of which Blavatsky, Olcott, Sinnett and Besant spoke in a significant manner. In that Steiner turned to his own Master, he raised the level of his independent authority and was in a certain sense protected from the attacks of the other Masters.

One can naturally raise the question of why Rudolf Steiner, who until 1901 was a representative of individualism, now listened to the voice of a

"Master." In some ways the answer is simple: Just as one individual learns through communicating with other individuals, the spiritual researcher also learns through communicating. We do not follow such communications blindly, but with insight and understanding. We make what we have acquired our own. We remain individualists, but our field of vision broadens, just as it does with anyone who is introduced to new ideas and makes them one's own.

From June 18 to 22, Steiner traveled to Amsterdam for the congress of the Federation of the European Sections. The meeting was organized in the style of a scientific congress. As though in different departmental faculties, theosophists spoke about topics of natural science, comparative religion, the brotherhood of humanity, esotericism, etc. Steiner spoke in the "philosophical faculty" about "Mathematics and Esotericism," and showed that higher mathematics, with the concept of infinity, leads into the worlds of the spirit and thus is an important facet of esoteric schooling (35). The dominant figure at the congress was without question Annie Besant, who enriched the gathering with two lectures—"The New Psychology" and "The Being of Esotericism." Steiner wrote very positively about the congress and especially about Besant's lectures in *Lucifer-Gnosis*, calling attention to the impulse that—although in a still imperfect art—strove toward a "spiritualization of all civilization" (34).

At Steiner's invitation, Annie Besant arrived on September 15 to start a ten-day lecture tour through Germany. The trip took her from Hamburg through Berlin, Weimar, Munich, and Stuttgart to Cologne. Marie von Sivers, Rudolf Steiner, Mrs. Bright and Bertram Keightley accompanied her. Marie von Sivers translated the lectures, and Rudolf Steiner gave a summary of each lecture in German. In Berlin, Weimar and Cologne, Annie Besant spoke about "The New Psychology," and in Munich and Stuttgart about "Theosophy and Christianity." For members, she spoke about the work in the branches and about "The Human Being as Master of his Destiny." At the time, this trip was certainly quite important for the German theosophical movement. Not only did many of the members have the opportunity to speak with Annie Besant personally, they also experienced themselves as part of a worldwide movement. She also was able to reach the general public; the auditoriums were at times overfilled.

For Rudolf Steiner it was naturally important to make the best of this newly achieved attention. But before he could set out on his next lecture tour at the end of November, he gave a series of lectures for a small circle of about seven concerning "Planetary Evolution." In June and July, he had already spoken about this topic in single lectures and had published a number of articles concerning the evolution of the universe in *Lucifer-Gnosis*. In the series of lectures this topic was developed for the first time sequentially. This work created the necessary balance and anchor for the outer work. In November he then traveled to Nuremberg, Regensburg, Munich, Stuttgart, Karlsruhe, Heidelberg, Cologne and Düsseldorf. This meant that in the course of a year he had visited Stuttgart, Munich, Weimar and Cologne four times. He continued to travel in this manner in the coming years. In 1905, he was, among other stops, five times in Munich, and four times in Cologne, Stuttgart, Hamburg and Düsseldorf. He quite obviously wished to cultivate the theosophical work locally with some continuity. He did not appear sporadically, but regularly, giving at least one public and one private lecture, so that the diverse needs could be satisfied.

One cannot overemphasize the value of these trips for the establishment of the German section. Seen from the outside, the trips took an enormous effort, especially in the early years. Accommodations were difficult, either in poorly heated hotels or in the private quarters of well-meaning theosophists who then besieged Steiner from early in the morning until late in the night. Only his room at Duchess Kalckreuth's in Munich was warm and good. She and Sophie Stinde felt that he also needed to be able to rest at times. Steiner, however, valued the opportunity to speak with as many people as possible and almost never refused an invitation. Thus, in the early years of the section, almost all of the members became personally acquainted with him. Each of them had the opportunity to voice his problems and to ask for counsel. For his part, Steiner learned to know the members in conversations and consultations. This formed a tight net of relationships, acquaintances and friendships, the actual substance of the German section.

The Esoteric School, which was formally independent of the Theosophical Society, developed step by step in the background of the section work. The first esoteric lessons that Rudolf Steiner gave in his function as "archwarden" took place on July 9 and 14, 1904, in Berlin. In August, Steiner wrote a number of letters to members further afield, either accepting them into the Esoteric School or, as in the case of Michael Bauer, inviting them to join. During the winter of 1904/05, a small number of esoteric lessons were given. In the beginning of June 1905, a first newsletter was sent to the members of the school, formally outlining the requirements of the school. From October 1905, the number of esoteric lessons grew steadily.

In was, however, only in the following years that the path of schooling was presented in detail. In 1906, the students received a pamphlet with the title *General Requirements, which each person who wishes to undergo esoteric development must take upon himself*, containing a precise description of the six basic exercises. Rudolf Steiner proceeded with a great deal of care and mentored each student individually. A small circle of people came together within the German section who strove to bring theosophy to life within themselves. Through them, the section became ensouled.

It is characteristic of Steiner's work that at the same time as he was beginning to develop the work of the Esoteric School, he also began to publish a series of articles in *Lucifer-Gnosis* entitled "How to Attain Knowledge of Higher Worlds," later to become *How to Know Higher Worlds*. Steiner began working discretely on esoteric training with a small circle of people. At the same time, the principles of this work, the path of schooling, was made public. Steiner first articulated the path in *Theosophy*, in the chapter "The Path of Knowledge." Here one finds the first steps described systematically.

In the articles "How to Attain Knowledge of Higher Worlds," one finds a more personal style that comes perhaps most clearly to expression in the way the author addresses his readers. For instance: "If you have ever stood before the door of someone you revered, filled with holy awe as you turned the doorknob to enter for the first time a room that was a 'holy place' for you, then the feeling you experienced at that moment is the seed that can later blossom into your becoming a student on the esoteric path." "You can only achieve true knowledge if you have learned to respect this knowledge." "Create moments of inner peace and learn in these moments to *differentiate between what is and what is not essential*." "You must shed all prejudices." "Without healthy common sense, all your steps will be in vain." Here the spiritual teacher addresses his students not formally, but as friends, in a brotherly manner.

It seems as though Rudolf Steiner thus steps out of the choir of the otherwise unknown spiritual teachers. He speaks to everyone. *How to Know Higher Worlds* begins with the pregnant statement: "The capacities by which we can gain insights into the higher worlds lie dormant within each one of us." But Steiner also speaks in the name of all true spiritual teachers. "All true teachers of spiritual life are in agreement in regard to the content of these rules, even if they do not express them in the same words" (10).

Finally, toward the end of the book, the spiritual student is even addressed directly by spiritual beings. Both the "lesser" and the "greater" guardians of the threshold speak at length. The passage in which the "greater" guardian speaks begins: "You have freed yourself from the world of the senses. You have earned the right of citizenship in the suprasensory world" (10).

In this manner, Rudolf Steiner allowed himself to become an organ of expression for those beings who would speak to humans from out of the spiritual world. He writes in a letter what the publication of these texts meant for him. "Alone the responsibility weighs heavily on me. I have to consider every sentence, every phrase ten times in order to present the spiritual content that I have been entrusted to relate as precisely as possible, although I received it in a completely different form and language" (264).

In order to stimulate the qualities of soul and the sublimation of soul life that allows one to open one's soul to the spirit, it is not simply content that must be related, for instance the simple sentence: Reverence for the truth and for knowledge is an irrevocable condition of higher knowledge! It is much more important to find a language through which a certain mood of soul can be stimulated. Just by reading what are described as golden rules, and the exercises that are given, the sensitive reader should be moved by their meaning and develop the feeling without which any practice remains empty and void. In addition, it is important to find a balance between the individual exercises. The powers of discernment and judgment together with a healthy ability to stand in the world must unite with inner deepening and a sense for the revelations of nature. Through this union, a well-balanced soul life can become an organ through which the voice of the spirit can be clearly heard.

Although Rudolf Steiner laid the foundations of the anthroposophic path with *How to Know Higher Worlds*, in light of the individually different qualities of soul, he described the path to higher knowledge again and again in different ways. The articles "The Stages of Higher Knowledge" were printed in *Lucifer-Gnosis*. Later, in 1910, followed the chapter "Knowledge of Higher Worlds" in *Outline of Esoteric Science*; in 1912, "A Path to Self-Knowledge"; and in 1913, "The Threshold of the Spiritual

World." In 1923, Steiner published four further articles called "On the Life of the Soul," in which once again exercises were described. In addition to his writings, Steiner expanded on these questions in many lectures and described thus for the wanderer on the way to higher knowledge many paths and approaches.

CHAPTER 25

ATTEMPTS TO FRUCTIFY THE ART OF LIVING

On January 15, 1905, Rudolf Steiner gave his last lecture at the Workers' College. He spoke to an audience of about 1300 people. It was on the occasion of the fourteenth anniversary of the school's founding. Afterward he informed the council of the College that the scheming against him had reached a point that made a continuation of his work there impossible. Pale and disheartened, completely exhausted, he returned home. Marie von Sivers was shocked at his appearance. Just a few days later, Steiner wrote to her. "You should not have been concerned with my appearance on Sunday. That was no doubt just a reflection of the situation at the Workers' College. You know that I felt a certain calling for the work in these circles. Something has been destroyed that I truly did not want to see destroyed" (262). For six years Steiner had invested time and energy into the work there. He was personally connected to many of his students. These threads had now been torn. A field of practical, public activity had been taken away from him.

Rudolf Steiner had genuinely hoped that the proletariat movement would have developed differently given appropriate conditions. He saw here an opportunity for true social activism. He later expressed that if enough people had tried to work the way he had, different thoughts and ideas would have awakened in the heads of the workers, which then could have affected wider circles. This was 1905. The first clouds of the coming world war were visible on the horizon. It was the year of the Russian-Japanese war, the year of the first Russian Revolution, and the year of the first Morocco crisis. Such work would have been especially significant then. Following 1905, the events that "would lead to the world catastrophe that occurred in the second decade of the twentieth century" became sharper and more rapid.

Now that he was no longer able to work within the framework of the Workers' College, and aware of the dark clouds gathering on the horizon,

Steiner focused his efforts on turning the theosophical work in a socially practical direction. He wanted to do something to resist the snowballing tendencies of the time. He wrote in January 1905, "Step by step our time drifts into a style of life that makes necessary a concerted collaboration of all upward-striving forces. It would be necessary to pour our spiritual views into *everything*.... When I realize in whose hands the responsibility for our democracy has come to lie! It is not pretty!" (262). But with whom could one join forces? Steiner searched among his contemporaries. In 1905, 1906 and 1907, we find him searching for colleagues with whom he can bring theosophy into the realm of the practical.

His efforts to fructify daily work through spiritual impulses can be seen from various angles. One of the fundamental axioms from *How to Know Higher Worlds* is apparent in the striving to grapple with daily life.

> *Every insight that you seek only to enrich your own store of learning and to accumulate treasure for yourself alone leads you from your path, but every insight that you seek in order to become more mature on the path of the ennoblement of humanity and world evolution brings you one step forward.* (10)

Ideas become ideals that work on in us.

The theosophical efforts would have withered, and Rudolf Steiner would not have been able to progress along the path of knowledge, if he had not focused his energy on the transformation of daily life. Resolutely he followed this hidden law of those who truly understand: The spiritual world does not reveal itself to those who merely seek insight. An ongoing communion with the spiritual world is only for those who place their spiritual gifts in the service of human development and world evolution. Inspiration graces those who are actively engaged.

Another aspect of the path becomes apparent. It belongs to the "Requirements for Esoteric Training." The student is called upon to "feel himself to be a part of the totality of life" (10). In the face of the problems that come to meet us in life, we begin to consider to what extent we ourselves are at least partially responsible for these things. When we consider the criminal life, we will be led "to reflect that I have received something that was withheld from them—that my good fortune comes at their expense. It is then but a small step to the insight that, as a member or organ of humanity as a whole, I am jointly responsible, with all human beings, for everything that happens" (10). With such an inner posture, one ceases to merely criticize and instead looks for ways to make a positive contribution to the world.

From 1905 to 1907, Steiner made an astonishing number of differentiated attempts to become practically engaged. He was interested in the renewal and expansion of the therapeutic arts, in the "social question," in peace, and in human brotherhood. He addressed educational questions, women's suffrage, and nutrition. All of these questions could only be resolved through a spiritual understanding, through new forms of unprejudiced thought.

Steiner tried to make this clear in one example. He described the importance of charitable social institutions, and then went on to show that these institutions, when taken alone, intensify feelings of egoism and in the long run contribute to misery and poverty. Then he added, "These words may be taken at face value. One can only help individual people by giving them bread. One can only provide a large group of people with bread when one helps them gain a new outlook on life" (34).

A rightly understood spiritual worldview is for this reason the most practical thing of all. Too often, people are inclined to take the theosophical truths theoretically. This moved Steiner to present time and again the practical consequences of Spiritual Science. At the end of the pamphlet *Education of the Child*, which was published at this time, he warns explicitly of the dangers of a theoretical approach to Anthroposophy.

> Only when everywhere in theosophical circles the knowledge is penetrated to the point that it becomes important to make the teaching fruitful for every life circumstance in the widest possible manner and is not just a theorizing about it, then life will reveal itself to Spiritual Science. Otherwise, people will continue to consider Anthroposophy to be a kind of religious sect of individual peculiar fanatics. (34)

In working toward bringing theosophy into practical life, Steiner had his eyes on the goal of world peace. The first principle of the Theosophical Society was "to form the core of a general brotherhood of humanity without regard to differences of race, belief, gender or nationality." Steiner took up this ideal of human brotherhood energetically. In 1905 and 1906, he spoke a number of times about how theosophy awakens an understanding of human dignity. An understanding for the value of human life and individual dignity grows out of insight into the spiritual nature of the human being. This is the basis for true brotherhood (96).

Differences of opinion that separate and isolate individuals and groups of people become practically irrelevant in the light of such insights. It was out of this understanding that Steiner actively sought truly brotherly collaboration with the other theosophists. In 1904, France and England had agreed on the *entente cordiale*. Shortly thereafter, in July 1905, Rudolf Steiner traveled to London for the theosophical congress, where he gave a short address that he later summarized.

> It was during the period following the signing of the *entente cordiale* when everything was being viewed in the light of this agreement. I tried to characterize how in a movement like the "Theosophical Society" the goal could not be for theosophical truths to be disseminated from a single center. A center could only serve to provide a place where what now arises in all areas of the world can come together. And I closed with the words: If we build on the spirit, if we strive for a spiritual community in a truly concrete, positive manner so that the spirit that is generated here and there is brought together at the center of the "Theosophical Society," then we will create a new *entente cordiale*. (185)

The hope that the Theosophical Society would bring together all those who were striving spiritually in common understanding was based on the peace-bringing strength of the spirit. In 1905, Steiner viewed the Theosopohical Society as the genuine peace movement that could serve as a counterweight to the forces that were pushing toward war. "A truly peaceful society is one that strives for spiritual knowledge. The actual peace movement is the spiritual-scientific stream. This is the peace movement, because it rests on what lives in human beings and strives toward the future, the only things on which a truly practical peace movement can be built" (54).

In those years, Steiner viewed the worldwide collaboration of theosophists, which reached from India to America, as something that could work against the forces of war. It was this mission of peace that moved him to step away from the active push to separate from the Thesophical Society because of the conflict around Krishnamurti and the "Star of the East." In spite of all the imperfections, Rudolf Steiner valued greatly the homeopathic effects of such an earth-embracing collaboration.

His relationship to the leadership of the society was extremely loyal. Although he rejected any form of theosophical centralism, this was not a reason to cultivate a separatist or political stance. One only has to read Steiner's summary of his report to the members of the German section in the congress in London. Both Annie Besant and H. P. Blavatsky were acknowledged. He praised Annie Besant's lecture about "The Demands of Pupilship" without reservation and said about her, "Not as a form of idolatry, but from the spiritual content of the personality I became convinced that in her lives what can lead to higher spiritual worlds" (*Mitteilungen*, I, November 1905, compare also 264).

Steiner followed the ideal of a reciprocal give and take, a spiritual cooperation, in which he in no way had to play the central role. In a letter to Günther Wagner, he described how much this congress had meant to him, how he had experienced himself as a learner. He summarized the idea of such gatherings: "The congress was to be a center of spiritual life, which can then stream back into all corners of the world" (264).

Similarly, living theosophy should also be a center of spiritual life. Its streams should flow, either noticed or unnoticed, into life, giving it a new direction and new meaning. Healing ideas and practical thoughts should pass from person to person, be heard and taken in, and find their way into the then contemporary civilization and affect it harmoniously.

This was not illusory. During the first decade of the twentieth century, many people were convinced that things had to change. There were a multitude of movements trying to reform various fields of life. Health reformers wanted to bring about better nutrition, clothing and lifestyles; the school reform movement, a new form of education; and land reform, a new kind of ownership. Contradictory solutions and conflicting principles were publicized for women's suffrage, health, and the social question. Anyone who had even a halfway reasonable idea for change found an eager audience.

Steiner's difficulty lay in the fact that he did not have any set methods of particular solutions. He did not advocate any one-dimensional principles and had no simple answers to offer. It would have been easy to raise the head, heart, and hand to an educational principle, or to push for land reform as a solution to social inequality, just as it would have been easy to preach vegetarianism or raw food nutrition. Steiner was never concerned, however, with trying to bring about reform based on principles that intellectually made sense. He was convinced that all the activity around trying to reform things was basically just well-meaning quackery.

The basis for any improvement in the human situation is a comprehensive understanding of life—insight into the apparent and also hidden relationships. A few examples are given here.

The anthroposophic renewal of education did not originate in any sort of principle. It was not in the ubiquitous sense "child-centered," but rather originated in an understanding of the essence of childhood and human development. This understanding first had to be attained. Truly appropriate pedagogical methods can only be developed based on such understanding.

The first contribution Anthroposophy makes to such understanding lies in creating a quality of candor and ingenuousness able to overcome prejudice, sentimentality and antipathy. In Steiner's writings concerning the social question from these years we find, for instance, thoughts concerning the concept of "exploitation." In the general use of language, this concept is emotionally weighted. It is not a neutral, descriptive concept; it is a battle cry. This is understandable, but it leads to automatically connecting the concept to the notion that only the rich exploit the poor. To this Steiner remarked, "Whether I am rich or poor, I exploit each time I buy something that is underpriced" (34). Even the worker who buys things cheaply is de facto an exploiter. Today, in light of the exploitation of nature, such a clarification of the concept makes even more sense.

The next step, following the creation of this quality of ingenuous candor and leading into practical activity, is the emerging understanding of the true facts of life. Regarding the social question, the influence of a self-centered outlook can lead to the seemingly reasonable question: "Which societal forms have to be created to insure that each worker can receive the reward of his work *for himself*?" (34). The idea of justice seems to be behind this question. Each person should really receive what he or she has earned. "We count on the fact that the totality of a community would best thrive when the individual can take home the "full" or at least the best part of the profits of his work" (34).

At this point, one must turn away from the theories and examine life itself. In a society in which a division of labor is present, it is impossible to determine who has created what. The profits of labor in a modern society come about not through individual efforts, but through cooperation and collaboration. Under modern conditions, the individual is in fact better off than he "deserves" based on his labor. For this reason alone, we should demand that each should take home the reward of his labor. Steiner's "fundamental social law" was articulated with these relationships in mind.

> The health of a whole community of people working together is all the greater the less each one claims the fruits of one's own work for oneself—that is, the more one gives the fruits of one's own labor to one's fellows and the more one's own needs are met by the others, rather than by one's own work. (34)

Based on this, Steiner then proceeded to individual suggestions.

Steiner's thoughts and indications for practical life were for the most part not taken up in the years leading up to World War I. His thoughts on the social question were completely disregarded. Those few who did in fact read his articles took them as well-meaning idealism or as a sort of sermon. No one noticed that he had formulated one of the essential laws of a social organism.

Even the essay concerning the "Education of the Child" was met with little interest. Some zealous theosophists came to him for further suggestions about how to raise their children. Most of them were interested in concrete details—what color of clothing should the children wear; what should they eat. If one takes into account the number of suggestions concerning the art of living that Steiner made after 1919, the lack of interest among the early theosophists for such questions is regrettable. How much could have been done in the course of twenty years!

Renewal of the art of healing and medicine was especially important to Steiner at this time. There was a reason for this. On the one hand, the way that doctors understand the human being is expressed practically in the way they treat their patients. On the other hand, it has the greatest influence on how the general public views human nature. Nothing affects the general public's understanding of the human being more than medical opinion. At that time, in Steiner's opinion, the general approach in medicine—especially in pharmaceutical therapy—was based on trial and error. "That comes from a lack of intuition. Many aspects of modern medicine have arisen through this lack" (53). He was convinced that "it is absolutely necessary that studies such as medical studies be permeated with theosophical spirit. What is important is that theosophical understanding be united with science. The dilettantish natural healing can and should not be taken under our protection. That would be dangerous" (262). Already in 1905, Steiner had developed perspectives for an intuitive approach to medicine. However, he needed to collaborate with trained doctors.

He began to look for interested candidates among the theosophically oriented doctors. He visited Dr. Emil Schlegel in Tübingen. He had written a book titled *Reforming Medicine through the Homeopathy of Hahnemann* and had shown himself to be an unconventional, intuitively gifted doctor. In Kassel, Steiner met with Ludwig Noll and his brother-in-law, Otto Eisenberg. In Düsseldorf, he spoke with Felix Peipers. Schlegel, Noll and Eisenberg had by that time already found their own approaches and had no interest in what Steiner offered. Peipers was the only one with whom the beginnings of collaboration developed in the following years, in spite of what Steiner wrote to Marie von Sivers. "Peipers is fairly undeveloped. Medical school has led the poor man more into confusion than into clarity. He does want what is best. But he has not yet found an inner center" (262). Good will, however, brought Peipers to the point that in 1908 Steiner could begin to work on questions of color therapy with him.

On the whole, Steiner found almost no one in these first years who was interested in bringing theosophy to bear in such a way that its fruits could flow into civilization as a whole. Theosophy was probably for most people too new and unknown; one had to first get to know it better for oneself. Yet there were a number of individuals who wanted to be active, but because of their training and social standing could not work professionally; many upper class women and civil servants had found their way to theosophy. To meet the needs of this group, Steiner developed symbolic rituals with aspects of the rituals of the Freemasons. This need, of which Steiner spoke a number of times (28), must have become apparent early on and, according to the reports, was expressed quite emphatically.

The institution of these symbolic rituals has been the cause of some questioning over the years. The problem does not lie in the fact that Steiner used the forms of the Freemasons to meet the schooling needs of a group of theosophists who wanted symbolic instruction. The Freemason rituals speak directly to the imagination and the emotions and depict the various stages of esoteric development. The problem lies in the fact that Steiner bought the diploma that authorized him to lead the Freemason rituals from Theodor Reuss, a man with a questionable reputation.

One can almost feel Steiner's distress when he writes about this question in his *Autobiography*. He finally admits laboriously that he was taken in by a swindler. He starts out by describing how he had intended to connect with the existing forms out of a sense of respect for history. In this case, such a statement is curious. Steiner did not take up the forms used by the order that issued him the diploma. He developed his own rituals in the Freemason style. It is also difficult to understand why he paid Theodor Reuss good money to issue him a diploma that authorized him to act as a Grand Master. The Memphis–Misraim rite to which he linked his work was not an especially well-respected historical institution, although it did have, as many Freemason orders did, a legend tracing its roots at least as far back as the Templars, perhaps to the Essene scholars. The form that Reuss represented was an invention of the late nineteenth century. This was something of which Steiner certainly was aware. By 1906, he spoke only of historical concessions that he had had to make (256).

Steiner's actions seem even more remarkable when viewed in light of his letter to Marie von Sivers from November 30, 1905.

> The thing with the Freemasons is something we want to approach slowly, not rush into. Reuss is not a person one can count on. We have to be clear that we must be very careful in this situation. We are dealing with a "framework," not reality. At the moment nothing is hidden behind the scenes. The esoteric forces have *completely* drawn back. At the moment I am not sure if one day I will have to say: this cannot be done. I would ask that you not make a big thing out of this when you speak with people. If someday we are forced to say we cannot support this any longer, then we shouldn't get too involved. There are personal motives and personal vanities at play. The esoteric powers flee in the face of both. It is certain that at the moment it is of no significance to the esoteric powers that we do this. But I can't say anything specific about this yet. If we notice something improper during our next meeting with Reuss, we can act accordingly. (265)

The reason Steiner felt he had to link his rituals to the windbag Reuss could lie in the history of the Theosophical Society. Reuss represented the Memphis-Misraim rite in Germany as it was practiced by John Yarker. Yarker had accepted the founder of the Thesophical Society, H. P. Blavatsky, into his lodge. Blavatsky had not only accepted Yarker's approach, she had plans to collaborate with him in founding a form of theosophical Freemasonry. By connecting with this work, Steiner took up the work begun by Blavatsky. Given his thoughts at the time, one could easily conceive of such an intention.

Soon after the transaction with Reuss became known, Steiner came up against the opposition of theosophical Freemasons, who were well aware of the questionable nature of Reuss's freemasonry. Reuss was later responsible for the founding of the Ordo Templis Orientis (OTO), with which Steiner was not connected. This led to a number of accusations, as the OTO professed to the use of a variety of magical practices.

More important than the formal connection, which Steiner later viewed as questionable, is the content. Here we call attention to the fact that freemasonry is a form of ceremonial symbolism. It is not by chance that the imaginative language originates in the work of the mason. The work in the lodges is the preparation for what the Freemasons strive to achieve outside of the temple. The impulse for the work in the world is carried out from the lodge. This is explicit in the texts used by the lodges.

> May what the laborers on the temple of humanity call "strength" inspire me in my work. Let what you have learned work on when you leave the portal of this temple to return to your life outside; from your hearts shall flow into the rest of humanity what can shape hearts into bricks of the great temple; from your thoughts shall flow what can bind the temple together; from your will shall pour what may serve as mortar for the stones of this temple. Do only what genuinely springs from your heart, what you are led to by careful thought, and for what the strength of your will has steeled you. (265)

Thus the practical work of theosophy was brought to mind in a symbolic form: the members of the Freemasons were shown through the rituals that higher knowledge finally and ever again must lead to practical work in the world.

Circumstances did not allow Rudolf Steiner to become practically active in the social realm, in medicine, or in education in 1905/6. He did not find individuals among the members of the Theosophical Society who were able to work with him. In its place appeared the ritual practice of ceremonial symbolism. This was a preparation that would lead from the inner temple into daily life. In the years from 1910 to 1913, this path from imagination to reality was brought to artistic expression in Rudolf Steiner's mystery plays. Only later was it actually taken.

Chapter 26

THE THREE PATHS

From at least one point of view it was fortunate that Steiner could begin the symbolic, ritual work—of which he had spoken since 1904—in the first days of 1906. Here he had created a space completely independent of the other theosophical activities. In the *Mystica Aeterna,* as the lodge was called, he was neither a general secretary of the Theosophical Society nor one of the arch-wardens named for the Esoteric School by Annie Besant. Here he was his own master. In Freemasonry terms, he was a sovereign Grandmaster. This independent space would become crucial in the coming years. In addition, this inner circle added to the unity and stability of the society, underpinning Steiner's widespread recognition among the members.

The year 1906 brought a continuation of the travels Steiner had undertaken the previous year. In the autumn of 1905, he had lectured in Switzerland and now returned for two short speaking tours. At Whitsun, he traveled to Paris for three weeks. He now began to give longer lecture cycles. In Paris, he gave eighteen lectures, followed closely by cycles in Leipzig, Stuttgart and Munich. On the way he visited smaller groups. In all, he spent almost eight months away from Berlin in 1906.

In letters to Marie von Sivers, he would write that the lectures were increasingly successful. "Yesterday evening in Hamburg the auditorium was filled, and I intuitively felt that it went better than ever" (262). When he ended up staying longer in Zürich than originally planned, he wrote, "Yesterday was without question the best evening yet in Zurich. Even though bad weather and other circumstances kept many people away, the way the audience followed was remarkable" (262).

It was around May 20 that Steiner and Marie von Sivers set out for Paris. The idea was to hold a series of lectures for Russian friends there and other interested parties. The political situation in Russia had made it impossible to hold the lectures at an estate in the vicinity of Kaluga as originally planned. Margarita and Max Woloschin had rented a house in Passy on the Rue Renoir where at first a small circle of friends gathered to hear Steiner. Marie Steiner wrote, "The living room was packed with chairs, and planks that we had found in the garden were laid across the suitcases; some people sat in the entry. We had not been able to find someone to serve us. We took care of setting up and cleaning; meals were cooked in the kitchen in the cellar, where we entertained a variety of guests."

The French writer Édouard Schuré was present for every lecture and took copious notes that he later published. Among the visitors were the Russians Konstantin Balmont, Dimitrij Mereschkowski, Sinaida Hippius, and Nicolai Minski. There were heated debates and the most curious conversations in this circle. Mereschkowski interrogated Steiner like an inquisitor: "We are naked and poor and thirsty and yearn for the truth. Tell us the ultimate mystery!" Steiner replied, "If you can tell me the penultimate mystery." Mereschkowski, beside himself, cried, "And one can save oneself without the church?" (comp. Woloschin). In the middle of this course began the congress of the Federation of the European Sections of the Theosophical Society. Following the congress, the audience grew so much that the lectures had to be continued in the headquarters of the French section on Ave. de la Bourdonnais. Some of the French members viewed this as a "new German invasion" and did not necessarily welcome it.

In fact, almost no one concerned themselves with the *German invasion*. What caused the greatest stir at the 1906 congress was the situation with Leadbeater. Charles Webster Leadbeater, who was perhaps the most prominent esotericist in the Theosophical Society, had, on May 16, 1906, been called before a committee of the English section. The committee, chaired by Colonel Olcott, challenged Leadbeater to defend himself against allegations that he had been teaching boys to masturbate. He chose to resign from the society before he was expelled. During the congress, the breaks were filled with conversations concerning Leadbeater, his behavior and his credibility. An official letter made the whole thing more explosive and gave it unnecessary publicity. Annie Besant, who at the time was in Simla, India, wrote in a letter to the members of the Esoteric School, "I want to go on record saying that giving such instruction to men, not to mention innocent lads, deserves the sharpest censure. It distorts and perverts human sexuality, which man has been given to insure the continuance of the human race" (Tillet).

The Three Paths

In the history of the Theosophical Society, the Leadbeater crisis was in a certain sense a cause for alarm. In reality, the primary question in the situation was not the heatedly debated moral issue of onanism, but rather the choice of spiritual paths taken by leading theosophists.

It is quite remarkable that Steiner did not join in the general public indignation, although he was very critical of Leadbeater and seems to not have liked him. In a letter to the members of the German section he wrote that he had always rejected Leadbeater's esoteric methods and was not surprised by the current situation. But he did not believe "that anyone who trusted the methodological basis of Leadbeater's esoteric research had any reason to condemn him." There was reason to doubt Leadbeater's personal intentions (264).

He stated his views even more clearly in a letter to Annie Besant in response to her official statement of June 9.

> The whole thing appears to me from a much more profound aspect and in a deeper connection. I have to see the cause of all this misfortune in the peculiarity of Mr. Leadbeater's occult methods. These occult methods *necessarily* lead, in certain cases, to this or other mistakes similar to those evinced in Mr. Leadbeater's case, because such methods are no longer appropriate to the current stage of Western humanity. It need not always be the same mistake, but it can amount to similar things just as serious. These methods can only lead to a positive result if, standing behind everyone who enters on the path of development, there is the absolute authority of a *guru*—which is impossible in the West due to the general cultural situation. Western people can be led to the stage of psychic development at which Leadbeater stood only if the part of their guidance that can no longer proceed from the *guru* is replaced by a *mental* development that has reached a certain stage. And Mr. Leadbeater lacks this stage of development. In this case I do not refer merely to an intellectual philosophical training, but to the development of a stage of consciousness that consists of inwardly contemplative insight.... The Masters of the Rosicrucian School have elaborated the "path" that is the only one appropriate for a Western person in the current cycle of development. (264, pp. 247–48)

Thus it is that Steiner also wrote that, in his opinion, "Leadbeater was not guilty in the normal sense of the word of a 'moral failure.' He was a victim of his own method. What is being condemned morally by the public should be judged from the point of view of 'Where there is strong light, there will be dark shadows.'"

> It is not important that we condemn Mr. Leadbeater, as so many others have, but that we find the correct way to continue to work productively. This can only lie in acknowledging the Rosicrucian path as the appropriate one for European circumstances. (264)

This is the first time that the Rosicrucian School and the Rosicrucian path are mentioned in their connection with Anthroposophy. Steiner had spoken earlier about Christian Rosenkreuz in connection with freemasonry and the temple legend. Here he speaks of the Rosicrucian path as the path that is appropriate for the Westerner. And he indicates clearly that the path described by him in his articles "How to Attain Knowledge of Higher Worlds" is the Rosicrucian path.

For the German theosophists this came as a surprise. Some were naturally aware of and knew something about the Rosicrucians, yet it was not this fairly well-known, yet dubious movement of the late eighteenth century that Steiner was referring to. He named what he was doing and the path he represented the Rosicrucian School.

The situation with Leadbeater called for clear spiritual differentiation. Steiner took this step by examining the various esoteric methods. Until 1906, he had emphasized the unity with Annie Besant and presented his own approach without contrasting it with others. Now he explicitly developed the teaching of the three paths.

According to the available sources, Rudolf Steiner first spoke of the three paths of initiation in Leipzig on July 10, 1906. This lecture is poorly documented. He spoke of an Eastern, a Christian, and a Rosicrucian path. The lectures in Stuttgart on September 3 and 4, 1906, in which he again spoke of the three paths, are better documented. They are to be found at the end of the collection *Founding a Science of the Spirit*. Further presentations followed on September 19 in Basel, and on October 20 and 21 in Berlin. Later, he returned to the topic repeatedly in a variety of venues. His thoughts on the three paths can be found in written form in *The Stages of Higher Knowledge* and later in *Outline of Esoteric Science*.

Steiner called the essence of the Rosicrucian school "true self-knowledge" (95). Basically he picks up again on the theme with which he began the lectures on mysticism in October 1900. Now he expands upon it: True self-knowledge leads one beyond one's own narrow self (95). The first stage of the path he calls "study." Through study, one immerses oneself in the great thoughts of the world—for example, cosmology or cosmogony or the laws of evolution. "By following the rigorously strict chains of thought, we challenge ourselves to craft rigorously logical thoughts. This study also purifies our thoughts, so that we can learn to think logically" (95).

What Steiner indicates here in a general way he had described for Annie Besant as "the capacity to behold one's thoughts within." He then added that sense-free thinking, when grasped in self-knowledge, can serve as a reliable guide through all the stages of knowledge.

> If this is missing, Western people wander about *without a rudder,* regardless of whether they are moving on the physical or on a higher plane. At the present time when all higher human powers are so closely linked with the powers belonging to the lower levels of the sexual realm, a slip, such as Mr. Leadbeater's, can occur at any time. (264, p. 248)

We find ourselves confronted with the highly dramatic fact that Rudolf Steiner was compelled in light of the Leadbeater affair to designate his approach to inner schooling as the "Rosicrucian path." This did not directly affect the essence of the method. *How to Know Higher Worlds* originated in a Rosicrucian inspiration. But due to the fact that the method was now named and had been contrasted with two other methods, it took on contour.

In 1906, "study" is expressly named as a part of the path of inner schooling. What had already been indicated in *Theosophy* was now made explicit. In *Theosophy* (1904), forming a "thought-picture of the higher worlds" was described as "the first step toward individual spiritual vision." Steiner now systematically developed the idea that the independent path to higher knowledge requires that a person first form corresponding "thought images" in order not to be overwhelmed by the reality of the spiritual impressions. Clarity of thought provides security for human freedom.

Further, Steiner pointed out the changed relationship to the teacher or guru in the context of the Rosicrucian path. The Eastern path, which has a direct effect on the bodily organization, can only be followed under the close guidance of a spiritual teacher who gives a student the necessary correction and provides a strict context for the way the student lives.

The Rosicrucian path makes a new relationship to the teacher possible. A teacher is, however, necessary here, as well.

> A teacher must always be present at initiation. Serious initiation without a teacher does not exist. Whoever wants to make this assertion is as foolish as someone who believes that a child can be born without the union of both the male and the female. Initiation is a spiritual process of conception. (97)

On this path, however, the teacher becomes a guide who does not regulate a student's life but only gives indications for one's own schooling. Students can also find their own guidance in many things through "study."

Finally, Rudolf Steiner mentioned to Annie Besant the relationship between the forces used for spiritual research and the forces of human sexuality. He did not return explicitly to this question, only pictorially in that he compared the human being to the blossoming plant. When in blossom, the plant opens itself to the sun, which sends its holy spear into the flower. The human being is a plant turned upside down. The roots of the plant correspond to the human brain. The reproductive organs, the flower, are hidden in the lower part of the human body. Out of this arises the following image:

> Plants stretch their reproductive organs innocently up into the cosmos. Think about the transformation of this gesture at a higher level. Observe the animals and human beings. See how human beings cover what plants otherwise expose upward to the sun. And then consider this: a time will come when human beings should reach a level of development whereby all lower needs will have left their bodily organs. At this stage, they will reach toward the Sun with what corresponds to the calyx of the plant. Then all the drives will have been purified, all desire overcome. This transformation is called the Grail, or sacred chalice, in the Rosicrucian School. (97; comp. also 55 & 98)

The mystery of the Rosicrucian schooling is revealed in this picture. The pure forces of the will and of life that are hidden in the forces of reproduction open the spiritual student to the spiritual light of the world. Clarity of thought is the basis of this striving, but its true essence is pure love opening itself to the world. The spiritual schooling is based fully on those energies of life that are normally at work in human sexuality. It leads to a sublimation of these forces, to a soul consciously working with them. This is, however, only possible in the light of pure spiritual thought.

The Leadbeater affair gave Steiner cause to rearticulate the spiritual stream that he represented. It presented itself in new thought forms. The significance of this process becomes perhaps clearer when one thinks of how cutting and polishing change the nature of a jewel. The value comes into appearance as the stone is finished. In Germany, Austria, and Switzerland, Steiner spoke explicitly and consequently about Rosicrucian theosophy; in Berlin, Munich, Basel, Vienna, Düsseldorf and other cities, he described the specific nature of the Rosicrucian approach from a variety of viewpoints. Then in Munich, in 1907, following the Munich congress, he held the comprehensive fourteen-lecture cycle on "Rosicrucian Theosophy."

The decisive question for the international theosophical movement concerned Annie Besant's long-term position regarding Leadbeater. In the past, he had been her most important advisor in all esoteric matters. Now she was alone and at first indignant about his behavior. Who would replace him as her advisor on the esoteric? For a short while, she appeared to turn once again to the Indian teacher Chakravarti. But Leadbeater strove to have himself rehabilitated. He wrote regularly to Annie Besant, who finally began to view the occurrences of the spring of 1906 in a new light. Steiner's quiet analysis of the situation, although acknowledged, did not in the end find fertile soil.

At the beginning of 1907, a number of very questionable things took place in Adyar, which showed that Steiner had been correct in developing his work independently. On the evening of January 6, the elderly president of the Theosophical Society, Colonel Olcott, together with Annie Besant and Olcott's private secretary, Marie Russak, received a "visit" from the two "Masters," Morya and Koot Humi. The story goes that they declared that Annie Besant should be Olcott's successor as president of the society. The Masters returned on January 1. This time they reproached Olcott for his conduct during the Leadbeater affair and directed him to write a letter to Leadbeater, which should then be made public. The Masters continued to visit Olcott periodically until his death on February 17. These visits were reported to the members of the Theosophical Society and became a subject of discussion.

One can only speculate about what actually took place in Adyar in January and February 1907. One wonders who actually arranged the whole thing. Unfortunately, Steiner was quite reticent about the whole affair. He wrote to Marie von Sivers on February 25, "However things evolve, for the

T.S. the whole affair is devastating. Not necessarily so bad for the spiritual movement. Even the disintegration of the T.S. should not shock us at all. You have to understand, that I cannot speak about the details of the affair with the Masters in Adyar, even with you" (262).

Somewhat later, when the discussions about the matter had become somewhat more critical and George Mead had published his opinion, Steiner wrote to Marie von Sivers, "We can't continue to be silent about the humbug, when everyone else is trumpeting about it everywhere. If we do not make a timely statement, we will end up hollowing out the earth beneath our feet" (262).

The situation was quite difficult for him. He knew no better choice for president than Annie Besant. She, however, had taken the directions of the Masters to heart. Steiner could not take the position that the whole thing was a swindle without casting aspersions on her and the whole mythology of the Masters. In his official statement, he wrote simply that the words of the Masters concerning the choice of president should be ignored. And he added, "None of those individualities that we can recognize in supra-sensory experience would ever become involved in such matters as the impending choice of president" (264).

He supported electing Annie Besant to be president. However, in a letter to Anna Minsloff, a Russian theosophist, he wrote,

> Much more important than whether Mrs. Besant is chosen or not is that she herself is brought back to the right course. If no particular complications arise, then Mrs. Besant must necessarily be chosen. Of all the older members of the society, she appears until now to be the most suitable. (264, p. 264).

Annie Besant let it be known that she was absolutely convinced that she had been chosen by the Masters to take on the leadership of the Theosophical Society and that she planned to work as they directed. She wrote, "If we were to separate the society from the Masters, the society would die." Strangely enough, she didn't recognize that an election was impossible under such circumstances. Rudolf Steiner recognized that her view of the position would lead to difficulties and especially problems with the German section. He was outspoken about this (264). Still, he felt that Annie Besant was someone who took spiritual life seriously. Her opponents, on the other hand, were inclined to turn the Theosophical Society into a club for comparative religion or something similar. "There is a stream in the society that, if it came into power, would gradually smother all spiritual life" (262). Thus it was that he advocated for electing Annie Besant.

In the German section with some 600 votes, only 20 voted against her. In the Theosophical Society as a whole with 12,984 members, she received 7072 votes. 152 members voted against her and 5,780 abstained. On June 28, 1902, Annie Besant became the second president of the Theosophical Society.

Rudolf Steiner had to acknowledge the consequences of all these occurrences over the course of the previous two years. He separated the Esoteric School over which he had responsibility from the school led by Annie Besant. Following the Munich congress, there was a meeting between Rudolf Steiner and Annie Besant, who had come from India for the congress. In this conversation Steiner was frank about his respect for the older woman and presented again what he had written to her in his letters. He made it clear to her that it was without rancor but with amity that he now had to separate his school from the general Esoteric School of the society. On June 7, 1907, Annie Besant, who also had real respect for Steiner, responded magnanimously and in a written statement explained:

> Dr. Steiner's occult training is very different from ours. He does not know the Eastern way, so cannot, of course, teach it. He teaches the Christian and Rosicrucian way, and this is very helpful to some, but is different from ours. He has his own School, on his own responsibility. I regard him as a very fine teacher on his own lines, and also a man of real knowledge. He and I work in thorough friendship and harmony, but along different lines. (264, p. 239)

Following the Munich congress, Rudolf Steiner called a meeting of his esoteric students and told them about the separation of the schools. He asked each of them to decide which of the schools he or she would like to be associated with. He saw the new autonomy of the school, with its focus on the Western path, as a spiritual reality affecting not only the institution but also the reality of the spiritual plane (266).

In conjunction with the Munich congress, one has to recognize the fact that a spiritual stream, which up to now had received little notice as it prepared the new Western esotericism under the veil of the older, better known Eastern esoteric, now stepped forward and declared its independence.

The necessity for this step becomes apparent when one considers, among other things, the fact that Annie Besant resumed her collaboration with Leadbeater shortly after the congress. Already in August 1907, she was to be found in the vicinity of Dresden in Weissen Hirsch together with Leadbeater, the Indian teacher Jinarajadasa, Miss Bright and Mrs. Russak. They practiced esoteric chemistry and studied the nature spirits in the surrounding forests (Tillet).

CHAPTER 27

THE MUNICH CONGRESS: A CONFERENCE IN A ROSICRUCIAN TEMPLE

At the end of the theosophical congress in Paris, it was decided that the German section would organize the 1907 congress. It was no doubt an honor for the still young and relatively small section, but it was also a burden, financially as well as otherwise. In any case, the estimated budget of 5,000 marks did not begin to cover the costs. For Rudolf Steiner it was clear from the beginning that this conference should set a mark. At first, he perhaps thought only to give the artistic impulse a stronger presence. But in light of the occurrences described in the last chapter, he continued to revise his plans. Almost at the last minute, the decision was made to turn the venue into something that would at least indicate the archetype of a Rosicrucian temple.

First, Marie von Sivers took the initiative to perform a piece by Éduoard Schuré. She wrote:

> In September of the same year (1906) we visited Mr. and Mrs. Schuré in Barr in the Elsace. Schuré spent the days in anticipation of the evenings, when he could ask questions. These he had already written down in his notebook. The answers took the form of an intimate lecture by Dr. Steiner. Stimulating conversations took place during the walks to the ruins of the old castles, to Odilienberg, and to the Heidenmauer. It was there, as we spoke about the development from the ancient Druid mysteries to those of ancient Greece, that I found the courage to ask Mr. Schuré if we could perform his play about the Eleusian mysteries at the planned congress in Munich. Dr. Steiner had already agreed. Schuré was pleasantly surprised, but at the same time a bit fearful. (M. Steiner, *Schriften II* [Collected writings])

In October 1906, it was announced at the general meeting of the German section that the congress would be held in Munich. Only in this city were there enough people free to take on the preparatory work, which would demand a great deal of time and devotion. In response to a question from Mr. Hubo, Steiner went on:

> The task of the German congress shall be to bring everything together in inner unity. Art, music and language should resonate with the rest of the arrangements. It will seek to remind us of the ancient mysteries. To this end, the performance of a mystery play is planned. To what extent we will be able to do all this will, of course, depend on the circumstances. (*Mitteilungen*, IV, January 1907)

Marie von Sivers and Rudolf Steiner traveled to Munich in November 1906 to prepare for the congress. Steiner gave a series of lectures on the Gospel of St. John to lay the spiritual foundation of the congress with the friends in Munich. Together with Sophie Stinde and Duchess Kalckreuth, they sketched out the plan for the congress. The concert hall was rented. This hall was large and contained a stage. Most important, it was free of any form of decoration. They returned to Munich in December and January to continue the preparatory work. Primary responsibility for the preparations lay in the capable hands of Sophie Stinde and Duchess Kalckreuth. They worked very "quietly"—they did their work backstage, oversaw the technical organization, took care of the more than fifty coworkers, quieted the waters when necessary, and urged on exhausted seamstresses or actors.

During Christmas and the first days of the new year, Marie von Sivers and Steiner disappeared from sight. They went away without leaving an address where they could be reached, in order to be able to work in peace. Marie von Sivers probably began with the prose translation of the *Holy Drama of Eleusis* at this time, Steiner wrote. This kind of work was next to impossible when they were in Munich or Berlin. Steiner was constantly besieged by people asking for advice or help. They spent this time in Venice, which was not necessarily the best choice. "We interrupted the work for one or two walks each day. These were rich with impressions, but for the most part rather sad ones. The decay, the decadence was more apparent when" (in winter) "there was no brilliant sunlight bathing the ancient walls with its radiance, no deep blue sky cloaking Italy with its magic" (Rudolf Steiner Studies, I). For Steiner, who loved living by the open sea, it was nonetheless a time for thought and the gathering of new strength.

In January 1907, in a couple of stolen hours, Rudolf Steiner drafted the program for the congress. One passage illuminates his intentions especially well.

The Munich Congress: A Conference in a Rosicrucian Temple

Since the theosophical relationship to the world is a ideal of the future, it cannot be brought to complete manifestation in the present. It is perhaps possible, however, through the arrangement and composition of the events, to bring the theosophical leitmotifs throughout the congress to expression: concentration and transparency of the ideas, and peacefulness and inner focus.

Steiner consciously accepted the fact that the theosophical ideas would not come completely to expression. The imperfect presence of the future was more important to him than the tried and true. One has a sense of how Steiner draws the future near. He does not work from a set plan; rather, he feels his way as he goes, seeing just what can be done. It was Steiner's intention to give the conference itself a theosophical form, to go beyond the mere exchange of more or less abstract ideas. Theosophy was to be experienced, seen, and thus to become more real.

From April 6 on, with one short interruption, Steiner was present in Munich. He revised Marie von Sivers prose translation, bringing it into free rhythm, and then began with the rehearsals. He took on directing the play and designed all the scenery and costumes, which were made by the Munich theosophists. Marie von Sivers described the work.

> [Rudolf Steiner] worked in all the arts and with all the handwork, directed all the laborers—painters, sculptors, musicians, carpenters, drapers, actors, seamstresses, stage hands, electricians. If he'd had the necessary material and help, he would have created something fabulous in a short time—the temple of the future. As it was, he could only sketch out ideas. (284)

The rehearsals were fairly dramatic themselves. The two women who were to play Persephone and Hecate had to drop out—fortunately soon after the rehearsals began. One of them had to be taken to the psychiatric clinic. Other actors quit; some could barely manage to speak loudly enough. Marie von Sivers practiced constantly with the various players. She had to take special care of Alice Sprengel, who stepped in to take the role of Persephone. Ms. Sprengel would often simply fold her hands in her lap and give up. Others, like Dr. Felix Peipers, thanks to his natural dignity and carriage, proved to be perfect for his role. He played Zeus. Only in the last weeks before the congress was due to begin did it become certain that the performance would take place.

At this point, Steiner had the walls of the auditorium covered with red cloth and began to transform it into a "temple." This was a very costly undertaking. Steiner put it off until he was sure that the play could be performed. Then the auditorium was transformed with amazing speed. It must have made a strong impression on the participants to enter the completely red auditorium. For some it was not entirely pleasant. But Steiner set great store by this deep, strong radiant red. In his report of the congress, he explained the reasons why he had chosen this color more fully: The higher self should feel itself spoken to, challenged and elevated.

The seven apocalyptic seals, as they were described in the traditional Rosicrucian texts, were hung on large, round tablets. "Between each pair of seals stood a column. We were not able to sculpt the columns. But they are seen as true architectural forms and correspond to the 'seven columns' of the 'true Rosicrucian temple'" (284).

At the front of the auditorium, at the stage opening, there stood two additional columns. One was red, the other blue. There were four verses that belonged to these columns, in which four stages of spiritual elevation from pure thought to creative will were brought to expression. Finally, on the program, beside a drawing of a rose cross, were the initials E.D.N./I.C.M./P.S.S.R. These called attention to the three Rosicrucian phrases *Ex Deo nascimur, In Christo morimor,* and *Per Spiritum Sanctum reviviscimus.*

Thus, on May 18 at ten o'clock in the morning, the Munich congress began in a different way than any previous theosophical congress had— one entered a room that represented a spiritual temple. In addition to the lectures, recitations and music brought the artistic element strongly to expression, and at five o'clock in the afternoon on Whitsun, Schuré's *Holy Drama of Eleusis* was performed, a mystery play written to awaken memories of the ancient Greek mysteries.

Earlier theosophical congresses had been organized in the style of scientific conferences, with many lectures, working groups for the different disciplines and the accompanying debates. The Munich congress was permeated with the intense will toward artistic form. It took the form of a celebration that strove not merely to satisfy intellectual needs, but to elevate them and give them form. Theosophy should not get stuck in people's heads, costuming itself with the trappings of academia. It should struggle to come to expression and move people.

The Munich Congress: A Conference in a Rosicrucian Temple

Steiner took up the idea that theosophy was the seed of a new culture seriously. Every true culture leads to its own forms through which it reveals itself. One has only to call to mind the Middle Ages. The spirit and faith of medieval Christianity took form in the cathedrals and the village churches, in the monasteries and the chapels. Artistry was also apparent in small things; even at the beginning of the nineteenth century the things of daily life, including such things as door knobs, were given artistic form. For Steiner the time had come to find a new beginning of this form of artistic expression.

It was clear to him that the artistic offerings that had been attained in the short time available and with the available workers were far from being seasoned. He spoke about this openly. He was, however, also aware of the fact that everything has to begin somewhere. In the beginning, what is important is the spiritual intent not the perfect form. The painted columns, for instance, were not finished works of art, but they pointed toward possible artistic forms. The apocalyptic seals were technically simple, but they contained the seeds of inner life (284). Finally, Steiner was either courageous or bold enough to give the theosophical friends who wanted to work artistically relatively free reign. He was glad that so many individuals wished to contribute to the work. All in all, the multitude of theosophists who worked as artists, skilled handworkers, as lay people and helpers in the auditorium or on the organization created a social atmosphere that would continue to bear fruit.

There were more than 600 participants in the congress, the majority of whom were German. The rest came from England, France, Belgium, Holland, Scandinavia, Italy, Russia, Bulgaria and even India. It has been reported that the artistic aspects of the congress were met with scorn, irony and criticism by the foreigners—the English, the French and especially the Dutch guests. Directly following the congress, Marie von Sivers wrote to Édouard Schuré that a number of foreigners had come with feelings of antagonism (Rudolf Steiner Studies, I). It must have been quite easy to criticize specific aspects of the presentations. But Annie Besant, for instance, was *enthused* by the attempt to perform a mystery drama, according to Éduoard Schuré (Rudolf Steiner Studies, I).

It is to some extent understandable that the foreign guests, coming from different traditions, did in fact begin to sense the conflict that began to show itself there. For one, the custom to award Annie Besant the role of president of the congress was not observed. Marie von Sivers gave an account of the events. "The organizing committee for the congress, to which Dr. Steiner did not belong, insisted that the role of president not be given to Annie Besant, who took this for granted, but to Dr. Steiner. He had no choice but to accept and offered her the honorary chairmanship. It was a demonstrative gesture from the German section" (284).

It also became known that the Esoteric School had been split into two schools. Steiner requested that his students decide to which of the schools they wanted to belong. This led to a number of conflicts, especially in Holland where there were students of both Besant and Steiner. The differences between Steiner and Besant did not remain hidden, although the outer form was maintained. The older theosophists became aware that a new spirit announced itself, and the more sensitive could feel the rumblings in the depths.

On the whole, the congress did make a mark. Guests invited to a theosophical congress found themselves suddenly in the representation of a Rosicrucian temple; on Whitsun Rudolf Steiner gave a lecture about "Rosicrucian Initiation." Although he did not develop the idea of the three paths in this lecture, he did speak about the Christian and the Rosicrucian paths and emphasized that Rosicrucian initiation was the form of initiation "that enabled the individual to put to use all aspects of modern culture. It teaches us to understand spirit in matter. When one recognizes the relationship between even the most material object and the spirit, one becomes able to let the spirit flow into matter" (284). The incomparable modernity of the Rosicrucian path was proclaimed, and the audience was aware of this.

The direction and intention that was hinted at during the congress was presented in more depth and clarity in the fourteen days following the congress. The congress came to conclusion on Tuesday evening, May 21. On Wednesday, Rudolf Steiner began a series of fourteen lectures. In these lectures, he developed in brief an overview of Rosicrucian theosophy. With a few brush strokes, Steiner first described—as in *Theosophy*—the nature of the human being, the spiritual world and the working of karma, then went on to give the first comprehensive description of the evolution of the cosmos, beginning with the planetary stages and ending with the history of the earth.

What was pictured artistically during the congress in the seals and columns was now described in majestic imaginations, which in the clarity of their conception and their inner immanence went far beyond what had been described in the articles about the akashic record. The study of the seals and the columns led to pictorial understanding of metamorphosis in the development of the earth; the lectures presented a comprehensive picture of evolution.

In these lectures, through the clarity and power of the presentation, one could experience the spiritual contribution made by Steiner to this congress. One can imagine what an open, unprejudiced listener experienced. He felt Steiner's intense concentration and competence during the lectures and would have been amazed that Steiner was able to do this seemingly so easily following the exertions connected with the congress.

Marie von Sivers gave a picture of Steiner's personal life at this time in a letter to Éduoard Schuré.

> Each day brought something unexpected. Around 200 people remained in Munich for Dr. Steiner's lectures. They tore us to pieces. It was very difficult to get away. Toward the end, at 9:00 in the evening, there were still ten people waiting to be received. When we had to catch a morning train, as in this case, we packed between 2:00 and 6:00 in the morning, without having gone to bed at all. (Rudolf Steiner Studies, I)

The trip took them to Leipzig, where Steiner went directly from the train to give a public lecture. That was on June 8 and 9. He then traveled to Berlin for a few days, and from there on to Kassel, where the next series of lectures began on June 16.

It is noteworthy that in Kassel, where the members had agreed among themselves to be more considerate of him, he once more picked up the Munich themes. He spoke again about Rosicrucian theosophy, in a less difficult manner and in freer variations. The audience was not large. There were only about forty people present, some of whom had also been in Munich. The repetition brought these sweeping new subjects home.

One would much love to know what Rudolf Steiner's own experience of this time was. Unfortunately, there are no direct indications or documentary sources. One can speculate. The fact that his letter to Annie Besant concerning the Leadbeater affair received practically no response no doubt showed him just how isolated he was among the leaders of the Theosophical Society. When the proclamations of the "Masters" in Adyar were made public, he saw the chasm opening and recognized how ridiculous the situation was. At the same time, he did not want to join the ranks of Annie

Besant's small-minded critics, who had nothing to offer but mundane common sense. He found himself alone among the theosophical leaders, without a real partner with whom he could converse.

Among his own students, the German theosophists, there were a number of people whom he could count on. First, of course, Marie von Sivers—who came closest to being a critical partner—then Sophie Stinde, Arenson, Unger, and Michael Bauer. Mathilde Scholl found herself at the time in crisis and was unable to help; the gifted, but also ambitious leader of the branch in Leipzig, Elise Wolfram, had just discovered her own significance. In short, there was a group of strong students, a hopeful group of people, but also a number of problems.

It is quite impressive how Steiner, outwardly now on his own, follows his own path. First he develops the teachings of the Rosicrucian path of knowledge. Then within the realm of spiritual knowledge, he develops the idea of the evolution of the cosmos, an inner experience of a majestic process of metamorphosis, which he brings to expression both artistically and imaginatively. Whoever experiences the inner lawfulness and consequence of this imaginative exploration can understand what was important to Steiner at the time. Inwardly, he held himself upright on the lawfulness of the universe and followed what emerged as necessity. The Dutch and French theosophists could think what they wanted, and the general lack of understanding could be widespread, but, in spite of everything, the path showed itself clearly in Rudolf Steiner's inner eye.

He did write about the challenges presented by the lack of understanding. In a letter to Marie von Sivers from Vienna, he wrote:

> There are many dumb theosophists. But the dumbest ones seem to be the leaders of the lodge in Vienna.... Prague is much better. The present visit there has proven to be in certain ways quite successful. Vienna is in every way a backward city; theosophy here is the essence of backwardness.... But for the moment we are not going to dwell on all of that. This time it will be necessary to have a day's "break" concerning lectures, especially those for dull-minded audiences. This alone is exhausting. You cannot begin to imagine how everything bounces back when one has to speak to such heads, as is often the case. (262)

One should not assume that Rudolf Steiner was at any time exclusively focused with his thinking and experience on theosophical questions. He followed political and economic news with great interest. Scientific developments were of special interest to him. In 1907, there are a number of important passages that show how he followed the tendencies in modern physics and chemistry. It was his view that the essential nature of the time came to expression symptomatically in such developments.

During the winter of 1907/8, Rudolf Steiner spoke ten times on the topic *Science at the Crossroads*. The venues were usually university cities like Basel, Strasbourg, Heidelberg, Uppsala, Bonn, Leipzig and Munich. He described in brief the ideas that had been developed out of research into the nature of matter over the course of the last ten years. Before the turn of the century, there was a general belief that the atom was the final, indivisible particle that made up the world. It was pictured as a small sphere. But around the turn of the century, this belief was challenged by the discovery of radioactivity and the decay of atoms. In his lecture on this topic in Berlin, Steiner built up to the following picture:

> It will become clear that what we see and hear is in fact real and that it is pure fantasy to think of a world of matter behind what we see and hear. This world of matter will turn to dust and decay. What is behind it will be acknowledged. What is and can be experienced will come into the foreground. One will recognize that an atom can be nothing else than frozen electricity, frozen warmth, frozen light. And one will have to go even further, to the recognition that it is concentrated, formed spirit that we find in everything.... Everything that is matter is spirit—is the outer manifestation of spirit. (56)

It is probably owing to the lack of a truly interested, capable audience that these themes, which connected the other lecture content of 1907 to contemporary science, were not taken further. Steiner could only give a very general idea that the popular notions of matter, which closed off the path to the spirit, were erroneous. But it belongs to the general character of the year 1907 that in addition to the conceptually clear, reliable path to spiritual knowledge that can take on practical form, Steiner also illuminated earthly circumstances in such a way that the spirit at work in them also became visible. The rule "above as below" was observed in this manner—in addition to describing the path into the heights, Steiner also indicated the path into the depths.

CHAPTER 28

BREADTH AND DEPTH

Following the critical and rapid developments that continued up to the end of 1907, 1908 appeared outwardly to be a time of relative quiet, a time in which regularity once more reigned. A closer look shows that the outer peace is somewhat deceptive. In addition to his ongoing work, during this time Steiner must have written a good part of *Outline of Esoteric Science*, which was then finished in the fall of 1909. This book presents a biographical riddle: When was it actually written? The first edition contained some 440 pages. The question becomes more cogent as one must assume that Steiner, who had already drafted a first, unpublished version, wrote the manuscript for the published version of *Outline of Esoteric Science* in 1908/9.

In addition to his work on what was to be one of the fundamental books of Anthroposophy, in 1908 Steiner gave six major lecture cycles, each usually consisting of twelve lectures. Among these were the lectures about the "Gospel of St. John" (given in Hamburg and Oslo), "The Apocalypse of John" (Nuremburg), and the "Egyptian Myths and Mysteries" (Leipzig). In addition, he gave another 180 lectures over the course of the year and traveled widely.

It is not only the amount of work that is astonishing. More fascinating is the fact that he did not merely articulate ever new, wider and deeper insights from his spiritual research, but that both *Outline of Esoteric Science* and the lecture cycles reveal an underlying degree of remarkable composition and form. Once one has discovered it, one can only regard Steiner's accomplishment with reverential awe.

Whoever has been faced with the challenge of articulating spiritual content knows how difficult and time consuming this task can be. It is different than with the articulation of other content. With this, the writer can to some extent let himself be guided by the external, temporal or logical context. He can appeal to the common beliefs of the reader. This is not the situation when one strives to depict the suprasensory world. The writer must not only explore, depict and compose, and summarize, he must do so in a way that provides the reader with the initial steps toward higher knowledge.

The work of presentation, the crafting of the text, and the architecture of the developed thoughts is one that demands an unbroken focus of will. Later, we find him gouging out the forms of the first Goetheanum or carving the statue of the representative of mankind. From 1907 to 1909 we see him shaping, carving, painting and crafting "in the spirit."

To return to the sequence of events: Steiner traveled constantly during this period. He visited a total of twenty cities, some of them two or three times. It is hard to imagine that he not only prepared his lectures while traveling, he also did most of his writing while underways. The travels were of two types—lecture tours and trips Steiner took to escape. At the beginning of 1907, Rudolf Steiner and Marie van Sivers had traveled to Venice in order to work in peace. After finishing the lecture cycles in Munich and Kassel in early summer, Steiner wrapped up his editorial tasks in Berlin and set off in the beginning of August on his first major trip to Italy. Five more such trips followed, the last in 1912. It is certain that Marie von Sivers was instrumental in convincing him to take these trips. Steiner remembered these shared journeys in his *Autobiography*:

> Now, because Marie von Sivers and I had to travel in connection with anthroposophic work, the treasures in museums all over Europe came within my reach. Consequently, from the beginning of the century—in the fifth decade of my life—I went through a higher training in art and related to that my perception of the spiritual development of humanity. Marie von Sivers was always at my side. With her fine sense of taste she partook of everything that I was able to experience when viewing art and culture, supplementing and sharing it. She understood how all these experiences flowed into what made the anthroposophic ideas mobile and alive. (28)

Steiner did not only visit the large museums and churches in Florence, Milano, and Rome, in the Uffizi Gallery, and the Sistine Chapel. He also found time to visit relatively unknown museums and monasteries, where he could observe the traces of the spiritual and psychological history of Western culture. He was especially interested in two themes—architecture and the development of painting from Cimabue up to Rafael and

Michelangelo. In southern Italy, he wandered through the ruins of the Greek temples in Paestum and Segest; in Rome, he viewed the Colosseum and St. Peters; and in Florence, the cathedral and the Campanile di Giotto. He took his time and let the various sites work on him at length. In Rome, he also went down into the catacombs and followed the subterranean passages to the site where the original Christians worshipped. "We were strangely moved today when we wandered through the catacombs, the scorned underground of Rome" (106). On later trips he also visited the cathedral in Palermo and the ancient Benedictine monastery at Monte Cassino, as well as other sites.

Rudolf Steiner rarely spoke immediately about the things he had experienced. It was only in the years 1914, 1916 and 1917 that he began to speak about the aesthetic and art historical questions that he had begun to study in 1907. In a tentative manner, he called attention to the pictures he had viewed. Probably the most significant thing for him was the artistic stimulation he received from the older works of art. "In the contemplation of the stylistic forms, the seed of what would become the forms of the Goetheanum sprouted within my soul" (28).

On his travels, Steiner always found time to observe the landscape and the people who lived in each landscape. In 1908, shortly after one of the stronger eruptions, he took the risk of climbing Mt. Vesuvius. The earth rumbled and quaked beneath him; suddenly, funnel-shaped holes appeared before him, into which fell ashes and volcanic debris. Such natural phenomena, like the Solfatara, which he mentioned a number of times, fascinated him. And from a number of his lectures, one sees that he also gained insight into the spiritual history of southern Italy (144).

In a letter to Éduoard Schuré, Marie von Sivers wrote that as soon as Steiner returned from his walks, he continued his work. During a fourteen day trip to Rome in 1907, Steiner would go out to visit the Lateran or St. Peter, then walk back to the hotel and after a quick snack return to his room, take the manuscript that he had brought along out of the big leather grip, and write, sometimes until midnight. The next day, he would visit perhaps the Stanzen in the Vatican, then return to write again in the evening.

In addition to these working trips came the trips in service of theosophy. In 1907/8, Steiner sought to widen the scope of his work. Up to the middle of 1907, his lecture tours were limited primarily to Germany and

Switzerland. In the second half of the year, he traveled to Prague and Austria, and in 1908 to Holland, Denmark, Sweden, Norway and Hungary. In Prague, Steiner met a circle of openly interested people who soon formed their own theosophical group under the umbrella of Steiner's Berlin branch and a few years later became the Bohemian section of the Theosophical Society. The situation was completely different on the trip through Austria. Vienna seemed to him to be the epitome of backwardness; he ironically named Graz the "capitol" of the Steiermark; and he called Klagenfurt an "Alpennest." "The nature on both sides of the railroad is majestic and beautiful, but the people..." (262). In spite of this, he visited Vienna and Klagenfurt again in 1908.

In March 1908, he made a lecture tour to Holland. On this trip, he no doubt visited the Maurithuis in The Hague and the Rijksmuseum in Amsterdam. This trip was tiring. The bad weather didn't help. In a letter to his parents, he wrote, "The weather here is terrible. It is cold and rainy. And Holland is quite unfriendly when it rains." But the climate seems to have been unfortunate in other aspects, too. As Steiner had remarked, the Dutch were especially dissatisfied by the changes at the Munich congress. Now he arrived in Holland for a series of lectures with themes closely connected to those of the congress: the Christian-Rosicrucian path to knowledge. Not only that. In contradiction to the usual theosophical notions, he described that in life after death, time does not flow forward, but that the dead experience a stream of time flowing backward (comp. 258).

The Theosophical Society had a rule in its charter that a general secretary from one country could not give lectures in another country without having been invited by the general secretary of that country. The official Dutch Society was so little thrilled by Steiner's visit that he was not invited by the Theosophical Society to return. It was only in 1913, when the Anthroposophical Society had split off from the Theosophical Society, that he was able to speak again in Holland.

His relationship with the Scandinavian countries developed in a completely different manner. Early in the fall of 1907, Steiner received an invitation, probably through Richard Erickson, to visit Scandinavia. The visit took place in late March and early April 1908, still winter in Stockholm. Although Steiner did not have the habit at that time of reporting about his travels, he spoke very warmly of his experiences in Scandinavia both in Berlin and, a few weeks later, in Nuremberg. In the relatively empty stretches—Sweden had at that time as many inhabitants as London—was the possibility "that the ancient Norse gods and spirits still can affect the spiritual environment. One can certainly say that for someone who knows something about the spiritual, it is in a certain sense so that finds the spiritual expressions of the ancient Norse gods at each and every corner. These were what the Norse initiates encountered in pre-Christian times" (102).

The trip went well and Steiner was invited to return at the earliest possible date. Three months later, he traveled to Oslo, which at that time was named Christiania. Theosophists from many parts of the world, individuals who had recognized Steiner's unique spiritual significance, gathered at the school in Nordstrand where Steiner was speaking. They had followed him into this pine-scented land with its fjords and islands. In the light-filled air with granite under their feet, Steiner found an audience that allowed him to venture beyond what he had developed up to that point. In "majestic pictures, he revealed the depth of the seemingly simple words of the Gospel of St. John."

Over the course of the next six years, Steiner returned to Scandinavia eight times. This alone speaks to the importance of this connection for Rudolf Steiner. Thus in 1908, we can identify the predominant north-south axis of Steiner's travels: From Berlin he travels to Stockholm and Christiania in the north and to Munich and Rome in the south. The west is blocked to him from 1908 to 1913. To the Russians, the representatives of the east, he could only speak in Helsingfors (Helsinki) in 1912 and 1913. He was not able to enter Russia itself.

Steiner was not only concerned with spreading Spiritual Science throughout Europe but strove also to intensify the work. He began his regular lectures in Berlin in 1908 with the remark that he would no longer speak at an introductory level for those who were new to theosophy. He would instead address the higher regions of theosophy; he would speak to those with an advanced knowledge of theosophy. "This too must be possible in a theosophical branch" (102).

He began a very detailed exploration of evolution of the higher spiritual beings and the spiritual-physical cosmos. One has the clear impression that he was working on themes from *Outline of Esoteric Science*, while at the same time speaking about corresponding branches of research and additions to the central work in these lectures. Whereas in

Outline of Esoteric Science, he described the path of world evolution in a linear, systematic manner, in these lectures he speaks also of by-ways. He speaks about how certain spiritual processes are connected with the human organism and how these are mirrored in mythology and in art.

Steiner developed these themes on three different levels for audiences in 1908. In his public lectures in Berlin he spoke in language that was accessible to everyone. He spoke of "the sun, the moon and the stars," "the beginning and the end of the earth," and about "heaven and hell." In his lectures for members, he described various aspects of evolution. In connection with the "Esoteric School," he gave indications as to how one could learn to understand and perceive higher knowledge on the path of inner schooling and experience. For students living in Berlin who visited all of the lectures—and there were quite a few—he cast ever new light into the infinite reaches.

In addition to the work at the two centers in Berlin and Munich, Steiner felt it to be important to give people living in other places the opportunity to intensify their relationship to theosophy. The way to do this was through the so-called lecture cycles. In 1906, Steiner had given such cycles in Paris, Leipzig, Stuttgart and Munich. These had shown that the eight- to fourteen-day immersions into theosophy were both supportive of a deeper understanding of theosophy and beneficial for the participants. It was helpful to immerse oneself completely in an ambiance of learning. In 1907, Steiner gave further lecture cycles in Munich, Kassel, Hannover, and Basel. These were also successful. The audiences came together in a mood of celebration. In conjunction with these gatherings there was almost always a lesson for members of the Esoteric School.

From 1908 on, these lecture cycles began to take on a new form. Through 1907, they were almost always a comprehensive introduction to theosophy. Their introductory character continued in 1908, but Steiner began to focus on specific themes. That year he twice gave an introduction to theosophy in light of the Gospel of St. John (in Hamburg and Christiania), once in Nuremberg with a focus on the apocalypse, and he spoke in Stuttgart and Leipzig about the universe, the earth and the human being in relation to Egyptian mythology.

Steiner began to gently specialize theosophy. Only after *Outline of Esoteric Science* had been published and a wide outline of Spiritual Science was available in written form did he begin to focus explicitly on special topics. His lectures on cosmology, the folk soul, and the different Gospels belong to this period.

The lecture cycles served as focal points for intensifying the theosophical work in different cities. For a time, it seemed as though the work in Leipzig was growing well. Steiner gave a number of cycles in Stuttgart, Basel, Kassel and Hamburg, which were also favored. Christiania was the Scandinavian city in which he gave the greatest number of lecture cycles. By the end of 1908, a whole theosophical landscape had come into being. In six cities, Steiner found increasingly independent colleagues among the members: Sophie Stinde and Duchess Kalckreuth in Munich, Carl Unger and Adolf Arenson in Stuttgart, Michael Bauer in Nuremberg, Mathilde Scholl in Cologne, Ludwig Noll in Kassel, and Richard Erickson and others in Cristiania. The work was centered in Berlin, where Rudolf Steiner returned regularly. Here a group of loyal helpers had formed around himself and Marie von Sivers, two of whom deserve mention: Johanna Mücke and Kurt Walther. By 1909, there were about twenty theosophists giving courses and lectures in the different cities.

On August 1, 1908, Marie von Sivers founded the Philosophisch-Theosophisch publishing house. Begun in the most humble circumstances, through the undemanding efforts of Johanna Mücke, it soon grew into a flourishing undertaking. It began publishing single lectures by Rudolf Steiner, then went on to publish entire lecture cycles. Members of Steiner's audiences had begun to scribe the lectures and courses. The number of uncontrolled transcripts in circulation began to grow. Marie von Sivers took the problem in hand. She insured that relatively conscientious stenographers were present to scribe the talks. In the beginning, she corrected the transcripts alone. Later, she sent them to Adolf Arenson and others to be read through and corrected. Beginning in 1908, therefore, a collection of Steiner's lectures became available. About thirty-five volumes appeared before World War I.

In 1909, Marie von Sivers wrote to Éduoard Schuré about her work as a publisher. "We have now started to reproduce Rudolf Steiner's lectures. Instead of one young woman, I have had to hire four....It has meant setting up a whole factory. We need machines, rooms full of closets and shelves for all this paper, and volunteers to keep everything in order.... We haven't yet been able to print anything, as Mr. Steiner doesn't have time to look through the proofs. How much easier that would make everything!" (Rudolf Steiner Studies, I).

Steiner's tone in these lectures strove to move the listeners and to lead them into the future. Contemplating evolution should prepare the soil in which further evolution can take root. The new should arise out of the old. For instance, at the conclusion of the second lecture in the Stuttgart cycle *Universe, Earth, and Humanity*, he said:

> Our time must not give birth to an ancient wisdom but to a new wisdom that does not look backward but forward, prophetically, apocalyptically forming the future. We can see an ancient wisdom, preserved in the mysteries of past cultural epochs. Our wisdom must be an apocalyptic wisdom, the seeds of which we must sow. We need once again a principle of initiation in order to restore the original connection with the spiritual world. This is the task of the theosophical movement. (105)

Rudolf Steiner wrote *An Outline of Esoteric Science* to insure that the principle of initiation would become a general principle of the development of civilization. As *Theosophy* did, *An Outline of Esoteric Science* begins with a presentation on the nature of the human being, but this time from a different point of view. The chapter is titled "The Makeup of the Human Being" and describes in a new way the process of transformation through which humanity passes, in that an individual begins to transform himself out of the "I." In this context, for example, memory is described as a specific capacity of the "I."

As beings gifted with memory, individuals learn, step by step, to grasp the past and make it their own. Through the forces of memory, people learns to recognize the wisdom of the world from which they come. These forces of memory are then challenged to the extreme in the chapter "Cosmic Evolution and the Human Being." Looking back over the evolution of the world through the stages of "Saturn," "Sun," "Moon," and "Earth," a picture is developed of the four steps in the creation of the world in which we live. Anyone can recognize these four stages of evolution in the physical, the etheric, the astral and the spirit, study them and, in doing so, remember them.

A close study of the world reveals it as a "cosmos of wisdom." Beginning with the architecture of the human body and reaching out to the boundaries of the solar system, the world shows itself to be permeated with wisdom. This can be studied in numerous ways. When it is taken up into the self and remembered, the self attains the capacity to carry this wisdom into the future. It can become active, borne by an unsentimental love. Thus, *Outline of Esoteric Science* closes with a look into the future:

> The "cosmos of wisdom" is developing into a "cosmos of love." Everything that the I can develop within itself must turn into love. The exalted Sun being we were able to characterize in describing Christ's evolution manifests as the all-encompassing example of love, planting the seed of love in the innermost core of the human being. From there, it is meant to flow out into all of evolution. Just as wisdom, which formed earlier, discloses itself in the forces of the sense-perceptible earthly world, in present-day forces of nature, love itself will appear as a new natural force in all phenomena in the future. This is the mystery of all future evolution: that our knowledge and everything we do out of a true understanding of evolution sow seeds that must ripen into love. The greater the power of the love that comes into being, the more we will be able to accomplish creatively on behalf of the future. The strongest forces working toward the end result of spiritualization lie in what will come from love. The more spiritual knowledge flows into the evolution of humanity and the Earth, the greater the number of viable seeds will there be for the future. (13, pp. 396–97)

That love is naturally present in the human being is revealed by the love of the mother for her child. A mother does not have to force herself to love her child. And when a mother truly comes to understand the child, this love is permeated with understanding and wisdom. For the doctor who is able to intuit what a patient needs, it is just as natural to transform his insight into practical help. Such examples aid one in recognizing how insight becomes help, which then becomes love.

> Beginning with the Earth phase of evolution, the wisdom of the outer cosmos becomes inner wisdom in the human being. Internalized in this way, it becomes the seed of love. Wisdom is the prerequisite for love; love is the result of wisdom that has been reborn in the "I." (13, pp. 397)

In *Outline of Esoteric Science*, the meaning of earth evolution is made visible. The human self takes hold of the wisdom in the world through the forces of memory. Through what was made possible by Christ, the self receives the strength to act out of insight born of this wisdom, out of the experience of the meaning of existence. Thus, through the conscious, insightful actions of the human being, the seed of love comes into being for the future. A "cosmos of love" is prepared for a distant future.

CHAPTER 29

THE ILLUMINATION OF THE CHRISTIAN MYSTERIES

In *An Outline of Esoteric Science*, the act of Christ—*the Mystery of Golgotha*—stands in the middle point of earth evolution. In Rudolf Steiner's life, this newfound understanding of the event at Golgotha, which came about only after hard inner trials and tribulations, was a critical occurrence. "It was decisive for my soul's development that I stood spiritually before the Mystery of Golgotha in a deep and solemn celebration of knowledge" (28). At this point in Steiner's life, at which the significance of this understanding takes on clarity, we can trace its development back to where it began.

The inner import of this understanding makes it clearly different from the ideas Steiner had spoken about in 1890 with the Cistercian priest Wilhelm Neumann. Such ideas are something different than the knowledge achieved through inner trials. Later, as is documented by passages from *Intuitive Thinking as a Spiritual Path*, his Nietzsche book and a number of his articles, he had rejected these ideas. In one passage from 1898, he wrote:

> We are entering the twentieth century with essentially different emotions than those of our Christian forefathers. We have truly become "new humans," yet those who have embraced this new view with their hearts are but a small community. We want to fight for our gospel, that a new generation can arise in the coming century—a generation that knows how to live and is satisfied, joyful and proud—without Christianity, without a longing for the hereafter. (33)

After the turn of the century, in 1901/2, Steiner tried to use his own soul-spiritual experiences to understand and experience what had lived in the ancient mysteries. In 1902, he then described the birth of the true self and the path of development that leads the self to the being of the cosmos and to the rebirth of the self out of the spirit. Led by his own experience, he described the milestones of this process of the birth of the divine seed in the individual, the stages of suffering, death, the passage to the underworld and resurrection—moments that make up an essential part of the mysteries. The inner experiences of the initiates were related in sweeping pictures. These images are also present in the Gospels and in the Apocalypse. The essential substance of the Christian mystery of death and resurrection became for Steiner a cognitive experience. The question arose as to how this mystery was reflected in history.

In 1902, Steiner still interpreted the images presented in the Gospels and the Apocalypse through what he knew of the mysteries of Greek and Egyptian antiquity: Christianity grew out of the mysteries, but the mysteries are in Christianity open for everyone to see.

> The Mysteries had been a hothouse plant, and their wisdom was granted to the few who were ripe to receive it. Christian wisdom developed as a Mystery whose content was vouchsafed in the form of knowledge to *no one,* but to *everyone* in the form of faith.... The secret of the Mysteries was brought by Christianity from the darkness of the temples into the bright light of day. The revelation of the ancient temples lived on, however, within the inner sanctum of its content of *faith.* (8, p. 170)

The interpretation of both the mysteries and Christianity is by Steiner in 1902 somewhat ambivalent. The image of the hothouse plant gives the exclusivity of the mysteries a somewhat questionable character, just as Christianity's popularity is also looked at askance, gained as it is through the fact that one cannot understand it. Basically, however, both Christianity and the mysteries have the same content. In Christianity, it is these mysteries that are revealed and made available to all.

This ambivalent interpretation of Christianity was to change in the next few years. In the revised edition of *Christianity as Mystical Fact and the Mysteries of Antiquity,* published in 1910, the ancient mysteries are presented as imaginative harbingers of the Mystery of Golgotha. The latter is seen as the central event in earth evolution.

This view matured in Steiner's thinking from 1903 to 1908, a time in which his religious surroundings, in as much as they existed, were predominantly liberal. This liberal theology, which had originated in positivist thought and began with the critical analysis of the traditional texts, had around 1900 reached a second stage of its development at which the interest in text analysis had started to diminished. Adolf von Harnack, a very cultured representative of this new direction, was inclined to view the three synoptic Gospels as an accurate record of Jesus's teachings—the significance of God the Father and the infinite value of the human soul. For Steiner, Harnack's interpretation of Jesus's life was an oversimplification of the Gospels and couldn't shed light on the universal significance of the Mystery of Golgotha.

Before attempting to describe Steiner's path toward understanding this mystery, it is important to have a sense of how he conducted research. He spoke a number of times about his approach. In 1925, in the foreword to the new edition of *Outline of Esoteric Science,* he wrote, "In spiritual cognition, everything is immersed in intimate soul experience; not only spiritual perception itself, but also the understanding with which the unseeing, ordinary consciousness meets the results of clairvoyant perception" (12).

Soul experience, the human soul and the development of the soul are the keys to spiritual knowledge. What is recognized in the spirit must take hold of the life of the soul and reflect itself in life (129). What Steiner in 1902 calls the mystical life is of immense significance. The *mystai*, the spiritual knowers, must themselves take in what they have understood. Rudolf Steiner uses the word *durchmachen*, meaning to go through it, to do it, to experience it. Spiritual recognition is not merely a viewing of higher worlds and distant times, but an experiencing, a living of spiritual content. It transforms the life of the seer.

What is beheld and experienced must also be understood. Thoughtful understanding is a special task for the one who experiences the spirit. One has to develop the proper thoughts about what one has experienced (2). This brings up another problem when one progresses from understanding to articulating what one has experienced. "But in order to make this understanding really possible, those who present spiritual perceptions must be able to cast them in the form of thoughts without having them lose their imaginative character" (13, p. 4).

The seer does not only have to bring his or her experience to complete consciousness and clarity but must also conceptualize them, present them in imaginative form and finally recognize them in the traces of history. Only a layperson in this field has the notion that this is a simple task. In fact, attaining spiritual knowledge is something that takes time and effort, something that must be approached along a variety of paths.

In a very general way, Rudolf Steiner described his experiences in the years from 1901 to 1907 or 1908 in his *Autobiography*. It was important to him to know this path as an inner one. "For me, the period between 1901 and about 1907 or 1908 was when I experienced, with all the powers of soul, the realities and beings that approached me from the spirit world. Specific insights developed from those more general experiences of the spirit world" (28).

How this is to be understood is apparent in the 1925 foreword to the twentieth edition of *An Outline of Esoteric Science*. Originally, Rudolf Steiner wanted in addition to the general presentation of the nature of the human being and the spirit world to include a special description of cosmic evolution as the last chapter of *Theosophy*, published in 1902.

> When *Theosophy* was going to press, the subject matter of this current book [*An Outline of Esoteric Science*] had not achieved closure in me as was the case with that of *Theosophy*. In my imaginations, the spiritual being of the individual stood before my soul, and I was able to describe it; but this was not yet true of the cosmic relationships that were to be presented in *Esoteric Science*. Individual details were there, but not the total picture. (13, p. 1)

Steiner first attained a spiritual understanding of the individual human being. The different aspects of the human being, including the higher spiritual members *manas* (spirit self), *buddhi* (life spirit) and *atman* (spirit human), stood before his inner gaze. He also saw the development of the soul through the reincarnation of the spirit and the wandering of the soul through the soul world and the land of the spirit. His point of departure was the inner understanding of the individual.

In *Outline of Esoteric Science* he presents, however, the spiritual nature of humanity and its process of development in cosmic evolution. "In 1909, I then felt that the prerequisites were in place for me to be able to produce a book that 1) cast the content of my spiritual vision in the form of thoughts to a certain provisionally adequate extent, and 2) could be understood by any thinking people who placed no obstacles in the way of their own understanding" (13, p. 4).

The presentations of 1909 are the foundation of everything that Rudolf Steiner developed later. From this point on, through his discerning perception of the cosmos and historical evolution, he developed further what had been laid out in *Outline of Esoteric Science*, although this book remained the basis for everything. His earlier written presentations of cosmic evolution that were published anonymously in *Lucifer-Gnosis* with the title

"From the Akashic Chronicle" are in comparison to *Outline of Esoteric Science* only preliminary studies. They can't be viewed as the foundation of what would become Anthroposophy. Missing in these early depictions is not only any mention of the Mystery of Golgotha, but also the explicit description of the effects of the luciferic and ahrimanic beings. Steiner had not yet found his own voice. This seems apparent when one reads a passage such as "The Lemurian Race." Steiner too was aware of the problematic nature of these early attempts. He wrote, for instance, in the introduction to the chapter about the lemurian race:

> Although the greatest possible care was taken when deciphering the akashic chronicle, I must emphasize the fact that these reports should in no way be seen as having a dogmatic character. Not only is reading of the things and events that lie so far removed from the present difficult, the translation of what has been seen and deciphered into modern language is almost impossible. (11)

These problems led Steiner in 1905 to distance himself from the then customary language, which he had also used up to this point. He remarked, for instance, that the word "race" would "lose all meaning" in the future, and that the word itself "was not a fortunate designation" (11).

This sketch of the way Steiner's language and understanding evolved will be the background of an examination of the development of his understanding of Christianity. In the context of his explorations of the akashic record, he researched also the life of Jesus. In 1913, he remarked that research into the details of Christianity was especially difficult. He thought this was due to the fact that he had not had a Christian upbringing.

> I want in no way to assert that I am at this time able to articulate precisely what is contained in the spiritual text. For I experience a number of difficulties and problems when I try to bring the images that pertain to the secrets of Christianity from the akashic record. It is difficult for me to concentrate these images to the point that I can hold on to them. I see it as a task given to me by karma to say this as I have. Without doubt, it would be much easier for me if I had received a truly Christian education as a youth. This was something I did not have. I grew up among freethinkers, and during my studies was also drawn to other freethinkers. My own education was scientific. And that makes it difficult for me to find the things about which it is my duty to speak. (148)

This decidedly non-Christian upbringing, for which Rudolf Steiner's father was primarily responsible, was, however, an important preparation for an unprejudiced approach to knowledge. "On the other hand, I think that because I was a stranger to Christianity in my youth, I am able to confront it more openly. I believe that since I was first led through the spirit to Christianity and the being of Christ that I am justified through my lack of prejudice and my open-mindedness to speak about these things" (148).

In his autobiographical lecture on February 4, 1913, Steiner spoke about his non-Christian upbringing in detail. And in the autobiographical sketch he did for Éduoard Schuré, he summarized it thus: "I did come to know the church services, as I had to serve as an acolyte, but I found true faith and religiosity by none of the priests with whom I was acquainted. In fact, I learned bit by bit to know the shadow sides of the Catholic clerics" (262).

The strong outer influences of his non-Christian surroundings cast a shadow into the young Steiner's life and made it difficult for him to grasp what he had once experienced as a child in the services and through the Latin liturgy. There was no one with whom he could speak of these experiences. Thus, the positive early experiences remained purely inner experiences, which the boy did not find mirrored in anyone else's soul.

In regard to a special theme, research into the mysteries connected with the holy grail, Steiner made further statements concerning the nature of his research. First he mentioned that in this case "the tracks disappeared. I had to search to find them again." Then he remarked that in his earlier lectures and books "the things I said concerning the name of the grail are among the least satisfactory" (149). Finally he casts light on the karmic mystery of such research:

> By esoteric research, one is guided step by step, often in connection with one's karma. And one does not know, when one encounters something that seems to be connected with something else, what will become of this in one's own soul under the influence of the forces that come out of the spiritual world. One often doesn't even realize that something one has received out of the depths of the esoteric world is related to a problem with which one has struggled for years. (149)

One can begin to see that Steiner first had to overcome obstacles and inner resistance on his path toward an understanding of the Christian mysteries. The difficulties arising from his non-Christian upbringing were only a part of the problem. The theological literature was like a hedge of thorns through which Steiner had to find his way. His library bears testimony to the fact that he did so. Secondly, the path upon which he was "gently" guided unfolded step by step. This corresponds to modern consciousness—it was not a path of revelations or euphoric pan-visions. Modern consciousness attains its insights step by step, testing them as it progresses. Cognition is gained in stages; it questions and strives to find which thought is appropriate and justified. The mystery of modern consciousness is depicted in the saga of Parsifal (144). Parsifal finds his way in stages and through crises. This is also the basis for Steiner's explanation of the meaning of the word *grail* for the students of the eleventh grade at the first Waldorf school. "Grail comes from *gradalis*, which means in stages, gradually. Parsifal's path is one of a series of stages, from his early dullness, through doubt to *saelde*" (W. J. Stein).

All that is left of the stages of Steiner's biographical path are the footprints, the traces we can find in his lectures and writings. These do not allow us to make absolutely certain assumptions about his inner experiences, but there are milestones that mark certain stations along his way. For the reader who becomes aware of them, they speak clearly. This clarity disappears when one tries to even out the differences in Rudolf Steiner's various statements.

One of the first very significant statements in this context is found in a notebook dating from 1924. In this entry, he jotted down autobiographical dates in preparation for a lecture. He noted, "1903 = the dawning of the Christian mysteries." The image of the dawn, which calls to mind the rising of the sun, points toward a slow process of realization lighting up his inner horizon.

There is one passage from 1903, a time in which the documentation is still somewhat sparse, that bears witness to this dawning. In his Christmas lecture on December 21, 1903, Steiner describes how, in the ancient mysteries and especially in the Egyptian mysteries, the birth of the light in the winter nights was celebrated. Then, towards the end of the lecture, he said, "What the Egyptians celebrated became a universal reality, a cosmic event." Then he added, completely in keeping with the approach apparent in *Christianity as Mystical Fact*, that Jesus carried the secrets of the temple out into the world. What follows has a different tone: "No longer is sanctity to be found in the temple alone; they shall find the kingdom of heaven, represented as the harmonious ideal of human destiny, within themselves.

They shall ascend the peaks where a balance is to be found between the changeable heart of the individual and the unchanging laws of the macrocosmos" (B 32). An amazing step! Jesus did in fact reveal the secrets of the mysteries. These secrets are no longer a matter of belief or faith; they have become cosmic facts.

About two weeks later, on January 4, 1904, Steiner spoke publicly about "Theosophy and Christianity" and stated that it was the task of theosophy to "recognize the truth" of Christianity (52). The nature of this truth he summarized at the end of the lecture. "I am with you each day until the end of the world." What Steiner proclaims is the contemporary Christ!

This critical shift has its own background. In 1904, Steiner referred a number of times to those spiritual individualities known in the theosophical movement as the "Masters," and whom he liked to refer to as "our spiritual guides." In a letter, he declared, "I have been directed to cultivate the Christian element." Then he specified this commission: "Christian mysticism, the interpretation of the Christian symbols, etc. It will be our task to persuade ministers, even Catholic priests, to embrace esoteric Christianity. They will then have to let the esoteric flow into their teachings" (264).

Otherwise very little has been passed down concerning the directions of the spiritual guides. The only person with whom Steiner seems to have spoken of this at length is Marie von Sivers. In a letter from 1905 that seemingly alludes to a previous conversation, he writes, "I can only tell you that if the Masters had not been able to convince me that, in spite of everything, theosophy is something important for this time, I would have continued even after 1901 to just write philosophical books and to speak about philosophical and literary themes" (262).

The direction of the spiritual guide does not mean that he relieved Steiner of the necessity to do his own spiritual research. The dawning of the Christian mysteries showed Steiner that the deed of Christ was an objective cosmic event. He went on to examine this active cosmic presence in the evolution of humanity. Without the help of the Bible or any sort of dogma, Steiner developed his ideas about the cosmic significance of Christ. On June 10, 1904, he spoke of the incarnation of Christ in the body of Jesus of Nazareth, saying that through this "the *buddhi* principle itself was present in a human body" on the earth. Thanks to this presence, the forces that strove to tempt humanity away from its proper path, which Steiner in 1904 still spoke of as "Rakshasas," were banned and conquered. He went on, "This would not have been possible if Jesus of Nazareth had not been the union of two natures: on the one hand, the ancient *chela*, who was completely connected with and could work on the physical plane, holding it in balance through his own forces, and, on the other hand, Christ himself, a purely spiritual being. This is the cosmic conundrum that lies at the roots of Christianity. At that point in time, something occurred in the esoteric regions. The enemies of humanity were banned. There is an echo of this in the story of the Antichrist, who was chained but would appear again if not confronted with the essence of the Christian impulse" (93).

Steiner differentiates clearly here between Jesus and Christ. Jesus is designated as a higher spiritual student, a *chela*, who, as Steiner later describes, "at thirty years of age" sacrificed "his life to the incarnating Christ" (B 60, p. 5). Christ bore the *buddhi* principle to the earth and incarnated it. According to *Theosophy*, the *buddhi* principle forms one aspect of the human organization. It is the fully transformed, spiritually permeated and spiritually guided life body, the life spirit.

In November 1904, Rudolf Steiner described these events in a different way. He mentioned that the "spark of the *buddhi*" can also come to expression in the spirit self, the spiritually transformed soul body.

> Then the individual becomes a teacher. Buddha, Zarathustra, Krishna, Moses, and Hermes were such teachers. These individuals were born to be teachers. If the *buddhi* influence reaches the *kama* [the realm of desires] itself, then later in life the Christ principle must enter the body that has been permeated with *kama*. This was the case with Jesus, who was only able at thirty years of age to take in the Christ. If we examine Jesus's development, we see that he had taken on karma due to the fact that *kama* was developed in him from the beginning.

Here we find the situation that the Christ principle that the *buddhi* incarnates penetrates more deeply into the human organization than it could in the great teachers. In their case, the *buddhi* principle did not penetrate the realm of desire but remained in the regions of the spirit. Steiner continued, "Because Christ desired to become a brother to humanity, he had to enter a body that bore the burden of karma. The body prepared for the incarnation of Christ; the *buddhi* principle was formed by a *chela* of the third degree of initiation (Zarathustra). This body was formed as a dwelling of a divine being" (B 69). Steiner revised this description in 1909 and said that the body of Jesus of Nazareth did not in the usual sense bear karma. But in 1904 he had already recognized the connection between Jesus and Zarathustra.

In the lecture notes cited here, which appear to be reliable, Christ is described in the terminology of Indian cosmology. He is designated as a *dhyanian* being, or angelic being. "The *dhyanis*, who live on a higher plane and who throw the sparks of the *buddhi* gradually into humanity, are called in a higher sense Buddhas or in Christianity Christos.... These are the true gods" (B 69). Thus the Christ was seen, heard and experienced initially as a God among other gods. This is a way of thinking that was also present among the earliest Christians. They spoke of Christ as the king of the angels. The difference between Christ and the other divinities lies in the force that makes it possible for him to penetrate earthly and human nature much more deeply than the others. "Jesus Christ is the first *lunar pitri*, filled with the *buddhi*, the union of God and man. One has also to take into consideration that in the case of Jesus the *buddhi* divinity has entered life most deeply" (B 69).

Such passages provide insight into the dawning of the Christian mysteries. Steiner experiences Christ's divinity although he is not yet able to grasp it in its entire depth. He describes the liberating nature of the deed of Christ and mentions the incarnation of Christ into the body of Jesus. The latter is understood to be a later incarnation of Zarathustra. The understanding that Christ works from out of the generation of divinities, seen here as angels, was revised in 1911. Steiner clarified and accentuated how Christ was different than the other divinities and showed that he originated in a completely different realm than the other gods (129). Each presentation provides a piece of the puzzle.

These ideas, which reflect the different stages of Steiner's understanding, were shared in a small, intimate circle. Among Mathilde Scholl's papers were notes from this time, describing the gatherings. They took place in Marie von Sivers's apartment and were attended by a very few women who were well versed in theosophical literature—Countess Kalckreuth from Munich, Helene Lübke from Weimar, Mathilde Scholl from Cologne and Marie and Olga von Sivers.

One finds in Steiner's lectures during the spring of 1906 an interesting attempt to describe Christ in a different way. This attempt remained an isolated episode through which Steiner was confronted with the fact that listeners and readers inclined to be literal could easily misunderstand him. It is, in fact, in this case important to pay attention to the intention, not one's own ideas, and not to try to illuminate the text using ideas that Steiner later developed. The lectures were on the topic of "Lucifer." In these talks, Lucifer is presented as the bringer of light, the bringer and mediator of knowledge, as the liberator, similar to the Greek myths of Prometheus. This is easy to follow. But Steiner adds, in order to better characterize the luciferic principle, "This does not oppose, but rather augments the Christ principle. Together they form a unity, just as all the seemingly opposing natural forces do for those who recognize nature and the universe" (54).

In another lecture he formulated the following: "Early Lucifer was spoken of as the other pole, the one who brought light to humanity. Two forces must be active on the earth—Christ, the bearer of love, and Lucifer, the bearer of the light. For humanity, light and love are the two poles. Human beings now live under the influence of these two polar forces" (97). In a third lecture, he expands on this theme. "These are the two streams present in humanity. The one stream desires only to be blest, the other wishes light in the process. Those who are afraid of knowledge consider Lucifer to be evil. But for the others, Lucifer is the bearer of the light, the bringer of light" (97).

In 1909, Rudolf Steiner took these ideas up once again but in clearly different form (comp. 113). In 1921, he annotated the text and explicitly requested that the reader note that he used the name "Lucifer" in this context to signify the bringer of the light.

His presentations from 1906 raise the question of whether they were not the expression of a still incomplete understanding of the Christ. Later, he did speak of the divine light of Christ, saying that it not only warmed the hearts but also illuminated the heads. The light of Christ brings warmth or love and insight or knowledge.

Shortly after Rudolf Steiner gave the above-mentioned 1906 lectures, the Leadbeater affair, which was described earlier, shook the Theosophical Society, and Steiner felt compelled to differentiate his work from the Eastern stream promulgated by the society. By articulating the nature of Rosicrucian theosophy and drawing a line between the Rosicrucian path that he taught and the Eastern approach, he emancipated himself from the noteworthy—but in many ways luciferic—stream of H. P. Blavatsky and Annie Besant.

On May 31, 1906, after the decision had been made to make a clear separation between the two approaches, Steiner gave a lecture in Paris. Éduoard Schuré's notes document that Steiner began the lecture by saying, "Christianity plays a unique, incisive and essential role in the history of humanity. It is, let us say, the central moment, the turning point between the involution and the evolution" (94).

Schuré's notes have the lecture ending with the following thoughts: "The new science of the spirit teaches, as the Rosicrucians did, about the inner Christ in each person and about the future Christ in humanity as a whole" (94).

Thus in the second half of 1906, Steiner reached a new level of understanding concerning Christ. Up to this point, he had not spoken of the Mystery of Golgotha, nor had he spoken of Christ as an exalted sun-being or as the son of God.

According to the existing documents, Steiner first used the term "Mystery of Golgotha" in a lecture on December 2, 1906. It is, of course, possible that he had coined and used the phrase at some earlier, undocumented point. What is important in the present context is that this lecture strikes a new chord and that the Mystery of Golgotha is seen literally from a new perspective. Steiner began the lecture by connecting to the ideas that he had previously developed—that Christ brings the possibility and the strength to humanity to receive the *buddhi* principle—then goes on to speak of the Mystery of Golgotha from a cosmic perspective. "If, from a distant star, we were able to watch the evolution of the earth through many thousands of years, we would see a time in which Christ worked upon the earth in such a way that the entire astral was permeated by Christ. Christ is the spirit of the earth, the earth is his body. Everything that lives upon the earth that sprouts and grows is Christ" (97).

Rudolf Steiner had spoken in a conceptually similar manner a few weeks earlier. In a lecture cycle on the Gospel of St. John, he described Christ as the representative of the "great consciousness of the earth" (94) and at the end of the cycle called him the "sun" that illuminated humanity.

> You could never see the Sun if you had no eyes. Who created human eyes? The Sun created them. Christ is the Sun, which the human soul shall take up into itself with the help of what allows us to see Christ. The Gospel of St. John is this eye. This eye would not, however, have been able to see without the true Jesus Christ, who first opened the

eyes of his disciple, the one who loved his Lord, and who he himself awakened, his intimate pupil. (94)

This motif of Christ as the spiritual sun that illuminates humankind and permeates the earth would be developed further in the coming years. Directly following the 1907 Munich congress, Steiner gave the major lecture cycle "Roscrucian Theosophy." The relationship between Christ and the sun is spoken of explicitly, not metaphorically, in its cosmic significance.

> In examining the sun, we must take into consideration its body, the body of the planetary sun, with ego-spirits that are spirits of fire, and with a sovereign of the sun, the most highly developed of the sun spirits, Christ. During the time that the earth was the sun, this spirit was the central spirit of the sun.... When the earth became the earth, this spirit had reached the summit of its development and remained with the earth after uniting itself with the earth through the Mystery of Golgotha. (99)

Steiner spoke again about the Gospel of St. John a year later in Hamburg. Here he presented this idea in a sweeping imagination in which all the motifs that he had developed up to that time were brought together in a comprehensive picture. Once again he spoke from the perspective of an observer located on a distant star following the evolution of the earth during the Mystery of Golgotha. This observer would have noticed the colors and forms of the earth's aura *before* the Mystery of Golgotha.

> Then he would have seen how at a certain point in time the colors of the aura changed. What is this point in time? This is the moment in which the blood flowed from the wounds of Christ Jesus on Golgotha. The entire spiritual make-up of the earth changed in this moment.... In this moment, as the event from Golgotha took place, the force—the impulse that earlier reached the earth from the sun through the light—began to unite with the earth. The union of the Logos with the earth brought about the change in the earth's aura. (103)

In this lecture the picture is brought to the audience of the Mystery of Golgotha as a cosmic event, one that does not only affect humanity but that transforms the entire earth and opens her path into the future.

In 1907 and 1908, Rudolf Steiner developed another idea that would be essential for the future: the insight into the double nature of evil, the oppositional forces. This insight, which plays a fundamental role in what

Steiner presents in *Outline of Esoteric Science*, is not found in the articles that form "From the Akashic Record." He articulated it for the first time on January 1, 1909, in a lecture in Berlin and would deepen and refine it constantly in the coming years. His thoughts on this subject would have to be the subject of a separate research project. It will have to suffice to say that Lucifer can be understood to be the force that would draw humanity away from the earth and tempts human beings toward hubris and pride, whereas Ahriman chains thought to matter and lets the world of the senses appear to be the only reality. The effects of both forces continue beyond the threshold of death. Materialism leads to isolation after death; and Lucifer hides the inner truth of the soul world that originates in the spiritual world.

In *An Outline of Esoteric Science*, which was finished in 1909 and published at the beginning of 1910, Rudolf Steiner describes the Mystery of Golgotha as the overcoming of these two inimical forces.

> At that moment in the life of Jesus Christ when his astral body first contained everything that Lucifer's intervention can conceal, he began to appear as the teacher of humanity, and human evolution on Earth began to be implanted with the potential to take up the wisdom that will allow the gradual attainment of Earth's physical goal. Moreover, at the moment when the event of Golgotha took place, the other possibility, which can allow Ahriman's influence to be turned toward the good, was implanted in humanity. From this point onward, human beings can take with them into death what frees them from isolation in the spiritual world. This event in Palestine stands in the center, not only of humankind's physical evolution, but also of that of the other worlds to which human beings belong. (13, pp. 273–74)

Such passages contain the essence of Steiner's Christology. He confirmed this in the preface to a new edition, released shortly before his death in 1925.

> Since the time when the imaginations presented in this book first merged into a complete picture in my soul, I have constantly been developing my ability to perceive the human being, the historical development of humanity, and the cosmos. But the outline I offered in *Esoteric Science* fifteen years ago remains unshaken as far as I am concerned. Everything I have been able to say since then, if inserted into this book in the right place, seems only to elaborate on that outline. (13, p. 8)

With the articulation and publication of the basic tenets of Anthroposophy in *Theosophy, How to Know Higher Worlds,* and *Outline of Esoteric Science,* another chapter of Rudolf Steiner's life comes to a close. It was a period during which he was predominantly active as a teacher of Spiritual Science. From 1909 on, other forms of activity, the seeds of which were apparent earlier, appear in addition to his teaching.

1910 also brings a new phase in the development of Steiner's Christology. Having explored and sketched out the wide-reaching cosmic connections and consequences, Steiner now turns toward the mysteries of incarnation, the events in Palestine, the individual gospels and the connection of all these mysteries with human nature. The results of this research, which come to detailed expression in the lectures concerning the fifth gospel, cannot be adequately presented within the framework of this biography. One must study them in context to do them justice. What follows therefore is but a sketch of some of the indicative aspects.

In *Outline of Esoteric Science,* Rudolf Steiner had already described a particular crisis in the evolution of humanity that led to fundamental changes in the make-up of the human being. That part of the human being in which the human formative forces that provided ongoing rejuvenation were at work was withdrawn from the influence of the human soul, which had come under the influence of Lucifer. "One part of the life body remained outside of the physical body. It could be guided only by higher beings, not the human 'I'" (13). As human evolution continued, this truly human part of the individual remained under the protection of higher beings who had taken up abode on the sun (13).

In 1909, Steiner explained that since this period of crisis there has existed a special being in the form of a soul that has remained pure. He called this being—the essence of pure human formative forces—the Adam-soul. According to his descriptions, this pure soul incarnated into the body of the Jesus child described in the Gospel of St. Luke. Earlier, around 1904, Steiner had arrived at a different conviction: that a representative of human development who had passed through many earthly lives and attained a high level of spiritual development was incarnated in the person known as Jesus. In 1909, he explains that the Jesus child described in the Gospel of St. Matthew, the child visited by the three kings, was an incarnation of Zarathustra. He goes on to describe how at about the age of twelve, the reincarnated Zarathustra leaves his body and then lives on in the body of the child described by Luke. Thus, a seasoned being who has developed himself in the course of many incarnations becomes the steward of the purest forces of childhood present in the child whose story is told by St. Luke. Just before the baptism in the Jordan River, the being of Zarathustra leaves the body of Jesus of Nazareth, into which, at the baptism, the being of Christ now enters (comp. 114 & 123).

These presentations, which still cause many people consternation today, were, in 1909, incredibly risky. One of the people present during the lectures about "The Gospel of St. Luke" recalls, "A tremendous excitement was felt in the audience—one can scarcely imagine what it was like today—when Steiner revealed these secrets for the first time. Not everyone was immediately convinced; there were at that time unbelievers and skeptics,... individuals who only gradually found a relationship to it" (Treichler).

With presentations like those concerning the two Jesus children, Steiner was trying neither to increase the degree of the miraculous in the world nor to raise the complexity of the anthroposophic teachings. Insight into the pureness of the forces that form the human being is necessary in our time. Over the course of the next few years, Steiner returned repeatedly to the topic of the pure nature of these human formative forces and described how these forces that form and shape the human being are also present in each small child. Until roughly the third year of life, small children are under the guardianship of Christ. Through His guidance, the human being attains human form. A child learns to stand upright and to walk, so that later she can put her skills to work for others; she learns to speak, so that she later can communicate with others; she learns to think, so that she can join with others in a shared experience of the spirit and learn to understand the world (comp. 15). The Christ-mystery works on through these metamorphic stages in contemporary humanity.

Rudolf Steiner expanded on these ideas in 1913. He explained how what is present as the essence in the individualized Adam-soul accompanies humanity as a true creative force and permeates and rejuvenates each individual each night. Then he goes on to describe how this being works into the healing forces of the human being. Although these forces normally are not pure, but mixed with other aspects of the human organism, they are the forces that allow us to awake refreshed in the morning (146).

In 1914, in a final step in this sequence, Steiner turns to the cosmic prehistory of these human formative forces and describes how, in distant times, Christ gave them their form through three pre-Christian moments of sacrifice. In this manner, in the years leading up to 1914, a Christian anthropology came into being. In the senses, in the soul and in the bodily organs, Rudolf Steiner discovers the presence of the active Christ, which comes to expression in the walking, talking and thinking of the small child (comp. 149 & 152). Thus, a Christological approach to understanding human nature arose that showed the presence of Christ's activity in the development and the formation of the human body and soul.

Apparently independently of these anthropological studies, Rudolf Steiner began generally in 1909 to deepen his understanding of the human being. He sketched out, for instance, for the first time what was still a fragmentary study of the senses. Titled "Anthroposophy," this study described the suprasensory processes that take place in the physical senses. In addition, he explored the forces that give the human being form. In 1911, he gave a more comprehensive presentation of these themes in Prague in a series of lectures titled *An Occult Physiology* (128).

The reader of these lectures and fragmentary sketches can follow how Rudolf Steiner's research led him to probe the depths of the human organization and how he found new ways to speak about and envision these questions. The viewpoints that in the years leading up to 1909 led him to ever-new heights of understanding, he now applied to earthly conditions. His Christological research led him to understand the mysteries of the life of Jesus and the events in Palestine; the anthropological explorations showed him the path to an understanding of the physical human being.

At the same time, the human soul is described with growing depth and imagination. In 1909, Rudolf Steiner described the dramatic nature of the different human soul forces in lectures about "The Mission of Anger," "The Mission of Truth," and "The Mission of Devotion." In 1910, he sketched out a *Psychosophia* in a series of four lectures, in which the formation of mental images, desires, the act of forming judgments and the process of perception are described so movingly that one seems to see them appear before one's inner eye. After 1909, Steiner's anthropological descriptions attain an extraordinarily concentrated imaginative quality.

Here it must also be mentioned that the research was for Steiner extremely time consuming and difficult. Since 1909, he had planned to put the results of his research into the senses and the human form into written form. He began to write—the first ninety pages of the manuscript had already been set by the printer. Then problems began to arise with his research. Although Steiner thought that the publication of *Anthroposophy* was needed and important, the work came to a standstill and finally, notwithstanding a number of separate studies, broke off entirely. This was in spite of the fact that he had reduced his lecturing in order to be able to focus on the planned book.

Anthroposophy, Psychosophy, and *An Occult Physiology* form a bridge between the higher insights of Steiner's Christological anthropology, daily experience and the knowledge of mainstream anthropology. Steiner once indicated that they "were a serious, worthy foundation of our spiritual stream" (115). This foundation was extremely important.

Hidden in these anthropological explorations are significant insights into the path of higher knowledge. Within each individual are the sleeping yet active pure human formative forces. These lead to higher vision. The book *How to Know Higher Worlds*, which leads one into the "Garden of Readiness," begins with the words "The capacities by which we can gain insights into higher worlds lie dormant within each one of us." These dormant capacities are in fact the true, higher self that experiences the world. These forces of pure spiritual life need a guardian to ensure that they do not go astray in our world until they find higher guidance, as the individuality of Zarathustra guided the pure Adam-soul. The knowledge and orientation that one can find today in the anthroposophic work of Rudolf Steiner have this task: To experience consciously the pure human formative forces that would awaken in our time, to protect them and to guide them through the world. This is what one could call the Zarathustra impulse of Anthroposophy.

Let us return at the end of this chapter to the point at which it began. Toward the end of the above-mentioned lecture from June 3, 1913, Rudolf Steiner posed the question of why he did not speak of the things he had mentioned in this lecture back in 1909 when he first spoke of the child Jesus from the Gospel of St. Luke. He answered, "That is due to the manner in which these things were discovered." He explained that his insights had arisen through observation, and that the esoteric observations "had only later been permeated with human understanding." Initially only "the basis of an understanding of the truth of the two Jesus children" was present. "The rest had revealed itself on the foundation of this initial basic understanding" (146).

Chapter 30

THE MYSTERY PLAYS

In retrospect, it could appear as though Rudolf Steiner allowed himself to be led by two themes for many years: the transformation of the human being as it appears in Goethe's "Fairy Tale," and the dramatic arts. With the performance of the first mystery play, these two themes came together, and out of this union the entire anthroposophic art impulse was born. Thus, the first Goetheanum was created to provide a worthy venue for the performance of the mystery plays and gave birth to anthroposophic architecture. Steiner painted a stage set for one of the plays, planting the seed for further explorations in the field of painting. In connection with the plays, eurythmy was performed for the first time. And Adolf Arenson composed the "musical interludes."

The motif of drama comes to meet one in the idea of knowledge, in the way Steiner understood it. He once jotted down the following on a loose piece of paper:

> One should not wish to disregard the drama of knowledge in favor of the grammar of knowledge; and fear should not hold one back from plummeting to the depths of what is individual. One climbs out of this chasm in the company of a multitude of spirits and experiences them as soul mates; through this, one is *born* out of the spiritual world but has embraced death, becomes oneself the destroyer of what has become, brings this to expression in spiritualized form, and is present in its destruction. (40)

Here we find the drama of knowledge sketched out *in nuce*. Whoever has gained a sense, perhaps only through Steiner's descriptions, of the reality of the path to knowledge knows that gaining anthroposophic insight is a dramatic undertaking.

From about the time he was twenty-eight onward, Steiner cultivated a lively interest for drama and the theater. In 1898, he described the impression that a play by Gunnar Heiberg made on him. "When I saw his 'King

Midas' ten years ago in Vienna, I went half crazy. I left the theater in an uncontrollable Heiberg frenzy. I could not go home. Full of enthusiasm, I sought out the next pub, asked for paper and ink and stuttered words onto paper. 'The harbinger of a new day' is what I wrote about it" (29). Carried by such enthusiasm and a comparable interest, he immersed himself in Berlin's theater world, especially from 1897 through 1900, and was for two years the editor of the *Journal of Dramatic Art*. Drama appeared to him to be "the literary vanguard of the present" (29).

No other art form can bring the forces of destiny to expression as a play can. No other art form offers as many possibilities for the presentation of individuals, events and interrelated series of action. It was under these auspices that the dramatic was born in the form of the Greek tragedy, in which the actions of gods and human beings were united with the lawfulness of destiny. Rudolf Steiner wanted to reconnect with this archetypal motif of Western civilization when he staged the "Mystery of Eleusis" in Schuré's reconstruction during the theosophical congress in Munich. This play also called to mind the nature of the Greek mysteries. In the penultimate passage in his *Autobiography*, Rudolf Steiner recalled this attempt, "Thus a connection, however slight, was established with the ancient mysteries; but the main thing was that the conference included artistic work. It pointed to the will to never allow spiritual life into the society without an artistic element" (28).

In 1909, Steiner repeated this attempt by staging Schuré's *The Children of Lucifer*. In the address that preceded the world premier of this piece, he spoke about another aspect of the intentions connected with this artistic presentation. Dramatic presentations "on a stage that represents the world" is the place of practice for true action. Through art, we find "with the most certainty, the opening through which we can slowly penetrate the practical branches of life with our way of doing things" (113).

Without question it would be one-sided to view art merely as place of practice for true action, as a didactic exercise, and thus eradicate its innate value. Yet Steiner found in Schuré's plays, of which he spoke quite highly, a body of work that seemed especially well designed for this sort of exercise. Only in a private conversation with the artist Margarita Woloschin did he speak openly about why he had chosen to stage Schuré's plays.

> Then I asked him why he had staged Schuré's play in Munich. "I find it to be as lacking in artistry as a bad print." "I am glad that you find

it to be inartistic. I do too. But I certainly couldn't stage the naturalistic plays of Gerhard Hauptmann!" He held Hauptmann to be a very gifted dramatist, "but in this case it is not what the people needed." I suggested, "Couldn't one then perform Aschylos or Sophocles?" "With these actors? Of course not! I have too much respect for these spirits to perform their work with the available people. Forgive me," he continued, "you are a contemplative person but I have to be active. And I have to work with what I have." (Woloschin)

In this conversation we see another form of the theme of taking action. For Steiner, the staging of these pieces was a form of action; he brought his coworkers into movement, he tore them out of their own thinking, and he awakened their activity by his own example. These dramas were, in fact, what the Greek word originally meant—they were events, happenings, action. There is a resonance between this connotation of the original Greek and the original meaning of the Indian word *karma*, or *karman*. It also signified action or deed. Thus the deed and destiny, drama and karma flow together in this undertaking.

In addition to the motif of drama itself, we meet the theme of human transformation as Goethe poses it in his "Fairy Tale" from the *Tales of German Emigrants*. Steiner was still twenty-eight when he first encountered the "Fairy Tale" in 1889. It must have held a similar fascination for him as the theater had. He seems certainly to have spoken about it with his Viennese friends—Paula and Richard Specht, Friedrich Eckstein, Rosa Mayreder, and others. When he arrived in Weimar, he researched what was available concerning the "Fairy Tale" and reported on his findings in letters, calling attention to earlier conversations.

In his work with the "Fairy Tale," Steiner turned often to Friedrich Schiller's letters *The Aesthetic Education of Man*. Schiller poses the question as to how the individual can bring himself into harmony with the higher ideal that each individual can experience within himself. His idea of a centered state of soul, the aesthetic state in which a person is entirely human, led Steiner to ask if there wasn't a state of consciousness "that revealed the truth in the essence of the objects" (28). It was no less a question than "human consciousness coming to an understanding with itself," as he says in a later passage (28).

Steiner recognized that Schiller's conceptual construction, which placed the aesthetic state between the two poles of spiritual and natural necessity, must have appeared too simplistic for Goethe. Steiner describes Schiller's ideas as profound, "but far too simple when it comes to actual soul life, where deeply rooted forces flare up into consciousness and then vanish after having affected other, equally fleeting forces. These processes are dying away even as they are arising, and abstract concepts are suitable for comprehending phenomena that have a somewhat longer duration. Goethe sensed the truth of this and placed pictorial knowledge in his fairy tale, as opposed to Schiller's conceptual knowledge" (28).

Quite early on, Rudolf Steiner realized that the "Fairy Tale" was not simply an imaginative description of the transformation and initiation of the human soul forces. It was the reflection of a much larger process. On November 30, 1890, he wrote to Richard Specht:

> I have had to put aside for the moment my exegesis of the fairy tale. I have stumbled on something extremely important in my study of it, which I have to work through in depth before continuing. At the moment, I *can't* say anything more. One thing is certain: Goethe's entire credo is contained in this piece. One cannot begin to explain it before living through specific aspects of what took place quietly and invisibly in Germany during the period from 1790 to 1820. I am following a very special trail. (39)

We can assume that this led him in time to an understanding of the spiritual background of the "Fairy Tale," which he first spoke about in 1924.

Rudolf Steiner first presented his interpretation of the "Fairy Tale" before the Goethe Society in Vienna on November 27, 1891. The only documentation of this lecture is in the form of a report. Missing in the report is a theme that played a central role in his second presentation on this topic in the form of an article published in the *Review of Literature* on August 28, 1899: "Die and become." This indicates that his understanding of the "Fairy Tale" took a significant step forward in the course of these eight years.

In his *Autobiography*, Steiner's remarks about this article, which was written for Goethe's 150th birthday, are noteworthy. In this article, he wanted for the first time "to express the esoteric content that lived within me publicly." And he added, "The 'Fairy Tale' lived within me as esoteric content. The article was written out of an esoteric mood" (28). In spite of this, Steiner described the article as "still minimally esoteric"—he did not think that his readers could have taken any more.

Only after the esoterically interested circle of people around the Brockdorffs had asked about spiritual content would Steiner speak "in a completely esoteric manner" about the "Fairy Tale" (28). The soul drama presented in the "Fairy Tale" opened the door to Steiner's anthroposophic work.

Goethe made two contributions to the beginning of a modern science of the spirit. Following his example, Steiner was able to lay out and demonstrate the methodological aspects of the dramatic reality of understanding; the spiritual content of the "Fairy Tale" enabled him to speak directly out of the spirit. In subsequent years, Steiner used the motifs of the "Fairy Tale" to awaken the souls of his audiences, especially in introductory lectures. The pictures allowed him to speak freely and without being dogmatic about the core of the new esoteric—the mystery of becoming human. All other topics were less suitable for the furtherance of the new approach to spiritual knowledge. Purely scientific themes would not have resonated with many listeners; religious topics would have scared others away and would have led to misunderstandings; and the purely theosophical would only have fired the interest of very few.

For Steiner himself, the pictures brought to expression the spiritual reality that provided the foundation of Anthroposophy. This, however, strove toward greater clarity and concreteness. Following the 1907 and 1909 performances of the Schuré dramas and the accompanying formation of a circle of amateur and professional actors, in the winter of 1909/10, Marie von Sivers began to ponder the question as to what would come next. Toward the end of December 1909, as plans were being made for the coming year, she wrote to her friends in Munich, Sophie Stinde and Duchess Kalckreuth:

> Yesterday I asked the Doctor to decide, as there had been so many requests. He said that he would like once again to begin the course [in Munich] with a theater performance. I said that the ladies in Munich were probably still recovering from their efforts from last year and asked if it couldn't be done in Karlsruhe, Stuttgart or Frankfurt. For instance, if we were to do "Iphigenia on Tauris," we could do it anywhere. Then the Doctor said that he would like to present Goethe's "Fairy Tale" or perhaps repeat the "Mystery of Eleusis." The "Fairy Tale" would need so many sets and costumes that it would be difficult to pull it off anywhere else.... Now, you have to think about this all carefully and don't sacrifice yourselves if you don't have the strength.... We will probably arrive in Munich either before or toward

the middle of July, and we would have to have the performance ready a week or two earlier than last year, since we have to be in Bern at the beginning of September. It is also possible that through this the artistic enthusiasm of our members is intensified and we could risk collecting for a theater. (Rudolf Steiner Studies, I & B 17)

This letter mentions nothing about a mystery play. At this point, Rudolf Steiner wanted to "present the 'Fairy Tale.'" Marie von Sivers no doubt pictured a dramatization of the original text. At the same time, the wish to build a theater appears in the background. These two things changed quickly. Steiner's idea of staging the "Fairy Tale" turned into the staging of the first mystery play, of which three more would follow. When he wrote the fourth, he intended to continue the dramatic sequence. Marie Steiner spoke of other plays that Steiner had in mind. The idea of building a theater turned into the building of an independent center for higher learning. The end of 1909 and the beginning of 1910 brought the dawning of a new future that would only take form gradually.

The first half of 1910 brought completely different tasks. Rudolf Steiner gave four major lecture cycles: "The Gospel of St. John" in Stockholm, "Macrocosmos and Microcosmos" in Vienna (119), "Manifestations of Karma" in Hamburg (120), and a series of lectures concerning the European folk souls in Kristiania (Oslo) (121). He traveled continuously. He spoke in the following cities: Norrkoping, Lund, Strassburg, Freiburg, Karlsruhe, Heidelberg, Mannheim, Pforzheim, Berlin, Kassel, Dresden, Weimar, Frankfurt, Wiesbaden, Dusseldorf, Cologne, Bonn, Koblenz, Elberfeld, Essen, Stuttgart, Munich, Klagenfurt, Rome, Palermo, Hannover, Bielefeld, Bremen and Copenhagen. In all, he lectured in thirty-eight different cities.

Traveling first from north to south, then south to north, he spoke of the manifestation of Christ in the twentieth century. His gaze is focused on the future. He speaks of the decisive nature of the 1930s, and from Stockholm through Europe to Palermo, he proclaimed the need to prepare for the most important event of the century. He spoke of the fact that the ability to behold the etheric world of life would awaken in the human soul and with it the capacity to experience Christ's presence within this world. He calls attention most strongly to 1933—thirty-three years after the end of the time of darkness (*Kali Yuga*)—when this new ability would first appear. At the same time, he warns:

This will increase for the next 2500 years after the middle of the twentieth century. Enough people will have themselves had a Damascus experience that it will be a recognized and accepted phenomenon. We are pursuing Spiritual Science to ensure that these still weakly developed capacities do not go unnoticed—that those individuals who have these gifts are not written off as fools and dreamers but will be understood from a small group of people who will see to it that in their own circles human ignorance does not brutally trample these tender seeds to death. (118)

Rudolf Steiner often turned his attention to the danger that "one might roughly trample to death the seeds that will spread new capacities across the earth" (118). When one reads this today, one can hear the sound of the soldiers marching, drowning out the great mystery of our time. One can see the "rough feet" trampling the tender seeds.

Although Steiner was inwardly completely engrossed by these themes and their challenges, in his rare moments of freedom, his imagination returned ever again to the performance planned for Munich. He sketched out scenes and possible stage directions in his notebooks. In the earlier notes the characters are still named Lily, human being, and the man with the lamp. At the end of June, Steiner returned to Berlin from Oslo and began a first draft. The "Fairy Tale" became a play, the imaginary figures became people conversing, and the riddle of the story became a riddle of the soul. The first drafts reveal much that is unexpected and completely original, things that were later lost as he prepared it for the stage.

Then Steiner traveled with Marie von Sivers to Munich. Sometime around July 7, the actors and actresses gathered in Duchess Kalckreuth's and Sophie Stinde's large living room and spoke about the play, in which "the idea of reincarnation would appear on the stage for the first time." Steiner characterized the different roles and assigned them to the people present. Then he spoke about the content of the play. To their surprise, the cast learned that Steiner had not yet begun to write out the parts.

Rehearsals began at ten o'clock the following morning in a gymnasium, and Steiner began, describing as he went, to read the first act—the dialogue between Sophia and Estella. The actors copied their parts out of Steiner's notebook. On each of the following days, Steiner would bring the continuation that he had written during the preceding night. Later, Elisabeth Vreede began to type and make duplicates of the text. Steiner revised the parts as needed during the rehearsals. Marie von Sivers, who had taken on the role of Maria, was given her last dialogue during the general rehearsal. "Isn't it true," said Steiner, "it would be nonsense to write a play before there was going to be a performance" (Errinerungen).

The mystery play that had been written during the night and rehearsed the next day is much more than a dramatization of Goethe's "Fairy Tale." The characters are people who have a shared history and a shared destiny. So, for instance, the two will-o'-the-wisps from the "Fairy Tale" appear in the play transformed into the two scientists Dr. Strader and the philologist Dr. Capesius, two completely different characters. The story content also took on a new dimension, becoming the dramatic representation of soul-spiritual development and trials.

The cast found the assignment of the roles to be successful. Marie von Sivers played Maria, a role that she embodied into each and every syllable. Mieta (Marie Elisabeth) Waller played Johannes. Steiner did not hesitate to cast a female in a male role. Dr. Felix Peipers, tall and dignified and with a noble voice, played Benedictus. Very few roles were played by professionals. Max Gümbel-Seiling was cast as Dr. Strader, and Otto Doser as Capesius.

Rudolf Steiner directed the work. He characterized the different roles and recited the parts, but he didn't give the actors strict directions as to how to play their roles. To the actor playing Ahriman, he said merely, "Speak broadly." And Lutz Kricheldorff, who had the role, added, "To the best of my memory, he never once corrected me" (*Reminiscences of Rudolf Steiner*). That was certainly in keeping with Steiner's intentions. In 1909, with the performance of Schuré's *Children of Lucifer*, he explained that what they had hoped for was "that we could achieve unity without anyone having to place himself in the kind of machinery within which speaks the commander's voice and the commands are carried out" (113). He repeated this in 1910.

> The way our dear friends here work together to create what they have created may be seen in some ways as an example not only for the anthroposophic work but perhaps also for the working together of humankind. Especially because it would diverge from any true anthroposophic sensibility to take command of this kind of work. Progress is only possible when each of our friends is engaged wholeheartedly. (122)

This doesn't mean that Steiner didn't pay attention to details. He concerned himself with the scenery, the costumes and the lighting. It has been related that the vestibule in the first act of *The Guardian of the Threshold* had to be repainted three times before it had just the right hue of indigo. "Indigo seems to be a color that is difficult to define" was Steiner's remark. He accompanied the actor with the role of Dr. Strader to the costume studio of the tailor Mück to choose the colors and pattern. Steiner chose a light orange velvet, because the right color wasn't available in regular fabric. Many of the other costumes were produced under the genial guidance of Imme von Eckardstein, who played Lucifer from 1911 on.

Most mornings, before the rehearsals began, Steiner visited the Schrannenhalle, where the painters Hass, Linde, and Volkert oversaw the construction of the sets, backdrops and other props. The canvasses were spread on the floor of the large light-filled room. They were painted with large brushes attached to long poles. Other helpers sewed the backdrops, kneeling on the floor. Still others were working on supports or experimenting with the delicate veil curtains that were needed for the scenes in the spiritual world. Rudolf Steiner went from group to group, encouraging them, making suggestions and, as the story is told, enjoying the fact that they were all hard at work in harmony with one another. Marie Steiner captured the liveliness of this time:

> It was the most beautiful time of the year, these theater days in Munich. During this time we were allowed to concentrate completely for about two months on one thing. We rehearsed during the days, and at night Rudolf Steiner wrote the parts of the play that had already composed itself within his thoughts. In between, he visited and oversaw the work in the various workshops in which, following his directions, people built sets and props, painted, sculpted, sewed and embroidered. The rough designs on which the craftsmen and artists oriented themselves flew from his fingertips. Thus he wandered among the workers, and everywhere he appeared the seeds began to sprout—new life emerged. The enormous canvasses that would become the backdrops lay heaped in the attic of the Schrannenhalle. He sketched out the sizes and the ornaments for the columns of the Temple of the Sun, the underground temple, the cloudlike forms of the spirit regions, the cliffs, the boulders and crystals of Ahriman's kingdom, the enchanted pictures of Lucifer's dominions. (*Reminiscences of Rudolf Steiner*)

In the background—unobtrusively and quietly—Sophie Stinde and Duchess Kalckreuth took care of feeding and housing the volunteers, managed the finances and organized everything. Each year their task grew larger and more difficult. In 1909, the *Children of Lucifer* was performed for around 600 visitors. In 1910, this drama was performed again on August 14, and then on August 15, the *Portal of Initiation* premiered. In 1911, *The Holy Drama of Eleusis* was performed, as well as the *Portal of Initiation* and the second of Steiner's mystery plays, *The Soul's Probation*. In 1912, there were over 1000 people present, and in addition to the two mystery plays presented the year before, Steiner's third play, *The Guardian of the Threshold*, was performed. By 1913, the audience had grown so large that Steiner had to reject the idea of performing another of Schuré's plays. *The Guardian of the Threshold* and Steiner's fourth play, *The Soul's Awakening*, were each performed twice.

There was a plan to produce a fifth play in 1914. Originally, they thought to perform it in the newly built center in Dornach. When it became clear in the springtime that the building was not going to be finished by July, they set a tentative performance date for Christmas of that year. Marie Steiner later said that the fifth play, which was never written, would have been set in Greece, in Delphi, at the Castalian spring and in the temple of Apollo. The outbreak of World War I on August 1, 1914, destroyed these plans. Toward the end of 1922, Rudolf Steiner revived the idea of performing the plays in the now nearly finished Goetheanum. In his papers, the draft of an announcement was found. In August 1923, all four plays were to be performed four times each (259). This plan had to be abandoned following the fire that destroyed the Goetheanum. The mystery plays were performed again in 1928 and 1929 after Steiner's death, at the opening of the second Goetheanum, this time under the direction of Marie Steiner. All four plays were performed together for the first time in August 1934.

Rudolf Steiner explained a number of times that the scenes that unfold in these plays were neither construed nor thought out. He wrote them the way they showed themselves to him and only understood some of what was in the plays later, an understanding that he then added as commentary. The individual development of a number of people stands in the center of these plays. The individual signature of these developments was the most important for Steiner. This focus on what was individual is clear in the character development: Felix Balde is clearly related to the herbalist Felix Koguzki; Professor Capesius has aspects of Karl Julius Schröer; and Doctor Strader, in the quality of his inner struggles, draws from the figure of Gideon Spicker.

In Goethe's "Fairy Tale" we find the image of the hawk, which, following the direction of the old man with the lamp, takes a mirror, soars high above the earth and catches the first rays of the sun to awaken the sleeping Lily, thus initiating the procession to the temple. In *The Portal of Initiation*, the hawk appears transformed in the role of Theodosia, the clairvoyant. She speaks the message that sets the characters in this play into movement along their path. It is a message that Steiner proclaims from this point on.

> But now the time draws near
> When earthly man shall be endowed
> With the new power of sight.
> What once the senses could behold
> When Christ lived on the earth,
> Will be perceived by souls
> When soon the time has been fulfilled.

Steiner speaks here of a reality that had not appeared above the horizon of the time. All told, the mystery plays are pieces of spiritual realism. Their intention is to depict spiritual realities. Steiner expressed this himself when he said that the content of the plays was "much more intensive, closer to life, more real, because it was more individual" than what he could express in more general terms.

> In a book like *How to Know Higher Worlds*, one can only speak about human development in a way that is more or less applicable to each and every human being.... That means that no matter how concrete such a presentation is, it takes on a certain abstract—one could even say theoretical—character. One thing we have to keep in mind: Development is not simply development in general! There is no development in and of itself, no generalized development; there is only the development of this or that or a third or fourth or the thousandth person. There must be as many processes of development as there are people on the earth. (125)

Later, commenting on his work, Steiner called to the attention of his audience, for example, the role of Johannes Thomasius and in 1913 explained, no doubt to the amazement of his listeners, the stages of the path that Johannes had taken.

> If we only consider *The Portal of Initiation*, and focus on Johannes Thomasius, we see that he does not progress very far at all. He doesn't progress beyond what one could call imaginative soul experiences with all their one-sidedness and errors. Everything that is presented here is subjective.... This is indicated in a fairly tangible manner in that it is clearly described in all the scenes that...Johannes...is on stage. We have to think that everything that happens takes place within his soul as a form of imaginative knowledge. Even if he appears to speak words in the temple at the end of the *Portal of Initiation* that are objectively valid, we must keep in mind that in various temples there are people who speak of things that they have not yet embodied. (147)

In a draft for the afterword to the fourth mystery play, Steiner developed this thought further. "In the *Soul's Probation*, the soul-spiritual occurrences are emancipated from Johannes's inner life. He no longer lives merely in the subjective; he is immersed in life processes and experiences their spiritual aspects and relationships.... In the *Soul's Probation* the shared experience of the spiritual world begins" (44).

Only in the *Guardian of the Threshold* does the transition into the objective world begin (147). The relationships become more complex and difficult. The last scene gives a view into the future that shows that each individual human who matures to a state of objectivity has a task to fulfill "in the temple."

Following these preparations, the developing human beings in these plays enter practical life. The "Temple of the Sun," which provided the spiritual background of the developmental paths depicted in the first two plays and that appeared in a metamorphosed form as the "Temple of the Mystics" in the third play, does not appear openly in the final play. The first scene opens in the office of a lumber mill. A secretary and an office manager enter and begin to discuss the future development of the mill, soon to be joined by both Doctor Strader and Johannes Thomasius. A whole new spectrum of difficulties arises and Benedictus, the spiritual guide of this group of humans striving for inner development, can no longer be pictured "as merely standing above his pupils, but woven through his own soul destiny in the soul experiences of the others" (14).

These brief remarks must suffice to show that the spiritual realism of the mystery plays leads from subjective spiritual heights into earthly reality. In the Rosicrucian mysteries are presented the prophetic vision, the image and the goal of a long path of development. In the *Soul's Probation*, existential struggles of the soul are placed in the middle point. In the *Guardian of the Threshold*, Johannes Thomasius has reached the point of his development where he shall take hold of the outer realities. In the *Soul's Awakening*, a solid grounding for practical work is attained, and the corresponding crises and failures arise. This was a prophetic indication of the path of development that the anthroposophic movement would follow in the coming years.

CHAPTER 31

SEPARATION FROM THE THEOSOPHICAL SOCIETY

The story is related that in 1889 Helena Blavatsky told a small group of theosophical students that the true reason for the Theosophical Society was to prepare humankind to receive a teacher of humanity who would appear in the twentieth century. She indicated that this would take place in the latter third of the century. Annie Besant publicized these thoughts and during a talk in Chicago in August 1909 said, "We expect him to appear in the Western world, not in the East as Christ did 2000 years ago" (M. Lutyens). C. W. Leadbeater had actually a few years previously already identified this teacher in the being of Hubert van Hook, the son of the general secretary of the Theosophical Society in the United States.

When Annie Besant spoke in Chicago, she was not yet aware of what had taken place in Adyar since she had left India the previous April. Charles Webster Leadbeater, who thanks to Annie Besant had been welcomed back into the Theosophical Society and who had returned to Adyar in February, had discovered two young Hindu boys, Krishna and Nitya, on the beach. He assured the boys' companions that Krishna had an especially large, beautiful aura and would become an important spiritual teacher. One of the companions, who knew Krishna well and had tutored him, found this to be outrageous, as he believed Krishna to be somewhat backward. But Leadbeater was not to be put off. He predicted that Krishna would have an illustrious future—and in this he was proven right.

Leadbeater was soon given responsibility for the education of Jiddu Krishnamurti, born on May 11, 1895. Struggling through tears, he and his brother were prepared for their future careers. At the same time, Leadbeater began to "research" the previous lives of the boy and the individuals connected to him. In Leadbeater's writings on this theme, Krishna was named "Alcyone," Annie Besant was called "Heracles," and Leadbeater, "Sirius." Finally, Annie Besant got wind of what had taken place in Adyar and was informed that the much spoken of "Alcyone" was, in fact, Krishnamurti.

On January 10, 11 and 12, 1910, Krishnamurti was "initiated" with Leadbeater presiding. In April, a series of Leadbeater's articles entitled "Rents in the Veil of Time" began to appear in the *Theosophist*. In these, he presented Krishnamurti's/Alcyone's previous lives back to 23,650 BCE as well as the lives of those individuals connected with him. Later, the "Lives of Alcyone" was published, and soon it was considered a mark of theosophical attainment to have one's name appear in the *Lives*. Naturally, even outside of Germany there were a large number of prominent theosophists who either harbored doubts as to the seriousness of Leadbeater's "research" or found the whole thing completely ridiculous: *In the Lives, in the Lives, I've had all kinds of husbands and wives*. But in general, the whole thing was fairly successful in theosophical circles and the cult around Krishna grew. Finally, on January 11, 1911, the first anniversary of Krishna's initiation, George Arundale founded the Order of the Rising Sun, which shortly thereafter became the Order of the Star in the East (OSE). This order, which was to prepare the coming of the great spiritual teacher, produced widespread propaganda. Whenever possible, national representatives of the order were appointed and national groups were formed.

In the spring of 1911, Annie Besant traveled to Europe with Krishna, Nitya, George Arundale and others. On May 8, the anniversary of Helena Blavatsky's death, she gave a talk in the London headquarters of the Theosophical Society and indicated that Christ would appear through Alcyone as he had 2000 years earlier in Jesus. She called this Christ "Lord Maitreya," a bodhisattva.

Rudolf Steiner became acquainted with Annie Besant's still relatively unformed plans and intentions at the latest during the congress in Budapest in June 1909. Annie Besant, who did respect Rudolf Steiner's work, wanted to include him and made the suggestion that he consider himself to be the reincarnation of John the Evangelist and play an important role in what was to come. Steiner politely declined and added, according to his own account seven years later, "There can be no question of any willingness on my part to be anything else within the context of an esoteric movement than to be connected with German culture—only with German culture, within Central Europe" (167). In addition, during the time they were both in Budapest, Steiner attempted not only politely but with all the respect due to the presiding president to point out the dubious and risky nature of her plans. And at that time, in June 1909—the last time he was to see Annie Besant—he had reason to believe that she would take his words to heart. For his part, Steiner wanted to avoid any unnecessary dissent. The German section was now just seven years old and needed time to develop.

In 1909, when talk of the differences between his path and that of Annie Besant arose, he remarked, "Besant and Steiner seem to get along quite well, even if they are traveling along different paths." And he recognized during the congress "the sweeping intuition and depth of feeling" in Annie Besant's lecture entitled "The Christ, Who Is He?" He dwelt on this lecture, interpreting and deepening certain passages in a very positive manner. Concerning one point, however, he noted the difference in their approaches. "One can completely agree with the view that the Christ—concerning the manner and timing of this, my insights diverge from those of Mrs. Besant—will reappear and be recognized by those who are prepared. We should, however, lay emphasis on the preparation rather than on the reappearance" (Mitteilungen, January 1910).

Steiner's published remarks from the general assembly of the German section as well as in the *Mitteilungen* show quite clearly that he was earnestly trying to have things develop peacefully, to work quietly and not to disturb the striving for understanding, although he was certainly aware of the questionable nature of Annie Besant's plans.

In any case, the outer symptoms of the impending conflict were barely visible in 1910. In October, Annie Besant wrote a long positive article about Rudolf Steiner for a series entitled "Theosophical Worthies" in the *Theosophist*. The article concluded with the words "Long may he live to guide the people whom he enlightens, and to carry his message through Europe." And in March 1911, a very positive review of the English translation of *Theosophy* appeared in the same publication.

At the same time, the differences between Leadbeater/Besant on the one side and Steiner on the other did not go unnoticed. While Annie Besant was speaking of Krishnamurti as the *vehicle* of the coming Maitreya, Steiner was speaking of the reappearance of Christ in the etheric. His presentations met with understanding in Central Europe and in Scandinavia. It seems as though Annie Besant's followers began to raise the question as to how Steiner's influence could be contained. A first step in this direction took place in Switzerland, where Steiner was also active and where the branches in Basel, Bern, Lugano, St. Gallen and Zurich considered themselves to be part of the German section. The three branches in Geneva, however, were connected with the French section. A plan was made to form a separate Swiss section. The three Geneva branches were reorganized into seven branches, the number needed to form a national section. In January 1911, Annie Besant announced in the *Theosophist*:

> Our eighteenth national section was acknowledged on November 29, 1910. Our Swiss brothers felt that it was necessary to form their own section, instead of remaining part of the French section as was allowed by our founding president. Thus we now have a T.S. in Switzerland that is responsible for the area covered by the Swiss Republic. We wish our youngest brother well. (*Theosophist*, January 1910)

The "brothers" in Geneva had not, however, gone about things in a very brotherly manner. They had not made any attempt to come to agreement with the five already active German-speaking branches (which had more members than the seven artificially created Geneva branches). These would not have agreed under any circumstances, as they wished to remain connected with the German section. The formation of the Swiss section, encompassing the entire Swiss territorial region, served no purpose other than limiting Steiner's influence among the members of the Theosophical Society. The German-speaking branches protested the move, a protest that Annie Besant could not ignore. Behind closed doors, however, there was now some talk of an unwarranted German expansion. Seemingly, Annie Besant had managed to overlook the fact that by the formation of the German section in 1902 at which she had been present, the Lugano branch had been counted as a part of the new section, without any disagreement. Neither was the connection between the German-speaking branches and the German section any less reasonable than the connection between the French-speaking branches and the French section. Before 1910, no one had thought to question these arrangements.

In June 1911, Annie Besant appointed Wilhelm Hübbe-Schleiden to represent the Order of the Star in the East (OSE) in Germany. On July 4, 1911, he wrote to Steiner to inform him of the appointment. At the same time, Mrs. Besant appointed Dr. Hugo Vollrath, who had been expelled from the German section for good reasons with her agreement, to be the managing secretary of the OSE. Rudolf Steiner received news of these appointments in Munich, where he was engaged in preparing the performances of the mystery plays. Since Steiner did not have time for extensive correspondence, Hübbe-Schleiden asked his friend Ludwig Deinhard to speak with him. Steiner and Deinhard finally met on July 25. The next day, Deinhard wrote to Hübbe-Schleiden:

> Steiner's position concerning the order is the same as the one you described in an earlier letter as the only reasonable one. He said, "What Mrs. Besant does outside of the T.S., whether it be the forming of an order or anything else, does not concern me as the general secretary of the German section. I cultivate my Rosicrucian movement and work to win my followers over to the idea of esoteric development."...He was not at all bothered by the fact that you let yourself be named as the representative of this order in Germany.... "The order itself," said Steiner, "seems to be something that will never be taken seriously in Germany. One should try to awaken interest here for it because it contradicts completely German thought and sensibility. Whoever joins it will not be taken seriously by reasonable people. No one takes Dr. Vollrath seriously." Thus, Steiner's response. (Klatt)

In addition, Deinhard warned his friend about the position he had accepted and described his impression of his conversation with Steiner.

> In any case, he doesn't take Leadbeater's esoteric research seriously. Steiner didn't say a word about all the talk of the reappearance or non-reappearance of Christ's spirit. That he views the young Alcyone as a competitor—Steiner did not make this impression at all. He sees Alcyone as nothing more than a young man who, in spite of his thirty... previous incarnations and his initiation in the esoteric world, at the moment still has to learn enough to be able to do something in this world. (Klatt)

Toward the end of the letter, Deinhard urged his friend to resign this position as the public representative of the order so as to protect his reputation. Hübbe-Schleiden did not follow his friend's advice. As one of the founders of the Theosophical Society in Germany in 1884, he now saw himself called to support "this universal movement with a vision for the future" (Klatt).

From September 16 to 19, 1911, a theosophical congress was planned. It was to take place in Genoa. Everyone expected that a discussion of the pertinent questions would take place during this gathering, especially an open dialogue between Rudolf Steiner and Annie Besant. On September 10, Steiner received a telegram from the general secretary of the Italian Society, Otto Penzig, informing him that the gathering would not take place and requesting that he inform the German members accordingly. Steiner sent a telegram to Penzig asking the reason for the cancellation. "I have acted on the strict orders of the president and the secretary of the congress," Penzig replied. Annie Besant claimed later that she had not cancelled the congress, merely her attendance. Whatever the case, it is strange that Annie Besant, who reported constantly on all her activities in the *Theosophist*, is completely silent concerning the cancellation of the Genoa gathering. This abrupt and seemingly unwarranted cancellation led to a certain discontent, especially as a number of theosophists, not only from Germany, were already on their way to Genoa.

While the activities of Annie Besant and the Order of the Eastern Star were meeting with opposition in larger and smaller groups outside of Germany, there was growing interest for what Rudolf Steiner had to say. This didn't pose a problem in Scandinavia, as the Scandinavian sections were, for the most part, closely connected to his work. There were, however, supporters of Steiner's spiritual direction as well in England, France and Holland. Active in France were Alice Sauerwein, Éduoard Schuré and Eugene Levy; and in England, Harry Collison and H. J. Heywood-Smith. In 1911 and 1912, the Danish baron Alfons Walleen-Bornemann was especially active, not only in Denmark but also in England. He met with all sorts of difficulties and the opposition of the representatives of the Order of the Eastern Star. Annie Besant complained about his aggressive manner in a letter to Steiner on January 4, 1912, and requested that he rein in his followers (Unger). The existing documentation suggests that the actions of both parties were less than productive and that Baron Walleen, in contrast to Steiner, made the mistake of entering into an ideological discussion.

The looming conflict reached a new level during the general assembly of the German section, when the motion was made to rescind Dr. Vollrath's expulsion. The German members were taken aback by this motion, especially as it was accompanied by a tactless letter from Dr. Vollrath and they thought that he would use the section as a stage to propagate the work of the order. A number of members considered at that time the founding of a new society, and Steiner found himself having to quiet the insurrectionists in his own circles. He took the stage at the general assembly just after Baron Walleen had described the obstacles that he had met during his trip to England and, in connection with this, voiced the idea of founding a new society. Toward the end of his talk, Steiner said that most important for him was that the individuals "who play a leading role in our theosophical movement share the opinion that we must hold onto the society for as long as possible! This is what makes it difficult for me to support any initiative that would harm the society in any way....The destruction of the society as such is at this time certainly not what is called for—positivity is called for. And as far as this is concerned, it is more difficult to be positive than it is to be negative" (264).

In spite of Steiner's words of warning, the supporters of a new society founded a *Bund* on December 16, 1911, which gave itself the task "to unite all those who wish to cultivate Rosicrucian Spiritual Science." They wanted to achieve this with an organization "that was founded on trust and responsibility, without a written charter but rather through trying to approach what in the spiritual sense can be called a hierarchical order." In addition, the declaration stated:

> Neither in its form nor in its content does the *Bund* have anything to do with the Theosophical Society; its members may be members of the Theosophical Society or not; it does not wish to endanger the existence of the German section in any way; it has not been founded in opposition to anything, but out of the intent to positively support the cultivation of a specific spiritual stream, Rosicrucian Spiritual Science, and it strives for a form that corresponds to the content of this spiritual stream. (*Mitteilungen*, March 1912)

The reason for the formation of the *Bund* was clearly to form a group to which both members and non-members of the Theosophical Society, regardless of their nationality, could belong. The meetings of the *Bund* were open to the extent that representatives of the Adyar-based approach to theosophy were also able to attend. For example, Dr. Otto Schrader reported on and provided his own commentary to the discussions in the *Bund* in *Theosophy* (December 1912). All in all, the *Bund* remained a very loose-knit organization that neither issued membership cards nor collected dues and soon, as Rudolf Steiner noted in 1921, "progressed gradually from a gentle sleep into social extinction" (76).

During the time that these events were taking place in Germany, Annie Besant appointed John H. Cordes, a native Austrian and Krishnamurti's guardian, to be the national representative for Germany on the international council of the Theosophical Society, which convened in Adyar. She requested that he contact Dr. Hübbe-Schleiden, Dr. Vollrath and Bernhard

Hubo in Hamburg. In January, Cordes wrote to Hubo, "Could you help me obtain short news items for publication and as much private, intimate information as possible?...If you choose to honor me with private matters, I shall handle them with absolute discretion" (*Mitteilungen*, December 1912).

This requested was directed to the wrong party. Although Bernhard Hubo, who was responsible for the branch in Hamburg, had been somewhat skeptical concerning Steiner at the founding of the German section, he had changed his assessment since then. Hubo responded to Cordes, expressing first his surprise over the fact that Cordes was appointed to represent the German section without having contacted Steiner, the general secretary of the section, and obtaining his agreement. He was also outraged at the thought that he should provide Adyar with any sort of personal or intimate gossip. "Things have truly gone too far when the central headquarter of the Theosophical Society takes steps to develop a network of spies!" (*Mitteilungen*, December 1912)

Representatives of the *Bund* met on February 20 and 21 in the branch's house in Stuttgart. Rudolf Steiner stayed in the background during these deliberations. He wanted to see what initiatives were living in the members. However, he gave a lecture on each of the two evenings. These lectures focused on the significance of the ideas of reincarnation and karma for modern life. He showed how humanity, faced with increasingly complex relationships, could find an inner orientation through these ideas so that it would not be necessary for each individual to have a guide standing at his shoulder "telling him to turn to the right or to turn to the left" (135). Then he sketched how important the ideas of reincarnation and karma are for the creation of new communities.

> The way in which an anthroposophist thus works to bring forth a new culture must live in his consciousness. A feeling for the intensive significance of reincarnation and karma in life is something that can sustain a community regardless of the outer circumstances. Those individuals who can be united through such an inner feeling understanding can find each other only through Anthroposophy. (135)

This appeal was at the time not really understood, nor was it recognized. Those present were preoccupied with other problems. But it still shows clearly the intent that Rudolf Steiner wished to bring to bear in the formation of a new, anthroposophic society.

To clarify the situation with the Theosophical Society, in March 1912 Rudolf Steiner wrote a long letter to Annie Besant, to which he later referred. He explained "that I certainly did not presume to have the right to tell her what she could or could not do in regard to the 'Order of the Eastern Star,' something with which I had absolutely not concerned myself. Neither did I raise any objections to her appointment of Dr. Vollrath. What came to expression in the annual meeting of the German section merely confirmed the fact that Mrs. Besant,... by ignoring the opinions of the general secretary of the section, had essentially voiced a vote of no confidence" (*Mitteilungen*, December 1912).

In spite of this, on May 8, Annie Besant wrote to Mathilde Scholl, the editor of the German section's newsletter. In this letter she articulated her position in regard to discussion concerning Dr. Vollrath during the annual meeting and his appointment as the German secretary of the Order of the Eastern Star. She denied knowing anything about the reasons for his expulsion from the German section or about the pamphlet he had published critical of Steiner. She claimed that she would never had suggested Dr. Vollrath as secretary had she known these things.

Her statements did not reflect the actual truth of the matter. Vollrath had turned to her with his complaints on December 1, 1908. She had responded on January 1 and March 18, 1909. She knew about the situation both through Steiner's reports and through Vollrath's letters. She should certainly have felt obligated to read Vollrath's pamphlet before appointing him to a position of responsibility. In any case, she should have been aware that the appointment of Vollrath, a notorious troublemaker who Ludwig Deinhard described as "spiritually abnormal" (Klatt), would be seen as an affront in Germany.

Annie Besant's letter did have the desired effect among the non-German members. Steiner was now viewed as a troublemaker. In Germany, however, where the circumstances were known, her defensive protestations of innocence only caused more discontentment.

The conflict continued to smolder until June 19, 1912, when Wilhelm Hübbe-Schleiden poured oil on the coals and let loose the flames. He held a lecture in Hannover entitled "Message of Peace." In the first part of the lecture, which Hübbe-Schleiden immediately published, was much talk of brotherhood and peace and that any potential differences had been carefully ironed out. Then he accused the German section of dogmatism and intolerance and opined that the section was run in a manner similar to that of the Catholic Church (Hübbe-Schleiden). This is brought especially clearly to expression in the afterword to the lecture. The stance of the new *Bund*, he says, can be compared "to that of the Jesuits.... The Anthroposophists believe blindly in the revelations of their teacher, Dr. Steiner. Theosophists do not believe in the infallibility of any one person. There is no one-sided dogmatism in the Theosophical Society; it is not a place of infighting or discord. The Theosophical Society strives for complete spiritual freedom and independence, for brotherly love, for peace and happiness" (Hübbe-Schleiden).

Hübbe-Schleiden could expect resonance for his ideas from a number of places, for there were in fact a number of dogmatic, intolerant followers of Rudolf Steiner. There was also, as shown by the formation of the *Bund*, a tendency toward hierarchical forms. Hübbe-Schleiden, however, saw things from a somewhat narrow perspective. Dogmatism and a tendency toward adulation also held sway among the followers of Leadbeater, Besant and the members of the Order of the Eastern Star. Neither the order nor the Theosophical Society were free of hierarchical forms. A perusal of Annie Besant's lectures and writings gives one a wealth of material for the study of personal idolatry and hierarchical structures. What was infamous about Hübbe-Schleiden's piece was the comparison with the Jesuits, who were believed at that time, even among educated people, to be capable of all types of evil.

Following Hübbe-Schleiden's attack, Rudolf Steiner finally spoke out. Until then, he had been silent concerning the Order of the Eastern Star and had not responded to any of the attacks on his work. Toward the end of a lecture for members on June 20, 1912, he spoke about his concerns. These words are characteristic of Steiner. First he spoke about the fundamental principle that guided him and, originally, had also been an important motto in the Theosophical Society. It had to do with the truth, and with the striving toward objectivity and truthfulness. He reminded his listeners "that it is very difficult to bring this elemental gesture of theosophical striving to expression in theosophical action" (133). Here Steiner called back to mind the old theosophical motto "No creed is higher than the truth," which in Germany at times was expressed in Goethe's words: "Wisdom is only to be found in the truth."

Steiner then spoke of all the talk about tolerance that erases all differences, which allows the most contradictory statements to stand beside one another without any further explanation. "It is quite easy to say that all opinions are equal in the theosophical movement. This remains an empty phrase if it is not taken seriously. And it is then especially an empty phrase when the opinions of others are not presented in an appropriate manner." Then he explicitly addressed the accusation that Anthroposophy was specifically tailored to fit the German character. He countered this attempt at relativism—which glorifies one's own work while at the same time imprisoning what one dislikes in narrow nationalist borders—demeaning Anthroposophy as a German idiosyncracy. "It is something for humanity as a whole, as mathematics are, not something for a single nation. To present what we are doing here as being merely for one country, a narrowly defined territory, is an untruth" (133).

It is noteworthy that Steiner speaks here of methodology. He does not argue the truthfulness of the subject content; he demands rather that one not distort another's views and that one not immediately demean the knowledge that another has gained. If each insight is relegated to the level of opinion, no dialogue is possible and everything dissolves into a tasteless mass of differing viewpoints. On top of that, the point of departure for any dialogue is the ability to understand the other's ideas and the capacity to articulate them correctly, not simply to attack what one thinks the other said.

Toward the very end of the lecture, Steiner spoke about the Order of the Eastern Star. He compared this initiative with other societies and orders. In Steiner's words, there are "many different societies and associations in the world—societies for the peace movement, for vegetarianism, abstinence societies, and so on. These are all goals that one can work for." On the other hand, to form "a society or order for the arrival of a future savior" was as grotesque as forming a society "for the coming of a 'Bismark'" (133). He did not speak against Krishnamurti nor did he belittle the possibility that Krishnamurti might someday incarnate an important individuality. He spoke only of the founding of the order as utter nonsense.

In contrast to many of his followers, who emphasized the difference between his teachings and those of Mrs. Besant, Steiner turned his attention to those aspects of the conflict that could be generally understood. He did not enter a debate as to whether Christ would appear in the etheric or through Krishnamurti. He expressly refused to enter such a debate and remarked, "Anyone who is acquainted with the sciences knows that there are things that can be debated. But there are things that cannot be debated, where if someone else has a different opinion one must say, 'He just doesn't know what it is all about'" (133).

Later, he would also emphasize these two questions: the question of intellectual honesty and truthfulness and the question of method and process. In accordance with the charter of the Theosophical Society, he also rejected all forms of dogmatism. The Order of the Eastern Star was formed around a dogma: that Krishnamurti would be the bearer of a future spiritual teacher, the Maitreya or Christ. In Steiner's opinion, this dogmatic approach could not be reconciled with the charter of the Theosophical Society. He opposed any attempt to reorganize the TS to make it more amenable to the goals of the OSE, as had been done in Switzerland, or by forming branches of the Theosophical Society that were based on the teachings of the order.

Hübbe-Schleiden's "Message of Peace" and Steiner's response to his accusations brought the conflict into the open. Shortly thereafter, in June 1912, Steiner traveled to Munich to prepare the coming performances of the mystery plays and to write the third of the dramas. The next seven weeks leading up to the performances were extremely trying, as Rudolf Steiner was under pressure from all sides. Already in the beginning of May, during a conference in Cologne, he had been approached by a group of individuals from Holland, England and Belgium who rejected what the OSE stood for. On July 1, Marie von Sivers reported to her friend Mieta Waller, "The outer circumstances have probably never been more difficult for the Dr. than they are this year. For weeks now, each morning brings more bad tidings."

Steiner was able to finally write the first scene of the third mystery play on July 27, only three weeks before the first performance!

In spite of this, they were able to finish with the rehearsals and staging by August 18, and that summer they put on a total of four plays—Schuré's *Divine Drama from Eleusis* and the three mystery plays, *The Portal of Initiation, The Soul's Probation,* and *The Guardian of the Threshold.* During this period, Rudolf Steiner also wrote the book *A Path to Self-Knowledge.* In the personal realm, Marie von Sivers's mother was on her deathbed. Marie and her sister, Olga, cared for her.

Following the performances from August 25 to 31, Rudolf Steiner gave a series of lectures entitled "About Initiation." During this time, in the morning on August 27, 28 and 29, about 800 people gathered to consider the future of the *Bund*, which was to be formed anew. In the course of the discussions, Marie von Sivers, Michal Bauer and Carl Unger argued for the necessity of remaining within the Theosophical Society in order to transform it. Theosophists from outside of Germany took the position that the *Bund* was necessary to insure that the form of theosophical teaching brought by Rudolf Steiner could be heard in other countries. A number of voices were raised against the formation (Otto Schrader from Adyar, Josef Elkan from Munich and Alfred Ostermann from Colmar).

Rudolf Steiner was present during these discussions but did not take an active role. According to the reports published in the *Theosophist*—which are only questionably accurate—he only spoke out twice, both times with clarifying statements. He must have, however, suggested the name *Anthroposophical Society* for the new association at this time. The *Bund*, as Steiner pointed out years later, never did become a social reality; it remained a rather diffuse, indefinite organization.

Alexander Strakosh, who noticed Steiner's restraint during these meetings, wrote in his memoirs, "From this point on, he expected us to take the initiative." And, in a way anticipating future developments, he added that Steiner would have been most gratified if the activity of the new association had grown out of its own intentions and he had been left free to present his own research in it. "We were burdened by the fact that we were not able to fulfill his wishes. They were not personal wishes, but arose out of the task that he had been given" (Strakosh). In fact, Steiner had hoped that the members of the association would not trouble him with all the decisions but would develop their own abilities through reciprocal counsel and help. He was also of the opinion at that time that the active members would work much more productively with what he developed as Spiritual Science and come to the point of being able to develop further what he, for example, presented in *Outline of Esoteric Science* (comp. 156).

Rudolf Steiner stayed on in Munich until September 7 to be available for conversations with his esoteric students. After a short holiday with his friend Moritz Zitter in Tyrol, he traveled to Basel, where he gave a series of lectures on "The Gospel of St. Mark" from September 15 to 24. Dutch friends who arrived late for the course reported that they had received a telegram informing them that the course had been cancelled. Some overzealous member of the OSE had tried to "save" them from attending Steiner's lectures.

In the course of the lectures, Rudolf Steiner emphasized, among other things, that the conflict, which was becoming increasingly public and more heated, not be seen in a false light. Repeatedly during these lectures—as well as in the course "The Bhagavad Gita and the Letters of St. Paul" that followed in Cologne and later in "The Esoteric Significance of the Bhagavad Gita" given in 1913 in Helsinki—he showed that it was not a conflict between Eastern and Western spirituality. Anthroposophy acknowledged the teachings of the East and did not diminish their value at all.

Neither did Steiner wish to fight against the OSE or its teachings. He simply presented the insights into Christian mysticism that he had acquired since his lectures on "Christianity as a Mystical Fact," lectures given before he had assumed the position of general secretary. He left it up to his audience to form their own judgment.

Steiner thus stressed repeatedly that there were other grounds for the conflict. He fought against having his teachings and views presented erroneously, against the attempt to hinder the work of the German section, and he fought against the way Annie Besant was very cleverly misrepresenting the situation, cloaking her statements and views in veils of tolerance and brotherliness and spicing them with condescending platitudes.

At this point, the other side took recourse in something that if he were to counter it, Rudolf Steiner, while perhaps not putting himself in the wrong, would certainly appear to be intolerant. A new branch was founded in Göttingen. The members applied to Steiner for admittance into the German section. Steiner refused to sign the charter and defended his decision in a long letter to the applicant, Dr. Hübbe-Schleiden. He explained his refusal by saying "that the art in which you have represented theosophy in the recent past is regarded by the German section as contradicting its intentions and being inimical." Toward the end of the letter, he wrote:

> Collaboration is impossible with individuals who *do not* wish to acknowledge another point of view (in this case, the one taken by the majority of the members of the German section), but refuse to admit it, preferring rather to accuse the others of dogmatism, etc. This is not a question of the standpoints themselves, but rather of the way of working. For this reason, in the name of the German section, I must deny your application to admit the branch into the section. (Klatt)

Separation from the Theosophical Society

A second application was submitted by a group in Leipzig. The situation was somewhat different. This group had already been admitted by Annie Besant as an independent group connected directly with Adyar. They had not wanted to be connected with the German section.

It was, however, clear that neither Hübbe-Schleiden nor the group in Leipzig had a desire to work with the German section. Inasmuch as the applications were in earnest, their intention was to build a voting block in the German annual meeting. For anyone following things from afar, the refusal to admit them could be viewed as willfulness, especially as Hübbe-Schleiden was one of the representatives of theosophy in Germany.

He immediately informed Annie Besant and tried to win over his old friends in Germany, among them Ludwig Deinhard and A. W. Sellin in Munich. These and other occurrences—for instance, Annie Besant's formation of an Austrian section—caused a stir among the German members. Mathilde Scholl traveled at the end of November to Berlin to speak with Marie von Sivers about which course to take. Marie von Sivers indicated that Rudolf Steiner had done everything that was possible for him to do and now awaited initiatives from the members. Mathilde Scholl first contemplated traveling to Adyar for the annual meeting to represent the German section there. Then she considered that it might be worthwhile printing a documentation of all the various stages in the escalation of the conflict. She did neither.

Steiner returned to Berlin from Munich on November 30, 1912. Mathilde Scholl shared her thoughts with him and suggested that he call the council of the German section to Berlin for a meeting that coming Sunday, December 6. "Dr. Steiner listened to everything I had to say without expressing either support or rejection. I then asked him, 'Will you be here next Sunday, Dr. Steiner?' He replied, 'If you carry out your plans, I will be here.' Then he left the room" (Meffert).

The council members gathered in Berlin on December 6, reviewed all the documents pertaining to the situation, and decided to send a telegram to the recording secretary of the Theosophical Society and an open letter to all the general secretaries. The key passage in the telegram read:

> Basing upon the recognition that the president has continually and even systematically violated the highest principle of the T. S.—"No religion higher than the truth"—and has abused the presidential power in arbitrary ways, thus hindering positive work, the executive

> committee here assembled, after the minutest examination of documents, can only see in the resignation of the president the possibility of further existence of the society.

This telegram was meant to be read at the annual meeting in Adyar and bore the signatures of all twenty-eight members of the executive committee, but not Steiner's. Groups in Austria, Switzerland and Italy sent similar telegrams to Adyar. The general secretary of the Scandinavian groups resigned in protest.

In her address to the general assembly, Annie Besant spoke about the unfolding events.

> In one section out of twenty-two, there is trouble—the German. I say in one section only, because the trouble in India is not from the section, but only from a handful of individuals. The German general secretary, educated by the Jesuits, has not been able to shake himself sufficiently clear of that fatal influence to allow liberty of opinion within his section. His repeated refusal to authorize admissions of individuals and of lodges, on the definitely stated ground that they did not work in the method of the German section, have been laid by me before the general council.

To eliminate any possible misunderstandings, she wrote in the *Theosophist*:

> The T. S. faces an organized attack led by the most dangerous enemies of independent thinking and freedom of speech: the Jesuits.... In Germany, they are striving to secure the predominance of Christianity in the T. S. and to turn it into a Christianizing sect. By doing this, they wish to push the T. S. into the East.... Any means are justified to secure the glory of God. The *Black General*, as the leader of the order is called, has agents everywhere. Attacks are in process in many parts of the world. Money flows like water. In a single day, the mail brings news of attacks in Rome, Stockholm and Hong Kong. It is very interesting to follow. One is reminded of the words of warning "The devil is come to you with great anger, because he knows that his time is short." (*The Theosophist*)

This brought the rumors of Jesuit influence in Steiner and his friends, which had been circulating for some time and had been first publically voiced in Hübbe-Schleiden's "Message of Peace," into the light of day and gave them a documented basis. For Annie Besant, this apocalyptical picture that she had conjured up out of nothing served to legitimize an ultimatum to Steiner. It was dated January 14, 1913, and notified him of the withdrawal of the section's charter. She gave two reasons: first, because he had refused to admit the two branches in Göttingen and Leipzig, and second, because the executive committee of the German section had taken the position that membership in the OSE was incompatible with membership in the T. S. She gave Steiner a period of several weeks to respond.

In the meantime, the *Anthroposophical Society* had been founded, without ceremony, in Cologne on December 28, 1912. Everything that followed were but the consequences. On February 2, 1913, a last gathering within the context of the German section took place. During this meeting, the response of the executive committee to Besant's ultimatum was agreed on. It stated that they could see no need to retract anything and in light of the president's actions felt themselves to be expelled. Especially the lies concerning Jesuitism had made any further dialogue impossible. These lies did, however, have an unexpected positive effect. They led Steiner to speak at length about his life.

The first general assembly of the Anthroposophical Society was held in Berlin from February 3 to 7. The core of this society, which grew quickly, was the German section of the Theosophical Society. Leadership of the new society lay in the hands of Marie von Sivers, Michael Bauer and Carl Unger. On March 7, 1913, Annie Besant signed the charter of the German section over to Dr. Hübbe-Schleiden. Steiner was now relieved of his earlier duties and could speak freely. In an article for the *News for the Members of the Anthroposophical Society*, he wrote at length about the history of the conflict. He focused on the accusations made by Hübbe-Schleiden in a publication entitled "Thoughts on the Separation of the Anthroposophical Society from the Theosophical Society."

Here we encounter a side of Rudolf Steiner that is, for the most part, unknown. He refutes Hübbe-Schleiden's accusations with incredible sharpness, documenting his points with passages from their correspondence and giving a picture of the real pretensions and views of this veteran of the Theosophical Society. Steiner felt that it was important for the healthy development of Anthroposophy and the Anthroposophical Society that Hübbe-Schleiden's accusations not go unchallenged.

In March 1913, Steiner was able once again to speak in Holland. At the beginning of the lecture series, he spoke at length about the events that led up to the separation from the Theosophical Society, which at that time had much support in Holland. He concluded with the words, "In spite of all the bitterness and pain, I experience what has happened as something extremely liberating, especially from the narrowness that has been so troublesome in the life of the Theosophical Society since the Munich congress of the European sections" (27, 1st ed.).

For Rudolf Steiner, this feeling of liberation was linked to the hope that a wider sense of life that could be the source of new impulses would be possible in the Anthroposophical Society.

CHAPTER 32

SURROUNDED BY ARTISTS: 1907–1918

The first decade of the twentieth century was a period rich in artistic renewal and experimentation concentrated in a manner that is seldom in history. This era of new forms and ways of working, seeing and hearing appeared as a European movement centered in Berlin, Vienna, Munich, Paris and Moscow, and also in Italy and Scandinavia. Of course, this burgeoning of the modern art movement had its predecessors in Turner, van Gogh, Cezanne and others; at the turn of the century, however, this artistic revolution had become a general phenomena. It was the artists themselves who carried this movement forward against the predominant artistic sensibilities and the market, which only began to notice the new direction somewhat later.

Although there were many groups and associations of artists, of which the "Blue Rider," the "Bridge" and the "Storm" are only the most well-known, each artist developed his or her own individual style. It is understandable that artists, striving to transcend the boundaries of tasteful aesthetics and the expression of individual gifts, searched also for spiritual direction and orientation. Quite a wide circle of them encountered Anthroposophy and were stimulated by the encounter.

It is not possible to document each of these encounters today, but there is, for instance, solid evidence that Wassilij Kandinsky studied both *Theosophy* and *How to Know Higher Worlds* and gained not only ideas for his theory of color from them but also inspiration for specific paintings. There are indications of this study in his book *The Spiritual in Art*. Steiner, for his part, valued Kandinsky's originality and would have liked to see him become a member of the Anthroposophical Society, but Kandinsky chose to follow his own path. One of his students, however, discovered Steiner quite early. This was Maria Strakosch-Giesler. Among those who attended Steiner's lectures in Munich was also Alex Jawlensky, who strove for a quality of mystic experience in his painting. In Holland, Jacoba van

Heemskerk and Marie Tak van Poortvliet heard Steiner speak in 1913 and joined the anthroposophic movement. It is also astonishing that Piet Mondrian was inspired by *Theosophy* and sought to become acquainted with Steiner.

Steiner was quite open to these new directions in painting. He supported them whenever he could. When one member of the society mentioned his difficulties with modern paintings, he replied, "It is just a new limb on the ancient trunk of art" (Strakosch). He recognized in it the striving to emancipate oneself from the model and the outer objects. On the other hand, he did not believe that abstract painting would have a long future. Art needs content. Already in his first unpretentious attempt in 1911, when he designed the backdrops for *The Soul's Probation*, there is a hint of this new content.

Steiner's work underwent a lively debate in certain Russian literary circles. We mentioned the presence of the Russian poets Balmont, Mereschkowski and Minski during the lectures in Paris in 1906. Andrei Bely commented on the situation in Russia in 1911 in a letter to Alexander Bok.

> After returning to Russia, we frequently received news of Steiner. One person after another returned, fascinated with him. In Moscow, in the vicinity of the symbolists, was an absurdly weird group of Steinerites. Ever more frequently, word spread through Moscow concerning *the latest news about higher reality*; in the astral atmosphere of Moscow, astral paperboys sold the *Cosmic Evening Chronicle*. There was talk of revolution, talk of symbolism and talk about the end of the world. (B 89/90)

The groups met in close proximity to the "Musaget" publishing house.

The interest in Steiner among artists mirrored Steiner's own interest in art. Before World War I, the anthroposophic movement had a primarily artistic orientation. This reflected Steiner's own intentions. He had, after all, spent the years around the turn of the century moving in the artistic-literary circles of Berlin and had, since the Munich congress in 1907, actively supported artistic work in the theosophical movement. Scientists were rare in the anthroposophic movement before 1914. The industrialist and technician Dr. Carl Unger was an exception. We must also take into consideration that Rudolf Steiner's closest colleague during these years, Marie von Sivers, was an artist, who sacrificed her own artistic career to carry the work of building up the theosophical–anthroposophic movement, thus giving the movement a flexible, non-bureaucratic style. In the early years of the development of the anthroposophic work, the opportunity to work artistically was rare. Even after she took on the trainings for eurythmy and speech after 1914, she had to put a good deal of her energy into the society, the publishing house, and the publication of Steiner's work. Through all these things, however, wafted an artistic wind.

In Munich, too, the center of the anthroposophic art impulse, Sophie Stinde put aside her own landscape painting to support the growth of the anthroposophic movement. Her group soon drew other artists in. The sculptor Ernst Wagner joined them in 1906 and remained a personal student of Steiner's until 1914. Walo von May, a friend of Wagner's, also became acquainted with Anthroposophy through him. There was also a very promising sculptress, Cecile Peiper, who worked in Munich from 1908 to 1920 and has since been unjustly forgotten.

Three other painters placed their skills in service to the artistic striving inspired by Rudolf Steiner. Hermann Linde, Hans Volkert and Fritz Hass took on the unenviable work of painting scenery for the mystery plays. Imme von Eckardstein, a talented painter, created costumes for the plays and painted pictures of the zodiac for the 1912/13 calendar. Hermann Linde moved to Dornach in 1914 primarily to work on the small dome in the first Goetheanum and later painted a series of twelve pictures illustrating Goethe's "Fairy Tale." Thus, in Munich at that time there grew a whole "nest" of anthroposophic artists.

When the artistic design in the Goetheanum began in 1914, other artists came from various parts of Europe to help. The sculptor Edith Maryon came from England; the painter Arild Rosenkranz came from Denmark; the painter Lotus Péralté (Countess Paini-Gazotti) arrived from France; Richard Pollack-Karlin came from Prague; the painter and graphic artist Thadeusz Rychter and Frantizek Siedlecki came from Poland; and from Russia came Margarita Woloschin—all recognized artists.

Unfortunately, we know little about the details of Rudolf Steiner's work with these artists, except that it was intense. Only Margarita Woloschin has written about how Steiner would visit the artists in their studios to discuss their work, make suggestions, and answer questions. One passage from Woloschin's journal is given here as an example of these visits.

> Dr. Steiner came into my workshop—without knocking, as he usually does. He suddenly seemed to grow, as it were, behind me. "Can you

paint this?" In his hand he held a drawing of an Egyptian initiate, with an angel and an archangel above him. When I asked, "Herr Doktor, how should I paint it?" he replied, "I want you to be completely free." I asked him about shadows and the role of light and dark in painting. "Darkness should not be applied as shadow, but rather to call forth a quality of soul—for instance, for something that calls forth the feeling of a deepness, like a deep well. The paintings should not create planes, they must create spaces of color in order to make the walls disappear." (Woloschin)

His memorial talks for his artist-friends who had passed away give insight into his relationships with the artists. He spoke in memory of Sophie Stinde, Hermann Linde, and Edith Maryon. He spoke words of heartfelt gratitude for their work, unwavering acknowledgement of their efforts, and deep awe for their achievements. It was primarily the artists who dedicated themselves selflessly to the anthroposophic work and who brought their artistry not only to expression in their own work but also in social action. Sophie Stinde was known to have had an eye for the needs of her colleagues; she often helped where she could, quietly and often anonymously. In the difficult atmosphere that was present in Dornach during the war, Hermann Linde was a mediator, a person who could smooth things over and bring people together. The social effects of the artistic work could be seen in the lives of these individuals.

It is easier to follow the tracks of anthroposophic influence in the literary arts than it is in the sculptural arts. Here, too, there was an outer circle of individuals who had some fleeting contact with Anthroposophy, among them Franz Kafka and Max Brod, who both heard Steiner speak in Prague in 1911. Among the poets and writers who became involved in Steiner's work were, in addition to Éduoard Schuré, Albert Steffen, Christian Morgenstern, Andrei Bely, Manfred Kyber, Alexander von Bernus and, for a time, Friedrich Lienhard.

It is evident that Rudolf Steiner valued any true artistic work greatly. He recognized in artistic imagination an inner capacity that was related to the soul forces underlying spiritual research. He often called attention to artistic works that strove to present the spiritual in an artistic form. In doing so, he was never narrow-minded or pedantic. He enjoyed wandering through the very different landscapes of the soul revealed by different writers; his interest was focused primarily on the artistic striving, not on the merely aesthetic qualities, which were masterfully handled by many contemporaries. For instance, in 1910, he praised Schuré's book *The Great Initiates*.

> We often confuse our own views on Goethe, Shakespeare or Dante with what their contemporaries were capable of understanding in regard to the spiritual forces that were brought into the spiritual evolution of humanity by such individuals. And, especially as anthroposophists, we must be conscious of the fact that during their own time in history, people are least able to recognize how powerful and strengthening the spiritual works are for the souls of their contemporaries. If we consider that the future will judge things much differently than the present is able to, then we can surely say that the publication of *The Great Initiates* will one day be viewed as something tremendously important for the spiritual content and the spiritual depth of our time. (122)

For a contemporary reader these sentences raise, of course, a number of questions that can at first only be answered by pointing out that Steiner, as we saw in regard to Marie Eugenie delle Grazie, was never stingy with praise. In this case, he did not merely praise Schuré, he produced *The Holy Drama of Eleusis* and *The Children of Lucifer*. He had also intended to stage Schuré's *Soeur Gardienne*. This was not possible due to the amount of work that was involved in preparing to build the Goetheanum.

Perhaps most important, Steiner concerned himself intensively with Schuré. Between 1906 and 1912, he visited him regularly at his country house in Barr in Alsace. Together they hiked over Odilienberg, Steiner gave private lectures for him, and he drew up a short autobiography and other writings—the famous *Documents du Barr*. In 1914, they visited Chartres together. He was one the few people with whom Steiner spent so much time.

A sharp observer would have noticed that Steiner did not cultivate Schuré's acquaintance without any rationale. Andrei Bely wrote, "He understood how to pay tribute to the vanity, which was unrecognized and therefore not to be tamed; he would pass the seventy-year-old Schuré around at the lectures that he attended like a stuffed capon" (Bely).

The bridge to Schuré was Marie von Sivers. Schuré had first brought theosophy to her attention; their correspondence dated back to 1900. She translated his writings into German, maintained contact with him until 1914, and it was probably thanks to her initiative that Steiner produced

Schuré's plays. She clearly had a relationship of destiny with Schuré. Steiner's relationship to Schuré cooled during World War I. They met again in 1922, during the *French Course*. The aged Schuré attended the course and daily, as Emil Bock remembered, one would "see him walking back and forth with Steiner in front of the Goetheanum, immersed in friendly conversation" (*We Experienced Rudolf Steiner*).

Rudolf Steiner's encounter with Christian Morgenstern was surely one of the most enjoyable and important encounters of his life. Morgenstern's inner path had led him directly to Anthroposophy. Even before meeting Steiner, he had independently studied the Gospel of St. John in an anthroposophic manner and on November 6, 1908, he wrote to his bride Margareta, "I think that when you have fully understood the fourth Gospel, I will have also ceased to be a riddle to you" (*A Life in Letters*). A few days later, on November 10, he noted, "Yesterday I had a strange, mystical thought: why Nietzsche was only a harbinger, not an end, a fulfiller, a—Buddha" (ibid.). These words indicate what Morgenstern sought the direction of his questions and his striving.

Ten weeks later, on January 28, 1909, Morgenstern heard Steiner speak at the House of the Architects in Berlin. The lecture was about Tolstoy and Carnegie. Morgenstern knew immediately that he had found the man whom he had sought, and he attended Steiner's other public lectures. In the beginning of April, he heard that Steiner was going to give a series of lectures for members in Dusseldorf and asked if he might attend. Steiner spoke about "The Spiritual Hierarchies and their Reflection in the Physical World (Zodiac, Planets, Cosmos)." Morgenstern listened with all his soul and in the winter of 1913/14, he put his impressions into the words:

> He spoke. And as he spoke appeared in him
> The Zodiac, Cherubim and Seraphim,
> The star-like sun, the wandering of the planets
> From place to place.
> All this leapt out, born on his voice,
> Was glimpsed, a spark, a cosmic dream,
> The heavens wide seemed invited down
> Through his word. (*Writings and Letters* II)

Steiner recognized Morgenstern's experience directly, without outer mediation. In 1914, he recalled Morgenstern's manner, "If one considers Morgenstern's mood of soul, his entire mood of soul, one sees that it would hardly have been possible to have a better prepared, a more completely attuned soul join us as was Christian Morgenstern's when he became connected with us in 1909" (261).

In May 1909, Morgenstern followed Steiner to a lecture series in Oslo, where Steiner spoke about the Apocalypse. Morgenstern wrote to his bride first about the mileu in which he found himself. "I have been tossed back and forth. The outer appearance of the movement troubles me. Anywhere that people gather together foolishness begins to blossom like a weed, even in the most beautiful garden. I have to say to myself: Foolishness within the theosophical movement is still ten times better than foolishness outside of it" (*A Life in Letters*). Soon, however, he could report that he had shared a meal with Steiner and Marie von Sivers, and that they had spoken of Nietzsche and Lagarde. His experience intensified as the course drew to an end.

> Yesterday, May 15, he spoke in an especially spellbinding manner about our own cultural epoch, the coming epoch (in the Apocalypse called the community of Philadelphia—brotherly love), and the following one. He is truly a great leader and there is no shame in following him. He exudes an infinitely pure spirituality and an infinitely spiritual purity. (*A Life in Letters*)

Mogenstern followed Steiner to the congress in Budapest and then to Kassel, where he attended Steiner's lectures. But then his health forced him to retire to the Black Forest to rest and recuperate. In August, he was in Munich to see Schuré's *The Children of Lucifer* and stayed on to attend the following lecture cycle. After this, the steady deterioration of his health due to tuberculosis forced him to spend his time far from the centers of anthroposophic activity, in Obermais/Meran, and in Arosa and Davos. His wife, however, traveled when she could to hear Steiner's lectures and returned to relate to him what she had heard. Finally, in September 1910, he was able to travel to Bern to hear Steiner's lectures on "The Gospel of St. Matthew." "Fourteen magnificent unforgettable days. The Gospels blossom in this light like the rose gardens" (Bauer). During 1911, he was once again unable to attend any of the gatherings. His wife, Margareta Morgenstern, brought him the news from Munich.

In 1912, Rudolf Steiner stopped in Zurich when he returned from Italy to spend a day with Morgenstern. It was a day spent in conversation. Morgenstern was only able to speak softly, with great effort. Steiner told him of his travels in Italy, spoke of Giotto's frescos and—what struck Morgenstern most strongly—of a sunrise in Umbria. Morgenstern spoke with his eyes and his smile, and he gave Steiner a packet of poems, which bore witness to his deep connection with Anthroposophy.

In August 1913, already marked by death—yet both psychologically and spiritually absolutely present in spite of his frailness—Morgenstern was brought to the sanatorium run by the anthroposophic doctor Felix Peipers. He was able to attend the last Munich performances of the mystery plays *The Guardian of the Threshold* and *The Souls' Awakening*. He wrote his friend, the actor Friedrich Kayssler, who could not find any connection to Steiner's plays—a long letter in which he begged for understanding.

> Steiner dramas are not *plays*, they *mirror* spiritual worlds and truths. Although burdened with much of the baggage of an early work, a beginning, they usher in a new epoch of the arts. This epoch is still far away; centuries could pass before there are enough people who want this spiritual art that in every city mysteries of this kind can be offered and received—but here in the *Portal* is the historical beginning, here we are present at their birth. (*A Life in Letters*)

From November 22 to 24, Christian Morgenstern was able to travel to Stuttgart, where Steiner was lecturing. On November 24, Marie von Sivers gave a matinee performance of Morgenstern's poems. Rudolf Steiner gave the introduction in a manner quite characteristic for him. "For each poet, there is something in the world that is sacred, something that no one else can approach the way he can. For the gods have created for each such soul a lonely, isolated place in the cosmos from which all others are excluded unless the poet himself leads them there" (Christian Morgenstern, *The Victory of Life*).

And Steiner, who was often asked by the members of the Anthroposophical Society if there was anything they could do for him, said toward the end of his talk: "It will always give me great personal pleasure when many souls have found new depth through what our movement can achieve in this realm, when many souls open for a true and beautiful acceptance of Morgenstern's poetry. And if one or the other of you wish to do something for me, something in which I can take pleasure, you can best do so by being open for what we are about to give you a few good examples of and by being willing to listen into it with your full understanding" (ibid.).

Christian Morgenstern was able to attend one more series of Steiner's lectures, the Leipzig cycle on "Christ and the Spiritual World and the Search for the Holy Grail" (150). He was fever-free during these days, and Marie von Sivers once again recited some of his poems before the lecture on December 13. For the first time, his unpublished poems were recited. They were later published in *We Found a Path*. In his introductory talk, Rudolf Steiner characterized these poems.

> I would like to say that to the highest proofs of the inner kernel of truth and validity that our soul seeks belongs the fact that we see spring out of the spiritual ground poetry from such depths of heart and heights of the spirit as precisely that of Christian Morgenstern.... When I let such a poem work within my soul, I have within me something more than just this poem—something, of course, that all true art also has. I wish to say the word: "This poetry has an aura." A spirit flows through this poetry, penetrating and weaving through it, a spirit that radiates out of the poetry, gives it the deepest inner strength and can stream out of this poetry into our own soul. (Christian Morgenstern, *The Victory of Life*)

During the last three months of his life, Christian Morgenstern lived in Meran, working on the collection of poems titled *We Found a Path*, which he dedicated to Rudolf Steiner. He was able to correct the proofs before passing out of this life on March 31, 1914. Due to a fortunate set of circumstances, Rudolf Steiner, who had been called to Dornach for pressing consultations, was able to speak at his friend's funeral on April 4 in Basel.

Following Morgenstern's death, as the eternally creative individuality was no longer fettered by the limits of bodily existence, the fruits of Morgenstern's heartfelt spiritual research became apparent to Rudolf Steiner. In May 1914, he spoke about what had become apparent to him in the spiritual world, without naming any names.

> In the individual of whom I am thinking, who passed away just a few weeks ago after years of suffering, a world of cosmic imaginations formed itself during his long illness, freeing itself as it were from the body as it approached death. As the illness progressed and the body wasted away, a world of imaginations—cosmic imaginations—arose out of the withering body. This individual has now passed through the portal of death, and the imaginations have begun to glow with a wonderful beauty, so that they can be perceived in the

spiritual world as a wonderful piece of spiritual art, like an artwork that has been created out of the cosmos. (*Christian Morgenstern, the Victory of Life*).

Steiner spoke of Christian Morgenstern often in the years that followed. He would speak of him as a guardian spirit of the building under construction in Dornach, but he also drew attention to the further unfolding of Christian Morgenstern's work in the spiritual world. In honor of the first anniversary of Morgenstern's death, he said on Palm Sunday 1915:

> We can say that the arrival of the soul that was incarnated in Christian Morgenstern in the spiritual worlds was for these worlds a remarkable event, in a certain sense an epochal event.... We can glimpse in the land of the spirit a gathering of souls that have passed through the portal of death and have borne with them to an exemplary degree the most important cycles of earthly existence into the spiritual worlds. Christian Morgenstern's soul entered this circle, a soul that was prepared inwardly with an inner urge for Spiritual Science, or to put it more succinctly, for the language of the spirit—a soul that strove to experience the spiritual, the suprasensory within the earthly, that strove to experience the force in the soul that both enlivens and enthuses earthly human beings....
>
> We can name several of the outstanding individuals of the last century—Fichte, Schelling, Hegel—who have entered the spiritual world through the portal of death and speak thus. We investigated the earth's mysteries with our earthly understanding, but our understanding remained barren for what now surrounds us; barren and empty has remained within us that can provide answers to this great and vital question: What is the nature of the living human being in the lands of spirit? Insight into the true nature of human beings was brought into their circle by the spiritual being who was incorporated as Christian Morgenstern. Moreover, Hegel and Fichte could then say: We tried to find a way to explain the secrets of the earth. Yet in the entire spectrum of concepts that we brought forth from our earthly understanding, from the depths of earthly knowledge, the question that poses itself here was not answered. What is the human being? What truly is the human being in relation to the cosmos? Then a human spirit appeared among us, a human star, and explained it to us through what being human is, through what one brings, through what one had prepared for the heavens while still on the earth. (*Christian Morgenstern, the Victory of Life*)

These words of Rudolf Steiner indicate that his encounter with Christian Morgenstern was one of the most important encounters in his life. Outwardly, their meetings were seldom and brief. Morgenstern did not belong to the group of people with whom Steiner was constantly involved, the people he had to counsel, to comfort or correct, those with whom he had to spend much of his time in discussions. For Morgenstern, it was enough to hear Steiner speak and to read what he had written. The listening and reading allowed him to commune fully with the spiritual teacher. Steiner revealed himself completely to the listening Morgenstern. He was not really dependent on outer contact, although it certainly moved him deeply to speak personally with Steiner. The encounter between the spiritual teacher and the poet was primarily a purely spiritual encounter, an encounter on the plane upon which Steiner was actually at home. For Steiner, the experience of being seen and understood must have been one of true joy. Through the poems in his last collection *We Found a Path*, Morgenstern became also in earthly life a witness for the importance of Anthroposophy.

Steiner's encounter with Andrei Bely (1880–1934), who no less than Morgenstern also spoke out for Anthroposophy, but whose significance as an anthroposophist was only recognized in the German-speaking countries some 60 years after he first met Rudolf Steiner, developed quite differently. Bely was nine years younger than Morgenstern and nineteen years younger than Rudolf Steiner. He lived in Steiner's proximity for four years, first in Berlin and Munich, following Steiner to the various lecture cycles, and then in Dornach, where he worked on the building of the Goetheanum. He dedicated himself to Steiner as a pupil, or, perhaps more accurately, an apprentice, and Steiner knew that Bely could see him for what he was.

Andrei Bely, whose given name was Boris Bugaieff, was a very talented individual, in some ways more gifted than Morgenstern. By the time he met Steiner he had already published a number of poetic works, among them *The Silver Dove*, and, in 1912, when he joined "this thing of Steiner's," he was still working on his novel *Petersburg*. During his time with Steiner, Bely went through periods of deep crisis. His notes entitled "Material for a Biography (intimate)" give insight into these critical periods.

He was able, however, to distill out of these crises the memoir *Transformation of Life*, his certainly very personal, if one wishes, subjective memories of Rudolf Steiner, which he wrote in 1928/29. This book describes a multitude of individual observations that Bely, thanks to his sensitivity, his openness and his education, was able to make. Out of this array of observations arises one of the most personal pictures of Steiner that has ever been drawn.

No doubt some of the anecdotes that Bely relates second-hand deserve the label "good inventions," but Bely is a storyteller. He tells a story, perhaps at times relishing a bit of gossip. But which of the other of Steiner's multitude of pupils even tried to capture the image of Steiner during a lecture? Who else wrote of the inner experience of listening? For instance, how Steiner in the lectures for the members called upon ever-higher forms of attention and empathy, leading his listeners to a shared experience, a shared seeing of the imaginations, to the point that they could perceive that about which couldn't be spoken. Where else do we find such frank reports of the way Steiner scolded, loved, encouraged? For his part, Steiner recognized Bely's genius. He described Bely's work, *Rudolf Steiner and Goethe in the Contemporary Worldview*, which was published in 1917 in Moscow and has yet to be translated, as an "outstanding book" (B 89/90).

We also have Bely to thank for insight into the way Rudolf Steiner worked with his personal pupils, how he counseled and guided them. In the beginning, he had Bely visit him weekly and tell him about his work with the meditative exercises. Then these meetings grew ever less frequent and Bely finally describes how he came to discover the guidance and counsel he needed when listening to Steiner's lectures. More than anything, we find reports about how Steiner encouraged independence, originality and imagination. Bely confesses openly that his development also had its points of regression, that he was only able to save himself through his research work on Steiner and Goethe.

On top of that, we have Bely to thank for an excellent description of the Dornach milieu in 1914 and 1915. He tells of his sufferings within this milieu but also sketches pictures of those students of Steiner he most loved: Michael Bauer, Sophie Stinde, and Carl Unger.

In 1916, Bely returned to Russia. In the early years of the Russian Revolution, he was very active in Anthroposophy. He gave numerous lectures and initiated a plan to perform the mystery plays in Russia. In 1922/23, he was once again in Germany, wrestling with deep inner conflicts, and on March 30, 1923, he spoke for the last time with Rudolf Steiner. He returned soon after that to the Soviet Union, where in the meantime the Anthroposophical Society had been banned and he had been denounced.

He continued to work quietly on anthroposophic questions. In the period from 1924 to 1926, he wrote his principal work, *A History of the Becoming of the Self-Knowing Soul*, and in 1928/29, *Verwandeln des Lebens*. He died on January 8, 1934. The latter work appeared in German forty years after his death.

The third writer that should be mentioned here is Alexander von Bernus. Von Bernus first met Rudolf Steiner in 1910 in Munich, where he often stayed, and in the ensuing years gradually grew closer to him. In 1912/13, during a critical juncture of his life, he turned to Steiner for guidance. Steiner visited him on February 27, 1913, at the cloister in Neuburg by Freiburg that was at that time in von Bernus' possession. Nothing is known about the conversation they had, but shortly afterward von Bernus wrote to his friend Melchior Lechter, "This man bears within him such deep love and charity that one would sacrifice everything for him. He is also in fact one of the few great clairvoyants now alive" (Sladeck).

In August 1913, von Bernus, who had not followed the details of the building plans for the Goetheanum, offered Rudolf Steiner a piece of property in the vicinity of the Neuburg Cloister big enough for the projected building. Steiner thanked him but had to decline his offer, as Dornach seemed chosen by destiny to house the new building. Von Bernus, who strove to deepen his understanding of Anthroposophy, wanted to find a way to actively support Steiner's movement. Late in 1915, he decided to publish a quarterly, in which anthroposophic writers would also come to word, but which would not be explicitly "anthroposophic." He began without having spoken with Steiner, and when he approached the first prospective anthroposophists was met with a certain amount of mistrust. A few days later, however, one of those with whom he had spoken returned and told him of the conversation he had had with Steiner about von Bernus's proposal. "I will tell you what he said about it word for word: 'When someone finally has an initiative, you can't just throw a wrench in the works!'"

Thus, in the middle of World War I, *Das Reich* (*The Kingdom*) was founded. Articles by Rudolf Steiner and other anthroposophic writers were included in each edition. But—and this was the intent of the publisher—they appeared in conjunction with pieces by Richard Benz, Theodor Daubler, Walter Hasenclever, Alfred Mombert and Rainer Maria Rilke. Von Bernus hoped to gain understanding and recognition for Anthroposophy in German cultural life through a culturally diverse quarterly.

The members of the Anthroposophical Society were astonished and somewhat taken aback to see their master in such company. There was some consternation concerning the undertaking. It caused Steiner to take his anthroposophic friends to task. One should be excited about this initiative. The publication is a sign of goodwill and should be supported regardless of one's opinion of any single piece of writing. "I was very disappointed to hear that Herr von Bernus had received stacks of letters from our members voicing their disapproval of what had been printed" (174b). To von Bernus, he wrote, "Don't pay any attention to what the people write; do what you think is correct" (Sladeck). He remained faithful to von Bernus and contributed articles for each of the eight editions of the journal. In response to von Bernus's request, he wrote an extensive commentary on *The Chemical Wedding of Christian Rosenkreutz.*

In Novemebr 1917, von Bernus opened in Munich an art gallery also named *Das Reich.* The first exhibition was of the work of the anthroposophic graphic artist Karl Thylmann, who had been killed during the war. Rudolf Steiner, Ernst Uehli, Albert Steffen and Hans Wohlbold all spoke at this gallery, along with a number of non-anthroposophic speakers. But Alexander von Bernus, in spite of his efforts, had little success and received, as did Rudolf Steiner, little appreciation. Albert Steffen related that Steiner spoke to him before a lecture in Munich saying, "In spite of all our efforts, Spiritual Science is not being taken up. We are on the verge of a terrible catastrophe." And Steffen added, "His eyes spoke of enormous suffering" (*On Spiritual Paths*).

Until 1918, it was primarily artists, painters and writers whose work spoke of the fertile nature of Anthroposophy and who formed the small contingent of striving individuals who embraced Rudolf Steiner's impulse and freed him from his loneliness. Their mobile, individually creative spirituality took hold of the vitality of Anthroposophy, and they tried to support Rudolf Steiner through their work.

CHAPTER 33

BUILDING

The twentieth century bore witness to a number of connections between philosophy and architecture. There were thinkers who strove to build and give form to things, and there were architects who wrestled with philosophical principles. Ludwig Wittgenstein, one of the most influential Western philosophers, was also an architect. In 1926, he designed the Stonborough Residence in Vienna. He worked through each detail of the house. On the other hand, the architects of the Bauhaus school as well as Le Corbusier developed their own philosophies. The desire to transcend the merely conventional in architecture in order to achieve a new quality of style is symptomatic in these strivings. In the case of Wittgenstein and the Bauhaus architects, this new style was inspired by natural science and technology. Functionality, faithfulness to the materials, and clarity were their mottos.

Rudolf Steiner's architectural impulse must be seen as a remarkable example of this struggle to bring forth a new style. He not only designed the first Goetheanum in a completely new, freely formed style—and then just ten years later the second Goetheanum in very different style—he also designed a series of houses, an art studio, a boiler house and a transformer house, each with its own original look. Taken together, these buildings bear witness to an extraordinary architectural imagination. Steiner's architectural work, which began in 1913, had a certain history that we will examine briefly. First some thoughts concerning his general intentions.

When Rudolf Steiner returned to Berlin after the Munich congress in 1907, he prepared a short report for the members detailing the intention of this gathering. In this report we find the following remarks: "Theosophy can also be built: it can be built architecturally, in education and in the social realm. The Rosicrucian principle is to bring spirit into the world, to do productive work for the soul" (96).

When Steiner spoke here of building, he meant any kind of practical work, work for others, or socially productive work. "Building" is thus a metaphor for work that serves to transform the world. Steiner was not primarily interested in putting up buildings, but in bringing inner work to outer expression. In his talk about the Munich congress, he also said, "It strove to show something about our theosophical work that I have repeatedly emphasized—that theosophy should not only be a matter of personal pondering or a living-into-oneself. Theosophy should take hold of practical life, should be a question of *Building*, a question of working one's way into all the various aspects of practical life" (96).

"Spiritual Science should not and does not intend to bring forth couch-potatoes or strangers to life; it will bring forth people of action, who are able to step forth into the world" (96).

Steiner did not simply have normal business in mind when he spoke these words; he was envisioning an activity of cultural reform and transformation. And all culture needs form, style—something that in this day and age of formlessness and the lack of style is sometimes difficult to understand. Steiner had articulated this idea relatively early, in 1905, in a letter to Marie von Sivers.

> Our ideal should be to create forms that are the expression of inner life. For in a time that cannot envision forms and then create them out of this imagination, the spirit must dissipate, become a nonexistent abstraction. Abstract spirituality must encounter reality as a mere aggregate of matter barren of spirit.... Until people begin to have a sense that there are spirits alive in fire, water and the earth, there will be no art that can bring this wisdom to outer expression. (262)

Here it becomes apparent how Steiner continued to keep his earliest convictions alive. In reading Goethe, he had discovered the statement "Thus style rests upon the deepest foundations of knowledge, upon the very nature of things, in as much as we are permitted to recognize this in visible, tactile forms" (HA, vol. 12). Steiner added his comment to this insight. Art brings cosmic lawfulness to appearance in the work of art. A work of art "thus appears as a miniature universe" (1-b). This idea, rooted as it is in Goethe's way of understanding, emerges as the fundamental idea behind Steiner's architectural impulse.

From 1907 until 1913, through his spiritual, inner work Rudolf Steiner developed the strengths, intuitions and insights out of which the

Goetheanum would arise. He also gave indications of specific form elements; but, as with the mystery plays, which he only began to write as the performances were clearly in sight, the concrete architectural gesture began to form itself in the summer of 1913 and then was further developed in the following fall and winter. And just he had performed Schuré's plays before bringing the mystery plays to the stage, two building projects were undertaken in 1913 that can be seen as preparation for the Dornach project.

In 1907, one of the basic form elements, the idea of *evolution*, visible in the seven painted capitols displayed in Munich, was evident. This was a formative gesture that in this way had practically never been present in architecture before. Only in the frieze of the Parthenon and in the depiction of the history of the Church on Romanesque and Gothic cathedral portals are sculptural presentations of a temporal evolution to be found. These sequential historical images do not, however, capture what is, since Goethe understood evolution specifically as the process of the coming into existence—the formation and transformation of a single being. In the seven pillars, this evolution of a single being becomes the primary formative gesture of the interior space and, in addition, the lawfulness of the seven-stage metamorphosis. The fundamental principle of all developmental processes that take place in the stream of time is brought to artistic expression. Through these ideas of evolution and metamorphosis, Goethe appears as the godfather of this new style.

In a lecture on January 23, 1920, Rudolf Steiner spoke about how he came to the second primary motif in 1908—the two interpenetrating domes. In them comes to expression the elemental gestures of speaking and listening, from revelation and the taking in of what is revealed. "Two cylinders, not completely closed, covered by two, partially open domes, express the twofold nature of what would reveal itself and what accepts the revelation. And the predominant nature of the two domes will indicate to those who approach the building that there is something here that is sheltered, veiled—but something that should be revealed" (*Architecture, Sculpture and Painting*).

The social aspect of the architectural gesture can be recognized in the harmony between these two primary form elements. In the auditorium are representatives of the self-directed evolution of humanity. They take in the revelations, which come to meet them from out of the spiritual as the future goals of this evolution, and gain through these revelations strength for their own further development. The social gesture becomes imaginatively apparent. This was also extremely important for Steiner, as he was convinced that social life could not flourish without artistic imagery. "What the human being is, and through what means an individual can place oneself truly into social life, can only be grasped when one is able to raise oneself to imaginative conceptualization" (ibid.).

It is interesting to follow how this initially purely conceptual architectural impulse gradually came to manifestation, with Steiner feeling his way, in building projects on which he was asked to participate. In 1908, E. A. Karl Stockmeyer, stimulated by the motifs for the columns at the 1907 Munich conference, began to experiment with architectural forms that incorporated the columns and created a small building in Malsch, near Karlsruhe.

At that time, however, it seemed as though there could be no question of realizing Steiner's ideas, which called for a building of a certain size. Yet on a light summer evening in Norway, a young woman approached Marie von Sivers and suggested building a "temple" for Rudolf Steiner's work. Among the Dutch participants at the Munich congress, there were a few who did respond positively to Steiner's intentions. Among them were Ita Wegman, Elisabeth Vreede and Marie Elisabeth Waller, who was then twenty-four years old. They all had gained some idea of what was striving to come to life in the interior architectural motifs displayed during the congress.

Marie Steiner-von Sivers related the rest of the conversation.

> I had to acquaint the young woman—it was Marie Elisabeth Waller—with everything that was connected with such a project. She then realized that it could only be one piece of a larger project. But she wanted me to tell her what could be done in the area of art. We found ourselves in agreement and gained Rudolf Steiner's support. The result was the performance of Éduoard Schuré's *Children of Lucifer*, and, a year later, we were able to experience the first of Rudolf Steiner's mystery plays, *The Portal of Initiation*. (*Nachrichtenblatt* 1925)

Marie Elisabeth Waller played Johannes Thomasius; Marie von Sivers was Maria.

Marie Elisabeth Waller was one of the people in Steiner's vicinity who preferred to work quietly. Outwardly she belonged to the circle of people who, as long as Rudolf Steiner held the reins, was not often spoken of, but who donated a good deal of money for the anthroposophic work. Together with her sister Oda Waller, she took on a good part of the financial burden of the performances of the mystery plays. She also contributed large sums of money to the building of the Goetheanum and later for the Rudolf Steiner-Halde, yet she never asked for any form of special recognition.

Both Rudolf Steiner and Marie von Sivers recognized the special qualities of this young woman. She shared a house with them from the winter of 1908/9 until she was married in 1924, first in Berlin on Motzstrasse 17, then in Dornach in "Villa Hansi." After their marriage, Rudolf and Marie Steiner named her as the heir of their entire estate—with the exception of the publishing house that belonged to Johanna Mücke—in the event that both of them were to die. In that case, she would have also inherited all of Steiner's copyrights. Marie Elisabeth Waller was the one who convinced Rudolf Steiner to paint the dome of the small cupola himself and who officially made the suggestion to name the building, which had until then been called the "Johannesbau," the "Goetheanum."

Although she was not directly involved in founding the "Johannesbau Association," which was formed in early April 1911 in Munich, Mieta Waller was one of the people who were instrumental in making this step possible. The association was registered on May 9. The seven regular members at the time of registration were Sophie Stinde, Countess Pauline Kalckreuth, Dr. Felix Peipers, Count Otto Lerchenfeld, the painter Hermann Linde and an architect, Schmid Curtius. Mieta Waller's name did not appear. By July 8, the association had acquired a well-placed building lot between Germaniastrasse and Ungererstrasse. Following the performances of the mystery plays in August, Dr. Peipers gave a presentation of slides showing some details of the planned building. Following this presentation, Count Lerchenfeld spoke about the financing of the project. Without the obstacles that soon arose, ground would have been broken for the building by Christmas of the same year.

During the time that these preparations were under way in Munich, the Stuttgart anthroposophists had pushed ahead. One member had donated 50,000 marks, and steps were taken immediately to build a house for the theosophical work in Stuttgart. Ground was broken in January 1911, and the house was opened in October. Since the Stuttgart members had not imagined that Rudolf Steiner would have significant ideas about the design of the branch house, he was only able make suggestions concerning the color scheme of the various rooms, although in a special room in the cellar of the house, the column motifs, which had been shown in Munich, were placed, for the first time, on structurally bearing stone pillars. Seen from outside, the Stuttgart house was another solid bourgeois residence.

Rudolf Steiner participated in planning and design work only if he was asked to. In 1911, he gave few suggestions concerning the planned Johannesbau. It appears that he even remained somewhat removed from the Munich project. Later he asserted that he would rather have founded a bank than be involved in building a theater.[*]

There were also other pressing concerns for him in 1911. His most important colleague, Marie von Sivers, who had exhausted herself in the theosophical work, was taken seriously ill at the beginning of the year. From a purely practical standpoint, Steiner depended on her help. She held all the threads of the organization in her hands, oversaw the publishing house, and also shielded him from importune visitors and questions. From an inner, spiritual point of view, she was even more important to him. He counted on her judgment. There were things that he could only speak of with her. In any case, he recognized a "wink of fate" in her illness. He put his outer activities, his travels, on hold for a time in order to help her regain her health. He also recognized that he needed time for his own inner work. His half-finished book *Anthroposophy* waited on his desk, and the spiritual world indicated to him "that this work should appear as quickly as possible" (262).

Toward the end of March, during the time that the Munich friends were preparing to form the building association, he traveled with Marie von Sivers, accompanied by Mieta Waller, to Istria on the shores of the Adriatic Sea. They rented a house in the idyllic village of Portorose, where Marie von Sivers could regain her strength. In spite of her illness, she did accompany Steiner to Bologna for a philosophical congress, where he gave a lecture on the philosophical foundations of theosophy. It was there that she began the slow path back to health.

Rudolf Steiner remained in Portorose until the end of May, traveling only once to Munich at the beginning of May to view the building site and to begin preparations for the summer's performances. His first detailed indications on the design of the building probably originated at this time.

---

[*] From the unpublished address at the founding of the company, *Der Kommende Tag* [The coming day], in Stuttgart, March 11, 1920.

For the most part, however, he left all the design work and planning in the hands of the architect, Schmid-Curtius, who drew up all the plans and prospects that exist from this time.

Rudolf Steiner was concerned at the time with the inner aspects of esoteric art. He worked on the *Theosophical Calendar 1912/13*, and later, after returning from the general meeting of the Scandinavian section in Copenhagen, on his book *The Spiritual Guidance of the Individual and Humanity*. He could not, however, make any progress with *Anthroposophy*. Before traveling to Munich to begin rehearsing for the summer performances, Rudolf Steiner and Marie von Sivers sojourned for roughly three weeks in Veldes, now Bled, and arrived in Munich in the middle of July, partially rested and strengthened and ready to take up work again on the plays.

Following the summer performances and the lecture cycle "From Jesus to Christ" held in Karlsruhe in early October (to which many theosophists traveled in a special train), many of the participants went on to Stuttgart for the dedication of the new house. Rudolf Steiner spoke kindly of the intentions that guided the friends in Stuttgart, offering some thoughts concerning the color scheme and honoring the artistic ideas, although he himself no doubt viewed the "red roses blossoming in the light of electric flames along the cross that had been placed on the front of the lectern" with mixed feelings. Marie von Sivers took the opportunity of addressing the gathering before Steiner's lecture on October 16. She warned them to not forget in their joy for the beautiful new Stuttgart Center the goal of building a school for Spiritual Science in Munich, and she requested that the other branches place this goal before their own individual interests.

Soon after this, the Johannesbau Association officially introduced itself to the members of the German section of the Theosophical Society, stating that it was necessary to create an appropriate setting for the mystery plays and for the lecture cycles. "The idea of a school for Spiritual Science is the necessary consequence that must be drawn from the conveyance of the spiritual knowledge with which our time has been honored." One can hear Rudolf Steiner in the background. Not a temple, not a theater—it was a school for Spiritual Science that was to be built.

On December 12, at the annual general meeting of the German section, Rudolf Steiner presented the ideas that informed his architectural impulse for the first time to a larger audience. In this lecture, one meets a third fundamental motif of the planned building. "Out of what Spiritual Science can give us, we must find the way to create an interior space that through color and form and other artistic qualities is at once closed and yet in each detail is so that the closed interior space is not truly closed but challenges us with our eyes, with our feelings and sensation, to pass through them." He then summarized this in the motto: "To have walls and to have no walls" (286). He repeated this idea a year later and said that one should be able to enter the cosmos, into the infinite, in different ways, from any place in the building (286/36).

At this point obstacles began to arise. The plan was to lay the corner stone on February 27, 1912. But the authorities refused to issue a building permit and demanded a series of changes. The ceremony was postponed until May 16, but there still was no permit. After giving a lecture cycle on "The Gospel of St. Mark" in Basel in the second half of September, followed by the first eurythmy course, given not far from there by Lory Smits, Rudolf Steiner, together with Marie von Sivers, traveled to Dornach for a respite. Dr. Emil Grosheintz had offered to let them use his country house for a few days of rest and relaxation, as Steiner was completely exhausted.

The hill—on which, in 1499, in a bloody battle the Swiss confederates had defended their freedom from the empire—was peaceful and lonely. The trees had begun to don their fall colors. Marie Steiner wrote:

> Dr. Steiner must have experienced remarkable things that night. He came out of his room deeply disturbed and it was apparent that he had to shed a heavy weight from his soul. With effort, he brushed the dark shadows from his forehead. We went out for a long walk, in order to see the countryside from the heights above us. It was difficult to master the steep, often pathless ridges and we returned late, completely exhausted. Everything happened in a strangely penetrating, imaginative manner that had a symbolic quality. (Letters and Documents)

During these walks, as Rudolf Steiner later recounted, he imagined how one would be able to see the building from all sides and how beautifully it would stand there in the open.

Some days later, Steiner, who originally had planned to travel to Austria, visited Dr. Grosheintz in Basel and asked him, "What are you planning to do with this property?" Grosheintz recalled that when he bought the land he had said to his wife, "The future will show me just why I had to buy so much land." They went on to speak of the difficulties that the project was encumbered with in Munich. Grosheintz knew "that Dornach didn't have any building regulations," and Steiner added, "Basel has a positive theosophical karma." And then, significantly, Steiner made the statement that he would soon repeat: "We do not have much time." Grosheintz replied, "If you need that property, it is there."

In February 1913, after the building authorities in Munich had refused once again to issue a building permit, a group of Swiss friends—Professor Gysi, Frau Hirter-Weber, and Frau Schied—took steps to acquire the additional land needed to build in Dornach and contributed it to the Johannesbau Association. After visiting the site again on May 16, Rudolf Steiner become very actively involved in the process. He recommended that they bury the plans for the Munich project and build in Dornach.

On May 18, 1913, he brought this recommendation before the members in Stuttgart, speaking with uncharacteristic emphasis of its necessity. First, he made it clear that neither the churches nor the political authorities were blocking the building permit; it was the Munich Arts Commission "that has thrown a wrench in the works!" He then continued to say that the artistic impulse that reigned in Munich was one that was dying. "A new culture would never be able to find a place within what is in the process of dying. Right where one would expect the most blossoms is something that is dying, and the new cultural impulses must acquaint themselves with the fundamental premise: Let the dead bury the dead—you, however, shall follow me." His final words pointed to the necessity that the building "under the present circumstances must be completed quickly. I do not emphasize the word *quickly* lightly, my dear friends!" (*To the Members of the Anthroposophical Society, Concerning the Johannesbau*, Munich 1913).

Three weeks earlier, Steiner had written to his mother and siblings, to whom he sent money, "And the war continuously threatens to begin" (39). He followed the political developments in Europe with great concern. The crises that followed one another ever more quickly and the ineptitude of German politicians, supporting such projects as the railway to Baghdad, led him to fear the worst (Polzer-Hoditz). Strangely enough, he did not speak of these things with his anthroposophic friends, although he did with his mother, and perhaps it was not only the political situation that moved him to hurry.

In the months following his address to the Stuttgart members, the entire building project—that had in the meantime been granted a permit for Munich—was gradually restructured. The first three-dimensional model, dated May 1913, was simply of a double cupola supported by two cylinders. The whole thing was then placed upon a concrete pedestal, which Steiner called a ramp. Then, in addition to the East–West axis in which the cupolas lay, following the suggestion of Max Bezinger, wings in the north-south axis were added at the intersection of the two domes. These first designs of the outer architecture were done in collaboration with Rudolf Steiner. Schmid-Curtius, the architect, had then to lay out the footprint, taking into consideration these very general design elements and, in doing so, to take care in laying out the concrete pedestal to accommodate the columns and the bearing walls. Only after the performances of the mystery plays and the lecture cycle that followed was Steiner able, in September 1913, to begin work on a more detailed model.

This brought about the necessary change. Rudolf Steiner described the situation looking back after ten years in Dornach.

> I considered myself to be merely the representative of those who had taken up the initiative to build. I believed that I had to concentrate my energy on the development of the inner spiritual work of Anthroposophy and was thankful for the intention of creating a home for this work. In the moment, however, that the initiative began to come to realization, the artistic design became a question of the inner spiritual work. I had to devote myself to this design work. (36)

The moment of realization was September 1913. Rudolf Steiner began work on the building design, first with rough, general sketches, then in detail. In Munich, a large wooden model that one could slip into was completed. It was immediately shipped to Dornach, where Steiner later continued to work on it. He arrived in Dornach on September 15, returning from a short visit with his friend Moritz Zitter in Kitzbühel. On September 17, he laid out the exact placement of the building, following which they immediately broke ground. On September 19, Steiner wrote to Alexander von Bernus, who had offered him a building site near Heidelberg that destiny had brought him clearly to Dornach. "Each day more spiritual reasons appear before my soul that show the rightness of the things that were to a certain extent thrust on us from outside. Thus I can no longer have anything against laying the foundation stone here tomorrow, after sunset. And this, in an esoteric sense, is for me a responsibility that lies quite heavily upon my soul" (Bock).

The next day, a trench for the foundation stone was dug and its concrete foundation was finished. Rudolf Steiner now took over leadership of the project. He designed the foundation stone: two pentagon dodecahedrons made of copper. He wrote the document that was to be placed in it. The ceremony began at 7:30 p.m. on September 20, 1913. Mercury appeared "as the evening star in Libra." One of those present, Ludwig Polzer-Hoditz, wrote:

> On this evening a few members gathered on the hill in Dornach. A circular trench had been prepared to lay the foundation stone in; an improvised stairway with nine steps led down to where the foundation stone was to be placed. The placement had been calculated so that it would lie directly under the speaker's podium when the building was finished. The foundation stone was in the form of two pentagon dodecahedra connected to one another, one larger than the other. It was made of copper. The document, which Rudolf Steiner wrote in memory of the ceremony and which was to express the significance of this moment and the reality of the building for all time, was sealed in the foundation stone. Before the ceremony began, a bonfire was lit. It was pouring rain. Some of us held burning torches. We stood in a close circle around the trench. Rudolf Steiner approached. He first called out to the hierarchies, then in the address that followed, he gave a short overview of the historical spiritual development up to this day, the twentieth day of September—1880 years after the Mystery of Golgotha, 1913 years after the birth of Christ.... Twelve red roses and one white rose were laid upon the foundation stone, then it was laid into place with straps forming a cross. (Polzer-Hoditz)

This ceremony did not only mark the laying of the foundation stone for the Johannesbau. Imaginatively, it also marked the striving toward a new mystery culture in a materialistic time. The seed of a new willingness opening itself to the reality of the spiritual beings was to be planted in the stream of human development. Rudolf Steiner concluded the ceremonial gathering with torchlight and pouring rain and with the words:

> The consciousness that lives on in us from this evening shall ignite in us the striving to gain understanding of the new revelation that has been given to humanity. The human soul thirsts for this new revelation, but she will only drink of it when, fearlessly, she gains belief

and trust in what the science of the spirit avows and what will once again unite what has had for a period of humanity's evolution to be separate: religion, art and science. (245)

The idea of a building that would open itself on all sides in different ways, whose walls would be no walls at all, was at once the symbol of the development and striving of those souls, who from the depths of their hearts were willing to open themselves to the spiritual in the cosmos, to receive the new revelation that was apparent in the spiritual world.

Two days later, preceding the re-forming of the now expanded Swiss Johannesbau Association, Rudolf Steiner indicated that he recognized the voice of destiny in the developments that had led up to breaking ground on the hill in Dornach, a destiny "that perhaps will only reveal itself gradually." For many antagonists, the building would become a stumbling block. In fact, the true difficulties were yet to come (*Schicksalszeichen*). These were prophetic words. Perhaps it is important to note that neither Rudolf Steiner nor Marie von Sivers, if the minutes are to be trusted, were present at the first general meeting of the Johannesbau Association that followed.

As construction began in Dornach—the woodworking shop was built and the foundations were poured—Rudolf Steiner traveled to Oslo. This journey to the North and the revelations that he shared concerning the Fifth Gospel there illuminate the ritual deed of laying the foundation stone. One gazes upon the new revelation that Steiner had spoken of when dedicating the foundation stone. To the extent that the anthroposophic impulses unite themselves with and become visible upon the earth, new dimensions of spiritual knowledge become accessible.

Before and with the laying of the foundation stone, Rudolf Steiner had felt the burden of esoteric responsibility; he also found it difficult to speak of the Fifth Gospel. He spoke explicitly about the inner resistance that he had had to overcome. In Oslo, for instance, he said:

> You will perhaps better understand what I mean with the word overcome if you will allow me a personal remark. It is very clear to me that in the spiritual research, to which I have devoted myself, many things are at first extraordinarily difficult to extract from the spiritual text of the universe, especially things of this nature.... I do not presume at all to state that I am today already able to articulate precisely what presents itself in this spiritual text. I experience it as difficult

and arduous to bring images that pertain to the secrets of Christianity from out of the akashic record. (148)

Andrey Bely experienced the five lectures in Oslo with great attentiveness and described them in a completely personal manner. With his inborn sensitivity, he sensed the special nature of these lectures that, as Bely aptly noted, framed the building of the First Goetheanum. He compared these lectures with those that Steiner had given in August 1913 in Munich.

> In Munich, there were about 2,000 people; in Oslo, between 200 and 300. They were graced to be present when the Doctor revealed for the first time the pinnacle of what he had to say about Christ. And as for himself—I have never experienced the like. Usually he arrived for a course certain about what he had to say, with the content planned out across the days. His engagement grew within certain segments, spontaneous insights joined themselves to the prepared content. Always his certainty brought forth the first word; he would raise his arm above the lectern like a pianist above the key council.
>
> I can say, in this sense, that he "appeared" for a lecture course.
>
> It was different in Oslo. In Munich, he "appeared," strong and in control of himself, while here he almost plunged in, leapt—in the direct not metaphoric use of the word—to the lectern. He was somehow unkempt, with his unruly hair straining off to the side....
>
> The Doctor was a great teacher; he was the master of dozens of techniques. But at that time, none of them were at his service. There was the dumbness of Zacharia, the aureole of the teacher shattered before us. A "teacher" could never speak the way the Doctor spoke then. That was the way a *brother* spoke who was not concerned about having mastered the content in order to present it in an orderly manner. What he had brought with him weighed down upon him; the teacher could only helplessly point toward what he had brought and had to even lean on us in view of the enormous discrepancy between his own personality and the theme. (Bely)

Given that these are Bely's personal experiences and interpretations, one thing, however, is certain. Steiner spoke here differently than he usually did—not as a teacher, but as a witness. Assja Turgenieff, Bely's companion, added:

> The lecture cycle on "The Fifth Gospel" began on October 1. The hall with its banal decorations and the doves painted on the ceiling disappeared gradually during the lectures. The doves fluttered off, and

> something like the dome of heaven, inhabited by beings of light, settled down upon us. And below gathered those who one could not see, but whose presence could be felt. In the middle stood Rudolf Steiner, so delicate and fragile in his black jacket with his gaze opening wide on what he beheld. (Turgenieff)

From Oslo, Rudolf Steiner traveled to Bergen. He discovered the slate in the Vossian quarries, and thus what would cover the roof of the Goetheanum. He returned by way of Copenhagen to Berlin. On October 24, he then returned to Dornach for four days in order to concern himself with the building and to address some of the details. During his stay, the machines with which the wood for the building would be prepared were delivered to the woodworking shop.

During the next six months, Steiner traveled a total of eight times to Dornach, returning each time to Berlin and to speak of the Fifth Gospel in other German cities—Nuremberg, Hamburg, Munich and Cologne. At the close of the year, he spoke in Leipzig about "Christ and the Spiritual World: The Search for the Holy Grail" and began to touch upon the topic of Christ's sacrifices before the Mystery of Golgotha, a topic he then spoke about in February in Berlin; in March in Stuttgart, Pforzheim and Munich; in May in Paris; and in June in Basel.

The emerging building was thus cloaked in the spiritual atmosphere of the new revelation of Christ. Each time Rudolf Steiner returned to Dornach, he had once again borne witness to the reality of Christ "out in the world" and led people to a new quality of experience. Friedrich Rittelmeyer, at that time not yet a member of the Anthroposophical Society, was invited by Steiner to attend the Nuremberg lecture. He experienced the evening as one the most remarkable of his life.

> Rudolf Steiner stood before us—because I sat in the first row, I could observe his facial expressions closely—and spoke of the life of Jesus as a young lad growing up. He gazed out over the gathering, as though he was focused on the images that he had before him. He described these pictures attentively, with great care. "I'm not quite sure that the sequence is correct, but this is how it appears to me," escaped him from time to time. Or: "For all my efforts I have not been able to find the name of the place; there must be a reason that it seems to have been extinguished." The devotion with which he spoke was in no way inhibited. He stood completely upright there before the extraordinary. A pure spirituality filled the space. (Rittelmeyer)

Building

It was cold and wintery, the ridges were covered deep in snow, when Rudolf Steiner returned to Dornach for his fourth working visit on January 27, 1914. The wood framing, golden in the sunlight, marked out the small cupola. The blows of the hammers rang out clear and rhythmically from the structure. There were a total of 250 people working on the site. During this time, the first anthroposophic coworkers began to arrive. Edith Maryon, Assja Turgenieff and Andrey Bely were the first of what would grow to be a whole host, most arriving in early summer to work on the building.

Rudolf Steiner spent these days in meetings and working on models of the main entrance and the interior, both of which the architects Schmid-Curtius, Moser, Aisenpreis and Bauer needed to continue. Marie von Sivers wrote to her friend Mieta Waller on February 2:

> Now I must be a source of inspiration, as the Doctor terms it; sit silently beside him while he works…. It was certainly pleasant, the few hours when we could sit there alone, but usually there is such a hubbub in the workshop that it makes one dizzy…. The other inspirational hours are spent in the model—it's like being in the cellar. The Doctor works diligently under the one cupola. Living waves of form, made of wax, flow out of one another; under the other cupola, I sit uncomfortably with Hamerling's hymns and inspire until I grow stiff. Today I emancipated myself to some degree and wrote letters. Yesterday, we sat under the cupolas until midnight. (Letters and Documents)

After a short stay in Berlin and Hannover, where he spoke once again about the Fifth Gospel, on February 17 Steiner was once again in Dornach to continue work on the models. Construction moved ahead briskly. The small dome had already been sheathed; the arches for the large dome had been raised. There was some concern because of rather significant cost overruns. Finally, on March 11, 1914, the work of carving the capitals began. The unfinished capitals of both the large and the small cupolas, coming directly from the woodworking shop, were set up in the still raw cement rooms at the east end of the ground floor. Each of the different woods had its own color and smell. Calmly, with no sense of hurry, Rudolf Steiner showed his coworkers how to carve. Hour after hour, he stood there, balanced on two wooden boxes, guiding the gouge with one hand, swinging the wooden mallet rhythmically with the other, removing chip after chip of the tough wood until the first form of the Saturn capital began to appear. The onlookers grew tired of standing, but Steiner worked on. Now and again he would climb down off the boxes, look at his work, compare it with the model, then continue.

The general work of carving began the next day. Most of the members who had come to help had to take a first break after about half an hour. There was almost nothing to see; it looked as though a mouse had gnawed a bit on the wood. The beech, oak, cherry and elm were tough. Steiner had showed them how to let rhythm take the place of strength and how to work slowly and steadily. Many of the helpers learned quickly. Led by experienced artists, small groups formed around each of the capitals and pedestals, gradually bringing the various forms into appearance. Even then, in the middle of March, there must have been well over fifty people, men and women, at work carving. Rudolf Steiner was happy to see so many members of the Anthroposophical Society at work on the building. More people arrived over the course of the next few months to work at carving the architraves and other forms. One would often see Steiner among the carvers. He showed them the art of shaping the forms: The convex planes were to be worked as flat as possible, the edges would appear out of the planes, and round humps were "astral fat" and were to be removed or avoided.

The topping-out ceremony took place on April 1. Rudolf Steiner was not present. He did appear on the next day, called back for an urgent meeting. The situation had grown so critical that Rudolf Steiner even postponed a lecture in Berlin, something he otherwise never did. Up until this point, Steiner had pushed to have the building completed by August 1. The consultations on April 3 showed that this deadline could not be met and, on top of this, the unions were using the pressure to meet the deadline to increase their demands. On April 14, in Vienna, Rudolf Steiner had to inform the members that the usual summer festival would not take place in the coming summer, "because the next such gathering should take place in the Johannesbau, and the construction work is going to take longer than originally thought. There is reason to hope that we should be far enough along toward the end of this year to arrange a dedication ceremony for the new building" (153).

Difficult inner problems in the Anthroposophical Society brought Rudolf Steiner back to Berlin at the end of April. They were caused by a Norwegian, Marcello Haugen, who had caused a good deal of distress especially among the ladies in the anthroposophic movement and finally had to be expelled from the society (B 105). Steiner also wanted to hold the lecture that had been postponed from April 2. Toward the end of this lecture, he spoke for the first time publically about the building being raised in Dornach. An increasing number of people were becoming aware of the fruitful impulse alive in anthroposophic Spiritual Science.

> One sign of this is the fact that we are able to build a university for Spiritual Science in Dornach near Basel. It is not the intention to concentrate Spiritual Science in one place. Rather it should bear witness that Spiritual Science can bring forth creative architectural, sculptural and painted forms and bring them into harmony in such a building. This building should be an example that Spiritual Science is capable of taking hold of life directly. (63)

In May, Steiner was able twice to spend several days in Dornach. The columns had been raised during his absence and the architraves were waiting. Once again, in addition to many other things, he worked with the artists, who were doing the carving, and called their attention to the double curved surfaces found in flowers: "Study the plants! The etheric forms in people and animals are adulterated; in the plants they are pure" (Turgenieff).

After visiting Paris and Chartres at the end of May, Rudolf Steiner returned to Dornach and stayed until July 31. One of the reasons for this long sojourn was that difficulties had arisen and some mistakes had been made. There were errors in purchasing wood, errors in certain measurements, errors in setting up the exterior forms—all errors that cost a good deal of money. For this reason, Rudolf Steiner began the first lecture that he gave in the woodworking shop with the words:

> One thought that will often be present in us in connection with this building is the idea of the responsibility that we must have in light of the sacrifices of the friends who have made our work here possible. Those who have acquainted themselves with how large the sums have gradually grown will understand that the only equivalent for such sacrifice must be a strong sense of responsibility that can ensure that what one can hope for from this building is, in fact, achieved. (286)

In the lectures that followed and then continued in the fall, Rudolf Steiner illuminated the idea of the building from different sides. He spoke of the place of the Johannesbau in the development of architecture, how it was envisioned as the outer shell for the words that would be spoken inside, and how its sculptural forms should lead one to the spirits of movement.

At the same time, whenever he spoke about the project, he emphasized that it was only a beginning, the first attempt to find a new style of architecture. He said, for instance, at the dedication of the Glashaus, "Perhaps this building will not achieve all that we strive for; we are only able to raise the first, primitive beginnings."

That it was necessary to build was certain for Steiner given the critical nature of the time, the recognition that the world was threatened by war. He spoke on June 17, just nine days before the assassination in Sarajevo.

> When the conception of such works of art will find successors in the general culture, then those people who enter through the doors of these buildings, who let themselves be moved by what speaks through this art,...these people will never treat their fellow human beings unjustly, for from the artistic forms they will learn love, they will learn to live with their fellow human beings in harmony and peace. Peace and harmony will flow into their heart through the forms.... A true healing of evil to good will in the future for human beings lie in true art, sending a spiritual stream into the souls and heart of humans, causing these hearts and souls,... if they are inclined to lying, to stop lying; if they are inclined to disturb the peace, to stop disturbing the peace of their fellow humans. Buildings will begin to speak....
>
> Today people are gathering in conventions to negotiate world peace. They believe that what passes from mouth to ear can truly bring about peace and harmony. But conventions will not create peace and harmony. Peace and harmony, a situation that is worthy of humanity, will only then begin to flow, when the gods begin to speak to us.
>
> When will the gods begin to speak to us? (286)

The two lateral wings were raised roughly at the time of these lectures. In the middle of June, work was begun on raising the architraves onto the columns. On June 17, the Glashaus, the studio to the north of the main building, became available for engraving the colored glass for the windows. On June 20, they began to cover the roof with the Norwegian slate. At this time more than 150 members of the Anthroposophical Society were at work on the artistic forms, work that was done exclusively by the members.

Building

On the morning of June 29, the painter Hermann Linde, who was at work on the preparations for painting the large cupola, brought the morning paper from Basel to the building site. When Rudolf Steiner arrived at the studio, he showed him the headline that reported the assassination that had occurred in Sarejevo the day before. A witness said, "I will never forget the expression on Rudolf Steiner's face at that moment. Enormous dread and grief lay in his wide open eyes, and he said, 'Now the catastrophe is upon us'" (Boos-Hamburger). Assja Turgenieff recalled that, in the following weeks, Rudolf Steiner had spoken again and again, serious and questioning, with the coworkers about the danger that threatened, as though he were waiting for something—an answer, a deed.

In spite of the tense politic atmosphere, Rudolf Steiner left in the middle of July for a two-week trip north to Norrköping, in Sweden. There, in a quite rural setting, he drew together the essence of his Christological studies in four lectures, "Christ and the Human Soul." From a historical perspective, these four lectures seem to be the summary of his pre-war Christology. It was not that Steiner simply referred to what he had said in early lectures, but, building on what he had developed previously, he placed the capstone on what had gone before. His later Christological studies belong in a new chapter. He returned then to Dornach by way of Stralsund, Hamburg and Berlin.

In Dornach, he spoke on July 26 about the creative powers of the colors that bring forth forms. Toward the end of this lecture, he called attention to the growing activity of those who were inimical to the anthroposophic spiritual stream. In the various local newspapers, since the work began, there had been a series of disparaging articles about the building, about Anthroposophy—which was termed "Buddhist Theosophy"—and about the anthroposophic colony. Steiner had replied to these articles in February in the local daily newspaper (35). Now that the building was visible from afar, these attacks had begun to increase. This filled Rudolf Steiner with "anguish." But "if we take into consideration everything in Europe's present situation that fills us with anguish, the anguish for our own movement is but a small one" (286).

In these last weeks of peace, with all the architraves resting upon their columns, Steiner was able to test the future acoustics of the auditorium, although the scaffolding was still standing. It seemed apparent that the room would have the anticipated resonance, and that both the spoken word and music would sound the way Steiner had expected (174a).

Although the political crisis had grown more acute, Steiner responded to an invitation from Helene Röchling to travel to Bayreuth for a performance of Wagner's *Parsifal*. On August 1, 1914, the day on which the German military mobilization began, Rudolf Steiner and Marie von Sivers attended the performance. Marie Steiner reported:

> The shock reached us in Bayreuth. It was an afternoon performance. Kirchhof sang Parsifal. As soon as it was over, he had to leave to be mustered in. We drove all night in an open car.... The night was pale, ghostly. The armed bridge and track guards were extraordinarily distrustful—we were unkempt, wild-looking in the wool jackets and caps that we had hastened to buy, and we had no passes. Rudolf Steiner's friendly, winning way overcame all the difficulties; without him things would have gone differently. The border patrol was quite gallant! Where have you come from? From Bayreuth. Ah, these must be your costumes? Yes. Then it was over, the barrier was closed behind us.... It was the worst day in Rudolf Steiner's life. I had never seen him so dejected. (*Nachrichtenblatt* 1925)

During Rudolf Steiner's short absence, the scaffolding, which would later have to be put up again, had been taken out. Temporary lighting had been installed. Margarita Woloschin told how she had lingered in the hall as the sunset and the evening darkened. Suddenly, the electric lights came on, casting a stark light on the architrave. Steiner came into the room, studied the sculpted forms, and said, "It has to be quite different; it hasn't yet come alive." Then, after studying them in silence, "We will have to go over everything again" (Woloschin).

But how? The war had thinned out the ranks of coworkers. Only twenty-five men were left in the woodshop. Switzerland had also mobilized. Not only most of the German workers, but also a large number of the Swiss, had been mustered in. This was also true of the anthroposophic coworkers. There were fewer resources to carry on the work, construction slowed and the project was drawn out. Finances became a major worry. The real costs had left the estimates far behind by the spring of 1914. Then came the costly errors of the actual construction. Finally, at the general assembly of the Johannesbau Society on December 31, 1914, the chairman had to admit that "until now the war has cost us 100,000 Swiss francs. In addition, many of the gifts were in the form of stocks and bonds, and these have lost much of their value." Grosheintz estimated the losses at 250,000 Swiss francs. Almost half a million francs were missing from the money that had been donated, which had been estimated to cover the costs of the entire project. Up to that point, not including the cost of the site, 2.6 million francs had gone into the project. There was enough money left to continue for several months, but it was apparent that it would run out in the course of the coming year. How could the work continue?

IMAGES, PART TWO

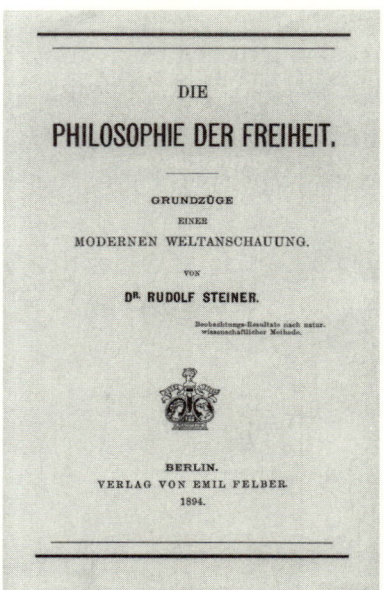

Above: Rudolf Steiner, 1892; Die Philosophie der Freiheit, 1893 (see chapter 16); below: Friedrich Nietzsche, 1890s; and Elisabeth Förster-Nietzsche (see p. 178).

Above: Fritz Koegel (1860–1904); Rudolf Steiner, 1896; below: Anna Steiner-Eunike (1853–1911), whom Rudolf Steiner married (see pp. 138, 209, 214); Ernst Haeckel (1834–1919), an eminent German biologist, naturalist, philosopher, physician, professor and artist (see pp. 59, 211).

Above: John Henry Mackay (1864–1933); Rudolf Steiner, 1901; below: Marie von Sivers; and Helena Petrovna Blavatsky, or "HPB" (1831–1891), cofounder of the Theosophical Society (see chapter 23).

Above: Annie Besant (1847–1933), president of the Theosophical Society (Adyar); Adolf Arenson (1855–1936); below: Carl Unger (1878–1929); Arenson and Unger established the important anthroposophic branch in Stuttgart (see p. 275); and Michael Bauer (1871–1929).

Above: Sophie Stinde (1853–1915) and Duchess Pauline Kalckreuth (1856–1929); see beginning p. 276 on the roles of these important women; below: the 1906 congress in Paris for the Theosophical Society European Section (see chapter 26).

Above: Rudolf Steiner in Mark Landin, Germany, 1906, probably with Eliza von Moltke on the left (the center woman unknown); Édouard Schuré (see chapter 27); below: the Theosophical Congress in Munich, 1907 (see chapter 27).

Above: The Munich Theosophical Congress, 1907; below: Rudolf Steiner with Annie Besant, 1907; Rudolf Steiner with Marie von Sivers in Stuttgart, 1908.

Rudolf Steiner, 1908

Above: Rudolf Steiner in Stockholm, 1910; Christian Morgenstern (1871–1914); below: Assja Turgenieff (1890–1966) with Andrei Bely (born Boris Nikolaevich Bugaev, 1880–1934)

*Above: the first model of the building in Munich;
below: rendering the building complex in Munich (Carl Schmidt Curtius)*

*Above: construction of the Goetheanum, February 1914;
below: workers atop the partially finished Goetheanum*

Above: Rudolf Steiner with the model of the Geotheanum, June 19, 1914; below: model of the interior; and carving the column capitals.

Aerial view of the Goetheanum

Above: Lory Maier-Smits (1893–1971); Rudolf Steiner gave her the first course on the basic elements of Eurythmy in September 1912 (see chapter 34); Tatiana Kisseleff (1881–1970; see p. 424); below: Marie and Rudolf Steiner, 1915.

Chapter 34

WARTIME IN DORNACH

As mentioned, it seems that Rudolf Steiner had already had a sense that war was approaching in 1913. He had not, of course, foreseen exactly what would happen. What made the war seem inevitable was, in his estimation, not only the political tension and the increasingly frequent crises, but also the practical materialism and worship of Mammon that had taken hold among such a large part of humanity. In April 1914, he described the rapidly growing consumer-based production as a cancer and remarked, "This tendency will continue to grow, until it—you will understand why in a moment—destroys itself" (153). In other contexts, he spoke of the war as the consequence or the karma of materialism, a volcanic eruption of forces that had been focused in the wrong direction, and an attempt to come through crisis to catharsis.

For Steiner, war was on the horizon, but his push to have the building finished by August 1 (the day war was declared) was not connected with his anticipating that it would begin around this time. He clarified this point a number of times, pointing out that even esotericists can be surprised by events. On September 30, 1914, looking back on the situation in July of that year, he said that at the beginning of "July we could only say that we would gather in Munich and afterward, when we then parted, that we could expect to be confronted with events of great significance" (174b). During the first half of July, Rudolf Steiner still reckoned that the lecture cycle "Inner Reading and Inner Hearing," planned for August 18 to 27 in Munich, would take place. It was only on July 20 that he became aware of a significant change in the realm of the soul that pointed toward the events that followed (174b).

When Rudolf Steiner returned to Dornach from Bayreuth on August 2, the world had changed drastically for him, too. Assja Turgenieff recalled, "At the outbreak of the war, Dr. Steiner was downcast, shaken. It was depressing to experience these times with him; one read their pain in his eyes. He experienced it much more deeply than we did but was, however, better able to bear it" (Turgenieff). Outwardly, the war placed limitations on Steiner's freedom of movement. Permission to travel between Germany and Switzerland was granted only after much effort and thanks to good connections; Steiner was also able to visit Austria three times during the war. The other European countries were closed to him, and even after the war it was at first very difficult to visit Norway, then Holland, and finally France and England. During the war, political surveillance of Steiner's lectures began and, in Württemberg, it continued on after the war had ended.

The war brought for many years the great lecture cycles to an end. These had been an important instrument for the deepening and development of Anthroposophy. Now Rudolf Steiner spoke in Dornach on the weekends—Saturday, Sunday and Monday; in Berlin, he spoke at the branch on Tuesday evenings; and he continued the public lectures at the House of the Architects. When he could get permission to visit other German cities, he gave lectures both for the public and for the members. The content of the lectures changed as well. In October 1914, Steiner pointed out to the members in Dornach that it would be naïve to imagine "that the earnest strength that is needed to say something substantial in the field of spiritual science can still be brought to bear is such times as those in which we live." He added, "The highest truths cannot be spoken into the storm" (156). Finally, the esoteric lessons and the ritualistic gatherings were ended, because during war any secret gathering in a closed circle would have been misunderstood and caused distrust. Thus, during the war, Steiner was without his most trusted colleagues, a circle that in spite of all its problems was still an important part of Steiner's work.

The lectures held during the war contain, in addition to presentations from Steiner's own spiritual scientific research, explorations of questions pertaining to aesthetics, art history, history, and critiques of various aspects of his time. In these, Steiner didn't speak of new spiritual discoveries, but focused on the healthy observation of phenomena and occurrences. The art history lectures as well as the expositions on Faust contain a rich, exemplary collection upon which one can school oneself.

Only a very reduced crew of workers remained in Dornach. Steiner's primary concern was that "construction [should] not reach a standstill" (157). Those remaining at the site drew more closely together. Representatives of the different countries gave one another a hand and focused their energy on the building. Cannons could be heard in the distance, and at night the floodlights from the Isteiner Klotz swept over the landscape. Everyone expected that the French armies would cross through; the first course that Rudolf Steiner gave was a first-aid course.

The harmony among the workers was, of course, threatened at times. There were representatives of the different factions at work on the site. They thought differently than each other and had different sensibilities and sources of information. In 1915, after an initial period of unity, a certain amount of chauvinism became apparent. The shared work helped, as did the artistic work that Steiner initiated and supported—eurythmy performances and plays, through which human interactions were cultivated.

In Tatiana Kisseleff, Rudolf Steiner had found someone to take up the eurythmy. After having to leave Russia for political reasons, Kisseleff had studied law in Paris and Lausanne. She began to follow Steiner's work in 1911 and was one of the first to take up the new art form. Before the war broke out, she had moved to Dornach and had begun giving eurythmy courses. This was the beginning of a development that Rudolf Steiner could support fully.

Steiner had, as was mentioned above, given a first course in eurythmy in August 1912 for the then eighteen-year-old Lory Smits. This course, consisting of nine lessons, focused on the elemental gestures of the alphabet and the basic choreographic movements of eurythmy. This eurythmic "spelling" had been taken a step further in 1913, and a first demonstration took place on August 28 following the performances of the mystery plays in Munich. Further demonstrations followed in Cologne, Leipzig, and Berlin. From time to time Rudolf Steiner had given further explanations and there was soon a whole bevy of young ladies who had dedicated themselves to the new art. Tatiana Kisseleff's arrival in August 1914 brought an artist to Dornach with whom Steiner had been able to work intensively on the forms of eurythmic expression. In 1914 and 1915, the systematic development of eurythmy began. Tatiana Kisseleff functioned as the teacher, and most of the painters and sculptors joined her to form a stage group.

At Christmas and again at the end of December, a scene from the first mystery play and the Christmas celebration had been presented in eurythmy. In 1915, regular performances began in the Goetheanum woodworking shop: at Easter, "Easter Night" from Goethe's *Faust*; at Whitsun, the Ariel scene; and in July, a selection of poems from Goethe and Morgenstern. On August 15, as part of a conference to which about 300 people came in spite of the war, the "Redemption" scene from the second part of *Faust* was performed. The "Prologue in Heaven" came on August 19, and on August 29 the "Twelve Moods" verses that Steiner had written for eurythmy were premiered.

Rudolf Steiner had begun in 1908 to look for someone who would be interested in developing this new art. In response to Lory Smits's request for a form of dance or gymnastics, he began to work on the basic elements of what would become eurythmy. The goal was to bring to visible expression the invisible movements of the human etheric body. The spiritual etheric of language was to be made visible. When a person speaks, it is not only his or her physical larynx, tongue, lips and teeth that are active; language is the outer manifestation of a suprasensory movement. On October 7, 1914, Rudolf Steiner had touched on these relationships at the end of the lectures "Inner Reading and Inner Hearing."

> The world of form rules over the physical body; the world of movement rules over the etheric body. The movements that are innate to the etheric body must now be discovered. The human being must be guided to bring to expression in the gestures and movements of the physical body, movements that are natural for the etheric body....
>
> This is what is attempted in eurythmy. It will show us that human beings when they move are truly a link between the cosmic letters, the cosmic sounds and what we use in our human letters and sounds in our poetry....
>
> In brief, we can define eurythmy as the fulfillment of what the human etheric body naturally requires of the human being. (277a)

It is no doubt symptomatic that the cultivation of the harmonizing eurythmy exercises, based as they are on unified choral movements, were intensified at a time that the Dornach membership was undergoing a difficult crisis. It had some history. Marie von Sivers and Rudolf Steiner had planned for some time to marry. Because of the excess of work, they had simply not gotten around to it. Steiner had written to his mother in April 1913, "Since there was so much to do this winter, the plan with Miss von Sivers, of which I spoke to you when I last visited, could not go any further; but we are still thinking about it for the future. She was very happy when I told her that I had spoken of it with you" (39).

After this letter, a year and nine months would pass before the "plan with Miss von Sivers" was put into action. Rudolf Steiner and Marie von Sivers were married on December 24, 1914. This marriage, which came after twelve years of loyal, intensive collaboration, affirmed and placed openly in the public, did not change anything in the way they lived, but it did deeply disappoint one specific woman who had had—seemingly without justification—other hopes. Alice Sprengel had helped during the Munich performances since 1907, and in that connection the relationship had been nurtured and she had been supported. Now, in her disappointment, she joined forces with a man named Dr. Heinrich Goesch and his wife. This threesome, which rarely came to work on the building, set the strangest rumors about Steiner in circulation. Steiner, who became aware of the absurdity of the situation, initially responded with a series of lectures about problematic esoteric developments. Then, after the climate had also been charged by other occurrences, the storm broke out. On August 20, Rudolf Steiner received a letter from Gertrud and Heinrich Goesch in which they accused him de facto of practicing black magic and suggestion and of not acknowledging any form of critique (253). As proof, Goesch pointed out Steiner's way of shaking hands. According to him, this handshake allowed the recipient to be magically manipulated. Steiner read Goesch's letter to the gathered members on the following day. When a few of them tried to put in a good word for the Goesch's, Rudolf Steiner and Marie Steiner left the room.

The next day, Michael Bauer handed Rudolf Steiner a written vote of confidence signed by some 300 members. Steiner then spoke at length about the situation on August 22. He differentiated between the pathological behavior of Dr. Goesch and Alice Sprengel's tragic confusion. The latter distanced herself in 1916 from Goesch, then fell under the spell of Theodor Reuss and became, as far as is known, a member of one of Reuss's orders in Ascona.

Andrei Bely recalled this period in Dornach, a period in which his own personal crisis also reached a climax.

> From the end of July until the middle of November 1915, Rudolf Steiner fought on a number of fronts simultaneously: he fought against our indolence; he took steps to insure that the Swiss government did not acquiesce to the demands of certain intelligence agencies to have us deported; he fought against various spiritual streams that

were undermining his "Dornach" with both open and veiled accusations (Jesuits, Protestants, various esoteric societies); he battled with the middle-class thinking that threatened to encircle him and with the specific pathologies of the Anthroposophical Society; he struggled with the lack of money and people who were able to finish the building; he fought for the young against the old, and he brought a measure of restraint to our challenging approach "in spite of the old!"—I will spring over the period during which this stall of Augias was cleaned. Bauer, Marie Steiner and Sophie Stinde (until her death) stood courageously at his side. (Bely)

These events are reflected in the lectures Steiner gave during this period. At times he chose not to speak of these things at all, but to focus on carefully crafted, thoughtful, methodological explorations. He commented on a brochure by F. von Wrangel on *Science and Theosophy*, and then spoke about "Esoteric Movements in the Nineteenth Century"; later he spoke about the poetry of Gutzkow, Krasinski, and Julius Mosen and about Theodor Fechner.

The opposition against Rudolf Steiner that became visible at this point continued on into the subsequent years. It is worth noting that the attacks first came from a series of individuals who were not just members of the society, but were also members of the esoteric school and the symbolic Freemason rituals. In addition to Heinrich Goesch, who continued his attacks on into the early '20s, Max Seiling, Ernst Bold and Erich Bammler soon appeared on the stage with various pamphlets and brochures. In these and in articles in such journals as *Psychic Studies, Theosophy,* and *Prana,* appeared a flood of nonsense and garbage about Rudolf Steiner. Respectable critics found themselves in the position, as they put it, of being able to quote these "typical renegades" with only the greatest care (Heyer).

During this time, unnoticed by those around him, Rudolf Steiner was in the process of preparing another major undertaking.

When he began in the summer of 1913 to plan the actual building of the Goetheanum, he did not work the design out in all its details. He kept himself open for what would show itself as the work progressed and for what others would bring to his attention. For instance, he willingly followed Max Benzinger's suggestion and added the two side wings.

Many details concerning the interior architecture, including plans for painting the small cupola, were still undecided in the fall of 1914. Late that autumn, the Danish painter Arild Rosenkrantz left his home in

England to come to Dornach. As all new helpers did, he first joined the crews working on carving the forms in the building's interior. But Steiner soon decided that this work was not good for the painter's hands and moved him into the glass engraving studio. There Rosenkrantz showed Steiner the sketch of a piece that he planned to do for a church in London. It was a crucifixion scene with Christ surrounded by angels. Steiner thought the approach was too traditional and offered some suggestions. When Rosenkrantz then a few days later showed him another sketch, Steiner is supposed to have answered, "You have to paint that in the small cupola." The next day Steiner spoke to him about his idea of depicting Christ between the two oppositional forces. In this collaborative back and forth, the first depiction of Christ for the small cupola, which was done by Rosenkrantz, came into being. It was later replaced by one that Steiner had painted.

Among the first group of artists that arrived in Dornach in February 1914 to help with the building was the English sculptor Edith Maryon. Illness forced her to return to England from April through June, but by the beginning of July, she was back in Dornach. The extraordinary quality of her work must have become apparent quite quickly. Rudolf Steiner asked her in October to come to work in his studio and discussed with her the task of designing a large sculpture for the niche at the east end of the stage. In the following weeks, Maryon began the design process. First she made a small model out of wax and modeling clay, the second of which led Steiner to suggest corrections. She then made a larger model that incorporated Steiner's suggestions. This was roughly 35 inches high, made of plaster of paris, and remains in existence. Steiner then made a fourth model, to which he added an additional motif. The design continued this way in an ongoing sculptural dialogue.

After eight months of work, Steiner was ready to speak about the emerging sculptural composition at a lecture for members given in Linz on May 15, 1915. He managed to give his listeners a remarkably clear and detailed picture of the piece, which was to show "the relationship that exists in the world between the three forces Christ, Lucifer, and Ahriman" (159). The first large model, more than six feet high, was finished in the summer of 1915. Before it was completed, Steiner had prepared studies for the heads of Christ and Ahriman for the large sculpture, which was to be about thirty-three feet high. One of the first people to see these models was Friedrich

Rittelmeyer, who visited Steiner in the studio in the summer of 1915. He contemplated the head of Christ at length. He could feel the strength and significance of this attempt especially at that time. There is nothing all-too-human about this visage—through the human features one can experience the cosmic magnificence.

For Rudolf Steiner, who had lived since May 1914 in a house that he had christened "Villa Hansi" and where he had a small room that served as both a study and a bedroom, the studio became from 1916 on the center of his life. It was here in the workshop that he would receive the innumerable visitors of the coming years, individuals seeking his guidance or help. It was here that he worked on the great sculpture of the representative of humanity. It was here, if anywhere, that he was at home. In Edith Maryon, he had found a guardian of the workshop, someone who took care of the smallest things conscientiously and quietly.

Rudolf Steiner needed this oasis of artistic work that, in addition to Villa Hansi, provided him with his own work space, especially because during the war ever greater burdens were placed on him. The most bitter and, in this connection, worst loss was the death of Sophie Stinde. She had coordinated the artistic work of the building and had taken care of the helpers. She died on November 17, 1915, during a visit to Munich. After taking charge of the work in Munich from 1904 on and carrying most of the responsibility for the Munich performances beginning in 1907, she had moved to Dornach in 1914, became chairperson of the building association and freed Steiner from many of the project's technical details. She had worked quietly, never placing herself in the foreground. In many of the memoirs that describe the early Dornach years, she is not even mentioned. But her work was a true blessing for Steiner. After her death, a great deal of the work came to rest on his shoulders as her successor in the building association, Dr. Emil Grosheintz, was a dentist in Basel and not able to take over many of her responsibilities. Steiner's attempts to find someone to replace her came to nothing.

Thus, the first war years brought Rudolf Steiner burdens, obstacles and a series of personal difficulties, most of which arose through the tactlessness, the delusions and the wishful thinking of some of the members. In the artistic work that had grown in intensity in many areas, he found a field in which he could live and be active. Even in the turbulent years of the 1920s, he was to find new strength for his work through artistic activity.

Chapter 35

THE DESTINY OF CENTRAL EUROPE

At some point after August 20, 1914, Rudolf Steiner received word that General Helmuth von Moltke, the commander of the German general staff, wished to speak with him. Steiner had been acquainted with his wife, Eliza von Moltke, since 1904 and, although Helmuth von Moltke did not share his wife's spiritualistic inclinations, he had learned to trust Rudolf Steiner and his spiritual approach and had read a number of his writings. Steiner responded to the General's request and set off to visit him. The trip took him through Stuttgart and Mannheim, where he made stops to insure that his ticket would not reveal exactly where he was headed, then on to Coblenz, where the headquarters of the general staff were at that time.

In connection with the general mobilization on August 1, 1914, Moltke had experienced drastically the Emperor's lack of certainty. After giving the order at 5:00 p.m. for mobilization for the next day, a few hours later he had tried to rescind this order, which had already set in motion the painstakingly planned deployment of the troops on the western front. The scenes that followed had brought Moltke to the point of despair and had crippled the already fragile health of the sixty-six-year-old general. Now he turned to Steiner for personal help and inner guidance.

Steiner documented this meeting, which took place in a private residence, laconically. "I saw General von Moltke only once in the month of August, on August 27, in Coblenz. We spoke only of purely human matters. The German army was still victorious" (24). We can assume that in this conversation Rudolf Steiner had given Helmuth von Moltke, who bore the entire burden of responsibility for Germany's war efforts, inner support. He made no mention in this conversation—as he did later in a number of letters—that the genius of the German peoples "stood there with his torch raised high in a promise of assurance" (Moltke II). He protected him. Perhaps Steiner gave him at this time the encouraging words of the meditation:

> The power will conquer,
> The power predestined by fate
> For the folk, which
> With spirit protection,
> For the welfare of humanity,
> Wrests light from the battle
> In Europe's heart.

Younger readers may perhaps be astonished that Rudolf Steiner would have spoken words of encouragement to the commander of the German military, that he would have tried to give him confidence and hopes of victory, even indicating that he had been placed by destiny in this position (Moltke II). One could recognize a historical archetype in this dialogue, the dialogue that took place between Krishna and Arjuna on the battlefield in the first book of the Bhagavad Gita; but one could not fail to notice the difference between the transcendent wisdom of Krishna and Steiner's empathetic gesture.

One would be even more astonished to hear from Steiner that in 1916, in the middle of the war, just after von Moltke's death, he had been willing to open a news agency in Zurich to give the German's position a fair hearing in the international press. In the middle of June 1916, Lieutenant Colonel von Haeften, who had for a time been von Moltke's adjutant, recommended that Steiner be entrusted with this task.

> I was able to point out to someone (von Haeften) that it would be impossible to achieve anything within the framework of the old news agencies. Things had progressed to the point that, on a Tuesday,...I was told: There is every indication that you will be able to move to Zurich in the next few days to open the news agency. The next day I received a letter of rejection from general headquarters pointing out that there were so many people in Germany waiting for such a position that it was impossible to take an Austrian into consideration. (338)

This passage indicates clearly that Steiner initially proposed and pushed the idea of a news agency and that he was completely prepared to work in publishing to support the forces of Central Europe. It must have been incredibly important to him that a differentiated, authentic image of Germany emerge in the international press; such a position would have endangered his position in Dornach.

The questions could arise: Can an "initiate" become so deeply enmeshed in earthly battles? Must not a wise person refrain from taking sides? Is such a one not concerned primarily with the well-being of all humanity? If we truly wish to understand Steiner's position here—which in many ways is symptomatic—and not merely write it off as an "urge to play politics" or mere patriotism, we must look at the situation somewhat more closely.

From a historical distance, it is easy to see that different peoples have different characters and different tasks. We can consider the Greeks and the Romans. An unprejudiced approach will recognize that the former had a cultural-historical mission in the development of philosophical questions as well as in the evolution of architecture, sculpture, and drama, in which the human form and human destiny mirror one another. No less obvious is the fact that the Romans developed social and legal forms, as well as a legal system, which played a definitive role for centuries throughout much of Europe.

Setting aside ethnic anecdotes, it is more difficult to recognize that the various European peoples, even today, have both differences in character and in their tasks. One can, however, when considering the path of European history, recognize the role of the Italians in the development of the classical form of the Renaissance, that of the French in the blossoming of the Age of Reason, and how the English and the Scots influenced the development of modern science and took steps toward the realization of certain social forms—for instance, the division of powers and parliamentary process.

Steiner had first spoken about the character and task of the various peoples in lectures concerning the mission of the different folk souls in 1910. Understanding the nature of the folk souls became critical following the outbreak of World War I, because in this war national consciousness and the way the other nations were viewed played a central role. Rudolf Steiner, in any case, viewed the European war from this perspective, and his primary concern was for the destiny of central Europe. Although it was possible to say that the Italian, French and English cultures had to some extent fulfilled their tasks, it was a different story with Germany and Austria. The fulfillment of what they had to contribute to the further evolution of humanity was still to come.

In 1884, in one the earliest surviving articles, the twenty-three-year-old Steiner had articulated what he saw as the task of the Germanic people.

He wrote that the threads of the other European cultures came together in Germany as though in a point of intersection, in which the grand motifs of the other peoples were to be internalized and developed further. For instance, what Darwin had established scientifically was brought into a conceptual unity and a personal experience by Haeckel. Steiner also hoped that Germany would be able to find a governmental form in which "reason held the highest office" (30). Thus, already by 1884, he saw central Europe and especially Germany as having a double task: The deepening and internalization of European culture on the one hand and, on the other, the creation of social relationships, which were informed by a sense of the value of human life.

In 1910 and 1914/15 Rudolf Steiner articulated these ideas more concretely by saying that "the striving toward individuality" comes to expression in a unique manner in central Europe.

> And with the phrase "striving toward individuality," we cannot only characterize the Germans but must also take into consideration a number of other central European peoples. They all share this striving toward individuality. Regardless of their outer differences, we find it in Czechs, in East Slavs, in Slovaks, in Hungarians, and we find it at the other pole of Germanic culture, in the Poles. (287)

It was for this reason that Rudolf Steiner had spoken of the "I"-character being present especially in the folk souls of central Europe, and it was in light of this that he saw the specific task of central Europe as being the challenge to develop a culture that rested upon individual intention, an "I"-culture. By saying this, he did not mean to suggest that it was something better or more elevated than, let us say, the pragmatic, matter-of-fact quality of the conscious soul that one could observe in the English. This comes to clear expression in the following characterization of the "I."

> In the "I" is that element of the human soul that has to come to grips with itself. For this reason, there is a brooding tendency, a tendency to be preoccupied with oneself. Although the Germans have waged and will continue to wage all sorts of wars, the characteristic battles are those that Germans have fought with other Germans in order to bring what is within the "I" to expression. If one follows these battles, one finds a true reflection of the battles that take place within the "I" of each human. (287)

As mentioned, Steiner was convinced that Central Europe stood at the beginning of its own unique mission. He articulated this in the oft-quoted words: "The German spirit has not brought to completion what it is to craft in the becoming of the world" (64). Rudolf Steiner thus speaks repeatedly in 1914 and 1915, especially in public lectures in Germany, of the task of Germany. In contrast to other contemporary speakers, he did not speak of this in relation to the German—or rather Prussian—military tradition, from Friedrich the Great down to the elder Moltke, nor in relation to Scharnhorst or Bismarck. Rather, he spoke of the spiritual stream that led from Jakob Bohme and Angelus Silesius to Goethe, Schiller, Fichte, and Hegel.

> We can follow the continual development of the Germanic soul to the German spirit. We see the German spirit in its very beginnings, the seeds beginning here and there to sprout and reveal within them the promise that the heights, which are implicitly present, must still be scaled, that these cannot be destroyed but must evolve, because they belong to its innermost being. (64)

It was in this manner that he viewed German development to be an essential aspect of the evolution of humanity. A decisive factor in the future of humanity would be the development of a culture born of the "I." In many lectures given throughout 1914 and 1915, Steiner spoke as an advocate of this aspect of Germany's significance and tried to call his listeners' attention to the true nature of the German mission.

Here we have reached a very difficult chapter of this story. In light of the subsequent historical developments that took place from 1917 until 1919, and especially then from 1933 until 1945, some of Steiner's statements from 1914 and 1915 appear highly questionable. To gain a historical understanding, one must, however, place oneself within the time period and attempt to see the situation as it appeared then. Rudolf Steiner had, even within the Theosophical Society, emphasized the fact that he understood his task as being one that lived within the Germanic context, and that he viewed himself as a representative of the Germanic spirit. In 1914/15, he saw the true inner Germanic gesture, and thus one of the—if not *the*—key factors of the future of humanity existentially threatened.

Outwardly, this threat appeared to be against the German Reich and the Austro-Hungarian Empire. Inwardly, something quite different was being threatened. It had to do with whether the transformative forces of the "I," working out of the spirit, would be able to play a role in the historical development of human culture. Working out of the spirit—through pure thinking or true intuition—had been Steiner's theme at least since the publication of *Intuitive Thinking as a Spiritual Path*. Early on, he had recognized the fact that such a striving would be met with grave resistance. Other forces of the soul oppose the free expression of direct personal spiritual experience. The tendency is to foot one's thinking and action on rational principles, success-oriented pragmatism, and the tendency toward mystical feelings or emotional euphoria.

The resistance of these soul forces against the intuitive qualities of initiative drawn from the spirit by the "I" is quite significant. Reason pours scorn on the "I" and the forces of intuition and accuses it of being irrational; pragmatism shunts the "I" aside and orients itself on the practical outcomes; mysticism conjures forth murky values, on behalf of which it takes action and speaks.

In his booklet *Thoughts during the Time of War—for Germans and those who do not believe that they have to hate them* (1915), in which he took no "fundamental esoteric knowledge" into consideration (186 & 24), Rudolf Steiner summarized the 1914/15 lectures and tried to awaken first the Germans to the true essence of the Germanic mission. He took the ideas and biography of Johann Gottlieb Fichte as a starting point and showed how this one German had conceived of life and action born out of the suprasensory and how he had lived in accordance with this conception. Using Ralph Waldo Emerson's words, he illustrated how the being of the "I," which looks toward the whole, had come to expression in Goethe. If one combines the inner gesture that comes to expression in these two thinkers, one gains a sense of what Steiner meant when he spoke of impulse born of the "I." In Fichte, we find a reverence for the suprasensory and the will to action; in Goethe, a sense of the whole—a substantive knowledge of the sensory–supersensory that can lead the will toward meaningful action.

Steiner went on to show, from a wide historical perspective, how the forces of the soul that resist this cultural impulse of the "I" have over the centuries stifled the emergence of this impulse in Germanic culture (159). The Thirty Years War, during which forces from all sides of the compass gathered to destroy the emergent spiritual blossoming that had begun in Germany, is a possible example of this. Steiner did not use this as an example in the 1915 booklet. He quoted Ernst Renan, who in

1870 had spoken of "a war to annihilate the German race" (24). He also called attention to the works of Chomiakow and Danilevsky, who spoke of Russia's global mission (24) and in whose writings he discerned the manifestation of "the Russian aggressor's instinct cloaked in the idea of the historical mission of Russia" (24).

Among the English, he discerned the presence of an ideal focused on what is practical. "A purely political form of reason focused on practical consequences must calculate what danger is posed to England if Germany were to vanquish Russia and France" (24). Moreover, Steiner illustrated the historical politics of England by pointing out how they had come to rule the oceans of the world. "How did England's political ideal come to expression when another European power found itself moved by the forces of history to extend its influence on the sea? We need only to ponder how this political ideal attacked Spain and Portugal, Holland and France, as these countries took to the sea" (24).

There was no similar driving force to be found by the Germans "that would lead in a comparable manner to the present war," according to Steiner, as he had been able to discover with the French and the Russians (24). But "the Germans could have predicted that this war would be waged against them at some point. It was their duty to prepare for it. Opponents claimed that taking those steps to fulfill their duty was actually a cultivation of their militaristic tendencies" (24).

Toward the end of the document, Steiner turned his attention to the historical necessities that had arisen out of the long present tendencies within the various peoples and wrote:

> As the various forces that have been described as being inimical to "Europe's middle" united themselves to put pressure on the middle, it was inevitable that this "pressure" would color the way the Central European peoples viewed international events. The events of the summer of 1914 took place within a specific historical context. This context was such that the forces at work within the different ethnicities responded to the events and took hold of them, removing the decision of what would come of them from the sphere of normal human judgment and placing it in a higher context, one in which universal historical necessities influence the path of human evolution. (24)

This document was written in the early days of July 1915. In a lecture given on November 10, 1918—immediately after the collapse—Steiner reflected on the situation out of which this document arose. He remembered that he had not immediately understood the situation that had arisen following the defeat of the Germans on the Marne River. "I am not afraid to admit that I did not recognize immediately after the defeat on the Marne that truly those things had to happen, which now in fact have taken place" (185a).

In other words, in September 1914, Steiner was not at all clear that the war would end with a German defeat. This only became clear to him after he had published the booklet mentioned above. After the true nature of the situation became clear to him, he forswore the planned continuation of the booklet and then took every possible step to insure that no further editions of the booklet be published. It was not that he thought what he had written was in some way amiss. As late as 1923, he countered the critique of the book that had arisen in anthroposophic circles sharply, saying that the writing of this document was his own work. (258). But—as he said in 1919—the most important thing is not that what is voiced is right in an abstract sense, "but that something is done or not done in the right moment" (186). Steiner changed the way he worked and the initiatives he took to meet the realities of each situation.

It is now possible to follow quite clearly the way Steiner spoke about the war, especially in public lectures changed through the winter of 1915/16. Take for instance the lecture given on December 16, 1915, titled "Fichte's Spirit Here in Our Midst." In this and other lectures around that time, it is noticeable that all mention of the defense of Germany is missing. Instead, the lectures are more discursive and descriptive. Rudolf Steiner tells long stories from Fichte's life and from the lives of late nineteenth century Austrian figures. These lectures lack the earlier clear intentionality; the audiences are free to form their own intentions based on simple facts. Steiner summarized the topics of these lectures in his book *The Riddle of Humanity*.

In this book, Steiner turns his attention to the way in which the Germanic national character influenced German and Austrian thinkers. Yet the theme of the German spirit, the spirit of the Germanic peoples, is never brought to the forefront. One can have the impression when reading these portraits of individual spiritual work that Steiner placed some importance on reminding the Germans and Austrians of exemplary, deep, yet to some extent forgotten thinkers. He saw in the work of these spirits "nourishment for the soul," something that his contemporaries were deeply in need of (169). He took great care with the formulation of his thoughts in this book. "We will see whether what has been written in this book—in which I have sometimes taken two days to write a sentence that covers a quarter of a page in order to stand behind every word, every phrase—will in fact be read, or only read as badly as previous books have been" (169).

The hunch that moved Steiner to write in this way proved to be true. *The Riddle of Humanity* was one of his least-read works.

During December 1916 and January 1917, Steiner spoke in Dornach again about the historical context and what had led to the war. The situation had once again changed critically. On November 21, 1916, Franz Joseph, the Austrian emperor, had died. His successor, Emperor Otto, and the foreign minister, Count Ottokar Czernin, were weighing the possibility of a special peace treaty for the Austro-Hungarian Empire. On December 12, the leadership of the German Reich issued a declaration of peace. The United States was asked to inform the Allied forces that Germany was prepared to enter into peace negotiations. The Allies refused. Lloyd-George wanted to continue the "Knock-out policy" until Prussian militarism had been completely annihilated; Aristide Briand, the French president, declared that in light of the threat to freedom even the use of the word peace was blasphemy. On December 21, the American president, Woodrow Wilson, wrote to the warring and neutral parties suggesting discussions concerning the conditions of a peace treaty. These negotiations continued without success until January 31, 1917, when Germany informed the United States that beginning February 1, German U-boats would wage war against Allied shipping without restraint. This declaration cleared the way for America to enter the war.

The lectures given in Dornach during the winter of 1916/17 need to be read against this background. In contrast to his earlier lectures, Steiner looks in detail at the historical chain of events and the patterns of diplomacy. It is evident that he put a good deal of effort into studying the facts. His library bears witness to this. There are several yards of books on the outbreak of World War I. Naturally, he also studied the journals, something for which Basel was the ideal location. Emil Leinhas, who would later become the general director of The Coming Day, had the opportunity to visit Steiner often during the war years. He recalled, "Rudolf Steiner followed the political and military events during World War I in detail and with great attentiveness. He informed himself daily of the news, and paid attention to what the foreign and domestic politicians were saying and how the press was reporting events. He waited for anything that might give a glimmer of hope that the catastrophe of war was coming to an end" (Leinhas).

Based on this wealth of knowledge, Steiner gave a total of 25 lectures concerning the war and the events accompanying it and expanded on many of the facts by indicating the esoteric realities that lay at their source. Before America entered the war and the beginning of the Russian Revolution, he clearly did his best to cast the circumstances in a light that would show what was justified in the fighting of the Central European powers. A good summary of his thoughts concerning this are to be found in his lecture of January 8, 1917 (174). He certainly hoped that his spiritual efforts would be perceived somewhere, and that they would be brought to fruition.

In these lectures, Rudolf Steiner defended the Central European powers, especially against the in-no-way-gentle propaganda of the Allies. But he was also concerned that these things be seen in an appropriate manner historically. He rejected carelessly assigning specific moral concepts—such as freedom or justice, which applied to human individuals—to peoples. Instead he spoke of the need to develop a feeling for what is tragic in history. He spoke here of the tragic in its highest, formal sense and remarked that one must introduce the truly tragic "as a category, a concept in the evolution of humanity." Otherwise, one "always [arrives] at the simplistic judgment: this or that could have been avoided" (174).

There are also things voiced in these lectures that reach far into the future. In the lecture from January 15, 1917, Steiner speaks of the bilateral division that arises when one attempts to create an economically based global hegemony. Each time one ruling power arises, there will be another that arises in opposition to it. "There must always be a bilateral division. And that this has been brought into the situation in one fell swoop is a huge, a gigantic idea of the esoteric brotherhoods I have spoken of" (174). At that time, Steiner spoke of the British Empire and Russia as the two poles of this bilateral division. After 1945, for at least the forty-five years of the Cold War, the split existed between the Soviet Union and the United States. The groundwork for this was laid in 1917 by America entering the war and by the Russian Revolution. The storm gathering on the horizon would not only obliterate Germany as a spiritually independent power, it inaugurated the decline of Europe.

The statements that began in 1914 and that can be interpreted as pro-German came to an end in the 1916/17 lectures concerning the war and the contemporary political situation. In this context, there is something one must pay attention to. During the war, Rudolf Steiner never spoke publicly about German politics or about German politicians and military leaders. Within circles of members, he also only did so sparingly and quite late in the war. When he returned, however, to Berlin in February 1917, he spoke to a small group of trusted friends increasingly critically about German politics. Friedrich Rittelmeyer recalled how he had called attention to the fatal effects of the burned earth politics after the retreat to the so-called Siegfried position and how, in the summer of 1917, he became horrified over the lack of concrete recommendations for peace. The "peace" treaty negotiated at Brest-Litovsk caused him to despair. "Things will now sink completely into chaos!" (Rittelmeyer).

No one can deny that in the first war years, Rudolf Steiner was wholeheartedly on the side of the Central European powers. We have tried to show that this was not due to any form of simple patriotism. He knew the significance of Central Europe for the future development of human civilization. But from the beginning, as was expressed clearly in the lecture of October 29, 1914, he opposed moralizing about the historical and political developments. In this connection, he quoted Schiller's "World history is the universal judge." He continued, saying, "Let us say for the moment that the violation of Belgium's neutrality was an injustice. Who is going to be the judge? Whoever thinks as Schiller and Goethe did would answer: World history! This is the judgment that German history will have to accept" (64). He reminded his listeners of Bismarck's famous words, which were spoken in 1866 in response to requests that he take steps to punish Austria: "We are not called upon to be judges, but to push forward a German political agenda; Austria's rivalry with us is no more punishable than our rivalry with Austria is" (64).

It is quite remarkable to realize that Steiner continued with this line of thought even after Germany's defeat. On November 9, 1918, just after Germany's collapse, he spoke again of the intrusion of German troops into Belgium and called his audience's attention to the new situation.

People can judge things however they wish. In war, success means victory and the lack of success means defeat—means that a military operation does not achieve its objectives. Then it is totally understandable that from the moment—I say this completely openly, even though there is the danger that such a statement may strike some as odd—that the advance into Belgium brought no results and was completely demolished at the battle of the Marne, this advance was unjust. Some people, lacking in imagination, may look at this askance, but I have never judged it differently. (185a)

In 1918, Steiner remarked, again quite ingenuously, "In Berlin, as there is everywhere in the world, there is a party of warmongers. They have influenced things through their own instruments" (185a). He spoke as well of a "Viennese party of warmongers" (185a). He would also soon speak of the complete breakdown of German and Austrian politics, although he continued to maintain that the *German people* were not responsible for the war (338). However, Steiner drew a sharp line between the German people and the German government. He condemned German politics "unceasingly" (24). Concerning the "guilt" of the German people, his position after 1918 was that "it is the guilt of a people that does not think politically, for whom the intentions of its 'leaders' are hidden as though wrapped in an opaque veil, and that, because of its non-political nature, could have no notion that the continuation of these politics must lead to war" (24).

This does not speak highly of the political intelligence of the Germans but probably does capture the tendency of many Germans to look at world politics in terms of black or white, right or wrong, and to apply middle class values to global issues.

Although Steiner's personal appraisal of von Moltke didn't change after the war, the way he characterized the general's situation did. In May 1919, Rudolf Steiner wrote a foreword to von Moltke's memoirs and described him as a tragic figure condemned by his own destiny and his military way of thinking to lead the German troops in a war that could not be won (24). Then, in 1921, he spoke of the lessons von Moltke had learned in the spiritual world after his death and the insights he had gained. "It was not possible to achieve victory in September 1914. The spiritual capacities to use such a victory as a positive developmental step were not present in Central Europe" (Moltke II).

Two years later, he spoke again from this perspective. This time his presentation was graver, with a pictorial quality born of the spirit.

> In 1914, we had been abandoned by the gods. We allowed ourselves to be driven by spirits striving in different directions. All Europe was caught up in this pushing and pulling in all directions. It was as though a whole mob of ahrimanic beings with opposing interests had settled into the Rhine. Then there were the others on the Weichsel, who had joined forces with Eastern demons. All of this had an effect on human souls. It was not possible to have done anything other than what took place. (Moltke II)

Von Moltke describes an immense arch that leads from the hopes present in 1914 to the bitter recognition voiced in 1924. Rudolf Steiner appears to have traveled this path himself. We can follow inwardly how, in 1914, out of a sense of reverence for the German folk spirit, he did all he could to nurture and anchor the presence of this spirit in the hearts and souls of his compatriots. We can see how he strove to bring to life for his listeners the stream of light and warmth that flowed from this folk spirit, how he called attention to the destined necessity of the emergence of a culture of the human "I," and how he tried to defend this culture against the opposition of other forms of spirituality. We see then how, as the war developed, he began to discern what in fact took place as a result of the battle of the Marne. The tone of his lectures changed toward the end of 1915, and he expected his listeners to take up and act on what he presented. Then, at the turning point of the war, in the winter of 1916/17, he undertook to present his insights once again, supported with a rich array of facts and illuminated with the depth of esoteric understanding that was possible for him at that time. He hoped that these insights would be able to have an influence in the decision-making. These hopes were for naught.

Finally, in 1918, he was faced not only with the collapse of the German Reich, but also with how masses of people let themselves be deluded by the abstract, impractical world of ideas that came to expression in Wilson's Fourteen Points. He recognized that the spirit of the Germanic peoples had lost almost all possibility to develop effectively. With this recognition, he decided to work to realize the ideas of the threefold commonwealth that he had begun to develop in 1917. Following the war, he called attention to the oppositional forces at work within the Germanic people, something he had not spoken of in 1914 in order to give the folk spirit the opportunity to bring its goodness to bear. He spoke of the leaders of German politics and their spiritual deficits unambiguously. He recognized that a German victory would have been impossible, because the spiritual competence to work productively with the consequences of such a victory was missing in Germany. "World history is the universal judge."

CHAPTER 36

THE IDEA OF THE THREEFOLD HUMAN ORGANISM

In Berlin on September 10, 1917, Rudolf Steiner finished a book with the title *Riddles of the Soul*. Toward the end of the book, in the sixth addendum, is a short, fourteen-page chapter entitled "Requisite physical and spiritual relationships in the human being." As introduction, Rudolf Steiner mentions that this chapter contains "the results of thirty years of spiritual scientific research" (21). In the following pages, an attempt will be made to outline the path and extent of this research. What Steiner develops in the sixth addendum is the idea of the threefold nature of the human organism, the central idea of Anthroposophy. It is the core of Steiner's work—his most original, most personal research.

Other essential aspects of Steiner's Anthroposophy are interwoven in this pivotal concept. The entire scope of the anthroposophic approach to anthropology and psychology are inherent in it. Steiner's insights into the nature of uprightness (walking), talking, and thinking only become completely understandable within this context. His work on the significance of the first three years of life also finds its fulfillment. Through Steiner's work on the threefold nature of the human organism, his thoughts concerning anthropology based on an understanding of reincarnation and karma takes on a new concreteness. At the same time, this idea leads toward a new understanding of the human being's relationship to the heavenly hierarchies and to the Holy Trinity.

Much of what Rudolf Steiner developed over the years in connection with Anthroposophy can be found in one form or another by other thinkers. Paracelsus taught of the distinctions between the physical body, etheric body, astral body, and "I," although he used different terms, a teaching that perhaps can be traced as far back as Aristotle. Dionysios Areopagita developed the essential teachings concerning the hierarchies. The idea of the seven-stage evolution of the earth can be found in the work of Blavatsky, and, as Lessing indicated, the idea of reincarnation is as old as humanity.

Yet all of these, as well as many other aspects of Steiner's Anthroposophy, acquire their specific anthroposophic gesture and, as we will try to show, their center, through the idea of the threefold nature of the human being.

Before we begin to trace Steiner's research, we will take a quick look at the idea itself. In *Riddles of the Soul*, Steiner takes the three aspects of the human soul—thinking, feeling, and willing—as his point of departure. "The bodily counterparts of thinking (mental picturing) are to be found in the processes of the nervous system, with its extensions into the sense organs on the one hand and into the internal organization of the body on the other" (21). Thinking, however, when we consider its content, is to a great extent independent of the brain and the nervous system. The physiological processes in the brain and along the nerves simply mirror the activity of thinking or forming mental images. "Nerve activity is what is not sense-perceptible in the life of the nerves, but its presence is proven necessary by the meaning behind what is sense-perceptible" (21). This can be observed when examining the eye. With our senses we can perceive the lens, the iris, the retina and the visual nerves. What is apparent to our senses can only be understood when we grasp its meaning. We are able to grasp and interpret details through the direct experience of sight. Because we can experience light and darkness, we become able to understand the dilation of the iris; the experience of sharpness and blurriness provides the basis for understanding the changing curvature of the lens. In each case, it is our experience that allows us to come to an understanding of the naked physiological realities. From the side of the spirit, our mental imaging is permeated by the forces of imagination. Generative, pictorial cosmic thoughts are at work behind the shadowlike reality of our mental images. Both in dialogue and in one's own thinking and contemplation, one can notice how a well-chosen image stimulates and brings vitality into the process. Careful observation reveals that much of how we orientate ourselves in thinking rests on imagery.

Feeling, the totality of the wave-like movement of sensation and emotion, must, according to Steiner, be sought in "the rhythm of life that is centered in breathing and closely connected to its rhythm" (21). Feelings such as sadness, joy, tension, excitement, disappointment, and others affect this life rhythm. They intensify it or deaden it, speed it up or slow it down, deepen it or flatten it. In general, we still have only a vague understanding of the connection between the highly differentiated rhythmic organization and human feeling. Feeling, for its part, is permeated from the spiritual with what Steiner terms *inspiration*. He does not use the term in its ubiquitous sense. What Steiner speaks of here is the vitalizing force that takes hold of an individual from his first to his last breath and influences a person's emotional life in the manner described by Goethe in *Faust*. "The wonderful feelings that gave us life grow rigid in the din of daily life." We are placed in a direct, unmediated relationship with the world though the forces of inspiration in feeling; they connect us with the world, letting it live within us and us within it.

For Steiner, the will revealed itself to "be, in a similar manner, based in the metabolic processes."

> For seeing consciousness, our willing, which toward the body is based on metabolic processes, streams from the spirit through what in my writings I call "Intuition." What manifests in the body through the— in a certain way—lowest activity of the metabolism corresponds in the spirit to the highest: what expresses itself through intuitions. (21)

We take hold of our surroundings thanks to the intuitively guided will.

This threefold view does separate the human being into three disparate parts. In the living organism, these three realms of activity constantly interpenetrate one another. All action is accompanied by mental imaging and is connected with feelings—so, too, do nerve activity, rhythmic processes and metabolism accompany and affect one another reciprocally.

The following can only serve to sketch out the path Steiner took to arrive at an understanding of these threefold relationships. Perhaps, however, it can stimulate one or another reader to a deeper independent study of this theme.

In his *Autobiography*, Steiner noted that during the 1880s, in connection with the sensible/suprasensory form of which Goethe speaks, he had glimpsed "the threefold nature of the human organism in a still sketchy, imperfect form." It appeared clear to him that the soul-spiritual aspects of the human being came most clearly to expression in the human head. "On the other hand, I had to recognize the limb system as that aspect in which the sensory/suprasensory remained most hidden." This remark is quite important, as it emphasizes the actual question at hand. Steiner is looking at the relation of the spirit and the soul to the body, and how differently spirit and soul come to living expression in the three systems.

This also explains why there is no mention of this idea in Steiner's annotations to Goethe's "First Sketch of a General Introduction to Comparative Anatomy." The simple differentiation of the three parts of the animal body structure that Goethe developed there has little to do with what Steiner grappled with in developing his concept of the threefold nature of the human organism. His focus was on human nature; his approach must be modified for a study of animal nature and adapted to each species since the activity of the spirit in the animal kingdom is completely different from the activity of the spirit in a human being.

During the ten years after 1885, Rudolf Steiner had ample opportunity to observe the different aspects of the spiritual in life. He was especially drawn to the manner in which the past spirituality of a previous earthly life comes to expression in the present. In observing people like Fercher von Steinwand, Ernst Haeckel or members of the circle around Marie Eugenie delle Grazie, he recognized how the gifts that an individual had acquired in a previous life showed themselves "when a strong impression resonates further and becomes a sort of living memory, in which all the important outer aspects of a person's life disappear and what is usually thought to be 'unimportant' begins to speak clearly."

Clearly the primary problem of the years from 1885 to 1895, the problem foremost in Steiner's thoughts, was that of human freedom. This question centered on the polarity between the independence of intuitive thinking from the nerve-sense system, on the one hand, and, on the other, the will that is liberated through the moral intuition to flow forth and take hold of the body. Connected to this were studies of the stages of consciousness that showed how the soul/spiritual frees itself from the natural processes (30 & 4). The idea of pure perception as *non-patterned sequences in time and space* that Steiner develops in *Intuitive Thinking as a Spiritual Path* and in *Truth and Science* contains implicitly the decisive idea of the independence of thinking from the nerve/sense organization. In the descriptions of the nature of thinking as a universal force—of which we become aware, not "because of its outward flow from the center of the world, but at one point on the periphery" (4)—we can glimpse the independence of the human organization. This is also explicitly stated in *Goethe's Theory of Knowledge* (2).

Following Steiner's *Autobiography*, we see that in the years after 1896, he articulated a new way of viewing the world in which thinking no longer is merely used to explain the beings and life that one encounters. At this stage of consciousness, thinking now grasps the universal processes in their relationship to one another. One series of occurrences appears as a riddle, another as the answer to the riddle: "Through this the truth of the idea is experienced that *the Logos, wisdom, the word* holds sway in the world and all that is connected with it" (28). The relationships between the sweeping cosmic imaginations, which had been up to this point grasped conceptually, show themselves pictorially, and their innate wisdom begins to speak. This is essential for understanding the threefold nature of the human being, because the relationships that come to expression in the human organism can be grasped only imaginatively.

These first years in Berlin are a time of trial for Rudolf Steiner. "At that time, I had to rescue my spiritual worldview through inner storms that took place behind the scenes of my everyday experience" (28, p. 188). Following this period of inner turbulence, he was able to present the fundamentals of an understanding of the threefold in a new, more objective manner. The first piece in which these fundamental ideas are systematically presented is *Theosophy* (1904), in which the human being comes to expression as body, soul, and spirit. This is the framework for everything that follows: understanding the threefold nature of the human being hinges on grasping the way in which body, soul and spirit interact in the three systems.

The question can arise: How were these things researched? In *Intuitive Thinking as a Spiritual Path*, the method was one of inner observation based on scientific method. The difficulty with this approach lies in bringing the observations to a true inner picture rather than abstracting them into ideas upon which one speculates. For this reason Steiner speaks about *observing* thinking, not thinking about thinking, something he expressly warns of (6). Inner or soul observation is based on fully conscious inner activity—for instance, the conscious development of a thought. One then brings this process back to life through memory and observes it again. Just as one can step back from an object in space and gain a different perspective, through memory one can step back from an event and see it anew. The passing of time makes it possible to observe calmly. With the passage of time, the observation of an inner process, when the activity of soul is completely conscious, can be as "objective" as the observation of a spatially separated object. To be precise, in this situation time does not actually play a role; it is overcome by memory.

In later years, new dimensions of this manner of research become evident. In 1918, Steiner described his suprasensory research method with the following words: "I do not like to speak about personal experiences when I speak of matters concerning spiritual research; *but all these things are personal experiences taken to the point of objectivity*" (Goetheanum, 1941). If one pays attention to the way Steiner expresses himself concerning spiritual research, one often finds phrases like: one has to live through it and do it; one must immerse oneself in it and become one with it. In spiritual research, it is important that this is experienced in complete consciousness. Then they can be remembered and examined with waking consciousness. Research into matters of the spirit reveals itself as a completely conscious experiencing of the suprasensory with the full breadth of one's humanity. How this happens can become clear in what follows.

In August 1905, Rudolf Steiner drafted the chapter in *How to Know Higher Worlds* in which he speaks of the "separation of the personality during spiritual training." He begins by describing how in daily life certain experiences immediately call forth actions. "Someone enters a room, finds it to be stuffy and opens a window. One hears his name called out and turns to find who is calling. One is asked a question and provides the answer" (10). These examples illustrate how in normal life the soul forces work together in an unmediated manner, how an experience calls forth an action. In the course of spiritual training, these automatic responses are slowly overcome through control of thought, independent impulses of the will, attention to the emotions, etc. "In the spiritual development of the individual the threads that bind the three basic [soul] forces together break.... The organs of thinking, feeling and willing free themselves from one another" (10). Soul observation first becomes possible through inner development, until the differentiation of thinking, feeling and willing, which is spoken of, becomes a reality for the inner experience. The spiritual researcher must consciously mediate their connectedness through his own "I" forces, and through the inner struggles that accompany their separation learn to know thinking, feeling and willing in their essential beingness.

This is—characteristically for Steiner—not yet enough. The knowledge that is won in this manner must be critically examined. Challenging one's own experiences is one of the key elements of spiritual research. Mainstream psychology has identified other ways to differentiate the life of the soul. Rudolf Steiner in turn questions his own results. With some justification, one could regard what we call thinking as a curious collection of activities. A conscientious observation of the totality of what we know as thinking initially shows it to be an aggregate of mental images, imaginations, memories, words, sentences, associations, insights, prejudices, fantasies and so on. In light of this variety, one can lose the concept of thinking. With what justification can we speak of thinking? A spiritual researcher must pose himself such questions. For Steiner, the consequence of such questioning was to address the mental image and the activity of forming mental images, which he does in *Riddles of the Soul* and again in the beginning of *The Foundations of Human Experience* (1919).

In an extensive process of examination, he explores and works experimentally with other conceptual approaches that suggested other ways of looking at the differentiation of the forces of the soul. In an exceptional manner, he took the research of the philosopher Franz Brentano as proof for his own ideas. This was not a random choice. As a thinker, Franz Brentano had conscientiously examined the question of the differentiation of the soul forces. In his *Empirical Psychology* (1874), his exploration led to a "classification of psychic phenomena." Brentano differentiated between three different activities of the soul: mental imaging, judgment, and the phenomena of love and hate. It is fascinating to see to what extent Steiner was willing to work with Brentano's approach.

In his lectures about "Psychosophy" (1910), he took Brentano's suggestion as his point of departure, adding only, in no way in contradiction to Brentano's conclusions, the phenomenon of perception, and then went on to show how Brentano's differentiation could be made to bear fruit through an anthroposophic approach. Rudolf Steiner described how in the process of forming judgments, the "I" brings itself to expression, how perception is connected with the physical body and the senses, and how the activity of forming mental images flows forth out of the etheric and is guided by the astral through the forces of love and hate. One arrives at such a differentiation if one takes a purely inner-psychological point of view as Brentano did: the will does not show itself by normal observation in the inner soul life. Usually the will is only perceived as action. In this manner, Rudolf Steiner questioned and pondered the results of his research. He observed the life of the soul from various points of view and steered clear of any dogmatic position.

Toward the end of 1905, Rudolf Steiner began for the first time to describe systematically the three stages of higher knowledge in the magazine *Lucifer-Gnosis*. The last of these articles was written in 1908. But a fully rounded presentation of the stages of "Imagination, Inspiration and Intuition" first appears in *Outline of Esoteric Science* (1910). Of course, Steiner had used the term intuition when describing Goethe's approach to knowledge. In the introduction to the first volume of *Goethe's Scientific Writings*, he spoke of the intuitive concept (1-a), and in *Goethe's Theory of Knowledge* (1886), he speaks of "intuition" and the intuitive concept (2). The idea of intuition then found its clear, systematic expression in *Intuitive Thinking as a Spiritual Path* (1893).

It seems evident, that the idea of intuition, which can be endlessly deepened and expanded upon, was for Rudolf Steiner the actual point of departure for his own higher knowledge. On the one hand, it is through intuition that in contemplating the nature of organic life the idea of the type can be grasped; on the other hand, in the realm of human morality, the moral impulse. The stages of higher knowledge evolve out of it as though out of an embryonic cell, until they are finally to be recognized as essential aspects of the individual human being.

In their highest spiritual form, imagination, inspiration and intuition stand in relation to the higher hierarchies and to the Trinity. In the most concentrated form, this connection between the higher human being living through imagination, inspiration and intuition and the hierarchies is presented in the *Anthroposophical Leading Thoughts* of 1924 (26). Yet already in 1907, during the Munich congress, the trinitary motif of the three Rosicrucian phrases—*Ex Deo Nascimur, In Christo morimur, Per Spirituam Sanctum reviviscimus*—was present, although in a very reserved manner, visible only in the program and as initials on one of the apocalyptic seals. From 1909 onward, these three phrases would come to play a central role in anthroposophic esotericism.

By 1909 at the latest, the fundamental teachings of spiritual science, which were the framework and the conceptual prerequisites of the threefold idea, had been formulated. In 1904, the idea of the threefold nature of humans—spirit, soul and body—had been articulated in a new form. In 1905, thinking, feeling and willing were described as the three essential forces of the human soul. From 1905 through 1909, Steiner developed his teachings concerning the higher stages of knowledge (imagination, inspiration and intuition), and in 1907 Rudolf Steiner began to speak about the trinitary cosmic process, which comes to expression in the Rosicrucian path, as the core of his own esoteric work.

Listing these dates does not mean that these insights first arose at this time for Steiner. He lived for many years with his thoughts, and some of them took on new meaning for him after 1904. The dates show us when Steiner felt the thoughts were ready to be spoken, to be placed in the world.

A more pictorial presentation of what has been sketched out here could find its seed in the following thought. Usually, one thinks of a human being as he appears before us in an earthly form. From an anthroposophic point of view, what is being perceived are the physical, etheric and astral bodies of the human "I." That is, however, not the entire human. A human being does not only consist of what appears in earthly form, but has also a suprasensory aspect, which lives in the period between death and birth. We come to an image of the whole human being only if we include this suprasensory being, which evolves himself as he wanders time and again through the cosmic spheres from incarnation to incarnation.

Theosophy is based on this idea. The notion of the human being in his or her totality is outlined in the chapters "Reincarnation of the Spirit and Destiny" and "The Three Worlds." A second fundamental exploration of this theme comes in *Outline of Esoteric Science*. In a great tapestry of ideas, the human being in his or her entirety becomes visible. Given, these first sweeping imaginative discourses are in conceptual form. And especially the ways the higher members of the human being are connected with the bodily organization are not laid out in concrete detail.

But beginning in the autumn of 1912, Rudolf Steiner began to describe the path of the cosmic individuality through the spheres of the stars and planets in increasingly concrete images. These descriptions climax at Easter 1914 in the Viennese lectures "The Inner Being of the Human Being." Here Steiner takes the inner being of the earthly human, which expresses itself in thinking, feeling, and willing, as his starting point. He then goes on to show how these three soul forces blossom and are further developed in conjunction with divine spiritual beings after death. The soul forces, which have unfolded their activity during earthly life, are freed from the focal point of the body, expand into the peripheral cosmos, are reformed and guided by the cosmic realities until they pass through the "cosmic midnight," completely transformed, and turn toward a new life on earth.

Through magnificent imaginations, Rudolf Steiner describes how and what the human spirit experiences in life after death—how one's entire being is woven from the divine. The first two lectures end with the words: *Ex Deo nascimur.* The third and fourth lectures speak of how Christ leads human beings through the door of death, and how he accompanies each human through the heavenly spheres to the point of cosmic midnight, insuring that the individuality remains unified. "If we understand this process of development correctly, we must say: We die into Christ. *In Christo morimur*" (153). In the last two lectures, the focus is on the descent from the spiritual world. The role of the spirit in the path toward a new birth becomes apparent: *Per spiritum sanctum reviviscimus.*

Here, the relationships between the threefold human soul life and the realities of the spiritual cosmos become gradually evident; thinking, feeling, and willing are presented in their cosmic dimensions. Rudolf Steiner picked up on this theme a number of times—in 1915, in the lectures "The Forming of Destiny and Life after Death"; then beginning in 1922 with "Philosophy, Cosmology and Religion"; continuing on to the November 1923 lectures "The Suprasensory Human" in den Haag; and then the karma lectures and the talks for the members of the School for Spiritual Science in 1924.

When viewed from this perspective, the human being is not narrowly defined by space and time. In each human being, there are higher beings present, as are the forces of the past and of the future. This seems self-evident if one contemplates the nature of memory or the questions of special gifts, of wishes and hopes, and that of destiny. Rudolf Steiner focused, however, on much more complex temporal relationships in his research into the threefold nature of the human being. There is, for example, the statement that the human head—the focal point of the central nervous system—is a transformation of the bodily organization of the previous life, a transformation that takes place between death and rebirth. This has great significance for the nerve-sense system. It rests within the security of the skull; the capacity to form mental images rests upon the certainty of the unchanging past.

In trying to understand the biographical development of Steiner's research, the question arises as to when he came upon these insights. We do know when Steiner spoke about this transformation of the head for the first time. It was in 1911 in the lectures about "Esoteric Physiology."

> We have to recognize that the formation of the skull is a work of art. We must also discern in the formation of the skull something that is uniquely individual, an individual quality that is the expression of the history of the "I" in a previous incarnation. We see that even this formation of the bone, apparent in the skull, has been removed from the influence of the "I"—the "I" can no longer influence it in the current incarnation.... The human skull bears witness to how the individual was in his last incarnation. Whoever thinks it paradoxical that anyone would be led to something living when he perceives an object that has been formed in a certain manner does not have any justification when presented with some other formed object to try and form a picture of the living forces that formed it. (128)

What he means is that just as one knows when one sees a shell that it once housed a living creature, one can also see in the forms of the skull the forces of the individual from the last incarnation. The skull is the image of the "I" now past.

In March 1911, we find Steiner speaking of these relationships as though they were self-evident, as though he is speaking of something that he has been acquainted with for some time. Did he first discover this relationship in the period between 1880 and 1890? In January 1915, when speaking of the artistic principles of this process of transformation, he touches for the first time on precisely how this relationship occurs. He begins by describing again how the head is the transformation of what was the rest of the body in the last incarnation. The bones of the head come into being through inversion, or reversal, of the long bones of the limbs. This is the first time he articulates the principle of inversion. The long bones of the body must be turned, like a glove, inside out to become the flat bones of the skull. This cannot be thought of as a mechanical process, but rather as a complex tapestry of interrelated forces (275).

In 1911 and 1915, Rudolf Steiner spoke of this process as though in passing. In 1916, in a public lecture given on April 15 at the House of the Architects in Berlin, he began to explore this principle in depth. The ideas, now conceptually well worked through, were developed systematically in relation to Goethe's teachings on metamorphosis. It is not possible to summarize this lecture here, which runs forty-five pages in the print edition. Steiner touched on many different aspects of the threefold nature of the human being. One central thread concerns the nature of time and stages of development, both in the physical and in the realm of the soul. This allows us to differentiate between forms that are "older" or "younger." Finally, Steiner formulated "that magnificent, very significant principle."

> In the inner formative forces—note: *inner* formative forces—of our heads, we have the formative result of what was prepared within the rest of our organism, with the exception of the head, in our past life; and in what is being formed in the rest of our bodily organism now, we have the seeds of the formation of our heads in our next lives. (65)

This insight would make it possible for science in the future to differentiate between what is influenced in the growth of the human body by the stream of inheritance and what is formed by the human individuality.

In this lecture, the connection between the concept of the threefold nature of the human being and the reality of reincarnation is made explicit. Not quite one year later, on March 15, 1917, interestingly again in a public lecture, Rudolf Steiner gave the first coherent presentation of the threefold nature of the human being. The content of this lecture was what would later be published as the sixth appendix to the book *Riddles of the Soul*. He summarized his thoughts on the subject:

> The relationship between the human soul and the human body is such that the entire soul is related to the entire body, not merely the nervous system. Here I have characterized for you the beginning of a new approach in science that, supported by the ongoing discoveries of natural science, if these are viewed in the appropriate manner, will bear fruit. (66)

The path from research into the nature of the cosmic individual and the principle of reincarnation is, however, not the only path Steiner followed when researching and laying the conceptual foundations of the idea of the threefold nature of the human organism. The research path that led him into the heights had to be balanced by one that led him into the depths. From 1909 on, in addition to the cosmic aspects of human existence, he also worked toward an ever deeper understanding of the earthly side of human existence. This research is only partially conveyed through Steiner's lectures. It is possible that at that time there was not sufficient interest in these questions among the members of his audiences.

The beginning of this research period is, however, clearly marked. In conjunction with the eighth general meeting of the German section of the Theosophical Society, Rudolf Steiner gave four lectures with the title

"Anthroposophy." He began by characterizing what was meant with the term. Theosophy had raised itself to the heights of universal knowledge, but it "was in danger of not being able any more to see the earth below its feet" (115). Anthroposophy did not find its point of departure in the lofty heights, but remains "as it were, in the middle" (115). Whereas theosophy strove to let what is divine in the human being speak, Anthroposophy could be characterized in this way: "Place yourself in the middle, between God and nature; let the human within you speak about what is higher than you and lights up within you, and about what reaches up into you from below—then you have Anthroposophy, the wisdom that is spoken by the human being" (115). Following this introduction, Rudolf Steiner spoke about the different ways to study the human physical body, focusing on what he termed anthropology, which is almost exclusively concerned with the physical body and the physiological processes—the opposite of the theosophical approach. Then he once again characterized Anthroposophy.

> If one does not look out into the world but rather into the human organism and comes to an understanding of the individual organs, the physical body, etheric body, astral body, sentient soul, mind soul and consciousness soul, the way the human being is today—this is Anthroposophy. In Anthroposophy, we also have to take our point of departure from the lowest in order to find our way step by step to the highest. (115)

The consequence of this is: "In Anthroposophy, we must begin with the human senses when we begin with the physical plane. It is only through them that the human being knows anything of the physical, sense-perceptible world" (115).

This is why Rudolf Steiner began with an exploration of the senses. His presentation of his understanding of the senses is biographically extremely interesting. Initially because—keeping in mind the stand of research into this area in 1909—it begins with an enrichment of scientific anthropology. Instead of the then recognized six or seven senses, he described ten senses—in addition to the usual five senses plus the sense of balance and of warmth, he spoke in this first presentation of the sense of life or well-being, the sense of movement, and those of language and thought. Secondly, his work on the senses proves that Steiner was a true spiritual researcher, not merely a common clairvoyant or given to philosophical speculation. His path of research can be followed, the breakthroughs and errors recognized.

When he first spoke of the senses in 1909, Steiner rejected the notion of a sense of touch, which he would later include in a catalogue of the senses; a sense for the ego of another person was also missing. This indicates that he did not proceed in a speculative or combinatory manner, trying to make things work out with the beauty of the cosmic twelve. He only arrived at the full spectrum of twelve senses through a careful analysis of the totality of human experience (206). One can also substantiate through one's own work Steiner's descriptions of the inner aspects of sense perception, which arise out of an imaginative conceptual approach, and differentiate between the specific qualities of the various fields of perception. Inner observation leads to the recognition that it makes little sense to speak of perception in general terms; the experiences of seeing and hearing, or smell and warmth are quite different from one another. Each of the senses allows us to enter deeply into a specific quality of the world; through each of them we gain a different relationship to the world around us. These discoveries and the precise descriptions of new realms of sense perception are quite literally sensational. It is hard to understand that modern phenomenology, which was developed in those years by Husserl, Scheler and their students, has taken no note of them.

At this point, Steiner decided to write about what he had termed *Anthroposophy*, to pull together in a book not only his work on the senses, but also descriptions of the inner aspects of the life processes and other elements of human existence. He began to write and drafted a number of sketches. At some point in the future when Steiner's notes have been published in their entirety, it will be better possible to get a true sense of the struggles Steiner endured to come to a clear picture of the senses and thus, also, to understand what he had intended in speaking of Anthroposophy. Many difficulties arose. Of them, he said, "I was not able to continue because I wanted to write it entirely in the style in which I had begun, and my own stage of development at that time did not allow me to find the right language" (Oct. 2, 1920; 45). On another occasion, he spoke about difficulties with the content. "I had at that point presented as much of Anthroposophy as I had acquired through my spiritual research.... In writing, something new arose."

It was necessary to continue with the explorations and research. A year passed, in which Steiner pursued new research and made further attempts to articulate the results. "The time came when I said to myself:

To bring things to the kind of conclusion I must have after a year,... it is necessary to develop more precisely a certain kind of mental imaging, to develop imaginative, inspired thinking." As he proceeded, it became clear that knowledge of the nerve-sense system, which was at the core of his work with the senses, had to be expanded, so that the relationships between the senses and other organs—for instance, the kidneys—could be understood (45).

It is possible to date these efforts more exactly. The content of the book *Anthroposophy (A Fragment)* was half finished in November 1910 and had been printed. But although it was extremely important to Steiner, he could not finish it. He spoke of this in a letter from February 1911.

> Thus it has happened, for instance, that the first half of my *Anthroposophy (A Fragment)* has been printed since last November, yet I have not been able to continue it, because it was impossible to bring the truths that have presented themselves to me spiritually to paper. Yet I know from the spiritual world that this work should be published as soon as possible. (262)

No doubt hoping to make further steps along this path, in March 1911 Steiner held a series of public lectures, "Occult Physiology," attended by a number of doctors. In these lectures, he was able for the first time to explore in depth the inner organs of the human being. He received the transcripts of these lectures in May in Portorose and intended to revise them for publication. He noted in the margin, "The Prague lectures that I gave between March 18 and 28 need to be published immediately. There are real dangers looming if this does not happen" (262).

Although he only gave a few lectures in the spring of 1911 and spent nine weeks without visitors in Portorose and Veldes, helping nurse Marie von Sivers back to health, neither of the two projects—*Anthroposophy (A Fragment)* or *An Occult Physiology*—moved closer to publication.

It was not a lack of undisturbed time, as was so often the case, that hindered him. The difficulties were of a conceptual nature and were not so easily solved. It is thus not surprising that in his next series of lectures, given in Kristiania (Oslo) in 1912, Steiner once again addressed questions of human physiology and experience, but this time from another perspective. In these lectures, he spoke of the various research methods, highlighting the dangers and the obstacles, then went on to say that the path of an "esoteric aspirant" to an understanding of the human "I" did not lead through introspection or mystical deepening, but rather through an understanding of the *human form*. "To help us get over this difficult point, just take the term 'human form' the way it is meant—what comes to meet us in the world.... For much of our experience the human form, the human *Gestalt*, proves to be the expression of the individual human being" (137).

Taking this perspective, Steiner calls attention to twelve aspects of the human form, which show its relationship to the forces of the zodiac. His depiction differs from descriptions known since the Renaissance of the relationship between various parts of the human body and the zodiac. In the present context, however, Steiner's depiction is only the preface to further explorations. In the following lecture, he said, "What appeared yesterday to be a relationship between twelve parts in fact groups itself into three humans, and we have to understand that the human being is, in fact, comprised of three humans" (137).

The comprehensive presentation that followed gave a highly complex description of these three humans, each of which is in turn comprised of seven members. The knowledge of the three seven-membered humans, according to Steiner, was known in esotericism as the *mysterium magnum*. The relationship to Steiner's later developed idea of the threefold nature of the human being is evident toward the end of the lecture when he speaks of the threefold relationship between thinking, feeling, and willing.

> In normal life, these three things—thinking, feeling, and willing—are bound together in the "I"-consciousness. But although they play into each other in daily consciousness, they drift apart as soon as we take a first step into the realm of higher consciousness.... This is the other side of the *mysterium magnum*. When individuals take the real step and cross the boundaries of their own consciousness, they separate the unity of their "I"-consciousness into three. Likewise, the seeming unity of the human form, if we observe it more closely, separates into three seven-membered humans. Both our "I"-consciousness and our outer form are a unity that separates out into three humans.... These are two sides of a multifaceted *mysterium magnum*" (137).

Examples like these show how Rudolf Steiner worked toward an understanding of the threefold nature of the human being. He followed a variety of cognitive paths in doing so. He examined the human senses that led him to explorations of the bodily organism and to esoteric research of the inner organs. He placed the human form in the center of his esoteric research and was led to insight of the threefold nature of the human body and to its connection with thinking, feeling and willing. At the same time he followed other paths of research—the unified nature of the nervous system, the polarity between blood and nerve, and others. He followed the physiological research of his contemporaries quite closely, and during the war he drew on their work to deepen and clarify his insights into the threefold signature of the human being.

There is a third series of connections to take into consideration in relation to the development of Steiner's research in this field. Before reciting the Foundation Stone meditation at the new founding of the General Anthroposophical Society in 1923, Steiner gave an introduction, at the beginning of which he said, "It was possible to perceive the threefold nature of the human being, through which the individual can in a new way bring to new life in his entire being—in spirit, soul and body—in the words "Know Thyself." It was possible to perceive this for decades. It ripened for me only in the last ten years amidst the storms of the war" (260).

There is a riddle in these words. We can to begin to fathom it by asking: Why was it only possible in the preceding decades to perceive these threefold relationships? Why was it not possible to recognize them centuries ago? Aren't these relationships based on physiological realities that, since they have been present, should have allowed the recognition of the threefold?

There are three possible answers to this last question. First, one can imagine that the threefold relationships couldn't be perceived because they had been veiled in some mysterious manner. In Steiner's work, there does not seem to be any mention of such a veiling. Such a thing is also difficult to imagine. Second, one may think that it was only the spiritual evolution of the questions asked in the research that made it possible to discern the threefold. Even then, these relationships would have had to have been perceptible. Third, it is possible that the threefold relationship ripened fully only in the nineteenth century. There are indications in Steiner's work that point in this final direction.

In connection with the threefold social order and historical developments, Rudolf Steiner spoke of humanity's crossing the threshold to the spiritual world—without noticing it directly. He illuminated this statement by calling attention to the individual's crossing of the threshold on the path to higher knowledge.

You can read how the individual begins to trifurcate as he enters into the spiritual world. You can read this in *How to Know Higher Worlds*. The interpenetration of thinking, feeling and willing, which is the natural state within the world of the senses—you could read the chapter from the *Guardian of the Threshold*—thinking, feeling and willing separate when one enters the suprasensory world. Generally, humanity goes through this today secretly, under the threshold of consciousness. There a threshold is crossed. People go through this triarchal separation inwardly *in a manner that is different from how things once were*. The observation of the passing of humanity through a certain threshold shows one that threefolding the social organism is dictated to us from out of the spiritual depths of existence. (19, comp. also 192)

Over the course of the nineteenth century, the spiritual make-up of humanity shifted or—perhaps better said—it went through a transformation. There were other very sensitive individuals, contemporaries of Steiner, who also at least felt the incredible change that took hold of humanity. Max Scheler, a philosopher who Steiner held in high esteem, had the impression that a new age was approaching and thought that the change that was becoming ever more noticeable was "not only a transformation of things, conditions, the institutions, the basic concepts and forms of art and almost all the sciences—it is a *transformation of the human being himself*, his inner configuration of body, drive, soul and spirit" (Scheler).

In his unique, concrete manner, Rudolf Steiner had spoken in 1913 about this transformation, pointing out that the human being had undergone a physiological change in the previous centuries. In ways that were not recognizable for mainstream physiology, fine structures formed in the cerebral cortex and later throughout the human organism through which new forms of memory became possible (152; comp. also 152; 190).

What is described here concerning the bodily development of the human being in the period from roughly 1400 to 1900 holds true in an even more significant manner for the evolution of humanity as a whole. This process of evolution, which takes place over long periods of time, is not merely natural in the narrow scientific sense. There are spiritual impulses that are at work here. Beginning in 1911, Rudolf Steiner spoke of the effects of the Christ impulse in the individual and in humanity as a whole in such a manner that the way this impulse works to form the human organism casts light on the connections we have been following. In the book *The Spiritual*

Guidance of the Individual and Humanity, he described how in the first three years of life three things are learned that have a formative effect on the bodily organization of the growing child. First, the child learns to stand upright and walk; the soul, which gains through this step an orientation in space, takes hold of the bodily organization and transforms it. Second, the child learns to speak, to articulate inner experiences, to name the things around him or her, and in doing so, takes hold of the formation of the larynx and breathing. Finally, the child develops a life of thinking and questioning and so takes hold of the formation of the brain.

It is easy to see that walking, speaking and thinking have a relationship to the will, to feeling and to thinking. Learning to stand upright and walk is the most elementary and powerful expression of the will; born on the rhythmic waves of the breath, a child's speaking reveals a strong emotional quality; and the child's questioning is the beginning of what later becomes thinking. To a certain extent, we can say that in the first three years of life, a child crafts the foundations of his or her willing, feeling and thinking.

The most significant statement in this context is Steiner's indication that these colossal, eminently wise developmental steps reveal the activity of Christ. "To recognize the forces at work in childhood development is to recognize Christ in the human being.... A truly clairvoyant self-knowledge leads the modern human being to the insight that forces that emanate from Christ are to be found in the human soul. In the first three years, these forces are active without the human being having to do anything" (15).

These statements call on us not merely to view the formation of the human organization nor the development of the threefold structure of the human organism in a naturalistic manner. The threefold structure appears to have a divine origin.

That this idea has certain validity is apparent in the content of the lectures that Rudolf Steiner gave concerning the deeds of Christ before and after the Mystery of Golgotha. They were published in *Christ and the Spiritual World: And the Search for the Holy Grail* (149) and *Approaching the Mystery of Golgotha* (152). The lecture held in Pforzheim on May 7, 1914, is especially notable. Only during this lecture did Rudolf Steiner speak the four mantric metamorphoses from the beginning of the Gospel of St. John. It is also only here that he describes the deeds of Christ before the Mystery of Golgotha, how Christ had in earlier times three times infused the archetype of the human being that accompanied humanity through its evolution, each time making possible new formative aspects (152). The first gift with which Christ imbued the human archetype was the impulse to uprightness. The second transformed the life organism of the human being is such a way that speaking and language were transformed. The human being could then not only express his or her own pain and joy, but became able to "grasp the objective." The third infusion led to a further transformation of human speech—language became a medium of understanding between humans.

Rudolf Steiner continued his presentation by calling attention to how Christ, through the Mystery of Golgotha, was able to both save and transform human thinking. Human thought became able to receive divine life, and the life of this divine thought can become the light of the human "I" (152). This was not the end of Christ's deeds for humanity. In present times, the ongoing working of Christ is preparing a further transformation of the human soul. After "the Christ impulse [flowed into] the attainment of uprightness, language and thinking," in the future "the Christ impulse will slowly permeate the forces of memory" (152). Steiner described the future effect of the Christ impulse on memory.

> He is not yet in them. When the time comes and he is within them, when the impulse of the Christ does not only live in human understanding, but when it flows forth over the entirety of human memory, then one will no longer have to learn history through external documents, because the forces of memory will expand. Christ will live within these memories. (152)

If we summarize the path taken here, we can perhaps answer the question as to why Rudolf Steiner mentioned in 1923 that the threefold nature of the human being could only be recognized in the preceding decades. Only when humanity crossed the threshold in the middle of the nineteenth century did the trifurcation of soul life become deep soul reality. Toward the end of the 1870s, the inner organ that served spiritual memory had developed to the point that it could be accessed by an evolved humanity. These two events made knowledge of the threefold possible.

If one follows the chain of thought that Steiner presents in *Outline of Esoteric Science*, it is through the forces of memory, which transcend time, that we see the genuine activity of the human "I" (13). Thanks to memory, a person is able to pull together the soul experiences of thinking, feeling and willing, forming a center with which he or she is able to proceed through the flow of time with inner continuity. The threefold nature of the soul's life finds its center in the force of memory.

The force of memory—its continuity, universality and objectivity—is, however, also jeopardized. It is for this reason that the present is the time when the Christ impulse begins to permeate the forces of memory. Rudolf Steiner believed that this took place in relation to the reappearance of Christ in the etheric.

> The Christ event now approaching us—not in the physical world but in the etheric, and connected with the first kindling of the power of memory with the first kindling of the Christ-permeated memory—will be such that Christ will approach humankind as an angel-like being. We must prepare ourselves for this event. (152)

Based on what has been examined here, we might say that the threefold reality of human nature is the expression of Christ's activity, and that it can only be perceived through the light of the etheric Christ permeating the forces of memory. This idea casts light also on the meditation given by Steiner in 1923 at the Christmas conference as the foundation stone of an anthroposophic society. In the first three stanzas of this verse, the attentive listener is led to experience the threefold nature of the human being. The Foundation Stone contains, however, a fourth stanza, which speaks to the divine light, the Christ-Sun. The light of Christ permeates and embraces the experience of the threefold reality.

Rudolf Steiner remains silent concerning the path that led to these experiences. With this in mind, we will steer clear of idle speculation. Immersing oneself in what has merely been sketched out here concerning Steiner's research does give one a sense of the immense reach of the path he must have trod.

CHAPTER 37

THE THREEFOLD SOCIAL MOVEMENT DURING THE WAR

When Rudolf Steiner traveled on February 2, 1917, from Dornach to Berlin, he became a witness to a dramatic change in the fortunes of the war that took place over the ensuing months. After the collapse of the peace negotiations in December and January 1916/17, Germany had begun unrestricted U-boat attacks. The hope was that this new strategy would cut Britain and France off from much-needed supplies coming in by sea. In an immediate response, the United States terminated negotiations with the German ambassador in Washington and broke off diplomatic relations. Two months later, the United States declared war on Germany. Worker unrest in Petrograd climaxed on March 8 in outright revolution. On March 12, a provisory government took power, and on March 15, Czar Niklaus II abdicated. In April, Lenin traveled through Germany, Sweden and Finland to reach Petrograd and then, in November, to lead the Bolshevist revolution. Rudolf Steiner recognized signs of a historical watershed in the United States' entry into the war and the overthrow of the government in Russia. But for the moment he could only observe the course of events in silence.

By the beginning of the summer of 1917, it became apparent that the ruthless U-boat attacks had not achieved their goal. Under the leadership of General Petain, France had mastered the military challenges it had faced in the spring and the let-up on the eastern front that was expected after the Russian Revolution did not occur. In fact, on June 30, the Russian army began the so-called Brusilov Offensive. Confusion and contradiction spread throughout the most important German political circles. Initially, the focus seemed to be on Chancellor Bethmann-Hollweg. The military command, the nationalists and the conservatives wanted to replace him with a more malleable figure, and the political left supported him halfheartedly only because they had no other candidate for the post. A governmental crisis appeared imminent. The volatility of the situation increased sharply on July 6 when one of the delegates, Matthias Erxberger, who had been a supporter of the expansionist war policies, spoke to an audience of several hundred in the Reichstag. He gave a stark picture of Germany's situation at the time, pointing out that the U-boat offensive had not achieved its goals, the Allies were well supplied while Germany was not, and the presentations made by the military command were erroneous, so there was no choice but to come quickly to a peace agreement and give up any thoughts of annexation. The frank nature of his talk sent shockwaves through the nation. Intense but contradictory political actions took place throughout the country with the effect that, on July 14, Bethmann resigned and was relieved of his post and on July 19, the German parliament passed a peace resolution.

Rudolf Steiner was in Berlin at this time and able to follow the symptoms of inner decay and collapse closely as they progressed from day to day. Friends like Alfred Meebold and Emil Leinhas, as well as other sources, provided him insight into what was going on behind the scenes. He was able to experience how the enthusiasm of 1914, which had had no spiritual roots, ebbed and then appeared again as its own counterpart. He saw in spirit the lack of any higher perspectives or true ideas in German politics as a threatening vacuum and he saw how each side pushed what they thought to be "real politics" in cynical, shabby fashion.

Among the anthroposophists often in Berlin at the time was Count Otto Lerchenfeld (1868–1938). He had been a member of the Anthroposophical Society since 1907, was active in both the Munich productions of the mystery plays and in the building project, and had excellent political connections. He was a minister of the Bavarian court; and the Bavarian ambassador and delegate to the German parliament, Count Hugo Lerchenfeld, was his uncle. The Bavarian consulate was frequented by a number of the leading political figures of the time. Count Otto Lerchenfeld was able to keep abreast of the negotiations and debates either through direct conversations or through the reports of his uncle. He was thus able to see more deeply into the events, doubly so because his uncle had an extremely clear view and spoke quite openly with him. His journals captured his impressions from those days.

> It is not possible to just stand and watch! There is a muddle of rulers—the cabinet, the chancellor's administration, the ministry, the

military! Order—counter order! Our consulate is like a dovecote—ministers, statesmen, the few diplomats that still remain—half of the parliamentary delegates come in and out the door. Uncle Hugo is only to be seen at breakfast, if then. He looks as though he's been beaten over the head, completely overworked. Most of the others who come and go look the same, but they all try to pretend as though everything is in order. (Boos)

With these impressions and on the edge of despair, Lerchenfeld visited Steiner in the Motzstrasse, describing the situation as he saw it and sharing his personal concerns. Rudolf Steiner listened to what he had to relate, then asked him to return the following afternoon for a longer conversation. During this afternoon session—it must have been around June 20—Steiner developed the idea of the threefold social order and spoke about some of the specifics that could be conceived based on this idea. The possibilities that Steiner opened through his presentation changed Lerchenfeld's mood completely. "Was for three hours with Dr. Steiner in the Motzstrasse. I can see the solution for everything. *Know* that no other solution is possible." He returned lighthearted and, with a spring in his step, crossed through Tiergarten, in central Berlin, to the Bavarian consulate.

Steiner had for years observed with great concern how inept, even awkward, German politics were and how both the actual events and the moral-spiritual aspects of political life were judged erroneously. There was a tendency to retreat behind legalities and fabricated rights. The Entente on the other hand had fought a skillful propaganda war using events like Germany's invasion of Belgium or the sinking of the *Lusitania*, while at the same time emphasizing that it was not for one's own country that one fought, but for humanity, democracy, freedom, and the rights of the minorities. When the United States entered the war, the battle to sway international opinion entered a new phase. Woodrow Wilson, then president of the United States, took the stage as a moral judge and turned what had been a war between European powers into a war of ideologies. He brought his country into the war to protect the forces of democracy throughout the world. He stood up for the liberation of the peoples and spoke of a war with neither winners nor losers. In the course of the war, after Lenin and Trotsky proclaimed the goals of the Soviet Union, Wilson's first utterances metamorphosed into a program with fourteen points. This fourteen-point program gained a great deal of popularity, as did Wilson.

The middle-European powers had nothing to compete with it except their own belief in the power of their weapons.

Thus, the first point in Steiner's conversation with Lerchenfeld had to do with the necessity of Germany finding some way to counter this propaganda. He had no qualms about calling what he was about to describe a "middle-European program" (24). Up until this point, Germany and the other warring countries had spoken about the objectives of the war. In Germany, these debates had centered on the question of annexation. With one remark, Steiner swept these notions from the table and pointed out how treacherous the lack of truly positive statements is in international politics. In the first memorandum that Steiner drafted following the conversations, it was written: "We middle-Europeans seem at the moment to shy away from declaring our will to the West, while the West is literally smothering us with declarations of its will. By doing so, the West creates the impression that its concern is for the health of humanity and that we are threatening these strivings through such things as militarism" (24).

The Central-European program that Steiner suggested was to be a "program of human liberation" (24); his focus was on individual freedom, since it was only individuals, not peoples or nations, who could be free. For this reason, he wanted to place "all matters of jurisprudence, education and spiritual life" in the realm of "individual freedom." "The State relinquishes the responsibility for courts, schools, churches and so on to the various professional and ethnic associations. This is naturally not a case by case decision, but limited to a specific period of time" (24).

This suggestion was focused on a very real, concrete situation, namely on the colorful mix of ethnic groups in eastern Europe and the Balkan countries, where many different peoples lived not only alongside of one another but also with one another. Take for instance the city of Lemberg, which had a population of Poles, Ukrainians, Russians, Jews, Germans and even Armenians. Any normative approach would by necessity lead to repression of the minorities in such circumstances. Up to World War I, there had been attempts by the ruling parties to force their own language on other ethnic groups. The Prussian government had tried to force the Polish-speaking population to use German in their schools and as the official language; the Hungarians had pushed a radical program of spreading the Magyar language; and there were similar attempts by other groups in the Balkans, in Poland, and in Russia.

If one places the responsibility for legal matters, language, education and culture in the realm of individual freedom, one cannot "be afraid of the *complete freedom* that comes to expression in federal autonomy for ethnic groups."

> We find such federalism modeled in the relationships between the German states. It is to a certain extent the modeled that has been crafted by history for what must be developed in Central Europe: a fully emancipated federalist form for all the aspects of life that are rooted in the individual.... A healthy form for these relationships will only be found when national feeling arises out of freedom, not freedom out of nationalism. If one strives for the former, he places himself in the stream of global historical evolution. If one chooses the latter, he works against this evolutionary stream, causing new conflicts and wars. (24)

The question of minorities that became a problem throughout middle-Europe after 1919 and recently resurfaced in the break-up of Yugoslavia shows the validity of this remark. Although Yugoslavia appeared to have a federalist government, it was not rooted in individual freedom and cultural autonomy. The southern Slav federation recognized only the freedom and rights of the various ethnic groups, each of which tried to use the national government and the various ministries as tools through which to gain power and privileges. The lack of cultural autonomy came to expression with a vengeance in the "ethnic cleansings" that accompanied the war between the peoples of what had been Yugoslavia. As Steiner formulated his thoughts during the summer of 1917, he placed individual freedom and the limitation of governmental power against the anticipated consequences of an approach based on ethnic self-determination that would of necessity lead to the repression of minorities.

Thus the idea of the threefold social order came into play as a counterproposal to the plans proposed by Wilson and the West. Besides the autonomy of the legal, educational and cultural spheres, the threefold approach also put limits on what was to be decided democratically. "A purely democratic parliament would only address matters that are truly political or that have to do with the military or the police" (24). A democracy that was limited in this manner would develop "of necessity in a conservative manner"; the evolution of the Social Democrats was the best proof of this.

Economic decisions would also have to be uncoupled from politics and placed in the hands of a special economic parliament, and a "form of senate would be elected out of the three bodies, whose responsibility it would be to guide political-military, economic, and legal, pedagogical, and cultural matters and oversee all the things they have in common, including finances" (24).

In this memorandum and in the conversations with Count Lerchenfeld, the topics of the then current political debates also appear. A number of politicians were pushing for a revision of the German constitution approved under Bismarck. Their goal was to have the chancellor elected by the parliament, not appointed by the emperor alone. The appointment by the emperor would merely be the formal recognition of the parliament's choice. The discussion centered on the shift of power away from the emperor and into the hands of the parliament. Steiner was skeptical of this tendency. He thought it could work in England but that "German and Austrian undertakings would not become more intelligent simply because they were decided by a gathering of some 500 delegates instead of a couple of statesmen. One cannot imagine anything more discouraging than the superstitious belief that the adoption of their democratic model, in addition to everything else we have acquired from England, will have a magical effect" (24).

With such statements Steiner sought to catch the attention of the probably quite conservative recipients of the memorandum. He did, however, voice his own beliefs (compare 185). Steiner, who never cast his vote in an election and who fervently supported human rights and the well-being of the workers, was not a believer in democracy in the modern sense of the word. Being able to vote had no meaning for him; he was concerned with individual freedom. He looked upon any form of ruling power skeptically.

Just as important as the positive impulse that came to expression in the threefold commonwealth was, in Steiner's eyes, the need to rebuff the accusations made by the Triple Entente that Germany had invaded the surrounding countries and thus bore full responsibility for the outbreak of the war. This very difficult question, which is still debated today, occupied Steiner's thoughts time and again. In October 1921, he spoke about it with the French journalist Jules Sauerwein. The interview, published in *Matin*, caused some uproar, as it pointed out the lack of guidance and planning in the German leadership.

If we ignore for the moment whether Steiner was correct in his assessment of why the war began, we can recognize in the tenacity with which he pursued the topic his sense for politically important questions. In fact, the idea that the Germans alone were to blame for the war, as it was laid out in the Treaty of Versailles—which was used to justify reparations for the costs of the war—became a key piece of German nationalist propaganda after 1919. To challenge this unilateral assignment of guilt, Steiner demanded at the very beginning of his memorandum "an unvarnished" report of the events leading up to the outbreak of the war.

What he meant by an unvarnished report, Steiner explained later, was that there should be a simple report of what took place, step by step, hour to hour. Such a report would shed light on the chaos and lack of direction in Berlin at the time, but would also show just how surprised everyone was by the sequence of events. This was by no means a harmless proposal. One of the people with whom Steiner discussed these ideas in 1917 knew immediately that a report like this would lead of necessity to the abdication of the Kaiser (186 & 185a). Rudolf Steiner hoped more than anything that a straightforward documentation of the events would show that the initiative to begin a war had not originated in Germany, but that the leading German politicians had been the victims of a widespread misjudgment of the actual situation. At the same time, he warned against including any doctrinaire viewpoints or dubious contentions, such as the claim that the English King Edward VII had attempted to surround Germany. He rejected this and wrote, "The truth is that England has for many years understood how to pursue a political path that reflects the actual European situation and seems favorable to England, a political path that exploited the dynamics of the nations and peoples in a rather scientific manner. Only in England did politics have a completely objective, unified character" (24).

With remarks like these, Steiner cast light on the different political styles and attempted to call attention to various important threads in international politics that had gone unnoticed.

By the beginning of July 1917, Steiner's consultations with Count Lerchenfeld had progressed to the point that Lerchenfeld was ready to try to contact a number of people in positions of power. According to Count Polzer-Hoditz, Lerchenfeld used his connections to contact Prince Lichnowsky, the last German ambassador to England, Albert Ballin, director of the Hamburg-America shipping line, Maximilian Harden, the editor of the

Future, as well as others. All of them excused themselves from a meeting. Then Steiner sent Polzer-Hoditz a telegram asking him to come from Austria to Berlin. But by the time he arrived on July 13, the governmental crisis was approaching its climax, and Steiner could only inform him of the refusals.

Over the course of the next few days, Steiner shared his thoughts on the threefold commonwealth with Count Polzer-Hoditz and worked through the content of the memorandum with him. This was not to remain mere words, said Steiner, but should as soon as possible be published as the basis of a middle-European peace program by someone with an international reputation. On July 18, they traveled together to Munich, where Lerchenfeld had arranged an interview with the last German ambassador to Washington, Count Bernstoff. Steiner's ideas did not appear to impress Bernstoff. On July 20, they returned to Berlin, where Steiner began work on a second memorandum for Holzer's brother, a leading member of the Austrian emperor's cabinet.

This second memorandum, written some two weeks after the first one and tailored for a specific individual, has a very different tone. At the very beginning, a "Mr. W. Wilson" is cited, whose words, "if they had been written by a literary friend of humanity" one could easily "acknowledge as self-evident" (24). But:

> Wilson's words are not those of a literary friend of humanity. They are the banners for the actions for which the Americans have armed themselves and that the Entente has pursued in middle-Europe for the last three years. The fact is that middle-Europe must fight against what lies behind these banners that proclaim succor for humanity and the liberation of the ethnic groups. The Entente and Wilson *say* for what they appear to be fighting. Their words have the *force of propaganda*. This force becomes ever more dubious....
>
> For the real goals of this program—not counting the moral glitter—lie in the exploitation of the instincts of the middle- and eastern European peoples, to make these peoples through moral and political pressure economically dependent on Anglo-Americanism. Spiritual dependence will follow as a certain consequence. (24)

In this tone, with none of the restraint present in the first memorandum, Steiner went on to speak of the impending threat of the hegemony of the Anglo-American peoples and their domination of middle-Europe, and finally to emphatically outline which ideas and proclamations would be necessary and decisive for middle-Europe.

The second memorandum was given to Count Polzer-Hoditz on July 22, and Steiner hoped that Count Arthur Polzer-Hoditz, advisor to the kaiser of Austria, and who people thought would be named the next foreign minister, would make use of the program that he had outlined. Count Ludwig Polzer-Hoditz related taking leave of Steiner:

> When he realized that I was nervous and restless due to the weight of my responsibility, he said in the most gracious manner, "Just be calm. One must also be able to watch how a people is crushed. If what I have shown you to be a possibility of salvation does not come to pass, a series of catastrophes will follow. What does not come about through reason will have to happen after the great changes that will occur; cosmic will demands it." (Polzer-Hoditz)

Polzer-Hoditz spoke with his brother on July 24 about the second memorandum and on July 26 was able to present to the prime minister of Austria, Ernst Seidler, the first memorandum. Both attempts led nowhere, although in his memoirs Arthur Polzer-Hoditz spoke of how he had studied the memorandum in depth and had recognized that Steiner's suggestions were not only reasonable, but also practical.

In Berlin, Rudolf Steiner was also active. Quietly, without anyone noticing, he found occasion to speak with a number of individuals who had the influence to affect the course of events. He related this without naming any names. "I gave what I had written to a man—not only one, a number of men, but I will only mention one as a case in point—who then wrote to me months later. That was a good sign, for he had studied the things in depth, had truly made an effort and had also spoken with me about them." (185a).

The man, who was a privy councilor, raised the strangest arguments against the threefold approach; he said that it would make economic wars and social-democratic politics impossible.

Perhaps the most important, although not the most promising, conversation was the one that Steiner had with Richard von Kühlman (1873–1948), who was at that time the German foreign minister. Their meeting must have taken place sometime between August 1 and September 25, 1917. Steiner mentioned this conversation briefly a number of times. In Stuttgart on April 21, 1919, in presenting the activities of the movement for a threefold social order that had begun in Württemberg, he said:

> I told Kühlman, "You have the choice to be reasonable and listen to what needs to happen in the evolution of humanity...or you will be heading into times of revolution and cataclysm." Instead of reason, we received the treaty from Brest-Litovsk. Just imagine what would have happened..., if in response to the Fourteen Points, the voice of the spirit had spoken amidst the thunder of the cannons. All of Eastern Europe would have understood. (192)

Later, Steiner complemented this remark, adding that his suggestions had at that time been understood, but his listeners "had not been able to bridge the chasm between intellectual understanding and true action" (330).

Rudolf Steiner returned to Dornach toward the end of September. He had invested an immense amount of time and energy trying to set the necessary wheels in motion and entering into dialogues in the most unlikely settings. He was not personally distressed but had reached a point of deep objective disappointment that his attempt to raise a spiritual wall to block the West and open a path to the East had found no practical echo. He took leave of the Berlin members on September 25, saying, "I was only able to hint today at many things and had to leave much unsaid that, however, will reveal itself in your souls when you reflect on what was said here today. In any case, you will have noticed one thing: that I wanted to speak seriously, with bitter earnestness and it is in this manner that I would like to conclude these lectures for the moment" (176).

Steiner's efforts could not be continued from Dornach due to both the censors and the need to respect Swiss neutrality. Rudolf Steiner didn't return to Berlin until January 20, 1918. Probably soon after he arrived, he met with First Lieutenant Hans von Haeften, who was still the head of the "Military Department of the Foreign Ministry" and a close associate of Ludendorff. Von Haeften, however, also maintained close contact with a group of south German liberals who at the time were quietly supporting Prince Max von Baden's candidacy for the chancellorship. The speaker for this group was a colleague of von Haeften's named Kurt Hahn, who later founded the Salem School. Obedience bound von Haeften to Ludendorff; reason drew him toward the south German liberals.

Steiner spoke at length with von Haeften, who was interested to hear what Steiner could tell him about the situation in Switzerland and what could be learned from there. In the course of their conversation, they also discussed the planned springtime advance of the German army.

> The conversation reached a place where I said something like: I don't want to put myself in the position that someone could accuse me of wanting to get involved in questions of military strategy but rather prefer to speak from a perspective that would not give anyone cause to imagine that this possible military dilettantism was at issue. I said that Ludendorff could possibly achieve everything he could ever dream of with a springtime offensive; but even then I thought it to be a ridiculous idea. I mentioned three reasons for this. (174b)

The three reasons, which Steiner did not mention, were certainly of a general, political nature. In any case, his arguments were brought forth in a context that was becoming increasingly critical. A number of Germans—Alfred Weber, Robert Bosch, Friedrich Naumann, and the union leaders Karl Legien and Adam Stegerwald—planned to intervene against a springtime offensive and were demanding in addition an official German statement to the effect that the sovereignty and integrity of Belgium would be restored immediately after the end of the war. Prince Max von Baden also supported this action. Von Haeften, who had already become acquainted with the ideas of the threefold social order and understood its implications, recognized Steiner as an important ally in this initiative and introduced him to Prince Max. In 1921, when speaking in Oslo, Steiner recounted his meeting with Max von Baden, who he visited in Karlsruhe in January 1918.

> During our conversation, this personality remarked upon how important it would actually be to have a psychology of the European peoples. The chaos into which we sailed would demand that those who wished to step forward and provide some degree of leadership had some insight into the forces at work in the different European folk souls. And he regretted that it was not possible to work out of an understanding of the various folk souls when dealing with public affairs. I replied that I had developed such a psychology of the folk souls in a series of lectures here in Oslo and later sent him a copy of these lectures with a foreword that reflected the then current situation. It did not, however, help. (209)

Of course, Steiner also spoke with Max von Baden about the springtime offensive and, most importantly, about the threefold social order. He even stated his willingness to rework his ideas in light of the changing situation, even though it was "already quite late" (185a). And Prince Max understood what Steiner was speaking about. In his memoirs, in which he does not mention the meeting with Steiner, one finds the following: "It was not correct to leave the war of ideas only in the hands of Wilson and Trotsky; we had to place an independent, well conceived program for the new organization of Central Europe that took into account the realities of this region up against the clichés coming from the west and from the east" (Max von Baden).

In this connection, he also speaks of the task to work to liberate and help reorganize Eastern Europe. He accused the German journalists and diplomats of being crippled by fear, of lacking any practical political intelligence and of being seen as mere idealists. But even Max von Baden could only rise momentarily to the occasion. For the most part, he dealt with secondary problems and became so caught up in these battles that he was unable to find a path from understanding to action. When he later became chancellor for a few weeks, it was too late.

Rudolf Steiner had no inclination to play a political role. He held himself completely in the background knowing that, as a spiritual researcher, he had other tasks. But the lack of understanding that came to expression in the actions of Germany's leaders struck him as dangerous and a source of objective distress; it revealed the spiritual condition of the German upper class, which wanted nothing better than to hold on to the past and, right up until October 1918, could not imagine anything other than slight modifications to the traditional order. "One fundamental aspect of our fast-paced time is that people think so terribly slowly" (181).

Steiner never seemed to mind holding conversation after conversation trying to find supporters for the threefold social order, although he probably knew that these conversations would not lead anywhere. He never asked himself if he was going to be successful; he felt it to be his duty to speak about what he had come to understand, to work for this insight. The possibility did exist that it would open a door for social change. Friedrich Rittelmeyer relates, "I often saw Rudolf Steiner returning exhausted from these conversations with Germany's leaders. One of them said to him, 'You may be right. But I'm not the man to do it.' 'You have to be the one to do it' was Steiner's reply, 'for you are in the right position'" (Rittelmeyer).

"Rudolf Steiner had absolutely no personal wishes. He would have been entirely happy to remain in the background and selflessly help those in positions of responsibility" (Rittelmeyer).

The "fatal" treaty of Brest-Litovsk, signed in March, destroyed any remaining possibility of coming to a reasonable peace agreement. Rudolf Steiner turned his attention to other tasks.

CHAPTER 38

PREPARATIONS FOR THE POSTWAR PERIOD

In March 1918, Rudolf Steiner, who had published at least one new book a year since 1910, began to rework a number of his earlier publications. He began in March and April with *Intuitive Thinking as a Spiritual Path: A Philosophy of Freedom* and *Goethe's Worldview*. In May and June, he wrote "Goethe's Standard of the Soul," in which two of his previous pieces appeared in a new form. In July, *Theosophy* was revised and one chapter was markedly expanded. Finally, toward the end of July, Rudolf Steiner began to rework *An Outline of Esoteric Science*, a task that was not finished, however, until May 1920. Moreover, four other works that had been out of print were revised, receiving new forewords or afterwords. The 1912 lectures on the Gospel of St. Mark were published for the first time, with a foreword that emphasized the particular circumstances of 1912. The lectures on the Gospel of St. Matthew were also sent to the printer at this time. This insured that, shortly after the war had come to an end, most of Steiner's written work would be in print and, in addition, that whatever capital the publishing house still retained was sensibly invested in inventory.

In the years just before as well as during the war, a number of young academics had found their way to Anthroposophy. Some of those who encountered Steiner before they turned thirty were Dr. Caroline von Heydebrand, Dr. Friedrich Husemann, Dr. Oskar Schmiedel, Dr. Karl Heyer, Dr. Karl Schubert, Dr. Roman Boos, Dr. Maria Röschl, Dr. Herbert Hahn, Dr. Walter Johannes Stein, Dr. Eugen Kolisko, Dr. Hans-Erhard Lauer, Emil Bock and Dr. Eberhard Kurras. It was foreseeable that another generation of academics would soon join this group, all of whom had come to know Rudolf Steiner before 1918.

It was important that the fundamental philosophical works from Steiner were available, for these provided the conceptual structure with which to defend his work in an academic setting. For this reason, Steiner began with the revisions of *Intuitive Thinking as a Spiritual Path* and *Goethe's*

Worldview. These two books were written in that mood of soul that arises out of intentional individualism and a feeling of protest against the legacies of the past. In the years from 1892 to 1900, for instance, Steiner had revered Max Stirner and his philosophy of radical egoism, and in a letter to John Henry Mackay, one of Stirner's students, Steiner had gone so far as to say that the second half of *Intuitive Thinking as a Spiritual Path* was in complete agreement with Stirner's *The Individual and His Property* (39). Steiner revised his view of the relationship in 1914 in *The Riddles of Philosophy*. But although he set different accents from 1903 onward, the basic concept of his work remained the same.

It is important for an understanding of Steiner's life and in trying to gain a sense of how he saw himself to recognize that Steiner never deviated from the fundamental epistemological path that he laid out in his philosophical writings. Many of Steiner's earlier statements can be misunderstood and given too much attention if one loses sight of his philosophical questions.

In a lecture given on May 25, 1921, Steiner delineated both his point of departure and the direction of his questions. "The source lies absolutely within the modern scientific worldview. Whoever works his way through the unfortunately rather long list of my writings will be able to discern that my point of departure was never to be found in religious problems.... The starting point was never of a religious nature, it was always the scientific worldview that I grew into as a young man" (B 116). Theological questions and problems were for Steiner personally something quite foreign. He did not view religion as part of his task. He once remarked to Friedrich Rittelmeyer in 1917, "In my life's work, I must concentrate on the esoteric. Otherwise I won't be able to come through. Religion is your task" (Rittelmeyer). Although such a statement must be taken with a grain of salt, it does show clearly where Steiner did *not* see his task. It's for this reason that he was justified in writing in the foreword to the 1918 publication of his revised *Intuitive Thinking as a Spiritual Path*: "Only ill-will could find in these changes occasion to suggest that I have changed my fundamental conviction" (4).

Going through the revisions, the reader can notice that the fifty-seven-year-old Steiner writes in a milder, more differentiated manner than the thirty-two-year-old Steiner. He doesn't want to antagonize anyone, especially on account of literary formulations. For instance, he no longer terms the moral processes "products of nature" but rather "universal products." But he maintains the stance that morality comes into being within and through the individual; for if it were the product of any form of non-human influence, there would be no possibility of freedom.

It is also possible to observe how carefully and with pedagogical sense Steiner now writes. In the first edition, he wrote fresh from the heart, going straight to the point. "I do not check to see if my action is good or evil; I do it because I am in love with it" (4). In the edition from 1918, he takes into account possible misinterpretations and writes, "I do not work out mentally whether my action is good or bad; I carry it out because I love it." And by way of explanation, he adds, "My action will be 'good' if my intuition, steeped in love, finds its right place within the intuitively experience-able world continuum; it will be bad if this is not the case" (4). The tone of joyful, vehement protest has disappeared.

The new edition of *Goethe's Worldview* incorporated most of the text of the first edition, those parts that dealt with Goethe's thought, with only minor changes. The two chapters, however, that dealt with the Platonic worldview underwent more major revision. In 1897, Steiner had charged that the Platonic view sundered the world as a whole into two parts, in "the mental picture of a world of illusion and in another the world of ideas, which alone reflected true, eternal reality" (6). This separation must lead to the question "How do the ideas and the things of the sensory world come into connection with one another?" This "completely superfluous question" took the spiritual evolution of the West in the false direction. Philosophers—with the exception of Aristotle and Goethe—did not realize that the idea is directly present *in* the world and that thoughtful research is in actuality a process through which these ideas are brought to conceptual expression through observation, action, experimenting and inner re-creation. The Platonic view, however, brought the "evil eye" (6), which made the sensory world appear worthless and without spirit. An endless number of humans were thus blinded to the true relationship between ideas and experience. Steiner did not deviate from this fundamental stance in 1918. By allowing it to be reprinted, he showed that the striving to experience the idea in the sensory world remained and would continue to remain important.

In the first edition, Steiner continued forthrightly, "In order to completely blind people for this relationship, Platonism joined forces with Christianity. This religious creed with its faith in an afterworld is simply a folksy form of Platonism. It raises a personal being modeled after the human image to the creator of the universe. The church fathers simply placed the Platonic world of ideas into this being's spirit" (6). In the 1918 edition, Steiner expanded on this and presented it in a much more differentiated manner. He writes, for instance, that the Platonic stream was "strengthened in the course of the development of Western thought, owing to a one-sided understanding of Christian truths" (6). Platonism doesn't come under such stark criticism, and the idea of a "genuine Christianity" appears (6). Steiner has become milder; he still articulates the core of what he wrote in 1897, just not quite as bluntly.

Personally, 1918 was also a year in which Rudolf Steiner worked through his own past. It was a year of looking back at where he had come from. He traveled at the end of May and the beginning of June to Vienna, then on to visit his mother and siblings in Horn. From there he went on to visit Count Polzer-Hoditz in Tannbach, ending up finally in Prague. In Vienna he visited his old friends Rosa Mayreder, Frau Breitenstein and others. For several days he traveled around the city in a "Tages-Fiaker," in order to visit old acquaintances. Maria Strakosch invited Viennese artists to her studio, where Steiner spoke about art and creativity and remained for the subsequent conversations, immersing himself again in the atmosphere of the Viennese art scene. In Horn he visited his eighty-four-year-old mother for the last time. She died that Christmas.

On June 7, he traveled through Linz to Tannbach, Count Ludwig Polzer-Hoditz's estate. The Count led him on long walks through the forests and ravines and along the brooks to hidden springs. That Sunday, they went to Mass together, after which Rudolf Steiner celebrated a Rosicrucian ceremony in one of the old rooms of the castle. He left for Prague on June 11. There, too, he took time to revisit the past. He spent a long time gazing out on the old city from the windows of the council chamber in the Hradschin. He visited the ancient venerable library in the Strahov Monastery and, on June 17, he visited the Charles Castle with a small group of local anthroposophists. Here he found the last traces of Charles the Fourth's spirituality in the reconstruction of the Grail chapel that he had had built in the castle's vaulted chapel.

It is certainly no coincidence that during this year of reflection and finding his place in the historical moment of the present, Rudolf Steiner also focused on the discipline of history itself, its science, and its methodology.

History had always interested the scientist in Steiner. As a student, he had read Rotteck and Tacitus, he extensively annotated the history of Goethe's color theory, and he had lectured on history during his tenure at the Workers' College in Berlin.

From the beginning of his anthroposophic work, a deeper understanding of history, recognizing the deeper impulses that reveal themselves throughout history, was an eminently important aspect of Steiner's work. We meet this in the books *Mystics after Modernism: Discovering the Seeds of a New Science in the Renaissance* (7) and *Christianity as a Mystical Fact* (8). Even in these early works, the method of anthroposophic historical research can be discerned. A historian must bring what the mystics, the evangelists and the mystery traditions relate to inner experience in order to plumb the depths of their historical worlds. The key to historical understanding is crafted by the soul as it awakens itself and experiences within the struggles that have come to expression in the course of historical development.

On October 18, 1903, at the general assembly of the German section of the Theosophical Society, Rudolf Steiner lectured on the nature of esoteric historical research. In connection with the majestic cosmogony developed by Blavatsky, he developed the goals of such research, which was finally to show "how the *unified spirit* of the universe plays into the destiny of humanity, how the life of this spirit flows into the higher self of the great leaders of humanity to make itself known to humanity through these channels" (34). Steiner's summary of this lecture indicates that the goal of the lecture was not to lay out a methodological approach, but rather to plant the seed of a comprehensive, spiritual picture of history. Continuing in this vein, a year later he gave four lectures on the legends of Prometheus, the Argonauts, and Sigfried, and on the Trojan War.

Thereafter, the topic of history stepped for a time into the background. Only in the extensive, introductory lecture cycles did Steiner give an overview of cosmic evolution, which always concluded with a short look at the evolution of culture. In 1910, he developed the idea of cosmic evolution and in roughly 30 pages gave a well-grounded presentation of the development of culture from the time of Atlantis to the present.

In the New Year's period of 1910/11, seven years after his first lecture on esoteric history, Steiner revisited the topic in a series of six lectures on "Esoteric History." He first described the cosmic historical path of great individualities through a series of incarnations and the influence of the hierarchies in the course of history. The remarkable thing about this presentation is that the spiritual evolution is presented in connection with historical figures. Directly thereafter, there followed a series of presentations in public lectures given in Berlin about Zarathustra, Hermes, Buddha and Moses and a lecture about Galileo, Giordano Bruno and Goethe. All of these lectures show in a very pictorial manner how historical developments were born through great individuals or how history revealed its deeper character through them. These presentations continued in the winter of 1911/12 with lectures about the prophet Elias, about Copernicus and his time, as well as with a presentation of the development of the prophets. In the summer of 1911, Rudolf Steiner published the slender, but important book *The Spiritual Guidance of the Individual and Humanity*.

During the subsequent years, the topic of history no longer remained in the background of Steiner's work—the events of the time offered rich opportunity for historical reflections. But in the autumn of 1917, a new approach to understanding history began, which was refined during 1918. Steiner began with a lecture in Zurich in which he spoke to the question as to how the study of history can become a science. In other sciences, the facts are explained and understood. A zoologist can explain, among other things, the functions of the various animal organs, the growth of the animal, and with some accuracy predict how the animal will behave; but when deepened, a zoological study can advance to a true understanding of the animal. All effort in history, however, goes into reconstructing the basic facts and exhausts itself in relating what has been reconstructed. It only progresses to being able to describe what happened and thinks that this suffices as science. Everything that arises as an "explanation" is contested and bears the character of mere interpretation. Following this introduction, Steiner raised the questions: "What is it in the human being that bears a relationship to what we call historical development? What part of the human being participates in this development? How does being woven into this process affect the human being?" (73).

Some months later, he articulated the questions slightly differently in Berlin: "This is where we must begin, if we wish to examine history and its mysteries in the light of Spiritual Science. We must deal with these questions: Can we discover the object of history within the context of our general consciousness? And, do we actually know what we are trying to understand when we turn our attention to history?" (67).

The actual historical impulses that form historical development are hidden behind the historical facts. They do not live primarily in the consciousness of one's ideas, but rather in the depths that one cannot see clearly with full wakefulness. The historical impulses arise out of the realms of feeling and willing, where the human being dreams and sleeps.

> This insight is the shocking result of turning one's attention from the human being toward what reveals itself in historical development. It shows us that we cannot use the mental pictures that hold sway in our outer, fully conscious life to understand in any way what lives in history. For what one personally experiences in daily life is experienced in waking consciousness. But what history is, is in no way present in the wakefulness of daily life. History is not experienced in wakefulness, it is dreamed. History is the majestic dream of the development of humanity. It never enters into normal consciousness. (67)

This is a significant statement. It indicates that even someone living in the present can perhaps attain a narrow overview of the factual events taking place—that one can dream and sleep into the actual history, the genuine transformations that are taking place. Who can actually claim to know and fully understand what has taken place in the last twenty years? If we read the work of modern historians with this question in mind, we recognize the helplessness of the authors when they try to answer questions concerning the larger picture and where these developments will lead.

A true understanding of history can only be achieved through the higher forms of knowledge—imagination and inspiration. Rudolf Steiner calls attention to significant attempts to approach these deeper dimensions of history. In this connection he often mentions Herman Grimm, who lived with the idea of writing a history of the ongoing imaginative stream at work in traditional life. In the imaginative—the myths, fairy tales and legends that surface out of the semi-conscious and cast waves upon the surface of human consciousness—lives something of the historical dream of humanity. The voice of universal historical development speaks more clearly in the legend of Percival and that of Faust than in the records of many parliaments or conventions.

The closed curtain of the facts that progress from day to day, from year to year, which a historian must with care and patience reconstruct out of archives and collections and then present as history—these are merely the corpse of history. "To the inner soul content of history that is only dreamed by humanity in the course of historical development, outer historical facts are not just a body containing death within it, it is rather a body that is already dead, one from which the soul has already departed. That means that the soul is never in the outer historical facts!" (73).

At best, historical facts, the events, are windows for a gifted historian through which he can catch a glimpse of the deeper impulses, symptoms through which something can speak as does the meaning of a book through the letters. To read these letters, however, a person is needed in whom lives the forces of history, not some logical cipher machine. This was clear to Steiner quite early on. He wrote in 1896, "Only one can write history who searches in the characters and events of history for what hides behind the mere facts. In order to do so, one must live a powerful life of one's own. The driving forces of personal influence can only be observed within oneself" (1-e).

By 1918, Steiner would no doubt have expanded on this statement and have said that the research historian would have to immerse himself in such a manner in the stream of those forces that craft history that he would have to wrestle with the spiritual beings, the impulses, and forces himself. This was the kind of struggle that Steiner had engaged in since 1907, but especially in the summer of 1917.

After working through the methodological problems in the period from autumn 1917 until early summer 1918 in five lectures, in the fall of 1918 Rudolf Steiner embarked on a series of historical lectures. Of special note are the exemplary lectures on "Historical Symptomatology," which focused on the fundamental questions of the time and the symptomatological method. In the first five lectures of this course, Steiner explores with large brushstrokes the symptomatology of the development of the consciousness soul, which comes strongly to expression in the realm of science and technology up to the then present, and then went on to characterize perspectives of its further development.

Steiner's diagnosis of the present appears most explicitly in the lecture of October 25, 1918. In the middle of the nineteenth century, as the proletariat had just begun to form and had not yet become class conscious, at a time when the industrial and capitalistic forces in Germany were still in their childhood and the aristocracy had lost much of its respect, there was an opportunity for the middle class to restructure the social relationships in ways that reflected the need for free forms of self-administration. It was the opportunity to structure social relationships in a brotherly or sisterly manner, especially since by 1845, looking back on the French Revolution, one would have learned how not to go about it. The window of opportunity extended from roughly 1845 until the end of the liberal period in 1879. The middle class, however, were not awake to the possibilities that presented themselves. Nothing was done. Instead of a healthy social development, powerful pathological tendencies appeared, for instance imperialism, which began its death march in the 1880s, or anti-Semitism, which at roughly the same time began to poison people's minds as a form of racist ideology.

When the czarist regime collapsed in 1917, middle-class circles under the leadership of the lawyer Kerenski came to power. "What happened there? What happened was that the social revolutionary Mensheviks had no ideas. They were in the majority, but they had no ideas. They had nothing to say about humanity's future. They had all sorts of ethical sentiments in their heads, but no one can find the true impulses that can lead humanity further with ethical sentiments" (185).

The lack of ideas formed a powerful spiritual vacuum that was filled by the Bolshevists. Lenin and Trotsky knew exactly what they wanted; they had concrete plans: a peace treaty, the dispossession of the industrialists, and distribution of land. This all had to happen immediately. With this program, they could take up the power that lay orphaned in the streets. In other words, the middle class had not taken up its task. The then present situation, which was already struggling with the forces of nationalism, imperialism and industrialism, was made even more difficult. Steiner viewed Bolshevism as an extremely dangerous force.

In this situation, one could not hope for things to right themselves on their own. Two elements were needed: genuine ideas for the future and conscious spiritual-social striving. Steiner saw himself as a person who in this situation, after things had progressed in the wrong direction for the last forty years, could not only offer ideas out of spiritual insight that could provide direction, but also had to do so. And, in addition, that he had the task to help individuals see soul-spiritual aspects and practices for social life. This he does in the already quoted lecture:

> A much more intense idea of what it means to be human, an idea that takes hold of one deeply, must arise out of the spiritual and begin to

live in social life.... The only thing that can bring healing to humanity—I mean humanity, social life, together—has to be a genuine interest of one person for another. What is unique to the time of the consciousness soul is the isolation of people from one another... This separation must have a counter pole, and this counter pole is the cultivation of an active interest from person to person. (185)

This interest exists in a mood of "positivity." Instead of judging, and often condemning, others based on personal sympathy and antipathy, the challenge is to develop interest and understanding for what Steiner, using a term he borrowed from Goethe, called "malformations." A deep interest for the difficult and pathological can "be a source of infinite clarification for the deepest riddles of existence" (185). This was how Rudolf Steiner saw the spiritual situation of the world at the end of World War I. The path into the future could only be forged through extraordinary new forms of behavior and ideas that transcended what was given naturally.

Rudolf Steiner appeared—speaking in the small circle that gathered in the Dornach cabinet shop—as a messenger for a future that would grow out of insight, out of an experience of the ideal, and out of individual initiative and replace the old self-replicating historical path. As a leitmotiv through all the lectures of this period was the call not to fall into pessimism, but to awaken.

CHAPTER 39

STRUGGLE FOR THE THREEFOLD COMMONWEALTH

When the old order in Germany collapsed at the beginning of November 1918, Rudolf Steiner changed the tone, the content and the intensity of his lectures. A woman who attended the lecture he gave on November 8 in Basel gave her impressions:

> Yesterday evening, in his last public lecture, Dr. Steiner, in a manner hitherto unknown, sounded a trumpet call, through which the worlds of light cried into our ears: Wake up! The good city of Basel trembled right through to the Rheinbrücke. People sat there uncomfortably, and when the storm was past, they stared with eyes wide open and quizzical expressions at the man who walked through the auditorium to greet friends and acquaintances. They had more likely expected him to ascend directly through the ceiling with a flaming sword in his hand and disappear into an endless expanse of light. (J. M. Bruinier, *Chronik*)

This wake-up call continued through the lectures for the members in Dornach that followed. He spoke openly and strongly about the things he had had to leave unsaid over the course of the last years for fear of losing any chance of continuing his work in Germany. He was, after all, an Austrian with a "Russian" wife. Now he spoke of Wilhelm II, Kaiser Franz-Joseph and the Russian Czar Nikolaus II as insignificant figures; industrial and financial powers were the actual drivers in what had happened (185a). Concerning Ludendorff, about whom he had spoken openly in trusted circles, he now declared tersely, "Lundendorf brought about Bolshevism in Russia. He thought that he could only come to a peace agreement with the Bolshevists, no one else. Not only is the catastrophe that came over the German people in many ways the fault of a single person's efforts over the course of two and a half years, the catastrophe in Russia is also connected to the grotesque errors of this man" (185a).

Steiner's words were a signal. He explained what it meant to a well-meaning anthroposophist, who had spoken with a representative of the old order at the beginning of 1919, and had managed to convince the man—a well-placed official in the Foreign Ministry—to invite Steiner to Berlin. Steiner didn't even bother to answer the telegram and told the man who had arranged things sometime later, "I never answered your telegram. One cannot deal with these people any longer; their time is past" (Leinhaus).

The initiatives, which Rudolf Steiner now embraced, came from the other side of things. During the war, he had been extremely discreet with his political actions. The anthroposophists had never been privy to his undertakings. We still don't know exactly how it happened, but a copy of Steiner's memorandum found its way into the hands of a certain Major Fessmann, an officer in German intelligence, and from there into the possession of the Stuttgart anthroposophist Emil Molt. Molt was a man who had started out with nothing and worked his way up to become the part-owner and operator of a cigarette factory. He was at first astounded by what Steiner had quietly attempted to bring about and then felt himself, based on what he had read, called to also do something; for him the memorandum "became his destiny" (Molt). He realized that as an anthroposophist he could—no, must—take hold of the destiny of the time.

On Saturday, November 9, 1918, Molt was on a business trip to Zurich when he heard about the collapse of the German government. Instead of returning home immediately, he traveled to Dornach to hear what Steiner would have to say about the situation. He arrived just in time for the evening lecture and heard the words that moved him so deeply. "No one of us can know when he will be called upon to give counsel or to affect change.... It will be necessary in the future that one goes to meet what occurs with open eyes and an awakened consciousness" (185a). Molt's response: "That was the only possible answer for me" (Molt).

This sequence of events is symptomatic. Rudolf Steiner gave no directives; he awakened his listeners and encouraged initiative. Alfred Meebold also pointed this out in an unpublished memoir.

In October 1918, he had the opportunity to observe Steiner as he painted in the small dome of the first Goetheanum. After a long silence, Steiner suddenly turned to him and said, "We are now going to have a revolution in Germany."

"Yes, I know," I replied.

"Then you can prove whether you are really men or not."

As he said this, he laughed with enjoyment. I felt very uncomfortable. I asked how I was to understand that.

"You have to stand up and speak."

I rejoined, "It will be a witch's kitchen. What can one speak about?"

"You just have to stand up and begin. The right words will come," was his answer.

Then he returned to his painting, but just a few minutes later he turned again and repeated, "Yes, then you can prove whether you are really men or not."

In the weeks that followed, Emil Molt, Carl Unger, and Hans Kuhn began to take initiative in Stuttgart. They developed the grand idea of creating an industrialist's coalition in Württemberg to create jobs for the soldiers returning home from the war. Molt especially became politically active in various contexts. One day, when he was visiting the factory, Speidel, the foreman, mentioned to him that the son of one of his colleagues had been recommended by his teacher for the *Gymnasium*. Molt felt instinctively the emotional impact this had on his foreman and had the idea of creating a school for the children of the workers.

For the time being, however, his days were taken up with questions of local politics, the idea of the industrialists' coalition, socialization and the food shortage. Molt returned to Dornach for November 23 and 24 to consult with Steiner. And Steiner, no doubt due to Molt's presence, spoke for the first time to the members in Dornach about the threefold social order and went into some detail concerning social forms.

During these conversations, and those that followed them in December, Molt asked Steiner about concrete possibilities of bringing the threefold idea to realization. In response, Steiner wrote down the notes concerning socialization found in Molt's papers (24). Another, albeit also incomplete picture of the questions posed to Steiner at this time can be found in the notes made of a similar meeting, which took place on January 27. Emil Molt, Hans Kühn and Roman Boos quizzed Steiner about the details of the threefold social order. They spoke about banks, money, currencies and taxes, socialization, factory management, payments to entrepreneurs, ownership and credit—all themes that were not in the foreground of Steiner's thoughts at that time.

In the middle of this questioning, Rudolf Steiner suddenly spoke about what he was thinking and hoping for. "We must first use the money we have to found independent schools, in order to teach people what they need" (Molt).

This indication of a concrete possibility was at first not noticed by the others present. They were so immersed in their own problems, questions and ideas that they neglected to hear what Steiner was talking about. The second topic that he mentioned concerned the necessity of a full disclosure of the occurrences leading up to the war.

Rudolf Steiner had sometimes let his discomfort concerning questions about the individual details of social life shimmer through. Already in 1917, he had written about the problem. "It is thus obvious that the speaker restrains himself from going into particular details. In the case of truly practically conceived impulses, these details resolve themselves in action. Only a utopian can think things out in detail, but the ideas that arise out of his abstractions cannot be practiced" (24).

Following his experience of the conversations that took place between November 1918 and January 1919, during which he was asked again and again for concrete suggestions regarding far-ranging reforms, Steiner spoke again about the problem of isolated solutions and reforms, although he well knew that the well-meaning questions concerning the details of the threefold approach would not disappear so quickly.

> You can certainly ask the question: How shall this or that be done? For the most part, these are the wrong questions for the phase of the work in which we now find ourselves. The spirit of what lives in the threefold approach could be described in the following manner. There could be, for example, just to focus on something, the best possible system of taxation. The challenge today is not to figure out what the best possible system of taxation is; the challenge is to work toward a threefold structure. And as the threefold commonwealth becomes an ever-more concrete reality, the best system of taxation will come into being through the threefold practice. (189)

Although the well-meaning questions went against his grain, he still didn't want to completely disappoint the questioners. When Emil Molt after many discussions finally realized "it is beyond our capacities to build things up from scratch," he requested that "things be inaugurated by the spiritual author himself." This was naturally not what Steiner had hoped for, but he agreed with the condition that they first prepare a certain stage for his work. He could write a draft of a call to action. If it were signed by about 100 people, it would be possible to set a movement in action with Stuttgart as its center (Molt).

Rudolf Steiner spoke about this situation a number of times later in his life. In the unpublished part of his lecture of May 25, 1921, he emphasized that the threefold movement came about when a number of people approached him after the war to ask about his thoughts on the future of social life. "I was asked; people came to me. I mention it explicitly because it tends to be overlooked, and because usually things are presented in such a way that I appear to be a fanatic, an agitator who forced the things on people." In 1922, in Oxford, he spoke even more clearly and said, concerning *Toward Social Renewal,* the book he had written to support the threefold movement, that friends from Stuttgart had requested that he write it. "I did not write it on my own accord; it was requested that I write it" (302).

This book was not something that Rudolf Steiner was able to toss off. The work on the "Appeal to the German People..." alone took him a good deal of time. It was six days after he agreed to write it that he was able to hand it over to Molt, Boos, and Kuhn. They began immediately to recruit helpers and collect signatures. They were quite successful at it. Some of those who chose to add their signatures to the document were Hugo Sinzheimer and Wilhelm Vershofen, both members of the German National Assembly; Professor Hans Driesch, Walter Goetz and Paul Natorp, all well-known scholars; and artists such as Herman Hesse, Wilhelm Lehmbruck and Jakob Wassermann. Rudolf Steiner must have been gratified to discover also the signatures of Gabriele Reuter and Marie Eugenie delle Grazie.

During a lecture on February 15, Rudolf Steiner made the Dornach anthroposophists aware of the appeal, told them how it had come about, and said that he had had a number of conversations in recent days concerning the question "How can one find the path to understanding"—or, "Is it in any way still possible to find a path to understanding before something utterly catastrophic occurs?"

One finds an important key to understanding the threefold movement in the way Rudolf Steiner answers this question. One can also experience a good deal about Steiner's thinking and the position he takes.

> The last questions cannot be raised by anyone whose thinking is rooted in reality. For he does not create hypotheses concerning what is possible or what is not possible, but takes hold of the things he believes have to be done. If one would embark upon a path, he must take the first step. And no one should believe that even if the first step appears to be different than the goal one has set for oneself, that the first step was unnecessary. The first step of a journey can only cover a very short distance. (189)

In addition, Steiner continued, it is only important that one doesn't end up going backward, that one doesn't get sidetracked, but that one has enough strength of will to stick to the direction that one has chosen, and with open heart and mind to find ways to connect with what is actually there.

This intent to find ways to connect with the given reality is accomplished in remarkable ways. Before Steiner announced the beginning of the threefold movement in Dornach, he held four public lectures in Zurich in early February that focused on the social question. Directly following these lectures, while the response of the audience was still fresh, Steiner began to write what would become *Toward Social Renewal* while staying in a hotel in Zurich. During the time that preparations for the threefold movement were being made in a number of cities in Germany, especially Stuttgart, Rudolf Steiner gave a total of 18 public lectures in various cities in Switzerland to awaken interest in the threefold idea. He wanted it to be known in Switzerland, his de facto home, what it was he was going to be fighting for in Germany. It was important for him to stay in contact with a whole spectrum of people as he wrote *Toward Social Renewal*—with workers and scholars, and with politicians and industrialists.

During a stay in Bern he met with Kurt Eisner—the then prime minister of Bavaria and just fourteen days before Eisner was assassinated—to speak with him about the publication of documents pertaining to the outbreak of the war. During the same stay, he attempted to speak with the German ambassador about the same question. Most important, he listened to the discussions that followed his lectures in order to better understand the inner obstacles facing the threefold idea.

During this period of preparation, Steiner did not forsake his other obligations. At the end of 1918, he decided with Tatiana Kisseleff that public performances of eurythmy should be prepared. Zurich was chosen as the first venue. The Swiss painter Walo von May designed the cover of the program. The colorful drawing portrayed the idea that everything is in movement. On February 24, 1919, after an introduction by Rudolf Steiner, the program began with words from the first mystery play: "The weaving being of light." The first presentation was received with a surprised silence. But then the applause began, and grew. The press gave contradictory reviews. A second public performance took place in Winterthur on February 27, the third in Dornach on March 13. The first public performance of eurythmy in Germany took place in Stuttgart on May 25, 1919, in the middle of the hottest battles concerning the threefold movement.

Once the preparations had been completed and *Toward Social Renewal* was being printed, on April 19, *Still Saturday*, Rudolf Steiner called the Dornach friends together for a farewell address in which he mentioned, among other things:

> I do not want Anthroposophy to remain unproductive, especially in this realm of social challenge, or that you simply view these things as two separate undertakings that progress alongside one another. I'd like you to recognize that the one carries the other and to be conscious that the people, who never wanted to listen to any deepening of the way we view the world, are naturally not suited to understand the social impulses spoken about here. But then one has even a greater obligation, if one has grasped the anthroposophic foundations, to do something to help people understand. Today is not the time to ask at each opportunity about this or that detail. Whoever asks constantly about the details just wants to continue along the old path. It is not important at this juncture to have figured out all the specifics. It is a matter of the great, important brushstrokes of this new impulse reaching out across the world.... Feeling oneself placed within the time will have to be the fundamental gesture that allows ideas and ideals that have grown from the anthroposophic soil to permeate what they now must. (Nachrittenblatt 1943)

When Rudolf Steiner set out for Germany on Easter Sunday 1919, the situation there was incredibly tense and, what is often forgotten, even more turbulent than during the collapse of the German government in November 1918. On March 31, a general strike was called in Württemberg, crippling all public services. There was street-fighting in Stuttgart, Cannstatt and Esslingen. So-called security companies suppressed the workers' movement. On April 7, when the strike finally collapsed, sixteen had been killed and another fifty injured. On that day in Munich, the Republic of the

Councils was declared; volunteer troops gathered to break up this movement. In the Ruhr region, 300,000 miners were on strike, and many people expected a new wave of revolution. Steiner did not hesitate to cast himself into this whirlpool.

The members of the threefold movement had made progress in Stuttgart. The Stuttgart *Tagblatt* had published Steiner's Call to Action on March 5. On March 21, the committee—Emil Molt, Carl Unger, and Prof. Wilhelm von Blume—made a public presentation in the auditorium of the city garden. It was an impressive evening, especially as Prof. von Blume, the author of Württemberg's charter and not an anthroposophist, spoke clearly and understandably about the threefold social order, pointing out also the destructive nature of the old order. Hans Kuhn, a young anthroposophist, had come into contact with members of the radical USPD during the critical days of the general strike and had awakened their interest in threefolding. Emil Molt had spoken about the threefold idea both among his workers and in the Democratic Society in Cannstatt.

When he arrived, Rudolf Steiner, who seemed to be fresh and rested, asked for reports about what had been happening. The discussion soon turned to the question of whether the proletariat, who had shown themselves to be open to the new ideas, should be the primary focus of the threefold propaganda. Steiner warned against narrowing the movement in this way and emphasized the importance of cultivating interest for the work among the middle class, among other things because their position would have an effect on the workers. Above all, the focus was to be on gaining support to realize the threefold social order.

On the evening of April 21, Rudolf Steiner spoke to the members of the Anthroposophical Society. In addition to the Stuttgart members, there were a large number who had come to Stuttgart from other cities to help the threefold movement. Steiner tried to show how human thinking had not kept pace with the enormous changes that had taken place in the last decades. The challenge was to develop a new form of social consciousness. He developed this idea further on April 23 and May 1, pointing out that humanity had unconsciously crossed the threshold, on the other side of which people were called upon no longer to simply let social life and history run their respective courses, but to craft these out of consciousness and insight.

The next morning there was a meeting of the committee with the guests who had arrived from throughout Germany, Austria and Scandinavia;

some had had quite adventurous journeys. During the discussion, the full range of the problems that each of them had brought along became apparent. The debates covered topics including international politics, who was to blame for the war, questions of currency and socialization as well as practical matters.

That evening, April 22, Rudolf Steiner spoke to the signatories of the Call to Action. The auditorium in the Stadtgarten was filled to the last seat. Following Prof. Blume's opening remarks, Steiner took the approach he had taken in the first chapter of *Toward Social Renewal* and spoke about the fundamental contradiction of our time. He said that in the present, which is ruled by thinking in the areas of technology, economics and politics, spiritual life is weak; it is experienced by people ideologically, as an illusion, not as a living reality. To craft a healthy, sustainable social life for the future, it is necessary to untangle the knots that rule social life at present and to separate it into the three autonomous sectors, each of which are governed by different laws. Spiritual/cultural life, if liberated in this manner, can become strong enough to guide the development of new social forms. This idea reflects one of the core biographical threads of Steiner's life: to act out of understanding. The threefold movement was to create the possibility of a social life born out of understanding and insight, the basis for human freedom.

A lively discussion followed the lecture. It ended in the formation of the Society for a Threefold Social Order. Emil Leinhas, Max Benzinger, Hans Kuhn and Theodor Binder joined the Committee, which now became a seven-member working group. They met again on April 24 with the visiting representatives. Rudolf Steiner chaired the meeting. In the discussion, which focused among other things on the participation of the village populations in the threefold movement, E. A. K. Stockmeyer reported that he often met the objection that threefolding would relieve the state of its power. Steiner remarked quite simply, "But that's what we want!" thus voicing a fundamental aim of the threefold approach. Montesquieu had developed the idea, based on a tripartite separation of power, that the three powers would balance and control one another. Steiner was concerned with overcoming power that arose out of the political decisions through which a state gained influence over spiritual and economic life, thus benefiting certain programs or groups and not giving others equal chance. Overcoming power is one of the central pillars of threefolding. People, human insight and ideas should govern, not wield power. Instead of mechanistic regulations, decisions should be made in dialogue, publicly.

In the days and weeks that followed, Rudolf Steiner spoke in Stuttgart and the neighboring towns, primarily to the workers in large factories: the Waldorf-Astoria Cigarette factory, the Bosch plant, the Daimler works, the Del Monte packaging plant, and the Werner & Pfleiderer factory. He gave public lectures in Stuttgart, Esslingen, Cannstatt, Feuerbach, Ludwigsburg, Waiblingen, and in Upper and Lower Türkheim. The lectures took place in smoke-filled auditoriums, in the Dinkelacker Brewery, in a railroad repair shop—with Clara Zetkin—and in the factories themselves. In addition, there were regular meetings and talks with important personalities. He and Emil Molt visited Robert Bosch, whose response was reserved. The other "threefolders," with Emil Molt at the fore, also worked tirelessly so that the idea of threefolding would find its way into public consciousness, especially into the discussions of the workers.

As usual, Steiner did not speak excessively about his personal feelings during this time. He did, however, write on May 10 to Edith Maryon, the keeper of the sculpture studio in Dornach. "Every day there is a lecture to give, followed by discussions. It is somewhat trying for an aging organism, and I would be happy, if now and again, I could exercise other body parts on our artistic activities, rather than just the larynx. This is just how things have to be. And since the day before yesterday, it appears that people begin to understand me somewhat better than has been the case. But that can also change" (263 and 1).

Following the collapse of the government in November 1918, the quickly formed workers' and soldiers' councils had played a significant role, but during the National Congress of Councils in December, the majority of the representatives gathered there decided to support the earliest possible election of a national assembly mandated to draft a new constitution. With this vote, they distanced themselves from the council system. What remained was the idea of factory councils. When Rudolf Steiner arrived in Stuttgart, there was a workers' council. During the general assembly of the workers' councils from the larger Stuttgart region, a motion was made to have Steiner speak at the next meeting. On May 7, he addressed the assembled representative of the workers' councils and explained the basic ideas of the threefold social order. His appearance at the meeting, if we grant credence to the social-democratic press, did not meet with the approval of the party leaders. They could not, however, hinder Steiner from accepting the invitation to address a gathering of the workers' committees from the largest Stuttgart companies the next day. He spoke about the workers' councils. "Just let the councils come into being and don't mess it up with any kind of laws governing them. They have to establish themselves first; they have to establish themselves in each factory. But during this period of transition, they have to insure that they can be entirely independent of the bosses and the foremen. They must be independent" (331).

Following this statement, which makes it clear that Rudolf Steiner envisioned a spontaneous self-organizing rather than a regulated movement, he made the suggestion that the workers' councils in the large factories in any given region unite, and finally, to let the functions of the councils become evident based on how they constituted themselves. Once the general direction became clear, ideas that were appropriate for the work would arise out of the work.

In the discussion, during which a growing sense of understanding and agreement arose between Steiner and the workers—as he reported to Edith Maryon—words with a brisant character were spoken. Looking back at the situation from last November, Steiner remarked that at that time the councils didn't know what they actually wanted; ideas for positive action were missing. "This shows that it is important not merely to run around like hypnotized chickens following the question: How do we come to power? But to ask: What are we going to do with the power? I always have to ask: How are we to act?" (331).

As the old forces collapsed, the challenge was to use the power the workers already had to simply form councils and take up the economic tasks that were asking to be addressed. Naturally, the councils could not merely be social decorations but would have to take up real tasks (331). This was language the workers could understand. They asked Steiner to continue working with them.

Rudolf Steiner was well aware that he could not accompany what he appeared to have set in motion quietly. Before he continued his work with the workers' councils, he shared his views on the council movement in a public lecture attended by a primarily upper-middle-class audience in the Gustav-Siegle House. He called attention to the wonderful fact that many people were not willing to simply let things take their course, but had joined forces to work together. "People have stood up, people who in different ways in the councils, human councils, want to take the future into their own hands, who out of their own initiative, their sense of humanity, out of their own human willing, want to take hold of what is evolving" (330).

> Today it is not possible—this is what the striving toward a system of councils shows us—to impose any form of social structure from above. The only possible way at present is to work together with all those people who are striving to create this system of councils, to cultivate an exchange of opinions and experience concerning truly human questions. (330)

This lecture ended with a moving scene. Siegfried Dorfner, a well known leader of the USPD in Stuttgart, spoke up as "a member of the proletariat." He spoke first about the class conflict that had grown over the previous decades despite all attempts to overcome it, and the fact that the classes had become deadly enemies. Then he continued:

> Now, Dr. Steiner has shown that nothing healing for the future is to be found in the parties. He said only a strong will, new thoughts and action can save us from the chaos. And you, honored listeners, have applauded Dr. Steiner enthusiastically. Now I'd like to share with you that in these last weeks in all the meetings the proletariat of all the parties—socialists, independents, communists—have found themselves in complete agreement with Dr. Steiner and have applauded him even more enthusiastically than you have. They have resolved to demand that Dr. Steiner be called to take part in the administration. Ask yourselves: Is this not a bridge? Do we in fact now have no possibility of uniting ourselves? We workers reach out to offer you our hands [loud applause]; we take our stand on the basis of threefolding and the class struggle will disappear. In freedom and equality, we can be brothers. If we can work together like this, Germany will not go under. In spite of everything, we will move toward a wonderful future! (From a Stuttgart newspaper; compare *Die Drei* 1985, 661)

This gives us a glimpse of Rudolf Steiner's deeper striving. He hoped to stimulate at least a part of the German people—the workers and the middle class—to spiritual and practical activity. He wanted to overcome the fatalism and the obedience to authority, to call into life a people's movement through which the workers and the middle class could take their lives and destinies into their own hands. He hoped the practical work would create an opening for spiritual impulses.

Steiner's support of the council movement should not be construed as support for the *council system*. He was not interested in the councils themselves or in the theories that stood behind them. He was interested in people willing to take an active part in the developments of the time and in his collaboration with these people. And he found these collaborators in the council movement.

Within a month, with few resources and a very small number of coworkers, the movement had become remarkably successful. At the same time, from this point on, the oppositional forces became active—at first tentatively, but then with ever-increasing aggression. The movement experienced setbacks, and the threefolders made mistakes of their own. Toward the end of May, Hans Kuhn, the office manager for the Threefold Association, circulated a flyer—"Attention Manual Laborers! Attention Spiritual Laborers! Attention Manufacturers!"—which called for the formation of factory councils, using inflamed rhetoric and with a demagogical style. Steiner had focused on providing guidance to the workers who had already formed councils, on creating actualities that would have had to be accepted. The wild proclamations of the flyer brought on the necessary opposition of the factory owners, who now resolutely set a counter-course and issued their own proclamation opposing the statements in the flyer.

The leftists and the union activists also viewed an independent council movement with suspicion. The party leaders, who had distanced themselves from the rank and file through their political tactics, felt that they were losing their influence. They didn't want the spontaneous formation of factory councils. Their goal was to pass a law governing the formation, the operation and the powers of the councils. They now did their best to hinder the grassroots movement.

Rudolf Steiner described the situation with a great deal of restraint in a letter to Edith Maryon on June 4, 1919.

> Everything would naturally be much easier if, in addition to everything else, one did not always have to deal with the misunderstandings that are constantly arising. Everything one says is turned into something quite different as soon as it is repeated. People attack one from all sides simply because they have been misinformed. There is a strong tendency to want to make everything fit into the party organization. Whenever anything arises that has nothing to do with the parties, they make it into something other than it is. This is not only

true of the opposition. Even those who look positively on what I have presented do it. It makes the real work very difficult. (263 & 1)

The involvement in the council movement caused an imbalance in the threefold action. There was the danger that the threefold movement was becoming too narrowly focused, although the threefold approach, as it was intended, only made sense as a whole. Rudolf Steiner pushed to create a cultural council to augment the factory councils. The cultural council was to take action to insure autonomy in the realm of cultural and spiritual activities and support an independent, self-governed school and university system. Although a number of eminent artists like Thomas Mann, the painter Hans Thoma and the conductor Fritz Busch signed the petition to form such a council, it never really got off the ground. On June 22, 1919, Rudolf Steiner spoke about the efforts to form a cultural council in a lecture for the members of the Anthroposophical Society. "We've been muddling along on the thing for the last three weeks and there is still no movement" (192).

A third initiative that met with a lack of success was Steiner's attempt to contribute to a clarification of the events surrounding the outbreak of the war. He thought the publication of the record that General Helmuth von Moltke had kept for his wife would be helpful. He hoped that by publishing an honest and frank account of the events leading up to the outbreak of hostilities for the non-German world, Germany could win back some of the moral credit it had lost and knew that the threefold movement could not succeed without this. On May 3, 1919, he asked Eliza von Moltke for permission to publish her husband's records.

For a number of reasons, this was not the best of ideas. The papers ended with these remarks: "I have made these sketchy records without recourse to notes or other documentation. There may be some errors concerning dates, etc. I was also quite ill when I wrote them. They are intended for my wife and shall never be made public."

Still, Steiner recognized the full import of the problem concerning who was to blame for the war. And Moltke's record was the only document he had on hand. It bore eloquent witness to the confusion in Berlin at the beginning of the war and appeared thus to disprove the thesis that the German leaders had worked with a clear sense of purpose to bring about the war. For this reason, Steiner made the effort during these intensely busy days to write an extensive, explanatory preface to Moltke's document.

On May 28, as Steiner was preparing to send Eliza von Moltke copies of the first print run, he was dismayed to learn that some anthroposophists had already obtained copies from the printer the day before. Emil Molt was one of those who had visited the printer. Thinking that he was being helpful, he took the pamphlets directly to the Prussian embassy and delivered them into the hands of the ambassador, Hans Adolf von Moltke. He in turn immediately notified family members, the Foreign Ministry and the General Staff. Pressure was brought to bear to forbid publication. Eliza von Moltke was taken to task by the family patriarch and the permission to distribute the pamphlets was withdrawn.

On June 1, General von Dommes, who had been part of the General Staff in 1914, came to meet with Steiner to insure that Moltke's notes would not be published. With this goal in mind, he asserted that they were incorrect in three places. Steiner asked von Dommes if he was willing to make his statement under oath. Von Dommes agreed without hesitation. Steiner later described the exchange. "He noticed nothing of what I went through as he spoke. Every word prejudiced—rigid, inflexible judgment, as though the war had not occurred" (Moltke II).

Since the three points of which von Dommes spoke have not been reliably documented, it is practically impossible today to judge whether or not his claims were justified. Rudolf Steiner did not believe so and later remarked, "I am completely convinced that the three points were correct, for they were also psychologically correct" (174b). But at that time he feared they would use every legal means at their disposal to prevent publication, thus robbing it of any positive effect. He finally agreed to let the entire print run of 50,000 be pulped—costs to be absorbed by the von Moltke family. All his efforts were of no avail.

By the middle of June, it had become apparent that the threefold movement was not going to lead to any form of outer success. Count Ludwig Polzer-Hoditz, who was visiting Stuttgart at this time, reported the following to his friend Walter Johannes Steiner after a meeting with workers' representatives on June 17:

> I stayed for supper with Kinkel and experienced a terrible pessimism from Dr. Steiner. He said, "Your experiences up till now have not been good; the coming ones won't be any better. One can't do anything with the leaders of the socialist parties; we would have had to gain the support of the masses much more quickly, before the leaders

got involved. Then the workers would have continued to follow the committee. Now they are afraid of the party heads."

Still, Rudolf Steiner did not give up. He continued meeting with the workers' representatives until July 23, although the discussions with workers became increasingly difficult. He lectured ceaselessly in Stuttgart, but also in Göppingen, Heilbronn, Weil im Dorf, Ulm, Mannheim and Schwennigen. His experiences are captured in the draft of a letter dated June 28.

> We would without doubt make good progress with the proletariat if the party leaders were not so resolved to pull the carpet out from under our feet. The proletariat is more obedient to them than the Catholics are to the leaders of their church. And the middle class sleeps the sleep of the soul, lets itself be awakened now again to support proclamations, and is completely in the hands of the puppet masters whose only means are those that oppose the spirit. Everything together will bear evil fruit. (B 27/28)

During July it became clear that a breakthrough for the threefold approach in the short-term could not be expected. The ubiquitous habits of thought and feeling resisted the completely different art of thinking necessary for understanding and acting courageously on Steiner's ideas. Although in July the threefold movement outwardly intensified its efforts—the weekly *Threefolding of the Social Organism* appeared, at first in a run of 40,000 copies; Carl Unger, Ernst Uehli, Kurt Walther, Adolf Arenson, Emil Leinhaus, and Emil Molt were active lecturing in Stuttgart and the region; and *Toward Social Renewal* had sold some 30,000 copies since May—Rudolf Steiner began again to speak about anthroposophic topics in the more narrow sense in his lectures. He wrote to Edith Maryon in Dornach, "In recent days, in addition to the other kind of lectures, I have also given some anthroposophic ones. One could even say there is more openness for these than for the others" (263 & 1).

Rudolf Steiner had gained many experiences through this initiative. He had had to recognize that in spite of the war, the old ideas and values lived on unshaken, especially in the middle class, and that otherwise well-meaning individuals could not understand the intensity with which he fought for his ideas or his closeness to the workers (192). He had seen his collaborators, most of whom had come from middle-class backgrounds, make mistakes. At the same time, he had seen a number of anthroposophists—although they were actually not prepared for political work and had become involved with Anthroposophy because of quite a different soul mood—plunge courageously into the fray. There were soon a number of local threefolding groups in different German cities, many of which became quite active. But no one had risen into a position of leadership, able to take over the guidance of the movement from him. During the entire campaign, this weight rested solely upon his shoulders.

Other tasks awaited him, however. He was needed in Dornach; and in Berlin, where he had had to cancel the lectures planned for January, the anthroposophists hoped to see the leader of their branch once again. He had been away for a year. The eurythmists, who had now performed for the first time in public, were waiting for new impulses and direction. More than anything, the next concrete challenge, the founding of the Waldorf School, was knocking at the door. Thus in early August, Steiner had to bring his personal efforts for the threefold movement to an end and focus on the other tasks awaiting him. This is not to say that he no longer contributed to the threefold work. He wrote regular articles for the *Threefold Journal*. In October 1919, he held a series of lectures in Zurich entitled "Social Future." And in 1921, he gave two courses for speakers who wanted to work in the threefold movement. But he retired from frontline political action.

This undertaking, in which he entered public life as a political figure, was a risk for Rudolf Steiner. It was a bit of a two-edged sword as far as his reputation went. On the one hand, it made him a public figure. He became a topic of discussion as well as a subject of caricatures. On the other hand, his work gave rise to a number of misunderstandings and new opponents. At this time, a torrent of books, pamphlets and articles attacking Steiner began. And spiritually—or, one might say, esoterically—the step into the battles of the day was also not without a certain risk. He had to give himself over to events, processes and ways of thinking that focused his attention on outer, material problems. He experienced these tendencies to seek orientation on materialistic facts rather than on ideas as a lead weight. In the course of the movement, he sensed ever more strongly how little his audiences were able to raise themselves above the mundane questions of the day to ways of seeing that would open perspectives for a social future. He later summed up the campaign as follows:

One would venture to say that when we speak of the threefold social impulse, the campaign was a test whether Michaelic thought has grown strong enough to enable one to feel how such an impulse flows forth directly from the formative forces of time. It tested whether Michaelic thought has grown strong enough in enough individuals. And the results were negative. Michaelic thought is not yet strong enough in even a small number of individuals to be felt in the wholeness of its time-shaping force and power. (223)

Rudolf Steiner was speaking of the tendency for thinking to get stuck one-sidedly on material facts. Michaelic thought, of which he spoke in 1923, is born out of pure thinking, opening itself to the spirit—the spiritual reality of humanness and the spirit in nature—and leading to action imbued with spiritual meaning. In the first article Rudolf Steiner wrote for the *Threefold Journal*, he characterized Michaelic thought's counter-image.

The destructive superstition has settled into the proletariat that everything to do with the sphere of rights and that of culture arises as a natural necessity out of economic systems. Large numbers of non-proletariat have also fallen prey to this superstition. What has developed over the last centuries as a phenomenon of our time—the fact that cultural and political life are dependent on economic relationships—has come to be seen as a natural necessity. No one recognizes the truth of the matter: this dependency has plunged humanity into the catastrophe. Now one imagines, superstitiously, that all we need is a different economic system, one that can give birth to a different political and cultural life. (24)

An act was needed to balance this tendency, a visible initiative founded in reality. Rudolf Steiner returned at the end of the Threefold Campaign to the intention he had spoken of the past January: "With the money that we have, we must found independent schools, to teach people what they need." He turned his attention to the founding of the Waldorf School, a school whose spiritual/cultural life would be focused not on economic concerns or governmental requirements, but would find its orientation through insight into the needs of the developing child.

Chapter 40

THE INDEPENDENT WALDORF SCHOOL

As Emil Molt recalled in his memoirs, he had never seen Rudolf Steiner happier than on August 19 when he picked him up in Freiburg and drove with him through the valley of the Elz, by Haslach and Freudenstatt, to Stuttgart for the beginning of the teachers' course in preparation for the opening of the Waldorf School. Other contemporaries related that they had never seen Steiner as joyful and radiant as on September 7 at the celebration for the opening. Whether this joy was unique to this occasion must remain an open question. The inauguration of a new pedagogical impulse was something Rudolf Steiner had striven toward for many years. It grew out of the innermost core of Anthroposophy. He felt it to be a field where Anthroposophy could have a practical effect on the time—certainly a reason to be joyful.

He had spoken about pedagogical questions for many years. In 1907, he published the booklet *The Education of the Child from a Spiritual Scientific Point of View,* in which he sketched out the basic ideas of an education guided by the developmental stages of the growing child. But in the period from 1907 through 1918, the response to this book was disappointing. Although he was often asked by anthroposophic parents for educational advice—what children should eat or what clothes they should wear—the central ideas of the book were for the most part ignored. Still, his pedagogical interest never waned, and he often brought up educational questions in his lectures.

The impetus to found a school arose not from reading Steiner's lectures but out of the immediate needs of the time. As was mentioned, Emil Molt first thought about founding a school in November 1918, following a conversation with one of his foremen, but his attention was taken up by other, more pressing problems. But then in March 1919, Molt had brought a young anthroposophist to Stuttgart to provide general education courses for the workers. His name was Herbert Hahn. After some initial difficulties, the talks were well received. On April 23, just three days after he arrived in Stuttgart, Rudolf Steiner spoke to the roughly 1000 employees of the Waldorf-Astoria cigarette factory about the fate of the workers, who, having been excluded from higher liberal education, could only develop a part of their human potential. Following the lecture, there was a meeting of the factory council that Rudolf Steiner also attended. During this meeting, Emil Molt voiced his intent to found a school and asked Steiner to lead the effort. Molt, a deeply practical man, also mentioned that he had set aside 100,000 German marks from the previous year's profits. He later acknowledged that he felt somewhat sheepish when Steiner remarked dryly that this was a nice enough sum.

Two days later, the first serious discussion concerning the school took place. Following quite a trying lecture for the workers at the Daimler factory, Rudolf Steiner returned to his apartment to meet with Emil Molt, Herbert Hahn, and Karl Stockmeyer, who had been brought in by Molt to work on the creation of the school. Stockmeyer, who had been involved with Anthroposophy since 1907, was a science and mathematics teacher in Baden and involved in the school reform movement. At the beginning of the conversation, Rudolf Steiner spoke about questions Herbert Hahn had raised, then developed tentatively his thoughts concerning the new school. In doing so, he spoke of such large classes that Stockmeyer was inclined to withdraw from the initiative. Rudolf Steiner, however, requested strongly that he stay involved, and in the following weeks Stockmeyer began to work out an operational plan for the school.

As soon as the decision had been finalized to go ahead with the school initiative, Rudolf Steiner, Emil Molt and Karl Stockmeyer met with the social-democratic Minister of Culture Heymann and presented him with the plan for the new school on May 13. Heymann liked the idea that through a "capitalist" the idea for a "comprehensive school" for students of the various classes was to be realized and, due to the fairly loose educational laws dating back to 1836, was able to grant the school a license in but a few weeks.

At the same time, Rudolf Steiner began—still tentatively—to sketch out his ideas for a new school in a series of three lectures for members of the Anthroposophical Society. The central ideas in these lectures were that the teachers would approach their teaching from an intuitive understanding of human development, that the content of the classes would guide children into the real world, that the trend toward specialization would have to be overcome, that they would have to find a path to a living understanding of nature and a sweeping sense of history, and, finally, that the school would be self-governing. And even at this point Rudolf Steiner called for doing away with the ubiquitous schedule, calling it "a death trap for everything that is truly pedagogical" (192). He later achieved this to some extent through the introduction of lesson blocks.

Emil Molt took up the search for a schoolhouse and finally found a piece of property on the Uhlandshohe, where a well-loved Stuttgart restaurant was for sale. He visited the property on May 30 with Rudolf Steiner, who noticed the uncultivated area behind the building and the "red wall" of rock at the far edge of the grounds. He remarked that students would be able to make wonderful geological observations there. Molt acted immediately. He used almost his entire private assets and bought the building and grounds for a sum of 450,000 German marks.

Even more important than the fortunate purchase of the property on the Uhlandshohe was the task of finding the right teachers. Since Rudolf Steiner had been responsible for the development of the anthroposophic work in Germany and had spoken with most of the members, he knew most of the people who could be asked to join the faculty. Among those he brought to Stuttgart, in addition to Herbert Hahn and Karl Stockmeyer, were Paul Baumann, a musician, the eurythmist Elisabeth Baumann, Dr. Caroline von Heydebrand, Dr. Rudolf Treichler, Dr. Walter Johannes Steiner, Johannes Geyer, as well as four other teachers, all of whom left the school before Steiner's death either for personal or health reasons.

Before the inaugural course for the faculty began, Rudolf Steiner traveled back to Dornach for twelve days to work with the colleagues there and deal with questions concerning the building project. Soon after arriving, he gave a lecture on August 9 concerning the relationship between questions concerning social life and education. In it, he built a bridge from the ideas sketched out in 1907 to the present. He described how the young child up to the age of seven sculpts his or her bodily organism through active imitation and how this sculptural process, if the imitation is good, gives the body an inner structure so that it doesn't place obstacles in the individual's path as he or she grows older. Healthy imitation is the basis of freedom. Freedom is only possible if one is sovereign in relation to one's self. In a similar manner, the child from ages seven to roughly fourteen needs teachers who can lead one imaginatively to an understanding of the world. In this period of life the teacher must be a true authority: Just as the grapevine needs a pole to climb up on, a child in the second period of life needs a mediating authority to look up to. The experience of looking up to someone in this way metamorphoses into a sense of justice strong enough to embrace the rights of others. Following puberty, when a young person has become sexually mature and can experience the possibility of a sexual relationship, the challenge becomes transforming this special form of love into a general feeling of love for humanity and interest in the world. Interest and insight rooted in love can become the foundation of brotherhood among adults (296).

He continued to speak of further challenges facing education at the time. Technological intelligence was increasing rapidly, bringing with it the tendency to follow one-sided interests and, finally, to conceive of evil: human intelligence had already acquired a clear tendency toward evil. The intellect should, however, not be stifled, but "in the future those who understand these things will need courage to give oneself over to the world of the intellect because of the temptation toward evil and the possibility of error inherent in it" (296). Teachers and educators must learn to understand and take these relationships into consideration in order to cultivate in children the possibility of a love for what is good, which is born out of the Christ impulse.

All told, the thoughts that lay behind the founding of the Waldorf School when the teachers came together the evening before the beginning of the course were of great magnitude, rooted in a deep sense of humanity. In his introductory talk that evening, Rudolf Steiner said the new school would have to be a true cultural deed, which could reform the entire educational system. Without question, compromises would have to be made, but no one should lose sight of the actual goals.

He described the school as a true republic of teachers, in which each would be fully responsible for what he or she was doing. Independent pedagogical initiative, born of a true understanding of human nature, would be the deciding factor in the life of the school—not rules and regulations, policies and procedures. For the teacher, it was important to cultivate a living interest in everything that was happening in the time. "We have to find the enthusiasm we need for the school and our work through interest in the world." Out of the needs and challenges of the time that "are both larger than one can imagine" must be born the courage to act (293).

The course for the teachers began on August 21. At 9:00 a.m., Rudolf Steiner began with a lecture on general anthropology followed, after a fifteen-minute break, by one more specifically focused on methods of teaching. That took them up to around 11:30. In the afternoon, from 3:00 p.m. to 6:00 p.m., there was a seminar session with exercises and discussion. The course ran fourteen days, ending on September 5.

Steiner's enthusiasm for the school initiative is not outwardly apparent in these lectures. His joy, inner support and enthusiasm are metamorphosed in the unbelievably concentrated lectures, the practical suggestions and in the exercises for the teachers. In the center of the course stood the lectures on the nature of the human being—a description of the threefold human being from three points of view, an in-depth overview unlike anything Rudolf Steiner had done before or was to do after. The teachers gained through these lectures the beginnings of a living understanding of the human being, an understanding that could allow them to respond pedagogically out of the depths of their experience (291). Steiner summarized the course from two different angles soon thereafter when speaking in Berlin. He said the task is to found a pedagogy "that reckons with the fact of reincarnation in the development of the child's soul." The educator "must have a fine sense for the signature of a previous incarnation in the growing child" (193). At the same time, the challenge is to teach in anticipation of the tasks and challenges of the future. "What is crucial is that we teach prophetically, that we anticipate the challenges that the next generation will face. This has its place in the world" (193).

In this sense, remembering and anticipating, the teacher must bridge the past and the future, weaving them together with the task of bringing the stream of the future in the present into a healthy relationship with what appears in the present as the fruit of past incarnations. To meet this challenge, the teacher needs a living feeling for and an intuitive sense of what lives and strives to unfold in the students he or she meets each day.

On September 7, following the fourteen-day course of preparation and inspiration for the young faculty—the average age was thirty-two—the Independent Waldorf School was ceremoniously opened in the Stadtgartensaal in Stuttgart, a building that was destroyed in World War II. There were roughly 1000 people present for the occasion: the 250 pupils with their families and relatives, people connected with the Waldorf-Astoria Cigarette Factory, others who were active in the threefold campaign, and a large number of anthroposophists.

The ceremony began and ended with music by Bach. To open, Paul Baumann played the Prelude in C major from the *Well-Tempered Clavier*, and an aria for the violin closed the festivities. Following welcoming words spoken by Emil Molt, Rudolf Steiner addressed the audience and spoke, among other things, of what the founding of the school meant for him. "For me...it was a sacred duty to take up what lived in the intention of our friend Mr. Molt regarding the founding of the Waldorf School in such a manner that this school could become the expression of what one can believe to have gained from Spiritual Science in the present time" (298).

The "sacred duty" of which he spoke is that connected with all pedagogical work, and he went on to ask:

> Is it not a most sacred, religious duty to cultivate the spiritually divine that appears anew and reveals itself in each human who is born? Is not this rite of education a religious rite in the highest sense of the word? Do not all our most sacred, inner sensibilities, especially those imbued with religious feeling, need to flow together in the rites that we celebrate on the altar of education as we strive to bring forth the seed of the divine spiritual that would reveal itself in the development of the child!
>
> Science coming to life!
> Art coming to life!
> Religion coming to life!
>
> This is finally education. This is finally teaching. (298)

Recitations, singing, and eurythmy followed Rudolf Steiner's address. Karl Stockmeyer spoke for the teachers, Mr. Saria for the workers. After the festivities, the pupils paraded through the city and up the hill to the school on the Uhlandshohe, where they were divided into classes and introduced to their teachers. The faculty rounded up the day at a performance of *The Magic Flute* in the Great Hall of the Staatstheater.

The founding of the Waldorf School was for Rudolf Steiner a sacred rite in the manner described above, one to which every elder generation is called. In the opening address, he also spoke of the "art of education and teaching," calling upon the teachers to be "the artistic teachers of the human being becoming" (298). This is one of Steiner's biographical motifs, which can first be found in the lecture "Goethe as the Father of a New Aesthetic." Artistic action is not to be found in the realization of an ideal, in that an ideal is merely impressed on reality; rather, it takes the reality of the situation as its point of departure and strives to bring what lies hidden to expression.

Thus, he rejected training children to live up to any given ideal. In his next to the last course on education, held in Arnheim in 1924, he spoke about this explicitly.

> The child is given to us to be educated. If we place ourselves upon an anthroposophic foundation in our teaching, we do not look at the child and think: there is some social or other ideal of humanity and it is our job to help the child to develop in such a way that he or she becomes ever more the expression of this ideal.... For anyone who truly wishes to teach out of an anthroposophic understanding, this is in no way a viable point of departure. One cannot begin with an idol. An abstract picture of humanity is something construed, it is nothing real. (310)

He went on to describe how a teacher observes a child; how a child comes toward one in the first days of life with undefined features and uncoordinated movements. If one follows the child's development, one sees how the child's physiognomy becomes increasingly defined and gradually brings the child's soul life to expression on the surface, and, a little later, one can notice how the child's movements become more coordinated and harmonious. The true educator lives in a perceiving, devotional relationship with the child. Steiner continued:

> One must ask, with a sense of sacred devotion, *What is working its way to the surface?* The teacher's heart and attention is led back to what is unique in each human being, to the soul-spiritual that was there in the soul-spiritual, pre-earthly world...and one says to oneself: Child, now that you have passed through birth into earthly existence, you are among humans; before you were among divine spiritual beings. What once lived among divine spiritual beings has come to earth to be among humans! One can perceive the divine in the child in the process of becoming. One feels oneself to be standing in front of an altar. But here there is a difference. On the altars one is used to in religious communities, people make their sacrifices to the gods, in the hope that their sacrificial gifts rise up into the worlds of the divine. Here one experiences an altar reversed: divine beings let their

stream of grace descend as divine spiritual beings, that these divine messengers might become human upon the altar of earthly existence! In each child, one beholds the unfolding of spiritually divine cosmic order—how God works in the world. (310)

The presentation ends with a remark that teachers and educators must understand themselves to be servants of this unfolding, the helpers of what works its way to expression in the features and movements of the child. They are there to care for what they first become acquainted with when they stand before the child.

To those who do not know Steiner well, it might appear that the strong religious motif connected with the anthroposophic pedagogical impulse brings a sentimental, even regressive quality into education. This would be a fundamental misunderstanding of Steiner's intentions. What he describes as the "sacred rite" of pedagogy is for him a description of what we are asked to do in education. The statement that the children are "messengers of the divine" is not a platitude, but an observation.

The Waldorf School has a unique place among the anthroposophic initiatives. First, Steiner took on the guidance of the school and grappled with all the duties and challenges that this leadership entailed, especially all personnel questions. In doing this, he strove to attract people with real talent—true individualities. He was more concerned with the individual than with his or her personal beliefs. He brought two teachers, Hannah Lang and Hans Rutz, onto the faculty who were not anthroposophists. The conversation that took place between Rudolf Steiner and Hans Rutz when the latter applied for a position in the new school is quite instructive. After being welcomed by Steiner, Hans Rutz said, "I can tell you right from the beginning, I am not an anthroposophist; I must have full spiritual freedom!" (*Lehrerkreis*). Rutz became a Waldorf teacher.

Just how fortunate Steiner was in his choice of teachers is reflected in their spiritual productivity. Many of them were not only active as speakers and public representatives of Waldorf education but also authored books and articles. It is worth noting that it was not only the academically trained colleagues—Hermann von Baravalle, Ernst Bindel, Erich Gabert, Herbert Hahn, Caroline von Heydebrand, Eugen Kolisko, Erich Swebsch, Walter Johannes Stein, Martin Tittmann and Rudolf Treichler—who took time to write. Both Hedwig Hauck, the handwork teacher, and Count Fritz Bothmer, the gymnastics teacher, wrote about their work; Paul Baumann wrote songs for the students; and Max Wollfhügel, in addition to a number of paintings, created an oeuvre of board drawings, while other teachers wrote plays for their classes.

Rudolf Steiner also encouraged the teachers by giving them special tasks and inviting them to lecture or give courses. When he was asked to give educational courses in Switzerland, England or Holland, teachers from the school also spoke about their work, and Steiner never failed to honor their efforts and to mention the work of the colleagues in his own lectures and reports. He praised highly the talk Caroline von Heydebrand gave during the autumn congress in Stuttgart in 1921 and wrote about the lecture she gave on April 22 in The Hague. "The pedagogical impulse lives in each one of her sentences, just as it does in her work in the Waldorf School in Stuttgart" (*Goetheanum,* vol. 1). He delighted in the younger colleagues like Hermann von Baravalle, who joined the faculty as a twenty-two-year-old and was given the honor of speaking at the opening of the Goetheanum in 1920. Baravalle also spoke in Torquay at the last pedagogical course Rudolf Steiner gave, supporting Steiner's presentations with his own observations. In a similar manner, Steiner gave other colleagues opportunity to grow through specific tasks—Dr. Kolisko, Dr. Schubert, Dr. Schwebsch, Dr. Hahn, and Dr. Steiner, to whom we will return later.

Rudolf Steiner also spoke quite forthrightly and frankly about mistakes made by various colleagues. After the pedagogical conference in 1923, he admonished them for "emphasizing the negative, critical elements." "One can certainly swing a big club; I don't have anything against that. But it can't be with a negative slant." During the same discussion, he noted that the speaker had neglected his actual topic (300 & 3).

It was through the teachers' meetings and by visiting classes that Rudolf Steiner maintained his involvement in the school. There are transcripts of a total of seventy teachers' meetings led by Steiner. It seems that he visited classes on at least 140 days. The regular visits to the classes made it possible for him not only to mentor the teachers and give them suggestions for their work—he also learned to know the children. One of the most remarkable things about the transcripts of the teachers' meetings is that he seems to have recognized each child who was mentioned. Over the course of the five years that Rudolf Steiner was able to be involved in the school, over a hundred children were spoken of in the meetings. These moments, when the child was placed in the middle of the faculty's consciousness, were the heart of the meetings. Some children came up four or five times. In time, all the children were also examined by the school doctor, Eugen Kolisko, who was able to introduce observations concerning the children's constitution and health.

Steiner's example set the tone for the work in the meetings. His motto was that each teacher had to find an intense relationship to each child by learning to know and understand them.

> Work psychologically! If you think about it, you will understand what I mean. You shouldn't get stuck on the idea that the children need to achieve this goal or that goal, but rather ask yourselves what the children can achieve based on their psychological constitution. Work completely out of the children! You can only get in the habit of this if you cultivate a true striving to understand the child in all of his or her different variations. Each child is interesting!...
>
> To understand psychologically how the children truly are is something one can only achieve through a difficult path of study. This is something I think we must focus on after this first year: Learning to understand the children. Don't take it upon yourselves to think that they should be like this or that. (300 & 1)

It is often apparent in the teachers' meetings how Rudolf Steiner defended the children against the judgments and notions of the teachers and the parents. He repeatedly counseled the teachers to deal with certain misbehavior with humor. He also pointed out the consequences of false conclusions on the part of the teachers. "It is a catastrophe if the children believe the teachers do not see the truth. We cannot be complacent about this; we must see to it that the children do not think we are judging them unjustly. If they believe this, we needn't be surprised when they act up" (300 & 2).

In one case a girl in the sixth grade, whose parents didn't live in Stuttgart, ran away from the people with whom she was staying, because, among other things, the mother had spoken about her disparagingly. Rudolf Steiner defended the girl.

> Are we an institution for the sole purpose of the appreciation of good children? The children are not how one thinks they would like them to be. The story just proves that Ms. N., with whom she is staying, has no notion of the child.... We have the task of educating the children, not to merely treat well-behaved children. This situation shows that we can't send children to Ms. N.... It is really annoying that someone would say something like that about a child. 'Strumpet' is

so inane that it is impossible to find a word strong enough to describe it.... The girl has an excellent character. (300 & 3)

In situations like these, Rudolf Steiner was always an advocate for the children; he usually understood the mischief and tomfoolery, poor performance and lack of interest quite well, and he reminded the teachers of their responsibilities as well as pointed out their failures. In many of the missteps of the students, he recognized errors on the part of the teachers.

All in all, the development of the school went well. It began in 1919 with twelve teachers and 256 students in twelve classes. By 1924, there were forty-seven teachers and 784 students in twenty-three classes. Beginning in 1920, the upper classes were added, and, because of the large number of students, parallel classes had to be formed. The faculty began to expand during the course of the first year. Dr. Eugen Kolisko came from Vienna to join the faculty as the school doctor; he also taught, developing a new approach to teaching chemistry and giving classes in human development. Dr. Karl Schubert, also from Vienna, took on the task of developing a class for children in need of extra care; Helene Rommel taught handwork; and Edith Röhrle and Nora Stein came to teach eurythmy.

During the first two years, the teachers' work was enthused by the pioneering situation. There was a special magic in this new beginning. Rudolf Steiner was, however, aware that such an undertaking as risky as creating an independent school would constantly need new impulses. In many ways the Waldorf School was the only school in the educational reform movement—as a non-anthroposophist put it—that brought new impulses in every aspect of education. Not only was it a coeducational school and not only were there block lessons, but with eurythmy, practical skills classes, handwork (for boys, too!), and gardening new courses were also introduced. English and French were taught beginning in the first grade. New teaching methods had to be developed to make this possible. Teachers taught independent of textbooks. They each had to develop their own syllabi and curricular materials. In addition, they governed the school themselves.

This was not only new and exciting, it was arduous and demanding. Rudolf Steiner faced the challenge of constantly rekindling the enthusiasm. He did this not only in the teachers' meetings but also through lectures that he gave exclusively for the teachers. At the beginning of the second school year, he gave four lectures, now published as "Deeper Insights in

Education" in *Balance in Teaching*. These lectures contain, when compared to the introductory course held a year earlier, completely new content and perspectives. During the teachers' meeting that followed these lectures, Steiner called the faculty's attention to the fact that the spiritual research behind the content presented both during the introductory course and the lectures they had just heard had in no way been easy, and that what he had presented must not merely be accepted on authority.

> We are just at that stage of the evolution of humanity where it is essential that a greater and greater number of impulses of freedom should be brought into the world by people mature enough to do so. If we work as teachers should, then what will bring progress into the world from the realms of the spirit must on no account be received by way of any soul-compelling authority. Ideally, everything must be received on the strength of goodwill and the listener's insight and the feeling that the person who is speaking has something to say. (300 & 1)

Through such remarks concerning his own position as a spiritual teacher in the faculty, Rudolf Steiner indicated, on the one hand, how he understood this position and, on the other hand, he made it clear that he was dependent on the willingness of his colleagues to listen. The esoteric impulses of Spiritual Science were thus given to a specially selected yet completely free circle of people.

At the beginning of the third school year, Rudolf Steiner again gave a series of lectures for the teachers. This time there were eight lectures focused primarily on questions of how to structure the lessons, how to work with the block lessons, the inner relationship between the various lessons, and the question of a spiritually appropriate approach to teaching science. At the end of these eight lectures, Rudolf Steiner turned to the good spirits guiding the school, saying:

> Help us, bring living spirit among us, let it pour into our souls, into our hearts, that our work might be good. If you can bring to feeling experience what we speak about at the beginning of the year, then you will also have an intuitive sense of the intention connected to these presentations. Therefore, let me place a short meditation at the end of these lectures. The meditation should be: "We wish to work, by letting flow into our work what from out of the spiritual world strives in soul-spiritual and bodily ways to become human within us." (302)

Rudolf Steiner hoped that the core faculty of the Waldorf School would become an organ of the spiritual world. One can picture in this community of individuals, which strove to raise itself to the spirit and to work out of the spirit, the archetype of a truly modern community. The faculty was without question a worldly community—not a monastic order with strict rules and continuous oversight, not a brotherhood of shared vows, separate from the world, but a group of free individuals, each of whom approached life in his or her own manner.

This freedom also had its problems and a shadow side. Although after two years Rudolf Steiner was able to say "that the methods and the methodological approach in teaching has made notable progress" (302), he also had to admit that although the children appeared to have understanding for what was being taught in any given moment, "it has not reached the level where what is taught lives on, that it becomes a part of the child's being, so that they can bear these things with them into life the way we sometimes earnestly tell them to" (302).

What bothered Steiner the most was the tendency by a number of teachers to constantly lecture the students, interrupting their flow of instruction only to pose apparently Socratic questions, most of which addressed banalities. Clearly these teachers had no idea of the method of teaching through discovery, or they didn't know how to apply it. The students sat through these monologues with separate roles—primarily in the upper classes—listening passively and awaiting for every lesson to bring a new sensation. "This is what is actually being cultivated. They are not learning to do anything, just to take things in" (300 & 2).

In March 1922, there was an inspection by the school department. The teacher complained bitterly to Rudolf Steiner about the lack of understanding and the criticism from the inspectors, and they discussed the possibility of confronting them through a publication or newspaper article. Six months later, Rudolf Steiner received the report submitted by the inspectors to the Ministry of Education. He spoke about it in the next teachers' meeting.

> Reading this report was very unpleasant for me. From what you had told me, I was under the impression that the report was written in an openly unsupportive, censorious manner. The report is well-meaning! I have to say that everything I read was right on the mark—for instance, that we aren't concerned when the children continuously

copy one another's work. *What is written in this report is true, that is what is so bitter!* You gave the impression that he had been critical and unsupportive. But the report is written in such a way that it is clear he doesn't want to harm the school. It is natural that he writes as though we are ruining the children. Then it's clear we will have to deal with the consequences when what is, in principle, sound is applied badly. What is good must also be applied well. What we need is a certain enthusiasm, a certain inner engagement. This has disappeared little by little. (300 & 2)

Rudolf Steiner was in no way inclined to reject justified criticism of the school, no matter where it came from. On the contrary, he knew what the problems were and took the criticism seriously and made no attempt to deflect it by pointing to higher considerations.

This remained apparent in the ensuing years. He spoke frankly and quite openly to the colleagues, who, to some extent, were living in a world of noble illusions. One of the teachers was, for instance, told the following: "I had so little approval for what you were doing in your lesson that I find myself unable to take responsibility for it. You have to excuse me for speaking so frankly since you have disappointed me in this. After having visited your class, I cannot take responsibility for what is happening there" (300 & 2).

The question of discipline was of special concern over quite a period of time. In the summer of 1922, Steiner was forced to admit that the faculty "was unable to handle" the upper classes (300 & 2). They had not been able to connect inwardly with the students, who had "become too much for" the faculty (300 & 2). He faced a similar situation a year later. He told the faculty that it was necessary to live the idea of the Waldorf School "with greater excellence and character."

> We must not deceive ourselves about the fact that our students (this is a trade secret) know too little to support our claim that the Waldorf school provides eighteen-year-olds with what they need to have learned. They do not know enough. It has not been possible to achieve our goals with a large enough number of students. (300 & 3)

It is characteristic that Steiner approached the problem from a spiritual perspective. To overcome the crisis, he called the teachers' attention to how they were preparing their lessons. He requested time and again that the teachers prepare themselves intensively. The lesson content must be so well prepared that the teacher does not have to concentrate on it and can focus all his or her attention on how it is presented (300 & 3). For this reason, as long as Rudolf Steiner was involved in the school, he made sure that the teachers had enough time to prepare. A language teacher, for instance, according to Steiner, had enough to do when teaching 16–18 hours weekly.

Under in-depth lesson preparation Steiner did not include only the factual preparation of the content. This was something, in his opinion, fairly easy; sometimes he gave teachers a course that lay beyond the boundaries of their own expertise asking, for instance, a natural scientist to teach history. He was more concerned that the lesson content truly come to life in the teachers. Teachers had to be convinced and enthusiastic about what they presented. Everything depended on such enthusiasm, born of a sense of the significance of what was to be presented. Teachers who lived with what they were bringing to a class created—whether they tried to or not—expectations that served to give the students guidance. Students perceive from the soul how earnestly a teacher lives with the subject and behave accordingly.

> The question of discipline is primarily one of good, methodological preparation. This applies to all the subjects and classes. It is a question of preparation. Perhaps we must look at the question of whether there is enough time to prepare. It is possible, as many have said, that there is not enough time for proper preparation, but this is the problem. We can simply acknowledge that in the Waldorf school in-depth preparation is needed, that one has difficulties with the content when standing in front of a class. The students become aware of this immediately and feel that the teacher has no authority. That's where the problem begins. (300 & 3)

Another difficult problem had to do with the challenge of re-seeing the lesson content from an anthroposophic perspective. The Waldorf School was not founded to merely pass on the materialistic perspectives of the time to the students. Anthroposophy was there to help students, for instance, come to true observation and through this to understanding of natural phenomena, to an understanding that led into the inner realities of nature and its formative forces. Dr. Eugen Kolisko was working on developing such an approach to chemistry. All the teachers faced the challenge of transforming the lesson content. There was, however, the danger that Anthroposophy could simply, in a completely unpedagogical manner, be used as lesson content. From Steiner's perspective, this missed the mark completely (300 & 2) and it pained him when such things surfaced. He spoke about it to one teacher: "Herr X, there are some things that you just mustn't misunderstand. I was flabbergasted when you began to speak about the *Chemical Wedding* today in class. I said that you could do this for yourself, to get an idea of the development of spiritual life. But you just laid it all out there in class" (300 & 2). And a little later: "The other danger is that one becomes too anthroposophic, like Herr X. I was sitting on needles hoping that yesterday's visitors wouldn't think the history lesson had become too religious. It is not okay to just give history a religious orientation. That's what the religion lessons are there for" (300 & 3).

Steiner took a stand whenever he noticed that "too much Anthroposophy was being brought into the lessons" (300 & 3). The Waldorf School was not meant to be a parochial school; Anthroposophy was only to be present in the methods and in the transformation of the lesson content aimed at making the content more approachable and understandable for the children.

Another point that concerned Rudolf Steiner had to do with organization and governance of the school. This had two sides. The school had been organized as a republic of independent teachers, in which each teacher gave freely of him- or herself in the lessons and took responsibility for what took place there. School governance in a narrower sense had a specific form—there was an administrative council and questions were worked through in the faculty meetings. In all administrative questions, Steiner was very careful to work within the structures and processes that had been put into place. Beyond this, the most important thing for him was that the teachers could work harmoniously with one another. He didn't expect "that everyone would like everyone else equally." But when it came to the basic human questions, "Pure harmony must rule here" (300 & 2).

When he noticed at the beginning of 1923 that there were cliques and ill will arising among the colleagues, and as in the teachers' meeting unpleasant undertones became audible, he tried to initiate an open dialogue. He pushed them to select a committee mandated to make a recommendation as to how the school should govern itself. At the next teachers' meeting, the committee presented its suggestions and proposed a three-person administrative council. No sooner had this been presented, when another teacher spoke up and suggested a fourth member of the council. Rudolf Steiner facilitated the discussion concerning this new suggestion. It was clear that he wanted the colleagues to speak frankly and truthfully. It was clear to him that the suggestion to expand the three person council was in no way naïve and pointed to the underlying politics alive in the faculty. At first he hoped that the colleagues would recognize and voice the effect of this suggestion to expand the council. When this did not occur, Steiner emphasized sharply the formalities of the process and requested "that we learn to speak responsibly. What is on the table is that the committee was newly chosen. We can expect that this committee made its recommendation after weighing the options responsibly.... We don't want to cast their work to the wind! But that is what happens when a counter-proposal is made and the faculty gives a vote of no-confidence. Accepting Y's proposal is a vote of no-confidence for the committee" (300 & 2).

It was inconceivable for Steiner that the conflict would be swept under the carpet simply to maintain the appearance of harmony. He pushed for an honest discussion. "There are things going on in the background and underground, I have no doubt about that." He pointed out that it was not possible to avoid disharmony by closing one's eyes. "Is it impossible for people to say, 'Look, I have this or that in my heart against you'? It doesn't hurt anymore; it wouldn't make you not want to work together. Why shouldn't we speak the truth among ourselves and still continue to value and respect one another?" (300 & 2).

The situation was brought to a close using parliamentarian forms. The recommendation of the committee was discussed and brought to a vote point by point. Finally, a vote was taken concerning the recommendation as a whole, since, in Steiner's words, it wouldn't hurt "to accustom ourselves to a certain precision by applying the parliamentary forms. We need this precision among ourselves" (300 & 2).

Although many things improved, there were problems and difficulties throughout the period Rudolf Steiner would be involved in the school. As someone who lived with very little sleep, was full of initiative and was energized by the work he did, Steiner found it hard to understand when some teachers began to show signs of tiredness. At one point he said to the faculty, "You're stuck in your seats; you're tired. An individual can't be tired if he is to live in the spirit. To be tired is to be uninterested."

He was also disturbed by the lack of moral contact between the upper school teachers and the students (300 & 3), and that the lecturing had not ceased but in fact increased (300 & 3). He intended to give a new impulse

(300 & 3), and during the last meeting he would be able to have with the Waldorf School teachers, in September 1924, he announced that, during the first week of October, he wished to give a series of lectures concerning the moral aspects of education and teaching (300 & 3). During the same meeting, he remarked that in light of their intellectual and spiritual development, the students seemed to have been brought quite a distance and that they were deeply connected both with the school and with their teachers.

In fact, the Waldorf School, in spite of all its difficulties, was a model that sparked a good deal of interest. Given the situation at the time, this interest did not make itself apparent in the teachers' colleges, among the tenured professors, or by the educational authorities. It arose among the teachers themselves. There was an exception to this. In Basel, Switzerland, the Department of Education invited Steiner in 1919 to give a lecture on *Spiritual Science and Education.* Following this lecture, a group of about 60 teachers got together and asked him to give an entire course about Waldorf education. This took place in Basel from April 20 to May 11 for teachers from the city and the surrounding region. The course was received warmly. At the end, the speaker for the participants thanked Steiner and remarked that if he were the head of the Swiss Department of Education, he would make Dr. Steiner the head of the teachers' college, for Steiner had the right spirit to enthuse and get these young teachers going.

There were two further pedagogical courses in Switzerland: in 1923 in Dornach and in 1924 in Bern. Teachers from the Waldorf School made contributions in both courses. In 1923, Caroline von Heydebrand, Hermann von Baravalle and Walter Johannes Steiner were there. They did not only make their own presentations, but were available throughout the course for questions and discussions. In this they created a bridge to Rudolf Steiner's work for many Swiss teachers. The presence of these teachers who had put Steiner's thoughts into practice was proof for the colleagues from the Swiss public schools that it was possible to realize these sweeping thoughts in a human context. Eugen Kolisko joined his colleagues during the 1924 course. Once again, the discussions showed that Waldorf education was of great interest to the Swiss educators.

The fruits of this work became visible only after Steiner's death. In Switzerland, the anthroposophic educational impulse was developed further in very original ways, especially methodically.

There was also interest for Steiner's educational work quite early on in England. The English educator Millicent MacKenzie, professor at University College in Cardiff, traveled with a large group of interested teachers and educators to Dornach at Christmas 1921 to attend a specially arranged course of sixteen lectures. During this course, Caroline von Heydebrand, Walter Johannes Steiner and Ernst Blümel, from the small school that had been formed at the Goetheanum, each gave two demonstration lessons. As a result of this conference, Rudolf Steiner received an invitation to speak at Oxford the following summer.

In Oxford, something took place that had not happened to Rudolf Steiner during the entire tenure of his work in Germany. His lectures were held in the venerable town of Oxford, with its rich past and wealth of traditions, in an academic setting. The conference was held under the patronage of the English Minister of Education. Professor Findlay, a well-known psychologist, made the introductions. And an entire committee of honoraries, to which both Professor MacKenzie and a principal named Jacks belonged, greeted Steiner ceremoniously in their gowns. The English press reported on the conference at length. The *Manchester Guardian* summarized the results of the conference. "Our complicated, ponderous civilization demands a richer and freer flowing in of foundational spiritual impulses. Such a carrying in of the spiritual can take place only through the new individualities who are born into the world and who can fully develop their abilities there" (*Manchester Guardian*, Aug. 31, 1922).

Other newspapers, such as *The Nation, The Athenaeum,* and *The Oxford Times*, published similarly ingenuous reports. Toward the end of the conference, a committee for free education and pedagogy was formed with the goal of founding an English Waldorf school; and a school in King's Langley decided to incorporate ideas of Waldorf pedagogy. Although the realization of these took some time, it was clear that the anthroposophic educational impulse had reached England.

After the successful conference at Oxford, Rudolf Steiner was invited to return to England for educational lectures in 1923. This Holiday Conference took place in Ilkley, Yorkshire. Once again, a number of teachers from the Waldorf School accompanied him. Caroline von Heydebrand, Julie Lämmert, Hermann von Baravalle, Karl Schubert, and Erich Schwebsch spoke, and Steiner was able to report with satisfaction, "The Waldorf teachers have been very successful with their evening lectures and discussions" (263 & 1). Concerning his own intentions he wrote, "I do my best to let a living picture of what a Waldorf lesson is like come about through my lectures. It appears that there is a good deal of understanding" (263 & 1).

It pleased Steiner to no end that the president of the conference, Margaret Macmillan, was an active, practical educator who had, on the one hand, in Deptford near London built up a home for around 300 children out the most impoverished circumstances and, on the other hand, just published a book entitled *Education through Imagination*. Rudolf Steiner was deeply impressed by this encounter. In an article for the *Goetheanum*, he described Margaret Macmillan and her work. "She strives to observe the unique details of the child's inner life with true pedagogical genius. The book is a treasure chest of wonderful observations of the child's soul and of pedagogical tips derived from these observations. A chapter such as "The Child as an Artisan" can only be read with the deepest satisfaction" (*Goetheanum*, vol. 3).

On the trip back from Ilkley, he took time to visit Macmillan's home and described what she had been able to achieve with the abandoned children she had taken from the street. "You can see, as the care begins to take effect, spiritually alert, happy, healthy, decent young human beings in the different classes. It is just as pleasing to watch these children play as it is to watch them at learning, eating or at rest."

About Margaret Macmillan, he wrote, "To hear this woman speak about the social challenges concerning the education of the children of the poor is a powerful experience" (*Goetheanum*, vol. 3).

Unreserved acknowledgement for every aspect of Macmillan's work speaks out of each line of the article. Without any question, the visit to Deptford, where 300 years earlier Shakespeare had performed for Elizabeth I and where he could sense the spirit of Macmillan's sister Rachel, who had died in 1917, in each and every room, made a deep impression on Rudolf Steiner.

He spoke to the Waldorf teachers in a more differentiated manner about her work. He recommended that every teacher read her book. He called attention to the excellent empirical descriptions of psychological phenomena and added:

> The upper layer of the soul, in as much as the soul brings forth imaginative forces, is presented in a very interesting way. An excellent

description of the soul of the child, yet she doesn't know the forces out of which it arises. I believe that when the underlying ideas are provided out of Anthroposophy, what has been described could be illuminated nicely, and that anyone who is working anthroposophically can discover many things in this book. (300 & 3)

Rudolf Steiner almost never spoke about the new education movement. He never mentions names like Georg Kerschensteiner, Berthold Otto or Maria Montessori in his lectures, and we do not know whether or not he was acquainted with their writings. He does mention the Jena pedagogues Theodor Vogt and Wilhelm Rein and speaks positively of the organizer of the conferences on artistic education, Alfred Lichtwark. On a visit to Haubinda, he spent time in a Lietzian boarding school, but was not impressed by what he saw.

It is an open question as to why Steiner did not find a connection to the best representatives of the new education movement. We can find a partial answer in his interest in Macmillan's work. He could connect with her work because she had a well-founded anthropological approach toward understanding the soul of the child, even though it was largely descriptive. He focused primarily on this anthropological aspect of her work; it was only certain methodological inventions that failed to interest him. Steiner's intention in the development of Waldorf pedagogy was not to present new methods and principles; he strove to develop an educational approach based on an in-depth understanding of the nature of the human being and human development.

In 1924, Rudolf Steiner gave his last pedagogical course in England for the teachers of a planned school outside of London. They were the last pedagogical lectures he gave before he died. In the last lecture, given on August 30, 1924, he summarized the fundamental ideas of his pedagogical approach in a very short and simple way:

Formative education = before the change of teeth;
Enlivening education = between the change of teeth and puberty;
Awakening education = following puberty. (304a)

The school that was in planning and for which these lectures provided a spiritual preparation did come into being. It opened in 1925 and was the first Waldorf school in the English-speaking world.

The Independent Waldorf School

On September 9, 1923, a small school began in The Hague. At first, there were only three teachers with a total of ten pupils. Steiner visited the school from November 14 to 17, 1923, to meet with the teachers and visit their lessons. He expressed interest in individual children and took steps to insure that the teachers received a real salary. They had been working for nothing. In the summer of 1924, he returned to Holland to give a course on Waldorf education. Here he spoke for the first and only time in a public lecture series about the significance of an understanding of karma and destiny in education, in order to show how such an understanding can live within the educator's consciousness and bring insights that can help prevent illness and support health. The Waldorf school movement in Holland grew out of the seed that was planted here and expanded further after World War II.

In Germany, where in addition to the school in Stuttgart two further initiatives, in Hamburg and in Essen, had begun, both of which Steiner could only guide from afar, the first large education conference took place in April 1924 in Stuttgart. There were some 1700 participants. These were Rudolf Steiner's last public lectures in Germany, and they were received extremely well. The applause at the end of the conference went on and on, and many teachers left with impressions that remained with them for the rest of their lives. On the stage of the Gustav-Siegle House sat the teachers from the Waldorf School, and in front of them the slender form of Rudolf Steiner, who was already quite ill. He spoke, however, with fiery energy and ended the lectures with the verse:

> Bind yourself to matter
> And souls as dust will scatter.
>
> Find yourself in spirit,
> And human beings are united within it
>
> Behold yourself in humanity
> And worlds are built that gods began.

As Steiner's health deteriorated, he was unable to travel and was confined to his studio in Dornach. He was only able to advise the teachers in certain personnel questions. Students from the school sent examples of their work to him on his sixty-fourth birthday. He thanked them in writing. On March 25, 1925, he wrote to the faculty of the Waldorf School, saying that all the decisions, of which until now he had been part, would now have to lie in the hands of the faculty. In this letter, we find the sentence: "The Waldorf School is a worrisome child, but it is also a symbol for the productivity of Anthroposophy within the spiritual life of humanity" (260a).

Although there were many things in the Waldorf School that gave rise to worry, much had already been achieved. Primarily, the faculty had grown inwardly to the point that Steiner could hope they would be able to guide the school out of the spirit of anthroposophic pedagogy. With a second official letter, he placed responsibility for any further school wishing to work with the Waldorf approach in the hands of the Waldorf School faculty. They took this responsibility seriously, investing time and effort selflessly for as long as possible. Steiner's death gave the teachers impetus to deepen their own work. When the school authorities visited the school again in October and November 1925, they were quite positively impressed.

> Anyone who comes in contact with the Waldorf school recognizes immediately that a unique group of teachers is leading this school. Their connection to one another appears to be exemplary. They serve each other in love; each radiates energy and receives energy in return; there is no indication of trivial in-fighting, jealousy, or envy....
>
> The students sincerely love their teachers, who, rejecting all forms of physical punishment, work to form the body, soul, and spirit of each child entrusted to them through love, goodness, and wisdom and their own exemplary actions. (*Nachrichtenblatt*, 1926)

The incredible effort that Rudolf Steiner invested in the new pedagogy had begun to bear fruit. We can't forget that Rudolf Steiner was never able to work with a circle of individuals as intensely as he worked with the teachers of the Waldorf School. He gave roughly forty lectures exclusively for them. There were also seminars, the teachers' meetings and, in addition, the three science courses with forty-six lectures. Teachers had the opportunity to participate in conferences in Dornach, Stuttgart, The Hague, and Vienna, and some of them contributed to the large pedagogical courses. They were able to experience Steiner's educational thinking in different contexts. Thus, the new pedagogical impulse became rooted in many hearts. For Rudolf Steiner, anthroposophic pedagogy was not only something important to him, it was a field of work where he could give his best because what he had to bring was met with interest and understanding.

After Rudolf Steiner's death in 1925, the number of Waldorf schools grew gradually. Before they were closed by the Nazis in 1938, there were sixteen Waldorf schools, eight of which were in Germany. In 1969, fifty years after the founding of the Stuttgart school, there were eighty schools worldwide. By 1996, there were over 600. Today, there are some 1500 schools worldwide in settings as different as the Upper Eastside of Manhattan and the townships of South Africa.

Chapter 41

COMMERCIAL VENTURES

The commercial ventures that were initiated in 1920 present us with a number of riddles. It is not easy to understand Rudolf Steiner's position in this connection. When it became clear in 1924 that the business would have to be liquidated at considerable loss to the shareholders, Rudolf Steiner wrote a letter to the shareholders of the Futurum, Inc., saying, "Why did I ever say 'yes' to these ideas? Because if I had done anything beyond warning them of the possible outcomes, those who took the initiative would perhaps now say we could be providing the Goetheanum with a steady stream of income. I *had* to give them the opportunity to show what they could do" (260a).

He also wrote that he felt the people who had come to him with the idea had abandoned him, and concerning his position as chairman of the council: "It was with the greatest reluctance that I agreed at that time to serve as the chairman of Futurum, which was not one of my initiatives. I received no support from the initiators of this venture. My warnings fell on deaf ears" (260a).

The warnings that Steiner voiced before the founding are well-documented. He reminded them just before the formation of The Coming Day [*Der Kommende Tag*] of the words he had spoken when Emil Molt first approached him with the idea of such a commercial venture. "I have to say, I am not as worried about obtaining capital...as I am about finding the people who will be able to work with it in appropriate ways" (unpublished address).

In the same vein, Oskar Schmiedel recalled Rudolf Steiner speaking with his employer Dr. Roman Boos, a Swiss lawyer who was involved in the plans to found the Futurum Company. "You will not be able to find the people you need." Dr. Boos answered, "Yes, I have them already." Steiner did not reply and let Dr. Boos do as he chose (Zeylman's, *Wegman III*). In other words, Rudolf Steiner recognized quite clearly the central challenge that would live on, accompanying the new venture. And he didn't merely let the initiators do as they chose; he invested a good deal of time and energy and put his own name on the line to help this highly risky venture succeed.

But why? With this venture, Rudolf Steiner gambled not only his own reputation but also the relatively large sums of money that people invested based on their trust in him. Shouldn't he have at least slowed things down, or even withdrawn his support as he clearly seems to have recognized the shakiness of the undertaking? The reason given in 1924—that it was necessary to give the initiators opportunity to show what they were capable of—doesn't really answer this question and is not entirely convincing, since Rudolf Steiner did not only warn and speak out against proceeding, he also supported and encouraged the initiative. In any case, it doesn't explain why Steiner became so deeply involved with something that, in his own words, he did not want to be involved in.

There is no question that Rudolf Steiner, out of an initiate's consciousness, tried to give his coworkers freedom to work and gain experience. Did he also feel obligated to take responsibility for them, to accompany and guide them on the paths they had chosen? Had he misjudged certain people? Were there other considerations that took precedence, which pointed to the necessity of founding such initiatives?

On October 12, 1919, after the opening of the Waldorf School and his first trip to Berlin and Dresden since the end of the war, Rudolf Steiner gave a remarkably serious lecture in Dornach, in which he spoke of the decadence and decline of the old forms and emphasized that future progress for humanity was only possible through strong cultural impulses. Toward the end of the lecture he called attention to the Goetheanum, which was still not completed, and said:

> It's not going to work if we continue to make do with small steps, if we don't work consciously to convince humanity of the need for a new spiritual culture. This alone can be the origin of a new social culture. Social culture can no longer be drawn out of economic relationships, it must be impressed upon the economic relationships from out of the spirit.... The Dornach project should actually be viewed as the point of departure for a great worldwide movement, which is completely international and embraces all aspects of spiritual life. (191)

When Rudolf Steiner had finished speaking, Emil Molt stood up and addressed the audience, which for the first time since the war contained friends from Scandinavia and England. He suggested that they form their own commercial ventures to provide the necessary funding to support the work at the Goetheanum. Steiner's response pointed out the lack of people who could do this.

But Molt's suggestion was discussed further in the ensuing months, and, in November 1919, Rudolf Steiner drafted a paper outlining "Leading Thoughts for a Planned Venture." In these leading thoughts is a key to understanding Steiner's relationship to this initiative. They begin with the word *necessary*, a term that must be seen against the backdrop of the time.

In light of the failure of the threefold movement to achieve any of its outer goals and the slow deterioration of the political and economic situation in Germany, Rudolf Steiner spoke on October 3, 1919, about the critical situation in Germany. "For Central Europe it is a question of life or death, the life or death of the folk culture" (191). In the October 12 lecture mentioned above, he summarizes a longer passage, saying: "The earth has entered into its period of decadence and the civilization that still remains is deteriorating with it" (191 & 121). Something with the forces to form something new had to be placed in contrast to these tendencies of decadence and decay, not only for the Goetheanum, not only for Central Europe, but for the world as a whole. This is where the term *necessary* arises. "What is necessary is the creation of something like a bank with the goal of serving commercial and spiritual initiatives whose goals and practices are aligned with an anthroposophic worldview" (24).

He recognized the necessity of creating a type of bank through which capital would be made available for certain initiatives and ventures. It was not meant to operate with a focus on maximizing its profits, but was to serve the initiatives and provide the needed guidance and counsel. "The banker should see him- or herself less as a lender and more as a person involved in business who can assess the magnitude of an undertaking in need of financing and, with a sense of the realities involved, set up the framework within which it is possible for the undertaking to succeed" (24).

The ventures that would be supported by the bank would in turn work together and support each other associatively. Within these associations, spiritual life would need to be cultivated in such a manner "that people with appropriate abilities would be brought into positions where they can use their abilities in a socially productive manner." The financially healthy organizations should help carry those that only later "will bring the spiritual seeds planted in them to economic flower." The idea was, for example, to support and advise someone who had an idea that promised to lead to economic profit and healthy social results.

Rudolf Steiner was, however, also thinking about the Goetheanum. It had been founded at a time when there was still, to some extent, old inherited wealth available. These funds were no longer there; a new form of financial support had to be found.

> Support for what is central to the anthroposophic movement has to be placed in the center. For example, the building in Dornach will not in the beginning be able to support anything, but it will produce enormous wealth, even financial wealth, at some point in the future. We have to awaken people's understanding that they can support the work here with a clear economic conscience if they can be patient when it comes to returns. (24)

It is important to keep in mind that the Goetheanum was not conceived as a church supported by the tithes of the members. Steiner expected Anthroposophy to become economically viable in various fields and "that individuals connected [with the Goetheanum] would initiate ventures that could support themselves, provide salaries for those who carry them and still have something left over to help cover the budgetary deficit always connected with a spiritual initiative" (24).

In the "Leading Thoughts" there are a number of additional remarks that indicate that Steiner hoped through founding this bank-like venture to seed a new, healing economic culture, The Coming Day and the Futurum, Inc. were to be such organizations. If one takes the goals Steiner describes for these ventures, it is easy to understand why he thought it would be difficult to find the right people.

On New Year's Eve 1919, there was a meeting in Stuttgart to discuss the founding of such a bank-like venture. During this meeting, at the request of Emil Molt, Rudolf Steiner decided to become involved in the founding and become chairman of the advisory council. He spoke about the change of direction that this step represented on March 3, 1920, during a study evening on social threefolding. After the failure of the threefold movement in 1919, it became necessary to find other ways to convince people of the practicality of the threefold idea. "We must at least make the attempt with institutions that are conceived primarily as financial institutions… to create models through which people can see that our ideas can be realized practically and desire to emulate them, because they can believe what is in front of them even if they couldn't believe what we thought we were telling them so convincingly" (unpublished).

Steiner was interested in a new economic culture and the founding of The Coming Day was to be a step in the creation of such a culture, one that would fight against the one-sided focus on profit and profitability, where individuals and companies would work together objectively, advising and supporting one another and then also including the consumer. On March 11, before the stock company was founded, he emphasized that the entire venture would rest on the people who became involved. The challenge was to not focus on the impersonal, on certificates and recommendations, and to not simply try to implement programs, but "to recognize in a circle of individuals the productive gifts and abilities, to [work with] the living stream of life."

The Coming Day, a stock company formed to support economic and spiritual values, was formed on March 13, 1920, in Stuttgart with a start-up capital of 300,000 German marks. Rudolf Steiner invested 20,000 German marks, so he was not simply involved in the principle. The company attracted further capital relatively quickly. On September 16, the working capital had reached ten million German marks, and by April 1922, it had reached a total of fifty-three million German marks. When noting these amounts, one must keep two things in mind. In 1920, German marks still had some value: forty marks equaled one dollar. Inflation increased first in 1922 and then became astronomical in 1923. Although inflation was definitely a problem, The Coming Day soon had considerable resources in the form of factories, goods, real estate, etc., at its disposal, resources that retained their value in spite of the inflation.

At first Konradin Hausser, Hans Kuhn, and William Trommsdorf were given responsibility for the operations. Of these, Konradin Hausser proved later to be a successful businessman. But all in all it quickly became apparent that the three men were out of their depth. During the first year, Eugene Benkendorffer was hired as general director, but he too was replaced in September 1921 by Emil Leinhas. The rapid changes in the leadership of the company indicate that it wasn't the money but the people who were the primary problem.

It is naturally easy to criticize people after the fact. It is important, however, to recognize that most of those who became involved in this venture found themselves facing completely new challenges for which they were not prepared. The fact alone that, instead of a patriarchal, dictatorial organizational structure, they were trying to work collaboratively and make all decisions as a team was a completely new way of working for them and the cause of much irritation. There was no one there who had any experience in working collaboratively. The burden of responsibility came to rest squarely on Rudolf Steiner. He found himself continually having to coordinate, give advice and guide the decision-making processes. These burdens did not merely affect him outwardly. In 1924, he mentioned, without pursuing it in depth, that certain things that had been born out of the womb of the Anthroposophical Society had brought "also inwardly in an esoteric sense a difficult time" over the society (240).

If we take these remarks seriously, they give us some indication of Steiner's personal situation. Already during the threefold campaign he had written Edith Maryon, "There is much work that weighs upon me. It is work, in which each detail must be thought through" (263 & 1).

This seemingly innocent remark shows that Rudolf Steiner had to spend time thinking about the outer work; it made significant demands on his time. These demands grew after the founding of The Coming Day. The use of time and effort is not only of outer significance. In a lecture given on June 24, 1920, in Stuttgart, two months after the founding of The Coming Day, Steiner spoke about the problem of time and pointed out that the truly valuable work was suffering.

> It suffers mostly because it always seems necessary to have endless debates about decisions that could be resolved in half an hour, because things are allowed to get mixed up in the discussion that shouldn't be there. If you were to stop wasting time, you could probably do what you now do in ten hours in one hour. In today's so-called practical life, time is beaten to death. And what is caused by this beating time to death is that the thoughts get torn asunder. One actually has the feeling...that one is constantly in a noodle factory, where the thoughts that should be focused and concentrated are always being pulled apart like the noodle dough.... It is dreadful to encounter these thoughts that have been torn asunder, what we call today practical life. (197)

This description, which is symptomatic for the situation in The Coming Day until the end of 1923, shows what Rudolf Steiner experienced personally. He could also have said: Time for my own work is constantly being stolen from me. The experience of the fragmented thinking that ruled the meetings and discussion was exacerbated by the fact that it left too little time for spiritual work. Steiner noted that it was necessary to fight for a balance "between life in meetings" and the spiritual work that was the basis for everything.

> We will not be able to do this, however, if things continue as they have, if people come and tell me, "Something terrible has happened again; there is someone who had a bad opinion of everything and is a bad influence on everyone else." That may be, but it has not yet happened—although these things happen constantly when I am here—that I have been able to follow up on something like this and have the second person tell me the same as the first one. And when I reach the fifth or sixth person, they tell me exactly the opposite of what the first person said. I am simply relating the facts. I don't want to criticize anyone. I am not scolding or praising anyone, but this is how it is. What has to grow in our anthroposophic work is an absolute sense of the truth. It is very difficult to continue to work in this context if there is not a strong foundation of truth—direct, real truth. (197)

It is not as if Rudolf Steiner's colleagues were dishonest or deceitful. They experienced the events, of which they were a part, differently and often neglected to reflect upon their own experiences and interpretations of the events and to let the facts themselves speak. In any case, the differences between his colleagues took up more of Steiner's time; he had to clarify the events and accusations in private conversations with the individuals involved. In addition, there were the running operational questions, which were at times also difficult.

Steiner was concerned that the new venture would devour both his time and energy and that of his colleagues', as well as "the spiritual movement from which it sprang." Early on, he called attention to the dangers posed by the forays into practical life. "But if we don't mange to bring about change in certain areas, they will devour the original source of the anthroposophic movement. And then in accordance with the will of those who have become responsible for this spiritual movement, we will have a new form of materialism in that the spiritual movement is cast off. Spirit needs to be cultivated if it is not to die" (197).

With the words "original source of the anthroposophic movement," Rudolf Steiner is also referring to himself (240). From a spiritually realistic point of view, Steiner's decision to connect himself intentionally—with clear consciousness—with these outer tasks was also a spiritual reality. Steiner referred to this a number of times, although with a great deal of reticence. He once voiced the situation that he was not able to do his own work because people were constantly bringing him detailed questions, then making decisions concerning the primary problem, leaving him to pick up the pieces in a neverending flow of meetings (*Aufbaugedanken*). Concern for these outer tasks, however, came to demand so much of Steiner's time that he finally spoke up and said:

> This is not being voiced simply to complain about these things, but because individual forces are being used up that should be working on other tasks. Of course, we have to do these things if no one else is going to do them. And since they take time, it is clear that the spiritual work is going to suffer and won't be brought to the level it should achieve. (*Thoughts on Construction*)

This is one aspect of the esoteric difficulties that overcame the anthroposophic work due in part to the expansion of the outer activities. The anthroposophists left Steiner with responsibility for everything, with all of the problems—and Steiner accepted this responsibility because he understood what would happen if no one tried to shore up the work of the anthroposophic ventures. This led to his spiritual forces being used up by worries about money, the conflicts that flared up among his colleagues, and the problems that arose through their lack of competency.

Although this appears to have been evident to Steiner, he continued to allow himself to become involved in these projects and to place his capacities at their disposal, even though ever since the anthroposophic work had begun to bear fruit in more outward activities, he had had to shoulder the lion's portion of the responsibility. As chairman of the advisory council, he was certainly not obligated to concern himself with all the details, but he did so. For, as he mentioned in 1920, "we have embarked on undertakings that must not fail, that must succeed. There can be no mention of the possibility of failure; we have to say: They will succeed" (197).

He acted upon this conviction. When it was necessary to acquire properties for The Coming Day, he traveled throughout Württemberg accompanied by a team of real estate experts to view various properties that had been put up for sale. He pondered where and how anthroposophic insight could be helpful. He suggested developing a medicine to fight the outbreak of hoof-and-mouth disease that was affecting the cattle in that part of Germany, giving indications on how to prepare the medicine, and was involved in the first trials in Dischingen. He helped put together a selection of works for the publishing house connected with The Coming Day and wrote the foreword for the catalogue. In Switzerland, he traveled to Bönigen to inspect a cane and umbrella factory that was to be acquired by the Futurum, Inc., then on to Bern for further business meetings. Much of Rudolf Steiner's work was not documented, but we can assume that he paid as much attention to the details as he could. This all took place alongside his other activities: his visits to the Waldorf School, meeting with representatives from anthroposophic study groups from near and far, the eurythmy rehearsals, his speaking tours. He wrote to Edith Maryon from Stuttgart on June 23, 1920. "What is missing is a team of goal-oriented, skilled people. Such people are almost impossible to find. An undertaking of this magnitude, as we have begun here, weighs heavy upon the soul; it doesn't matter if one is more tired or less tired. Some things just have to happen" (263 & 1).

Besides laying the foundation for a more humane economic culture, the second goal connected with the founding of The Coming Day was to "support spiritual values." To achieve this goal, Rudolf Steiner financed scientific research, a therapeutic clinic in Stuttgart, and, at times, the Waldorf School through The Coming Day. The work in the research institute was focused on physics, chemistry and life science. In supplement to the company's prospectus in December 1921, the research projects in physics were described. It had been possible through the development of sensitive apparatus to "discover new chemical phenomena, especially in the field of photo-chemistry, which behave similarly to earth magnetism and static electricity. This experimental research illuminates the connection between earthly processes and those in the universe and could under certain conditions soon be of the utmost practical significance."

In the chemistry department, work was being done on producing more radiant colors and the development of a peat fiber for textile production. It is characteristic that Rudolf Steiner encouraged this work enthusiastically and often visited the research institute, which was close to the Waldorf School. Unfortunately, most of the projects never progressed beyond their early phases, because, in Steiner's opinion, they were not pursued with enough energy (259).

The life science work that was headed up by Lili Kolisko did achieve more significant results. She has related how Rudolf Steiner supported her work. Once they faced the challenge of finding a certain phenomenon on microscopic samples. Steiner examined the various samples and discovered in one the phenomenon they were seeking. Lili Kolisko recalled that at first she was unable to recognize the phenomenon and Steiner had had to teach her how to find it and even photograph it. She received ever-new indications from him, which she followed up on with enthusiasm and persistence and which led to, among other things, her developing a chromatographic method through which otherwise invisible phenomena could be made visible (*Gäa Sophia*).

The work of the clinic and therapeutic research institute that was opened in Stuttgart in the summer of 1921 was "not to be in opposition to the justifiable views of modern medicine, but rather an enhancement of the same." On the one hand, the clinic served a large number of patients who were ill or otherwise in need of medical attention. It was also a research facility for the development of new medicines. There were four doctors who joined the clinic: Dr. Otto Palmer, Dr. Ludwig Noll, Dr. Felix Peipers, and Dr. Friedrich Husemann. Steiner visited the clinic regularly, participating in the consultations and a large number of therapeutic indications. The medicines that were developed in this manner were produced at a larger scale in Schwäbisch Gmünd, the home of what would later become the Waleda factory.

Steiner was, however, not content with the work of some of the researchers or the Stuttgart doctors. For instance, he requested that the doctors write a medical *vade mecum*. It was never written. In Steiner's opinion, the doctors, although they were certainly well qualified, lacked the spiritual energy and strength to rise above the crowd. He spoke his criticism frankly beginning in 1922 and even, in the case of Dr. Friedrich Husemann, published it. We will return to this somewhat later. Steiner experienced the tentative nature of the doctors' work and their inclination to seek the approval of mainstream medicine in opposition to him personally. He wrote to Marie Steiner, "There has been more blatant opposition from the doctors than from anyone else in the society" (262). And he reproached them for "wagging their tails for the scientists." "We don't need to have any pretensions that the professors at the university will praise our *vade mecum*" (259).

After it became apparent that, due to the economic difficulties of 1923/24, the commercial ventures of The Coming Day would neither be in a position to support the spiritual/cultural initiatives, nor would they be able to inaugurate a new business culture, and because the research work in physics, chemistry and medicine was not progressing, Rudolf Steiner withdrew from the stock company, although it was not doing at all badly from a financial perspective. At the end of May 1923, he wrote to the members of the Anthroposophical Society in Germany that the ventures "had [arisen] in an absolutely justifiable manner out of the intentions" of the initiators. It was understandable that they wished to "see me involved in the leadership of these institutions. I obliged them although I was aware that taking on this obligation would divert me for a time too strongly away from my own task of cultivating the core of the anthroposophic work. Now I find I must be firm in saying that from here on I can only work within the core of anthroposophic life with its artistic and pedagogical manifestations" (259).

During 1924, a number of gifts made it possible to separate the most productive areas of the spiritual/cultural initiatives, such as the Waldorf School, the biological research institute and the pharmaceutical concern, from The Coming Day, and to place the clinic in Dr. Palmer's name. Following these steps, The Coming Day was liquidated, which meant that the commercial ventures that had become a part of this venture were, for the most part, returned to their former owners.

The Swiss company Futurum took quite a different course. In Stuttgart, the situation was such that there were anthroposophic entrepreneurs like Emil Molt, Emil Leinhas, Jose del Monte and Carl Unger with concerns that could cooperate with one another. This was not the case in Switzerland. Emil Molt and Dr. Roman Boos first had the initiative to found Futurum. Boos was a lawyer with some background in economics but without any business experience. Later it became clear that he was not completely healthy; phases of extreme activity were followed by deep depressions. Beginning in the summer of 1920, he headed up the secretariat in Haus Friedwart and at thirty-one found himself in the middle of everything that was happening in Dornach.

It is not easy for a historian to reconstruct the events surrounding the founding of Futurum. We have to assume there was a wish to have a financial instrument able to support the work at the Goetheanum outside of

Germany, where the currency was becoming increasingly worthless. It isn't clear, however, whether Roman Boos had Steiner's approval for his plan to found a stock company or informed him after the fact. Arnold Ith, who later headed up the company, recalled that Roman Boos asked him at the beginning of 1920 if he would be willing to lead a bank-like venture. Ith, who at that point was the editor-in-chief of a Bernese newspaper, declined. Boos didn't back off. He sent Ith a copy of Steiner's "Leading Thoughts," which were mentioned above. In the middle of February, Boos visited Ith in Bern and got him to agree to come to Dornach to discuss the question. The meetings ran over three days. Ith recalled later:

> On the third day, I met alone with Rudolf Steiner in his studio. I had not been able to decide whether to accept the position I had been offered to head up the new venture. Dr. Steiner asked me, "How old are you now?" I replied, "Thirty years old." He responded, "If someone had offered me such a position when I was thirty, I would have accepted it joyfully." At that point, I decided to take on the responsibility that was being offered to me. (*Nachrichtenblatt*, 1965)

Two months later, on April 26, 1920, Rudolf Steiner spoke in Basel in conjunction with the annual trade show and announced that in Switzerland a company patterned after The Coming Day—to support commercial and spiritual/cultural initiatives—was in the process of being founded (334).

From the middle of March to June 7, Rudolf Steiner was in Dornach, then until the end of July in Stuttgart. While Steiner was away, the Futurum stock company was incorporated in Dornach under the auspices of Roman Boos. Boos had managed to recruit a number of experienced businessmen, among whom was Johann Hirter, the president of the council of the Swiss National Bank in Bern, to be members of the council of the new company. Rudolf Steiner was named *in absentia* as president of the council, the person legally responsible to head up the work. Roman Boos was chosen as vice-president.

There are documented indications that Rudolf Steiner was not in agreement with these decisions. He said himself that he had accepted the presidency of Futurum, an initiative that did not originate from him, "with the greatest reluctance" (260a). Albert Steffen recalled a conversation in 1922, in which Steiner remarked that he had never wanted to initiate this venture (*On Spiritual Paths*). Pieter de Haan related that Steiner had complained that no one had asked him if this was what he wanted, and he "had to comply"—if he hadn't it "would have failed from the get-go" (*Mitteilungen*, 1982).

On the other hand, the fact is that Rudolf Steiner let himself be convinced by Roman Boos to open the Goetheanum and begin the "high school" courses and gave him free rein in planning the festive program. On the evening before the ceremonies to open the Goetheanum, September 25, 1920, Rudolf Steiner gave a talk, during which he spoke not only about the history of the anthroposophic work, but also about Roman Boos, praising his work.

> Dr. Boos, the founder and leader of the Swiss Threefold Committee, is more than anyone else the one who had the strength and initiative to bring about the work we will begin tomorrow.
>
> One would have to, in a certain sense, be completely convinced of the necessity of enriching all scientific, artistic, and social life through Anthroposophy. One would have to be armed with the ingenuity to wed absolutely clear, crisp thinking with the intuitive sense that what flows through the stream of Anthroposophy can truly bring to science what is needed. Then one must have the kind of holy fire that enables one to serve such an undertaking. This has happened in a manner, for which we cannot thank him enough, through our friend Dr. Roman Boos, and we have him to thank for these anthroposophic university courses, which we will begin tomorrow.
>
> Naturally, it would not do to forget all those who have contributed richly to this venture and worked to make it possible, but a driving force must be present in everything. And this driving force, I'd like to say, must be a social impetus. This is what we have had with this undertaking, and I could only wish that we could have many more initiatives with Dr. Boos; then we would certainly make some progress! (*Blätter für Anthroposophie*, 1955)

When one reads these words today, spoken as they were without the slightest restraint, it is difficult to imagine that Steiner was not in agreement with Boos's actions at the time they were spoken. Nevertheless, anyone who is familiar with Steiner's inner position knows that it was less important for him to be in complete agreement with everything his colleagues were doing; he focused on the enthusiasm, the intention, and initiative, which for him was sacred. He supported the initiatives of his students even if he was not completely in agreement with them. In *Intuitive Thinking as a Spiritual Path*, we find the maxim: "To *live* in love of action, and *to let live* in understanding of the other's will, is the fundamental maxim of *free human beings*" (4, p. 155).

It is also possible to assume that Rudolf Steiner had in some ways become resigned. He pointed out clearly that the Goetheanum had not been consecrated, merely opened, because the work done in the university courses did not reflect its true intention. He resisted ceremoniously opening the Goetheanum (36). But one thing is certain: He did not try to block Roman Boos's activities. Those who heard him speak must have had the impression that he completely supported Boos's work.

Like The Coming Day, Futurum was able to raise quite a bit of money quickly. The problem was how to use the money wisely. Profitable companies had to be acquired. To do that quickly was difficult, and it was here that the problems began, although Steiner also reviewed the companies in question. An old knitting factory, an umbrella and cane factory, an import/export company for southern fruits, a glue factory, a packing company, and a company specializing in office equipment were acquired. In the case of a number of these concerns, the calculations were completely off. Molt wrote of the situation with the import/export company. "The administrative director was frivolous, and the export of oranges and lemons to Denmark resulted in loss upon loss. Most of the produce was rotten by the time it arrived" (Molt). The sum paid for the office equipment company was too high and sales languished in the poor market conditions of Switzerland at the time, the packaging plant had almost no customers, and the umbrella and cane factory had to close shortly after Futurum acquired it. In short, the commercial enterprises were losing money.

At the end of May 1921, Roman Boos fell into a deep depression and had to resign his position in Futurum. On June 28, 1921, Johann Hirter, who could assess the situation correctly, also resigned.

The two pharmaceutical laboratories in Arlesheim where anthroposophic medicines were developed, the clinic that Ita Wegman had founded on her own in June 1921, and the publishing house at the Goetheanum where the weekly *Das Goetheanum* was published had also been incorporated into Futurum. In Stuttgart, Rudolf Steiner had insured that these spiritual/cultural initiatives received financial support. The directors of Futurum had little sense of the significance of these initiatives, which were in many ways financially sounder than the commercial ventures. They had thus to grow on their own merits. The clinic took out bonds, and Ita

Wegman raised the initial capital for the "International Laboratories AG" (ILAG), which later became Waleda.

In March 1922, things came to a head. During the annual general meeting of the company the directors, Arnold Ith and Emil Oesch, resigned after reporting on the desolate situation of the company and left the meeting. Rudolf Steiner, as president of the council, suddenly found himself alone, as Emil Molt, who also had had a leading role in the company, was not present for the general meeting. The situation became dramatic. Finally, a new council was formed comprised of Willy Storrer, Willy Stokar, Edgar Dürler, Karl Day and two men who had been on the council—Ernst Gimmi and Christian Krebs. Rudolf Steiner resigned as council president.

Ita Wegman, director of the clinic, immediately took the initiative, dissolving the connection between the clinic and the laboratories and Futurum and, by issuing new stock, expanded both concerns. It soon became clear that Futurum would have to be liquidated. What became apparent was that the company had used up most of its resources. A number of the stockholders renounced their claims in favor of the Goetheanum; others received stock in ILAG. ILAG, which later became Waleda, separated itself from the clinic, issuing stock valued at 450,000 Swiss francs. This was exchanged for Futurum stock, so that the laboratories shouldered most of the burden of the liquidation. It is worth noting in this transaction that a concern, which arose out of anthroposophic initiative, made good the losses that ensued when the purely commercial ventures folded.

It is also important to take note of the fact that the members of the Anthroposophical Society made significant sacrifices through the liquidation of both The Coming Day and Futurum. In the case of the former, funds were made available to support the Waldorf School and the research work in Stuttgart; in the case of Futurum, to cover the liabilities brought on by the directors of the company. By doing so, they helped Rudolf Steiner out of a very unpleasant situation, which had come about due to his respect for others' freedom and initiatives. His understanding of his role as a spiritual leader, who lived in trust of his colleagues' initiatives and sense of responsibility, forbid him taking command. In 1924, he looked back on the situation and said:

> It came about after 1918 that the situation was used by all sides to do one thing or another. If I had said, "This must not happen," today it

would no doubt be said, "If he had let it happen, we would be surrounded by flourishing projects."

For this reason it has been the case throughout time that the leader of an esoteric movement let what his followers wanted to do prove itself and let the reality of the situation speak through the facts. This is the only possible way to convince anyone. It also had to happen in this situation. (260a)

Although this process was painful for Rudolf Steiner, in the long run the impulses, which had been given in anthroposophic research, in medicine and in therapy, bore fruit many years later, and fifty years after the first attempt to form a "bank-like" concern, this idea has been taken up in different countries. The ideas and impulses, which were to bring about a new form of economics, did prove themselves. The seed that was planted then has begun to bear fruit today.

Chapter 42

THE NEED TO COMMUNICATE IMPULSES FOR CULTURAL RENEWAL

In the middle of June 1920, Rudolf Steiner read the first volume of Oswald Spengler's book *The Decline of the West*. This book, which at the time was discussed widely, especially among young academics, impressed him deeply and he spoke about it often over the course of the next three years. Like a cool scientific observer, Spengler foresaw in his diagnosis the complete decline of Western culture toward an end in widespread barbarism.

Steiner responded immediately, speaking about Spengler's book in a public lecture in Stuttgart on June 15, 1920. If everyone were to think that Western culture was doomed, "then it will in fact be doomed! That's why I believe this is a terrible book. Anyone who is infected with these ideas, which are taken in with honest intentions, must become a servant of this decline out of the utmost depths of one's soul. One must wander on paths of the soul that lead into the abyss" (*Drei Gegenwartsreden*).

Directly upon his return to Dornach, he spoke about Spengler's book to the members there. Again he emphasized that one must take this book, which had been inspired by a scientific mode of thought, seriously. "It would be frivolous to view such things superficially" (198).

The doomsday diagnosis from Spengler was neither new nor a surprise. In a number of early articles from the 1880s, Steiner too had described the tendencies toward decline apparent at the time, but he did not number among those who could only praise the past and disparage the present, and he certainly wasn't a prophet of doom. His work was dedicated to renewal, and although, especially after 1917, he had warned that certain tendencies threatened to lead things into chaos, he did so in order to call attention to the need for new spiritual impulses in civilization. In reading Spengler, he recognized immediately that the unredeemable position taken in this book would hasten the decline. No doubt Spengler was one among many symptoms, but it was the destructive nature of the time that came to expression through him. After the second volume of the work appeared in August 1922, Steiner addressed it in three in-depth essays (36).

From the very beginning, Rudolf Steiner wanted to place the possibility of action out of freedom up against one-sided scientific thought focused on casually necessary processes. One needed to counter the enormous pull of what was in decline with something more than simple idealism. The threefold impulse was not focused on any specific reform, but rather on the renewal of social relationships through insights originating in the spirit. Since the beginning of 1920, he had warned "that the present poses humanity questions that can only be answered out of a science of initiation" (196).

The necessity of impulses for modern culture arising out of a science of initiation became a key theme in his lectures. He repeated often:

> I have tried to show how in the course of human development humanity has reached the point where it needs...a science of initiation. This means it is necessary that the academic branches of human cultural life become permeated by this Spiritual Science, and, secondly, that the way we think and feel about the nature of being social becomes permeated by the feelings and emotions that arise in the human soul out of a consciousness that there is spiritual revelation, suprasensory revelation—one needs but to turn toward it. (196)

When Steiner spoke for the first time about Spengler's book in Dornach on July 2, 1920, this theme was also apparent. "Today, whoever makes the effort to truly become acquainted with what lives in social life, politics and in culture life, and recognizes the forces of decline inherent in it, will have to admit, if he is aware of Spiritual Science as it has been spoken about here that healing is only possible if the wisdom of initiation streams into human development" (198).

These words were not merely meant diagnostically. He had suggested to certain anthroposophists, who seemed suited to the task, that they train themselves as initiates (Tautz). Now that the Goetheanum was well on its way to completion, it was imperative that Steiner have a circle of individuals surrounding him who were seriously striving toward initiation. He could prepare the members of this circle and, in inner attunement with them, give the work at the Goetheanum the direction it was meant to have.

Rudolf Steiner made an attempt to re-institute the esoteric training he had put to rest at the beginning of the war. Details of this attempt were not documented. But members of the Anthroposophical Society were invited on Sunday, February 9, 1920, to participate in an esoteric lesson. In a very earnest lecture given the preceding evening, Steiner tried to shake up his listeners and closed with the remark that—pictorially spoken—no one would have any bread if it were not possible to re-found the earthly institutions out of the source of a new spirituality. "Think about it. It is a very serious situation" (196).

Apparently the announcement concerning the reinstitution of the esoteric lessons led to widespread discussion and criticism. It seems that some individuals wished to invite people who had no objective interest. Steiner found himself having to point out at the beginning of the lesson that he had at the very least hoped the older members would refrain from the otherwise ubiquitous forms of discussion and criticism. There was a lack of the necessary earnestness. A second esoteric lesson was held on February 17. Following this lesson, Steiner put the attempt to rest.

The facts speak for themselves, and Steiner undoubtedly spoke about his reasons for discontinuing the lessons only to a few trusted colleagues. There is a second series of events related to this. In the summer of 1920, after the seating for the Goetheanum hall had been completed, the time had come to open the Goetheanum. It was unthinkable that they could let the still unfinished yet now usable building simply stand empty. Curiously enough, what seemed obvious—that Rudolf Steiner would take this in hand, create a program and invite speakers—did not occur. Instead he handed the initiative over to Dr. Roman Boos and gave him complete freedom in organizing the event. Steiner had apparently decided to hold himself back completely in order to see how firmly rooted Anthroposophy had become in the people around him.

Roman Boos enthusiastically organized the entire conference. He invited the speakers, worked to formulate the themes, and determined the program for a three-week long series of higher education courses. There were more than thirty speakers involved, each of whom was to talk about his field. There was time set aside for discussion, but the arts were pushed into the margins (comp. Kühne & Lauer).

A new generation of anthroposophists appeared at this conference. Only three people who had been involved since the early years—Elisabeth Vreede, Adolf Arenson, and Carl Unger—played an active role in the courses. Most of the speakers were representatives of a middle generation who had become members of the Anthroposophical Society between

1907 and 1914. Among the youngest speakers were twenty-seven-year-old Eugen Kolisko, twenty-four-year-old Rudolf Meyer, and twenty-two-year-old Herman von Baravalle.

Rudolf Steiner had apparently insisted that there was to be no talk of "consecrating" the Goetheanum; the courses marked the "opening" of the building. Lili Kolisko remembered the "opening ceremony" on September 26, 1920. "Whoever had the fortune to be present at the opening was certainly left with an enduring impression. The music from the organ and orchestra that rolled like waves through the room, the festive anticipation of the almost thousand people, the sea of colored light, the wonderful murals on the cupola and the words of Rudolf Steiner, which sounded forth out of a deeply moving place" (Kolisko).

The opening must, in fact, have been a deeply moving event. Marie Steiner gave a recitation, and Roman Boos, Richard Seebohm, Emil Grossheintz, Emil Molt, and Carl Unger all spoke. Rudolf Steiner gave a short address weaving science, art and religion together again. He began with the words: "My heart is moved to speak these first words in this Goetheanum. For the solemn goal that this still unfinished building will serve in the future stands before my soul" (*Waldorf Nachrichten*, vol. 3).

What no one at that time noticed was that he spoke neither of his joy nor satisfaction that the building could finally, after the seven-year construction period, now be used. What stood before his mind's eye was the goal the building would serve in the *future*! Later, after the Goetheanum had burned, he admitted that something in him had "resisted ceremoniously opening the Goetheanum himself on the occasion of the higher education courses. The program of talks offered then was not appropriate for such an occasion. It should have happened in conjunction with an event that was completely in harmony with the idea from which the building originated. This never happened" (36).

The opening of the Goetheanum was a painful process for Steiner. In a number of the lecture cycles and in the evening discussions, he experienced a disharmony between the usual style of discussion in the scientific community and the forms of the Goetheanum.

> Owing directly to the lack of harmony I've described during the first conference, the Goetheanum is closely tied to the destiny of the anthroposophic developments of recent years. The first lecture series revealed itself as something that did not arise organically out of the

same source as the building. It was something that was brought into the purely anthroposophic space. What happens in the outer reality of human interaction does not always take the path of what is required out of the inner conditions of a spiritual context. (36)

If we translate these words, through which he expressed his feelings and experiences with a great deal of restraint, into a concrete situation, we see Rudolf Steiner sitting in the front row of the great auditorium listening to the lectures. Time and again, he experienced not only harmony with the forms of the space around him in the words of the speakers, but also the dissonances between word, thought and the interior of the building.

> I let my spiritual gaze wander over the way the interior architecture, the painting and the sculpture corresponded to what the speakers proclaimed from the lectern. And I discovered (it wasn't necessary at that time to mention it to the people) that everything that in the best sense of the word was an anthroposophic tableau, that was spoken out of Anthroposophy, agreed most wonderfully with the style of the building. But with quite a number of the lectures, there was the feeling that these should actually only be given once a series of auxiliary buildings have been built following designs that correspond to these specialized studies and presentations. (257)

Most important, the Goetheanum, as the independent School for Spiritual Science, was not meant to serve general scientific endeavors, not even Goetheanism. It was to be a place of spiritual schooling, of initiation. He sensed that the building was in danger of being diverted from its actual task.

Rudolf Steiner let little of his concerns come to light. Toward the end of the course, he did request that the satirical "The Song of Initiation" (40), which he had written in 1915 during a crisis of the society, be included in the eurythmy program. This could have been a sign for anyone who was acquainted with Steiner.

Rudolf Steiner gave six lectures on the *Boundaries of Natural Science* during the first higher education course. When compared to the lectures he gave before the war, a number of significant differences are apparent. During the years before the war, he was able to speak to audiences where people were open to taking in grand spiritual vistas, the results of spiritual research. Drawing on his own experience, Steiner spoke of spiritual beings, Christ, and the life of the soul after death. During the first higher education course and in the public lecture series that followed in 1921 and 1922, he found himself speaking to people who were more scientifically oriented. Thus, the lectures on the *Boundaries of Natural Science* became a methodological introduction to anthroposophic research. He led his listeners to the boundaries experienced in natural science and scientific thinking, and then went on to show how anthroposophic knowledge crossed these boundaries. In addition, he gave three talks about the Dornach architectural impulse and one together with Marie Steiner on the art of declamation.

As a whole, the higher education courses did not, in Steiner's view, show that all the contributors had been able to live up to the expectations posed by Anthroposophy and the times. Yet he did not waver from his efforts to bring anthroposophic insight into civilization and to widen the perspectives of scientific thinking, even though it was clear to him that he lacked capable colleagues. For example, during the higher education course, he made the suggestion to found a World School Association to support anthroposophic pedagogy on a wider scale. "The Waldorf School is wonderful; but founding the Waldorf School has really accomplished nothing in this field. It is just a small beginning. Just the beginning of a beginning. The school has really only been founded if in the next three months we manage to lay the groundwork for ten further Waldorf schools" (*Menschenschule*, vol. 46).

He suggested founding, for instance, such a World School Association in Holland. It could work to awaken interest for the new pedagogical impulse in Western Europe and raise the needed funds now no longer available in Germany. The intention behind a World School Association was not only to raise money for further Waldorf schools, but to create a financial basis for a free spiritual/cultural life, and, especially, to support the work at the Goetheanum.

Steiner spoke again about this idea in Holland in February 1921. He emphasized that the Waldorf School should not come to be thought of as an isolated school stuck away in some pedagogical corner, existing merely "at the mercy of the government." This impulse would only then bear fruit when anthroposophic pedagogy was brought out openly into the world in a large way. The idea met with no echo, rather "concerning the need for a World School Association..., even in the widest circles, everyone continues to sleep a gentle sleep" (76).

During the last week of the higher education courses, an Association for Anthroposophical University Studies was formed. It was focused on university students and kept contact with the anthroposophic student groups that formed on various campuses. Here, too, Steiner encouraged the participants to think big. "In conclusion, I wish to ask that you do not undertake these things in a separatist or sectarian manner, but with largesse. Do not turn anyone away; include everyone who wants to participate. The only determining factor should be the will to honestly engage in the kind of work we want to do" (217a).

The association was given an office in Stuttgart and made efforts to come into contact with the various student groups, but the work never really came to life. It is, perhaps, however, due to this work that about 800 students attended the anthroposophic higher education courses in Stuttgart in March 1921. Rudolf Steiner spoke about "Observing Nature, Experiment, Mathematics and the Stages of Knowledge in Spiritual Research." He wrote about his lectures in a letter to Edith Maryon. "All in all, the students who are present have been quite receptive. But one always has the feeling that in such a short time one can give people so little that it is very difficult for them to form their own judgments. And that is what is really important" (263 & 1).

Participants at this course remembered Steiner attending most of the events and, when things got difficult, stepping into the discussions. He participated in discussions concerning the theory of relativity, Asian painting, and synthetic geometry; he gave an extemporaneous talk on Dante and added a lecture concerning the outbreak of World War I into the schedule.

A third course followed in April in Dornach. The theme was "Anthroposophy and the Special Branches of Science." Reflecting on the lectures given during this course, Steiner noted that the lectures given by anthroposophic scholars showed "definite progress" when compared to those given in the fall of 1920. But the evening discussions were, in his opinion, "terrible" (*Aufbaugedanken und Gesinnungsbildung*).

Although he was forced to acknowledge, based on the feedback that was given in the discussions, that such courses were apt to call forth misunderstandings, because the younger participants came in the hope of finding Anthroposophy—not anthroposophically embellished science—Steiner continued to place himself at the service of his colleagues' intentions. Three further courses followed: the lectures on *Anthroposophy, the Roots of its Knowledge and its Living Fruits* during the Stuttgart congress entitled "Cultural Effects of the Anthroposophical Movement" from August 28 to September 7, 1921; the "Anthroposophical Higher Education

Course" from March 5 to 12, 1922, in Berlin; and the "*Anthroposofisch-Wettenschappelijke Cursus*" from April 7 to 12, 1922 in The Hague. One could also add the "West-East Congress" that took place from June 1 to 12, 1922, in Vienna to the list of large presentations of anthroposophic work to the general academic community.

These courses were not planned and organized by Rudolf Steiner but by active anthroposophists who were convinced that they had to present Anthroposophy as a spiritual focus, which embraced all the various fields of knowledge publicly. From the report Rudolf Steiner gave of the Berlin course (81), it seems apparent that he saw clearly how questionable this undertaking was. On the other hand, he was able to note after the Stuttgart congress that the earnestness with which anthroposophic speakers—primarily Caroline von Heydebrand—addressed contemporary questions had made a deep impression on the more than 1600 participants.

Based on the experience gained after two years of these courses, Steiner spoke about them to representatives of the younger generation in February 1923. "I won't say anything at all to question their value. But these courses were a misunderstanding. You were not looking for what was spoken in them. You were seeking Anthroposophy itself. Those scholars who entered the Anthroposophical Society earlier couldn't understand that. They wanted to unite their academic work with Anthroposophy. *You* could not accept that" (217a).

His academic colleagues wanted to bring Anthroposophy as science to the world; Rudolf Steiner saw other tasks. Although he had stepped back from the threefold campaign in Württemberg in August 1919 and no longer involved himself in the daily struggle for these ideas but left this work to others, the necessity of social threefolding remained unchanged in his soul. He engaged himself openly in the work through articles he wrote for the threefold journal and with lectures on various topics pertaining to social threefolding. As was mentioned above, the commercial ventures were to be models for anthroposophic social practices.

From the summer of 1919, political life had perhaps not become more stable but was definitely less mobile, and it was difficult—if not impossible—with the limited resources available, for the threefold movement to find a point of leverage. There were naturally a whole range of questions to which one could speak, but no one was paying attention. In November 1921, a last possibility opened up to gain an audience. Moritz Bartsch wrote a letter to the office of the Threefold Association in Stuttgart for a group of Schlesian anthroposophists in Breslau. He asked if it would be possible for the threefold idea to play a role in the upcoming vote concerning the national status of Upper Schlesian. In March, a vote was planned to determine whether the region would henceforth belong to Poland or to Germany. Either way would bring tension to the area, leaving an ethnic minority dominated by the ruling majority.

Rudolf Steiner was at the office of the association when the letter arrived and Bartsch's request was passed on to him. Karl Heyer recalled his response: "Dr. Steiner was extremely positive about the initiative of the threefold group in Breslau. He was strongly supportive. I remember how he then and also later explained that it was our task to take a stand with social threefolding where decisions were pending that would provide solutions to contemporary issues. If we could bring threefolding into the discussion in places, upon which the eyes of the world were focused, the world would see the threefold impulse" (*Mitteilungen*, 1962).

In spite of all the negative experiences, and in spite of the minimal chances of success, Steiner embraced this new possibility without hesitation. He was focused on the task and the goal, not on possible objections and reasons to hesitate. He immediately asked Karl Heyer and Dr. Guenther Wachsmuth to draft an appeal for a threefold campaign in Upper Schlesian. But he pointed out that only people living in Schlesian should be involved in the campaign.

The next day, Steiner returned to the office to read through the draft. He was not satisfied with it and proceeded to quickly draft the appeal that he had envisioned. His draft ended with a concrete proposal rejecting either a German or a Polish outcome.

> Upper Schlesian rejects the connection with either of the boundary countries until such time as an understanding for social threefolding has been awakened. The region will organize itself with self-governing economic concerns and self-governing spiritual/cultural endeavors. Unity between the two will be found through a provisory, local legal and policing organization with powers limited to the region. It will remain in this form until the entire European situation has been clarified. (B 93/94)

In other words, Upper Schlesian was to organize itself as an autonomous region in accordance with the threefold impulse. Spiritual, cultural and linguistic decisions, as well as the courts, would be placed within the realm of individual freedom enabling Poles and Germans to live peacefully with and beside one another. The important Upper Schlesian industrial concerns would be given to neither Germany nor Poland.

The campaign began in January, after Steiner had given the handful of Upper Schlesians who were designated as speakers an overview of the historical situation. The threefolders, who traveled from city to city and into the villages in pairs speaking enthusiastically and courageously about their ideas, did not have an easy time. The situation had already become poisoned by the ethnic tensions. A number of newspapers took up their ideas, and they would have perhaps been able to achieve some success if they had gotten started earlier. By this time, they found themselves in a witch's kettle, battling the bitter resistance of both ethnic groups and the Catholic church, which—as was reported—reacted with a wave of hate, especially in response to a series of articles from Roman Boos entitled "Jesuitica" that appeared in the threefold journal.

In the end, the Upper Schlesian campaign became the source for bad feeling throughout Germany. On March 4, 1921, the article "Traitors against Germany" appeared in the *Frankfurter Zeitung*. It accused the Threefold Association of supporting Polish interests. "Whoever does not vote for Germany, even if he merely abstains, works for Poland. The situation is clear; everyone must decide. Thus Steiner and his people are in fact propagating Polish propaganda, just as though they were being paid by Poland to do so" (B 93/94).

This article was picked up by papers throughout Germany and fanned the flames of criticism, which had grown through innumerable articles, pamphlets and lectures by Steiner's opponents over the course of the last two years.

Independently of the campaign in Upper Schlesian, there had been discussions a year earlier, in the spring of 1920, about how it might be possible to awaken interest for social threefolding, given the lack of success of the first threefold campaign. Repeatedly the idea came up that Rudolf Steiner should give a special training for speakers. At first, neither funds nor the people seemed to be at hand. In the beginning of 1921, Steiner's *Threefold Social Order* appeared in a large new edition with a new foreword by the author. In the foreword, he addressed the misunderstandings he had encountered concerning social threefolding in a straightforward, clear way.

Following this preparation, Steiner finally gave a course for speakers from February 12 to 17, 1921. The number of participants is not documented, but according to one account there were about fifty people there. The trainees were slated to speak at venues throughout Germany about Anthroposophy and social threefolding directly following the course. Unfortunately, there is nothing documenting this undertaking. There is no mention of it at all in the journal *Dreigliederung der sozialen Organismus*! There is an indication in a lecture from Steiner on March 11, 1921, that the campaign did take place. He seemed to have placed a good deal of hope in this "strong foray" and said, "The goal of the lectures was, on the one hand, to show how anthroposophic spiritual science could address the great cultural tasks of our civilization and then, out of this, to show how an anthroposophic conviction would affect social life" (203).

At the time he had no doubt only received a few positive reports of the campaign. Later, in 1923, after he experienced the effects of the campaign in Germany, he arrived at a devastating verdict. "There was this speakers' course I gave before a horde was turned loose on the German public. Look at the echo that this invasion caused! Some of the things that were concocted out there surpass everything in their grotesqueness" (259).

Even if one takes into account that the sharpness of this remark may to some extent be colored by the difficulties of 1923, its meaning cannot be overlooked. The last attempt at a widespread campaign to further understanding of the threefold impulse caused a good deal of damage. Although there were no doubt excellent lectures given by some of the speakers, the general response was completely negative.

Steiner celebrated his sixtieth birthday during the lecture campaign. He was in Holland again for the first time since the war had ended, and on February 27, the day his birthday was celebrated, he was in The Hague. He had forbidden any kind of bourgeois celebration; the day was to be a day of work. That morning he spoke to the local anthroposophists, in the afternoon he gave an introduction for a eurythmy performance, and in the evening he gave a public lecture on education, teaching and social issues. In response to birthday wishes spoken before the lecture for the members, he said, "The times in which we live are so grave that it is in no way appropriate to think about personal matters now" (203). He then thanked the "honorable chairman" and came to the point. He spoke about the seriousness of the time, the way it tested one, and the not readily apparent challenges that it posed.

The seriousness of the situation had also begun to affect Steiner personally. Building the Goetheanum in Dornach had made Anthroposophy visible to the world in quite a striking way. Since 1914, when this building project was getting underway, voices had been raised opposing Anthroposophy. In the beginning this was more or less harmless, and they could not be heard above the noise of the war. From 1915 on, a number of ex-anthroposophists—Heinrich Goesch, Max Seiling and Erich Bamler—began to attack Rudolf Steiner personally. In the summer of 1918, a Jesuit named Otto Zimmermann published two articles in *Stimmen der Zeit* attacking Steiner and Anthroposophy. In July 1919, the congregation of the Holy Officium in Rome issued a writ forbidding Catholics to read theosophical books or to join any form of theosophical association. Pope Benedict XV ordered this decision publicized. It was generally interpreted and applied to include anthroposophic books and the Anthroposophical Society.

From the beginning of 1920, after Steiner and Anthroposophy had become widely known through the threefold campaign in Württemberg in 1919, the attacks increased. Rarely a week went by without denigrating articles, pamphlets or lectures. The spectrum of opponents reached from the political far right—Dietrich Eckhart, Adolf Hitler and Erich Ludendorff—to the intellectual left, represented, among others, by Kurt Tucholsky and Ernst Bloch. There were representatives of the churches as well as university professors, and even self-appointed wise men like Duke Hermann Keyserling. There were opponents of Anthroposophy who traveled around the country like Arthur Drews, who lectured in cities from Cologne to Constance. In Dornach, Catholics held what amounted to an "Anti-Theosphy Conference," accompanied with music from the choir of the Arlesheim cathedral.

Some of the writings criticizing Steiner's work were quite objective and serious, such as the pamphlets by Friedrich Gogarten and Georg Hauk. In other cases, a "stand was taken" against Anthroposophy without any regard to facts. The writers claimed Anthroposophy was a mix of the mystical and the Eastern Indian, not anything new, but in any case questionable and bad for one's health. Some of it was secondhand, based on claims made by others of Steiner's opponents. At times, the attacks became intense, with Steiner being openly harassed and slandered. In the German nationalist circles, the most common accusation was that Steiner was Jewish and all of Anthroposophy an insidious Jewish plan. Others accused him of being a priest who had broken his vows. The slander reached a certain climax in the articles published by Max Kully, who was apparently kept well informed of all the Dornach gossip. He wrote about it at length, especially in the second half of the pamphlet *The Secrets of the Temple in Dornach*. One theme that was picked up on by certain right-wing opponents of Anthroposophy was the accusation that Steiner had used esoteric methods to influence the commander of the German general staff von Moltke, brought about the defeat on the Marne, and was thus primarily to blame for Germany's defeat in World War I.

These claims and accusations traveled quickly. Before a lecture on February 28, 1920, in Amsterdam, flyers were distributed entitled "Dr. Steiner, a swindler like no other," written by a Dr. K. H. J. de Jong. Soon after, Kully printed a segment of de Jong's rantings in one of his pamphlets. The attacks made the rounds from Dornach to Holland, Oslo, and Stuttgart with some regularity and made Steiner's work increasingly difficult.

The October 1920 edition of *Der Leuchtturm*, a newspaper published by Karl Rohm, predicted the burning of the Goetheanum. "Spiritual sparks like streaks of lightning snaking toward the wooden mousetrap—there are enough of them at hand and Dr. Steiner would have to be very clever to be able to calm the waves and prevent a real spark from one day bringing the glory of Dornach to an infamous end." Steiner remained aware of these things and knew well that the hidden threats had to be taken seriously since the mood had been so badly poisoned by the frenzy of attacks on the anthroposophic work (203).

A number of Steiner's colleagues took up the torch. Eugene Kolisko, Walter Johannes Steiner, Karl Heyer and Carl Unger, just to name a few, publicly refuted what was being said against Steiner both in their writings and in lectures. Steiner also took a stand against the false accusations in public lectures by speaking about his own background, his training and the development of his ideas. But a number of his opponents like Max Kully, Arthur Drews, Hans Liesegang and Jakob Wilhelm Hauer had little interest in the facts. Their only interest lay in destroying Anthroposophy. During Hitler's dictatorship, Hauer, a professor at the University of Tübingen, believed finally to achieve his goal with Himmler's assistance and through a series of "reports" and letters denouncing Anthroposophy. It seemed as though nothing was too questionable to use in the attempt to discredit Steiner's work.

Rudolf Steiner's sixtieth birthday was also the occasion for a public acknowledgement of his work. Friedrich Rittelmeyer, at the time minister at the New Church in Berlin, in spite of being ill managed to publish a collection of essays entitled "On Rudolf Steiner's Life-Work," honoring various aspects of Steiner's life and work. The authors wrote courageously and openly, without any trace of propaganda or dogmatism. The book was a success, and shortly after it had been published—a seldom occurrence with such books—there was need of a second edition. Steiner was quite moved by the efforts of his friends and later remarked that this book was the best representation of the anthroposophic work at the time (259).

Something similar was attempted within the Anthroposophical Society. A monthly journal called *Die Drei* was founded to bring anthroposophic work into academic circles. Steiner allowed the lectures from his 1909 Munich cycle, "The East in the Light of the West, the Children of Lucifer and the Brothers of Christ," to be printed in the journal as he had edited them and showed thus that he was quite willing to publish lectures given for the members about esoteric topics, as long as he'd had the opportunity to go through the transcripts and correct any errors.

CHAPTER 43

A BROADER UNDERSTANDING OF HEALING

The striving to widen the notion of what healing is belongs alongside the social threefold campaign, the inauguration of a new impulse in education, and the renewal of the arts in the attempt to bring cultural renewal through a science of initiation. Steiner had to tackle this challenge differently than he had in founding the school. There he was able to pull together a number of gifted teachers, acquaint them with the fundamentals of anthroposophic pedagogy, and then guide them in their work. In contrast, anthroposophic therapy was developed in dialogue and collaboration with doctors.

As early as 1905, Rudolf Steiner had been on the lookout for doctors who were interested in expanding their understanding of healing. Then, in 1908, he gave Felix Peipers the first indications for work in the field of anthroposophic therapy. Beginning that same year, he also began to work off and on with Marie Ritter. She produced her own medicines and, at Steiner's suggestion, began to work on a mistletoe preparation for cancer. The quite effective "photo-dynamic" remedies that she produced played a certain role in anthroposophic circles from 1908 to 1914, yet Ritter was not a doctor but a naturopath, who found remedies to heal certain sicknesses in her own unique, inimitable manner. Steiner was, however, not merely interested in developing remedies; he wanted to develop the general foundations of a rational approach to therapy.

When the Munich building project was moved to Dornach in 1913, Rudolf Steiner made himself a note on a scrap of paper: "Dr. Peiper's sanatorium is to be built in Canton Basel Land as a part of the Johannes-Bau project." A center for the development of therapeutic practices was envisioned as part of the School of Spiritual Science from its inception. The war put a stop to these plans, but, in 1917, Rudolf Steiner gave Ita Wegman, who had now been trained as a doctor and was practicing in Zürich, indications for the production of another mistletoe remedy for cancer that she prescribed with some success.

In the winter of 1919/20, the chemist Dr. Oskar Schmiedel, who had worked on the Goetheanum in 1914 and returned to Dornach when the war ended, began to produce remedies under the direction of Dr. Ludwig Noll, a homeopathic doctor. One of them was a flu remedy called Infludo. Schmiedel was not entirely satisfied merely producing homeopathic remedies. He was more interested in genuinely anthroposophic pharmaceuticals.

Because of his own questions about possible remedies, Oskar Schmiedel's interest was sparked when he heard Steiner say during a public lecture in Basel on January 6, 1920:

> Diseases are caused by something. But more important than knowledge of the cause is the process of healing.... Spiritual Science also has something to say...about medicine. Although it is most often denied, the fact is that many thoughtful individuals who have completed their medical studies find themselves in a state of deep despair when they find themselves let loose on the suffering masses, because then it becomes apparent what challenges the human organism presents human insight when it passes from health to disease, and how little is to be gained from the knowledge and methods of a purely scientific approach in trying to meet these medical challenges. (334)

These sentences questioning the validity of a purely natural scientific approach to medicine reflect Steiner's experiences since he first became acquainted with the therapeutic nihilism of the Viennese medical school. Within him lived the certainty that the substances and processes described by science became completely different in the human body. Even in the plant and animal worlds, the substances and their processes were drawn out of the realm of chemistry and physics and placed in a new context. In the human organism, these substances and the way they relate to one another were brought into the realm of ego activity and removed one step further from the laws governing the physical world.

Just as important was the conviction that the primary challenge in medicine is not to determine the causes of an illness, but to find the path to a cure. Diagnosis is certainly important and necessary, but the diagnosis does not alone point the way toward healing. The necessary therapy becomes apparent when one can gain insight into by what means the processes that have come out of balance can be brought back into a healthy relationship with one another. Steiner pointed this out first in 1905 and remarked that the experimental approach to developing cures reflected a lack of intuition (53). Now, in 1920, he went further:

> Spiritual Science must open the possibility of an intuitive medicine. Whoever is able to grant this Spiritual Science credence will understand that today I could only sketch out in generalities, somewhat abstractly, a path toward an intuitive approach to medicine, but also how some of what I've been able to say has already been developed and is just waiting for the official representatives of medical knowledge to come to the insight that it has to be taken up. (334)

After Steiner had then remarked how he would truly love to speak about these things with people who had a good understanding of the questions, Schmiedel took the initiative and asked if he really would like to give a course for doctors. If yes, Schmiedel would like to arrange it. Steiner requested that he organize the course in collaboration with a well-known doctor and suggested the founder and director of the Iselin Hospital in Basel, Dr. Edwin Scheidegger.

This attempt to inspire a wider understanding of the nature of therapy belonged to efforts in 1920 to bring the fruits of spiritual knowledge to bear in the general culture. In this case, the question was not medicine alone. Doctors and therapists did not merely relieve pain and heal disease. The popular understanding of human existence was colored to a great extent by medical understanding. Medicine has a greater effect on an individual's view of himself today than does philosophy. Steiner had experienced this during his time in Vienna, especially during his time with the Specht family. Whether a human being is merely a natural organism or a spiritual individual who can take hold of and effect the body is for the general public in many ways determined by how medicine is viewed.

The first medical course for 35 practicing doctors and therapists took place on March 21 in Dornach. With only three exceptions, all the participants were active in the field. During this course, Steiner took a different approach than he had with the teachers. There he had followed a clearly structured, easily grasped, systematic concept and developed the content of the lectures himself. In contrast, in the first lecture of the medical course, he asked the doctors to note down their questions and interests and hand them in to him. And during the last lecture, he reflected: "These lectures are very difficult for me—then where shall I begin?" (312). Following the introduction, Steiner spoke out of a living inner picture, seemingly without a systematic concept. One participant reported: "As we had been trained in clearly defined anatomical concepts, it was difficult to follow the metamorphoses of what is alive. We came up against grave inner resistance" (Deventer).

As Steiner mentioned at the beginning of lecture 15, in the opinion of a "very competent" observer these lectures were among "the most difficult of all the anthroposophic lectures to understand." Even Steiner had to admit that this was true "to some extent" (312). But as he pointed out pictorially, only through a description of the processes one had to grasp spiritually could one begin to understand the living and gain insight into healing.

In the afternoons, different doctors, among them Prof. Otto Römer, Dr. Edwin Scheidegger, and Dr. Eugen Kolisko, reported on their own work. Dr. Ita Wegman spoke briefly about her work with cancer patients. One afternoon, everyone took the tram into Basel and they were given a tour of the Iselin Hospital by Dr. Scheidegger. The possibility of creating their own institute was very present. Ita Wegman asked Hilma Walter, another doctor, if she would be interested in working with her to found a new sanatorium. Walter said yes. And on one of the last days of the course, Wegman wrote to Ludwig Noll, the most senior of the anthroposophic doctors, asking if he would join her in opening a sanatorium in Dornach or Arlesheim where they could work closely with Steiner on developing an anthroposophic medicine. Noll did not take up her suggestion. But the participants of the course issued a statement demanding the creation of a "medical-scientific research institute."

It seems clear that Rudolf Steiner was searching for a doctor with whom he could work to further anthroposophic medicine. He knew from his own experience how difficult it would be to find someone. The ideas that were propagated in an official medical course of study created "resistance" (262) against contextual relationships, which could be understood through spiritual research. He also didn't think that other established medical groups, such as the naturopaths, would be of much help.

In the summer of 1920, Dr. Noll did come to Dornach to work with Oskar Schmiedel to develop remedies for production. Noll consulted regularly with Steiner and always returned to the laboratory excited and in good spirits. He always brought new recipes, which Schmiedel then, in collaboration with both Steiner and Noll, would refine and produce.

Here, too, is Steiner's desire to develop the new approach to medicine in collaboration with the doctors visible. He didn't only refuse to accept patients himself; he strove to find new forms of working together, as though the future of medicine was dependent upon what lived between the people involved. Thus he hoped that the work with Dr. Noll would lead to a productive collaboration and invested quite a bit of time and energy in it.

He was deeply disappointed when Dr. Noll failed to appear for the three lectures on "Physiology and Therapy Based on Spiritual Science" that were on the program for the first anthroposophic higher education course. He didn't even notify anyone that he wasn't coming. Steiner had to take Noll's place and ended up giving four lectures aimed not at doctors but for the general public.

From April 11 to 18, 1921, there was a second medical course for doctors, dentists and medical students. Steiner called this a supplementary course and focused especially on the way the four aspects of the human organism interrelate and the corresponding remedies. Concurrently, he gave a course on curative eurythmy. As in the first course, other doctors contributed lectures, and a series of discussions took place during the afternoons.

A remark made by Rudolf Steiner during this course sheds light on how he envisioned the work of the doctors. He didn't see them simply developing a diagnosis, then referencing a book to discover which medicine should be prescribed. He expected the doctors would, at least within the context of their field, be able to access a higher form of knowledge.

> Quite often during the imaginative contemplation of how an illness presents itself or of any complex of symptoms, one intuits the appropriate remedy. But one is then tempted to think about what one has understood, to measure it against outer scientific knowledge, and one finds one's initial intuitive response is false. This is a very normal occurrence for anyone who is able to undertake esoteric research, not only pertaining to therapy. When one reflects on one's intuition, one initially questions their validity. What becomes apparent through imaginative research and the intuitions that it leads to is always right if it, naturally, rests on solid understanding. But one's judgment must first raise itself to what one can discover in this manner. (313)

It is immediately apparent that this approach to therapy demands courage on the part of the doctor. The doctor must refuse to follow the generally acknowledged procedures, must have the courage to, after dutiful examination, rely on his or her own judgment, his or her own intuition, and then work to heal each case completely individually. This means the doctor must work to overcome the suggestive power of a purely scientifically oriented approach to medicine. This is not something everyone can or wishes to do.

Following the first course for doctors, preparations began to open two clinics. As was mentioned, one was the medical research clinic in Stuttgart. The Wildermuth Sanatorium on the Gänseheidestrasse was bought for this purpose through The Coming Day. After Dr. Noll elected not to take the position, Dr. Otto Palmer agreed to head up the work there. He had been connected with the anthroposophic movement since 1908 and gave up a thriving practice in Hamburg to take on the new task. "When I took on the leadership of the new clinic, I asked Dr. Steiner about my responsibilities. He replied, 'Build up a movement of two to three thousand doctors.' This answer was almost enough to make me lose heart, if it had not been accompanied and softened by well-meaning words that gave me courage again" (Natura, vol. 1).

This remark gives us some indication of the sweep of Steiner's ideas. The general cultural disintegration that made a correspondingly large countermovement that could disseminate the insights of initiation appeared necessary. This was one reason Steiner worked so hard to make the therapeutic clinic in Stuttgart viable. Rarely did he visit Stuttgart without visiting the clinic—to participate in the consultations, visit the patients and make recommendations. One would then see Steiner, always in his black frock, hurrying through the hallways with Dr. Palmer and another doctor with their white coats flapping as they hurried to keep up. He never hurried with the patients, but listened patiently to whatever they wanted to tell him. Palmer recalled, "Never did one hear the Doctor voice a judgment about the length of an illness, or whether it could be healed or not. Accepting the possibility of a cure was the doctor's first principle, and by giving patients courage and hope it was possible to strike a chord in the soul that could, in resonating, help with the healing" (Natura, vol. 1).

The clinic was also envisioned as a center where medical research could lead to the development of new remedies. Thus, in addition to Dr. Palmer, Dr. Noll, Dr. Husemann, and Dr. Peipers, at times Dr. Ederle and Dr. Knauer were involved in the clinic. Although Rudolf Steiner gave the work on the remedies his utmost attention and was always willing to address the questions the doctors raised concerning the effects of the various ingredients, he did not wish to cultivate interest in the new art of healing by advertising exciting new products. He believed it was necessary for a doctor to publish the methods and principles of an anthroposophically expanded view of the art of healing. In 1920, he had given Dr. Noll the task of writing a *vade mecum*, a guide for doctors. He hoped, after the clinic in Stuttgart had begun its work, that this would soon be published. Soon he had to acknowledge with disappointment that even with the resources of the Stuttgart clinic and although they had met a number of times to speak about the project, this was not going to happen.

The clinic in Arlesheim, which opened just weeks before the Stuttgart clinic, had a different genesis. It was founded through the initiative of Ita Wegman, who alone raised the money to make it possible. Wegman had begun her medical studies when she was thirty years old and already a student of Rudolf Steiner. After she finished her studies, she opened a practice with a clinic in Zürich. Even before she moved her practice to Basel in January 1921, she had purchased a house in Arlesheim where she planned to open a sanatorium. After she had added on to the house and with a little help furnished it, she requested that Steiner come and visit the new institute.

> My heart was beating madly as I showed him the rooms with their different colors—the examination rooms and the offices. What was he going to say? And I will never forget the moment when we walked out onto the balcony from the top floor to enjoy the beautiful view of the Vosges, and Dr. Steiner turned to me and gave me his hand, saying that he wished to work with me and how happy he was about the clinic. He gave it the name "Clinical-Therapeutic Institute" and wanted to begin immediately to work on a project with me. (Natura, vol. 1)

Steiner was certainly impressed with the care and attention to detail that had gone into the house. Ita Wegman had overseen everything, from the curtains in the patients' rooms to setting up the kitchen. More important, although the institute was small, it was well appointed, and all the work had been done without having burdened him with a multitude of concerns and questions. At first, all Steiner could do for the institute was to draw up a brochure as he was leaving again for Stuttgart. One passage from the brochure is worth documenting here, as it brings Steiner's intentions for medicine clearly to expression.

> Patients in this clinic will not be treated in contradiction to the tenets of modern medicine but in a manner that reflect a widened medical understanding. All patients will be examined carefully; medicines will be chosen with the greatest care and individualized for each patient.
>
> What is offered here is not a one-sided approach to treatment, as is usual in allopathic, homeopathic or naturopathic medicine. A complementary approach will be striven for in diagnosis as well as in treatment.

Next, Ita Wegmann acquired a house and appropriate laboratory space for Dr. Oskar Schmiedel, who had begun developing remedies in a very small wooden barrack near the Goetheanum. Since Futurum decided against financing this move, she raised the money herself, thus laying the foundation for what would later become the Weleda Company.

Soon it became apparent to Steiner that Dr. Wegman was able to understand his suggestions and bring them to realization. Whereas in Stuttgart the doctors took up his time with endless discussions and requests for theoretical explanations, she demonstrated both initiative and a sense for the practical. He came ever more often to the clinic in Arlesheim to participate in medical consultations. But it was only in 1923 that the collaboration began through which Steiner was able to accomplish what he had envisioned.

Chapter 44

ESTABLISHING THE CHRISTIAN COMMUNITY

As a ten-year-old, Rudolf Steiner had served as an acolyte during communion. Doing so, he had experienced the ritual as a form of mediation between the sensory world and the suprasensory world. "From the very beginning this was not merely outer form, but a deep experience" (28). This deep impression had accompanied Steiner in various metamorphoses, yet in the decades leading up to the turn of the century had receded into the background. His contemplations were primarily of a philosophic turn; even his religious ideas were expressed conceptually. Probably at some point in the 1880s he had written a "Credo—the Individual and the Cosmos," wherein he stated:

> There are four spheres of human activity in which the individual gives himself entirely to the spirit, surrendering himself entirely: knowledge, art, religion, and in loving devotion to another person in the spirit. Whoever lives not in at least one of these spheres, lives not at all. Knowledge is devotion to the universe in thinking, art in beholding, religion in feeling, love the devotion with the sum total of all spiritual forces to something that appears to us to be a worthy essence of the totality of the cosmos. Knowledge is the most spiritual; love, the most beautiful form of selfless devotion. For love is a true heavenly light in daily life. Devout, truly spiritual love ennobles our existence through and through; it makes everything that lives in us sublime. A pure, devout love transforms the totality of soul life into something that bears the character of the universal spirit. (40)

Rudolf Steiner experienced a quality of devotion that never left him, although it came to expression in different forms in the various phases of his life.

When Steiner began to develop anthroposophic Spiritual Science in the years following the turn of the century, he saw his task as lying primarily in the realms of knowledge and the esoteric. He emphasized often that

Spiritual Science was not meant to be a new religion and that he was not the founder of a new religion. Spiritual Science strove to delve more deeply through its research into the nature of the various religions, to help toward a new understanding of them. It did not, however, wish to in any way infringe upon the religious beliefs of the individual, but rather to help give these beliefs a more conscious foundation.

> No one should be turned away from his religious life through Spiritual Science. Thus one cannot assert that Spiritual Science is a religion.... Spiritual Science will simply include the totality of the world in its explorations, including history and what has entered historical development as spirituality. That for this reason religion is also examined does not in any way contradict what I have just mentioned. (35)

This reasoning was brought forth by Steiner often. In 1923, for instance, at the founding of the General Anthroposophical Society, he stated that anyone, regardless of his or her religious belief, could be a member of this society. These were not empty words. Steiner believed that religious practice was a blessing for human life; both the simplest and most refined individuals could find what they needed in such practices.

Although his spiritual research had led Steiner to the recognition that the spiritual reality of Christ formed the center and the fulcrum of human evolution, he nonetheless was adamant that other religious streams, such as Buddhism or Zarathustrianism, could with complete validation be included in this central evolutionary stream. For this reason, Anthroposophy could not disturb anyone's religious beliefs or practices. Any religious path, if followed in the proper manner, can lead a person beyond the limits of the self. Steiner was convinced, however, that the insights born of Spiritual Science could lead to an unrestricted deepening of human devotion.

In the fall of 1916 this conviction took on a new aspect. In public lectures in Basel and Zürich, Rudolf Steiner was of the hope that Anthroposophy would help guide people back to religion and religious practice, even to forms of Christian "ceremonial service" (Gädecke). Shortly thereafter, speaking on February 20, 1917, in Berlin, he warned the members of the Anthroposophical Society against using Anthroposophy as an alternative to religious practice and, making what he termed an "interlude" in the lecture, said:

> Spiritual Science can to a great degree and especially in regard to the mystery of Christ be a support, a foundation for religious life and

religious practice. One should, however, not try to make Spiritual Science a religion but be clear that religion, in its true aliveness, in its living practice within the community of humanity, fires the spiritual consciousness of the soul. If this spirit consciousness is to come to life within humanity, we must progress beyond abstract notions of God or Christ. One must ever again through religious practice, through the exercise of religion, which can of course take on different forms for different people, be immersed in a religious milieu. (175)

He spoke of the necessity of an individual religious life even more pointedly in a lecture on December 11, 1918, in Bern. "To be fully human, a person always needs to maintain a direct, individual relationship to the suprasensory.... He doesn't only need the relationship with the suprasensory that can be attained through Spiritual Science, he needs a relationship born of ritual and the sacramental.... Spiritual Science deepens spiritually what lives in the outer forms of ritual and confession" (72).

It is possible that Steiner was speaking to specific individuals when he spoke in this way. Attention has been called to the fact that Friedrich Rittelmeyer was probably present for the lecture of February 20. Perhaps the remarks concerning the cultivation of religious life were addressed primarily to him. However, if one reflects on the substance of the remarks, Rittelmeyer probably understood them to be an acknowledgement of his own convictions and understood them as an appeal to the anthroposophists present.

What led Steiner to speak of these things was initially his observation that an "urge toward ritual" had, in a variety of forms, become apparent among his contemporaries (184). More significant, however, was for Steiner what he perceived in the depths of the human soul. He spoke of an illness with which people had been inoculated that led them to deny God. He characterized this illness with an image from the life of St. Paul, who spoke of a thorn in his flesh and said, "This thorn will spread and become ever more of a problem" (182). Somewhat later, he spoke of a "defect" with which people were born and that could only be balanced out if they began to search for a path to Christ (193). He was especially concerned with the future development of human intelligence and recognized a tendency toward intelligence "becoming evil," which at that time was only in its early stages.

In religious terminology, Steiner was speaking of the reality of sin—the illness born of sin—and saw in the catastrophe of the war "just a glimmer of the storm that would break over humanity" (185). Without question, earnest, intentionally cultivated Spiritual Science with its corresponding conceptual orientation and the meditative search for higher knowledge were to be a barricade against these tendencies. But for both the anthroposophists as well as for those who did not turn to Spiritual Science, religious practice was a source of strength that worked so deeply into the soul, affecting even the life forces, that it could not be rejected. A person would be damaged in the totality of his or her being if not directly—through true faith devotion—connected with God.

This connection could exist in many forms. In connection with anthroposophic pedagogy, Steiner had spoken about how teaching could become a form of sacred service, that the "vocation of teaching could become a priestly vocation" (310). In the fall of 1918, when he was speaking publicly about a deepening of religious life through forms of ritual, he spoke the following to anthroposophists in Dornach:

> In the time of the consciousness soul, one must quickly become a person who is not merely trapped in the dry, abstract forms of natural science that petrify the entire human being... but can have a sense of a natural science that can become a prayerful beholding of what the Godhead, in divine symbols, spreads throughout the world to the satisfaction of human beings, and also in everything through which God tests humanity. When one has once again become able, sacramental, at a higher level to transform the laboratory... and the clinic into an altar,... then the time has arrived, which is demanded by divine evolution for modern soul development. (184)

The earnestness of the times and the course of human evolution thus made a renewal in science and its application necessary, which could take hold of the heart and the will and raise human action to a higher level of responsibility. Steiner envisioned a quality of inner, religious intent illuminating the work in the clinics, the laboratories, the schools and on the farms, as well as in contemporary religious life. In the years following 1916, when he began to focus on bringing the impulses of a science of initiation to bear in society, he tried to seed such impulses in the various fields of work—in education, science and medicine. But he also saw the necessity to offer help to those individuals who strove for a renewal of religious practice. Who were in the circle of people who also sensed this necessity and would ask for his help?

Among the anthroposophists there were a number of protestant ministers and two Catholic priests. The latter had often come to Steiner with questions. For one of them, Hugo Schuster, the priest in Basel, Steiner had translated the Latin mass into German and drawn up a burial service, which was used for a number of years, from 1919 on, at the burials of members of the Anthroposophical Society. After the priest had celebrated the ritual, Rudolf Steiner would give the eulogy. In 1919/20, Rudolf Steiner created a service for the children at the Waldorf School, followed at Easter 1921 with a special youth service. He responded, beginning in 1919, to requests for religious rituals because he saw the necessity of renewal in this realm. However, all these new ritualistic forms were cultivated initially in very small circles.

It soon became apparent that Steiner was absolutely willing to support such renewal on a much larger scale, and it appears that he recognized in Friedrich Rittelmeyer an individual who could lead a movement for religious renewal. Rittelmeyer was born in 1872 and had studied theology and philosophy at the universities in Erlangen and in Berlin. Following his studies, he went on to Würzburg, where he served as vicar while working on his Ph.D. His dissertation was on "Friedrich Nietzsche and the Problem of Knowledge." From 1903 until 1916, he served as minister in Nuremberg. He met Rudolf Steiner in 1911 and began an intensive and at first quite critical study of Anthroposophy, supported by Michael Bauer, who headed up the anthroposophic work in the Nuremberg. In 1916, Rittelmeyer was called to the pulpit of the New Church in Berlin, where he attracted a "select, well-educated" congregation (Bock).

Rudolf Steiner allowed Rittelmeyer, who was not a member of the Anthroposophical Society, to attend the lectures for members and, when he moved to Berlin, to bring others to the lectures. He spent a good deal of time with him, sharing among other things intimate details of his own life. During 1917 and 1918, at the end of his lectures, he would find Rittelmeyer and speak with him about the lectures. In February 1919, when Steiner was unable to travel to Berlin for his planned lecture series, he asked Rittelmeyer to stand in for him. Rittelmeyer recalled a conversation with Steiner during the years in Berlin. "Once, it must have been in 1917, I met him on the way to a lecture and walked with him. He began to talk and said, 'I have to focus my life's work on the esoteric. Otherwise I will not achieve what has to be done. The religious life is your task.' I understood this to be an encouragement to continue on my path. Today, however, looking back, I realize that this was once again a moment when I should have asked him for more specifics" (Rittelmeyer).

During 1920 and 1921, Rittelmeyer was recovering from injuries he received in a mountaineering accident and was only able to do a little work. He was able to pull together the book *The Work of Rudolf Steiner—Hope for a New Culture*, which he edited and, in part, wrote. His Nuremberger colleague and collaborator wrote an article about "Rudolf Steiner and Religion." The courageous stand taken by these two respected theologians gives the impression that their support could be counted on in a movement for religious renewal.

But the initial impulse for such a movement came from another side. In 1920, two students of theology and philosophy had asked Steiner for his thoughts on religious renewal. They had, however, kept his very positive response to themselves. It was only in May 1921, when these two students were together with a number of their colleagues, that the ideas came into discussion. One of them, Gottfried Husemann, drafted a letter to Rudolf Steiner in which they asked about possibilities for religious activities within the spiritual framework of the anthroposophic movement. When Steiner received this missive, he invited two of the students, Gertrud Sperri and Werner Klein, to meet with him on May 23. He first asked if it was not too early for what they had requested, at which Werner Klein replied, "Doctor, we have to do this!" Steiner expressed his willingness to work together with them and invited them to join him for a course at the next possible date—in the middle of the semester from June 12 to 16, 1921.

Among the students who came to the course was Emil Bock (1895–1959), who had become acquainted with Rittelmeyer in Berlin and through Rittelmeyer with Steiner's work. Rittelmeyer had introduced Bock and Eberhard Kurras to Rudolf Steiner; they had attended the lectures he had given for the members of the Anthroposophical Society in Berlin and in this way had found their ways into the anthroposophic work. When Bock heard of the planned course, he postponed the final theological exams, which had been planned for these days, and quickly became the speaker for the group and took on the organization of the course. On the fourth day of the course, a meeting took place with Rudolf Steiner to speak about the future. The participants of this first course wanted to reach out to others who were interested in religious renewal and invite them to a next course in Dornach.

They hoped to find about a hundred further participants. Steiner was supportive of all their suggestions and even added up for them what such a course would cost. "We have accommodations. But you have to figure four Swiss francs per day for each participant. If there are 100 participants, that works out to 400 Swiss francs per day, or 5600 Swiss francs for fourteen days. You'll probably need about 6,000 francs" (342).

In addition they spoke about questions pertaining to their studies, possible collaborators and an announcement for the course. After Steiner had been able to fathom the intentions of the various participants in a number of discussions and Emil Bock had drafted the announcement of their further work, Steiner warned them not to waste any time.

It is apparent that Steiner embraced this initiative readily. In contrast to the economic endeavors, concerning which he had pointed out the lack of suitable personnel, he recognized the energetic will of the theology students and saw in Emil Molt someone with the competence to act. He was able to discuss the future and make plans with them freely, in an open dialogue. In August 1922, he spoke to the members of the Anthroposophical Society about the impression the questioning students had made on him.

> Some time ago a number of young theology students approached me. They spoke of their inner problems and challenges in a manner that left the impression of great seriousness. This was because a certain psychic undertone resonated throughout their words. It couldn't be explicitly articulated, but it lived extraordinarily strongly in these young souls.... It is the case that this unarticulated undertone that came from these souls made a stronger impression on me than what they actually said. (B 110)

Steiner had thus encountered an earnest, strong-willed group of quite young people—the core group ranged in age from twenty to twenty-six—who were willing to place themselves on their own feet and found independent congregations.

The participants in the first course succeeded in finding other interested people. By August 1, there were sixty registrations. When the course began at the end of September, there were 110 participants. Hermann Heisler, a protestant minister, anthroposophist, and activist in the Threefold Movement, managed to bring together the necessary funds, and Bock and Gertrud Sperri organized the living arrangements to accommodate the participants at a minimum of cost.

The second course for theologians began on September 26, 1921, in Dornach and ended on October 10. During the sixteen days, there were a total of twenty-nine lectures followed by discussions. Rudolf Steiner had chosen the "White Hall" on the second floor of the south wing of the Goetheanum for this gathering.

Rudolf Steiner, who had as a child experienced the significance of the Catholic mass, faced the task of awakening within a group of predominantly Protestant theologians an understanding for an impulse of Christian renewal through cultic ritual. This was difficult, as most Protestant theologians had been trained in the tradition of the sermon and biblical exegesis. Emil Bock wrote about the course:

> Among the participants during the course in September were a number of theologians who had no idea that the kind of intellectual discussion that had become their life's context signified the death of religion. Through their questions, which were in no way genuine questions but discussion topics, they occupied our entire time together. We feared we would, instead of beginning with the creation of a new form of sacred ritual, be trapped in an intellectual preamble. We fought desperately in the conversations between events, during which the questions we wished to pose Dr. Steiner were formulated. (*We Experienced Rudolf Steiner*)

Steiner viewed this situation in its historical perspective. He experienced what was taking place as the expression of the modern worldview developed during the last 400 years and tried to open possibilities for as many as possible by casting light on new questions through his anthroposophic research, beseeching patience. Emil Molt wrote:

> Before the beginning of each session I went to meet Dr. Steiner at his studio and accompanied him over to the Goetheanum and up the many steps to the "White Hall." Beginning on the third day, I pleaded with him to give further lectures instead of continuing with the discussion periods that took place after each lecture. He just said, "Have patience; this is just one of the things we have to work through!" He took up the questions that were so irritating for us with great calmness, as though it were possible to cast anew an entire stream of humanity through personal empathy. (*We Experienced Rudolf Steiner*)

During the second part of the course, Steiner was able introduce to the participating theologians, slowly and carefully, the new texts for their sacramental work. This was possible primarily thanks to the then twenty-six-year-old Emil Bock, whose focus on the higher goals worked to keep the participants on course. Bock shouldered this task almost single-handedly, as Rittelmeyer had been taken ill and was unable to attend, and Christian Geyer, although he was present and full of wonder for the way Steiner handled difficult theological questions, did not take on an active role. For this gifted speaker, it was in no way clear why one would want to place a ritual rather than the sermon in the center of the service.

As the course progressed, a group of about sixty people was formed. They wished to continue to work in the way that had been laid out. The active core of this group was made up primarily of leading figures from the youth movement who had recognized that without spiritual content this movement was destined to disintegrate. They dedicated all their energy to questions of religious renewal. Steiner was happy to find a circle of women and men who could work independently and with whom he developed ideas in dialogue. Reflecting on this work, he said to teachers of the Waldorf School during a faculty meeting in November 1921, "Look, now there is this wonderful movement out of which came the course for theologians. It was held in a very esoteric manner. It held within it the seed of a new cult, a sacred ritual. This shows how at one people were with each other" (300 & 2).

The esoteric nature of the course is not to be found in special ideas or extraordinary communications from the spiritual world but in the resoluteness with which the young participants took up the work. By comparison the situation in the Anthroposophical Society made Steiner sad; there were few members with Bock and Rittelmeyer's capacities. And although he never hoped that the movement for religious renewal would not succeed, he did say to the leading members of the Anthroposophical Society in the beginning of 1923, "Think what it would have meant if you in the Anthroposophical Society had had the strength to take them in! Dr. Rittelmeyer and Bock, however, left" (259).

During the winter of 1921/22, Steiner seemed to have expected the formalization of the new community to proceed more quickly. When he met with the core group during the Berlin College Course on March 7, 1922, he urged them not to waste any time. He felt September 1922 to be the latest they could begin. At the same time, he warned them not to count on the anthroposophists in the beginning; they should interest other circles of people for their work.

The leaders of the young movement did quite a bit to bring their initiative to the public. During the Berlin course, one day was organized around questions of theology. Bock, Rittelmeyer and Geyer spoke. Steiner did not feel the lectures, with their one-sided focus on the collapse of the old and their narrow Protestant content, were successful and opined in a report of the course: "There were only hints that something would come from Anthroposophy, but what form it would take was never spoken about" (81).

After the general preparations had been made, Rittelmeyer, Geyer and Bock traveled to Dornach. Between July 21 and August 7, Steiner met with them seven times and worked with them on their questions. In one of these conversations, he suggested the name "Christian Community." In another, he sketched out the relationship between Anthroposophy and the renewal of the priesthood and the sacramental ritual. Emil Bock noted, "Anthroposophy makes the founding possible. The founding itself occurs entirely through us.... Anthroposophy prepares the soil then steps back."

Following these days in Dornach, the founding circle met in Breitbrunn on Ammer Lake for their final preparations. Here they received word that Christian Geyer had decided not to join the new movement, something that wounded Rittelmeyer deeply. Shortly thereafter, everyone gathered in Dornach where the forty-five future priests were welcomed hospitably. The oldest, Rudolf Koschützki, was fifty-six; the two youngest were nineteen. The three women who were present represented the beginning of a new era in which women, too, would be allowed to celebrate at the altar.

During the dialogues leading up to the founding of the Christian Community, Rudolf Steiner argued emphatically for an inner hierarchical structure for the new movement. Three individuals would be responsible for the guidance of the movement, one of whom, Friedrich Rittelmeyer, would don the mantel of ultimate responsibility. The decisions made by these three would be binding for the entire community of priests and their congregations. Due to Geyer's decision to not join the new movement, one of the three chosen to bear this responsibility was lost just before the founding was to take place. This was in Rudolf Steiner's eyes unfortunate in two ways: for the movement itself, but also because of the potential publicity it would bring. Many would welcome Geyer's decision to step back from the new initiative.

The founding of the Christian Community took place in a series of steps from September 6 to September 22, 1922, in the White Hall of the

Goetheanum where the group of future priests gathered. Rudolf Steiner joined them daily, giving lectures and working through their questions with them. After the positions of overall responsibility had been filled and the priests had taken their vows, Rudolf Steiner took them step by step through the new ritual. On September 16, 1922, Friedrich Rittelmeyer celebrated the act of consecration of man for the first time. By September 17, all the priests had been ordained. During the following days, they set forth the rules of their community. On September 22, the newly ordained priests were sent forth to begin their work.

Following the burning of the Goetheanum, Rudolf Steiner wrote briefly about this founding.

> At the end of September and beginning of October 1921, a group of German theologians, who bore within themselves the impulse toward a renewal of Christian religious life, gathered at the Goetheanum. What was achieved in the work we did together culminated in September 1922. What I experienced with these theologians in the small auditorium of the south wing belongs among the high points of my life. Together with a circle of nobly enthusiastic individuals, it was possible to tread a path that would guide spiritual knowledge into religious life. (36)

The priests have been silent about the actual founding ritual that took place on September 16. In their memoirs, a number have mentioned that it was practically impossible to speak of it. Rittelmeyer wrote, "The shared experience of the first community of priests belongs within the most sacred reaches of a temple, not in the public hallways."

Emil Bock emphasized that the founding was not a course in theology but the birth of a new sacred ritual. "Rudolf Steiner was there among us in quiet humility and devotion, yet at the same time in his full spiritual capacity. The time was ripe and our hearts were open; he was able to bring down to us from heaven what the spiritual beings, who were connected with Christ and served him, wished to bestow upon humanity. We were to go out into the world as bearers of a new form of priesthood" (*We Experienced Rudolf Steiner*).

Rudolf Steiner had, however, invited three individuals from the anthroposophic movement to be present at this hour of new birth: naturally, Marie Steiner, who had always been present at the important junctures in the evolution of Anthroposophy; Ernst Uehli, a member of the council of the Anthroposophical Society who gave free religion lessons on the Waldorf School and celebrated the children's services, as well as edited the *Threefold Journal*; and finally, Albert Steffen, the Swiss poet and editor of the weekly *Das Goetheanum*.

In 1938—in a eulogy for Friedrich Rittelmeyer—Albert Steffen wrote about this birth moment of the Christian Community: "It is not yet the time to tell the story of this historical moment" (Steffen). In 1919, a passage from one of Steffen's journals came to light. Dated September 16, 1922, it said:

> Today the first Act of Consecration of Man was celebrated on earth directly out of the spirit; the risen Christ was present.... I may say that Christ was there, for I beheld the resurrected light-filled life body as the words from the bread and wine were spoken. It is the first time I have beheld the being of Christ before me. The arms were spread and the head was illuminated. And I experienced then that he healed and made holy. He was there and is there. (*Notes and Studies for the Work of Albert Steffen*, Heft 12/13)

Chapter 45

POSSIBILITIES—REALITIES

In the middle of July 1921, Rudolf Steiner received a letter from Jules Sachs, one of the two owners of the famed concert agency Wolff and Sachs. In addition to concerts, the agency had since 1905 also organized lecture tours for speakers such as Ernst Haeckel and other scholars. In the letter Sachs asked if Steiner, in light of the growing interest in "things metaphysical," would be interested in speaking "in our largest, most elegant venue, the Philharmonic" in Berlin and then to tour other cities. Even before this lecture on September 15, 1921, which had sold-out days before, the fact that some 1600 people had participated in the Stuttgart congress "Cultural Possibilities of the Anthroposophical Movement" (August 28–September 7, 1921) showed the interest people had for the anthroposophic work and signified an opportunity for the movement. This was to become even more clearly manifest in the coming months. During the speaking tours that Wolff and Sachs organized in January 1922, during which Steiner spoke in twelve cities, and in May 1922, when he spoke in nine cities, the auditoriums were often not large enough to seat the numbers who came to listen to the lectures. In June 1922, some 2000 people attended the eleven lectures Steiner gave during the Vienna congress. The period from early autumn 1921 through the summer of 1922 was the time of Steiner's greatest public impact. During this time he spoke to more than 20,000 people.

For Steiner, the numbers of people who attended his lectures showed that a longing for Anthroposophy lived in very many people. He was concerned whether it was possible to truly reach individuals who were striving spiritually and to gain them as long-term friends of anthroposophic work. When he returned to Dornach from Berlin and Stuttgart in September 1921, he could, on the one hand, speak of the success of the Stuttgart congress, the excellent talks that had been given there, and point out that this congress was a milestone for the anthroposophic movement, yet, on the other hand, it had become clear to him that the Anthroposophical Society "was becoming an obstacle for the growth of Anthroposophy." He said that the anthroposophic movement had outgrown the society and spoke of the necessity for the society to grow into the movement (*Eastern and Western Culture*).

What he meant by this he had called attention to in Stuttgart three weeks earlier. During a meeting with the members of the Anthroposophical Society during the Stuttgart congress, Alfred Heidenreich, one of the leaders of the youth movement, spoke, saying that the task of the young anthroposophists was not only "to bring Anthroposophy to the youth movement, but it is also our duty to place our youthful energy in the service of Anthroposophy so that the corresponding deeds can come into being" (*News from the Central Executive Council*, I, November 1921).

Rudolf Steiner could quite well imagine what would happen if groups from the youth movement would attempt to participate in the branches of the Anthroposophical Society. He turned to the older, loyal members and called out to them:

> Now a representative of the youth has spoken! There are a good number of students among us, my dear friends! We must recognize as a historical moment the fact that members of such movements or groups have found their way to our Anthroposophical Society or our anthroposophic movement. We must feel how necessary it is for us to do everything we can to respond to what they can rightly ask of us. A great deal of hope for the success of our society rests with the student movement. (*Eastern and Western Culture*)

During his address, Steiner spoke almost harshly about what was needed. The remnants of the "theosophical societal allures," the sectarianism, and the old theosophical habits had to be purged from the society. He didn't avoid depicting these sectarian behaviors in a blunt but humorous way so that everyone present would understand exactly what he meant.

> In the old Theosophical Society, one found a certain pleasure in saying, "Somewhere, preferably in some far-removed, inaccessible place, certain individuals called the *masters* live. They are the leaders of humanity. They have guided the evolution of humanity for untold ages. All of us are in their care. We have to serve them." One found pleasure in a certain sense of contentment that this service brought, which was heightened by the fact that these *masters*

lived so far away that one never really knew anything about who one was actually serving.... One imagined, when one turned off the light...and sat down at a little table with one's head in one's hands, that in the service of these *masters*, one participated in all the important matters of the present day.... Specifically, one found satisfaction in sending out thoughts. This sending out of thoughts was taken up with great enthusiasm in theosophical circles. (*Eastern and Western Culture*)

During the following months, Rudolf Steiner spoke often about the youth movement. He explained to the Waldorf teachers, "The youth movement certainly has a suprasensory foundation. One must take it seriously" (300 & 2). "The youth movement is a cultural phenomenon of great significance" (300& 2). He also spoke to the members in Dornach in this vein and added, "The fact that members of the youth movement have participated in anthroposophic events, including the Stuttgart congress, and have resolved quite positively...to connect themselves with the striving of the anthroposophic spiritual stream is something I feel to be quite significant" (209).

At the same time he complained about the situation in the Anthroposophical Society, which had become overrun by cliques and lost a sense of hospitality. "The tendency to form cliques has found its way into the Anthroposophical Society and this tendency has taken over everything, sadly even the esoteric work" (300 & 2). In many cities, special groups had formed. Concerned mainly with themselves, the members acted mysteriously and—as Steiner had indicated—cultivated a strange doctrine of the "masters." If someone from outside the group wished to join them, an embarrassed silence ensued, as the outsider was not yet "ripe" for the secrets of the group; or the outsider was inundated with special revelations and warned away from anthroposophists who might think differently. In short, the society was riddled with a certain form of sectarianism. This was very disturbing and made it impossible for thousands of people, including those who belonged to the youth movement, to find their way into the anthroposophic movement.

It is characteristic of Steiner that he only mentioned the situation a few times, hoping that, having had this called to their attention, the members would take appropriate steps to rectify the situation. Even in public, he voiced his opinion of these things openly. In January 1922, during a discussion with English teachers who had come to Dornach to participate in a course on Waldorf education, he said:

> The anthroposophic movement is a factor in Central European culture today. It is a spiritual movement. We don't have an organization to steer or guide this movement. The Anthroposophical Society—this has to be said and it is important to recognize—the Anthroposophical Society is not able to carry the anthroposophic movement. The society has become so sectarian that it is not able to carry the anthroposophic movement. (303)

Two things confronted Rudolf Steiner. On the one hand, he was aware of a large number of primarily young people who truly sought Anthroposophy. On the other hand, he had to acknowledge that the Anthroposophical Society had not been able to overcome the bad habits inherited from its theosophical past and had in a sectarian manner blockaded itself from the world.

It is remarkable that in spite of this, Steiner continued to speak about the anthroposophic work in non-anthroposophic settings. At the end of November 1921, he traveled for the first time since the war had ended to Oslo, where he gave ten lectures either to the public or to groups not connected with the anthroposophic movement. Upon returning to Dornach, he reported at length about the work in Norway and spoke of the very successful eurythmy performance in the National Theater, of lectures he had given in the Nobel Institute, of a public lecture attended by 2,000 people, and of lectures for the National Economic Society and a group of theologians. He also spoke of a cruel attack in the Oslo newspapers, which, however, did not seem to impact attendance at the performance and the lectures. In summary, Steiner said that the anthroposophic movement "was making its way into the world" and that the practical work was stimulating a good deal of interest. "But at the same time the number of our opponents is growing enormously."

The first of the above-mentioned lecture tours organized by Wolff and Sachs followed soon after, in January 1922. It took Steiner through twelve German cities and ended in Breslau, where he was stuck for several days because of a strike by train employees. He had a similar experience on this tour as he had had in Oslo. The large auditoriums in each city were sold out, and public interest was high despite the bad press the tour received. It was an exhausting trip for Steiner, who had to rethink and present the same themes in each of the twelve cities, speaking without amplification to upward of a thousand people after uncomfortable days of travel.

When he returned to Dornach, he found other concerns waiting for him. The situation with the Futurum, Inc. deteriorated week to week. But there were also things that lifted his spirits. For the last six months, a weekly newspaper, *Das Goetheanum*, had been published in Dornach. The editor was Albert Steffen (1884–1963). Steffen was a poet, dramatist and writer who had gained recognition before he took on the editorial post. His first novels had been published by S. Fischer Verlag in Berlin. He had met Steiner in 1907 and recognized him as his teacher. From 1908 until 1920, he had lived in Munich, participating in the anthroposophic work there. With a great deal of earnestness, he had schooled himself as a poet and anthroposophist, and since 1916 had spoken out for Steiner publicly. Early in the summer of 1921, Steiner had suggested that he become editor of the new weekly. From the beginning, he had worked closely with Steiner, going over each number with him before it went to press whenever possible. In the latest edition from February 12, Steiner found that Steffen had simply and with great clarity reviewed a lecture that a Professor Chastonnay from Zürich had given in Basel attacking Anthroposophy. Steiner found Steffen's objective, unexcited review quite satisfying. He cited it as an excellent example of how to address opponents of Anthroposophy when he later addressed the members in Dornach.

The fact that Steiner immediately called attention to Steffen's piece indicates just how troubled he was by the growing opposition and how deeply he hoped that these attacks would be responded to in an appropriate manner. He concluded his thoughts on Steffen's review with the words: "On special occasions I would like to make clear that a fitting appraisal of what has been achieved within our circles—which also, of course, includes a fitting appraisal of what hasn't been achieved and what needs to be done—that such a fitting appraisal should have its place. If we are not attentive to the outstanding achievements coming from within our ranks, the movement will not be able to thrive" (Lecture from Nov. 2, 1922, unpublished).

After spending a good two weeks in Dornach, Steiner traveled again to Germany, first to Leipzig and Halle for public lectures on the nature of Anthroposophy, then on to Berlin for the university course, during which he held ten public lectures. At the same time, he made a point of insuring that eurythmy performances took place as often as possible. Through eurythmy, under the guidance of Marie Steiner, Anthroposophy should be brought to expression in a purely artistic form. There was one performance in Leipzig, and two more in Berlin. From Berlin, he traveled to Stuttgart for a brief visit to work with the teachers of the Waldorf School, who were in need of his help. With them, he spoke openly about the events in Berlin. "The organization in Berlin was absolutely impossible. Only an hour was scheduled for discussion. There was certainly the possibility for someone to say something extraordinarily dumb, but no chance to defend the topic.... Things were well planned to give anyone who wished to harm Anthroposophy the opportunity to do so" (300 & 2). Following these grueling weeks, the collapse of the Futurum, Inc. came to a head in Dornach. Deserted by the initiators of this endeavor, Steiner tried with the help of Ita Wegman and Albert Steffen to save whatever could be saved before leaving again on his next trip.

Once the borders inside Central Europe had opened again for Steiner in 1921, he made trips to Holland and Norway. In 1922, he was invited to go to England. Compared to the tours through Germany, this trip was almost a holiday. In any case, for the next two weeks, Steiner was able to immerse himself in a different, much less hectic world, a necessary respite after the debacle with Futurum. Before going to England, Steiner traveled to The Hague, where Ms. Droogleever-Fortuyn had organized a university course, to which she had invited, in addition to Rudolf Steiner, a number of scholars from Stuttgart, as well as Elisabeth Vreede. The Hague is a calm, stately venue; the gathering was small and intimate. There were a total of 200 students present. Some events had as few as sixty participants. Rudolf Steiner reported on his impressions of the contributions made by his colleagues in *Das Goetheanum*.

On April 13, accompanied by Marie Steiner, Mieta Waller and Edith Maryon, Steiner traveled to England. The first stop was London, where he gave two lectures. On April 16—Easter Sunday—he was able to give an esoteric lesson for a circle of dedicated English members. That afternoon he visited Miss Cross's school in Kings Langley. It was an astonishing place. The children who lived there took care of all the necessary tasks—from cooking and gardening to cleaning. "Thus children are truly guided into all aspects of life and learn a great deal" (Lecture on April 30, 1922, unpublished). During their visit, the question arose as to how anthroposophic pedagogy could be worked with in the school. Then they went on to Stratford-on-Avon for the Shakespeare festival.

During the week in Stratford, Steiner was a guest, participating in an event for which he held no responsibility, throughout which he could watch and listen and take in the work of others. Each evening he went to the theater. The comedies entranced him. During the performance of *Twelfth Night*, he had such a fit of laughter that even the actors found themselves caught up in it. He was not as impressed by the productions of the tragedies, but he followed the lectures accompanying the festival with great interest. He heard the poets John Masefield and Sir Henry Newbolt speak, as well as the dramatist John Drinkwater. The perfection in Sir Henry Newbolt's form fascinated him. As interested as he was in all matters to do with the theater, he listened closely when Lena Ashwell and Cicely Hamilton spoke about the difficulties in contemporary English theater. He was originally asked to give two lectures but was then asked to give a third, a sign that he was well received. He closed his account of this trip for *Das Goetheanum* with the words:

> I left England on April 25 convinced that there are people in England who see the cultivation and representation of Anthroposophy as a part of their lives' tasks and who have taken strong steps to make them so. I feel for them the same gratitude that I feel whenever I meet individuals who help support this work. Given the situation today, the fact that I as a German could find such support in London and Stratford was especially gratifying. (*Goetheanum*, vol. 1)

Following a full week in Dornach and meetings in Stuttgart, Steiner embarked on May 11 on the second of the planned Wolff and Sachs lecture tours. This was to take Steiner to nine cities. Following lectures in Leipzig, Berlin and Breslau, he was scheduled to speak in Munich on May 15. Even before Steiner departed from Dornach, it had become clear that something was in the works in Munich. A number of the local papers had begun to publish inflammatory articles about Steiner, saying that hopefully good German men would be found to insure that he would not tread the earth in Munich.

When Steiner arrived in Munich, he was met by Hans Buchenbacher, who informed him of the security measures taken on his behalf. A number of anthroposophists had traveled to Munich to serve as a human shield. The tour organizers had hired a number of boxers and wrestlers and placed them inconspicuously in Steiner's vicinity. The atmosphere was tense as the lecture began. When the lights went out in the middle of the lecture, leaving the stenographer's lamp as the sole light in the auditorium, Steiner continued speaking, clearly and calmly. After a short time, the lights came back on and there were no further disturbances until Rudolf Steiner returned to the stage after the end of the lecture to acknowledge the continuing applause. Then all hell broke loose. There were stink bombs and whistles. The anthroposophic friends rallied to Steiner and hurried him into a room off the stage. A general melee broke out in the auditorium, the boxers and wrestlers waded into the fight, and a number of people were injured. Finally, the anthroposophists gained the upper hand. The demonstrators marched off down Maximilianstrasse singing "Victoriously, we'll conquer France."

Rudolf Steiner left Munich the next morning ahead of schedule on a passenger train. That evening, he spoke in Mannheim. The next lecture was in Elberfeld, where there was once again, in Steiner's words, a "scuffle." Here, as in Munich, anthroposophists sprang into the breach to stop the troublemakers. Emil Bock was among those who blocked the door. In a letter to Edith Maryon posted in Bremen, Steiner wrote, "Everything went well in Mannheim and Cologne. In Elberfeld there was some disturbance, but it was dealt with quite well. I will tell you what happened in Munich. It was not exactly pleasant.... I am doing well; I have no free time since the trips are quite long and the trains leave early in the morning" (263 & 1). When he returned to Dornach, Steiner did not, as he usually did, report on the trip, his impressions and experiences. A eurythmist who had known him for almost ten years and was familiar with his expressions remembered his return.

> This trip must have been indescribably difficult and exhausting for him. I remember the impression he made on me when I first saw him again in the carpentry shop. He was standing there, backstage, wearing the white smock he always wore when working in his studio. It seemed as though he had grown thinner; his gaze was quieter, more serious. It was as though he had just returned from a great and dangerous battle. The few words he spoke about the trip, simple and reserved, strengthened this impression. (Dubach)

A week later he left Dornach again, this time to travel to Vienna for the East-West congress. It was a risky undertaking to organize such a gathering at that time in Vienna, where the postwar misery had reached a highpoint. People slipped through the streets like shadows; the currency had lost almost all of its value. But the weather was good, and Vienna was certainly the place to grapple with questions concerning the relations between East and West. The best speakers the anthroposophic movement had to offer had traveled to Vienna for this event. They were Swiss, German and Austrian: Albert Steffen, Herbert Hahn, Erich Schwebsch, Caroline von Heydebrand, Friedrich Rittelmeyer, Ernst Uehli, Wilhelm Pelikan, Emil Leinhas, Friedrich Husemann, Carl Unger, Karl Heyer, Eugen Kolisko, Walter Johannes Stein, Hermann von Baravalle, Ernst Blümel, and Karl Schubert. Rudolf Steiner was evidently more than satisfied with the contributions of his colleagues. He described Herbert Hahn's lecture on how the folk souls were reflected in the various languages as "extremely insightful," and he found Schwebsch's presentation over Brükner, with its North German undertones, extraordinarily heartening. Mischievously he characterized his Austrian colleagues by answering the question to which order of monks they would have belonged in pre-Theresian times in this way: "Our dear Kolisko would have definitely become a Dominican," Baravalle and Blümel Benedictine, Schubert a Piarist, and Steine a Cistercian.

He was especially heartened by the warm reception received by the eurythmy performances. He experienced this as an "epochal event." Steiner took the opportunity to present a poem by an impoverished poet living in Vienna who he had known thirty years earlier and arranged for the proceeds of the performance to be given to him.

Rudolf Steiner gave a total of eleven lectures during the convention, one about the building project in Dornach, five concerning "Anthroposophy and the Sciences," and five more about "Anthroposophy and Sociology." For the latter two series of lectures, he had decided not to use the word "Anthroposophy" at any time during the lectures. He held himself to this. During the last lecture, he gave an overview of social threefolding in which he rearticulated the idea based on his experiences and insights of the last few years from the point of view that well-founded decisions were to be made in each of the three social systems.

Just a few days before the conference began, Dr. Eugen Kolisko, who was the son of the well-known Viennese anatomist Alexander Kolisko, gave a lecture in the Viennese Medical Society. He spoke about "New Approaches to Pathology and Therapy" to an audience of about 400 and went into some depth about the causes and treatment of migraines. This lecture caused quite a scandal, the result of which was that Viennese academic circles did not attend the East-West congress. Steiner wrote to Edith Maryon that the commotion caused by Kolisko's lecture "had not been exaggerated..., but this time dealt with fairly gently by the press" (263 & 1).

During the congress, Rudolf Steiner had so much to do that he was unable to participate in the afternoon discussions. He attended the eurythmy rehearsals and had meetings with people who had traveled long distances to attend the congress. There were visits to be made, and even after the congress had ended there were crowds of people waiting at his hotel to speak with him. The author Max Hayek, one of Steiner's non-anthroposophic visitors, related how he finally was able to speak with Steiner late one evening. He had seen him that day at the lectern speaking about the Goetheanum. He had appeared "so young and pure, so strong and fresh and tireless."

> How alive this man was, how light and mobile! In his voice, through which he appeared to give himself without reservation, glowed the healthiness of a spiritually kindled organism; in his eyes burned the flames of victory of an unbendable will over matter!
>
> And now I stood before the same man.... My first impression was of the vehement imperative: Be brief, for this man is exhausted beyond words—he is more tired than a man can be.
>
> I stood before an old man, an old lower Austrian peasant. Yes, this was a true Austrian.... I saw an old peasant who had worked himself to death on his piece of earth and now stood before me, bent and empty, a good, good man who had put everything on the line and had given all he had to give. (*Blätter für Anthroposophie*, 1961)

On June 11, Rudolf Steiner spoke in Vienna to the members of the Anthroposophical Society about questions relating to the anthroposophic movement. He had spoken similarly on April 13 in The Hague, then on May 21 and 23 in Berlin and Stuttgart, about the spiritual situation that had developed. He called attention to the chasm that had opened between the deeply effective work in the branches and the public activities, characterizing the feelings of, for the most part, the older members, who might say:

> "Yes, we used to come more quickly along a much shorter path to knowledge and the impulses of the spiritual world, and in an inwardly more genuine way, entering quickly an experience of the spiritual

> world. Moreover, it really doesn't interest us whether something that lives on in our hearts in this way can be defended publically in clearly articulated and disciplined trains of thought." Many of these older members say, "This does not really interest us." And they experience it as something of a loss that the anthroposophic movement has not stayed with the old forms. (211)

This movement—Steiner continued—did not seek popularity and public exposure. The reality of the situation, the spiritual state of humanity, had made the public work necessary.

> And if you hear today what used to be spoken of in other forms couched now in scientific terms, this is not the fault of the anthroposophic movement; it is its destiny. The world has demanded this of us.... The challenge is not to bring Anthroposophy closer to the sciences, but rather to permeate the sciences with Anthroposophy. We have been able to experience with deep satisfaction that friends, who have been trained in the various disciplines, have joined us, who are able to articulate scientifically the seeds that have been present in Anthroposophy. (211)

A chasm had opened between these two forms in which Anthroposophy manifested. In The Hague, where the Anthroposophical Society was a small, insular group, Steiner had, in connection with this characterization, warned against attempting to enclose the anthroposophic movement in small sectarian circles. It had to be brought out into the public arena. In Stuttgart, however, the high seat of anthroposophic erudition, he warned of the mistaken thinking that "Anthroposophy can be spread along the byways of professorial erudition" (*The Fall of the Human Intellect*).

It is worth noting that Rudolf Steiner, although he saw clearly the gap between these two different ways of living with Anthroposophy, did not at this time appeal to the members to immediately bridge the gap, even though he had to concede "that because of this chasm our movement has taken ill, inwardly and outwardly" (*The Fall of the Human Intellect*).

Steiner did not fail to note that certain animosities had arisen between representatives of the two camps, but he concentrated on bringing attention to the chasm itself, and he challenged his audience to imagine what a person, who had been introduced to Anthroposophy through the public, more scientific presentations, would think if he suddenly found himself in a meeting of a branch where the meetings were held in the traditional esoteric manner. Steiner thought to resolve the problem through a certain feeling of tact and an understanding of the experience of others. He called upon the virtues developed in *Intuitive Thinking as a Spiritual Path*, insight into the other, and a moral sense of tact.

In the coming months, the situation did not, however, get any better. In fact, it got worse. In any case, it was soon after the truly noteworthy success of the Viennese congress, yet no one understood how to capitalize on this success. Steiner wasn't thinking of publicity but on the way the members interacted with those around them. He spoke about this on June 22, 1922, in the trusted circle of colleagues at the Waldorf School.

> We can't capitalize on this if we isolate ourselves, if we don't bring in some new blood. We are guilty of psychological incest among the active members. This becomes impossible after a time. We have to expand the circles; but every time someone is suggested, someone has reasons to reject him or her. We need new blood. Throughout the entire movement we need not to believe that we must defend ourselves, but that we have to bring in new people. (300 & 2)

He knew of enough examples of people who had been repulsed by a certain stilted narrow-mindedness. A few days later, he spoke to the members in Dornach. "The chapter titled 'The Arrogance of the Anthroposophists' is one about which one could write volumes, not merely a few articles" (*Thought on Construction*). Even as a child, he had had a lively interest in other people. Neighbors in Brunn am Gebirge, where he had lived for a time with his parents, remembered how he would run out to meet them. He couldn't fathom how anyone could lack this interest. In addition, he could in no way understand how anthroposophists could not engage themselves in matters concerning the Anthroposophical Society, or be interested in larger questions concerning the state of the world. To his great dismay, he now had to acknowledge that those who had encountered Anthroposophy in the large public congresses were being repulsed by the anthroposophists themselves.

Among those who were being turned away or turned off were the younger people. These young anthroposophic enthusiasts were by no means all members of the youth movement. There were also students who had no desire "to bed down in haystacks," and others who had of their own accord immersed themselves in anthroposophic studies on specific themes. A good number of these young anthroposophists gathered on the periphery of the East-West congress. Various ideas were discussed, plans made and rejected. Finally, three participants in these discussions managed to corner Rudolf Steiner. Around July 20, Fritz Kubler, Ernst Lehrs and Rene Maikowski met with Rudolf Steiner in his studio in Dornach. During this meeting, the idea of a "Pedagogical Youth Course" was born, a course that was to unfold in spiritual dialogue with Rudolf Steiner.

At that time, Steiner was looking ahead to the discussions he was scheduled to have in the coming days with Rittelmeyer, Bock, and Geyer about the founding of the Christian Community, and then the planned pedagogical conference at Oxford. Following the trip to England, there was a course for French speakers and then the work with the priests and the founding of the Christian Community. Steiner suggested beginning with a course for the younger generation on October 1 in the Anthroposophical Society's house in Stuttgart. He realized that he needed to begin the work with the youth as soon as possible.

A number of small occurrences soon showed just how necessary his involvement was. Since he was not going to be able to be in Stuttgart until October 3, he asked Ernst Uehli, one of the most prominent anthroposophists, to step in for him. The young people, however, declined to work with him. The Building Association of Stuttgart Anthroposophists was taken aback that their house was being used by these young people and sent them a bill for 42,500 German marks (roughly equivalent to $400 today). The bill was paid.

A new way of working evolved during the course. The eighty-three participants spent practically the entire day together in the Anthroposophical Society's house. Rudolf Steiner lectured, walking back and forth across the podium, but also met with different groups and individual for conversations and discussions, listened to them speak of the challenges they faced, and discussed questions concerning their lives and their studies. Marie Steiner gave a workshop on speech formation, during which Rudolf Steiner sometimes appeared to explain the exercises in more depth. Toward the end of the course, painting workshops were offered, and the participants were also able to enjoy two eurythmy performances.

In response to questions posed by some of the young people present at the course, Rudolf Steiner came back to a theme that he had spoken of a number of times between 1913 and 1919. Now it appears as a prelude to Steiner's work in 1923 and 1924: the battle of Michael with the dragon.

In the last lecture of *Becoming the Archangel Michael's Companions*, the image of the battle with the dragon appears with a certain expectant power. Steiner speaks to his young listeners directly, intimately. He characterizes the presence of the dragon in contemporary civilization, how in this age it approached humanity from *without*.

> But the dragon must be conquered. The only way he can be conquered is if we become aware that Michael, Saint George, also comes from without. Michael, Saint George, who comes to the battle in this way is nothing other than true spiritual knowledge. (217)

This spiritual knowledge overcomes, among other things, the notion that the so-called law of the conservation of energy and matter also applies to the human being, making him subject to the laws of physical causality. Steiner does not leave this first image standing there. He goes on to state clearly that human beings have to connect themselves with Michael.

> When one finds one's way into the spiritual fabric of the world, one finds that—at the end of the nineteenth and beginning of the twentieth century when the forces of the dragon culminate—Michael, with whom we can unite ourselves, has also become active. A person can, if one wants to, have Spiritual Science, which means that Michael truly finds his way from the spiritual heights into the earthly realms. But Michael does not pressure us to do so, for today everything must spring forth out of individual freedom. (217)

Spiritual Science is spoken of here as the entering in of Michael. Finally, Steiner spoke directly to the hearts of his listeners: "If we wish to become true educators, we must, in a certain sense—speaking now in an image—become Michael's allies as he advances" (217). When the teacher's insights spring from knowledge of the growing child, "we will craft for Michael a chariot; we will be able to become his allies." He continues:

> And you will best achieve what you strive for, my dear friends, if you become conscious that you wish to become Michael's allies. You will once more become able to follow a pure, spiritual being, a being who is not bodily present on the earth, and you will have to learn to place your trust in a person because he or she shows you the path to Michael. (217)

It is possible that the simplicity and openness of these words is connected with a request made by a number of younger, as well as older, anthroposophists during the youth course. They approached Steiner asking about a possible path to esoteric deepening and a form of community building born of the spirit. He responded positively to their request. Fourteen days later, he spoke with four medical students who were searching for a spiritual deepening of their studies. He showed them that the transition from the spiritual-moral to the physiological was to be found in the warmth organization of the human being. And he added that if they would bring him fifty or sixty young doctors he would say more about it. It wasn't possible to speak about such things to the older doctors (M. P. van Deventer).

Thus, two further groups of younger anthroposophists approached Steiner following the founding of the Christian Community and the renewal of the sacramental ritual, requesting forms of esoteric deepening. For him these questions from the younger generation were a sign that the time for public events—the congresses, higher education courses, conventions, and public lectures—the time to reach out to a wide public in order to reach as many people as possible, had come to an end. Already in the autumn of 1922, in the course for French speakers and then in the lectures for members in Dornach, he had begun to speak again in a new way of the great spiritual substance of Anthroposophy—the experience of the human soul in sleep and after death, the connection of the human being with the cosmos, and the efficacy of the Christ impulse.

It is apparent that this change and the intention to once more concentrate anthroposophic life and thought around the central themes of Anthroposophy did not catch everyone's attention. At the end of October 1922, the doctors in Stuttgart organized a week-long medical conference with lectures given by Rudolf Steiner, although he had had, as he said at the beginning of the first lecture, no intention at all of speaking at this conference. A few weeks later, the natural scientists at the Goetheanum decided to arrange a conference at Christmas. Again, although he had no interest in this conference, Steiner was expected to speak. He complained energetically to Lili Kolisko, "These people behave as though I were their shoeshine boy! They arrange conferences without asking me, give me the final program, and expect me to lecture. I won't let this happen anymore" (Kolisko). Only after the fact did the organizers realize that Steiner had something other than a scientific conference in mind (Schmiedel in: Zeylmans, *Wegmann*, III).

During this time, Steiner was burdened by a number of quite serious concerns. There was the question of continuing the work on the Goetheanum. The project's coffers were almost empty. Finishing the construction and maintaining the building cost money, and the coworkers and eurythmists needed something, albeit little, to live on. In October it became clear the funds would run out in the next few weeks. Rudolf Steiner decided to go on tour in Holland and England with the eurythmy ensemble. The performances were well received in The Hague and even in London, where the circumstances were more difficult, and Steiner was pleased by the interest shown in the new art of movement. But in both places he voiced his concern to the members that a heartfelt connection to the center in Dornach was missing, and he pointed out the consequences of this lack. "In the moment that the center in Dornach collapses, everything collapses" (*The Hidden Side of Human Existence*).

He also spoke about his perception of the situation. "Building the Goetheanum was begun with enthusiasm. This enthusiasm has disappeared in those who were most enthusiastic in the beginning. And today they have left me to worry about how things are to be continued" (ibid).

Actually, Steiner had felt that he had been left with all the concerns relating to the building when Sophie Stinde had died in November 1915. The members were happy with the Goetheanum. They enjoyed visiting Dornach, but almost no one stepped forward to help carry the burdens, which culminated in 1922 when the funds from Germany practically dried up.

A second concern that worried Steiner had to do with the Christian Community. A number of the priests who wished to found congregations in Germany had, against Rudolf Steiner's counsel, turned to the members of the Anthroposophical Society for support. News of this reached Steiner just as he returned from London. He recognized the danger that the Christian Community would grow to the detriment of the Anthroposophical Society. The rituals and the enthusiasm of the young priests attracted many of the anthroposophists. During a meeting with the faculty of the Waldorf School, Steiner remarked, "Those things that are connected with the noblest aspirations also bear within them the greatest dangers" (300 & 2).

The third of his primary worries at this time concerned the leadership of the Anthroposophical Society. In October he had written to Edith

Maryon that "the Stuttgart gentlemen are also losing connection with the anthroposophic movement. They sit in their chairs, play executives, and people don't want to pay any attention to them" (263 & 1).

He spoke more strongly to the Waldorf teachers:

> If anthroposophic life in Stuttgart was more harmonious, the school would also profit. Things have become worse recently. Morally, everyone shuts oneself in one's own chamber, and soon we will reach the point that no one even knows anyone else.... What individuals do must flow on into the others, into what gives the society strength—joyful recognition and acknowledgment of each person's contributions. Good will is lacking. A joyful, inclusive recognition of people's contributions is missing. Individual contributions are falling by the wayside. Speak of what can be acknowledged. The Stuttgart system: lack of acknowledgement. This cripples activity.... If I work and nothing happens, I am lamed. (300 & 2)

Because of this situation, Rudolf Steiner approached Ernst Uehli, one of the three members of the council of the Anthroposophical Society. He requested that the council in the course of the next few days concern themselves with the state of the society, that they, together with other Stuttgart anthroposophists, make suggestions for a consolidation of the society. Otherwise he would see himself forced to "continue to ignore the council" and turn directly to the members (259). Second, he asked Uehli, who had been present at the founding of the Christian Community, to speak to the members about the new religious movement.

It appears that Uehli did not recognize the urgency of these requests. Since the end of the war, the council had not taken up any initiatives of its own. There had not been a general meeting of the Anthroposophical Society since 1914. Between 1914 and 1922, they had written only one newsletter, which reported on the discussions that had taken place on September 4, 1921. No action followed these discussions. Since 1919, the society had been practically without leadership, and the branches had been left alone, isolated and without any real connection to one another. Rudolf Steiner had more or less ignored the council, which, in his view, had distinguished itself through inactivity. Uehli was surprised by the demand to take action, to take his position seriously. It was another fourteen days before he contacted Carl Unger, another council member, to speak with him about Steiner's request.

For Steiner, the experience of the inertia and of the lack of understanding around him was painful. His work produced no echo. On October 14, 1922, he was forced to give a lecture to the branch although he was so overworked and exhausted that he said at the end of the lecture that the time in Stuttgart "completely annihilated his forces," because he received no real help (218). A little later, during the medical course at the end of October, one observer, Dr. Kurt Piper noticed "his poor appearance—he looked drained, even bitter." He was deeply shaken when he saw how Steiner, at the end of a lecture, sat down at a table and stared out the window, a look of vast sadness in his eyes (*Anthroposophy*, vol. 4, No. 21). On December 11, Steiner drove in the company of Eugen Kolisko and Annemarie Donath through the snow-bound Black Forest to Dornach. The last hour of the eight-hour-long trip passed in silence. Annemarie Donath told of how the car bumped and shook as it passed over the appallingly poor road.

> Every couple of minutes, we were bounced up and hit our heads against the roof. To my dismay, I heard groans escape Dr. Steiner on several occasions. He must have been in terrible pain. I will never forget the moment when he suddenly—we were getting close to Basel—turned toward the window and pointed at the sun going down, blood-red over the snow-white landscape. With a strangely altered voice, almost broken, he said softly, "The sun." There was something in his voice and his gestures that brought the aging Faust to mind. (Dubach)

Albert Steffen, after seeing Steiner that evening at Kolisko's lecture, wrote in his journal, "He is very fragile and even had to support himself with a cane." Steiner had once told the Waldorf teachers: "If I work and nothing happens, I am lamed" (300 & 2).

After his return to Dornach, Steiner was faced with the preparations for the Christmas Conference of 1922/23. There were rehearsals for two major eurythmy performances. Steiner also directed productions of the Christmas plays, acting out the various parts for the performers and even expanding upon the traditional text by adding to the paradise play the role of the Star singer, a role he gave Karl Schubert. He enjoyed these artistic endeavors and they gave him new energy. One witness described how light and agile his movements on the stage were. The image of the archangel Michael, the spirit of the time, shone through the lectures Rudolf Steiner gave during Advent. Michael was described as the messenger of the gods who received the knowledge that human beings acquired and spiritualized within the earthly realm. "An approach to science, the anthroposophic approach that is able to spiritualize the earthly, spatial powers of discernment, to raise these into the suprasensory, works upward. It stretches, in a certain sense, its hands upward to grasp the hands of Michael reaching downward from above. For it is here that a bridge can be built between human beings and the gods" (219).

There are four distinct threads apparent in the events that took place at the Goetheanum that Christmastide. First were the artistic presentations: two eurythmy performances and the Oberuferer Christmas plays. Then there were the lectures given by anthroposophic scientists and a series of discussions in the White Hall. In this context, there were two unfortunate occurrences. One of the researchers, Dr. Hans Theberath, didn't appear for his lecture; a coworker at the pharmaceutical laboratory, A. P. Imrie, demanded to hold a lecture on the morning of December 31. His presentation was extremely confused and left his listeners with a very bad impression.

In the context of the science conference, Steiner held a series of lectures entitled *The Origins of Natural Science* (326). Referring to specific moments in the development of science, he explored one part of the history of humanity. He described how humanity had emancipated itself step by step from its original unity with nature and had come to the experience of confronting nature, then based on this experience had developed ideas about the natural world. Something new could come about out of the combination of the mere sensory reflection that nature had become and the inner, apparently subjective experience that gives human beings the possibility of freedom. Steiner summarized this lecture in his own words.

> Natural science has reached the point where it observes only what is corpse-like in nature. Anthroposophical Spiritual Science must find the corresponding original essence, which exists only within the human being but in earlier stages of the evolution of the cosmos were part of outer reality.... (326)
>
> This reflection, experienced within, reveals itself to be the original essential beingness. The human being experiences this reflection, lives into the reflection as one's own reflection, and transforms it into the seed of future realities. Out of our ethics and morals, which are born out of the physical world..., will arise the physical worlds of the future, just as today a plant develops out of a seed. (326)

Rudolf Steiner gave general anthroposophic lectures on December 23, 24, 29, 30, and 31. The one given on Dec. 30 stands out. In it, he spoke about how the anthroposophic movement relates to the movement for religious renewal, the Christian Community. It appears that, with this lecture, in light of the unsettling news that had reached him earlier, Steiner had pulled the emergency brake to stop the emigration of anthroposophists to the Christian Community. In fact, he was moved by "the greatest concern for the anthroposophic movement. This concern "was what pressed me to say what I did concerning the movement for religious renewal during my next to last lecture at the Goetheanum." He expanded on this description of his personal emotions, saying:

> I certainly would not want to criticize the movement for religious renewal in any way. It came into being through my own advice three and a half months ago. It is natural for me to look upon the success of this movement with satisfaction. There can be no doubt about this. However now, after three and a half months, I have to repeat the words I spoke in Dornach, words spoken not to those involved in the movement for religious renewal, but to the anthroposophists...and these words could not be understood except as a characterization of the following: One delights in the daughter, but one must not forget the mother, not forget that the mother must also be nourished and cared for. (257)

On the surface, Steiner's efforts at that time were focused on preventing members of the anthroposophic branches from abandoning the branches believing to have discovered the pinnacle of Anthroposophy in the rituals of the Christian Community. At a deeper level, something much more important was at risk: a distinction, which was made manifest in the two organizations, but that had to be made in the soul of each individual. Steiner spoke about this in his lecture on Dec. 30, 1922.

> The different systems of the human organism must work in a pure separation from one another. Only then can they work together correctly. Thus is it also necessary that the Anthroposophical Society remain unreservedly anthroposophic, not weakened by the new movement; that whoever understands what the anthroposophic movement is—its true significance—understands it not in a haughty, arrogant manner, but in a way that reflects the challenges of our time and would summarize it with the words "Anyone who has once found his way to the Anthroposophical Society does not need religious renewal. For

would the Anthroposophical Society exist if it was in need of religious renewal!"

But religious renewal is something that is needed in the world at large, and because it is so deeply needed, assistance was given to help it come into being. (219)

As could be expected, a number of the statements Steiner made in this lecture spread quickly with the effect that a number of anthroposophists distanced themselves quickly from the Christian Community. The lecture was a heavy blow for the fledgling movement; the young priests, who heard about the Dornach lecture in their congregations, were stricken.

For Steiner, it was most important that the path inherent in the Christian Community in contrast to that of Anthroposophy not be confused. He viewed the sacramental rituals of the Christian Community as a way to bring the divine into the earthly. What was striven for in Anthroposophy was something different: to raise the earthly, the sense perceptible, to the suprasensory (compare 265 & 257).

What is often overlooked is that in these lectures Steiner presented the anthroposophic path culminating in the conscious participation of the individual in the cosmic sacrament and the spiritual communion of humanity. Looking back, it is easy to recognize in the Christmas lectures of 1922 the prelude for the remarkable lectures on the seasons from 1923. In the beginning, Steiner calls attention to how the seasons were experienced in the ancient mysteries, how in earliest times the festivals accompanied the polarity within the breathing organism of the earth. In summer, the wise men gave themselves and their thoughts over to the great expanses of the cosmos; in the depths of winter, they sought the light within themselves and in the depths of the earth. These presentations culminated in the lecture of Dec. 31, in which the knowledge of the seasons was interwoven with human understanding. Steiner showed how what revealed itself in nature held within it the story of the earth's becoming and how the individual today, through the free and independent deed of creative thought, can find her way into the realities of the cosmos. The spiritual understanding thus engendered can become "a true communion, the beginning of a cosmic sacrament appropriate to modern humanity."

Toward the end of the lecture, Steiner drew together what he had presented in a verse, which he wrote on the blackboard standing behind the lectern. Those present received with this lecture—the last to be held in the first Goetheanum—a mantram, a meditative exercise, which bore within itself the path to spiritual communion, to a cosmic sacrament. Through this last lecture, the Goetheanum became what it was meant to be: a school for Spiritual Science.

One could imagine that, had the Goetheanum not been destroyed by fire, Steiner would have continued in this vein and the Goetheanum would have become the type of place it was meant to be. Performances of the mystery plays, for which the building had been conceived, had been planned for the summer of 1923.

Chapter 46

THE GOETHEANUM FIRE

At five o'clock in the afternoon on December 31, a eurythmy performance took place at the Goetheanum. It was to be the last such performance in the building. Every seat in the large auditorium was taken. Following Rudolf Steiner's introductory words, the curtain opened, revealing the space beneath the small cupola. The "Prologue in Heaven" from Goethe's *Faust* was performed. Three archangels appeared in gold, orange and purple, surrounded by the choir of angels. The words "The Sun intones, in ancient tourney" were picked up by the colorful movements of the eurythmy. Then Mephisto arose from the depths like a ghostly bat. "Since you, oh Lord, have once again drawn near..." Mephisto's words were mimed because, as Steiner explained in his introduction, a "devilish eurythmy" had not yet been invented.

The second part of the program was completely new, festive and humorous, and the conclusion was an uninhibited *Capriccio* by Reger. The performance was followed by the lecture mentioned earlier, beginning at 8:00 p.m., and ending at around 9:30. The audience left the building and went out into the night. It was Sylvester, New Year's Eve. The night was cool. The heavy rains that had fallen since Christmas had stopped that morning. The moon, all but full, could be seen between scattered banks of clouds to the south. The day, during which it has been told a certain amount of tension was apparent, seemed to be ending calmly. Rudolf Steiner had gone home to Villa Hansi.

The last visitors left the Goetheanum at 10:00 p.m. Shortly thereafter, the two night watchmen became aware of smoke in the Goetheanum. They immediately raised the alarm: "Smoke in the White Hall!" By telephone the call for help went out to Rudolf Steiner, Haus Friedwart, the eurythmy houses, the clinic and anyone else they could think of. Ernst Aisenpreis and Max Schleutermann were the first to respond. They rushed through the south wing of the building up to the White Hall. The room was full

The Goetheanum Fire

of smoke. Max Schleutermann, who tried to make his way into the room, couldn't get enough oxygen and passed out. He had to be carried out of the building. Aisenpreis confirmed that no flames were visible in the building itself.

The local anthroposophists came hurrying from all sides with fire extinguishers; Rudolf Steiner arrived at the building. He entered the building with witnesses to inspect the electrical installations. The lights were burning throughout the building; the fuses were still intact. He then went to the Heizhaus to check the temperature of the water returning from the Goetheanum's heating system. It was a normal ninety-five degrees Fahrenheit. Then he returned to the building and went to where the south wing met the main part of the building and the stairway that led up to the White Hall. The walls there were hot and smoke was coming out of cracks in the stairs. A hole was cut into the wall with an axe. The fresh air was sucked into the hole with a howl and the fire flared and spread with a fury. His voice heavy and barely audible, Rudolf Steiner said, "There is no hope."

On the outside of the wall where they had discovered the fire stood a scaffold with a ladder on top leading up to the roof. They discovered a hole up there, through which they could look down into the fire. What was needed to start the fire was probably brought into the space between the outer and inner walls through this hole. The fire must have smoldered for hours between the walls before it began to burn openly. It's assumed that it was laid around 6:00 p.m., during the eurythmy performance. The arsonist must have been familiar with construction of the building and known about the space between the walls.

While Rudolf Steiner was searching the building for the fire's location, other anthroposophists who knew their way around the building had climbed up into the space between the cupolas in order to fight the fire from above. But no water came from the hoses, there was too little pressure, and the rising smoke drove them back down. Others worked to save as much as possible from the building: models, furniture and machines. At 10:45 p.m., the fire departments from Dornach and Arlesheim arrived. By then, they were only able to fight the fire, which had spread extraordinarily quickly, from the outside. Orders were given to evacuate the building. The lights were extinguished. Soon the firefighters, who had been joined by the company from Basel, concentrated their efforts on trying to protect the carpentry shop, so that the heat from the steadily growing fire did not set these wooden buildings ablaze.

Rudolf Steiner stood there in front of the carpentry shop with Edith Maryon and Ita Wegman. Marie Steiner, who had difficulty walking, had remained behind at Villa Hansi. It was exactly midnight, and the bells in the nearby villages had begun to ring in the New Year as the flames broke through the roof of the cupolas. Rudolf Steiner spoke about this moment a year later. "The red blaze rose up into the heavens. Dark bluish, reddish and yellow lines of flame flickered within the sea of fire, born of the metal instruments that lay within the Goetheanum, a gigantic sea of fire with the most diverse colors" (260).

In another context, in which he described how the highest spiritual beings work within the small child while at the same time being integrally related to the various metals, he spoke of something that had become clear to him as he stood there and watched the Goetheanum burn.

> The earth was formed through the melting and heating of the metals in the forces of fire. We look back into ancient times as the earth was being formed: In the metals being melted by the forces of fire, we can see one thread of the earthly deeds of the Seraphim, Cherubim, and Thrones. We can see the beings of the first hierarchy at work, supported primarily by the Thrones. We gaze back into the ancient past, when the melting of the metals by the forces of fire played a unique role in the forming of the earth, when the Thrones were principally involved and the Seraphim and Cherubim quietly did their part. The Cherubim play the primary role in the child's learning to stand, to speak and to think. But we can always see the beings of the first hierarchy working in unity with one another, their work weaving together. (231)

The colorful flames that destroyed this center of the new mysteries, revealed many things to Rudolf Steiner and allowed him as well to grasp the meaning of another great fire, the burning of the temple of Ephesus, which was to bring the ancient mysteries to an end. He described this for the first time on December 2, 1923, summarizing his impressions by saying that the flames of fire were like "writing."

> Behold the Logos
> In the burning of the fire;
> Find the solution
> In Diana's house.

"The fiery Akasha of New Year's Eve spoke these words quite clearly along with many others" (232). Such remarks show that for Steiner the fire became an ocular through which a multitude of relationships became clear.

To those people who were standing near him as the colored glow of the burning metals rose out of the fire, he said, "You must not forget this moment!" (Müller). Soon he had to look on as the roof collapsed, leaving the columns jutting up like huge torches into the heavens. The white beech columns to the west stood the longest, until seven o'clock in the morning. During this time, Rudolf Steiner walked in ever growing circles around the building. He visited briefly with Marie Steiner in Villa Hansi. He was seen afterward walking bowed down and with heavy steps up the hill with Edith Maryon at his side. At some point, either at this time or a bit later, some ardent friends began to remove everything they could from the carpentry shop and from Steiner's studio.

The large statue, *The Representative of Humanity,* was taken apart and stacked behind the carpentry shop. When Steiner saw this, a cloud of displeasure crossed his face and he turned away wordlessly. Finally he, who with the greatest presence of mind had maintained order and organized the relief work, completely exhausted from the pain of the night's events, took refuge with Ita Wegman and Edith Maryon in a small barrack between the carpentry shop and the Heizhaus on the side of the hill behind the Goetheanum. There, he stood at the window and watched the fire. The catastrophe threatened to crush him.

Emil Leinhas shared his impressions of Rudolf Steiner during that night. "Dr. Steiner stood a bit apart. From time to time, he walked closer to the fire with slow, dragging steps. He had to watch how, after so many bitter disappointments, this work too, to which he had dedicated ten productive, difficult years of his life as well as all his love, was destroyed by the flames in a few fated hours. At no time did he lose his customary calm strength. But desperation and pain were etched upon his face. He seemed to be a thousand years old" (Leinhas).

Many years later, Assja Turgenieff spoke of how this night had changed Steiner. "The light, youthful laughter that earlier had often lit up Dr. Steiner's earnest countenance, his quick, light movements, his rhythmic stride—no one could walk as he did—after the fire we never experienced these again. A huge weight lay upon his shoulders. It took effort for him to stand upright, and his walk was labored."

In letters written from his sickbed to Marie Steiner, Steiner confirmed Turgenieff's observations. October 26: "As you know, I have been estranged since January 1923 from my physical body. *That* is why the ever-increasing care became necessary" (262). By emphasizing the word *that*, he points to the fire as the direct cause of his illness. In another letter, from October 15, 1924, he wrote, "I told you quite a while ago that the connection between the higher parts of my being and my physical body has not been complete since January 1923; I lost in a certain sense in spiritual life the immediate connection to my physical organization" (262).

Otherwise, Rudolf Steiner did not speak of his pain or of his personal experiences of that night. The first words he spoke to the gathered members were, "The greatest pain knows to be silent" (256).

He spoke only of what was, as he said during the fire: "Much work and long years." Later, to the members, he said, "The work that was done with so much love and devotion over the last ten years by many enthusiastic friends of our movement has been destroyed in a single night" (259).

His pain was in no way lessened by the fact that he had known from the beginning that the building was not created for perpetuity. On March 7, 1914, he had spoken of a time in which "not a single stick of wood from our Dornach project" would remain: "Everything will be destroyed and laid waste" (286). Oswald Dubach, one of the coworkers at the Goetheanum, had heard Steiner say during a public tour of the building, "This building will be a sacrifice to the flames. We are building it in spite of this" (Raab). And in January 1921, Steiner had been made aware of the arson threats, called them to the attention of the members, and appealed to them to remain watchful. He was unmoved by this knowledge or his foresight. He did not focus his prognostic abilities on the threats in order to ward off the threatened catastrophe, but kept himself focused on his work and the tasks lying before him.

Naturally, Rudolf Steiner's enemies took the opportunity to mock him. They reveled in the fact that the "clairvoyant" Steiner had not been able to foresee the disaster. He spoke about this to the workers at the Goetheanum. "We must merely take these enmities into consideration; we just have to think about how much enmity one needs for newspapers to print such tastelessness after the fact. Didn't the 'clairvoyant' Steiner see this coming? I won't even speak about the incredible stupidity of such things. But it is clear that there is a malevolent degree of bad feeling present when people feel it necessary to print such things" (259).

The challenge now was to continue the work without pause to keep the adversaries from achieving their goal. After Steiner had convinced himself on New Year's morning that, in spite of the water and smoke damage, the carpentry shop could be used and that the costumes for the Christmas play had been saved, he spread the word that the performances would precede as planned.

At the same time, he felt it was important to inform the public of what had happened in order to squelch any rumors. At 2:00 p.m., he received representatives of the *National-Zeitung*, a Basel newspaper, as well as other newspapers, at Villa Hansi and gave an interview in which he described the way events had unfolded and confirmed that "the facts point to an outside arsonist" (259). Then he announced that the work would continue without pause, that at 5:00 p.m. the Three Kings play would be performed, and at 8:00 p.m. there was to be a lecture. Finally, he answered the question of whether he would build again. "Without question," he stated, but he added it would be different, simpler, and not with wood. "But the artistic gesture will remain" (259).

At 5:00 p.m., Rudolf Steiner ascended the makeshift stage in the carpentry shop and addressed the members. During the performance that followed, the angel lost her voice for a moment but then overcame her sobs and the play from the holy three kings and Herodias was performed. At the end, the ensemble circled the room embracing all who were present. Before the evening lecture, Rudolf Steiner gave the audience a short summary of the events of the previous night and emphasized again that all the evidence pointed to arson. The circumstances in which it was held are not apparent from the content of the lecture, the sixth in the series concerning the evolution of the sciences.

The following days, weeks, and months were taken up with the task of cleaning up the ruins and with legal questions pertaining to the insurance. On January 3, the police decided after interviewing all the witnesses that it was indeed a case of arson. It was assumed that a man named Jacob Ott from Arlesheim had laid the fire, since he had disappeared that night. This assumption arose solely because he had been discovered missing after the fire and rumors had it that he had fled the country. In fact, Jacob Ott had died in the fire. On January 10, Ehrenfried Pfeiffer discovered bits of human bones in the debris of the small cupola. There was evidence leading to the conclusion that these were the bones of Jacob Ott. That was, however, not enough evidence to prove that he was also the arsonist. Rudolf Steiner always refused to answer the question as to the identity of the one responsible for the fire.

In the ensuing weeks, Rudolf Steiner took it upon himself to work through all the questions concerning the insurance. He took the risk of not hiring a lawyer. He dictated the necessary letters and was present at all the negotiations that led up to the final payment of 3,183,000 Swiss francs. Not counting the ideal and artistic value of the building—paintings, sculpture and the colored windows were all destroyed—the fire caused financial damage to the movement of 2 million francs, since the sum paid by the insurance company did not cover the actual value of the building.

Besides the damages that the bitter, irreplaceable loss the fire had brought, this night had also borne witness to the courage, initiative and solidarity of the anthroposophists; each, young and old, had done everything he or she could that night. Rudolf Steiner had also noticed this and addressed it explicitly. "On the night of the fire, as always, when action was truly needed, the members did not waver, but sprang into the breach in a way that did justice to every ideal" (259).

Chapter 47

STUTTGART 1923

When Rudolf and Marie Steiner traveled to Stuttgart on January 16, 1923, they ventured into a land that had been spiraling into an escalating crisis since the French had occupied the Ruhr region on January 11. The inflation of the past years worsened; in the succeeding months the currency would become worthless. There was unrest throughout the German Reich, unrest that led to open conflict in the fall of 1923. These events naturally also concerned the German anthroposophists. It is necessary to keep this in mind as we proceed.

Rudolf Steiner expected to be given constructive suggestions for the consolidation of the Anthroposophical Society when he arrived in Stuttgart. He felt it was self-evident that a number of members would recognize the situation and take steps to rectify it. When he had visited the school briefly on January 9 and 10 to greet visiting teachers from England, a group of seven Waldorf teachers had asked to speak with him. Thus, he returned to Stuttgart this time hopeful and was pleased to find a number of people gathered who wanted to take initiative (259). He met with this so-called "circle of seven" immediately upon arrival in the society's house on the Landhausstrasse. What critical aspects would the teachers have recognized? What solutions would they propose?

In addition to the problems mentioned above, a number of further questions had been long waiting to be addressed. Since 1919, the center of anthroposophic activity in Germany had moved from Berlin to Stuttgart. The north and east of the country had come to lie in the lee of anthroposophic activity. Before 1914, Rudolf Steiner had been able to hold the society together, give the members new impulses and a feeling of connectedness through his visits to all the various branches and groups. It had become impossible to do so after 1918. Branches, which he had visited often for courses and lectures such as those in Dusseldorf, Hamburg, Hannover, Kassel, Karlsruhe, and Nuremberg, never saw him again after 1918.

In other places, such as Munich, Leipzig, and Breslau, he only appeared for public lectures. He only irregularly made it back to the branch in Berlin that he had founded and led, as his time was taken up almost exclusively by the work in Dornach and by the initiatives in Stuttgart.

Instead of Rudolf Steiner, speakers from Stuttgart traveled now and again to various places in Germany. The newsletters of the Threefold Association and the Association of Higher Education were distributed. The branches were viewed as local centers for the threefold movement and they tried out of an old sense of loyalty to live up to the new expectations. However, the Anthroposophical Society itself lacked an inner sense of unity and an ongoing renewal of its objectives. As was mentioned above, there were no general assemblies, and the single newsletter that went out between 1914 and 1922 could do little to spark a sense of shared purpose. The anthroposophists living outside of Stuttgart felt as though they were being ruled by "Stuttgart," but not noticed. When they visited Stuttgart, they often met up against a self-absorbed bureaucracy, anonymous and cold.

The following institutions had been founded in Stuttgart: the Waldorf School, the stock company *Der Kommenende Tag*, the Clinical Therapeutic Institute, the research institute, which came out of the threefold movement, the *Bund für anthroposophische Hochschularbeit* (The Association for Anthroposophic Higher Science), the weekly newspaper *Anthroposophy* and the monthly journal *Die Drei*. In addition, there were two branches and a whole series of anthroposophic study groups. Some of these endeavors, such as the Waldorf School, absorbed those people involved almost entirely; others, like the Federation for Free Culture, existed only on paper. The two branches had little to do with one another. Carl Unger headed up one of them. He worked with a strict epistemological approach. Toni Völker, who was the leader of the other, strove to cultivate the esoteric. The Anthroposophical Society itself was pretty much non-existent. In any case, it lacked direction and leadership. No one had a sense of the whole.

The situation was exacerbated by the lack of human contact between the people connected with the various endeavors. The different groups, even single individuals, worked in isolation. Everyone left the others to work in peace, but took pains to insure that the lines of demarcation between the various fields of work were not crossed. Each was a king in his own castle.

When Rudolf Steiner met with the group of Waldorf teachers, it quickly became clear that they had no idea of the real problem. They hadn't grasped that the Anthroposophical Society, which needed to enliven, inspire, and unify everything, had no direction or guidance. The seven teachers had instead personalized the problem. Walter Johannes Steiner explained that the society's executive council had become a "joke." There was an especial animosity toward Carl Unger. They were of the opinion that because of his strict method and his followers, he squelched any independent sparks of life.

Rudolf Steiner recognized the danger of this personalization: Carl Unger, as the representative of an entire generation of anthroposophists, would be forced out of the executive council; a new beginning would be attempted although no one had gained insight into the true nature of the problem. This was something a majority of the older members would not condone. Steiner was also disappointed to discover that Ernst Uehli, who he had asked to take steps toward a consolidation of the society, had been so vague in communicating this request that nothing had happened. The result of this first meeting—if one is justified in speaking of results—was that Ernst Uehli resigned his position in the executive council. Carl Unger was invited to a meeting on the afternoon of the next day. These meetings were followed by a meeting of the so-called "Circle of Thirty." All of the meetings showed the tendency to want to solve the problems rhetorically with various slogans.

Some of the slogans stated that people need to meet one another, people need to trust one another, there is a need for active energy, and it is necessary to be fully conscious of the situation. These slogans, although they were well meant, were empty. Rudolf Steiner found himself forced to take a stand against the rhetorical solutions being suggested. He wanted the situation to be seen for what it was. "This presentation," he remarked after listening to one of the suggestions, "is like a little opiate. If we begin in this manner, without any clarity, we will have based our discussions on something that is not true" (259).

Struggling with the bitter understanding that even the best of the anthroposophists had not yet awakened to an understanding of the true nature of the situation, Rudolf Steiner returned to Dornach on January 18. Negotiations regarding the fire and the fact that anthroposophic life there had taken an unhealthy turn demanded his presence immediately.

He had spoken about what he thought was needed on January 14 to the members in Dornach, presenting it in the form of a picture. The picture was not an explicit metaphor; it needed to be contemplated and unfolded within the soul if one was to truly understand it. He reintroduced it in various forms later.

> Imagine, contemplate, meditate on the question of awakening. In this time, when the accusations literally pour in through the windows, many long for various forms of the esoteric. Yes, my dear friends, the esoteric is present. Take hold of it! But more than anything, what is esoteric within the Anthroposophical Society is the will to awaken.... This must take its place within the Anthroposophical Society. Then it can radiate outward and become the focal point for an awakening of our entire civilization. (259)

What Steiner pointed out with this picture is that our daily awakening includes more than merely opening our eyes and beginning to take part in what is going on around us. In addition to conscious observation and the capacity to see and recognize the totality we meet, awakening also brings a feeling of sensitivity for the situation, the will to do what is needed, and the willingness to come to an understanding with others concerning a situation and find forms of shared action.

On January 22, Rudolf Steiner returned again to Stuttgart. This time he was awaited by the "Circle of Thirty," now expanded to include about sixty individuals. In this newly constituted social context, he found himself having to explain to those present what had already taken place. He spoke again about the task given to Ernst Uehli and said he had expected steps toward a consolidation of the society to have been worked out. Then he added, "Otherwise I would feel forced to continue to ignore the executive council and to turn directly to the members to try and find ways to begin to consolidate the society" (259).

His use of the word *continue* suggests that he had already ignored the executive council. In addition, he hints here for the first time of the alternative he will initiate at the end of 1923—to go over the heads of the present executive council and take the leadership of the society into his own hands. Early in 1923, however, he still hoped that a new impulse for the life of the society would arise from the members. He emphasized that the solution was not to be found sitting around a table. It was not possible to simply dictate change. Any change would have to be rooted in the true intentions of the members. The period of conceiving and organizing projects had passed.

Once again, circumstances at the Goetheanum called him back to Dornach.

Returning to continue the talks in Stuttgart on January 29, he expected those who had been involved in the previous dialogues to voice concrete suggestions. He was disappointed. Suddenly Stuttgart's own internal conflicts were the subject of debate. He broke off the discussion of the value or lack of value of Carl Unger's work, while at the same time emphasizing that the executive council had done nothing at all over the last few years (259). Without accusing Unger directly, Steiner said, "These are methods of pure negligence, simply filling a position without taking any action. No action has been taken since 1919" (259).

After awhile, discussion began again concerning the work in the branches. He broke in, saying for a second time that there had been no guidance, no leadership since 1919. The individuals who should have been leading had not been conscious of the fact that they were to lead (259).

In the subsequent discussion, Steiner became increasingly explicit. In all the Stuttgart initiatives with the exception of the Waldorf School, where Steiner had been responsible for hiring the teachers, true talent had been driven off. Those responsible had indulged in spiritual incest (259). The work in the clinic and in the research institutes progressed much too slowly, the results were not brought to bear.

The next day, specific questions were addressed in detail, openly and frankly. The *vade mecum* for doctors, which Steiner had requested since 1920, had never been written despite all his help. The *Drei* had published a completely unproductive debate concerning atomism and a misunderstood phenomenological method. Steiner once again indicated the alternative of ignoring the Stuttgart executive council and going directly to the members (259). He spoke openly about what he had experienced in these meetings. "One could only wish that something positive would be spoken about with true warmth! That is what we need. And it is what is missing. A certain coldness rules here, a terrible coldness. This entire gathering has been excessively cold. There was no warmth to be felt" (259).

Completely exhausted, Steiner asked at the end of this meeting, which continued into the early hours of the morning of February 1, to be relieved of the problems the researchers and doctors had brought upon themselves. He needed to focus his efforts on the Waldorf School and the fate of the Anthroposophical Society.

He returned yet again to Stuttgart, for the fourth time since the beginning of the year, from February 5 through 8. It had become clear that there would be a delegates meeting in Stuttgart at the end of February. A letter had to be drafted, calling upon the delegates to respond to the invitation. Naturally, Steiner was asked for his thoughts and counsel. Yet, as in an earlier situation, he refused. "It makes no sense for you to say that I should give you counsel. All that happens is that what I say is repeated. I'm not accusing you. It just doesn't help. All that helps is what is rooted in the soul of the individual, rooted well enough to become reality and permeated with will (259).

He had to thus refuse in this situation to draft the positive aspects of the appeal to the delegates. Anything he wrote would be passed on as "One should!," "The Doctor has said...," or "One should not!" This horrified him (259). One observer noted that Steiner had said, "It would be damaging for me to articulate the positive points" (259). In another setting, Steiner laid out his reasoning. "It would not be right for me to issue any form of directive that would have to be followed. I have said that if the executive council is to have any meaning, it has to have an intentional direction that transcends the mere formalities. The contents of the executive council's will cannot equal zero" (259).

With a certain harsh persistence, he challenged the participants to be independent, to take initiative. He was convinced that individuals had to act on their own intentions. The discussions were, however, without result. One member of the circle even went so far as to suggest that they should return to the way things were before 1918. Steiner responded by asking whether it "was not possible to take a step forward rather than leaping into the abyss" (259). A return to the past was unthinkable for him. "We cannot re-create the way things were in 1918" (259).

Friedrich Rittelmeyer had been invited to participate in the meetings held on February 7. Rittelmeyer, who bore individual responsibility for a spiritual movement and was not mixed up in the Stuttgart quarrels, grasped the essential points quickly and brought them in a way they could be heard around the table. In spite of this, no progress was made. Upon his return to Dornach, Steiner reported that the meetings to date had been without result. However, in the next few days a letter was to be drafted and circulated among the branches (259).

When Rudolf and Marie Steiner returned to Stuttgart for the fifth time on February 13, the invitation to all branches to send representatives to a delegates' meeting had been printed and was ready to be mailed. The meetings focused on preparing the meeting itself. Steiner intended the meeting to be held with a certain formality and requested a chairman be named. After some discussion, Emil Leinhas was chosen. A member of the then sitting executive council, he had assisted Steiner in The Coming Day and, more importantly, during the liquidation of Futurum.

At the beginning of the meeting, the question was raised of whether consideration should be given to the personal sensitivities of this or that person. Steiner responded immediately. He had too often watched the tendency to dance around people's sensitivities and inclinations lead to ridiculous decisions. When he could, he had called attention to this at the time. His response was that the fact that personal sensitivities play such a prominent role is ruinous for the society, especially when they appear in other guises. "If we are going to start again to deal with the sensitivities, any new steps again become impossible. We have to start casting off the untruths and recognize: We can found a society of Philistines. Then we can take personal sensitivities into consideration. But in doing so, we will drive Anthroposophy out of the society" (259).

During these meetings, the delegates' meeting was prepared in detail, from the choice of the chairman to who would speak on what topic and in which way. The circle of those responsible would not find itself unprepared as it entered the difficult and unpredictable gathering.

The invitation had been held very open. Following Steiner's lead, the Stuttgarters had restrained themselves from putting out guidelines for the choice of delegates. "We wish to give you a free hand in deciding how to choose your delegates and in determining the number of delegates you would like to send. We would find it very good if all groups doing anthroposophic work, whether within or outside of the recognized branches, would send representatives" (259).

On February 23, Rudolf Steiner traveled to Stuttgart for the sixth and last of the preparatory meetings. On February 24, the plan for the coming four-day meeting was discussed for the final time. It would have to take place in the Gustav-Siegle House as roughly 1000 people, in spite of the difficult travel conditions and the galloping inflation, were expected from Germany, Austria and Switzerland.

The meeting began at 8:00 p.m. on February 25. Emil Leinhas's words of welcome were followed by a talk by Eugen Kolisko about the situation in the Anthroposophical Society. Kolisko's talk sparked a lively discussion that continued until after 11:00 p.m. Rudolf Steiner listened in silence. The next day, he was also quite reticent, speaking briefly only twice to voice his understanding of where the problems lay. On the afternoon of February 26, the meeting became enmeshed in an escalating debate on a point of order. The attendees resisted continuing with the planned presentations. Chaos threatened. Steiner spoke twice, each time briefly, and finally the participants agreed to listen to the presentations in order to insure that the following discussion would be based on a full understanding of the situation. Speakers then reported on the work of the threefold movement, The Coming Day, the Waldorf School, the clinic, the research institute, and there was a statement concerning the relationship to the Christian Community, the Association for Continuing Education, the youth movement and, finally, concerning opposition to the anthroposophic movement.

In the report that he gave of the meeting when he returned to Dornach, Steiner spoke positively of the heartfelt, deep words Albert Steffen had spoken, he praised the brilliant lecture given by Louis Werbeck concerning the literary opponents of Anthroposophy, and he mentioned the freshness in how Hans Büchenbacher spoke of his experiences and encounters as a new member of the society. He mentioned none of the Stuttgart coworkers in this manner.

He described the thoughts that moved him on February 27, after "extraordinary, wonderful things had taken place alongside of other things" a few days later in Dornach. "If this continues tomorrow—tomorrow was the last day—as it has until now, the delegates will leave one another much as they had come. For nothing had become apparent—naturally, there was much Anthroposophy; some of the contributions were excellent—of what lived in the people who were there.... It was a classic example of life in abstractions. And there was true chaos on Tuesday evening" (257).

It was probably during this period of chaos—which was not captured by the minutes of the meeting—that a situation developed that Rudolf Steiner later spoke about in Dornach, describing his perceptions.

> There was a moment when I actually should have said, "In light of what has just happened, I must end my participation in this society." For other reasons, this is of course not possible, now that the society has taken that into itself; one cannot retreat in the face of that. But if

the deciding factor had only been developed in the conference room in Stuttgart in that moment, I would have been completely justified in saying, "Now I must find another way to bring Anthroposophy into the world; I have to separate myself from the Anthroposophical Society." (257)

The thought that he would have to separate himself from the society, which had become a "severe obstacle" (259) for the further development of the anthroposophic work, accompanied him throughout 1923. It was not the only disappointment he faced that year.

In spite of his thoughts and feelings, Rudolf Steiner gave a lecture that evening of February 27 on the "conditions of forming anthroposophic communities" (257). He contrasted two images. In the first, he described the religious ritual through which the suprasensory is called into the realm of the earthly, reminding those who experience it of their life in the spirit. He contrasted this with the image of a "reversed *cultus*" (257), through which individuals raise themselves out of the earthly, out of the sense perceptible, through the senses and into the spiritual by awakening to the soul-spiritual nature of another human being. In this awakening for the soul-spiritual reality of the other, a community can be created.

Something of the central idea of the lectures Steiner would give in 1924 when he progressed from the experience of the soul-spiritual of the other to knowledge of the role of destiny in shaping the spiritual individuality illuminated this lecture. "If a true understanding of Anthroposophy is present, it leads not merely to ideas about the spirit, but to communion with the spirit. The consciousness of this communion forms community. Those communities, which destiny anticipates, will form. Their forming will be the effect of a proper anthroposophic consciousness" (257).

Toward the end of the lecture, Rudolf Steiner suggested how such a knowledge of the various karmic groupings could be practiced. He suggested separating the Anthroposophical Society into two groups: the "old Anthroposophical Society" and an "alliance of independent anthroposophic communities" (257).

The audience was completely unprepared for this suggestion, through which Steiner hoped to create space for the younger generation, especially those who came to Anthroposophy from the youth movement and other unconventional groups, and to alleviate the points of contention by differentiating between the streams of destiny. Thirty-year-old Eugen Kolisko was one of the speakers following Steiner. He had the courage to voice his feelings and spoke to the audience.

> We would have to carry all our hopes to the grave if such a split came about in the society. You must be very clear about the consequences. The new, independent society would not bother with these institutions. It is the last moment to come to some form of shared insight, and I believe it is my task to speak from the position that I have placed my entire efforts in the service of the institutions since I became a member of this movement. (259)

With his suggestion, Steiner sparked the resistance of one of the most active anthroposophists, a man he respected highly. This was not the only time it would happen. Kolisko's opposition was born of a fully justified feeling. Ten months later, Steiner would admit that his lecture had "contradicted all the fundamental pillars of the Anthroposophical Society" (260). At that time, however, a division of the society seemed to be the only possible solution.

When the meeting broke up at 11:00 p.m., groups of people continued to discuss the suggestion. The general mood was one of bewilderment. Steiner returned to his apartment on the Landhausstrasse.

> They came to get me at midnight. I was not quite ready to fall asleep—not quite—but they came to get me. There was a meeting taking place downstairs. On the way from the second to the first floor, I was held up by a sort of in-between meeting, so got to the meeting downstairs at about 12:45 a.m. It was immediately clear: the situation had been understood, it had been correctly understood. (257)

He spoke with this group of younger members until 2:15 a.m., and during the course of the next day, Steiner's suggestion was made clear to the delegates. Rudolf Steiner spoke: "Unity upon a spiritual scientific foundation comes about through differentiation, individualization, not centralization" (259).

A committee of the Independent Anthroposophical Society was formed and, although there was yet another organizational muddle, the gathering ended with another lecture by Steiner, in which he spoke once again about all the difficulties involved. In the report he gave after returning to Dornach, he pointed out "that things will have to be this way for a while. Not forever; one cannot determine how things will be for all eternity" (257).

Steiner was again in Stuttgart to lecture from March 6 through 8. On March 7, he met with the leadership of both societies. There is no written documentation of this meeting, nor of the next one, which took place on March 25. The only thing certain is that Steiner was bitterly disappointed. He wrote a confidential letter to Edith Maryon on the evening of March 25. "As far as the society goes, I have only one thing to say: I would prefer to have no more to do with it. Everything that the executives are doing disgusts me" (263 & 1).

And on May 11: "The A. S. sleeps on; there is no way to awaken it" (263 & 1).

On August 1, he is no less explicit. "I am well, but things are unbelievably terrible in the society. Impossibilities appear in every corner" (263 & 1).

When speaking to the members, Steiner was less drastic, less personal, but no less clear. He ended his lecture in Stuttgart on May 11 with the remark that the tendency to be asleep was the worst thing for the Anthroposophical Society. After the division into two societies, the groups, which had earlier disturbed each other's sleep, now slept peacefully beside one another (224).

What did Rudolf Steiner experience? He saw that there were a number of highly gifted people gathered in Stuttgart. Unger, Heydebrand, Kolisko, Schwebsch, Stein, Hahn, Baravalle and others had given proof of their abilities both in their disciplines and as speakers. Thus Steiner was quite satisfied with the art-in-education conference that had been organized at the end of March 1923. He told the teachers the conference had not only been "inwardly an extremely good presentation," but that it had also left a deep impression on the participants (300 & 3).

Speaking in Dornach, he gave a general characterization not only of the teachers, but also of the older Stuttgart coworkers—with the exception of Emil Leinhas—by saying, "When I travel to Stuttgart and something needs to be taken care of...I just need to push a button. The leading personalities have a fine understanding. They understand everything immediately; there is no need for long explanations.... It is absolutely clear for them. I just need to give hints. But they then rarely do it" (257).

One could consider this barbed characterization unjust. The coworkers in Stuttgart all worked in comparison to normal standards very hard. We can only begin to understand what Steiner experienced when we turn our attention to the spiritual scientific idea of the will. True will lives in the world, is directly connected to what is taking place and acts out of this connection. This will, alive in the world, is aware of the problems and imbalances within itself and acts out of the situation. It does not form abstract principles to cause justifiable actions, it responds to what it perceives to be necessary.

This is easily observed in the act of knowing. One can abstractly have the good will to listen to another person and force oneself to listen. This listening is fundamentally different from a listening born of a true interest in the other person. In true interest lives the will to understand and to help if needed or otherwise enter into action. Rudolf Steiner reported on a conference that had been held in Stuttgart.

> The Stuttgart contingent had high hopes for this conference. Yet in spite of their good will, it will certainly not lead to anything real. For this "good will" is not the spiritual force of the will, but rather the notion (illusion) that one has the will. These personalities have great capacities—which comes to expression, for instance, in the Waldorf teachers; in many ways, they even have a certain genius—but of the nature of the will [they have] only the "mental image of the will." They end up saying, "We have 'good will,' but we don't understand what we should do." Truthfully, they should be saying, "We have an excellent understanding of what we should do, but we don't have the will to do it." (263 &1)

Especially painful for Rudolf Steiner was the lack of protection from the attacks and accusations of his opponents in the months following the fire at the Goetheanum, in which he lost the home that had been created for his work. The campaign of the enemies of the anthroposophic movement had reached one of its low points before the fire at the "Conference of Non-anthroposophic Experts on Anthroposophy" that was held from October 29 to 31, 1922, in Berlin. The worst enemies of the movement dominated the conference. Dr. Heinrich Goesch, who had been expelled from the Anthroposophical Society in 1915, was one of the "experts" who spoke. He and others ranted about the sexual magic practiced by Steiner. He asserted that Steiner served a devil of the will, an "Asura"—that he practiced black magic and would assert undue influence, especially on women. Such idiocy, along with other sordid rumors, was taken in without resistance by the theologians and professors attending the conference.

Shortly thereafter, a report of the conference was circulated in which Goesch's talk about Steiner's personality was praised and termed decisive for the entire conference. Now it was clear that behind Anthroposophy was a diabolical force.

Friedrich Rittelmeyer took it upon himself to take a stand against this absurdity, which was beneath any accepted *niveau* and made any discussion impossible. He wrote a rebuttal for the weekly journal *Anthroposophy*. His language was elegant. Although he called gossip, gossip and the ridiculous claims made by Goesch and others he refuted, he stopped short of calling the lies, lies and the slander, slander. He maintained a civil tone.

The editors of the journal received a letter from a Dr. R. Lempp in response to Rittelmeyer's article. Lempp, a prominent pastor in Württemberg, wrote that the conference in Berlin was a *comprehensive effort to gain an understanding of Anthroposophy* and emphasized the importance of Goesch's presentation. The editors of the journal printed this letter with a footnote regretting that it had taken so long to get it too print and added a response from Rittelmeyer that began with the words "What is so pleasing about this letter...." and in which Lempp is addressed as "Dear Dr. Lempp."

Steiner, who read the anthroposophic journals regularly, discovered this exchange immediately and was deeply hurt by it. Since he was in Stuttgart at the time, he brought it to the "Circle of Thirty" and voiced his indignation openly. "This journal has become the voice of blackguards and moral liars!" (259).

He accused Rittelmeyer of taking a friendly approach with Lempp, of having handled him with kid gloves. At Steiner's cost. But he was most exasperated that no member of the "Circle of Thirty" had noticed the inappropriateness of the exchange and that he had had to bring it to their attention. Steiner was not at all shy of justified criticism, but he was very clear with whom one could enter into a discussion and with whom one should not. For instance, in 1924 he wrote a relatively sharp critique of a book by a Benedictine monk, Alois Mager, titled *Theosophy and Christianity*, in which he attacked various aspects of Anthroposophy. Steiner never shied away from an objective debate.

But in light of the manifold untruths and abstruse claims the highly regarded "non-anthroposophic experts on Anthroposophy" had been gullible enough to believe, these were people to stay as far away from as possible. Beginning in 1924, Steiner added a notice at the beginning of each of his published lectures saying that the content of the lecture would not be discussed with anyone lacking the necessary qualifications.

The chief editor of the journal *Anthroposophy*, Jürgen von Grone, was dismissed as a result of the exchange. The journal printed a series of articles and letters designed to smooth things over. But Rudolf Steiner felt personally maligned by the whole episode. He could not accept sacrificing the truth in order to maintain an appearance of politeness with the wrong people. He knew this lack of judgment placed obstacles in the path of his own work. At the end of a meeting in Dornach, he found himself having to say:

> To a great extent in the Anthroposophical Society, anything that has to do with me is regarded as trifling, insignificant. I'm allowed to say my piece, but then nobody does anything that is in any way connected to it. And when I am subjected to this kind of abuse in our own journals, our work will suffer. But this sense of my insignificance is already so widespread that such an accusatory letter can lie around in Stuttgart for three or four weeks, none of those responsible concerns himself with it, then it slips into the journal in conjunction with a glorification of the opponent and no one wants to take responsibility. (259)

After all this, it could come as no surprise that Rudolf Steiner began to cut back on the time he spent in Stuttgart. In May 1923, he announced that the demands of the anthroposophic movement necessitated a change in his working focus and he would be stepping back from his responsibilities in The Coming Day. He resigned his position as chairman of the council (259).

In spite of this, he found himself dealing with questions concerning The Coming Day until January 1925. He also continued to work with the Stuttgart institutes and, of course, the Waldorf School. But the only large anthroposophic conference that Rudolf Steiner put on in Germany in 1924 took place in Breslau, not Stuttgart. And after founding the School for Spiritual Science in 1924, he did not hold class lessons in Stuttgart.

CHAPTER 48

SPRING 1923: THE STRUGGLE TO REBUILD

Rudolf Steiner had good reasons to put so much effort into the consolidation of the Anthroposophical Society in Germany, although following the fire, he had more than enough to do in Dornach. The anthroposophic work had originated in Germany, and the society had the most members there. There were more than a hundred working groups with upwards of 10,000 members in Germany. He was afraid that if this work could not be consolidated, it would lead to a more widespread crisis in the society as a whole.

To isolate the German problems within the country, Steiner began to decentralize the structures. Until 1921, there had been in essence one Anthroposophical Society with a "central executive" based in Berlin. The office of the executive moved to Stuttgart in 1921. This central executive headed up the Anthroposophical Society worldwide. In 1922, the Swiss Anthroposophical Society with roughly 700 members was formed with Albert Steffen as chairman. By the beginning of 1923, it had become clear that the leadership in Stuttgart could only speak for the German section of the society. Following the delegates' meeting, the Anthroposophical Society in Germany, and the German Independent Anthroposophical Society both held the status of national societies. Four further national societies were formed in 1923. On January 8, Steiner had agreed to the formation of a French society under the guidance of Alice Sauerwein (259). In his letter to Sauerwein, Dornach is named as the center for the general anthroposophic work throughout the world.

In April 1923, he began work to stabilize the anthroposophic situation in Switzerland. From April 5 through April 12, he held public lectures in Bern, Basel, Zürich, Wintherthür, and St. Gallen with the title "What was intended with the Goetheanum? What is Anthroposophy?" These lectures show just how aware he was of public opinion. He began by speaking of the public's perceptions and opinions concerning the now-destroyed

Goetheanum and Anthroposophy, then led them a short distance on the anthroposophic path to higher knowledge. As he had in 1919 before the threefold campaign began, he thus insured that there would be understanding for his intentions in Switzerland, the home of the Goetheanum.

That was but a beginning. From April 15 through 22, he organized a course for Swiss teachers with the help of Walter Johannes Stein, Ernst Blümel, Hermann von Baravalle, and Caroline von Heydebrand. A number of Czech teachers also attended. Once again, Rudolf Steiner proceeded with utmost sensitivity. In the first lecture, he developed a picture of the challenges in education using the life of the widely respected Indian scholar Rabindranath Tagore as a backdrop. He continued with a lively description of the three essential steps in a child's development—achieving uprightness and learning to walk, learning to speak, and the unfolding of the capacity of thinking. Only then did he come to speak of Waldorf pedagogy.

The Swiss teachers experienced the presence of the Waldorf teachers, who shared what they had learned and discovered in the practice and were always available for conversations, as especially gratifying. On four evenings, Rudolf Steiner took time to describe in a vivid, concrete manner practical steps on the anthroposophic path to higher knowledge. A non-anthroposophic teacher wrote about the course in the *Bernese School Bulletin*.

> And every morning, when we could listen again to Dr. Steiner speak, we felt a bit closer to him and could understand a bit better what he had to say, in the manner he had to say it. Then we newbies would stand together and each day would ask with more insistence: "Why aren't more of our colleagues here?"...I spoke with many of the participants. I know of no one who had to leave disappointed. At the very least, I received unbelievably valuable ideas for my work in the school. There was much I didn't understand, especially about Anthroposophy...but...most everyone [thought]: "I came here in search of enrichment for my work in the school and that is what I have found bountifully." In addition, there was unhoped-for bounty for heart and soul. (*Goetheanum*, vol. 2)

A general meeting of the Swiss Anthroposophical Society began on the last day of this course. This proceeded quite harmoniously and pleasantly until Steiner appeared in the afternoon after giving the final lecture for the teachers' course. Although there was no necessity to debate individual points in the context of the Swiss society—the Futurum, Inc. debacle was not on the agenda—the situation in the society was no better here than elsewhere. Steiner raised the question: "What is this Anthroposophical Society? The people come together, they read lectures and what-not; it is naught but a collection of cliques!" (259).

The concern with internal questions, listening to or reading lectures aloud, and being given esoteric exercises did not seem to Steiner to be vital enough content for a society. These things could be done without any societal framework. "None of these are the tasks of the society" (259). He was deeply convinced "that it is necessary for the Anthroposophical Society to give itself real tasks, that it serve a real societal function, that it is thus something special in conjunction with the anthroposophic movement.... As long as this task is not present, the situation... will not change. On the contrary, it will continue to get worse" (259).

The general meeting had the opportunity to set an example, to show how the society could set itself a positive goal, could take on a task "that would generate respect." Opponents of Anthroposophy could not be effectively countered by refuting their writings, but in that real tasks were taken up. If the discussions that never resulted in any positive actions simply continued, it would make it "necessary for me to cease my activities for the Anthroposophical Society, to focus on my own personal work; I could no longer consider the Anthroposophical Society, which can't seem to decide to take up any real tasks, to be the context for my work" (259).

A good beginning would be for the society to take up the challenge of really supporting the initiatives, such as the clinic, that had arisen out of the anthroposophic work. In addition, it would be important to recognize and support the truly active, productive individuals in the society and give them the support they need. Here Steiner called attention to Albert Steffen's work.

Toward the end of the meeting, he called their attention to something else. A Swiss officer, Colonel Gertsch, had offered Rudolf Steiner an estate near Winterthur as a place to rebuild the Goetheanum. Steiner and Albert Steffen had visited the site on April 11. Colonel Gertsch had set the price for the estate at 1.3 million Swiss francs. In the discussion, it became clear that no one wanted to leave Dornach. Rudolf Steiner was also of this opinion, but he felt it would be impolitic and naïve to simply turn down the offer; the citizens of Dornach and the authorities in Solothurn should at least know that there were other options. As the discussion continued, it also came to light that there was a request from Stuttgart that consideration be given to building there. Finally, Albert Steffen was asked by the general meeting to draft a resolution saying that they would welcome efforts to rebuild the Goetheanum in Dornach, but it should be clearly stated that there were other possible locations, if unforeseen difficulties should arise. The meeting concluded with the passing of this resolution. It was to be continued on June 10.

In the meantime, Rudolf Steiner was to take two major trips. The first took him to Prague, which he visited for the first time since 1918. He gave two public lectures and two lectures for members, and there was a public eurythmy performance at what was then the German theater. The public lectures generated the most interest. More than 850 people attended the first lecture. Rudolf Steiner spoke in general about Anthroposophy, and then, after a lively discussion, continued with a short talk about the Waldorf School. The second lecture attracted more than 1200 people. The two branches in Prague—the one Czech, the other German, which usually worked separately from one another—joined together for the two branch lectures, in which the themes developed in the public talks were deepened.

After a short working sojourn in Dornach, the next trip took Steiner to Stuttgart, Berlin and on to Oslo. There, in addition to a series of public lectures, he gave a series of lectures in which he spoke about the spiritual life of the human being in the cosmos, Christ's effect on humanity, and the historical significance of the Mystery of Golgotha. In Oslo, it was also possible to hold an esoteric lesson for a small group of anthroposophists. This appears to indicate that the society in Norway had achieved a certain level of inner consolidation.

On May 17, the Norwegian national day of celebration, the Norwegian Anthroposophical Society was formed without any complications. Its intention was to unite itself with the center in Dornach when the time was right. Rudolf Steiner spoke with absolute satisfaction of the results of this trip to the north. He wrote to Edith Maryon, "Everything went well in Norway. From one Monday to the next, I gave thirteen lectures and had a number of other things to do" (263 & 1).

On his journey back to Dornach, Rudolf Steiner stopped in Berlin. It was to be his last visit. In a lecture for the members of the Anthroposophical Society there, he summarized many of the themes of the lectures he had given elsewhere that spring. Toward the end of the lecture, he touched on the cosmic and social significance of a future St. Michael's festival.

> If people could resolve in a dignified manner to hold a festival for St. Michael at the end of September, it would be a deed of the greatest significance. People would have to find the courage: not simply to discuss matters of social organization and the like, but to do something that would unite heaven and earth, to reconnect the physical with the spiritual. Because this would bring once again the spiritual to life in the physical, something could really happen among people, a mighty impulse given to further the development of our civilization and our entire life together. (224)

These words point to a possible task for the Anthroposophical Society: a contribution to a new culture of the festivals. Such an initiative could have at that time, in which such attempts were not unknown—ten years later they would be misused politically—found resonance. In his conclusion, Rudolf Steiner remembered once again the catastrophe of the fire and the flames that had destroyed the Goetheanum.

> Physical flames devour temples that are constructed with physical materials. The flames of true spiritual enthusiasm, true spiritual life, which must fill the temple, illuminate it with what flares up in the spirit, these flames cannot destroy the temple, they can only make it more glorious. Let us think of living Anthroposophy as those flames that will lead us ever further, just as the living spirit of Anthroposophy is there to lead us to a future of humanity that can resurrect what is now in such a state of decay. (224)

With these words Rudolf Steiner took leave of the Berlin branch, which he had founded twenty-one years earlier, and from Berlin itself, where he had begun his work twenty-six years earlier. Following a short working visit to Stuttgart, he returned to Dornach where he remained, except for three short trips to Stuttgart, until the end of July.

During his absence, a number of the Dornach members had taken up the initiative to rebuild the Goetheanum. Albert Steffen had contacted the anthroposophic groups in England, the United States, and Holland, as there was doubt that such a project could be successful unless everyone worked together. Ita Wegman had begun to raise money. In just a few days, she was able to raise 35,000 Swiss francs and hoped to soon receive more funds from friends in Holland. These activities led to discussions in anthroposophic circles worldwide concerning the new building project.

Wolfgang Wachsmuth, the head of the publishing house The Coming Day, had brought together a small group of members with the question of how to spiritually protect Rudolf Steiner from the barrage of accusations coming from all sides. Rudolf Steiner met with this group, about 15 individuals, at his home on the early afternoon of May 27. Albert Steffen made the following remark in his journal concerning the beginning of the meeting:

> He said, "If I had written what I have shared verbally, everything would be different. It could never have been so de-spiritualized. Groups would have formed, which would have behaved with reverence, due to the way it had been presented." Now he spoke of the lighthearted manner in which it had been taken up—on the other side, from the non-spiritual way one founded businesses. "This is how the notion of the spiritual, which is good, becomes distorted."

Maria Röschl reported it somewhat differently. "If what had been given in the ancient, esoteric contexts had been published, many cults would have formed throughout the world. Because it was not made public, it gave rise to hate and betrayal" (265).

Steiner also emphasized that this group had formed of its own accord and had not been called together by him. There were also others who could be included in the circle, some of whom were more spiritually advanced. After this introduction, there followed the esoteric instructions.

When the Swiss society resumed its general meeting on June 10, a meeting in which Rudolf Steiner participated mostly in silence, the first, tender fruits of these activities had begun to be apparent. Collaboration that bridged the national boundaries had begun. There were letters from groups in England, the United States, Italy and other countries offering to help with rebuilding the Goetheanum. Plans were being made to share observations of those who were attacking the anthroposophic work. Finally, an invitation was extended for an international delegates' meeting from July 20 to 23.

On the evening of June 10, Rudolf Steiner began with a series of lectures on "The History and Significance of the Anthroposophical Movement in Relation to the Anthroposophical Society." This *call to self-reflection* gave a historical overview of the development of the anthroposophic movement. In a humorous narrative, rich with anecdotes, Rudolf Steiner painted a wonderfully soulful picture of the path of the "homeless souls" who had sought spiritual content in the old Theosophical Society and in the circles of individuals who had gathered around Richard Wagner. He then spoke of Helena Petrowna Blavatsky's destiny, of the beginnings of the anthroposophic work, and then of the problems of the present times. The series ended with consideration of the specific nature of the anthroposophic impulse, which Steiner had made manifest through his philosophical writings, in conjunction with the work of Goethe and in contrast to that of Nietzsche and Haeckel. The series as whole formed a magnificent mirror, in which the audience could reflect on their own problems, questions and behaviors. Each of those listening was free to awaken his or her own impulses through this process of mirroring.

On June 17, the general meeting of the Goetheanum Association took place in the carpentry shop. Following the announcement of the payment of the insurance money and other formalities, Rudolf Steiner spoke, describing the situation in which they then found themselves. The building of the first Goetheanum was made possible through the pure sacrificial will of those who supported it. This sacrificial quality permeated every cubic centimeter of wood, every cubic centimeter of stone. Now they had received three million Swiss francs from those who not only had no interest in the Goetheanum, but were probably inclined to wish that it didn't exist. Perhaps one should give this money to charitable causes. That would not be plausible. But it was necessary to be conscious that the path about to be trod was a tragic one, that they would "cast themselves into the tragic." Steiner continued:

> This cannot be done in sleep. It must be done wakefully. One must plunge into the tragic with complete consciousness, knowing that one found oneself in a realm in which one could not do what is purely anthroposophic. One must be aware that whatever one must do, although it is not anthroposophic, must be balanced by an even stronger anthroposophic impulse. (259)

What Steiner said expresses his own approach to life quite well. He had always acted in accordance with the necessities and actual challenges rather than out of a purely idealistic attitude. How easy it would have been to say in certain situations: I'm not going to have anything to do with this, you should leave it alone, too; it is going to lead you into questionable territory, where you could get your hands dirty. He embraced the risks and the challenges, dared to move forward and tried energetically to create a balance to whatever appeared to him to be questionable. "If one weighs something, he does not remove some of what he is weighing to balance the scales; he adds weight to the other side." And further: "To desire that the earth be a peaceful place to rest, to only find it divine when it shows itself to be the way one desires it to be, can never be the attitude of a spiritual movement. That is not strength, but the lack thereof" (259).

The international delegates' meeting began on July 21, 1923. Albert Steffen chaired the meeting. Delegates from 15 countries were present to discuss how to finance the rebuilding of the Goetheanum and to make the necessary decisions. The situation was unimaginably difficult. At this point in time, because of German law and the devastating inflation there, no money would be received from Germany, the country that was home to the majority of the anthroposophists. During the gathering, Rudolf Steiner gave three lectures, in which he endeavored to lead his listeners along a path that would bring about a personal encounter with the being of Anthroposophy. Otherwise he contributed little to the discussions, saying only that the planning could only be based on firm pledges. He also pointed out that a building memorializing the first Goetheanum could be built for a sum of one to two million Swiss francs. It would be something of a high-end shed, like the carpentry shop, but built of concrete. One could also build something more elegant, but it would take more money, probably between four and five million Swiss francs. On Sunday, July 22, there were secured pledges for about 865,000 Swiss francs. It appeared as though there would be enough money available to begin with plans for a new building.

As far as Steiner was concerned, the situation remained completely open, in spite of the financial support. He had not been able to endorse much of what had been spoken about during the meeting. Thus he found it necessary on the evening before he left for England, just days after the end of the delegates' meeting, to ask the members in Dornach to think carefully "of how to overcome the sectarianism. Otherwise the Anthroposophical Society will sink ever further into sectarianism.... What should concern us is how to avoid sectarianism. I wanted to let this tone resonate again, because it is enormously important" (259). He defended this appeal by stating that during the delegates' meeting "strong tendencies" to become enveloped in a sectarian attitude had been apparent (259). Especially the German delegates had displayed this tendency (300 & 3).

Rudolf Steiner left Dornach on July 30 with many worries and questions. The situation in the Anthroposophical Society remained fraught with problems. With the exception of Marie Steiner, who had with sovereign independence and an uncompromising attitude nurtured both the development of eurythmy and speech formation, insuring that eurythmy had gained a certain repute in the wider world, there were few people who were truly up to the tasks they had taken on. Albert Steffen's conscientious editing of the weekly *Goetheanum* allowed members outside of Dornach to participate inwardly in what was being done in Dornach. Steiner supported this work with weekly articles, which continued during the entire time he was away. Ita Wegman, who ran the clinic in Arlesheim with an expert hand, had, in the months since the fire and with silent magnanimity, become much more engaged in matters concerning the society. Otherwise, he had loyal helpers like Emil Leinhas and very talented people among the Waldorf teachers, but almost no truly independent colleagues who could share with him the weight of the work—and practically no one with whom he could speak with complete openness.

CHAPTER 49

SUMMER 1923: ENGLAND

There is quite extensive documentation of Rudolf Steiner's trip to England and Wales in the summer of 1923. He wrote regularly to his English colleague, Edith Maryon, who lay ill in Dornach. He later spoke often about the trip, giving insight into his work and his impressions during his time there. Finally, in addition to the lectures and the talks that he gave, there are further reports from others about his stay.

The trip, which originally was to take Steiner through Stuttgart to London then on to Yorkshire, began with a blunder. At the border between Germany and Holland, he left the train to deal with customs regarding Marie Steiner's luggage and passport. He suddenly noticed the train containing his traveling companions Marie Steiner, Guenther Wachsmuth and Mr. Pyle leaving the station without him. He missed the boat to England and had to take passage on a boat from Hoek van Holland to Harwich the next day. He was met by George Kaufmann, a gifted translator who had translated a number of his lectures into English. Together they traveled through Cambridge and Ely and on to Leeds, at that time an industrial city with row upon row of poor, dust-covered houses. Deeply shaken, Steiner stared out of the train's window, then said to Kaufmann, "Look at the shape of these thoughts—it is truly hell upon the earth." Later in Dornach, he spoke again about the impression these cities had made on him, "where black houses, looking unbelievable, are lined up abstractly, one after the other, where everything looks as though the coal dust had condensed, and as it condensed formed itself into houses" (*The Tasks of Civilization*).

Rudolf Steiner thus made his way to Ilkley. At first, the area did not make a good impression on him. He reported that it was not especially pleasant. But during the two weeks he spent there in the valley between the two high moors, he discovered in a number of places the ruined remains of an ancient stone-age culture: Dolmen and the traces of ancient sacrificial altars. He climbed one of the hills near Ilkley. At the top, he found a stone in which a symbol, a swastika, had been carved. He spoke later of his impressions.

What does one read in this symbol, when he stands before such a stone? He reads the words that lived in the heart of the Druid: See here, the eyes of the senses behold the mountains; they behold the dwellings of people; the eye of the spirit, the lotus blossom, the rotating lotus blossom for which the swastika is a symbol, gazes into human hearts, into their souls. This unites me with the community with which I have been entrusted. Just as one would read the writings in a book, this is to some extent what one reads when he stand before a stone like this. (*The Tasks of Civilization*)

The depth to which this experience moved Steiner is apparent in the fact that two weeks later, he tried to capture what he had beheld in a pastel sketch he titled *The Druid Stone*.

It was in these surroundings that Rudolf Steiner gave the series of lectures titled "Contemporary Spiritual Life and Education." In fourteen lectures he developed the basic tenets of Waldorf education, beginning with Greek culture and education. Margaret MacMillan presided over the conference; Hermann von Baravalle, Julie Lammert, Caroline von Heydebrand, Erich Schwebsch and Karl Schubert gave lectures. There was a eurythmy performance by the children from the school at Kings Langley and a eurythmy course led by Edith Röhrle. It was all taken in with great interest by the English participants, and Steiner seemed to be quite satisfied and contented. He thanked the audience at length and ended with the remark: "I have tried to present Waldorf education as something that calls our attention in freedom to the deepest needs of humanity today. That you have accompanied these presentations with the will to understand is something that will live on in my heart and soul as a wonderful memory of this course" (307).

After the course was over, Rudolf Steiner traveled with his companions through the thickly populated industrial city of Manchester, then on to Penmaenmawr, on the Welsh coast. He was immediately taken by what was then a small town looking out over the ocean to the island of Anglesey. "No place could have been better for the anthroposophic conference this year than Penmaenmawr. One experiences directly the rich astral atmosphere that has had woven into it what flowed through the Druids, whose traces one can follow everywhere" (*The Tasks of Civilization*).

During these days in August 1923, the ever-changing weather—heavy rains and radiant sunlight—emphasized the vitality of this world, which appeared always fresh. The play of tides painted the sea and the sandbanks in ever new colors. After Steiner had described the area and its special characteristics in some detail, he came back to the trip from Ilkley to Penmaenmawr, noting that "it is truly something like crossing a threshold when one, coming from Ilkley, which lies in the immediate vicinity of the industrial areas and has only retained the fleeting traces of the ancient druidic times, arrives here where the immediate present is simply spiritual. Everything is spiritual. One can certainly say that Wales is the guardian of an extraordinarily strong spiritual life—it exists in memory of times past, but these are real memories" (*The Tasks of Civilization*).

It was Daniel Nicol Dunlop's idea to organize a summer conference in Penmaenmawr. Dunlop, a man with his own spiritual experiences, had become acquainted with Steiner a year earlier and decided to organize a conference, which would focus on the essence of Anthroposophy and eurythmy. Rudolf Steiner did not know Dunlop well and had little notion of his intentions. He wrote to Edith Maryon, with whom he spoken about Dunlop before leaving Dornach, during the early days of the course. "Dunlop speaks elegantly and advocates for Anthroposophy so that, if he had other intentions, he would be representing these poorly and Anthroposophy well" (263 & 1).

As the course continued, Steiner's respect for Dunlop grew. It became apparent to Dunlop that he could not gain a clear picture of the work in Dornach through reports by the official representatives of Anthroposophy in England—Irene Groves and Henry Collison. It was necessary to bring Steiner to England (263 & 1). Dunlop had resisted planning the entire conference in detail. It should grow out of what was immediately present. Only Steiner's lectures were scheduled—at 10:30 every morning. Everything else was planned just three days in advance.

Steiner was especially impressed by Dunlop's insistence that the essentials of Anthroposophy be placed in the center of the conference.

> In these lectures I can speak completely anthroposophically; in Ilkley, the approach was to speak about education so as not to irritate the audience too much while introducing them along the way to Anthroposophy. This was thought to be the proper approach by a number of our friends there. It is not my opinion. I know that our approach to education can only be understood if people first grasp certain anthroposophic concepts. I am actually quite happy when our conferences have the character that this one in Penmaenmawr does. Dunlop has made a great effort to make this possible. (263 & 1)

Steiner was especially gratified by the opportunity to develop the themes he was working with extensively in a series of thirteen lectures. He had given the lectures the title "The Evolution of Consciousness: As Revealed through Initiation Knowledge" (227). I would like to call attention to one aspect of the content of these lectures. In March 1921, Rudolf Steiner had spoken during a course in Stuttgart of the loss of an important document from around AD 350. "There is a problem here—I admit openly that I have not resolved this problem, but it can be traced further..." (324). In Penmaenmawr, he described the spiritual content of this epos, which had originated in the traditions of the ancient mysteries and described in powerful imagery the descent of Christ in the person of Jesus from Nazareth, showing how the presence of Christ would lead to a metamorphosis of the ancient mysteries of Demeter and Isis (227).

In spite of the full program—in addition to his lectures, there were five eurythmy performances as well as lectures by Hermann von Baravalle and Caroline von Heydebrand—Steiner had time to explore his surroundings. One afternoon, perhaps August 23, he went missing. A few hours later, he reappeared, grinning. He had climbed the steep mountain just south of Penmaenmawr with Guenther Wachsmuth. Wachsmuth related the story:

> It was one of those unforgettable experiences. He asked me to join him to climb the plateau above Penmaenmawr to visit some Druid stone circles. In spite of his sixty-two years, he climbed rapidly and effortlessly.... When we reached the cliffs high above the town, we found ourselves on a lonely plateau encircled by sharp peaks in the middle of which stood the mighty remains of a druidic circle. It was...a strange unique picture as, surrounded by the lonely solitude of this setting, Rudolf Steiner stepped into the middle of the stone circle. He told me to look over the edges of the stones in the circle at the mountain peaks in the distance, then described, with an intensity as though it were taking place before him, how the Druids had once sighted over the stones, fixing the constellations as they wandered through the seasons and experiencing the spiritual cosmos, the spiritual beings, and what they brought to humanity. (Wachsmuth)

Steiner also described this trek to the two outwardly unassuming, half ruined stone circles, which stood in a wide, shallow dip between the mountain peaks and remarked that the circles, although they did not intersect, reminded him of the floor plan of the first Goetheanum (*The Tasks of Civilization*; comp. also *Goetheanum*, vol. 3 & 228).

A couple of days later, they took an "official" excursion by car to Caernarvon and the island Anglesey. Marie Steiner and Harry Collison accompanied him. Together they visited the burial chamber at Bodowyr. Here, too, Steiner experienced the majesty of the past. He later noted that some of what was related in the Arthurian sagas had taken place on Anglesey, although the actual center of those events was to be found further south. He also noticed, however, the contemporary technological achievements and, in a written report sent to Dornach, mentioned the superb bridge over the Straits of Menai, built in 1826.

During the evenings, there were some open discussions during which Rudolf Steiner responded to various questions. Throughout the first evening, he spoke about the problem of anthroposophic sectarianism, mentioning that "it wasn't as apparent here in England." He stressed that there could be no question of "orthodox beliefs, or any form of belief" in the anthroposophic movement (259). No anthroposophic dogmas should be realized or illustrated through the arts (259). Instead of sectarianism, orthodoxy and dogmatism, it was desirable to develop a lively interest for the anthroposophic movement in the world. This was a bit bumpy. "Individual anthroposophists should have the possibility of informing themselves of what is happening here and there in the world in regard to Anthroposophy.... The Anthroposophical Society suffers because no one knows what is happening in other areas—there are no connections, no communication" (259).

Throughout the evenings, they spoke about sleep and the sensation of smell, about colors, eurythmy, language, and, on one evening, extensively about therapy. On the last evening, after thanking Dunlop for taking the initiative to bring the essence of Anthroposophy to expression, Steiner responded to a number of other questions. Apparently, someone had asked about the existence and work of higher human individualities. He refused to address this question, saying, "The Bodhisattva is already waiting, but enough human beings must first become able to understand him" (*The Tasks of Civilization*). Much had been revealed to the world that had not been taken up. In the future, when the world would be wrapped in a cocoon of wireless waves, spiritual understanding would be much more difficult, as it was in the days when the ruined sites around Penmaenmawr were being built.

Steiner described the conference in Penmaenmawr as one "of the most significant moments in the development of anthroposophic life" (*The

Tasks of Civilization). After the misery of the months following the fire, in Penmaenmawr, he met the spiritually independent figure of Daniel Dunlop, who, in spite of minor criticism from within his own ranks, had presided over the conference with largess and an unfailing sense for the essentials. This gave Steiner space to breathe.

He was also able to immerse himself in the world of the ancient mysteries, beyond the threshold of the modern technological world. Although the autos on the coast road to Bangor and Holyhead were noisy and stank, it was still an etherically vital world. The deeds of the ancient initiates, although their traces were outwardly barely evident, were present before him in the akashic record in magnificent, radiant pictures. Many themes from the ancient mysteries surfaced in his lectures. Ita Wegman perhaps also experienced this spiritual atmosphere, which lived in Steiner's surroundings and that he manifested in the present. He had asked her to join them, as he wanted to discuss certain medical questions with her, first in Penmaenmawr and later in London. She had not been able to leave the clinic for the entire course but was able to be there for the second half. She had the opportunity to speak with Steiner about medical questions before his lecture. During their conversation she said suddenly, "I want to experience a form of medicine as it was during the time of the mysteries!" (Zeylmans, *Wegman I*). This spoken desire to which Steiner did not respond explicitly at the time opened new doors and possibilities. Ita Wegman's remark indicated that she wished to unite her own medical work with the central mystery of Anthroposophy, just as in earlier times healers had united their work with that of the highest initiates.

Rudolf Steiner responded by sharing with Ita Wegman the threads of destiny at work in their colleagueship. She noted in one of her journals: "Penmaenmawr Karma completely revealed" (Zeylmans, *Wegman I*). Somewhat later, he captured the essence of their collaboration in the form of a verse through which spiritual beings spoke (Kirchner-Bockholt).

> Be full of understanding, bring completion
> To prosper his mission
> Whereof an image is manifest
> In his earthly achievement
> We need his far-flung spirit path
> He needs your being to accompany him.

The necessity of the collaboration between Ita Wegman and Rudolf Steiner is expressed in this verse. Throughout his life, Steiner had depended on specific individuals in fulfilling his endeavors, individuals who were more than mere helpers. He needed a soul quality that was dedicated and understanding. In 1896, he had written to Anna Eunike, "I do not believe that with the work I had to do I could have made it through this year without your loving care and understanding" (39). In 1903, he wrote to Marie von Sivers, "You understand me; that gives me strength—that frees my wings to fly" (262). Not long afterward he stressed his "brother in arms" relationship with her. "Shared believing is a positive force that works magnetically for us. You have given me this strength of shared believing through your understanding and we must give it to one another" (262). In fact, without the self-effacing devotion she brought to the work, he would hardly have been able to develop the anthroposophic work in Germany. Edith Maryon had also dedicated herself completely to working with Steiner on a specific task.

Now a new collaboration began to develop. At first, it seemed to revolve around the development of a therapeutic approach born of a consciousness of the nature of the mysteries. In truth, it gave Steiner the possibility to speak concretely about questions of reincarnation and karma. The fruits of the depth of understanding that came to meet him through Ita Wegman would become apparent in the coming year.

In the evening following his conversation with Ita Wegman, Rudolf Steiner spoke about the anthroposophic approach to developing remedies and therapies based on various ways to work with healing substances, using antimony, quartz and phosphorus as examples. Toward the end of the lecture, he mentioned the facility in which these methods were being practiced.

> The clinic in Arlesheim deserves special mention in this context. It is under the excellent leadership of Dr. Ita Wegman, whose work is such a blessing for this institute because she has what I wish to call the courage to heal. For when one considers, on the one hand, the complexities of nature out of which processes of healing must be drawn and, on the other hand, the incredible complexity of the health and illness in human beings, what is needed to be a healer, if one considers the enormity of this field, is the courage to heal. (319)

On September 1, most of the participants traveled to London, where the next day the Anthroposophical Society in Great Britain was formed with Harry Collison as general secretary. In his address, Rudolf Steiner gave important indications for nurturing the anthroposophic work. "No spiritual movement can flourish in our time that is a specialized movement of humanity. It is simply an esoteric law, let us say, that every truly productive sustainable spiritual movement embraces all of what is human" (259).

"As anthroposophists, we must be intensely interested in what is happening in the world. The world is interested in Anthroposophy; if we do but interest ourselves for the world, it will become our enemy" (259). Little more is known about the founding of the English Anthroposophical Society. Steiner never reported formally about the event. In the evening of that day, however, he spoke to the members in London, concluding with a mantram that "could be written into the soul of every human being striving to manifest the 'I.'"

> I gaze into the darkness.
> In it arises light,
> Living light.
> Who is this light in the darkness?
> It is my self in my reality!
> This reality of I
> Does not enter here my earth existence.
> I am but an image of it.
> But I shall find it once again
> When I, with good will for the spirit,
> Have passed through the gate of death.

For the English members, this mantra was a special farewell gift following the intense experiences of the previous weeks. Before his departure, Steiner gave two more lectures to a group of doctors. The finale of the journey was a very successful eurythmy performance at the Royal Academy. He visited Margaret Macmillan's school (described in Chapter 40), and then, on September 5, left England and returned to Dornach by way of Holland and Stuttgart.

IMAGES, PART THREE

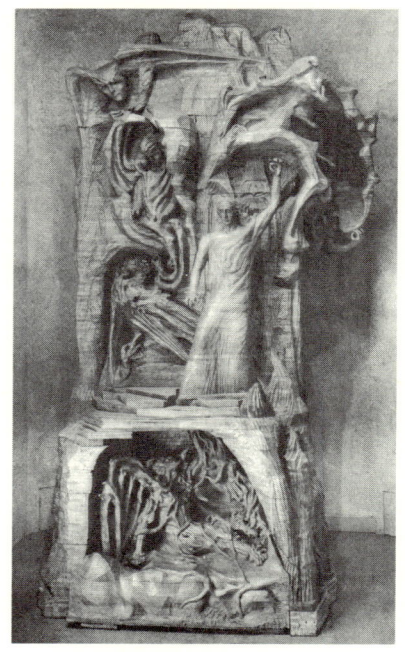

Above: Rudolf Steiner at work on the statue, The Representative of Humanity; *below: detail images of the central Christ figure.*

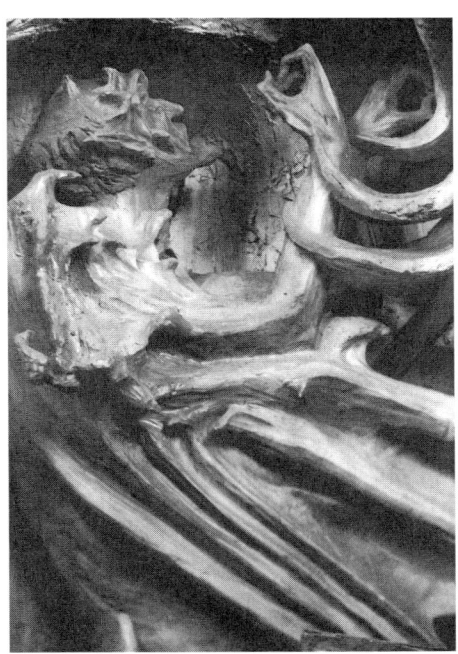

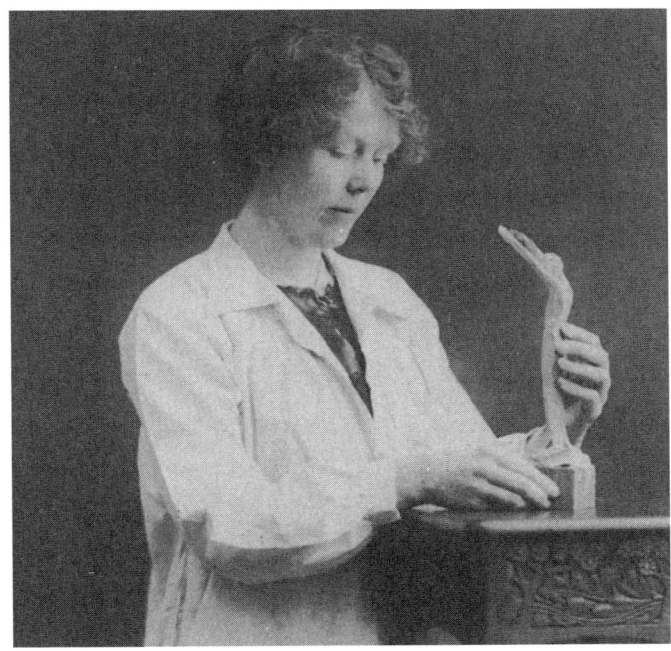

*Above: detail images of the Ahriman and Lucifer figures;
below: Edith Maryon (1872–1924), an English sculptor (see p. 428).*

Above: General Helmuth von Moltke (1848–1916); Franz Brentano (1838–1917; see p. 450); below: Count Otto Lerchenfeld (1868–1938); see pp. 391, 466); and Count Ludwig Polzer-Hoditz (1869–1945), who championed the threefold social idea and biodynamic agriculture.

Above: Berta and Emil Molt, who founded the first Waldorf school for the children of the workers at the Waldorf-Astoria Cigarette factory in Stuttgart; below: Herbert Hahn (1890–1970; see p. 478); and E. A. K. Stockmeyer (1886–1963; see p. 496).

Above: Caroline von Heydebrand (1886–1938; see p. 508);
Walter Johannes Stein (1891–1957; see p. 508);
below: Eugen Kolisko (1893–1939; see p. 513);
and Karl Schubert (1889–1949; see p. 516).

*Above: Lili Kolisko (1889–1976; see p. 539);
Rudolf Steiner (center) with medical coworkers;
below: participants of the second medical course, 1921.*

Rudolf Steiner met Ita Wegman in 1902 in Berlin, where she worked as a psysiotherapist. On Steiner's advice, she decided to study medicine in Switzerland and graduated in 1912. From 1912 to 1920, she worked as a doctor in Zurich, and in 1921 founded the Clinical Therapeutic Institute in Arlesheim (see p. 276 and chapter 43).

Emil Bock (1895–1959) with Friedrich Rittelmeyer (1872–1938), cofounders of The Christian Community and the movement for religious renewal; see chapter 44.

Above: participants of the East–West Congress in Vienna 1922; from left to right: Alfred Zeissig, Alexander Strakosch, Emil Leinhas, Ernst Uehli, Carl Unger, Count Ludwig Polzer-Hoditz, Walter Johannes Stein, Eugen Kolisko, Count Otto Lerchenfeld, and Ernst Scheiffele; below: Rudolf Steiner with Albert Steffen and Ernst Uehli during the East–West Congress in Vienna

Above: Rudolf Steiner, 1922; D. N. Dunlop (1868–1935; see p. 634); below: the Goetheanum burning, January 1, 1923.

Rudolf and Marie Steiner with Harry Collison (1868–1945) on the island Anglesey in Wales, August 1923.

*Above: Frederik Willem Zeylmans van Emmichoven (1893–1961; see p. 658);
Elisabeth Vreede (1879–1943), mathematician and astronomer (see p. 664);
below: Guenther Wachsmuth (1893–1963; see p. 664);
and Count Carl Wilhelm Keyserlingk (1869–1928; see p. 705)*

*Above: the participants in the agriculture course
in Koberwitz, 1924 (see p. 705);
below: Ita Wegman, Rudolf and Marie Steiner, and Elisabeth Vreede
amid participants at the 1924 lectures in Arnheim (see chapter 54).*

Top: Rudolf Steiner's first models of the second Goetheanum (see p. 757); center: the second Goetheanum under construction; bottom: the new Goetheanum opened with a conference of 2,000 participants in 1928.

Chapter 50

AUTUMN 1923: THE WAY TO DECISION

Steiner remained in Dornach for only a few days in the beginning of September 1923. He took the opportunity to speak about his travels in England and his encounter with the culture of the Druids. On September 13, he left for Stuttgart for a conference of the Anthroposophical Society in Germany. This conference, according to a number of remarks, disappointed him (259). He was concerned not only with the Anthroposophical Society, but with German culture in general to which Anthroposophy had a contribution to make. Before the delegates' meeting in July, he had spoken to the German delegates, warning them against naïve hopes for a "German victory" of any kind and stressing that Central Europe, from a spiritual point of view, still had critical tasks ahead. Then he added:

> The Anthroposophical Society would have the task of being awake to everything that is happening in the present. It would be easy to overlook the point in time that, one could say, is predetermined in history, when in many of the centers that surround Central Europe people recognize: Although our outer might has enabled us to achieve enormous victories against Central Europe, if we now do not want the earth to deteriorate spiritually, we must recognize Central Europe as a source of spiritual life. (259)

Steiner attempted to shake the German delegates, who had been behaving strangely, out of their narrow-mindedness and get them to recognize the task that lay before them. At the end of the disappointing conference in September, he spoke again about the development of Central European spiritual life. "Much of the spiritual life of Central Europe that seems buried away is awaiting a certain future. Not long from now in wide parts of the world, people will turn with longing to what even here is often rejected, to the older Central European spiritual attitude" (259).

After this introduction, Steiner's parting words to the conference participants took yet another turn. It could not happen that, when the world called for a resurrection of Central European spiritual life, there was no one in Central Europe capable of responding. "This would be the greatest loss for the world. It would be one of the worst catastrophes,...if the world were to turn to Central Europe...and no one could be found in Central Europe who understood what needed to be given" (259). After calling upon the Anthroposophical Society in Germany to be fully conscious of its task, Steiner departed the conference. The next day, during a meeting with the teachers from the Waldorf School, he remarked, "The four days were terrible" (300 & 3).

Once again he returned to Dornach for only a brief stay. After a night of keeping watch at the bedside of a dying child in the clinic, he left on September 25 for Vienna. During the days leading up to Michaelmas, he gave two public lectures and four lectures about "Anthroposophy and Human Feeling." He opened the latter with an immediately accessible meditation on the nature of Michael. "The forces of the dragon, striving to pull me downward, are at work within me; I do not behold them, I experience them as what would bring me unto myself. But I behold in spirit the radiant angel whose cosmic task was to besiege the dragon. I concentrate my soul life on this light-formed being; I let its light stream into my soul" (223).

There were difficulties around the eurythmy performance in Vienna. In most of the Viennese theaters, the stagehands were on strike. On September 27, Steiner negotiated with the employees at the Volkstheater to try and make the performance possible. "I tried my luck with the secretary of the employees. He was immovable. We ended up at the only theater in Vienna that had agreed to the demands of the workers and was thus not subject to any passive resistance. These negotiations took all Thursday morning" (263 & 1). The performance took place in the New Viennese City Theater. It was so successful that they had to return a week later to perform again. In between the two performances, the ensemble performed in Gmunden and in Salzburg. It was only through the Steiners' efforts that the performances were possible at all.

None of the Austrian members seemed to think that they could take on some of these arrangements. Steiner wrote to Edith Maryon "that our Austrian members are also asleep" (263 & 1). By the inaugural meeting of the Austrian national society, however, a wonderful rhetoric was presented in long, convoluted addresses of how, after twenty-one years, the society in Austria had finally come of age. Rudolf Steiner listened to it all in silence, and now and again his foot swung back and forth. He then responded, moving over the question of the society's coming of age with the remark that they should wake up, notice what needs to be done, and take initiative.

> This is what I have hoped to see in a society that has come of age.... Awakening means: To spark one's attentiveness for the surroundings, to collaborate in the world, to collaborate in achieving our great goals when our great goals come into consideration. Theoretical debates about now being twenty-one years old don't bring anything. What does it help to now be twenty-one years old? (259)

As he had done in London, Steiner spoke in Vienna to a number of doctors who had been invited for the occasion. Ita Wegman, who had also come to Vienna, had encouraged this gathering, and Dr. Norbert Glas had personally visited and invited the doctors Steiner had suggested. The short talk took place in the studio of Jo van Leers, who organized the distribution of the remedies being produced in Arlesheim. After Steiner's talk, people stayed on to speak with one another and Steiner conversed animatedly with various guests. Ita Wegman overheard him saying to one of the anthroposophists present, "I am going to write a medical book with Dr. Wegman." She was quite surprised since she had heard nothing of this plan. In Dornach, he soon announced this to the doctors at the clinic also. He had decided to embark on a collaboration with Ita Wegman, something new for both of them. He turned his attention to questions of therapy and healing and spoke, as he had in Penmaenmawr, in London and Vienna and a few weeks later in The Hague about fundamental principles of anthroposophic therapy. Once again he mentioned Dr. Wegman's "courage to heal" (319) and called attention to the close collaboration between the clinic and "the Goetheanum, our anthroposophic university in Switzerland" (319).

On October 3, he saw his siblings once more in Horn, then in the evening visited Rosa Mayreder, who noted in her journal, "He is especially genial. 'I could not have left Vienna without hearing your voice,' he said."

Two more trips were planned before Christmas. The first was to Stuttgart. He spoke with the members, gave three lectures for the teachers at the Waldorf School, visited the school and met with the teachers, and did what he could for the research institute and the clinic. It must have been incredibly exhausting. Emil Leinhas relates how Steiner's departure, originally planned for 4:00 p.m. was put off for one thing after the other until he was finally able to get away after 9:00 p.m. In contrast to his usual demeanor, he sat in silence throughout the trip, which was made without stopping, arriving in Dornach at 3:00 a.m. After arriving in Dornach, Steiner went straight to work, sitting in bed as was his wont. In those early morning hours, he wrote the first essay in *From the Life of the Soul*, which was to be picked up at 8:00 by a messenger to be taken to the printer.

The last of Steiner's twenty-two trips in 1923 took him to The Hague in Holland, where he gave several lectures and presided over the founding of the Dutch national society. This proved to be more difficult than first imagined. After the first preparatory discussions on November 16, Steiner wrote that everything was going well "except that the society here is in terrible shape—dissension, lack of identity, etc." (263 & 1).

On the evening before the founding, a number of the Dutch anthroposophists were sitting around the open fire in the living room of the hotel Oude Doelen. Pieter de Haan, Jo van Leer, Ita Wegman and Friedrich Willem Zeylmans were there, as well as a number of others. Zeylmans related:

> Dr. Steiner entered so pale and earnest and at the same time so sad that none of us ventured to begin a conversation. Finally, Dr. Wegman asked if something had happened. He spoke sadly, as though to himself. His words showed how difficult the experience was for him of the lack of understanding among the members, in spite of their personal good will, of the actual spiritual necessities. "The members do not want to... They have good intentions, but... What should I do...? Should I form an order?!" (E. Zeylmans, *Willem Zeylmans*)

The meeting to form the society took place on November 18. The Dutch had prepared a charter, which described the society as a "community of human beings...for the cultivation of true spiritual values" open to anyone who "has an authentic interest in the deeper spiritual forces" in the world and in human beings. Steiner recognized something sectarian, some exclusivity in such phrases. Who should decide what the *true spiritual values* were and who should assess *authentic interest*?

Later, in Dornach, he spoke about the founding, remarking that he had observed a tendency to want "the Anthroposophical Society to be something like an extended family that isolated itself from the outer world. It is somewhat like this with its current practices" (259).

During the meeting in Holland, he called on the Dutch to be "worldly" and hospitable. "In all earnestness: Try to become one with the world! That would be the best, the most important 'program!'" (259).

The not quite thirty-year-old Doctor Zeylmans von Emmichoven was chosen at Rudolf Steiner's suggestion to be general secretary of the Anthroposophical Society in Holland. After a shared lunch, Steiner said to him, "Keep in mind, you now have the full esoteric and exoteric responsibility for everything that happens in the field of Anthroposophy in Holland" (*We Experienced Rudolf Steiner*).

When Rudolf Steiner returned to Dornach, Marie Steiner traveled to Berlin to close up their apartment there. It had seen little use over the past years. It was a tedious task. The library had to be packed up, papers sorted, unnecessary ones destroyed. In addition, with the help of Johanna Mücke, everything had to be readied to move the Philosophical-Anthroposophical Publications to Dornach. The place that had for so many years been the center of Rudolf Steiner's work was to be abandoned, and everything was to be relocated to Dornach.

Up till now, there has been little discussion concerning the content of Steiner's lectures in 1923. It is not possible to summarize the very different topics in brief, or even to touch on all of them. A certain transformation in the way Steiner spoke during the year is apparent. It began in the second half of 1922 and became increasingly recognizable in the course of 1923. Seen from the outside, it is clear that he began again, as he had before the war, to give purely anthroposophic, thematic lecture cycles. Among these are the "French Course," "Philosophy, Cosmology and Religion," "The Spiritual Communion of Humanity," and the cycles given in Penmaenmawr and Oslo in 1923.

If we turn our attention to his further work, it is worth mentioning that he did a whole series of pastel sketches during the year. They were meant to serve as guides for the painting lessons at the Friedwart School and for the lessons Henni Geck was giving, but they also show that he enjoyed painting. This impression is strengthened by the blackboard sketches he did in conjunction with his lectures, especially in 1923. Time and again, he developed during his lectures very impressive imagery in just a few minutes. In this way, many of the lectures of that year became pictorial narratives, colorful and alive with form.

One can have the sense that Steiner, having lost the rich imagery of the paintings in the Goetheanum, began to paint new images with words. It is almost as if he was creating through these imaginative descriptions a new background for his efforts. He crafted magnificent word pictures of great beauty, especially after his return from Penmaenmawr, where the imaginative world permeated everything. He spoke through pictures and imaginations to his audiences.

One of the themes of these word paintings is the cycle of the seasons. In the beginning of October, he shared with his audience in Dornach the seasonal imaginations through which majestic, deeply contemplative images of the spirit of nature arise. These included the chemical processes of sulfur and calcium; the processes of growing, blossoming, and wilting; the formation of the clouds; and the formation of crystals appearing as a cosmic alchemy, in whose transformations the forces of the heavens ascend and descend—where in the background the mighty Archangels speak to human beings.

In the lectures that follow, those held between October 19 and November 11 in Dornach, he described in detail the animal and plant worlds in such a way that the eagle, the lion, the steer, the birds, butterflies, bats, reptiles and fish appear as revelations of the spirit at work in nature. The flight, the wings and feathers, the beak, and the claws of the eagle, or the developmental stages and process of metamorphosis of the butterfly from the egg to the pupae to the imago are described in rich contemplative imagery. The sense-perceptible appears as the concrete expression of the spirit in nature that speaks to humanity. In these lectures, Steiner read aloud out of the book of nature. Nature's letters became words that could resonate in the human being, and the various forms of the living world appeared as the human being spread out throughout nature: "The human being as the harmony of the creative, formative cosmic word."

Through these imaginative contemplations of nature, not through theories and ideas, Steiner led the way to an inner experience of the cosmic connectivity through and within which the human being exists. The relationship to the being of the world can be felt; the wisdom reigning throughout the cosmos reveals itself to human cognition.

When Rudolf Steiner resumed his lectures on November 23 in Dornach after returning from his trip to Holland, he focused on the approaching Christmas conference. The series of lectures over the next weeks about the evolution of the sacred mysteries were to bring to life in his listeners "what the anthroposophic movement can bring into being in the hearts of human beings. Then those, who will be sitting here as we approach Christmas, will truly have something to say in their thoughts about what, I would like to say, can happen in these last hours."

Expanding on the series of essays *On the Life of the Soul*, published in those recent weeks, he spoke in the first lectures about the inner path of schooling the soul that could lead to an understanding of the mysteries of the world. In sweeping steps, the soul was led beyond itself, out into the world, first into the realm of meteorological phenomena immediately surrounding it, then into the phenomena of the cycles of the day and of the year and, from the fourth lecture on, into questions concerning the substance of the earth. Quartz and the metals became organs of a way of knowing that discovered itself in the world itself. Then he led the audience into an exploration of the earth's distant past. One can have the impression that he was trying to take his listeners with him on the path to reading in the akashic record. It is important to note that, even in these more methodological lectures, his presentations were concrete, pictorial, and in constant relation to observable natural phenomena.

In the sixth lecture, Steiner began to speak of the actual theme of the series: the description of the ancient and most ancient sacred mysteries. In doing so, he returned to the topic with which he had in 1901/2 first begun to prepare the way for his anthroposophic work. The as yet unpublished lectures from this time, which served as the basis for the book *Christianity as a Mystical Fact* (8), show compellingly how he researched the thematic using the texts available at the time and supporting his arguments with carefully chosen quotes. In December 1923, he spoke completely freely, never taking up a book, never quoting printed works, directly out of his own unmediated experience of the sacred mysteries. His presentation began with the Ephesian Mystery of the Logos and its connection to cosmogony. (Somewhat later, during the Christmas of 1924, he expanded on this theme.) Then he gave three lectures on the sacred mysteries of Ireland. The dramatic nature of the novice's path to illumination was depicted through simple, easily accessible stories. On December 14 and 15, he told of what was experienced in the Grecian mysteries. In doing so he drew an arc from the cosmic insights that lived in the chthonian mysteries, over the mysteries of Ephesus to Plato and Aristotle, and ending with the esoteric knowledge of nature related by Aristotle to Alexander. The last three lectures, held in the days just before the Christmas conference, brought to the attention of his listeners the cult of Samothrace and the Rosicrucian mysteries, a path of initiation that strives to raise the seeker to an experience of the intelligence of the spheres through gaining insight into the nature of earthly substances.

In these days leading up to the Christmas conference, Rudolf Steiner unfurled these images of the ancient and more modern mysteries so that "those who are sitting here...may have something to say in their thoughts about what still can happen in these final hours" (232). In an artistic, imaginative manner, his listeners could picture how the initiates of earlier times had found the way from what was earthly to an experience of cosmic intelligence, and how everything earthly was the direct expression of concrete spiritual activity. In this way, Steiner planted the thoughts and feelings that "the anthroposophic movement can bring into being in the hearts of human beings" (232).

In these same days leading up to Christmas, Rudolf Steiner began, at the request of Albert Steffen and other friends, to write his *Autobiography*. The beginning of the first chapter was written on December 2 and appeared on December 9. Each week another installment appeared in the *Goetheanum*. The seventieth and last installment was printed on April 5, 1925. For Rudolf Steiner, this re-visiting of his life's path offered no doubt also the opportunity to reflect on his personal striving. Immediately before the Christmas conference, he wrote the passages in which he described his relation to geometry, and "the first unfolding" of an understanding of the spirit "that gradually evolved in me" (28). At the same time, writing these memoirs was a peculiar experience for Steiner. He wrote to Marie Steiner in Berlin: "I feel as though removed from the earth as I write these recollections of my life" (262).

At the same time as he was calling back to mind the life path of his own intentions, Steiner was also wrestling with the difficult question concerning the future of the Anthroposophical Society. In retrospect, it is clear that he decided to take over the leadership of the society. Five months after the Christmas conference, while visiting Paris, he spoke about one of the questions connected with this decision.

> It was a deeply momentous decision that I was faced with, also in regard to the spiritual world. It was a gamble. A gamble because it was possible that with the acceptance of the formal, outer position of leadership, the revelations from the spiritual beings, which we all rely upon,...could have diminished as I was being consumed by the administration of the society. (239)

In another setting, he spoke more explicitly. The spiritual powers that guided the anthroposophic movement "could have turned away" from it (240).

One can with justification say that Rudolf Steiner risked his spiritual existence with this decision. The choice of either stepping back from his involvement in the Anthroposophical Society or taking full responsibility for its further existence stood before his soul. It took him some time to come to a decision. When preparing for a lecture about the events in the autumn of 1923, Ita Wegman had written:

> It was shocking to see how he had been disappointed by so many people. People did understand what he wanted.... It had reached the point that Rudolf Steiner had considered leaving the Anthroposophical Society and working with a small circle of carefully chosen individuals. In the final hours, at the end of November 1923, he decided under great inner duress to take upon himself the leadership of the society. (Zeylmans, *Wegman* I)

This description is accurate and can be documented. Ita Wegman wrote in a letter to one of the members, who wanted to come with suggestions to Dornach, on December 2, 1923:

> It will be done differently than it has been with the forming of the national societies. Dr. Steiner will take charge of the whole process; he will, in fact, preside over and run the meeting as he sees fit. He will present the charter, and all the business of the international society will be administered under his direct guidance with the help of coworkers living here in Dornach, who he has chosen. (Zeylmans, *Wegman* I)

It is apparent that Rudolf Steiner had discussed the procedure with Ita Wegman and included her in his considerations. Even so, he had not made a final decision. On December 6, he wrote a letter to Marie Steiner, who was still in Berlin, saying that an unbelievable number of people were expected for the Christmas conference.

> Everything depends on the Christmas gathering, occurring on the first anniversary of the fire, being one that dignifies the occasion, and also on its numbers. If that were not the case, I think it would be better not to try and build again. In light of the bitter meetings in London and The Hague, I know it *can* go well here, but one must do everything possible to make it happen. (262)

In other words, Rudolf Steiner knew on December 6 that there was the possibility that the new formation of the society *could* go well. He also saw the other possibility, "to not try and build again," because without a functioning, sustainable society, building again would make no sense. Just how starkly these two possibilities were for him came to expression just before the Christmas conference was to begin. He had announced that he intended to take on the leadership of the society, and then remarked, "It is the case that things must be taken very, very seriously now. Otherwise, what I have often spoken of as a possibility will become fact: I will have to withdraw my support for the Anthroposophical Society" (259).

What had been put into motion in the weeks leading up to the Christmas conference was not an "irreversible decision" but, in Steiner's words, the second premise of a hypothetical judgment. The first premise was "If the anthroposophists will"; the second, "I can realize my intentions and take on the responsibility" (300 & 3 & 240).

How did Steiner, "after a difficult inner struggle" (260), come to make this decision? He gave a general answer to this question when he said that having contemplated the question at length as to how the society should function and having participated in the various meetings, he was forced "to accept that fact that I can only continue to participate in the work if I am chosen to be the actual chairman" (259). What he had experienced in the previous years was the failure of the responsible parties to actually lead the society. It had become absolutely clear that the society was not in the position to lead itself. For this reason, he had the *possibility* of taking on leadership. He wasn't taking the initiative away from anyone else. He hoped to find people among the members of the society with whom he could work productively, *if he could lead them*. To what extent he had actually considered withdrawing from the society is not known. Whether he had, as has been said, decided not to leave the society at the requests of Ita Wegman and Marie Steiner, and whether these requests had actually ever been voiced, is unclear. The only documentation we have for them is hearsay. One can assume that neither of them voiced such a request, but that Rudolf Steiner had had to decide to take on the risk of leading the society alone without any guidance even from the spiritual world.

In any case, in the weeks leading up to the Christmas conference, he did everything possible to make it a success. He attended eurythmy rehearsals, helped with the production of the Christmas plays, helped find accommodations for the many guests, and had the rooms in the carpentry shop opened up to accommodate the large number of participants, while at the same time dealing with the logistics of moving the publishing house from Berlin to Dornach.

Guenther Wachsmuth wrote about this period in his biography of Rudolf Steiner.

> During this time when things were taking shape, meetings of a small circle of individuals took place in a room in Rudolf Steiner's home. He laid out the plans for re-founding the movement, the society, the School of Spiritual Science, its esoteric task and the meaning and goals of the spiritual organism that was to be created. The plans and the decisions were made in collaboration with Marie Steiner, Albert Steffen, Dr. Ita Wegman and Dr. Guenther Wachsmuth. Later, Dr. Elisabeth Vreede was also asked to join. (Wachsmuth)

The date and the themes of only one of these meetings are known. It was the meeting on December 16 that took place at Steiner's home. There was probably a discussion about the program for the coming conference shortly before the meeting began. The program, which was printed in the *Goetheanum*, was dated December 16 but had been mailed out on December 14. There had also been a number of individual conversations. There don't seem to have been any other important discussions before the meeting. Albert Steffen wrote about Rudolf Steiner's meeting with Ita Wegman, Guenther Wachsmuth and himself in his journal.

> Dr. Steiner read the articles of the charter aloud and then told us how he imagined the configuration of the executive council. He: President. Frau, Dr. Steiner, and me: Vice-Presidents. Frau Wegman: Secretary. Wachsmuth: Cashier (Wachsmuth suggested treasurer, at which Steiner laughed and replied, 'The name doesn't change anything'). Then, the heads of the individual disciplines: Dr. Steiner, the entire school. Me, belles letters. Wachsmuth, national economics (he would prefer natural science, but Dr. Steiner said it would be a pity if he were not a mathematician).

This journal entry suggests that Steiner informed his closest colleagues only at the last minute of certain details. Elisabeth Vreede, who was named on December 22, wasn't even present. It is possible that Rudolf Steiner hesitated because he had hoped to have Edith Maryon join the executive council as the third woman, but her health prevented her from participating in the assembly.

On December 17, Rudolf Steiner made a model for the building to store the publishing company's books, which was to be built in the coming months, and spoke with Albert Steffen about the next edition of the *Goetheanum*. On December 18, he traveled by car to Stuttgart where he met Marie Steiner and brought her up to date on what had taken place in Dornach. Late that afternoon, he met with the councils of both German societies and announced his plans to re-found the society and chair it himself. The older colleagues realized that he had made this decision without consulting them and that what he had foretold in January had now become fact. He was going to go over their heads and turn directly to the members. It is understandable that they took this in silence (Lehrs).

In an account he sent to Dornach, and which Rudolf Steiner had printed in the *Nachrichtenblatt* on March 30, 1924, one of the German members, Dr. Hermann Poppelbaum, described the situation. "It was as though we had been freed of a great weight when, at Christmas, Dr. Steiner brought the focus of our work back where it belonged—to Dornach, into true anthroposophic substance. Of course, we had to admit that his taking over the chairmanship was the only possible course, while at the same time it was a verdict of bankruptcy for the work that had gone before, especially in Germany" (Lehrs).

On December 22, before the evening lecture began, Rudolf Steiner announced to the already quite large number of people who had arrived that he intended to take over the leadership of the society, and that Albert Steffen, Marie Steiner, Ita Wegman, Elisabeth Vreede and Guenther Wachsmuth would join him in forming the executive council of the new society. These individuals joined him on the podium for the duration of the conference as a "trial executive council." Throughout the conference, members and executive council sat face to face.

CHAPTER 51

THE CHRISTMAS CONFERENCE OF 1923

In his *Autobiography*, Rudolf Steiner mentions, among others, the Goethe scholar August Fresenius, who, as Steiner recalled, had in a "short, but significant article" explained the meaning of the remark by Goethe that the rough design of Faust had been clear to him *from the very beginning*. Most scholars took this to mean that he had, as a young man, already had a complete plan for the entire drama. Fresenius pointed out that in Goethe's usage, the phrase *from the very beginning* only indicated "that the first passages were clear to him as a young man and that only here and there had he developed some of the further details" (28). That Steiner wrote about this philological discovery, which "significantly illuminated Goethe's psychology" at such length, is worth noting.

What Steiner had in mind with the new-founding of the Anthroposophical Society was in this sense clear for him from the beginning. At the end of November and the beginning of December "came the great question: how to do *more Anthroposophy* in the future." Steiner prepared himself to address this question during the Christmas conference. This preparation is reflected in part in the draft of the statutes for the new society that he presented to Wegman, Steffen and Wachsmuth on December 16, and which were printed up for everyone attending the conference. During the discussion of each of the paragraphs, Steiner pointed out that he had put the utmost care into the way each point was formulated (260). It is possible to read from the statutes the conceptual direction with which Rudolf Steiner began the Christmas conference. From the new membership cards that would need to be printed to the establishment of the School of Spiritual Science with its three classes, it was all clear to him from the beginning. The first steps toward a new sense of direction in the Anthroposophical Society were clear in his mind's eye.

His decision to take initiative on his own and found the General Anthroposophical Society was crucial. Since 1913, he had let others take responsibility for running the Anthroposophical Society. He had worked as a teacher within the framework of the society but had held himself back in regard to all questions pertaining to the structure of it. He was not even a member. From 1918 on, he had worked with the initiatives and challenges that had been brought to him by a new generation of anthroposophists. He had dedicated himself to the campaign for a threefold social order, concerned himself with the commercial endeavors, given courses on education and natural science—whatever was asked of him. He had not taken his own initiatives but had responded to what was asked of him.

Especially throughout 1923, he had restrained himself from making any formative suggestions. He had participated in everything he could, and intensely present, often suffering, he listened and observed, accompanying the life of the society until it became clear that all that was left of his previous work was a heap of ruins (260). The society that had developed around him since 1912 was divided, the Goetheanum had burned down, and the commercial endeavors had failed. In the middle of December, when it became clear that some 800 people would be traveling to Dornach for the conference, Steiner left this stance of conscious restraint behind and decisively took charge of all matters pertaining to the nascent society. At every turn he gave clear instructions and resisted, with a conciliatory tone but unmistakable determination, any obstacle laid in the path of his impulse. From the moment he decided to take on the leadership of the society, he defined the tasks and determined the thematic.

The essence of Rudolf Steiner's intention for forming the society anew could be captured in simple words: *To ignite spiritual life and to consciously shape real life.*

Founding the society anew was not meant as a way to "realize" something thought out—a set of principles or ideals—but rather what was real needed to acquire a new form and to be raised into the light of consciousness. This reflects the way Rudolf Steiner spoke about Anthroposophy following the Christmas conference.

> Those who wish to discuss Anthroposophy must first realize that what they should say first is simply what the heart of one's listener speaks through itself. Never and nowhere in the world has initiation science intended anything but to say what the hearts of those who wished to hear were saying. In fact, in the most essential sense, the basic tone

of any anthroposophic presentation must be to state what lives in the hearts of those who need Anthroposophy. (234)

The statutes must also be understood in this context. They should articulate what from the hearts of those individuals who are in need of Anthroposophy is spoken. This is not at all easy to perceive. It is not the heart alone that speaks in the human being; other facets of his nature speak also. During the discussions concerning the various paragraphs, Steiner found himself having to clear away a good deal of thought detritus until Harry Collins, the English general secretary, spoke up on December 28, saying:

> You will forgive a very old member for offering some thoughts on these statutes. We have just reached paragraph 4. I do not believe that it can be our intention to improve on these statutes. Dr. Steiner had put a lot of effort into them and they are quite comprehensive. It seems to me that this discussion should be limited to questions concerning the implications and consequences of the various points. (260)

Resounding applause greeted the words of this representative of true English spirit practice. That day the other eleven paragraphs were passed as well as the statutes in their entirety. To insure that the parliamentary process, used as a way to heighten consciousness of the statutes, not be misunderstood, Rudolf Steiner pointed out in his first report of the formation of the General Anthroposophical Society, in the first edition of the newsletter *Was in der anthroposophischen Gesellschaft vorgeht*, that the statutes were not statutes in the usual sense "but the description of what can arise in a fully human, vital societal relationship" (260a). In Germany, where there was a tendency to theorize about such statutes, he repeated this emphatically, saying of the statutes, "They are actually not statutes at all, but the narration of what exists in Dornach and what the intentions are that live there" (260a).

One can also capture what was intended with the formation of this new society pictorially. In daily life, what lives in the depths of the heart is hidden; it lives as though underground in the human subconscious. But it is the true temple, in which the archetypes of human existence live. During the Christmas conference, Rudolf Steiner began to lift this hidden, underground temple into the light. Then, when he opened the view for the suprasensory temple, the independent School of Spiritual Science, he accomplished what Goethe had prophetically anticipated in the final images of his *Fairy Tale*. The temple was lifted into the full light of day.

The Christmas Conference of 1923

Rudolf Steiner did not only prepare the statutes and everything connected to them. He also prepared for what was announced in the program for Tuesday, December 25 at 10:00 a.m.: the laying of the foundation stone for the General Anthroposophical Society. People were somewhat astonished when they realized that the foundation stone of the new society would be laid before they had gone through the formalities of constituting the society. This sequence is important. It shows that the spirit took precedence and that the General Anthroposophical Society was founded by Rudolf Steiner out of the spirit; those present took up this impulse. This was voiced clearly by Steiner during his opening address the day before.

> The revelation of a spiritual reality has become discernible for humanity. It is not through earthly willfulness but by following the call that has been sounded from the spiritual world, not out of earthly willfulness but rather due to the presence of the magnificent images, which have been given from out of the spiritual world as a modern revelation for the spiritual life of humanity: this is the source of the impulse for the anthroposophic movement. This anthroposophic movement is not born of earthly considerations. This anthroposophic movement is in its entirety, including all its parts, in service to the gods, to the divine.... It is as such that we wish to let it live within our hearts. At the beginning of our conference we want to inscribe deeply into our hearts that this anthroposophic movement wishes to unite the soul of each individual who dedicates oneself to it with the elemental source of everything human in the spiritual world, that this anthroposophic movement desires to guide people to what is for the moment—in the evolution of humanity and for the earth—the last completely satisfying illumination. It can be voiced with the words, "Yes, that is what I am as a human being, as a human being wanted by the gods on earth and in the cosmos." (260)

These words anticipate the contents of the Foundation Stone verse, which Steiner had brought into spoken form in the weeks just before Christmas. At the outset of the laying of the foundation stone, he described these words as the summary of "the most important results of the last years" (260). He could also have said: The knowledge that I have struggled to attain during the last forty years has taken form in this verse. The essence of Anthroposophy flowed together into the Foundation Stone verse.

Yet it was more than simply the sum of Rudolf Steiner's work. In his lectures during the autumn of that year, he had presented anthroposophic insights in artistic, imaginative language. In the Foundation Stone, he brought the insights into the threefold nature of the human being, which he had described scientifically in 1917, into a "trinity of verses" (260). This "trinity of verses" could reveal itself to each person as a soul-spiritual path that led through the portal of the threefold nature of the human to the threefold forces of the trinity. The scientific recognition of the threefold nature became something new and different in the verses of the Foundation Stone. It became an artistic, meditative, spiritual life path that spoke directly to the human heart.

The Christmas conference had these two sides, both of which Rudolf Steiner prepared: the statutes, which described the life of the Anthroposophical Society, and the Foundation Stone meditation, which captured the quintessence of Anthroposophy, intensified through the artistic form. The life of the society was to unfold on the basis of the Foundation Stone.

On December 25, Rudolf Steiner stood before the 800 people who had taken place in the carpentry shop. The stage, which had been used as extra seating, was hidden behind a blue curtain. Punctually at 10:00 a.m., the doors to the carpentry shop were closed and bolted. Rudolf Steiner walked to the lectern and marked the beginning of the ceremony with three knocks. Following brief introductory words, he let the words of the Foundation Stone resound: "O human soul, know thyself in thy weaving becoming in spirit, soul and body!" (260).

The trinitarian forces of the heights, the periphery and the spirit respond to the words that three times lead the human soul to self-knowledge. In the forging together of human self-knowledge with the Father-Spirit of the heights, the Christ-Will in the periphery and the Holy Spirit's cosmic thought, the double-faceted Foundation Stone is formed in which human striving is sanctified by the Trinity. A fourth verse illuminated and permeated the Foundation Stone with warmth. The divine light, the sun of Christ that entered into the stream of history at the watershed of time, was called to mind (260).

> Light Divine,
> Christ-Sun!
> Warm thou
> Our hearts
> Enlighten thou
> Our heads,

> That good may become
> What we
> From our hearts would found
> What we
> From our heads would direct
> In conscious willing.

With the laying of the foundation stone, an ocular was planted in the life of the new society that, like an eye or an ear, would unite the human being with his archetypal forces. The future work was to rest on this foundation stone willing as it was to lead the human soul through self-knowledge to the spirit.

During the days that followed, Rudolf Steiner began the shared discussions each day by reading parts of the Foundation Stone verse. In doing so, he called attention to various compositional elements, clarifying the verse's meaning. During the final lecture, on January 1, 1924, the verse was read once more in its entirety. Thus was it woven into the fabric of the conference. On Easter Sunday 1924, the Foundation Stone verse was performed eurythmically with Marie Steiner reciting the words. In his introduction, Rudolf Steiner said:

> Such things must always be understood in the proper manner. All things like this have in the past tended to be viewed theoretically. People have not grasped that it simply does mean something—not only that there really are words of wisdom, but that they flow as a living force through the anthroposophic movement, spurring it on. When that happens, one cannot focus merely on the content of such words but must turn one's attention to the way these words flow through the anthroposophic movement. For the Goetheanum, today is the second step in the unfolding reality of these words. (260a)

As a whole, the Christmas conference had three stages. During the first days, attention was focused more on what had been achieved, on the past. On December 27 and 28, the conference turned to questions concerning the very present task of forming the society anew and then, during the last days, looked toward the future. Albert Steffen opened the conference with a lecture titled "The Destiny of the Goetheanum." Following the laying of the foundation stone and on the following day, the general secretaries of the various national societies and representatives of anthroposophic groups reported on what was happening in their region in order to give everyone a sense of the breadth of the anthroposophic work up to that point. The next two days were taken up with discussions concerning the statutes and their formal acceptance by the delegates. The last four days were dedicated to the future tasks, anthroposophic scientific research and the rebuilding of the Goetheanum. This path from the past to the future can also be recognized in the evening lectures Rudolf Steiner gave during the conference.

The formation of the General Anthroposophical Society, the center point of the conference, came about through the initiative of Rudolf Steiner "gazing upon the magnificent imaginations born of the spiritual world" (260). His impulse was to give the society form and content, to create a vessel wherein the anthroposophic movement could become social reality. On December 26, he spoke of aspects of the founding that went beyond these intentions. "At the present moment in history, the spiritual world wants something from humanity. It wants this something in various areas of life, and it is our task to follow this impulse from the spiritual world clearly and truly" (260).

With "clearly and truly," Steiner indicated the needed relationship to Anthroposophy—unabashedly, uncompromisingly anthroposophic. In various ways during these days, he had pointed out that Anthroposophy suffered when modern science was brought into it. Eurythmy would be ruined if it were to copy forms of modern dance; the medical impulse could only flourish if it were developed out of Anthroposophy.

Thus the individuals he chose for the executive council of the new society were people who had excelled in this and, just as importantly, had already worked in this manner. Marie Steiner had clearly been working in this way for the past twenty-one years. She had worked uncompromisingly with Rudolf Steiner to develop eurythmy and the art of speech formation. By 1923, she led this work independently and was regularly traveling with the ensemble, carrying this work out into the world. Steiner wanted originally for both she and Albert Steffen to be named vice presidents. She declined because it would seem strange for the public if the new society were to be headed up by a married couple. Albert Steffen was called onto the executive council not only because he was Swiss—with a nod to the country in which the Goetheanum had found a home—but more importantly because he had shown through his many initiatives how important the Anthroposophical Society was to him. He had accepted the role of general secretary of the Swiss Anthroposophical Society, become very active in support of rebuilding the Goetheanum, and, especially—which meant sacrificing his own poetic strivings—had taken on the task of editing and publishing the weekly journal *Das Goetheanum*. He had done this with a clear direction, good judgment and a sense of style, insuring that members throughout the world could be aware of the work Rudolf Steiner was doing in Dornach.

That Ita Wegman was called onto the executive council came as a surprise to most of the members. She had not yet begun to lecture at that time. She was by nature a woman of action, remaining silent even throughout the Christmas conference. She was known in the periphery of Dornach as the head of the clinic, a woman who cared intensely—and, if needed, without payment—for her patients. Rudolf Steiner recognized other aspects of her character. He knew how she had entered the fray during the Futurum catastrophe, helping to avert an even-worse disaster. He had seen her build up the clinic on her own. And he knew that she placed her enthusiasm and her "courage to heal" fully in service to Anthroposophy. At the end of November, they had begun an increasingly intense esoteric collaboration (260). Dr. Lili Vreede, mathematician and astronomer, had been invaluable in the work of the branch at the Goetheanum. She had built up the archive there and had often helped raise money. Finally, Dr. Guenther Wachsmuth had been working since 1921 in House Friedwart, managing the affairs of the anthroposophic work, organizing Steiner's trips and often accompanying him.

By choosing these individuals, all of whom lived in Dornach, Steiner formed a working council able to take initiative. He let himself be guided by real people, the ones who were present. By seating them facing the participants during the conference, he ritualized this formative gesture, explaining to the audience, "Today we are not dealing with principles, but with people. You can see these individuals sitting here before you, who are convinced"—that the work being done at the Goetheanum was being done well—"as those individuals who for a long time have been committed to working at the Goetheanum. You"—the participants in the conference—"have traveled here to found the Anthroposophical Society. You have declared formally that you are in agreement with what is being done in Dornach. By this declaration, the society is formed, out of personal, human intent; people join together with others, people don't declare their acceptance of paragraphs, which can be interpreted in many ways" (260).

It was certainly not intended that the members would simply attach themselves to Rudolf Steiner and the other members of the executive council. An "ongoing, lively activity" should stream out from the executive council. Every week, contributions in the newsletter would stimulate the work of the members.

> But you are aware that for the circulation of the blood you not only need centrifugal force, but also centripetal forces, forces that work back toward the center. We will have to take care that a number of members cultivate a soul affinity with the executive council on all matters that do not only pertain to the Anthroposophical Society in a narrow sense, but are connected with the entire spiritual life of the present in its connection with the Anthroposophical Society. (260)

He suggested that the representatives of the national societies—who he described in *this* context as a "robust outer executive council of equal value"—remain in constant correspondence with the Dornach executive council, and that they should write weekly letters about the happenings in their countries and their fields of work, *straight from the heart* (260). "In this way we can create for the Anthroposophical Society a fully free charter, based on unrestricted encounters" (260).

Part of his initiative was to bring a spiritual life born of personal communication into the society. In structuring the new society, he did not imagine a charter in the usual sense in which the rights, responsibilities and procedures were laid out. When he used the word constitution in regard to the society, it was analogous to saying of a person: he or she has a healthy constitution. The impulse of the Christmas conference was to call forth a living exchange, communication and unrestricted encounters—the elements of a spiritual circulatory system. Four weeks after the conference, he wrote in the newsletter, "Anthroposophy can only thrive as a living thing. The essence of its being is life. It is life flowing from the spirit. Hence it needs to be fostered by the living soul, in warmth of heart" (260a). And shortly thereafter: "Essential to Anthroposophy are the truths that through it become evident; essential to the Anthroposophical Society is the *life* that is cultivated in it" (260a).

Rudolf Steiner called the social tendencies that hindered life sectarianism and dogmatism. One of the peculiarities of the statutes is that he explicitly lists these two enemies of anthroposophic life: "The Anthroposophical Society is averse to any kind of sectarian tendency" (260a) and "A dogmatic approach in any sphere whatsoever does not belong in the Anthroposophical Society" (260a; comp. Beilage to 260).

Steiner included these two provisions in the statutes based on the bitter experiences of the past years. Sectarianism expressed itself in a lack of interest for the surrounding world, the lack of openness for the world, an attitude of soul that had finished wondering about the world before it had been truly experienced. It was the way of a know-it-all who derived just that knowledge, solely from books, that supported one's own prejudices. True interest for the world cannot exist without the love for what is revealed in the world. It feels itself to be one with the world. In this context, Steiner's statement that the Anthroposophical Society must be "a true society of the world" should not be taken geographically (260).

It is also worth noting that Steiner did not only reject dogmatism in the sense of rigidly following approved teachings, but everything dogmatic, any form of doctrinary teaching. This is why Anthroposophy cannot be understood as a compilation of fundamental tenets. The truths voiced by Rudolf Steiner are not true in and of themselves, but through the individual experience of their truthfulness.

There are two further hindrances to cultivating a true social, spiritual life that he mentioned repeatedly during the conference: bureaucracy and pedantry (260). He hoped that a feeling of tact would replace them. "One has to have a certain fine sensitivity for what is needed, when" (260).

The goal was to legitimately place the Anthroposophical Society in contemporary spiritual life. Anthroposophy was not to be trapped in the confines of the Anthroposophical Society, but stream out into the world, independent and without compromise. It was to be a "fully public" society. Its publications, like those of other public societies, would also be made public.

At the center of this public society, Rudolf Steiner formed the independent School for Spiritual Science as the core of its work.* Although the Goetheanum had had this designation for some time, it was understood in such a way that people thought of what was being done in terms of other institutions, only that the content was somewhat different. Steiner now

---

* Rudolf Steiner always wrote independent School and not Independent School. By writing "idependent" lower case, Steiner shows that it is not just a matter of a name, but that the School should really be free, independent.

returned to his original intentions to form a school for spiritual knowledge, in which the students would be guided toward independent spiritual insight. He had already mentioned his desire to work with students of the spirit in 1902. From 1904 until 1914, he had guided individuals in developing meditative practices within the framework of the Esoteric School, which was not a public institution. Now he announced publicly his intention to form a school, consisting of three classes with various special sections or departments.

In its conception, this school differed from the esoteric trainings that existed before the war. First, Rudolf Steiner conceived of and founded it independently, without linking it to any of its predecessors. He had indicated the direction of his thinking in 1920 when he revised the words of one passage from his play *The Guardian of the Threshold*. In the play the passage runs:

> And to this day all genuine mystic schools
> Descend directly from that earliest one,
> Which was established by the higher spirits.
> Humbly we cultivate within these walls
> What has been left us by our ancestors.
> Never will we assert that our own merits
> Deserve the offices that we now fill:
> The lofty spirit-powers choose by grace...

At the opening ceremony for the first Goetheanum, the verse went like this:

> Until now all genuine centers of knowledge
> Descend from the highest in the spirit spheres.
> In earnest seeking we all strive
> Toward true spirit-human inheritance.
> We will never speak of knowledge
> That does not bear the spirit's own seal. (40).

The independent school was created directly out of the spiritual world, not in connection with any outer tradition.

Second, from the very beginning the school was to consist of three classes, which students could move through according to their abilities. From 1906 until 1914, there had been different degrees within the Esoteric School and the "symbolic, ritualistic" (28) circle connected to it. These were regarded as "secret." They weren't spoken about publically, nor were they a formal part of the society. The members of this Esoteric School received "what, on the one hand, spoke to their thought life but in such a way that their feeling life was directly engaged in imaginative experience" (28). The new independent school was crafted in quite a different manner.

Third, the newly constituted school was divided into sections or departments. Through these the knowledge, which came to life in the spirit, could be directed into earthly practice.

In the final lecture of the Christmas conference, Rudolf Steiner gave a general sketch of the meaning and intent of the independent school.

> Dornach must be a place where it is possible to speak of all the important, immediate experiences in the spiritual world to those people who wish to listen. This must be a place where people find the strength to not merely hint in a speculative, dialectical, empirically modern scientific manner at the fact that here or there one might find traces of the spiritual, but, if Dornach is to live up to its challenge, it must be a place where one speaks openly of the historical developments in the spiritual world, of the impulses from the spiritual world that enter into natural existence and reign within nature. Here people must be able to hear of true experiences, of true spiritual beings. It must be the home of the school of true Spiritual Science. (260)

The scope of these words lived in the lecture cycle that accompanied the Christmas conference "World History in the Light of Anthroposophy." These lectures spanned the period from ancient Indian culture to the present. The leitmotiv was the inner nature of human development. The transformation of the forces of memory, the experience of death, the relation to nature, and the character of the sacred mysteries were described in sweeping images and through the destinies of key individuals. Rudolf Steiner harkened back to the time when, in the ancient Eastern mysteries, the gods themselves were present when the priest made their sacrifices. He described how, in the Greek mysteries, the presence of the gods in the mysteries was more pictorial, like shadows cast upon the wall. Ephesus stood on the threshold between the two and it was here, through the actions of Herostat, that the sacred mystery culture came to an end. He described how, in the period that followed, the cult of the personality intrinsic to the mysteries worked on in the destiny stories of specific personalities. He called attention to Aristotle and how he had taught Alexander the Great. Alexander was described as the one who brought the spirit of the penetrating, worldly, observation-based understanding of nature to Asia and

North Africa. Threophrast, on the other hand, brought Aristotle's logic to the West, where it served for centuries as the basis of higher education. Later, along various hidden streams, Aristotle's approach to understanding nature also found its way to the West. It blossomed in unique ways in Paracelsus, Basilius Valentinus, Valentin Weigel, Jakob Böhme and others. Finally, Steiner pointed to how, in the Rosicrucian teachings, the seed of a new knowledge of the human being came into being that was able to grasp the spiritual.

The audience at these lectures could experience that these historical excursions were in no way abstract, but that each word rang home. In the image of the ancient mysteries, in which the gods were present, the goal of the new mysteries arose within their souls. They could understand that in the future there will once again be such mysteries, in which the gods are present. The life of Aristotle, who schooled both the soul capacity for logical thought and cultured the will through the forces of perception, let them understand the task of uniting these two elements—beholding the spirit in thought and an experienced understanding of the spirit in the realm of perception. In this and various other ways, the lectures challenged them to self-knowledge.

Rudolf Steiner was in demand throughout the entire conference. He did not only preside over all the discussions, he took care of a multitude of details: from food tickets to the heating of the carpentry shop to organizing the collection of the blankets borrowed by participants at the conference. After the evening lecture on December 24, he spent time at the bedside of a critically ill member. In addition to the plenary sessions, there were meetings with the general secretaries, the Swiss school association, a discussion with the Swiss delegates, two lectures for doctors, as well as numerous other conversations.

On January 1, 1924, at 4:30 in the afternoon, there was a "Rout," a party in the carpentry shop. Sweets and beverages were offered, and Rudolf Steiner, who had just eaten a pastry, suddenly felt weak. He withdrew to a room behind the stage, where he collapsed with the words, "We are poisoned!" He summoned his strength soon after and that evening gave the final lecture of the conference. The next morning at 8:00 a.m., he wrote the fifth installment of his *Autobiography* for the January 6 edition of *Das Goetheanum*. At 10:00, he gave a lecture—quite uncharacteristically—sitting, due to his collapse the day before. At the very beginning he said, "One must be clear that the human organism is truly a closed system. To a greater or lesser extent, everything outside that system is a poison for the human organism. Everything that is outside of the human organism is actually a poison" (314).

These words made it clear to the doctors that he had not been criminally "poisoned," but that the pastry had disagreed with him. It did not seem to be necessary to say anything more about the occurrence at the time. Later, when he had had to retire to his sickbed, the rumor began to circulate that he had been poisoned in the usual sense of the word. In opposition to the rumor, he then wrote a notice for the bulletin addressed to the council in the carpentry shop, which stated: "There seem to be rumors circulating everywhere about the present failure of my physical bodily forces. In this situation, I would be much happier if the rumor mill had not found a place within anthroposophic circles" (260a, Beilage).

The same day he wrote to Marie Steiner, who was traveling with the eurythmy ensemble, "In addition, the anthroposophists are saying such nonsense about my illness. Versions are being circulated that are only apt to cause bad blood. Even poor P. Trinchero is being brought into connection with the whole thing" (262). Father Giuseppe Trinchero was an anthroposophist and Catholic priest. Later, in September 1924, Steiner gave him a special meditation. When he was staying in Dornach, the "good" anthroposophists regarded him with disbelieving wonder.

In actuality, Rudolf Steiner, whose health, at least since the fire, had been fragile, ate a pastry that, after the fatiguing demands of the conference, did not agree with him. The illness that had made itself known for at least a year and which would cause his doctors ever-growing concern to find an appropriate diet in the fifteen months to follow had taken hold of him.

The occurrence at the New Year's gathering, of which there are so many different accounts that the details are practically impossible to reconstruct, has also been interpreted as indicating that by taking on the leadership of the General Anthroposophical Society, Steiner had taken upon himself the karma of the society and that this karma had become manifest in the "poisoning." There is nothing in Steiner's statements about the occurrence to support this interpretation.

In the reports Rudolf Steiner made about how the new societal impulse was received by the members, one finds a fairly clear assessment. He first summarized these reports upon his return from Breslau on June 20, 1924.

> Reflecting on what has been attempted in various places—in Prague, in Paris, and now again in Breslau—I can say that what has streamed out from the Christmas conference, this esoteric impulse that flows through the entire Anthroposophical Society, the new quality that is there since the actual new founding of the Anthroposophical Society, has been taken up everywhere in a heartfelt, in a true, not only deeply satisfying, but in an extraordinarily ensouled manner; there is now truly a well-founded hope that since the Anthroposophical Society has gained its spirituality through the Christmas conference, that the executive council in Dornach is consciously working spiritually and that it can truly be noticed everywhere not only that the stream has begun to flow outward, but that the hearts of those participating reach out to meet the stream. (260a)

This rather convoluted statement seems to support the conclusion that Rudolf Steiner was quite satisfied with the way the impulse of the Christmas conference had been taken up. Even later, in September 1924, when over a thousand members had gathered in Dornach for various courses and lectures, Steiner reiterated this statement, saying that the anthroposophists had opened their hearts even more where the impulse of the Christmas conference flowed into their work (238).

This new impulse was well received by the members. The idea that Rudolf Steiner had taken on the "karma of the Anthroposophical Society" as though it were a burden of sin and that this had caused his death is a notion that would be more at home in an older, theological way of thinking. He had spoken quite differently about this series of events. He had become aware the year before the Christmas conference that the manner in which the Anthroposophical Society administered what arose out of his teachings did not correspond to the true being of Anthroposophy.

> With time it became clear that it was not something that could be reconciled with a true, authentic cultivation of the anthroposophic. Hence the necessity arose for me, who had up till then been the teacher of Anthroposophy, without any official connection to the Anthroposophical Society, to take on the leadership of the Anthroposophical Society together with the executive council in Dornach. Because of this, however, the anthroposophic movement and the Anthroposophical Society became one. And since the Christmas conference in Dornach, the opposite has become true: It is no longer necessary to differentiate between the anthroposophic movement and the Anthroposophical Society; they should be but one and the same. And those

individuals who have joined me in forming the executive council at the Goetheanum, they should be viewed as a sort of esoteric council. The role of this council can be characterized by saying, "To do Anthroposophy," whereas earlier it was only possible to administer what was taught through Anthroposophy. (240)

The Christmas conference was a turning point for the social context of the society. For Steiner the focus was no longer on teaching, but on doing and on leadership. He let the spiritual impulses living within him come strongly to the fore. Over the course of the fifteen months that followed, it became clear that he was willing to take his leadership role seriously, concerning himself with the most minute practical details.

Steiner spoke often of the "impulse of the Christmas conference" (240) or the "Christmas impulse" (240). In September 1924, when he spoke about the Christmas conference for the last time to the members, he said, "The Anthroposophical Society was to receive a new impulse through the Christmas conference.... And whoever wishes to be connected with this anthroposophic movement in a manner worthy of it must bear witness to the fact that the spiritual impulses also hold true for the Anthroposophical Society" (238).

With the use of the word *impulse*, he characterized what lived in his own efforts since he initiated the Christmas conference. He gave new impulses, spiritual impulses of the magnitude of those to be recognized in great historical events. This impulse can easily be described. Anthroposophical action should, from here on, originate in human self-knowledge attained through the Foundation Stone. Anthroposophical action should no longer orient itself on outer scientific thought, on pragmatic considerations, or on rational strategies, but be initiated out of a heartfelt consciousness. Steiner spoke in this vein during the final lecture of the Christmas conference. "If, during this conference, one has acknowledged this deep within one's soul, this Christmas conference will send a powerful impulse into the soul that the soul in turn can bear forth as a strong source of action, the kind of action that humanity needs today" (260).

That morning, the Dutch general secretary had spoken in a similar vein, saying that the challenge for the medical work was not to build bridges between mainstream medicine and the anthroposophic approach to healing, "but to establish a new kingdom in our hearts" (260). Rudolf Steiner picked up on these words of Zeylmans in his closing address and said:

More important than anything else that we take with us is the mood that we take from here, the attunement for the spiritual world that allows us to be certain that in Dornach a center for spiritual knowledge will be created. Hence what was spoken this morning by Dr. Zeylmans was quite beautiful, what was said about a field that will be cultivated here in Dornach, for the field of medicine that no longer can bridges be built from mainstream science to what is to be established here in Dornach. (260)

This tone was apparent even in the two public courses on education that Rudolf Steiner gave in Stuttgart and Bern in April 1924. He emphasized much more strongly than earlier that the mainstream scientific approach could provide no path to a true understanding of human nature or to a living pedagogy, and that true pedagogy could only grow out of a spiritual understanding of the human being (308 & 309).

The aim of the impulse of the Christmas conference was to form the society out of human experience, out of a spiritual understanding of human nature, to take an uncompromising stand for Anthroposophy born of self-knowledge, and to form everything anew out of this impulse. Steiner decided freely, after years of holding himself back, to take up this impulse in crafting the society. This signified a complete reversal of his earlier relationship to the society, although this impulse originated deep within the realm of his most elemental intentions.

CHAPTER 52

FOUNDATIONS

Following the Christmas conference, with the exception of three short trips to Bern, Zürich and Stuttgart, Rudolf Steiner remained in Dornach until March 26. On January 2, he began working with the medical section, giving a course for young doctors and medical students in which developed a new vocabulary to speak about the esoteric deepening of medical studies and the art of therapy. On January 6, after speaking of the difficulties of the esoteric path, he turned to the participants, saying:

> From this time on, from the period in time that began with the Christmas conference, a true change of direction needs to take hold in all aspects of the anthroposophic movement. And as you search for the right path in medicine, you must also participate inwardly from the very beginning in this process of transformation. The esoteric path cannot be merely a supplement. What is needed is a complete fulfillment of the life path through the esoteric impulse. (316)

The earnest esoteric thrust that was now to inform all the work going forward is perceptible in these words spoken at the very beginning of the work of the new medical section. It would resonate in one form or another throughout all of his lectures following the Christmas conference.

Steiner did, naturally, include in this new beginning what was still valid from the work of the past. In the first lecture for members after the conference, he turned his attention to the earth's most distant past and described how the seers of the ninth and tenth centuries had beheld the evolution of the earth from ancient Saturn to ancient Sun to ancient Moon. In the subsequent lectures, he followed the development from the mystery sites of the Middle Ages, through the forms of knowledge practiced by the true Rosicrucians, to the last of the mysteries, which had continued up to the beginning of the nineteenth century. The new impulse of the Christmas conference was thus united with the Rosicrucian stream.

Dated January 13, the first edition of the newsletter *News for the Members* appeared on January 11. It contained Steiner's report on "The Founding of the General Anthroposophical Society," including the Foundation Stone verse. Beginning on January 20, Rudolf Steiner wrote a weekly letter "To the Members!" as a way to nurture a constant line of communication between the Goetheanum and the members. In the early editions, following a historical overview of the anthroposophic work, he gave suggestions toward the cultivation of the soul-spiritual life in the society and a first orientation of the work in the independent School of Spiritual Science. Beginning on February 17, he started with the series of "Leading Thoughts." These made it possible for anthroposophic groups throughout the world to refresh their understanding of Anthroposophy step by step. A shared spiritual life began to pulse throughout the society; a shared consciousness arose, which bred a feeling of connectedness in which all members could participate.

In the center of the work, in Dornach, Steiner made it clear that now, after twenty-one years, what had been done needed to be reviewed, revised and renewed. On January 19, he began a series of lectures, "a sort of introduction to Anthroposophy." The older members in Dornach discovered to their surprise how Anthroposophy was reborn out of the fundamental questions of human existence in a comparatively elementary language. Concepts of the etheric and astral bodies were brought into connection with the cosmic forces, and Steiner described how the essence of the "I" appeared out of the metamorphoses of memory, unclothed and "spiritually naked" (34).

The Christmas conference impulse brought about a rejuvenation of the basic elements of Anthroposophy, transforming them from the more conceptual descriptions of the previous years to forms of objective experience. Through the "Leading Thoughts," Anthroposophy in this new form was made available to all the members, taking what was brought forth in the lectures a significant step further.

It was incredibly important to Rudolf Steiner that not only basic Anthroposophy be subjected to this process of rejuvenation. The work in the various special fields also received new direction. From February 19 to 27, he gave a course on eurythmy and music that was meant to "inspire a more inward grasp of tone eurythmy and eurythmy in general" (278). A second eurythmy course followed from June 24 until July 12. This focused on speech eurythmy. New guidelines were given for the original gestures and movements. In the newsletter, Rudolf Steiner wrote about the aim of this course.

> The participants in this course should not only have been challenged to better understand eurythmy, they should have experienced how all art must be carried through love and enthusiasm. The eurythmist cannot separate himself from his artistic creation and place it objectively before the aesthetic as can a painter or sculptor; he remains personally a part of his creation; one *sees* in him whether the artistic impulse lives in him as a divine cosmic reality or not. The eurythmist must present the artistic as a visible being through his own humanness in the immediate artistic present. (260a)

He also spoke differently in 1924 about anthroposophic pedagogy. Although he was not able to speak to the Waldorf School teachers about moral education as he had planned in order to deepen the impulse of the Christmas conference for the inner circle of the teachers, he was able to give four more public courses on education. The new quality that characterized Steiner's work in 1924 was present in these courses through the imaginative conceptual language that he used. In addition, he presented in two of the courses a path of teacher training through the arts, describing how, through certain sculptural exercises, the teacher could be led toward an understanding of the etheric body, and how, through music, language and poetry, he or she could begin to grasp the astral body and the "I" respectively. He summarized this completely new approach to teacher training.

> In the first period of learning, one learns through abstract logic to know the physical body. One then applies the forces of sculptural formation in intuitive discernment—one learns to know the etheric body. And in the third period, as physiologist, one becomes a musician and beholds the human being as a musical instrument, as an organ or a violin, seeing in the instrument the music made manifest. Thus one learns to know the astral body. And if one does not merely learn the meaning of words through memory but experiences the genius at work in them, he learns to know the "I"-organization of the human being. (308)

In each of these fields—in medicine, in eurythmy and in education—new ideas concerning training were brought forth, which, if they were taken up seriously, could lead to a transformation of the individual. The young medical students were shown an esoteric path to the art of healing, the eurythmists were enthused by the insight that a cosmic reality lived in their art, and the teachers were to be led to a feeling experience of the suprasensory aspects of the human being through artistic activity.

At the center of all these activities stood the independent School for Spiritual Science. Steiner described this school, its meaning and structure, in the second edition of the newsletter. This description reflects his true intentions concerning the establishment of the school. The alleged notes of Count Polzer-Hoditz documenting Steiner's intentions concerning the school—with a second class consisting of only thirty-six members and a third class with twelve members—have been shown to be a forgery. The indications originated neither by Rudolf Steiner nor by Polzer-Hoditz, but are the work of another man who was pursuing his own, very questionable aims.

In the first article concerning the School, Rudolf Steiner wrote that "a school with three classes would be incorporated into the general society," which "if possible, in the future would have to fulfill the esoteric strivings of the members" (260a). The spiritual researcher was charged with "bringing certain regions of his insights to ideation...that are accessible to ordinary consciousness." These ideas have a special character. "For each person who can bring them to life within his soul, they bear within themselves the proof of their own validity. Such ideas can be formed alone out of the mere ability to think; one can only craft them by casting what one has beheld in the spirit into their forms. Once they are there, however, anyone can take them in and discover their validity" (260a).

In the General Anthroposophical Society, one could learn the results of spiritual research in the form of such thoughts. Through the study and the emergent understanding of these thoughts, one entered the first stages of spiritual schooling. In the independent school, the teaching was to be different, done through "forms of expression taken directly from the spiritual world" (260a). "Here the work will progress toward ever higher esoteric levels. The 'school' will lead the participants upward into the realms of the spiritual world that cannot be expressed in the form of ideas. Here the necessity arises to find forms of expression for imaginations, inspirations and intuitions" (260a). The three classes were envisioned as working with different forms of expression through which imaginations, inspirations and intuitions could be grasped consciously.

Anyone could become a member of the General Anthroposophical Society. One only had to be interested in Anthroposophy and feel that an establishment like the independent school was justified. This was not the case with the school itself. Here Rudolf Steiner required the fulfillment of certain conditions. Each person who wished to become a member of the school needed to ask oneself "if he or she was in fact a person who wished not only to represent Anthroposophy in the world, but to embody it with complete courage and authenticity" (260a).

In addition, it was required that any member of the school who wished to undertake something anthroposophic would do so in agreement with the leadership of the school. "Whether it is the creation of a group or if it is something else, it must be done by the member in harmony with the leadership. This aspect of anthroposophic life is in fact centered on the leadership" (260a).

The School of Spiritual Science was not only called into being as a center for sequential esoteric training, but more importantly as a spiritual center that would give the anthroposophic work a shared focus. Between the leadership of the school and the members there was a "free contractual relationship" (260a). Rudolf Steiner committed himself to mediating authentic spiritual life to the members, for which the members also took on certain obligations. The leadership of the school was not obliged to work with members who did not take on these obligations. Rudolf Steiner let himself be guided by this reciprocal understanding; by September 1924, he had expelled twenty people from the school.

The esoteric of the School of Spiritual Science did not consist solely in the confidentiality of the lessons, although this was strictly observed, but on the unity in action. It was to be a community of shared will, a body that was aware of the shared responsibility and worked to live up to it. Steiner explained this at length in an article titled "In the Independent College the Human Element Should Make Itself Felt."

> This council is not interested in limiting initiatives in the different regions of the society. But it should be recognized as a necessity to bring whatever comes about in the society to the council's attention. The council can then harmonize what is striven for in one location or from a group of people with what from another side is intended. This council does not wish to work authoritatively "from above"; it will make it its task to keep an open heart and mind for everything that strives toward

realization within the membership. The council does hope that it can count on such understanding, and that members actively welcome it when it takes initiatives and wishes to accomplish something in keeping with the goals of the anthroposophic movement. (260a)

On February 15, Rudolf Steiner held the first lesson of the School of Spiritual Science in Dornach. Eighteen further lessons followed, the last on August 2. These lessons laid out a sequential path, casting light for the participants on the basic experiences made when entering the spiritual world. In the edition of the newsletter from April 20, Rudolf Steiner wrote openly about the content of these lessons, pointing out that in them "an overview... across the experience of the threshold between the sensory world and the suprasensory world" was presented. In language rich with imagery, he called to mind the steps toward the transformation of the inner self that raised one to knowledge of the suprasensory world (260a).

Rudolf Steiner also spoke to the members of the schools in Prague, Bern, Paris, Breslau, Arnhem, Torquay and London. He reported at some length on the two class lessons in Prague in the newsletter.

> In two gatherings of the first class of the general anthroposophic section I was able to place before the souls of those individuals who had decided to join the class the first steps of the striving to achieve suprasensory knowledge.... The number of people who could be admitted to the class was over one hundred.... It was deeply gratifying to gaze out on the souls of people I have long known from the Prague gatherings. In their eyes one could recognize the intimate connection they have with anthroposophic content in their lives. I became aware of many open hearts. (260a)

Here Steiner gives us some insight into what he experienced as a teacher in the newly formed school. It is necessary to expand somewhat upon this report. A further aspect becomes apparent in a letter written by Steiner to Ita Wegman in which he speaks of a disturbance during the second lesson given in Breslau. "The most impossible thing occurred. After we had already begun, the person responsible simply let a whole group of people come in. I was caught up in my part of things and did not notice this occurrence in the phys. world in time" (Zeylmans, *Wegman* I).

Originally, Rudolf Steiner had intended after completing the first series of lessons for the First Class to follow up with two more series after his trip to England in September 1924. They would have led directly to an experience of the ritualistic preparation of the anthroposophic movement in the suprasensory world at the beginning of the nineteenth century and of the suprasensory school of St. Michael from the fifteenth, sixteenth and seventeenth centuries. However, when he returned to Dornach at the beginning of September and realized that of the more than a thousand people gathered there for courses and lectures, many had never participated in a class lesson, although many of these hoped to do so. He decided to repeat the first lessons, in order that those who were just joining could also become acquainted with the beginning of the path. His illness made it impossible for him to complete the two planned additional series of lessons for the First Class, or to establish the next two classes. At the time of his death, the organization and content of the school was still incomplete, not only in regard to the lessons for the three intended classes, but also in regard to the work of the various sections. For a number of the sections envisioned at the time of the Christmas conference, Rudolf Steiner was never able to begin to establish the esoteric work in the different fields.

In paragraph 7 of the statutes of the General Anthroposophical Society, he had written, "The establishment of the independent School of Spiritual Science is the responsibility of Rudolf Steiner. He will appoint his coworkers and, should the occasion arise, his successor." This formulation intimates that Rudolf Steiner was not certain he would be able to name someone to take on the leadership of the school after him. The fact that he did not, in fact, name a successor indicates that he did not find anyone who could continue the esoteric work he began.

The day after giving the First Class lesson in Dornach, Rudolf Steiner began the work upon which he had originally, in 1902, hoped to base his efforts. At that time he had had the intention to re-focus the theosophical work toward practical karma exercises. The members were to have learned to read in the books of their own destinies and to understand the language of karma, so that each of them could find his or her individual path to self-knowledge. In 1924, twenty-one years later, he could at last begin to realize this intention.

In the first six lectures, Rudolf Steiner sketched out basic elements of the laws of destiny by describing the creation of karmic forces. Then, on March 8, 1924, he progressed to presenting exemplary individual destinies. That day, he sketched out three biographies without, however, going more deeply into their karmic origins. Those listening heard three short biographical sketches. The next day, he began to speak about certain aspects of their earlier lives.

He had in earlier years, in connection with the development of Christianity, periodically spoken about essential aspects of successive incarnations. Independently of the notions alive within the Theosophical Society at that time, he had, in response to an experience Marie von Sivers had had, spoken about the karmic connections and the incarnations of Elias. A description of the incarnations of Zarathustra followed in the fall of 1909. These presentations served to achieve a deeper understanding of Christianity. Later he had confidentially shared aspects of earlier lives with individuals—for instance, Günther Wagner and Helmuth von Moltke.

In 1924, an understanding of earlier incarnations became the central theme of general anthroposophic training. He spoke of the most recent past, exploring connections that had played on into the present and were characteristic for the spiritual life of the time. He wanted to achieve something completely new, to stimulate practical karma understanding. The first step in this direction consisted in becoming acquainted with individuals who had passed on recently or in the preceding decades. People have reported that it came as a shock to experience the idea of reincarnation not as a religious or historical notion but as a matter of practical life.

Introducing the first examples, which he stressed were to be viewed as examples, Steiner said:

> These explorations are based on observations that were made possible through the spiritual means that have been described and that can be read about in the anthroposophic literature. The only way to speak of such things is to narrate them. In this realm of exploration, one can only speak of what one has observed directly. In the moment one focuses one's attention from one earthly life toward another, previous life, rational ideation ceases. One can only behold. (235)

For this reason, he explained, when examining the life of this or that individual, one could be *led back* to the "next significant incarnation" (235). Or, one's gaze could fall upon something that was symptomatic that enabled one to look back (235). In his next lectures, he began to focus in on the specifics and the karmic symptoms that can lead one to the ability to explore earlier incarnations.

He had mentioned that he had thought about this sort of exploration for many years. In his *Autobiography*, he had written that "a number of observations of this sort" had revealed themselves to him when he was living in Vienna in the 1880s. They had been especially illuminating in his encounter with the poet Fercher von Steinwand. "In the play of his features and in every gesture, he made a soul being become apparent that could only have been formed in the beginning of the development of Christianity, when Greek pantheism was still present in this stream" (28). Steiner made his first "concrete observations of human reincarnation" around 1888. "Before this they were not distant, but they remained hazy, round, and did not take on sharp contours" (28).

This casts light on the fact that a number of personalities appear among the first detailed presentations of reincarnation in whom Steiner had been interested in the 1880s. The first was Friedrich Theodor Vischer, to whom he had submitted his essay "The Only Possible Refutation of Atomism" in 1882. Vischer, as Steiner often related, had thanked him for the essay. Also among these first examples were Eugen Dührings, with whom Steiner had become acquainted in 1881, and, especially, the destiny path of Eduard von Hartmann, whose publications he had followed since 1881 and with whom he had debated various philosophical questions. He had also studied the work of both Darwin and Haeckel at this time, both of whom are included in the first series of narrations. His detailed descriptions of the path to karmic understanding began thus with descriptions of people he had contemplated for more than forty years.

Not all, but many, of these first accounts are clustered around the origins of the then reigning scientific approach. Other accounts illuminate the political mentality of Wilson or the thinking of Marx and Lenin. There is a recognizable tendency of these accounts to focus on the ways of thinking at work in the contemporary events of the time. Those listening were certainly surprised to be confronted with the prevalence of Arabian influences in the spiritual tendencies of their time.

In these first karma lectures, Steiner also described a number of Anthroposophy's opposing spiritual streams, often with great understanding and sympathy. Taking Vischer as an example, he showed how in the course of Vischer's life this counter-current became the opposite of what he had originally intended. And Dühring was described with the greatest positivity, although as a twenty-year-old, Steiner had formulated the view that "his philosophy is the worst example of philosophical regression" (38). Steiner had never belied his awe for Eduard von Hartmann, neither had he skimmed over the abysmal differences that made real understanding between them impossible. His rejection of both Wilson and Marx is evident.

In the first series of karma lectures, Steiner had thus implicitly elucidated the karmic threads of the spiritual approach that had defined the recent past, colored contemporary thinking, and opposed Goetheanism and Anthroposophy. He addressed in this manner problems that had troubled him for over forty years. In 1918, he had sketched out the historically spiritual significance of the decidedly non-Christian Aristoteleanism and its Gnostic wisdom, which lived on in the Franciscan monk Roger Bacon and had its origins in the Academy of Gondischapur (184). In his lectures in March and April 1924, Harun al Raschid and other central protagonists of this spiritual impulse appear, and the work of the English Lord Chancellor Francis Bacon, the disseminator of a scientific approach to nature and societal questions, was brought to the audience's attention. This is a theme whose full significance would become clear in the lectures of the summer of 1924.

During the winter months of 1924, Rudolf Steiner attempted to craft the foundations for future work in two further areas. He founded the youth section and he made a model for the design of the second Goetheanum. Soon after the Christmas conference, it had become clear that younger people searching for Anthroposophy still did not have a place of their own in the society. He announced the formation of the youth section in the newsletter on March 9. In the first article, he turned to the "older members" saying that the youth had not turned away from them because they had grown old, "but because they had remained 'young,' because they had not understood how to 'age' correctly" (260a). He tendered the possibility to the youth, who were searching for esoteric substance, that they would find and experience the true human being in the anthroposophic esoteric. There were, however, at that time groups of young people who found absolute significance in their own youngness and experienced the notion of a broad-based generally human esoteric foreign. Turning to these groups, Steiner said that the executive council at the Goetheanum would not relinquish its view that "the eternal stream toward which the young people strove to discover flowed in the esoteric work of the Anthroposophical Society. It would be a mistake to believe that esoteric work received its true form only through youthfulness" (260a). Such words served to counter what was an essentially empty ideology of youth, while at the same time offering a positive alternative. In June 1924, Maria Röschl was called to the Goetheanum to head up the new section.

Rudolf Steiner had spoken about the plans for the new Goetheanum during the Christmas conference and had drafted a general architectural motif and a rough building plan. In the middle of March, he set aside three days to prepare a model for the building. Working almost without a break, he made a model from red modeling clay. The archetypal gesture of the first Goetheanum, which had found its form in the wooden building, was completely metamorphosed to meet the demands of a building constructed of concrete. The first building with its double cupolas was built as interpenetrating round structures; the auditorium of the new building was trapezoidal; and the stage, which at the Christmas conference had been envisioned as a semi-circular space, had become more or less rectangular. The metamorphosis of this archetypal gesture is only apparent in the outer elevations upon closer examination. The first architectural drawings based on the model were begun on March 26.

It was only after completing these foundational tasks that Rudolf Steiner could leave Dornach to begin to bring the impulse of the Christmas conference to bear in other locations.

CHAPTER 53

SPRING 1924

Three larger undertakings were planned before Easter, which came quite late that year—Easter Sunday fell on April 20. In Prague, Rudolf Steiner gave eleven lectures between March 28 and April 5. Directly afterward, he returned to Dornach to lecture and attend various meetings. On April 8, he arrived in Stuttgart for the education conference, where he gave five lectures, spoke with both the members and a gathering of young people, and attended innumerable meetings. On April 11, he returned again to Dornach, gave a class lesson upon his arrival, then a karma lecture the next day, and left on April 13 for Bern for another conference on education, during which he gave another five lectures, a lecture on karma, and another class lesson. On April 18, he returned to Dornach for the Easter conference and a full schedule, including a total of twenty lectures in the next ten days. On April 29, he was once again in Stuttgart, this time for the beginning of the sixth school year of the Waldorf School.

One can sense how Steiner, in spite of his illness, made every effort to carry the impulse of the Christmas conference into the world. The first trip took him east. As he had the previous Easter, he traveled to Prague. This time Marie Steiner and Guenther Wachsmuth accompanied him. He stayed at the house of Professor Adolf Hauffen and his wife, a man he respected highly. The work there began with a eurythmy rehearsal when they arrived—after traveling by night. That evening he gave the first of four public lectures; the next day, the first of the karma lectures for the members; on the morning of March 30, the first eurythmy performance; and that afternoon he assisted with the formation of the National Anthroposophic Society. There were three different languages spoken within the Czech society: Czech, Slovakian and German. The society was to be formed in such a way that the speakers of any of these languages did not feel discriminated against. The second and third lectures for the members followed that evening and the next day. On April 1 was the second public lecture; on April 2, he spoke before the eurythmy performance; and on April 3, he gave the First Class lesson held outside Dornach to almost one hundred participants. On April 5, he gave a second lesson. Thus it continued, day after day, until he boarded the night train to Stuttgart the evening of April 5 after giving the last lecture for the members.

During his stay in Prague, Rudolf Steiner gave advice to doctors, visited patients and received a number of visitors. But he also took the time to visit the Prague castle and wander through the city's used book stores. Guenther Wachsmuth accompanied him. It was important to Steiner to bring the impulse of the Christmas conference to life in the spiritual atmosphere that permeated Prague. He did so through the esoteric substance of the class lessons, through the new quality that breathed through the karma lectures, and through the four public lectures, which were accompanied by a eurythmy demonstration and two performances. His report on the trip in the newsletter reflected the gratitude he felt.

> A beautiful stream of earnest enthusiasm and eager devotion for Anthroposophy flowed out from our friends in Prague to meet what I had to bring. The Christmas conference at the Goetheanum has made it necessary for me to let the esoteric foundations of Anthroposophy speak ever more clearly through what I say. This found a heartfelt resonance among our friends there. (260a)

Rudolf Steiner left Prague with the night train on April 5. He arrived in Stuttgart and immediately continued by car to Dornach, where upon his arrival, he held a lecture for the members. On April 7, he did various tasks and attended a number of meetings—he also began to work on the watercolor painting *Easter*—then returned to Stuttgart for the education conference on April 8. Why didn't he just travel on April 6 from Prague to Stuttgart for the beginning of the education conference that evening? What made him add a stop-over in Dornach, an extra seven-hour trip?

Did he not want to allow too long a break in the series of karma lectures? Were there pressing things to be spoken through with the architects drawing up the plans for the second Goetheanum? Did his concern for the critically ill Edith Maryon or the ongoing work on the book on anthroposophic medicine bring him back to Dornach? We don't know. In any case, he arrived in Stuttgart on April 8, just before his first lecture was to begin, and stayed for only three days. Clearly, he had no desire to waste any time.

The five lectures on education during the educational conference in Stuttgart were the last public lectures he gave in Germany. The conference took place in Gustav-Siegle House, which was barely large enough to seat the 1700 participants, among whom were many teachers from the public schools. As was mentioned above, there was a new quality in the way Rudolf Steiner spoke. In his introductory lecture, he declared that true knowledge of the human being cannot be satisfied "simply with understanding the single person as he or she appears before us, as body, soul and spirit. It must strive to become conscious of what lives between people during their lives on earth" (308).

By calling attention to the mysterious, often unconscious back and forth that lives between people, these lectures introduced aspects of practical karma understanding. He described what lives between people.

> When a person encounters another person...sympathies and antipathies arise; we have impressions that tell us whether the other person is someone we wish to become closer to or not. We can also have other impressions. After the first encounter, we can say: This is an intelligent person; that is a person who is not so gifted. I could give other examples. They simply show that there are a multitude of impressions that wish to rise from the depths of the soul to the surface of consciousness that are suppressed in the naïve flow of daily life, but we can let them guide us in orienting our own lives in our encounters with others. It is also true that what we call compassion, which is one of the most significant sources of human morality, also belongs to this realm of non-conscious human understanding of which I speak. (308)

In the lectures that followed, Steiner described how an educator can achieve an experienced understanding of and the ability to work with what lives between people through a spiritually artistic training. On the morning of April 11, he ended his lecture series with the above-mentioned verse, the expression of an approach to education that could unite human beings. The audience thanked him for these lectures with a standing ovation that did not seem to want to end. He noted in his report on the conference in the newsletter that he had taken his cue from the mood of the audience and had spoken accordingly; for "some it was illuminating."

Otherwise, the time in Stuttgart was so completely booked that he was not able to be present for the lectures given by faculty members of the Waldorf School. He gave a karma lecture for the members of the society and met with representatives of the society and others. In the Waldorf School he was present at a long-overdue teachers' meeting and conferred with that year's twelfth-grade students. He took pleasure in a gathering with young people. "One could see in their faces how their youthful sensitivities flowed together with a feeling for Anthroposophy. This part of the education conference gratified me deeply" (260a).

Following his final lecture, which ended at 10:30 in the morning, he had planned to leave immediately for Dornach. The departure was delayed and he found himself having to prepare the seventh class lesson in the car. He arrived in Dornach just in time to begin the class lesson, which was scheduled to begin at 8:30 that evening. The next morning, he spoke to the workers at 9:00, and then drove to the clinic for a series of medical consultations. In the afternoon, he discussed the coming editions of the *Goetheanum* and the newsletter, and then gave another karma lecture for the members that evening.

From April 13 to 17, he was in Bern for a conference on education that had been organized on the request of teachers in the region. It was a continuation of the course for Swiss educators that had taken place in April 1923. The goal was to awaken interest among these teachers for anthroposophic pedagogy. In comparison to Stuttgart, the number of participants was relatively small. There was not as great an interest in educational reform in Pestalozzi's country. But Rudolf Steiner was pleased that what he presented was well received. "The gracious participation of the teachers present was proof that true understanding...came to meet what was brought. The fact that there were a number of non-teachers present shows that this is something that is experienced as meeting a general human need" (260a).

The seeds that were planted in Bern did take root and blossom in time. The anthroposophic school movement began after Steiner's death. The first steps were small, but it soon grew stronger and made valuable methodological contributions to the movement as a whole. It was up to Steiner to combine the pedagogical initiative with a deepening of the anthroposophic work. He held a karma lecture for the Bernese members, at the beginning of which he spoke emphatically of the Christmas conference impulse, and gave a class lesson for the members of the first class of the independent School of Spiritual Science.

Immediately following these conferences in Prague, Stuttgart and Bern, where Steiner had borne witness of the new spiritual impulse that had been born in the Christmas conference, he returned to Dornach for the Easter conference. In spite of the widespread social, political and financial difficulties of the time, a large number of anthroposophists made their way to Dornach, having heard that something completely new had begun to blossom there.

As the theme of the conference, Steiner chose Easter as part of the history of the sacred mysteries. He broke off the themes he had been developing in the karma lectures and once again took up those themes he had worked with in December 1923 and January 1924. By calling attention once more to the nature of the sacred mysteries, he hoped to deepen an understanding for what was intended with the Christmas conference and let this impulse resonate again, completed with the octave of Easter. The Easter festival was an opportunity—because of the Mystery of Golgotha—to reawaken in the hearts of the members a sense of the ancient mysteries, their decline, and the birth of the new mysteries through the Christmas conference. This took place on a number of different levels. The two presentations of the Foundation Stone verse through recitation and eurythmy, which Rudolf Steiner had prepared with Marie Steiner and the eurythmy ensemble, let the words of the verse become visible as moved and moving form.

In the four lectures, he presented the metamorphosis of the sacred mysteries. In the ancient mysteries, novices were guided to an understanding of the cosmos as space—"from the beginning of Christianity onward, the mystery of time took the place of the mystery of space" (260a). What had to be sought outside the earth before the Mystery of Golgotha could now, after the turning of the time, be seen as a historical event in earthly history. By reflecting once more on the path of the mysteries, a deeper interest in the meaning of Easter could be cultivated.

> When Anthroposophy strives for this deepened understanding, it, too, is permeated with the idea of the resurrection and becomes a witness of this event. What begins as an idea becomes a heartfelt conviction. The Easter conference at the Goetheanum wished to bring the impulse of the Christmas conference a step further in its development. (260a)

This was how Steiner presented it in the newsletter. In the final lecture during the conference, he had developed this idea further. The ancient cultures were based completely on the principle of initiation. The mysteries guided the spiritual life of the people. Over time, this powerful source of guidance stepped into the background; people were left to their own resources. In people living in the present, who have in no way attained full inner freedom, lives a dim, distant memory of what they experienced in past lives through the mysteries. The challenge that faces us in the present is to raise the fruits of the past into the light of consciousness and allow them to ripen.

> It is true that, if the impulse that radiated out from the Goetheanum through the Christmas conference, if this impulse truly comes to life in the Anthroposophical Society, the Anthroposophical Society, by leading into the three classes that need to be established—we have begun doing this already—will become the basis for the future blossoming of the sacred mysteries. The future mysteries must be seeded consciously through the Anthroposophical Society. (233a)

Taking the Artemis mysteries of Ephesus as an example, he described how the novice came to an experience of the cosmic etheric body permeated with planetary forces, what the content of these experiences were and how Aristotle later, as though echoing this initiation, could intuit and write about the "archetypal forms of designation," the Aristotelian categories. Today we must allow this "revelation of wisdom" that "rests in a kind of grave" to arise once more into the light of the world. "We are here, my dear friends, to once more make visible what has been hidden away!" This can't happen by simply uncovering the graves and digging up, as it were, what was laid to rest in them, but only by bringing into the light what lives in secret in the hearts of human beings. "Anthroposophy rests within the human heart. These human hearts must only learn to truly know themselves. We have to truly feel this to be led calmly and consciously—not instinctively, as it was in ancient times—back to the wisdom that radiated with living strength through the mysteries" (233a).

He showed how this was possible, taking the burning of the Goetheanum as a backdrop. The burning of the temple of Artemis transformed the spiritual substance of this holy place; it was carried out into the breadth of the living world to be rediscovered by Aristotle and Alexander as a natural fact. The substance of Anthroposophy that had been incorporated into the building had become a universal fact.

> The flames carried out into the expanses of the cosmos what had, more or less, been an earthly reality before. Since it was us who were

> affected, we are allowed to say in recognizing the significance of this catastrophe: Now we understand that we do not merely bear witness to an earthly reality, but a reality of the wide etheric world in which the spirit lives. The reality of the Goetheanum became a reality of the etheric in which the spiritually rich wisdom of the world lives. It was borne outward and we can now take in the Goetheanum impulse as though it flows into us from out of the cosmos. (233a)

Such words reveal something of the inspirational source of the new stream that flowed through the anthroposophic work. In the class lessons given for members of the First Class during the Easter conference, those participating could experience the practices of this new mystery school.

During the conference, Rudolf Steiner continued his work within the medical section, dedicating time for meetings with practicing doctors and with the medical students. During the last meeting with the doctors, two of Dr. Wegman's case studies from the book she was working on with him were presented and discussed, giving the doctors who were present the opportunity to experience basic principles applied to the daily practice. In his lectures for the medical students, Steiner gave indications for the doctors' inner development; the necessary treatment could be discovered through the inner contemplation of the patient.

> Through this approach, the inner will to heal is developed as the special soul mood needed by the doctor. The way the development of the will to heal has been presented in this course shows that it does not manifest itself as a separate—abstract—human capacity, but rather always appears individually in correspondence with the objective contemplation of the disease; it identifies itself in union with the knowledge needed to heal in each specific case. (260a)

Steiner strove in this manner to make the spiritual directly fruitful in practice. His indications were concrete and contained meditative indications.

On April 29, Steiner traveled once again to Stuttgart for meetings with the teachers of the Waldorf School and for the start of the sixth school year. His work with the teachers centered on the curriculum for the twelfth grade. On April 30, the pupils of the first grade were welcomed starting at 9:00, and at 10:00, Steiner spoke to the school community. At 12:00, he met with the students of the twelfth grade. That afternoon, he met for the first and last time with the faculty of the Stuttgart Eurythmy School, and, in the evening, continued his work with the Waldorf School faculty. The

Spring 1924

next day, questions demanding his immediate attention arose and he was forced to stay on through the day. It was late evening before he was able to depart for Dornach, where he arrived in the early hours of the morning to find a note from Ita Wegman informing him that his dear friend and close colleague, Edith Maryon, had passed away at 11:45 the night before.

Edith Maryon's death did not come as a surprise. Before he had left for Prague, Rudolf Steiner had asked Albert Steffen to give a eulogy if she should die before he returned. Now, on May 2, he entered the room where she had died. The life of this true friend stood in great clarity before his inner eye: a life of peacefulness and calm, a life of renunciation and devotion to Anthroposophy. He remembered the work they had done together on the sculpture that was to be the center point of the first Goetheanum, the day when he stumbled on the high scaffold and would have fallen into the depths below if she hadn't caught him, and he recalled the night of the fire, which caused her illness to flare up again. During 1923, he had written her letters whenever he was away from Dornach, which gave her strength and courage and kept the connection alive. Originally, he had hoped to have her join the executive council of the newly founded General Anthroposophical Society, but she had asked him not to. Instead, he appointed her head of the art section. He continued to visit her regularly after the Christmas conference, when she was confined to her bed, and shared with her the contents of the class lessons.

He was immersed in thoughts of her when he later came back to the studio, for which Edith Maryon had cared for so many years; he sat down in his chair, still immersed in his thoughts. His gaze fell upon the pieces they had worked on together, the Representative of Humanity, the eurythmy figures that had been conceived by Edith Maryon and that he had carried out, and on the tools that the sculptress had left behind. He remained lost in thought until finally turning to Albert Steffen, who was also in the studio and later described these moments.

The next evening, he spoke to the members in Dornach. He first memorialized Charlotte Ferreri, who had recently died in Milano, but then he interrupted the lecture in order to be present at the closing of Edith Maryon's coffin, which was to be taken to the crematorium in Basel. Fifteen minutes later, he resumed the lecture, speaking now exclusively of Edith Maryon. First he gave a characterization of her, describing her absolute dependability, her common sense, and her will that was in fact pure skill.

Most important, he described the nature of their spiritual collaboration—Miss Maryon had never placed any form of resistance in the path of the spiritual intentions he needed to realize, and she had never let her own personal considerations get in the way of the work but had placed her entire personal life at the service of Anthroposophy. This selflessness coupled with dependability and skill was irreplaceable.

Considering this loss, Rudolf Steiner chose to share with the audience exactly what the tendency toward personal self-aggrandizement within the Anthroposophical Society meant for him. When he took on the leadership of the society, he became responsible to the spiritual world for everything that happened within the anthroposophic movement. Taking on the leadership meant that he had to bear into the spiritual world everything that happened in connection with him.

> A person is working within the anthroposophic movement. He is working for the movement, but he weaves his own personal ambitions into what he does—personal intentions, personal qualities. Granted, one has these personal ambitions, these personal tendencies. But most people don't recognize them as personal; most people believe that what they do is impersonal, for the good of the whole, because they tend to deceive themselves as to the difference between personal and impersonal. This has to be taken along. And it leads to the most horrific setbacks coming from the spiritual world to the person, who has to bear these things whose origin is in the personal, into the spiritual world. (261)

These words are not entirely easy to understand. What does he mean? What occurrences does he have in mind? It is a riddle. Naturally, one can imagine that a great number of the members did not grasp the meaning of the Christmas conference and continued to behave in their private lives as they had before the conference. But it would be an illusion to expect anything else. The words must pertain to occurrences within the General Anthroposophical Society in which he experienced willfulness and personal aspirations.

One indication of his concern is to be found in remarks made first in Stuttgart, then again in Bern and in other places—that lectures or workshops offered within the context of the General Anthroposophical Society would not be recognized unless the organizers had first received the approval of the executive council in Dornach. A similar form of faithful camaraderie was also expected in all matters connected with the sections (260a). In the newsletter dated May 25, he finally announced that, in the future, individuals would be appointed who would be allowed to officially use the title "Anthroposophical Society" in conjunction with their work. Otherwise, this title could only be used with the agreement of the council. In a series of letters dated June 6, he authorized Adolf Arenson, Hermann von Baravalle, Moritz Barsch, Caroline von Heydebrand, Eugen Kolisko, Hermann Poppelbaum, Friedrich Rittelmeyer, Karl Schubert, Erich Schwebsch, Walter Johannes Stein, and Carl Unger as official speakers of the "Anthroposophical Society" (260a).

Other impressions confronted Rudolf Steiner's spiritual gaze in the first weeks of May as he continued the karma lectures, rehearsed a new eurythmy program for the tour that left with Marie Steiner on May 18, and finalized the building plans for submittal to the authorities. Ita Wegman, who worked intensively at this time with him, gave insight into his concerns. The spiritual forces opposing Anthroposophy had appeared on the spiritual horizon, derisive and threatening. They would unleash their power if the new impulse did not take hold (Newsletter, vol. 2).

When Rudolf Steiner traveled to Paris with Ita Wegman at the end of May to give public lectures and to speak within the context of the First Class, he mentioned this at the beginning of the first karma lecture. After speaking about the impulse of the Christmas conference, he continued:

> Connected with this—and I speak of spiritual realities here—is also the fact that very powerful hostile forces, demonic forces, are gathering against the anthroposophic movement. But we can hope that the strength of the fellowship that we were able to forge with the spiritual forces of good in the Christmas conference will in the future be able to drive these forces, these spiritual forces, that use human beings to achieve their aims from the field. (239)

Rudolf Steiner encountered the threatening presence of the demonic forces as he communicated the spiritual revelations and impulses that had become richer and stronger since the Christmas conference with reservation to the anthroposophists. He reported from Paris:

> It is possible to meet what lives as anticipation in the souls of the anthroposophists by casting off all reservations and presenting what lives in the revelations coming from the spiritual world directly. Generally, one can say that since Christmas it has been possible to

have the warmth of soul, which is so welcome when communicating anthroposophic insights, present in the lecture hall. (260a)

Although during his time in Paris he also received many visitors, spent an evening with the doctors, visited the small eurythmy school and spoke at the founding of the French Anthroposophical Society, he still found time, as in Prague, to visit important sites. He went to the Louvre several times, where, together with Ita Wegman, he viewed the statue of Gilgamesch in the Abyssinian collection, a statue of Alexander in the Greek collection, and spent quite a long time studying a painting by Benozzo Gozzoli that showed Thomas of Aquinas between Aristotle and Plato with a conquered Arabian philosopher at their feet. But even this was not enough. In spite of his failing physical forces, he went on to visit Notre Dame and Sainte Chapelle. In Dornach, he spoke of the work in Paris, emphasizing that the impulse of the Christmas conference in this city, which had been "through the ages a place of esoteric striving," "was felt with a deep inner sympathy. And this shows that as the living esoteric core of the anthroposophic movement becomes ever more apparent, the anthroposophic movement will perhaps finally find its proper course" (260a).

While in Paris, he received notice of a situation in which he recognized one symptom of the forces working against Anthroposophy. The widely known opponent of Anthroposophy, the minister in Arlesheim, Max Kully, had filed a complaint against Albert Steffen and Dr. Grosheintz for slander because of a passage in a book by Louis Werbeck, *The Christian Opponents of Rudolf Steiner*, which had been advertised in the *Goetheanum* and was being distributed at the Goetheanum. At first he was not disturbed by the message and wrote to Marie Steiner, "If I consider the situation, I don't believe that the court can do anything" (262). But when he returned to Dornach and read the offending passage where Werbeck spoke of lies, slander, perfidity, brutality, false accusations, etc., it was immediately clear to him that things were much worse than he had thought. He wrote to Marie Steiner, "When I returned home, I discovered the extent of the calamity. The passage in Werbeck's is such that the court will inevitably rule against it" (262).

Steiner counted a total of twenty-seven libelous statements in the text. He took full responsibility for the situation and, as chairman of the Anthroposophical Society, the responsibility for the distribution of the book. He appeared in court on July 30 and presented his own defense. As was expected, the court ruled against him, he was fined 200 Swiss francs and had to pay the court costs. In a further instance of the case in the Federal Court in Solothurn, he was insofar successful in that the court turned down Kully's demand for payment for injuries sustained. In Steiner's opinion, the publisher and the editor were more to blame for the situation than the author was. They should never have let the libel slip through. All in all, it was "quite a satisfactory ruling," because it allowed him to demonstrate that he would take all responsibility for whatever "happened within the context of the Anthroposophical Society" (260a).

After visiting Stuttgart in the beginning of June to confer with the teachers, speak to the parents of the students, and give a karma lecture for the members of the society, he traveled on to Breslau, accompanied by Elisabeth Vreede and Guenther Wachsmuth. They were joined along the way by Marie Steiner and the eurythmy ensemble. In Breslau, they were met by a caravan of automobiles and driven to the Koberwitz estate that lay south of the city.

In Koberwitz, which was administered at the time by Count Carl Keyserlingk, an agriculture course had been planned. This course had a history. In the context of his work with The Coming Day, Rudolf Steiner had concerned himself with the work on the farms that belonged to the endeavor. Sometime in 1923, Ernst Stegemann, a farmer who had concerns about the degeneration of the seed available for planting, contacted Steiner to ask for his recommendations. Stegemann had put Steiner's indications immediately to the test and had begun to speak of his experiences. Soon, Steiner was approached by other farmers. As Guenther Wachsmuth recalled, agricultural experiments had begun in Dornach in 1922, and in 1923, Rudolf Steiner gave directions for making the first biodynamic preparation. The preparation that had lain in the earth through the winter was unburied in the early summer of 1924, and Steiner had demonstrated how to ready the mixture and apply it to the land (Wachsmuth).

While these early experiments were being conducted in Dornach, Count Keyserlingk had met with Ernst Stegemann and they had decided to invite Steiner to give a course on agriculture. Steiner did not at first take the request seriously. Finally, Keyserlingk sent his nephew Alexander to Dornach with orders not to return until he had a definite date for the course. Steiner agreed to give a course at Whitsun 1924. Keyserlingk offered his Koberwitz estate as the venue for the course and invited all the participants to be his guests there.

The agricultural course was held from 11:00 a.m. to 3:00 p.m. from June 7 to 16, and an anthroposophic conference took place during the same period in Breslau, where Steiner gave nine karma lectures and two class lessons, and Marie Steiner gave a workshop on speech formation. There was also a eurythmy performance, and George Kugelmann's theater company performed Goethe's *Iphegenie*. More than 500 people were present at these lectures, which were the last lectures Rudolf Steiner gave in Germany. He also took the opportunity to address the younger members present three times. This daily schedule made certain—as Steiner once jokingly remarked—that he was never at a loss for something to do, especially since Dr. Lutz Engel brought him in a number of times for patient consultations, there were ongoing requests for personal conversations, and on top of everything, it was necessary to drive back and forth from Koberwitz to Breslau each day.

It was not easy for Steiner to give a course on agriculture. He wrote to Ita Wegman from Koberwitz that he had approached the course "with little hope" (Zeylmans, *Wegman* I), and he reminded the farmers at the beginning of the course that this was the first time he had attempted to do something like this. Later he remarked, "I am not sure that what Anthroposphy can contribute will satisfy us completely. But we shall make the attempt to speak out what Anthroposophy can contribute to our understanding of agriculture" (327).

In the course of the lectures, the opportunity soon arose to communicate the spiritual aspects necessary for the future of agriculture. Steiner began by contrasting his point of departure from that of mainstream agriculture. Whereas the materialistic approach focused merely on supplying crops with the necessary minerals, Steiner's approach focused on the care and cultivation of the living plant in its connection with quite differentiated cosmic forces. He described first the way these forces worked together with the earth, with the stones, and with water, air and warmth in order to show how the living forces manifest.

In the fourth and fifth lectures, he began to give the farmers concrete mixtures. In a very pictorial, concrete and understandable manner, he described the recipe for the manure supplement preparations, their preparation and application. Naturally, he gave the conceptual background of the mixtures, for the farmers should understand what it was they were working with. Through his descriptions, Steiner inspired respect and love for the plants used in these preparations. His descriptions of yarrow, chamomile and stinging nettle called attention to the living spiritual odor of these plants in a manner that must have awakened the keenest interest of the farmers. And his instructions for making and readying the preparations were so spiritually concrete that they could awaken a direct sense for the processes of the spiritual in nature.

In the discussions and question-and-answer sessions that followed the lectures, a lively exchange developed between the farmers with their practical questions and Rudolf Steiner, who usually answered the questions briefly and unequivocally. The way he answered the questions shows that his primary interest here was the practical application of the recipes and the art of using them. A research circle of farmers was formed during the conference with the hope that this circle would soon enter into a lively exchange with members of the section in Dornach. But the practical work would have to be started before it would make sense to speak of future plans.

Thus, in the later lectures, Steiner focused on practical questions and concrete details. He spoke about field prep and manures, dealing with so-called weeds and pests, the relationship of the insects to the plant world, the reciprocal relationships between fields, meadows and woods, and, finally, he spoke of the farm as an integral organism, "a sort of individuality," a living system, cyclic, in which everything carried and was carried by everything else (327).

The goal of the agriculture course was to kindle an experience of the spiritual processes alive in nature in order to counter the deterioration of the health of plants and animals by revitalizing the earth. Through a careful handling and preparation of the various forms of manure, the earth was to be given the quality of substance that would allow cosmic spiritual energies to flow into it. This cosmic vitalization should also serve to heal the earth and, through it, the plants and animals.

This impulse to find a life in harmony with nature that could understand the gestural language of the plants and the voices of the birds and could lead to an intimate encounter with the spirituality hidden in the trees, the rocks, the wind and the clouds could fulfill the deep inner longing of the *Wandervogel*. It can be experienced intensely in the talks Rudolf Steiner gave to the young people gathered in Breslau. He shared two old sayings with them: *In sal sit sapientia* [Wisdom rests in salt] and *Naturalia non sunt turpia* [Everything in nature is beautiful] (217a).

At noon on June 17, Rudolf Steiner left Koberwitz accompanied again by Elisabeth Vreede and Guenther Wachsmuth. They boarded a train in Breslau, settled in, and after a while Rudolf Steiner said, happy and satisfied, "Now this important task is also done!" (Wachsmuth). Perhaps, as they traveled through the wide Silesian landscape, Steiner gazed out the window and asked himself why this course had been held so far to the east. Koberwitz was, after all, some 500 miles from Dornach. On the trip out, he had remarked to one of his companions, Karl Lang: "The further East one goes, the more alive the landscape becomes" (Lang).

Toward midnight, they arrived in Jena. Rudolf Steiner wanted to visit the newly founded curative home Lauenstein there. He was welcomed there the next morning by the coworkers of the young establishment: Dr. Ilse Knauer, Franz Löffler, Werner Pache, Siegfried Pickert and Albrecht Strohschein. He was given a tour of the house and the garden and noticed gladly the wonderful location high above the city. Then he met each of the children cared for there and gave suggestions for their care.

Late that afternoon, he drove with his companions to Weimar, in order to visit once more the city where he had lived from 1890 until 1896. He gave his friends a tour of the city he had left twenty-eight years earlier. The next day, the journey continued by train to Stuttgart, where he met with the Waldorf teachers, and then by car to Dornach. That evening, he gave a long report of the events in Breslau and Koberwitz.

In these days of summer, when the sun reached its zenith, Rudolf Steiner also called the attention of those attending the karma lectures to nature, which showed itself in the full radiance of its foliation. He described how the earth and living nature, as well as the cosmos, were part of human destiny and how they spoke to humans through their formative gestures. Toward the end of the lecture given on June 22, he called out:

> From this point of view, why is the cosmos there? For the gods to have a means to bring the first form of karma to humans. Why are there stars? Why are there clouds? Why the sun and the moon? Why are there animals upon the earth? Why plants? Why stones? Why are there rivers, brooks, and streams? Why are there mountains and cliffs? Why is everything there, with the cosmos surrounding us? That is how the gods bring the first forms of our karma to us, depending upon what we have done. (236)

The practical side of the anthroposophic impulse, to comprehend the spiritual in nature and to care for it, was inaugurated in Koberwitz. In Dornach, Steiner expanded on this by showing that the cosmos was a part of the human being; it was through the cosmos that human karma revealed itself. And the cosmos awaits the day that this connection will be recognized. The words of Paul from the Letter to the Romans come to mind.

> All around us creation waits with great longing that the sons of God shall begin to shine forth in humankind. Creation has become transitory, not through its own doing but because of those who, having themselves become transitory, dragged it down with them, and therefore everything in creation is full of longing for the future. (Romans 8:19-20, Madsen trans.)

On St. John's, June 24, the eurythmists gathered in the carpentry shop for the beginning of the speech eurythmy course mentioned above. The elements of this new art of movement were reexamined and presented in new form. Marie Steiner wrote:

> We joined together for this course as though for a great celebration. People came with questions for Rudolf Steiner; we worked on things and revised them; we spoke of specific aspects, about which differences of opinion had arisen. It all had the character of a spontaneous, fresh improvisation. Drawings were quickly sketched on the blackboard; exercises to illustrate certain things were performed by the young ladies. Everything took place under the sign of dialogue and collaboration, not lecturing. (279)

The cultivation of the new art was very dear to Rudolf Steiner. Untiringly, he gave introductory talks before eurythmy performances and advocated for support for this artistic endeavor in letters to various members. His heart was with it. Humorously, as well as earnestly, he urged the members not to only attend his lectures, but also to come to the eurythmy performances. True Anthroposophy became visible for the audience during these performances.

The day after the beginning of the eurythmy course, a course for curative educators began. There were only twenty participants. Beyond the coworkers from Lauenstein in Jena and from Holle, a small home for children in need of special care connected to the clinic in Arlesheim, only a very few additional qualified individuals had been invited to attend. Within the context of this intimate circle, not only was it possible to develop general perspectives for the work with children in need of special care; children from the *Holle* and those that Steiner had observed in *Lauenstein* were also taken into consideration. The general principles could thus be individualized, and directions for the care of specific children developed. In this manner, Steiner's indications became especially keen and understandable. After the courses for eurythmy, pedagogy, medicine, and agriculture, this was the last course for the renewal of a specific field of work.

The establishment of the curative work was especially important for Steiner, who, from age of twenty-three to twenty-nine, had been a "curative educator" himself, caring for and teaching Otto Specht. He had received the three initiators of this movement, Fran Löffler, Siegfried Pickert and Albrecht Strohschein, during the Christmas conference and had invited them to join the course for medical students. During the Easter conference in Stuttgart, he had encouraged Strohschein to found the home in Jena. Now, with these twelve lectures, he took the time to help curative education get on its feet and, in doing so, fulfilled a thread of his own life that had accompanied him for many years.

CHAPTER 54

THE FINAL INTENSIFICATION: SUMMER 1924

After the seasonal zenith of the year and the first half year of inner reformation since the Christmas conference had passed, Rudolf Steiner turned to the outer organizational structures of the society. A special general meeting of the Goetheanum Association was called for June 29. In his opening address, Steiner pointed out that, in keeping with the impulse of the Christmas conference, there was a need to find a unified configuration to ford all the various activities. "This Christmas conference, my dear friends, was held to bring a fresh wind into the anthroposophic movement. We have to strive in the future to insure that the things do not drift apart, that in the future everything is guided in a unified manner out of the anthroposophic movement" (260a).

It was the need to build anew that drove Steiner to reorganize the society and the various peripheral activities at this time. He wished "to proceed with the new building as quickly as possible." (260a). He even hoped that by Christmas that year, gatherings could take place in the new building. To insure that the planning and building proceeded without any obstacles, the building association was to be combined with the General Anthroposophical Society and thus fall officially under his leadership, although he had been the de facto leader of the association for years.

He envisioned uniting all the practical endeavors of the anthroposophic movement under the umbrella of the General Anthroposophical Society: first "the General Anthroposophical Society in its narrower sense," then the Philosophical-Anthroposophical Publishers, the Goetheanum Association, and the Clinic in Arlesheim. These plans were approved without resistance by the special general meeting, and Rudolf Steiner, with the entire executive council, joined the board of the building association, remarking that he believed one could trust "the new board of the building association to carry out the decisions that were made" (260a).

It soon became apparent that merging the Goetheanum Association with the General Anthroposophical Society (GAS) was, in fact, no easy matter. The assets of the association would have had to be transferred to the GAS, which would have entailed paying rather high fees and taxes. The secretary of the local authorities, who had attended the general meeting as an observer, immediately called attention to this fact and pointed out that, in order to transfer the assets to the GAS, the latter would first have to be entered into the registry.

The uninterrupted series of events that were planned up to the time Steiner took to his sickbed made it impossible to accomplish these plans expediently. It was only in February 1925 that Steiner was able to proceed by coming up with a way of circumventing the formal difficulties. The building association changed its name to "General Anthroposophical Society," and its activities were incorporated into the work of the General Anthroposophical Society. We will return to this later.

Toward the end of June, a large number of anthroposophists had come from afar to attend Dr. Steiner's lectures. He responded to the presence "of so many friends wandering around the ruins of the Goetheanum" by offering a series of lectures. Between then and July 14, when he left Dornach again, he held, in addition to the running course and the lectures for the workers at the Goetheanum, six karma lectures and two lectures for members of the First Class. These lectures were "on an altogether different topic."

This "altogether different topic" was the karma of the Anthroposophical Society. After giving a general introduction of the topic in the first two lectures, in the third lecture he posed the questions: "What preconditions were needed for a soul to find its way to the Anthroposophic Society? What brought someone, for example, to search for his or her life path in eurythmy?"

In the lectures that followed, Rudolf Steiner answered these questions from various points of view. First, he called attention to the development of the individual soul in connection with Christianity, and then he spoke about the souls, which had together experienced—toward the end of the eighteenth century and during the first half of the nineteenth century—the mighty imaginations of a cosmic cultus as they prepared for their next incarnation. These experiences slumbered deep within the souls of those individuals who sought Anthroposophy. Goethe, too, had experienced something of these imaginations and brought them to expression in the fairy tale of the green snake and the beautiful lily. For this reason, the first of Steiner's mystery plays had the same structure as the fairy tale, although not the same content. The shared pre-birth experience of the cosmic imaginations had graced the souls with the impulse that led them to Anthroposophy and gave them the will to work out of Anthroposophy.

As he continued, Rudolf Steiner described two groups of souls that differentiated themselves clearly from one another. Both groups were present in the anthroposophic movement. The difference between the two groups lay in the manner in which each group sought Christ. Whereas one group sought Christ as Jesus upon the earth, in the other group lived a memory of the heathen experience of Christ in the cosmos, as the sun god. Finally, he posed the question of whether one should begin to wonder to which group he or she belonged. His answer was unequivocal. Just as the child comes at some point to understand which nationality he is—Polish, English, German, Dutch, etc.—in the future one must come to recognize to which group of souls one belongs. "And among those things that one should come to understand is that one should absolutely attain the self-knowledge that one belongs to this or that group of souls" (237).

The temptation to avoid having to make this decision by determining that one belonged to a mixture of the types, a transition form as it were, did not appeal to the audience. Steiner explained that these transition souls were people who constantly complained about the situation in the anthroposophic movement, who were picky and narrow-minded. Toward the end of this passage, he said:

> And by all means, we must—even if it comes to be a sort of examination of our consciences, an examination of the character of our consciences—we do have to get to the point where we can deepen the anthroposophic movement to the point that we can ponder such questions, and we can contemplate: In light of our suprasensory natures, how do we belong to this anthroposophic movement? (237)

Such statements make it clear Steiner's intention in giving the karma lectures. Everything was meant to be practical. In all aspects of these lectures, even the presentation of the destinies of significant personalities, he tried to awaken self-knowledge. He was at no time interested merely in increasing the amount one could know about these things, and certainly had no interest in esoteric sensationalism. These lectures were intended to make a deeper form of self-knowledge possible, first by enabling the recognition of one's inclinations and feelings in relation to exemplary personalities. Studying Francis Bacon or Karl Marx can give a person insight into him- or herself. Then, by describing the two types of souls, Steiner encouraged people to gain clarity about their own relationship to Anthroposophy, and, also, to gain an understanding that other ways of relating to Anthroposophy were also possible.

Before World War I, Steiner had given a number of lectures concerning the folk souls. These were intended to nurture "self-knowledge of the nations" and contribute thus to understanding between the different peoples. This was necessary "because the next stage in the destiny of humanity will bring all peoples together in a shared human mission to a degree that was not present earlier" (121). A common mission like this was only possible if each person was able to recognize his own task and one-sidedness and could learn to respect others. In this context, the karma lectures also had a practical role to play.

Rudolf Steiner had intended, after this series of six lectures on the karma of the Anthroposophical Society, which ended with a lecture on the School of Chartres, to leave Dornach on July 16 for the conference on anthroposophic pedagogy in Arnheim. But bad news arrived from Stuttgart. A liquidity crisis had arisen in The Coming Day owing to the economic downturn and the limitation on credit that had followed the German currency reform in November 1923. Although Steiner was no longer officially involved in the stock company, he rushed to Stuttgart on July 14 to help save whatever could be saved. He was no doubt most concerned with the spiritually productive endeavors, especially the Waldorf School, which was part of The Coming Day. In an initial meeting with the German stockholders on the morning of July 15, he found himself forced to request that the stockholders forfeit 35,000 of the 109,000 total shares. These shares corresponded to the value of the endeavors within the stock company that were doing spiritual work.

July 15 was a bitter day in Rudolf Steiner's life. He spoke about it to the members, calling to mind the original intention of these endeavors. "We perhaps buried the idea that was one of our most holy intentions—to create commercial endeavors that would serve the spiritual life" (260a).

They finally reached a solution. "The Waldorf School is provided the necessary resources. The Clinical Therapeutic Institute in Stuttgart is

The Final Intensification: Summer 1924

independent, an autonomous institution; Gmünd [the pharmaceutical company that would become Weleda] will remain with The Coming Day. The scientific research institute will have to be dissolved" (260a).

The Dornach publishing company acquired the part of the inventory that was the stock company's publishing business, taking all the books by Rudolf Steiner and a few from other authors. This solution was made possible by the willingness of the members of the society, many of whom had lost a great deal of their wealth in the post-war economic collapse, to forfeit their investments. It was not something they were able to do easily. The negotiations in Stuttgart continued through July 16. Rudolf Steiner was only able to make it to Arnheim late on July 17. Zeylmans related that when Steiner realized that the conference was to take place in a "holiday resort," he was somewhat deflated (comp. also 217a). Zeylmans and his friends, on the other hand, were shocked by how exhausted and ill Steiner appeared to be.

> During this conference, it was not possible to overlook how ill he was. It was disheartening to see just how exhausted he seemed when others were lecturing—Dr. Schubert, Dr. von Baravalle, van Bemmelen, Stibbe and myself—about education; I was also shocked to see how frail he appeared, how much weight he had lost. But in spite of this, nothing escaped his attention, and when he took his place at the podium, he was, as always, full of life, enthusiastic, effervescent—it was hard to believe that this was the same person. It was deeply moving to hear him speak in both the pedagogical lectures and in his talk for the young people about Schiller and Schiller's death; about the enthusiasm that devoured him from within; and about Schiller's heart, the physical substance of which had practically disappeared by the time of his death. One has to imagine that he saw before him that of which he spoke: the fire, which devoured the body. (*We Experienced Rudolf Steiner*).

The pedagogical lectures that he gave during this conference were spoken of above. In three lectures, he also spoke about anthroposophic therapy. If one reads the first of these lectures, one can recognize how Steiner, in spite of his fatigue, took his cue from the quality of consciousness alive in his audience and with incredible concentration and concise formulations described the anthroposophic path in order that the audience could understand how the anthroposophic approach in medicine proved its validity as a scientific, logical approach to healing.

As she had in Breslau, Marie Steiner gave courses in speech formation, so that three practical fields of anthroposophic endeavors were present in Arnheim: speech, education, and medicine. In his report of the conference, Steiner characterized the effect of Marie Steiner's work incisively.

> The healthy interaction of body, soul and spirit comes to expression through the artistic formation of speech. The body expresses whether it is able to incorporate the spirit in the proper manner; the soul reveals whether the spirit is alive in it; and the spirit is directly present in the way it affects the physical. Those who took part in the course on speech formation were able to *experience* directly the revelation of Anthroposophy in the activity of the human being. (260a)

The most moving lectures given in Arnheim were the karma lectures. After introducing the topic of the karma of the Anthroposophical Society in almost epic breadth in Dornach, in the three Arnheim lectures, he quickly recapped what was said in Dornach then took it a step further. In Arnheim, Michael was named for the first time as the teacher and impulse giver for the anthroposophic movement. The anthroposophic movement was spoken of as the Michael stream. Here he spoke also for the first time of the mission of this stream to nurture in a Michaelic sense the cosmic intelligence, which had become earthly, and to protect it from the attacks of ahrimanic forces. In Arnheim, he described the sequential leadership of the seven archangels, and he spoke for the first time of the Michaelic prophesy of the coming together of the aristotelean and platonic spiritual streams at the end of the twentieth century.

This Michaelic motif had been hinted at earlier, at a decisive moment in the movement. Following the separation from the Theosophical Society, Steiner had spoken in London on May 2, 1913, about Michael's mission. He repeated this description again on May 18 and 20 in Stuttgart, just after the decision had been made to build the Goetheanum in Dornach rather than Munich. For those who were able to listen deeply, it was clear that the spiritual insights of Anthroposophy were a gift of Michael (152). But in Arnheim, as in the months that followed, this became the central theme not only of Rudolf Steiner's lectures but also of his *Letters to the Members*.

The friends who were present in Arnheim experienced how he formed himself with the greatest energy to be the voice of this message, and how he summoned the strength to speak of the apocalyptic nature of the twentieth century. By revealing this esoteric understanding of Michael, he hoped to vanquish the adversarial forces, which wished to insure that the origins and objectives of the anthroposophic movement not become generally known. He battled these forces with the courage and the fire of genuine enthusiasm. In his talk for the young anthroposophists gathered in Arnheim, he spoke about what he was doing, although without pointing to himself in doing so.

> Grow inwardly to become one with the flames that are kindled today, so that the impulse of Michael may be realized! It can never become reality without the flames. But to be fired through and through, to live and work with this fire, one must oneself become a flame. Only the flames are not devoured by flames. If we can feel ourselves becoming flames that can't be burned by the fire, then we can in complete peace leave the physical heart behind as an empty sack, for we will have the etheric heart that understands that humanity has entered a new time: the life of the spirit. (217a)

In his report for the newsletter, Rudolf Steiner summarized the content and intention of the Arnheim lectures in brief.

> In the branch lectures, the way in which a recognition of the presence of the suprasensory in the evolution of humanity to an understanding of the tasks facing the anthroposophic movement was described. What we could call the "Michaelic" guidance of humanity in a suprasensory process in ancient times from the seventh century BCE up to the time of Alexander the Great and then again in the present was presented. Through such a presentation must be kindled the enthusiasm, which should permeate the life of the Anthroposophical Society. (260a)

What was presented in Arnheim cast a new light on the impulse of the Christmas conference. The members of the Anthroposophical Society became aware that the Christmas conference and what had led up to it had its origins in a Michaelic impulse. That this had to and could be voiced at this point was due to the spiritual battles that Rudolf Steiner waged at this time of life. These battles also forced him on his return trip from Arnheim and The Hague and again when he returned from England to immerse himself in the details of the problems faced by The Coming Day. The adversarial forces should be given no chance to slip in. That it was possible to speak about the esoteric nature of Michael was due to the fact that the Christmas conference impulse had, to a certain degree, become real.

In the Arnheim lectures, one can recognize how deeply Rudolf Steiner was connected with the spiritual stream of which he spoke. Since his days as a student outside Vienna, and then in Vienna itself, he had time and again encountered individuals through whom these spiritual movements—the School of Chartres, for instance—lived on in the present. Steiner often recalled the Cistercian priest and professor, Wilhelm Neumann, whom he had met in Marie Eugenie delle Grazie's circle. As he mentioned in Arnheim, following Steiner's 1888 lecture on Goethe as the father of a new aesthetic, Neumann had remarked "that it could not be understood other than to recognize that this man had a complete understanding in this moment for people living today and their connection to earlier lives on earth. Moreover, what he had to say about the relationship between two incarnations was correct—not at all wrong. However, he understood nothing at all but only said it" (240).

A few weeks later, in Torquay, Steiner recalled that, also during his time in Vienna, he had experienced, with spiritual intensity, the events in the world bordering the physical world, which was separated from it only by a thin veil (240). Thus, what one encounters in the karma lectures again and again is a strong autobiographical thread. Steiner was not teaching, he was narrating what he had experienced and encountered.

When Rudolf Steiner picked up the unbroken thread of karma lectures again in Dornach on July 28, he spoke again of the suprasensory events, which had posed the Anthroposophical Society its tasks, deepening and broadening his presentations and placing this theme ever more strongly in the center of his work. This sequence of explorations came to an interim conclusion in the beginning of August. On the trip from Dornach to Torquay, Steiner concentrated the essential thoughts developed in the lectures into the essay "In the Beginning of the Michael-Age" for the Newsletter. Anthroposophists throughout the world were introduced in this way to the content of the Dornach lectures.

The central theme of this essay is the karma of intelligence. Until the ninth century, people did not feel that they brought forth their thoughts themselves; the thoughts appeared as insights from a spiritual world, which were to be experienced in everything around them. At the height of the Middle Ages, however, the feeling began to spread that "I form the thoughts." Are thoughts revelations of the world or simply instruments through which the human being takes hold of the world? In earlier times there was a direct, unmediated experience in the belief that spiritual beings inspire the thoughts. "In ancient teaching, the being from whom the thoughts streamed into the things was named Michael. The name can remain. Then one can say: once, human beings received thoughts from Michael. Michael administered cosmic intelligence" (26).

In these sentences, Rudolf Steiner first formed the *idea* of Michael. It was not the traditional picture of Michael as dragon slayer that was brought to the attention of the members of the Anthroposophical Society. They were made aware of a spiritual being from whom "thoughts flow into the things." To find this being one must discover that there is a way of thinking that is in harmony with both the spiritual and the physical world—for instance, the form of thinking that Goethe worked to develop in his work with nature through which thinking becomes an *organ of perception* for what lives in nature.

In modern times, as humanity moved toward individual freedom, the thoughts "fell away" from Michael and entered the realm of subjectivity. The view that thoughts are exclusively subjective constructions formed to serve practical objectives such as the exploitation of nature or communication gained the upper hand. Those people, however, who were connected with Michael's guidance in earlier lives, can find one another again in the present in the Anthroposophical Society. They wish to remain loyal to Michael. This can only become a living reality when one learns to behold the thoughts in the being of the world, when one frees the thought from the abstraction of the subjective mental images in one's own head. When thoughts can be experienced throughout the entire human being, one can raise oneself to the realm of cosmic thought.

> [One can] turn one's attention to the spirit; there Michael comes to meet one and he reveals himself to have always been a part of the weaving of thought. He frees thought from the limits of the head; he opens the path to the heart; he sparks enthusiasm from within the soul so that one can live in soul devotion to everything that can be experienced in the light of thought. The time of Michael has come. Hearts begin to have thoughts; enthusiasm streams no longer from the dark reaches of mystical experience, but from thought-borne clarity of soul. To understand this is to take Michael into one's soul. Thoughts, which today strive to grasp the spirit, must flow forth from those hearts that beat for Michael, the fiery king of thought in the cosmos. (26)

The lectures Steiner gave in Dornach between July 28 and August 8 were a call to his listeners to fully embody a form of thinking that could connect them to the living beingness of the spiritual world. Such a way of thinking cannot remain mere reflection, as if shut up in "a small room." It takes hold of the depths of soul that participate in the cosmic pulse of life and leads to action.

Among the important matters that he had to address in Dornach at the time were the preparations for the rebuilding of the Goetheanum. On July 29, he drove to Solothurn to meet with the building authorities about the building permit. On August 4, representatives of Solothurn and Baselland came to Dornach to meet with the local authorities from Dornach and Arlesheim. They met in the Glashaus, one of the buildings from the original ensemble. Rudolf Steiner presented the model and explained the planned project. He was glad that the design had been welcomed by the local council and the citizens of Dornach. The Dornach council petitioned the cantonal authorities to grant a building permit.

During this time, Steiner also gave instructions to expand the carpentry shop to accommodate the visitors expected for the fall conferences. Finally, in collaboration with the architects Aisenpreis and Moser, he finalized the construction drawings for Ita Wegman's house and these were submitted to the building department. It had been Steiner's personal wish that Wegman, who had up till then slept in her office, would have a place where she could find refuge from the daily business of the clinic. He designed a simple, portable wooden house for her. When he returned from England, the house was finished and stood in the clinic's garden.

After finishing these tasks, Rudolf Steiner left Dornach on the evening of August 9, bound for England by way of Paris and Boulogne. It was to be his last major trip abroad. Driving through the night with Marie Steiner, Ita Wegman, Elisabeth Vreede and Guenther Wachsmuth, he arrived in Torquay at one o'clock in the morning on August 11. At the time, Torquay was a small, but quite famous bathing destination on the south coast of England in Devonshire. Neither Torquay, nor the conference venue, the local town hall, were comparable to the elemental world of Penmaenmawr, but just ten miles to the west rose the high heather-covered stretches of Dartmoor, rich with traces of megalithic culture.

In light of concerns voiced by the two primary organizers of this Second International Summer School, Miss Merry and Mr. Dunlop, about the

The Final Intensification: Summer 1924

growing fascination in England for spiritism, Rudolf Steiner had chosen to speak of "True and False Paths of Spiritual Investigation." The lectures took place daily from August 11 through August 27 at 10:30 in the morning. There was no lecture scheduled for Sunday, August 17. In addition, Steiner gave a course of seven lectures for the teachers of the school that was to be formed outside of London, three lectures for members, and two class lessons. George Adams-Kaufmann translated all of the lectures.

Led by Marie Steiner, there were five eurythmy performances. These were not attended by all the conference's participants, and the eurythmists had difficulty contending with the tastelessness of the atmosphere in the town hall. The performances did, however, excite those who attended them. Hermann von Baravalle, Elisabeth Vreede and Guenther Wachsmuth lectured in English. Once more, Anthroposophy, pedagogy and art came to collaborative expression.

In the main morning course of lectures, Rudolf Steiner developed the theme of the transformation of consciousness through the centuries, the development of higher forms of consciousness and various perversions in the development of consciousness. It is fascinating to observe how he responded to the mood of his audience and addressed these questions very concretely in relation to crystals and metals to the stages of human life, using examples of the fate of individual souls after death, or in relation to his shared research with Ita Wegman. After he had led his audience in ten lectures through the heights and breadth of spiritual scientific research, in the last lecture he returned to ordinary human consciousness, finally speaking quite explicitly of the path a contemporary anthroposophist could tread.

> What is then necessary? That one develops the outlook: We need to investigate what of the spiritual world must be investigated by those individuals who in their present incarnation can draw on strengths from earlier incarnations that help them bring forth what is necessary to do such research; the results of the research of this circle of people needs to be taken up by an ever-growing number of people in the form of ideas, be understood in the form of ideas; when the results of spiritual research are taken up by a healthy understanding, the groundwork is established for the conscious experience of the spiritual world. As I have often said, the healthiest way to enter the spiritual world is to begin by working with what has been brought to expression from out of the spiritual world. (243)

After warning about hurried attempts to gain access to the spiritual world by means of paths lacking illumination or the use of mediums, over whom one has even less control, and the urge to research everything immediately, he emphasized again the necessity of first gaining an understanding of the spiritual world by studying spiritual scientific ideas.

> If one believes that one is unable to gain such an understanding before being able oneself to enter the spiritual world, that person is in error. Another one of the false paths one can tread today is to say, "Why should the spiritual world be of any concern to me, if I cannot observe it myself." This is one of the largest, most dangerous, most apparent errors possible. A movement like the Anthroposophical Society must keep this error clearly in sight. (243)

This is one of his last, most incisive statements concerning the question: "How does one attain knowledge of the higher worlds?" He voices here, at the end of a series of lectures concerning true and false paths to the spirit, a legacy that has been present as a constant thread throughout his work. He articulated it once in December 1922.

> Today, we must consciously attain spiritual knowledge; note: spiritual knowledge, not clairvoyance! I have always stressed that clairvoyance can be achieved, but that is not what is important. What is important is to understand what comes to expression through clairvoyant research in ordinary healthy human consciousness, because it can be understood there. (219)

When speaking about the karma lectures, he pointed out that he wanted to show how individuals, as they passed from incarnation to incarnation, carried what they had attained spiritually in these lives from epoch to epoch. One can then understand that various forms of spirituality can be present at any given time. He also spoke to his audience in Torquay about his most immediate experiences in the spiritual world of the present. For months, it had been possible for him to speak openly and without reservation about karmic connections and the esoteric nature of Michael.

> This is one of the concrete things of which I have earlier spoken abstractly.... In fact, through everything that it was possible to give to the Anthroposophical Society since the Christmas foundation meeting, through the way I was allowed to work esoterically since that time—they are not new things, as one cannot discover something

> esoteric one day and speak about it immediately the next day, but they are old things experienced in the manner I presented to you—what has changed is that the demons that did not allow things to be talked about before must now remain silent. (240)

The stream of spiritual revelation continued and became increasingly intense both in Torquay and then in London. In increasingly comprehensive pictures, he uncovered the karmic dimensions of history.

Although the symptoms of Steiner's failing health were shockingly apparent to observers in Torquay, he took advantage of not having to lecture on Sunday to travel to Tintagel. It rained early that morning. Everything was veiled in fog. When they left at 8:00 a.m., Steiner predicted the rain would soon stop. The small group set off in three cars. In addition to the members of the Dornach council, there was Mr. Dunlop, Mrs. Merry, Mieta Waller-Pyle and her husband, among others. By the time they had reached Tintagel at noon, the sun had driven off all traces of the fog. They went on foot the last stage of the journey down the rocky cliffs of the coast, then up the cliffs of Tintagel. After returning to Dornach, Steiner spoke of his impressions that day.

> From the ruined remains of the castle—which, although it has completely collapsed, still made an enormous impression—one looks out on to the ocean. The ruin stands at the top of the cliffs with ocean on both sides. One can gaze out on the water in a place where the weather changes almost hourly and behold the shimmering sunshine reflected in the water; soon after, a storm blows up. If one views what is still happening there today with esoteric vision, it makes a fantastic impression. One experiences living, weaving elementary beings born of the light, the air—the effects of waves as they break against each other.

In these surroundings, he beheld the source of inspiration for the original Arthurian impulse that radiated out from Tintagel with a cultivating influence on Western Europe (240). He sent greetings to Albert Steffen, who remained behind in Dornach, faithfully holding down the fort.

> We come from the eloquent castle ruins. Once the ancient conquerors of the dragon sat here, strengthening the leaders might through the stars, the twelve.
> The castles lie in ruins. The astral morality is silenced; but spirit strength pulses around the crag and the power of soul imaginations storms from the ocean. The wrestlings of light and air change

magically, making themselves known to the soul still powerfully after three thousand years; and memory pictures from the elements."

After Torquay, there followed seven days in London. Steiner spoke to the members, to teachers, and to doctors and gave two class lessons. On August 26, a eurythmy performance took place at the Royal Academy of Dramatic Art. The anthroposophic impulse in various fields was thus also present in London. On August 31, Rudolf Steiner returned to Dornach, only to leave that night to travel to Stuttgart where he had to continue the negotiations concerning the future of The Coming Day, meet with Waldorf School faculty and with members of the previous year's twelfth grade. Upon his return to Dornach, the first day of work was dedicated to matters concerning the building project. The rest of the debris from the first Goetheanum had almost been cleared away and the building authorities had issued a new building permit. Decisions had to be made. The project was so large that these decisions had to be made carefully. According to Edwin Froböse, together with Ita Wegman, he did, however, dedicate a part of that afternoon to accept new members into the First Class of the School of Spiritual Science. A total of 261 members were accepted into the class in September 1924. When Rudolf Steiner began lecturing again in Dornach on September 5, there were over a thousand people present. There were actors and speech artists, the priest of the Christian Community, anthroposophic doctors, and a multitude of members who had come to Dornach for the karma lectures and the class lessons. Among them were many younger anthroposophists, who had found accommodation in makeshift quarters with straw pallets for beds, as well as some of Rudolf Steiner's long-time students. One of the oldest members present was Günther Wagner, who had been active in 1902 when the German section of the Theosophical Society was formed. Individuals from almost all of the different anthroposophic fields streamed together to be part of this conference. Missing were the teachers from the Waldorf School, as school was in session. In the newsletter dated August 17, courses had been announced for the theologians (six lectures from September 4 to 9), theologians and doctors (8 lectures from September 8 to 15), and a course in speech formation and the dramatic arts (September 2–15), in addition to the ongoing lectures for the members and the class lessons.

Steiner's lectures were to reach an unexpected climax in these three weeks. It was as though he wanted to give the members, the actors and

The Final Intensification: Summer 1924

speech artists, and the doctors and priests the greatest possible spiritual strength for their work. All the courses were extended—the course on pastoral medicine by three lectures, the course on drama by eight lectures, and the course on the apocalypse, given for the priests, by twelve lectures. The conference, which was originally planned to end on September 15, continued until September 23. In 1944, Marie Steiner looked back on these weeks.

> It was in September, twenty years ago that Rudolf Steiner, as though in a final glorious illumination of his spirit, drew on the last forces of his body, which had been all but devoured from the flames of suprasensory experience, and allowed an unimaginable wealth of spiritual gifts to flow through it to us. It was as though everything that he had done during his four decades of work to awaken humanity flowed together in a concentrated form. It was at once the ripe fruits of his work and a powerfully concentrated force for the future, which will be able to make the coming epochs spiritually fruitful. (Marie Steiner, *Collected Writings*, vol. 2)

Looking back, it is fully justified to recognize in these September courses Rudolf Steiner's legacy, which he gave his friends for their further paths. It would, however, be a mistake to think that he had spoken during these weeks with a sense that he was wrapping up his work. At this time he was full of plans for all the things that were still to be brought into being. A conference in Berlin and a course for the Waldorf School teachers were planned for October; the establishment of the independent School of Spiritual Science was to be continued; and the plans for rebuilding the Goetheanum constantly demanded his attention. He had also spoken of the possibility of a second youth course and of a course for nurses.

During the September conferences, he was focused on the spiritual revelations, the tasks, and on the people to whom he gave what he was able to give. There is no indication that he made any allowances for his health; one finds no cautious planning, no questioning the future. Like the beginning of the threefold campaign or the attempt to create commercial endeavors, he did not strategize, analyzing the possibility of failure. He didn't ask whether it would succeed; he simply did what the situation asked of him, fully and without question. He certainly did not have a cessation of his work in mind. That is apparent in the announcement, drafted on September 22 and printed in the newsletter dated September 24, 1924. "A series of lectures for the members is planned for Berlin from October 25 to 31.

Dr. Steiner will also give a number of talks for younger people, which will also be open to non-members." And the last lecture he gave for the workers at the Goetheanum ended with the words: "I have made a beginning of answering your questions. We want to continue next Saturday at 9:00 a.m., and I will answer more of your questions" (354).

The first course for actors and speech artists, which began on September 5, Rudolf Steiner gave in collaboration with Marie Steiner. Marie Steiner had already begun with the work on September 2. In addition to the actual participants in the course—the actors, speech artists and a few teachers—who sat in the front rows, some 600 people gathered for the lectures. Two professional actors, Gottfried Haass-Berkow and Georg Kugelmann, had brought their ensembles to the course. Among the other participants were Max Gumbel-Seiling, Otto Wiemer and Edwin Froböse. Marie Steiner had led them through the introductory speech formation exercises with a playful strictness and had spoken to them about recitation and declamation, about meter and forms of poetry. Ernst Weissert recalled, "One learned to admire and respect her sparkling spirit, her majestic manner, and her humor" (Reminiscences of Rudolf Steiner). In silence, the course participants awaited Rudolf Steiner's arrival on September 5. Friedrich Hiebel recalled:

> Punctually at twelve o'clock, he entered from backstage on the west side of the building, passed by us with slow, clearly flagging steps and stepped up on to the podium, supporting himself with one arm on the lectern.
>
> No one could overlook the fact that each day his steps were heavier as he passed by us; he could barely lift the soles of his shoes from the floor. Every step could be heard clearly, since even before he appeared absolute silence fell upon the hall.
>
> But each time he began to speak, after a few faltering sentences, his face grew radiant and alive. His presentations became livelier, his voice louder, his lecture more captivating. After an hour, he left the hall fully refreshed, as though borne along with wings, with an almost youthful lightness in his stride. (Hiebel)

What Hiebel described took place daily time and again in all of his lectures. Rudolf Steiner regenerated and rejuvenated himself in speaking. He took thus particular pleasure in the course on speech formation. He drew on a store of exercises—practiced for decades—and studies, and

The Final intensification: Summer 1924

he was easily able to illustrate his thoughts with many examples. He led the participants through aspects of speech formation, stage direction, to the art of acting. He presented themes of the course, the intent of which was "to progress from the tasteless naturalism to a new sense of style," in three articles in the newsletter. The second article ended with the following words:

> Marie Steiner has worked for many years to develop the art of recitation and declamation in such a manner that the artistic quality in speech formation can be experienced directly through her. She has made it possible for the anthroposophic work to flourish in this direction. She had the idea for this course and contributed her skills of recitation to it. Thanks to her initiative, a large number of stage artists found their way to the Goetheanum who, under her guidance, wished to learn what Anthroposophy has to give them. (260a)

Under these auspices, Marie Steiner went on to form a stage group at the Goetheanum comprised of the participants in the course who were not attached to an ensemble. The work was inaugurated on the day of St. Michael 1924. She named the group "Thespiskarren," for she said Thespis was the first to bring drama from the mysteries into the world, "and we wish to try to bring it back into the mysteries" (Froböse).

The course on the apocalypse for the priests of the Christian Community began on the afternoon of September 5. Reporting on this in the newsletter and in other contexts, Rudolf Steiner expressed his deep satisfaction with the work these priests had done in the two years since the Christian Community had been founded. "Since then, the community of priests for religious renewal has proceeded with great energy. Their activities have brought blessing and solace" (260a).

The daily religious exercises, the celebration of the Act of Consecration, and the struggle to proclaim Christianity had become a path on inner transformation and development. The wish had arisen among them to better understand the Apocalypse. Steiner had spoken about the Apocalypse in 1908 in Nuremberg in a course titled "Theosophy in Light of the Apocalypse." This was less an explanation of the Apocalypse than an introduction to theosophy. Steiner reported on the course with the priests:

> My spiritual path had made it possible for me to follow the footsteps of the voice of the Apocalypse. I felt that I could present this *book for priests* to the *priests* in a spiritually authentic manner. The Act of

Consecration stands at the center of the priests' work; what from the spiritual world can enter the world of humans by way of the ritual radiates out from it. The Apocalypse can rest in the center of the priest's soul; from it can stream into the priest's thinking and feeling what the sacrificial human soul can receive with grace from the spiritual world. This is what I thought of when preparing for this course when the priests came to me with their request. And it is in this sense that I have given it. (260a)

Because the Apocalypse also touches on future evolution and the manifestations of evil, Rudolf Steiner was not inclined to limit his lectures to a mere interpretation of the text. Present, past and future had to be brought into the light of the *secret revelation*. The deeply serious questions concerning the manifestations of evil had to be addressed. History and the future had to be spiritually examined. There is no doubt that Steiner's own research had taken him into this realm; indications of this are spread throughout his lectures. In the course with the priests he spoke very concretely—for instance, of the beast that would arise from the depths in 1933, and other things that pertained to the near future (346).

It must have been infinitely important to Rudolf Steiner to have the opportunity to give the priests a sense of their deepest mission and to sharpen their gaze for the decisions looming in the future. The almost inhuman tasks of the coming decades stood before him. In light of this approaching crisis, he wished to give as much as he could. Emil Bock recalled:

We coworkers of the Christian Community were in an especially good position to experience the tension that accompanied this stepping forward day-to-day. And not only because we were allowed to take part in all the various courses. We had come with the notion that Dr. Steiner, in addition to the course we received together with the doctors, would only have a little time to speak to us in concentrated form about the Apocalypse. Our course of the Apocalypse began on the first day and continued day after day even after the course on pastoral-medicine had ended. After two weeks of being so richly showered with gifts, I had the unpleasant task of asking Rudolf Steiner how much longer the course would continue. We all had congregations at the time that awaited the Sunday services. We had already had to inform them by telegraph that our returns would be delayed. His answer was: "Be patient for a couple of more days, then we will be able to see how long we will continue. (*We Experienced Rudolf Steiner*)

On October 2, after he had been confined to his sickbed, Steiner wrote to Marie Steiner about this course.

> The situation is that, on the one hand, the earnestness with which the priests work is truly gratifying; on the other hand, the work is so demanding because they need so much and it is so difficult to achieve their ideals. It is true that by the end of the course on the Apocalypse my forces were in a certain way completely exhausted—it took immense strength to reach the spiritual heights—and I didn't have the stream of individuals in need that the priests have. The lectures on speech formation did not tip the balance. (262)

The third course that took place during this time was the course on pastoral medicine. This was also sparked by a question posed by the priests, who had encountered a growing number of people in their ministry who had had extraordinary experiences. The question arose for the priests: How are we to understand our task in relation to these individuals? Where do the boundaries lie? When does it become a question for a doctor, not a priest? For this reason, the course took place under the auspices of the Medical Section. Roughly 120 people participated, most of them priests or doctors. Rudolf Steiner began by differentiating sharply between the task of the priest and that of the doctor. He warned of trying to mix the two, even though the sacraments were, in the hand of a priest, a form of healing, and the therapeutic efforts of a doctor could have a quality of the divine. Using examples, he described unusual or pathological configurations of the various members of the total human organism and how they come to expression in inner experiences. He indicated how one must learn to discern questions of freedom and responsibility in this context, how karma plays a role, and described where the tasks of the priests and of the doctors lay and how they could work together.

After the actual course had come to an end, he asked the doctors to stay. After the priests had left the room, he spoke again to the doctors. He first summarized what he had presented in the course in an imagination, which could symbolize the collaboration between the doctors and the priests: "The sacrificial chalice for the priests; the staff of Mercury for the doctors." And he added, "The esoteric doctors must learn once again to feel that he has the staff of Mercury" (318).

He then addressed the question of building community, pointing out that the priests already stood before the world as a community. It was more difficult for the doctors. "However, this community is also possible. This community must be practiced in the hearts of those who genuinely wish to connect themselves to the therapeutic practices originating at the Goetheanum. This community must find a much more inner band than that of the priests" (318).

He challenged the doctors, who were completely dependent upon themselves in their work, to find a way to unite, and out of a consciousness of this connection to join forces with sources of activity that he and Dr. Wegman were nurturing at the Goetheanum. "In order to take at least the first step, Dr. Wegman and I have decided initially to give a first esoteric impulse by creating an esoteric core that can naturally be expanded, but initially should be comprised of a number of practicing doctors who have taken the vows that are necessary for esoteric therapeutic work. The core group is comprised of Dr. Walter, Dr. Bockholt, Dr. Zeylmans, Dr. Glas, Dr. Knauer, and Dr. Kolisko" (318).

Thus, no doubt to the surprise of the other doctors within the context of the Medical section, a circle of individuals was formed who had taken the initiative to connect themselves to the work of the section. Had this differentiated process of building communities with specific foci continued, such inner core groups would have been formed in the various sections, each in its own manner.

Those who attended the many lectures, who stood in the stream of the many never-before-voiced indications, insights, and revelations, were overpowered. Kurt Magerstädt, a doctor who had sharply—perhaps even critically—observed Rudolf Steiner through the winter, and who had observed at Easter how his strength was failing, recalled his experiences during the September courses.

> And when we returned to Dornach in September, the month he gave over seventy lectures, and I was able to attend both the pastoral medicine course and the course on the dramatic arts, I had special opportunity to observe him. The question that arose was: How were *we* to bear everything that was offered there? The spirit flowed in unimaginable abundance. Every topic that he addressed appeared as fresh as the morning dew. Every aspect was completely new; there was no repetition, not in the language nor in his thought process. We were blessed with an ever over-flowing spring. We drank of it, never thinking that this would be the last time we were to experience our teacher in his earthly body. (*We Experienced Rudolf Steiner*)

The Final intensification: Summer 1924

The infinite might of Rudolf Steiner's presentations that can be sensed in the published lectures makes it difficult to imagine that between lectures and in addition to the courses, Rudolf Steiner was asked constantly for private conversations. There were endless meetings and people needing his counsel. Every day lines of people waited in front of Steiner's studio to ask him questions. He listened to each of them and invited innumerable people for private conversations. Whoever looks back on this, knowing what happened afterward, has to ask: Why didn't those friends who were aware of Steiner's weakening health form a protective shield around him, convincing the members to look elsewhere for solutions to their questions and problems? A possible answer can be found in a report Dr. Zeylmans wrote of these weeks. He described the state of soul consciousness in which many visitors found themselves at the time.

> In September 1924, all of us who had traveled to Dornach for new courses had the feeling that we were living well beyond the boundaries of our ordinary consciousness; we had been lifted up into another realm. We all appeared to be different; we saw and heard things that existed far beyond our normal limitations. When we met one another, we had to ask: Is that he? It was unbelievable and indescribable. One lived in a spiritual world of which one naturally had no command. There were moments during the last lectures of the pastoral medicine course when Rudolf Steiner radiated pure love and spirit so strongly that it was difficult to listen to what he was saying. It was no doubt an audience to whom he could give of himself freely. (*We Experienced Rudolf Steiner*)

Almost every evening of these sun-warmed late summer days, Rudolf Steiner spoke either to the members of the society or to the members of the First Class. They gathered in the large hall of the carpentry shop. In the first lecture, he spoke once more of the impulse of the Christmas conference, saying that from thereon "the spiritual impulses pertain also to the Anthroposophical Society" (238). Once again, as he had at Christmas, he stressed that in the future everything must be based on genuine human connections and that "Anthroposophy was at work in all the outer aspects. That needs acknowledgement of the real forces that must unite the individuals who come together in the society. These forces could not be forces created by any form of program or dogma that could be written up abstractly. In an esoteric sense the only thing upon which the Anthroposophical

Society can rest are the genuine human relationships present within it." Then he summarized this thought with the words: "The esoteric can only be taken up by what is genuinely alive" (238).

He attempted to awaken understanding for the difficulties posed by trying to create a new culture inspired by the impulse of the Christmas conference. People had grown used to other ways of interacting. He did not approach this challenge by speaking incessantly about the new culture that would hopefully permeate the society. What was necessary in this vein stood in his "Letters to the Members!" He preferred to communicate the new impulse through the content of his lectures. He hoped his audience would come to insights by listening to the karma lectures that could be realized in their own lives. Hence, he said at the beginning of these lectures: "Our friends will have the opportunity in the course of these lectures or elsewhere to learn to know what it means to actively work through on the earth what would today be revealed in the spiritual world. One should recognize the difficulties connected with this when an earthly administration is added to this communion with the spiritual world" (238).

The inner thread of these last ten karma lectures is to be found primarily in the *practical indications* that Rudolf Steiner gave. This is almost palpable, for instance, in the last lecture, given on September 23. The theme of the lecture is the difficulties of bringing spirituality into the intellectualism of the present time. Taking Karl Julius Schröer as an example, within whom lived a lofty, all-embracing spirituality attained in past lives, he presented these difficulties at length.

> Try to understand what I mean. Let us assume that there was a personality living in the second half of the nineteenth century who had a strong spirituality from his past lives. He would have grown into the contemporary forms of education, which were intellectual through and through. The spirituality that lives within this person would be so strong that it would come to expression regardless. But the intellectualism makes this impossible. This person was educated intellectually, experienced intellectualism in his society, in his vocation, everywhere; to the point that he could not bring to expression what lives within his soul. This would be a person about whom one could say, "Anthroposophy would be perfect for him." (238)

Rudolf Steiner gave similar descriptions of Gideon Spicker, Otto Weininger and others. His listeners were able to recognize as though in the mirror of the soul the problems they also had while listening to these detailed narrations. Naturally, most of those present had to struggle with the question of how to bring to expression what lived more or less hidden in the depths of their souls within the context of contemporary intellectual thought.

There was a second aspect. He spoke in these lectures about how specific individuals like Aristotle, Alexander, Bacon, Comenius and others were the bearers of certain spiritual impulses and intentional directions. He spoke of the struggles that had taken place in the suprasensory, the effects of Bacon's work, and he called attention to the souls that wished to cultivate intelligence in a Michaelic sense. These presentations were not meant to increase his listeners' knowledge of history but to cast light on the true nature of the present and the near future. Instead of a flat, one-dimensional understanding of the present, he hoped to bring a view of the relationships that would allow people to grasp the tendencies of the time from the point of view of reincarnation and to understand the role of Anthroposophy.

This way of understanding contemporary events was oriented less on the outer manifestations and more on the impulses that lived within the individuals involved. It was always annoying for Steiner when members would come to him to tell him that from this person or that person almost the same had been said as what Steiner was saying. The outer appearance of what was said little interested him. He followed the paths taken by contemporary scholars, examining the deeper intentions that arose from their ways of thinking. He had made the effort to trace the symptoms of the time in thinkers like Ernst Mach, Max Planck, Wilhelm Dilthey, Max Scheler, Franz Brentano and others to understand the actual spiritual basis of their work. He hoped, by describing karmic relationships, to make a similar understanding of the present possible.

> Anthroposophy has grown out of the spiritual life of the present. Although there are few similarities between the content of Anthroposophy and the spiritual life of the present, Anthroposophy has grown karmically in many ways out of this spiritual life. And one must take certain things into account that at first sight do not appear to belong to what is directly connected with Anthroposophy, but one must recognize these things in order to have a comprehensive sense of what aspects of the streams I have described have over the course of time played a role in the development of Anthroposophy. I did mention that one can only gain a true understanding for what takes place on the physical plane when one gains insight into what

lies behind these events, into what has been streaming from the spiritual world into these events taking place on the physical plane. And we must...once again have the courage to bring to life in the present the feeling from the ancient mysteries, which didn't merely connect physical events abstractly to a pantheistic, theistic religion or some form of spirituality, but that can follow the individual events, the quality of human experience in these events, concretely back to their spiritual sources and the spiritual beings. (238)

He spoke also of a third aspect. He spoke of his time in Weimar, saying that while he outwardly lived a very social life surrounded by many people, he had to pull himself out of that life quite energetically in order to seek the spiritual basis for future development. In this phase of his life, when he "had to experience quite strongly" the world that bordered directly on the physical world, he sought spiritual orientation (238). He found it in reading Schelling's later works, specifically his work on the *Divinities of Samothrace*. As he studied this work, he began to recognize, although "not quite clearly," (238) that this work, as well as other works, had been inspired by the individuality once incarnated as Tycho de Brahe who was now active in the spiritual world.

Following this story, he recommended to his listeners that they also use similar forms of support. "You will see that if you wish to have a true helper for your research into the future of the twentieth century who can guide you regarding the suprasensory world, if you need the impulses living in the suprasensory, it is the individuality...of Tycho de Brahe. This individuality is no longer on the physical plane, but it is always present and can give you insight into those things that concern the future of the twentieth century" (238).

The presentations he made in the karma lectures also had the objective of preparing those members who were ready for such questions and research impulses for the examination of their own lives and destinies. In every case, he modeled through his examples how one could gain insight into the ways karma works, and how one can be led to true insight when he, through the observation of insignificant details, becomes aware of the essentials. He expected that at least a part of his audience would be guided by these impulses to independent insights into the nature of destiny.

Toward the beginning of this last series of lectures, Rudolf Steiner had noted that since the Christmas conference, since the Foundation Stone verse had found its place in the hearts of the members, spiritual life flowed more richly and added:

> Take the significance of these words, which I have to speak based on my experiences in the last months, up into your hearts, my dear friends! By doing so we will be able in the future to give this spiritual foundation stone that we laid for the Anthroposophical Society last Christmas the right soil. What I wish to say in this introductory lecture shall point toward what I will share with you in the coming days. It shall point toward the fact that the anthroposophic movement in this critical period has essentially returned to its origins. (238)

And he recalled for the last time how he had hoped in October 1902 to begin the theosophical work with *practical karma exercises*. This had proven to be impossible. "What was then intended shall now become reality" (238).

The impulse to guide people toward practical karma exercises was intimately connected with another impulse: *to bring spiritual seekers along the path of self-development*. Thus, the karma lectures were interspersed with class lessons, a total of seven between September 6 and September 20. In a very concentrated manner, he recapitulated the contents of the first eight Dornach lessons. What was new in these lessons is that Steiner spoke about the class as the contemporary school of Michael, in which Michael was directly present.

In these last class lessons there were probably about 500 people present who were able to experience Rudolf Steiner as a spiritual teacher, who, imbued with the power of the spirit, could guide one on the path to self-knowledge—an inner knowledge that could lead from the understanding of the threefold nature of the forces of the soul across the threshold to the true human being whose origins lay in the spiritual world. The entire conference stood thus under the sign of esoteric deepening. It permeated all the courses and lifted the participants out of their ordinary consciousness.

The conference, which had included a total of seven eurythmy performances, came to an end on September 23. Rudolf Steiner gave the last lecture of the course on the dramatic arts, received the priests in his studio in the presence of the statue of Christ, and in the evening he gave a lecture for the members. The radiant, warm late summer days came to an end; the weather changed. On the evening of September 26—it was already dark and had started to rain—when the members began to make their way to the carpentry shop for the evening lecture, they met other friends coming down the hill who told them that the lecture had been cancelled. Some couldn't believe this and continued on to the carpentry shop where this news was confirmed. A meeting with farmers and the lecture planned for the following day were also cancelled.

During the afternoon of September 28, a Sunday, news circulated in Dornach that Rudolf Steiner wished to give a talk that evening, the evening before Michaelmas. The auditorium of the carpentry shop was filled to the last seat when Rudolf Steiner, cloaked in a mantle, entered supported by Marie Steiner and Ita Wegman. Spontaneously, everyone rose from their seats. When everyone was seated, Rudolf Steiner, after laying his mantle on the table, began to speak in a gentle voice. Toward the end of his talk, he said: "If in the near-future the Michaelic idea can come fully to live in four times twelve individuals—in four times twelve individuals who are recognized not by themselves but by the leadership of the Goetheanum—and if in these four times twelve individuals leaders arise to spark a celebration of Michael, then we will be able to gaze upon the light that from the Michael stream, and the Michaelic deeds will shine out upon humanity."

After only twenty minutes, Rudolf Steiner had to end his talk. He concluded with the *Michael Imagination*, a mantric verse, which were his last, great, earnest words to his students. Then he left the room, never again to be among the general membership.

Chapter 55

SICKBED AND DEATH

On September 30, Marie Steiner left for a longer tour with the eurythmy ensemble. She never spoke about what she felt as she left Dornach. It gave Rudolf Steiner solace to know that she was traveling into the world in service of Anthroposophy, while he was forced to stay in Dornach. He traveled with her in his thoughts and rejoiced in the reviews of the many successful performances. From his sickbed, he continued to draft choreographic forms for eurythmy presentations. Since Marie Steiner didn't return to Dornach until November 17 and Rudolf Steiner wrote to her regularly, we have a first-hand account of this period. On October 1, Rudolf Steiner moved from his room in Villa Hansi to his studio in the carpentry shop. The room in Villa Hansi was too small and the necessary baths could not be prepared there. Ita Wegman, who moved into an adjoining room, took responsibility for his care. The next day, he posted on the Dornach "Black Board" an announcement that, for some time, he would not be giving any lectures. He wrote to Marie Steiner, "Now I simply lie here and do not venture one step away from the warmth" (262). On October 3, at her request, Dr. Ludwig Noll arrived to help Ita Wegman with his medical care. On October 6, Steiner had to decide to cancel the conference that had been planned for the end of October in Berlin. That day he wrote Marie Steiner: "From a personal point of view, it would have made sense to have paid more attention to Dr. Wegman earlier on; she has long wanted me to get more rest. But, you know, it was my sense of duty to the higher spiritual powers that made me hold out until the September courses were finished. But, as I have said before, it isn't the courses, but all the demands people make in addition to the courses" (262).

The doctors were first able to cure a painful case of hemorrhoids that had robbed him of his freedom of movement. The treatments, which were very painful and kept Steiner chained to his bed, took about fourteen days. He reported to Marie Steiner that he was being taken very good care of. "But the care is annoying, and the treatments are painful. It is not a pleasurable hour when the two doctors arrive in the evening to give me my treatments. But taking everything into consideration, things are moving forward" (262). However, he was extremely weak and "kaput" (262). During the first weeks, he was only able to deal with the bare necessities. He could not bear visitors. Only Mieta Waller, then Mrs. Pyle, was allowed to enter briefly once or twice a day to ask if he needed anything. Albert Steffen came periodically to speak about the coming editions of the *Goetheanum*. But even as he lay there completely exhausted, he refused to let them take away his meetings with the architects concerning the rebuilding of the Goetheanum. But: "I have not even let Dr. Wachsmuth come to see me yet. He must bring everything to Ita Wegman, then get them back from her" (262).

He recovered very slowly. On October 13, he wrote that he had had a better night, but that the treatments drained him. Two days later: "The pain of treatments is difficult to bear" (262). A ray of hope was present on October 18. "Of myself I can only say that things are going slowly. One must have satisfaction in the fact that both Dr. Wegman and Dr. Noll joyfully remarked that I looked somewhat better today. So that is the way things are. The daily treatments are going to continue" (262).

A few days later he wrote that thanks to the ongoing treatments, he was doing somewhat better and had even let Dr. Wachsmuth in to see him. "There was no other choice. But he has to get used to leaving when I tell him that I can't continue" (262). Most people were difficult for Steiner at the time, Wachsmuth probably because he spoke so quickly and had so many questions he needed to ask.

On October 26, he mentioned that he was no longer chained to his bed, but could move around between his bed, his chair and the bathing room. "These are all my journeys for the present" (262). A few days later, he wrote that he felt much better, although everything was still progressing slowly. "Everything that originates from within me—for instance, writing something—is possible. But it is very difficult to respond to anything that comes from outside. There I must still be very careful" (262).

One can trace the resurgence of his writing abilities in the length of the articles he wrote for the *Goetheanum* and the newsletter. The installments of his *Autobiography* that he wrote for the *Goetheanum* had more than doubled in length by the beginning of November. The "Letters to the Members!" also became somewhat longer. On October 26, he published a review of Edmund Ernst's book *Reformation or Anthroposophy* and, in the Sunday edition of the *Basler Nationalzeitung*, an article on "The Rebuilding of the Goetheanum." On November 1, a second article, "The Second Goetheanum," appeared in the Basel newspaper and, in the *Goetheanum*, a lengthy review of Albert Steffen's play *The Four Beasts*. In the *Goetheanum* edition of November 9 was another review by Steiner, this time about a book by the Benedictine monk Alois Mager.

All his writing was done in the early morning. He wrote with a very fine, clear hand, practically without mistakes, the first draft ready to be published. Ita Wegman recalled:

> The transformation took place at about 5:00 a.m. His voice, which awakened me at this time, sounded different, strong and happy, somewhat impatient. It was time to hurry so as not to lose the precious moments. I rushed feverishly, knowing also how important this time was, got everything ready, and when he had drunk a cup of tea with a bit of lemon juice, he began to work. It was during this time that all the wonderful articles were written that were unexpected gifts for us. Without rest, he wrote until seven or eight o'clock, and then he wasn't tired but rather refreshed and awake. The rest of the morning was taken up with reading, taking care of necessary business, and receiving visitors. (*Newsletter*, 1925)

From the middle of November until February 23, when she left for another tour, Marie Steiner came to the studio every day at midday. In addition to many other things, they spoke about the eurythmy and recitation programs; sometimes he wrote a few explanatory words for the announcements. Thus, for the performance of February 1, 1925, he gave the title, "The Classical and the Romantic in Poetry and Music." Within the second part of the program was to be "Eleusis" by Hegel, a piece with which Marie Steiner had, following a suggestion by Rudolf Steiner, inaugurated our art of recitation in the very beginning of the anthroposophic movement. (277).

When possible, he received Guenther Wachsmuth at 11:00 a.m. to go through the correspondence, deal with administrative questions and review the requests for admission into the First Class. During the time he was confined to his room, over 300 new members were accepted with Rudolf Steiner's signature into the First Class. Wachsmuth, who had been the acting secretary of the society since 1924, described how Steiner would often make a whole series of decisions within half an hour. He would sketch out responses to requests that came in, giving a specific formulation of general guidelines for each individual case. There were times he also simply took the liberty of not answering at all. This silence was misinterpreted at times. "It sometimes happened that a visitor, in response to his question of whether he should do something and how he should do it, was told: 'Do it however you like.' The visitor would take this as an authorization, instead of noticing that such an answer could also be understood as a form of distancing oneself" (Wachsmuth).

From time to time the people who were working on the building project would come to present plans and sketches and to ask Steiner to give them guidance; Steiner stayed involved with the building project right up to the last days of his life. On October 31, he wrote to Marie Steiner, "The whole world has in the last few days demanded to know more about the new plans for the Goetheanum; they even want to receive pictures. I have done as much as my diminished strength will allow me to do" (262). From November on, the drawings were done following his suggestions. Albert Steffen visited regularly, not only to speak with Steiner about the *Goetheanum* and the newsletter, but also to discuss questions of literature with him. In the beginning of November, Steiner had a visit from Emil Leinhas. This visit dealt "with several questions concerning the liquidation of the *Kommenden Tag*. Rudolf Steiner was sitting in his chair wearing a house coat. I was shocked by his appearance. He was as thin as a skeleton. But he was completely aware of all the issues that needed his attention. He took a clear, explicit position on everything I presented. The meeting was short; I did not want to tire him any more than necessary" (Leinhas).

On November 11, Rudolf Steiner asked Ludwig Polzer-Hoditz, who was visiting Dornach, to come and see him. The reason for the visit was that Polzer-Hoditz had been taking care of Steiner's siblings, who lived in the Austrian village of Horn, and managed the money that Steiner sent to them. Polzer-Hoditz recalled that Steiner had spoken to him about his dead father and about the Michael School. "When I asked how I should hold the class lessons in Vienna and Prague, he replied with friendly emphasis, 'Do it as you think best'" (Polzer-Hoditz). The next day, Steiner wrote a letter to his sister on the occasion of her name day and reported: "Yesterday, Count Polzer-Hoditz visited me. We spoke about you. He will bring you some medicines" (39). It was a great relief for Steiner that he had a friend living not far from Horn whom he could ask for help.

At this time, the resistance against the rebuilding of the Goetheanum was reorganized. A number of dismissive articles were published in two newspapers, and, on November 23, there was a public demonstration in Arlesheim against the building project. Albert Steffen wrote, "During these weeks there were a number of brutal attacks by our enemies. Rudolf Steiner asked us not to concern ourselves with these goings-on. He seemed to pay it no attention whatsoever. But the fact was that his health deteriorated in those days to the point where he had to leave his chair and take to his bed" (Steffen, *Meetings*).

For this reason, from the middle of November on, Rudolf Steiner only wrote the installments of his *Autobiography* and the "Letters to the Members!" for the *Goetheanum*. During this time he wrote a verse, which offers unsettling insight into his own experience of the time (260a):

> You contradictory magic of life
> You shine in the night
> And the noble weaving of destiny
> Divine intention eternal might
> Pierces the forces of the adversary—
> Which spreads itself, tormenting my soul
> Crafting demonic misery
> Gliding toward me, serpent-like.

Albert Steffen recalled visiting him in the middle of December, to speak, as they usually did, about the *Goetheanum*. "When I knocked, I heard that he was feverish and wanted to turn around and leave him in peace, but was called back as I hurried down the path. Although the pain chiseled into his features was indescribable, his emaciated hands told a tale of even worse pain. As soon as he had given me the manuscript he had written for the *Goetheanum*, he gave me his hand in greeting. It was burning with fever" (Steffen, *Meetings*).

During these weeks of autumn as he lay in his sickbed, Rudolf Steiner wrote the chapters of his *Autobiography* that begin with the narration of his encounters with the artists in Weimar and lead up to his involvement with the Dramatists' Society (28). After Christmas, he began to write about what he termed his time of trial. In what we know today as chapter 22 of his *Autobiography*, there stands, like a center point among these passages, his characterization of the "turning point of the soul," which occurred when he was thirty-six years old. He wrote about it in the period from the middle to the end of November. He described how "the pure ideation of my previous life...drew back and what lives in the will stepped into its place," how the will also took over his spiritual knowing and how, in this will permeated spiritual insight, and "the stabilization of the spiritual individual in the spiritual world was infinitely intensified" (28).

This theme is expanded upon in the "Letters to the Members!" The essay "The Pre-Michaelic and the Path of Michael," which was written in the early days of October, concluded with three leading thoughts. "It is Michael's task to lead the human being back again on paths of will, whence he had come down when, with his earthly consciousness, he descended on paths of thought from the living experience of the suprasensory to that of the sensory world" (26).

In the following letter to the members, written on October 10, he characterized human consciousness since the fifteenth century. Humanity increasingly entered a realm in which a dead and deadening intellectuality held sway. One cannot remain unconsciously in this realm. The human being can in freedom follow Michael, the true anthroposophist. "Michael ascends again along the paths upon which humankind descended step by step in the evolution of the spirit, down to the exercise of the intellect. Michael will lead the will upward, retracing the paths wisdom descended to become intellect" (26).

In the letter dated October 19, which describes "The Experiences of Michael in the Fulfillment of his Cosmic Mission," Steiner addressed the problem of freedom from a cosmic perspective and the question it poses for humankind, whether they can in freedom find the path to Christ. In the leading thoughts he builds the bridge to *Intuitive Thinking as a Spiritual Path*, presenting the relationship between the impulse developed in this work and Michael's mission. "In my *Intuitive Thinking as a Spiritual Path*, the 'freedom' of the human being is shown to be an essential element of human consciousness in the present epoch. The cosmic dimensions of this 'freedom's becoming' are established in the descriptions of Michael's mission that are given here" (26).

The recognition and corresponding acknowledgment of an understanding of nature, its significance and its boundaries, which played a central role in Rudolf Steiner's life and thought from early on, is taken up again on

October 25 in connection with the activities of Michael. He had described the difference between knowledge of nature and knowledge of the human being in *Goethe's Theory of Knowledge* and stated that one could only gain knowledge of the human being "if one approached the spirit as a source of activity" (2). At that time he also opposed the attempt to "make the forms in which the spirit expresses itself, rather than the spirit itself, the focus of psychological research" (ibid). He had expressed similar views in the essay "Haeckel and his Opponents," in which he defended Haeckel against certain reactionary views. "*Because* observation of the way the spirit expresses itself is *self-observation*, it is one's own self that comes to expression in the spirit, not any form of external ratiocination" (30). A number of years later, he went on to describe the realms that open themselves to the self-observant spirit in his book *Theosophy*. Now, in October 1924, in addition to the way of thinking inherent in natural science, he calls his readers' attention to an encounter with nature illuminated by a higher level of self-knowledge.

> Today, one must speak about nature in the manner demanded by the evolution of the consciousness soul. One must take up into oneself pure natural scientific thought. But one should also learn to speak *about nature*—that means to *experience* it—in a manner appropriate to Christ.... Anthroposophy values correctly what natural scientific thought has learned over the course of the last four of five centuries to say about the world. But in addition to this, it speaks in another language about the nature of human beings and the evolution of the cosmos; it strives to speak the language of Christ-Michael. (26)

Those with an interest in biographical themes will note how Michaelic themes surfaced quite early in Steiner's biography. Now, toward the end of his life, what had been hidden comes to more complete expression in Steiner's descriptions of Michael. The "Letters to the Members!" cast a light on the biographical unfolding of Steiner's own mission.

By describing the essence and work of Michael from a variety of different perspectives, and by placing Michael's experience in a historical perspective, Steiner gives his readers insight into the spiritual source of inspiration for Anthroposophy. These letters to the members are an interpretation of the essence of Anthroposophy. The members could learn though the presentations of Michael how to understand Anthroposophy and to recognize what dangers threatened it. One could not have done justice to Michael simply by depicting him as preserving a center between two adversarial forces, or by saying that he served as a balancing point. He was much more concerned with the creative continuation of human development through the individual, who in thoughtful experience, independently and actively, could come to an understanding of the world in the depths of his or her own being. Both the ancient luciferic forms of mental imaging and the cold, strategic ahrimanic intellect could be overcome by such an active, creative development. The center, which was preserved by Michael, did not lie between two erroneous paths, but rather, in a certain sense, above both of them in a completely new developmental thrust.

The readers of these seemingly unsystematic letters were stimulated and guided to examine their own relation to Anthroposophy in the mirror of these portrayals of Michael. These depictions initially played out in majestic cosmic and cosmological pictures to the extent that, for instance, the reader of *Cosmic Thought in the Workings of Michael and in the Workings of Ahriman*, borne aloft on the wings of creative thought, could rise to the understanding of even greater imaginations.

> One of the imaginations of *Michael* is this: He holds sway through the *passage of time*, bearing the light of the cosmos as an essential part of his own being; crafting the warmth streaming from the cosmos as the revelation of his own being; and he holds sway in his *beingness like a world*, only affirming himself in that he affirms the world, as if guiding forces down to the earth from all parts of the cosmos.
>
> Contrast this with an imagination of Ahriman: He desires to conquer space as he passes out of time; he is surrounded by darkness, into which he sends the rays of his own light; the frost around grows ever more severe as he achieves his goals; he moves as a world that has contracted into a *single* being, himself, affirming himself only by rejecting the world; he moves as though he carries within him the sinister forces of dark caverns in the earth. (26)

From November 23 until Christmas, a series of presentations followed, depicting the efforts of Michael before the beginning of a new Michaelic epoch in relation to historical developments. These letters contain a wealth of information concerning historical figures and events from Michael's perspective, opening up possibilities for further research. Jan Hus and John Wicliff were described as people in whom the consciousness soul shone brightly. "Listening to the voice of Michael in their hearts, they proclaimed the right of the consciousness soul to rise to understanding of the deepest religious mysteries. They felt that the intellectuality inherent to the consciousness soul must be able to grasp in the realm of ideas what had been achieved in ancient times through imaginations" (26).

The individuals who gathered for the councils of Constance and Basel did not experience the emerging consciousness soul, nor could they find strength or certainty in the traditional ideas adopted by the intellectual or mind soul. Nicholas of Cusa alone appears in this context as an individual striving to achieve spiritual enlightenment by overcoming the forces of the intellect through the practice of *"docta ignorantia."* The last of this series of letters was written on December 14 and described the significance and limitations of Goethe (26).

In these presentations, Rudolf Steiner sketches out the difficulties inherent in the first stage of the development of the consciousness soul. The consciousness soul only awakens in the realm of the intellect, where the human being is bound to the body and his consciousness chained to the senses. Insight into the nature of the human being is lost, because the soul has not yet raised itself to conscious experience of the spirit. It does not recognize the presence of the spirit, neither within the soul's own being, nor in nature or history. Paracelsus and Jakob Böhme are exceptions. Michael's position in the cosmos becomes tragic; he respects individual freedom, yet depends upon human understanding.

> Michael's preparation of his mission for the end of the nineteenth century streams forth in cosmic tragedy. Below, upon the earth, there was often the greatest satisfaction with the effects of the new understanding of nature; the realms in which Michael was present were overcome by tragedy in the face of the obstacles placed in the path of a new understanding of the human being. (26)

As Rudolf Steiner wrote these lines, his physical strength was further diminished, he was constrained to his bed, almost unable to take any nourishment, and, as Albert Steffen recalled, feverish. Although completely lucid, he was unable to do even the simplest things. The intensity with which he had been able to write at the beginning of November was no longer possible. He could feel the construction noise from the Goetheanum site, which could be heard through the thin walls of the studio, with every bone of his body.

One must take his situation to heart. It was deeply tragic. Before his spirit stood everything that he wanted to do and would have been able to do it if his health had allowed it: the new building, the continued development of the School of Spiritual Science, and impulses for the various fields of work and aspects of life, for agriculture, medicine, education, and art. But he was only able to do very little. Thus he had to live through the tragedy of the spirit chained in his studio, unable to take hold of the plans and tasks awaiting him.

Anthroposophical life on the hill in Dornach, which had attracted over a thousand people the summer before, had slipped into a wintery quiet following Rudolf Steiner's collapse. On December 10, members gathered to celebrate Albert Steffen's fortieth birthday. For Christmas, some 200 anthroposophists from afar joined the local members, no doubt moved to some extent by questions concerning Dr. Steiner's health. There was no report from the doctors, but Marie Steiner did read his Christmas greetings "To the Friends of Anthroposophy now gathered at the Goetheanum." In it he reiterated that his physical forces had been exhausted during the fall presentations because of the demands that had been made on him outside of the courses. "That must all be accepted as fate (karma). To waste words telling you how painful it is for me to be physically separated from the work at the Goetheanum would be sentimental" (260a).

In the place of Rudolf Steiner's usual Christmas lectures, Marie Steiner read twice from the latest "Letters to the Members!," Albert Steffen gave a lecture on the work of Jakob Böhme, the Oberuferer Christmas plays were performed and there were a number of eurythmy performances.

Shortly before Christmas, Rudolf Steiner had received a letter from the chairman of the Swiss Historical Preservation Society, Dr. Gerhard Börlin. He suggested organizing an international architectural competition to develop a new concept for rebuilding the Goetheanum. Steiner's health kept him from answering the letter immediately, but on December 30, he wrote a long letter to Dr. Börlin, turning down his suggestion with the utmost politeness and stressing how much the possibility to be in Switzerland was appreciated. Toward the end of the letter, he did, however, address the efforts being made to stop the rebuilding of the Goetheanum and remarked, "The thing that disturbed me most about the claims of those opposing the rebuilding project was that the size of the building was a sign of pride, arrogance or even a desire for power. In

Sickbed and Death

fact, I am completely conscious that I am only acting out of the necessity of the situation" (260a).

It took terrific effort for Rudolf Steiner to write such a letter. But still, he did not turn the task over to Guenther Wachsmuth. It was only a question of choosing the right words; he wanted to personally make the effort to imbed the second Goetheanum in the proper manner into the social milieu. On January 1, a year after he had collapsed in the carpentry shop and two years after the burning of the first Goetheanum, his health took a critical turn. His doctors feared for his life. But he was soon able to resume his work.

Emil Leinhas, who was to represent Rudolf Steiner at the annual meeting of The Coming Day, recalled that he had been asked to come to the studio on January 2 at 9:00 a.m. When he arrived, Dr. Noll asked him to return at 12:00 p.m., as Dr. Steiner's heart was feeble, but he did wish to speak with him. When Leinhas returned, he found Steiner lying in his bed. Taking his place beside the bed, Leinhas suddenly became aware of just how critical Steiner's illness was, something that very few people knew. Rudolf Steiner asked him if, although he was the general director of the stock company, he could represent him and, when Leinhas had given his agreement, signed the necessary power of attorney.

From this point on, Rudolf Steiner was only able to have longer meetings with very few people. He was not able to meet with the Swiss building specialist Professor Ernst Fiechter, who wanted to publish a series of articles supporting the new building project and had come to Dornach on January 6 especially to speak with him about this endeavor. Steiner was only to see his ten-year-old son, Nick Fiechter, briefly. Nick had suffered severe trauma to one eye and had been brought by his parents to Steiner to seek help.

By January 10, in addition to the continuation of his *Autobiography* and the "Letters to the Members!," Steiner had also written the last foreword for *Outline of Esoteric Science*. Fifteen years after the first edition of this book, in this foreword Rudolf Steiner gave account of his spiritual research. He described the genesis of this seminal work, characterized the nature of the way of thinking that led to what it contained, and emphasized that everything he had written was the result of his own spiritual experience, not the reiteration of others' writings. Most importantly, all his insights had originated in a completely conscious, controlled research process.

During the second half of January, final preparations were made to register the General Anthroposophical Society and to incorporate the Goetheanum Association into it. Rudolf Steiner gave Guenther Wachsmuth charge of making the necessary arrangements with Mr. Altermatt from the Registry Office. He suggested incorporating the Goetheanum Association by changing its name to General Anthroposophical Society. By this means, both the lengthy procedure of registering the society formed at the Christmas conference and the substantial cost of transferring the assets of the Goetheanum Association into the new society could be circumvented. He was also convinced that the statutes of the new society were too unwieldy to be included in the registry. Guenther Wachsmuth recalled:

> Under his guidance, the points he deemed appropriate for the registry were summarized in a few paragraphs" (*Nachrichtenblatt*, 1950). There is no question that Altermatt oriented himself primarily on the old charter of the Goetheanum Association. Wachsmuth continued: "I gave this to Rudolf Steiner and remarked that it had quite a different style than the statutes of the Christmas conference. More than anything he was not pleased with the fact that in the registered statutes the council was to be voted for by the general assembly.... However, Rudolf Steiner said, "Let's do it the way it stands here. We can always change the text sometime in the future." (*Nachrichtenblatt*, 1950)

The last general meeting of the Goetheanum Association took place on February 8, 1925. Neither Rudolf Steiner nor Ita Wegman was present; the other council members were there. At 9:30 a.m., there was a preparatory meeting for the members. Wachsmuth informed them of the intended changes and told them that Rudolf Steiner had requested that the new statutes not "be published in the Newsletter, because they would only cause confusion. The statutes of the Christmas conference will continue to be valid for the members" (Hans Locher, in: *Mitteilungen aus der anthroposophischen Bewegung*, Easter 1980).

In the general meeting the new statutes, which would define all the outer legal relationships of the General Anthroposophical Society, were approved for submittal to the authorities. In the first paragraph, the GAS is named as the legal successor of the Goetheanum Association; in the second, the administration of the Goetheanum is listed as the third subdivision of the Anthroposophical Society. The executive council that was formed at the Christmas conference was voted in again unanimously (260a). The papers submitted to the authorities, which simply requested a name change for the Goetheanum Association, were signed by Rudolf Steiner and all the other members of the council (260a). After this change had been published by the Swiss Chamber of Commerce, an announcement was made in the Newsletter for the members of the Anthroposophical Society, informing them of the four subdivisions.

In the decades since Rudolf Steiner's death, these events have been interpreted in various ways. It seems to make sense to examine them in their historical context. Considering how careful he had been with the formalities during the discussion and approval of the statutes during the Christmas conference, it appears somewhat strange that statutes governing legal relationships between individuals would be decided upon at a general meeting of the Goetheanum Association without any official discussion and without the participation of the members. One can view this as a legal impossibility. Whoever is inclined to emphasize this completely misunderstands Steiner's intentions. The decision from February 8 had absolutely no impact on the Anthroposophical Society, which had been formed as an organ of the life of the spirit. The statutes that had been decided upon at the Christmas conference, which were concerned with something higher than merely regulating the legal relationships within the society, remained in force.

Although Rudolf Steiner viewed the statutes adopted at the Christmas conference as being unshakably earnest and important, he recognized that entering the revised statutes into the public record as being at best an acceptable concession to Swiss corporate law. He had spoken about his views on this question in other contexts. At the general meeting of the Johannes Building Association on October 17, 1917, he said:

> For this reason I do not place any importance in whether the building in named "Johannes House" or "ABC-House" in the statutes. These are not drawn up for us, but in order to represent our intentions to the outer world.... The anthroposophic movement can only attain its significance if its work rests upon living realities, upon the authentic, immediate living realities. My dear friends, whether the statutes are good or bad, or whether the names are good or bad, has absolutely no significance for the anthroposophic movement. What is, however, of the greatest importance to the movement is that it has members who take hold of the contemporary cultural developments vigorously and

with full understanding wherever they have the karmic opportunity and possibility. (Protocol for the Fifth Regular General Meeting)

He made similar remarks during a teacher's meeting when the teachers presented statutes they had drafted. "It is difficult for me to have a position on these statutes, because I have no interest in statutes. One can only act in the manner required by the daily challenges. Statutes are necessary for the outer world. They make our work look like something. That is why it is difficult for me to have an opinion concerning the statutes. They do not interest me. I do not believe that anything essential can be changed through statutes" (300 & 1).

In addition to these fundamental remarks concerning statutes in which he points out that they "are not for us, but to represent our work to the outer world" and that one can only act "in the manner required by the daily challenges," in February 1925, there is something else we must take into consideration. Hypothetically we could assume that if his health had allowed him to, Rudolf Steiner would have taken the time to structure the outer legalities of the General Anthroposophical Society in accordance with the legal requirements and that he would have had the general meeting of the society approve the necessary changes. But he lay ill, hoping that his health would return. He wrote to Felix Heinemann in Arlesheim:

> My health is still quite labile, and I have to search out the moments in which I can risk doing more than what the technicalities of the building project and the basic necessities of the administration require of me. I can only hope that by taking care in this manner my forces will once more be able to flow into the work at the Goetheanum. This is an existential necessity. (260a)

The question of the statutes that was dealt with on February 8 was but a simple administrative necessity that did, however, make some sense. On June 29, when he suggested the new inner organization of the society, Rudolf Steiner had recommended that he head up the newly integrated subdivision in order to expedite the building process. A letter written to Marie Steiner on March 5, 1925, gives insight into just how concerned he was with the project. "My health improves but slowly. And I *have* to be able to work again because, after everything that has taken place, if the building were not to be finished because of my health, the outcome would be disastrous" (262). In this context and with this urgency in the background, the

Sickbed and Death

decisions made on February 8 concerning the statutes appear plausible and readily understandable.

In retrospect, it seems as though Rudolf Steiner began in the next weeks to wrap up everything he had begun, to prepare for his no longer being there. This was, however, not his intention, it was more a question of destiny—events that either came toward him from the world or decisions that needed to be made as a logical consequence of what had gone before.

In February 1925, Emil Bock was sent to Dornach by the Christian Community to ask Rudolf Steiner a number of questions. At the time, Steiner's health was so bad that Steffen had noted in his journal: "there is absolutely no hope." Emil Bock had to pose his questions with Guenther Wachsmuth acting as the intermediary. Rudolf Steiner requested that Bock stay on. There was something he wanted to give him. Two days later, Wachsmuth handed him the text for the ritual appointment of the First Minister (*Erzoberlenker*) of the Christian Community. It was the last of the rituals he had promised the priests. Rudolf Steiner suggested that the priests be called together in Berlin for the service and that it take place just before the beginning of the conference that was planned for the end of February there.

He asked Marie Steiner and Guenther Wachsmuth to attend the conference in his stead. Marie Steiner traveled to Berlin on February 23. Her trip coincided with the beginning of a eurythmy tour that was to continue on through Danzig, Stuttgart, Heidenheim, Karlsruhe, Mannheim, then return again to Stuttgart. As Marie Savitch recalled, it was infinitely difficult for Marie Steiner to leave Dornach to fulfill this obligation. But Rudolf Steiner insisted "that the tour should not not be cancelled. And Marie Steiner had to assume the task of insuring that the activities out in the world not be brought to a halt" (Savitch). Friedrich Rittelmeyer was anointed as First Minister in Berlin on February 24, and, following Steiner's suggestion, Emil Bock was named as his successor. Wachsmuth had to give Steiner a report of this ceremony immediately upon his return to Dornach. He later recalled how deeply moved Steiner had been as he spoke (*We Experienced Rudolf Steiner*).

On February 27, 1925, anthroposophic groups throughout the world celebrated Rudolf Steiner's birthday. The students of the Waldorf School sent handmade presents to him in Dornach: pictures they had painted and pieces they had made in their handwork and shop classes. He thanked the teachers for their good wishes on March 15 and wrote:

> It is a great hardship for me to not have been able to see you for so long. And I must now place the responsibility for important decisions, in which I have quite naturally been involved since the school began, in your own hands. It is a time of being tested by destiny. I am with you in my thoughts. There is no more that I can do now, otherwise I risk extending this period of physical infirmity into eternity. (260a)

With these words he laid responsibility for the continuation of the school into the "self-counsel" of the teachers. A few days later, he had Guenther Wachsmuth inform the teachers that they were authorized to oversee all schools in Germany that wished to practice anthroposophic pedagogy (260a, Addendum). He thanked the pupils for their gifts and wrote, "Hopefully, I will be able to be among you again before too long" (260a).

Since the fall of 1923, Rudolf Steiner had worked with Ita Wegman on "that medical book," which was published with the title *Fundamentals of Therapy—Expanding the Art of Healing through Spiritual Science* (27). This collaborative undertaking did not only come to expression in the fact that Rudolf Steiner wrote one part of the book while Ita Wegman wrote the other. They worked collaboratively on the fundamental questions addressed in the book. It was a collaborative research project. Rudolf Steiner spoke about this in Torquay.

> This collaboration became possible because Ita Wegman not only has the kind of knowledge attained by today's doctors, but also the intuitive, therapeutic impulse that arises from the imaginative totality of the illness, enters directly into the spiritual world and from there guides the therapeutic relationship. That is where the path lies upon which one can research what I have spoken about here. We are thus striving through this work to develop an initiation medicine, which is in its essence an initiation science. (243)

Writing about the fundamentals of a medical approach whose origin lies in what becomes accessible through the path of initiation takes time. The anthroposophic understanding of human nature had to be formulated anew in order to achieve this goal. In this context, for example, the etheric forces are described as the forces that work in upon the earth from the periphery and that are modified by the effects of the stars (27). An understanding of remedies and the insights into the nature of substances upon which it was based needed to be presented through a number of examples. More than anything this first volume—others were to follow—needed to

Sickbed and Death

contain descriptions of certain characteristic illnesses and typical remedies. These questions became the focus of the collaborative process.

The book on which Rudolf Steiner and Ita Wegman had worked for the last year and a half was sent to the printer either at the end of February or the beginning of March. In March, Rudolf Steiner was able to make the last corrections. On March 28, he read through the last proofs and turned them over to Ita Wegman. "Something important has been given in this book" (*Nachrichtenblatt*, 1925).

After the General Anthroposophical Society had been formally registered, Rudolf Steiner asked seven Swiss individuals to head up the division concerned with the administration of the Goetheanum: Emil Grosheintz, Rudolf Geering-Christ, Marie Schieb, Marie Hirter-Weber, Luci Bürgi, Otto Rietmann, and Ernest Etienne. Among these individuals, all of whom had been actively involved in supporting the building of the Goetheanum, were also those who, in 1913, had purchased and then made a gift of the land upon which the Goetheanum had been built.

From his sickbed, Rudolf Steiner also made arrangements for his siblings. In the beginning of March, he heard that Polzer-Hoditz was staying in Dornach and asked to have him come to see him. Polzer-Hoditz recalled in his memoirs that Steiner, who lay in bed and could barely speak, had asked him to come concerning his sons' visas. A somewhat different picture of the visit is given in the last letter Steiner wrote to Marie Steiner on March 23. Earlier, Rudolf Steiner had given Polzer-Hoditz medicine for Steiner's sister, Leopoldine. In March, Polzer-Hoditz visited her again, and Steiner told Marie Steiner that he had brought bad news from this last visit. "My sister has gone almost completely blind" (262). He requested that Dr. Norbert Glas be called in to examine her and send him the diagnosis. Rudolf Steiner's last two letters, written on March 25 and 27, had to do with his ongoing concern for his siblings.

By the first weeks of February 1925, the continuing installments of Rudolf Steiner's *Autobiography* had reached the year 1902, the year his collaboration with Marie von Sivers began. The passage describing this beginning was published on February 14. Rudolf Steiner introduced his narration of the collaborative work with her with the following words: "Marie von Sivers was *the* one who, with her whole being, made it possible to protect our work from sectarianism and to give it a quality that placed it in the general culture and educational life." And he added, "Marie von

Sivers and I soon became close friends. Our friendship became the basis for extensive work together in a great variety of spiritual areas" (28).

Rudolf Steiner continued with his recollections of this time in the following weeks. Thus it happened that during the last weeks of his life, the beginning of his shared anthroposophic work with Marie von Sivers stood before his inner eye. It had not been easy for Marie Steiner to live with the increasingly intense collaboration between Rudolf Steiner and Ita Wegman over the course of the last few years. Ita Wegman was so entirely different than she was. Now she was forced to deny herself the opportunity to care for the person she loved the most. Trouble with her legs inhibited her from doing this. That they had spoken about this with each other is evident from a letter he wrote her in Berlin on his official birthday.

> I write you these lines at about the same time that you would usually be sitting at my side. Thinking about how beautiful it is to listen to you speak about your activities and to speak with you about various aspects of your work moves me deeply. And when I know that you have now and again been able to read in my *Autobiography* the description of our shared work, I feel deeply how closely connected we are. That destiny has brought other people close to me is simply the way destiny works. And my sickness has shown just how incisive this destiny can be. But you found the way to understanding; this is a blessing for me. To feel the unity of feeling and thinking in discernment is something I can do *only* with you. That I was not able to show you the last pages of the Steffen article before it went to the printer (yesterday) was a hardship for me. Then for myself, I find inner competence only in *your* judgment. (262)

He mentioned "our shared work" again on March 13, which, as he was just writing about it "appeared so beautifully before my inner eye" (262). Together with Marie Steiner he had built up the entire spectrum of anthroposophic work, had developed the anthroposophic speech arts and brought eurythmy into the world. Now, in 1925, Marie Steiner bore full responsibility for these branches of anthroposophic life, through which art was raised into the realms of the hierarchies.

For Rudolf Steiner it was necessary to develop the fundamental aspects of an approach to medicine originating in the path of initiation in addition to the work with the arts, something that was very close to his heart. Destiny brought about the esoteric collaboration with Ita Wegman, which, as could not have been otherwise, led to a rare soul-spiritual intimacy. Even if it was difficult for her, Marie Steiner had "found a way to understand this," and Rudolf Steiner could say to her: "That is a blessing for me." And, in what he wrote in conclusion, he was able to say to her that their relationship had not suffered at all: "Then for myself, I find inner competence only in *your* judgment."

His thoughts returned to Marie Steiner time and time again. He waited expectantly for news of the eurythmy tour and on March 20, he wrote to her in Stuttgart. "I gaze with wonder upon everything you achieve and with such devotion. In my thoughts I am with you" (262). But he also had to ask her to address the difficulties with the anthroposophic work in Stuttgart. She did so, but because of this had to remain in Stuttgart longer than expected and was only able to return to Dornach after he had already passed away.

Anthroposophical poets and poetry were also concerns of Rudolf Steiner at this time. He wrote to Marie Steiner about Kurt Piper, who had caused him some worry by publishing a number of concerning articles, saying that he had an "artistic, poetic nature"; "we don't have very many of these" (260). He asked her to speak with Piper. She contacted him and attended an evening recitation where Edwin Froböse recited a number of Piper's poems.

Insuring that the artistic productivity within the anthroposophic movement received appropriate acknowledgement had always been one of Rudolf Steiner's concerns. For this reason, in February and March he wrote a three-part article on Albert Steffen's early work. He had hoped to be able to continue this, but this was not possible. In the first paragraphs of these articles, he wrote of Albert Steffen:

> For *this* poetic spirit to enter in the proper moment with the characters of his dramas into the spiritual world, he did not need the help of any theory. He did not need to learn of the path into the spiritual world through Anthroposophy. But Anthroposophy can learn from him of a living, ensouled "pilgrimage" to the spirit-world.
>
> Such a poetic spirit must, if he is properly recognized, be experienced within the anthroposophic movement as the bearer of a message from the spiritual realms. That he has chosen to work within this movement must be experienced as a blessing of destiny. (36)

It seems clear that by writing in this manner about Steffen, through what he had written about Marie Steiner in his *Autobiography* and in the way he spoke about his collaboration with Ita Wegman, Rudolf Steiner hoped to awaken genuine respect for each other among his closest colleagues.

During this entire time, he hoped to regain his health. It was clear to both him and his doctors that one could no longer speak of a breakdown caused by overwork and exhaustion. His lack of appetite had intensified at times to a deep disgust at any form of nourishment. His entire digestive tract had ceased to function. Complete exhaustion followed any form of nourishment. In spite of this, he never lost courage. On March 5, as was mentioned above, he had written to Marie Steiner, "My health improves but slowly. And I *have* to be able to work again because, after everything that has taken place, if the building were not to be finished because of my health, the outcome would be disastrous" (262).

In a letter dated March 13, there is a sentence that seems to indicate that at this time he was able to eat a little. "It is completely understandable that the often high fevers, etc., have left me without any appetite and that for a time I could eat almost nothing at all" (262). On March 20, he wrote to Marie Steiner in Stuttgart, "The healing progresses slowly. Hopefully I will be able soon to continue work on the building model, so that the work is not hindered" (262). And on March 23 he wrote, "Everything progresses so slowly by me; I am actually quite desperate in the face of this slow progress" (262).

Perhaps at this point it would be important to say a few words about Rudolf Steiner's illness. It has been publicly stated that he died of stomach cancer (Brügge). In light of the way his illness progressed, such an assumption is fully understandable. But one of Ita Wegman's closest colleagues, Dr. Margarete Kirchner-Bockholt vehemently rejected this conjecture. And Ita Wegman had reported that Rudolf Steiner's etheric body was no longer able to work in the digestive organs in the appropriate manner. "The result was that these organs were subjected too strongly to the physical forces, which are forces of degeneration." (*Nachrichtenblatt*, 1925). In his recollections of Rudolf Steiner, D. N. Dunlop recalled, "A few weeks before his final illness, during the summer conference in Torquay, I spoke to him about my concerns for his physical health. He drew me aside, vigorously but with infinite friendliness, and made me aware that his situation could not be explained in terms of our usual notions of disease" (Meyer).

Albert Steffen, who visited Rudolf Steiner regularly throughout his illness, recalled this time:

> I visited him at five o'clock in the afternoon in his studio, where he lay in his sickbed. It is a tall room with skylights. Nothing of the earth looks in: no tree, no mountain, no house, only the light of the heavens. Sculptural and architectural models that he has made himself stand on the shelves along with some busts he has sculpted; at the foot of his bed, the noble statue of Christ, carved by his own hand, soars high above him. All around him are tables covered with books and manuscripts. (*Goetheanum*, 1925)

"Up to the last day of his life, his interest was for the entire world. In his studio, which he had not left for half the year, he had collected an entire library" (*Goetheanum*, 1925).

On March 14, Steffen presented Steiner his newest play, *Hieram und Salomo*. He had dedicated it to Steiner. During the days, Steiner spoke with him about the evolution of this legend. On March 20, Steffen asked Steiner to pose him a guiding question for his work on the *Goetheanum*. The next day, Steiner suggested that he find a solution to the question of why artists believed they would become less creative if they became anthroposophists. On March 25, Steiner reported joyfully of the successful eurythmy tour through Germany the troupe had made under Marie Steiner's guidance. "He also spoke of the publication of the medical book he had worked on with Dr. Wegman. The printer's proofs with his corrections lay on his bed" (*Goetheanum*, 1925).

The next day, Steffen found Steiner sitting in his chair. His hands, which had grown so thin, protruded from the wide arms of his housecoat. Their conversation of the previous days concerning worldview and poetry was continued and Steiner called a book about Shakespeare, written by his old friend Vinzenz Knauer, to Steffen's attention. "He spoke so joyfully and with such energy, one had the impression the crisis had been overcome." It was during these days that he asked to have his adjoining studio prepared so he could begin work again on the model for the second Goetheanum.

According to Ita Wegman's report, on March 28 Rudolf Steiner was very still, sad and silent. She recalled, "It seemed to me as though he had a difficult problem to solve. The forces of light in his eyes appeared weaker than usual." It is probable that he wrote, or at least finished, the last "Letter to the Members!" that day. This last missive is like a preview of what was to come in the twentieth century. It is titled "From Nature to Sub-Nature." In it, Rudolf Steiner characterizes the dangers of the technological age and the task that has arisen for humanity through the technological developments, which rob humans of a direct experience of nature and place themselves in its stead. "Humanity must find the strength, the inner cognitive power it needs to not be overcome by Ahriman in the technological culture" (26). And: "Today only very few people experience the decisive spiritual challenges that are emerging here. Electricity, which was praised after its discovery as the soul of natural existence, must be recognized as containing an inherent force capable of drawing from the natural world down into the world of the sub-natural. Humanity must not allow itself to be drawn along" (26).

At the time these words were being written, Europe did not yet find itself covered with a network of wires, radios were quite rare and information technology was still unknown. It was still the time of the steam engine; books were still set by hand using lead print. "The Leading Thoughts" accompanying this letter read like a prophetic orientation for the future.

> 183. In the natural scientific age, beginning in the middle of the nineteenth century, the cultural activities of humanity have gradually slipped down not only into the depths of the natural forces but deeper still into a region lying *below* nature. Technology becomes sub-nature.
>
> 184. This makes it necessary for the human being to find a fully experienced spiritual knowledge through which one can raise oneself just as high into the super-natural realms as one is drawn into the sub-natural through technology. One creates thus within oneself the strength one needs *to not go under.*
>
> 185. In the past, the conception of nature still bore within it the spirit with which the origins of human evolution are connected. This spirit gradually disappeared from our conception of nature; the purely ahrimanic flowed into it and from there into the technological civilization.

When Albert Steffen visited Steiner on the evening of March 28, the day these words were written, he found him once again in his chair surrounded by a deep silence, his eyes sad and still.

March 1925 was cold and foggy. It became quite windy in the last week of the month, and then the storms began. From the south and the west, the rain whipped against the walls of the studio. On March 29, Rudolf Steiner awoke in pain. "No work was done that morning. It was the first time. We spoke at length about the pain. There was no reason to be worried. The pains disappeared in the course of the day. He was extraordinarily still and patient that day and gave new suggestions for his care" (Wegman & *Nachrichtenblatt*, 1925).

At 4:00 that afternoon, the pain returned. Yet Rudolf Steiner asked again if the adjoining studio was ready yet for him to work on the model for the second Goetheanum. Both doctors, Wegman and Noll, kept watch throughout the night. Ita Wegman recalled the last hours of his life.

> At 3:00 a.m., I noticed a slight change in his breathing. I approached his bed; he was awake. He looked at me and asked whether I was tired. This question touched me. His pulse was not as strong as it had been, but much faster. I called Dr. Noll in order to speak with him about what ought to be done. Doctor was not astonished to see him there in the middle of the night and greeted him amiably. "I don't feel too bad," he said, "I just can't sleep." We turned the lights out again. At 4:00 a.m., he called me because the pain had reappeared. He said, "As soon as the day comes, we want to continue the treatment that I suggested."... Naturally, we didn't wait for the day to come but did what was necessary. But then the situation changed quickly—his pulse grew weaker, his breathing more rapid. And we had to experience how this life was gradually extinguished.... He went as though it were the obvious thing to do. It seemed to me as though the dice had been thrown for a last decision. When they fell, there was no struggle, no attempt to remain upon the earth any longer. He gazed calmly into the space before him for a time, said a couple of tender words to me, consciously closed his eyes and folded his hands. (*Nachrichtenblatt*, 1925)

Guenther Wachsmuth remembered, "The last moments of Rudolf Steiner's life upon the earth were free of any struggle with his body, free of any of the uncertainty that often accompanies death; his visage spoke of peacefulness, grace, inner certainty, and spiritual vision. He folded his hands upon his breast, his eyes, light-filled and strong, gazed into those worlds with which he united himself. When his last breath came, he closed his own eyes, an act that did not fill the room with the sense of something ending, but with that of a lofty spiritual deed" (Wachsmuth).

Marie Steiner, who had been called back from Stuttgart, arrived later that morning. At about 12:00 p.m., accompanied by Mieta Waller-Pyle, she entered the studio, where the other members of the council were gathered around Steiner's body. After a moment of silence, she asked to have

Emil Leinhas, who had accompanied her from Stuttgart, brought in. "She sat weeping, bowed down with pain at Rudolf Steiner's deathbed, holding his hand in hers. She held it out to me saying, 'It is still warm.'" Later, Marie Steiner discovered Rudolf Steiner's testament from February 19, 1907, which gave her the legal right to act in his name. "Whatever she does shall be done in my name." And she also read the words: "She shall view my death as something ordained by higher powers and not as anything mysterious. The events do have a connection, even if one is not yet able to understand it" (262).

EPILOGUE

A personal experience is the starting point for what I would like to say in conclusion. In the summer of 1953, I first visited Rudolf Steiner's studio. At that time, it was still very simply furnished. On a small podium, covered with a veil, lay the death mask. At that time I had already seen many pictures and sculptures of Rudolf Steiner and had heard stories about him that had called forth in me the image of a great man. When I raised the veil from the death mask, I discovered an elegant, finely formed head; everything about it appeared to me to be fragile and the lines of the faces spoke of tragic renouncement. All the majesty was transformed in the encounter with this last cast of Rudolf Steiner into pure spiritual intensity. The greatness became inner radiant passion; the majesty, subtlety. The indications of an impressive higher being that had been present in the sculptures and pictures paled before the death mask.

Over the years—I visited the studio regularly—I came to believe that one can better appreciate Rudolf Steiner's accomplishments when one takes into account the unpretentious circumstances of his early life and the fragility of his childhood constitution. In the 1876 picture of Rudolf Steiner's class at the Vienesse high school, one can find the fifteen-year-old Steiner on the right side of the second row from the back. Examining the other students, they seem larger and more fully formed. They are a bunch of sturdy young men gathered around their teacher Laurenz Jelinek. Compared to them, Rudolf Steiner seems slender, younger, and more delicate. Richard Specht recalled Steiner in the late 1880s: "Physically, he was so weak that he collapsed on the ground whenever one of us boys would throw himself upon him in a moment of love or exuberance" (*Neues Wiener Journal*, April 26, 1925).

Specht added, however, "Spiritually, he was full of energy." It was this spiritual energy that enabled him first to create his own cultural/spiritual world out of the simplest of beginnings, to struggle through the obstacles and hindrances, and finally to overcome his physical frailty. He wrote to his parents from Weimar, where he was often ill, struggling with coughs and headaches, that the climate there had "toughened" him, and added, "I think that when I return to Austria, this toughening will serve me well" (39). He worked to transform his own bodily constitution. Later, he was observed sitting for hours at a time at work carving the capitals in the first Goetheanum, working with the large gouges and heavy mallet, a task that tired others after half an hour or so. His once-high voice became a deep bass or baritone during his years in Berlin.

William Zeylmans recalled him in the 1920s:

> Rudolf Steiner is of average size, slender, almost delicate. This is quite apparent when one listens to him, because his voice is heavy and strong. It is a voice, the timbre of which is unforgettable. There is something in it that touches one deeply, as though the speaker bore with him the entire sorrow of humanity. Sometimes it is warm and embracing. The listening soul feels itself to be borne aloft into worlds inaccessible for normal consciousness. Then his voice grows more powerful. Words echo over the earth like the tones of a trumpet. Then again one hears tones of a deep inner gentleness, which moves the listener's soul and gives him the feeling that he is awakening into an inner world, radiant with hidden light. (Zeylmans)

His personal life was Spartan and humble. He preferred to live in small rooms; a narrow bed, a simple table and chair, and a rough bookshelf were enough. In conversation, he made his partner feel at ease; he was not a man of dramatic gestures. As did Nietzsche, he viewed politeness to be one of the four cardinal virtues that were most needed by modern civilization (221).

Just as out of the finely sculpted, extremely mobile, comparatively small body a powerful, musical voice rang forth, so blossomed out of what were originally rather narrow, limited surroundings first the philosophical, scholarly work, then the completely new artistic work, and finally the practical cultural work. Out of the impulses that became apparent to him in his struggles with the act of knowing grew first the elementary forms of a new approach to architecture, sculpture, literature and movement, and then, like a great, many-branched tree, the insights into education and medicine, for the renewal of agriculture and our understanding of social life.

The fire of youthful vigor and a constantly renewed source of enthusiasm remained with him as he aged. His entire life, right up to the last days, stood in the sign of a new beginning.

Epilogue

All these Rudolf Steiner's initiatives met resistance, opposition, and misunderstanding. Already in 1892, he had been designated by Ferdinand Tonnies as a Nietzsche fool, who had fallen prey to the aging philosopher's moral judgments. Later, Arthur Drews wrote that Anthroposophy was an indigestible mixture of willfulness, superstition and fantasy. From 1920 to 1923, hardly a week would pass in which Steiner was not the subject of a public attack. After the burning of the first Goetheanum, the eminent Karl Barth wrote, "It is with satisfaction that we have received news of the Goetheanum burning. [Emmanuel] Hirsch stated, 'The Lord has finally reached out his arm'" (Barth).

However, despite the enmity and the difficulties he had with those closest to him, and despite all the disappointments and setbacks, Steiner continued on his path without weakening. Yet it was not an inflexible "in spite of" that led him onward, but the ideas, the new impulses, the richness of his knowledge and his love of taking action. In 1892, in filling out the well-known questionnaire, he answered the question "Which vocation seems to you to be the best?" with the words: *Any vocation in which one's entire energy will be used to its fullest.* Steiner was always active, embracing new tasks, never exhausted spiritually. Certainly, following his widespread engagement in the European public arena after World War I, he began to focus his activities on his work with more intimate circles, to concentrate himself specifically on his anthroposophic work. Anthroposophy became again the middle point, what had arisen out of the anthroposophic work—the arts, education and medicine—was deepened, and impulses for a new approach to agriculture and curative education were given. The Anthroposophical Society was reformed and founded anew, and the sacred mysteries were renewed. From this perspective, Rudolf Steiner's creative activity climaxed in the years 1923 and 1924.

He was there for others to the point of complete exhaustion. And even as he lay ailing, he drew the forces to continue his work from an increasingly frail body that was practically devoured by the inner flames. He continued his work until the very last days of his life. In the last act of the fourth mystery play stands:

> His last thoughts were of the work
> to which he had in love dedicated himself.

THE COLLECTED WORKS OF RUDOLF STEINER

The German Edition of Rudolf Steiner's Collected Works (the *Gesamtausgabe* [GA] published by Rudolf Steiner Verlag, Dornach, Switzerland) presently runs to over 354 titles, organized either by type of work (written or spoken), chronology, audience (public or other), or subject (education, art, etc.). For ease of comparison, the Collected Works in English [CW] follows the German organization exactly. A complete listing of the CWs follows. Where possible, the current English titles are used; others are listed with approximate translations of the German titles. Other than in the case of the books published in his lifetime, Rudolf Steiner rarely supplied titles. Many of the German books have been published under several titles in English over the years.

For ease of identification and to avoid confusion, we suggest that readers looking for a title should do so by CW number. Because the work of creating the Collected Works of Rudolf Steiner is an ongoing process, new titles are published every year. To find out what titles in the Collected Works are currently in print, please check our website at www.steinerbooks.org, or write to SteinerBooks 610 Main Street, Great Barrington, MA 01230.

Published Written Works

CW 1	Nature's Open Secret: Introductions to Goethe's Scientific Writings
CW 2	Goethe's Theory of Knowledge: An Outline of the Epistemology of His Worldview
CW 3	Truth and Science
CW 4	Intuitive Thinking as a Spiritual Path: A Philosophy of Freedom
CW 4a	Documents to *The Philosophy of Freedom*
CW 5	Friedrich Nietzsche: Fighter for Freedom
CW 6	Goethe's Worldview
CW 6a	Now in CW 30

CW 7	Mystics after Modernism: Discovering the Seeds of a New Science in the Renaissance
CW 8	Christianity as Mystical Fact and the Mysteries of Antiquity
CW 9	Theosophy: An Introduction to the Spiritual Processes in Human Life and in the Cosmos
CW 10	How to Know Higher Worlds: A Modern Path of Initiation
CW 11	Cosmic Memory: The Story of Atlantis, Lemuria, and the Division of the Sexes
CW 12	The Stages of Higher Knowledge: Imagination, Inspiration, Intuition
CW 13	An Outline of Esoteric Science
CW 14	Four Mystery Dramas
CW 15	The Spiritual Guidance of the Individual and Humanity: Some Results of Spiritual-Scientific Research into Human History and Development
CW 16/17	A Way of Self-Knowledge: The Threshold of the Spiritual World
CW 18	The Riddles of Philosophy in Their History, Presented as an Outline
CW 19	Contained in CW 24
CW 20	The Riddles of the Human Being: Articulated and Unarticulated in the Thinking, Views and Opinions of a Series of German and Austrian Personalities
CW 21	The Riddles of the Soul
CW 22	Goethe's Spiritual Nature And Its Revelation In *Faust* and through the "Fairy Tale of the Snake and the Lily"
CW 23	The Central Points of the Social Question in the Necessities of Life in the Present and the Future
CW 24	Essays Concerning the Threefold Division of the Social Organism and the Period 1915–1921
CW 25	Cosmology, Religion, and Philosophy
CW 26	Anthroposophical Leading Thoughts
CW 27	Fundamentals for Expansion of the Art of Healing according to Spiritual-Scientific Insights
CW 28	Autobiography: Chapters in the Course of My Life, 1861–1907

Essay Collections

CW 29	Collected Essays on Dramaturgy, 1889–1900
CW 30	Methodical Foundations of Anthroposophy: Collected Essays on Philosophy, Natural Science, Aesthetics and Psychology, 1884–1901
CW 31	Collected Essays on Culture and Current Events, 1887–1901
CW 32	Collected Essays on Literature, 1884–1902

The Collected Works of Rudolf Steiner

CW 33   Biographies and Biographical Sketches, 1894–1905

CW 34   Lucifer-Gnosis: Foundational Essays on Anthroposophy and Reports from the Periodicals *Luzifer* and *Lucifer-Gnosis*, 1903–1908

CW 35   Philosophy and Anthroposophy: Collected Essays, 1904–1923

CW 36   The Goetheanum-Idea in the Middle of the Cultural Crisis of the Present: Collected Essays from the Periodical *Das Goetheanum*, 1921–1925

CW 37   Now in CWs 260a and 251

Written Works Released Posthumously

CW 38   Letters, vol. 1: 1881–1890

CW 39   Letters, vol. 2: 1890–1925

CW 40   Truth-Wrought-Words

CW 40a Sayings, Poems and Mantras; Supplementary Volume

CW 42   Now in CWs 264–266

CW 43   Stage Adaptations

CW 44   On the Four Mystery Dramas: Sketches, Fragments, and Supplementary Material on the Four Mystery Dramas

CW 45   Anthroposophy (A Fragment)

Public Lectures

CW 51   On Philosophy, History and Literature

CW 52   Spiritual Teachings Concerning the Soul and Observation of the World

CW 53   The Origin and Goal of the Human Being

CW 54   The Riddles of the World and Anthroposophy

CW 55   Supersensible Knowledge

CW 56   Knowledge of the Soul and of the Spirit

CW 57   Where and How Does One Find the Spirit?

CW 58   Transforming the Soul, vol. 1

CW 59   Transforming the Soul, vol. 2

CW 60   The Answers of Spiritual Science to the Biggest Questions of Existence

CW 61   Human History in the Light of Spiritual Research

CW 62   Results of Spiritual Research

CW 63   Spiritual Science as a Treasure for Life

CW 64   Out of Destiny-Burdened Times

CW 65   Out of Central European Spiritual Life

CW 66	Spirit and Matter, Life and Death
CW 67	The Eternal in the Human Soul: Immortality and Freedom
CW 68	Public lectures in various cities, 1906–1918
CW 69	Public lectures in various cities, 1906–1918
CW 70	Public lectures in various cities, 1906–1918
CW 71	Public lectures in various cities, 1906–1918
CW 72	Freedom—Immortality—Social Life
CW 73	The Supplementing of the Modern Sciences through Anthroposophy
CW 73a	Specialized Fields of Knowledge and Anthroposophy
CW 74	The Philosophy of Thomas Aquinas
CW 75	Public lectures in various cities, 1906-1918
CW 76	The Fructifying Effect of Anthroposophy on Specialized Fields
CW 77a	The Task of Anthroposophy in Relation to Science and Life: The Darmstadt College Course
CW 77b	Art and Anthroposophy. The Goetheanum-Impulse
CW 78	Anthroposophy: Its Roots of Knowledge and Fruits for Life
CW 79	The Reality of the Higher Worlds
CW 80	Public lectures in various cities, 1922
CW 81	Renewal Impulses for Culture and Science—Berlin College Course
CW 82	So that the Human Being Can Become a Complete Human Being
CW 83	The Tension between East and West
CW 84	What Did the Goetheanum Intend and What Should Anthroposophy Do?

Private Lectures to Members of the Anthroposophical Society

CW 88	Concerning the Astral World and Devachan
CW 89	Consciousness, Life, Form: Fundamental Principles of a Spiritual-Scientific Cosmology
CW 90	Participant Notes from the Lectures during the Years 1903-1905
CW 91	Participant Notes from the Lectures during the Years 1903-1905
CW 92	The Esoteric Truths of Ancient Myths and Sagas
CW 93	The Temple Legend: Freemasonry and Related Occult Movements: From the Contents of the Esoteric School
CW 93a	Fundamentals of Esotericism
CW 94	Cosmogony. Popular Esotericism. The Gospel of John. The Theosophy in the Gospel of John

CW 95	Founding a Science of the Spirit
CW 96	Origin-Impulses of Spiritual Science: Christian Esotericism in the Light of New Spirit-Knowledge
CW 97	The Christian Mystery
CW 98	Nature Beings and Spirit Beings—Their Effects in Our Visible World
CW 99	Rosicrucian Wisdom: An Introduction
CW 100	Human Development and Christ-Knowledge
CW 101	Myths and Legends: Esoteric Signs and Symbols
CW 102	The Working into Human Beings by Spiritual Beings
CW 103	The Gospel of St. John
CW 104	The Apocalypse of St. John
CW 104a	From the Picture-Script of the Apocalypse of John
CW 105	Universe, Earth and Man
CW 106	Egyptian Myths and Mysteries
CW 107	The Being of Man and His Future Evolution
CW 108	Answering the Questions of Life and the World through Anthroposophy
CW 109	The Principle of Spiritual Economy: In Connection with Questions of Reincarnation
CW 110	The Spiritual Hierarchies and the Physical World: Zodiac, Planets & Cosmos
CW 111	Contained in 109
CW 112	The Gospel of St. John and Its Relation to the Other Gospels
CW 113	The East in the Light of the West. The Children of Lucifer and the Brothers of Christ
CW 114	According to Luke: The Gospel of Compassion and Love Revealed
CW 115	A Psychology of Body, Soul & Spirit: Anthroposophy, Psychosophy, Pneumatosophy
CW 116	The Christ Impulse and the Development of "I"-Consciousness
CW 117	Deeper Secrets in Human History: In the Light of the Gospel of St. Matthew
CW 118	The Event of the Christ-Appearance in the Etheric World
CW 119	Macrocosm and Microcosm
CW 120	Manifestations of Karma
CW 121	The Mission of the Folk-Souls in relation to Teutonic Mythology
CW 122	Genesis: Secrets of Creation
CW 123	According to Matthew: The Gospel of Christ's Humanity
CW 124	Background to the Gospel of St. Mark

CW 125	Paths and Goals of the Spiritual Human Being: Life Questions in the Light of Spiritual Science
CW 126	Occult History: Historical Personalities and Events in the Light of Spiritual Science
CW 127	The Mission of the New Spiritual Revelation. The Christ-Event as the Middle-Point of Earth Evolution
CW 128	An Occult Physiology
CW 129	Wonders of the World, Trials of the Soul, and Revelations of the Spirit
CW 130	Esoteric Christianity and the Mission of Christian Rosenkreutz
CW 131	From Jesus to Christ
CW 132	Inner Experiences of Evolution
CW 133	Earthly and Cosmic Man
CW 134	The World of the Senses and the World of the Spirit
CW 135	Reincarnation and Karma: Two Fundamental Truths of Human Existence
CW 136	Spiritual Beings in the Heavenly Bodies and in the Kingdoms of Nature
CW 137	Man in the Light of Occultism, Theosophy, and Philosophy
CW 138	Initiation, Eternity, and the Passing Moment
CW 139	The Gospel of St. Mark
CW 140	Life between Death and Rebirth
CW 141	Life between Death and New Birth in Relationship to Cosmic Facts
CW 142	The Bhagavad Gita and the West: The Esoteric Significance of the Bhagavad Gita and Its Relation to the Epistles of Paul
CW 143	Experiences of the Supersensible. Three Paths of the Soul to Christ
CW 144	The Mysteries of the East and of Christianity
CW 145	The Effects of Esoteric Development
CW 146	The Bhagavad Gita and the West: The Esoteric Significance of the Bhagavad Gita and Its Relation to the Epistles of Paul
CW 147	The Secrets of the Threshold
CW 148	The Fifth Gospel: From the Akashic Record
CW 149	Christ and the Spiritual World: And the Search for the Holy Grail
CW 150	The World of the Spirit and Its Extension into Physical Existence; The Influence of the Dead in the World of the Living
CW 151	Human and Cosmic Thought
CW 152	Approaching the Mystery of Golgotha
CW 153	The Inner Nature of Man and Our Life between Death and Rebirth
CW 154	The Presence of the Dead on the Spiritual Path
CW 155	Christ and the Human Soul

CW 156	Inner Reading and Inner Hearing: And How to Achieve Existence in the World of Ideas
CW 157	The Destinies of Individuals and of Nations
CW 157a	The Formation of Destiny and the Life after Death
CW 158	The Connection Between the Human Being and the Elemental World: Kalevala, Olaf Asteson, the Russian People, the World as the Result of the Influences of Equilibrium
CW 159	The Mystery of Death: The Nature and Significance of Central Europe and the European Folk Spirits
CW 160	In CW 159
CW 161	Paths of Spiritual Knowledge and the Renewal of the Artistic Worldview
CW 162	Questions of Art and Life in Light of Spiritual Science
CW 163	Chance, Providence, and Necessity
CW 164	The Value of Thinking for a Knowledge That Satisfies the Human Being: The Relationship of Spiritual Science to Natural Science
CW 165	The Spiritual Unification of Humanity through the Christ-Impulse
CW 166	Necessity and Freedom
CW 167	The Present and the Past in the Human Spirit
CW 168	The Connection between the Living and the Dead
CW 169	World being and Selfhood
CW 170	The Riddle of Humanity: The Spiritual Background of Human History
CW 171	The Inner Development of Man
CW 172	The Karma of the Vocation
CW 173	The Karma of Untruthfulness: Secret Societies, the Media, and Preparations for the Great War, vol. 1
CW 174	The Karma of Untruthfulness: Secret Societies, the Media, and Preparations for the Great War, vol. 2
CW 174a	Central Europe between East and West: Cosmic and Human History, vol. 6
CW 174b	The Spiritual Background of the First World War: Cosmic and Human History, vol. 7
CW 175	Cosmic and Human Metamorphosis
CW 176	Aspects of Human Evolution / The Karma of Materialism
CW 177	The Fall of the Spirits of Darkness
CW 178	Secret Brotherhoods: And the Mystery of the Human Double
CW 179	The Influence of the Dead on Destiny
CW 180	Mystery Truths and Christmas Impulses. Ancient Myths and their Meaning. Spiritual Beings and Their Effects, vol. 4

CW 181	Earthly Death and Cosmic Life
CW 182	Death as Metamorphosis of Life: Including "What Does the Angel Do in our Astral Body?" & "How Do I Find Christ?"
CW 183	The Science of the Development of the Human Being
CW 184	The Polarity of Duration and Development in Human Life: The Cosmic Pre-History of Humanity
CW 185	From Symptom to Reality in Modern History
CW 185a	Historical-Developmental Foundations for Forming a Social Judgment
CW 186	The Challenge of the Times
CW 187	How Can Mankind Find the Christ Again? The Threefold Shadow Existence of Our Time and the New Light of Christ
CW 188	Goetheanism, a Transformation Impulse and Resurrection Thought: Science of the Human Being and Science of Sociology
CW 189	The Social Question as a Question of Consciousness: The Spiritual Background of the Social Question, vol. 1
CW 190	Impulses of the Past and the Future in Social Occurrences. The Spiritual Background of the Social Question, vol. 2
CW 191	Social Understanding from Spiritual-Scientific Cognition: The Spiritual Background of the Social Question, vol. 3
CW 192	Spiritual-Scientific Treatment of Social and Pedagogical Questions
CW 193	The Esoteric Aspect of the Social Question: The Individual and Society
CW 194	The Mission of Michael: The Revelation of the Actual Mysteries of the Human Being
CW 195	Cosmic New Year: Thoughts for New Year 1920
CW 196	What Is Necessary in These Urgent Times
CW 197	Polarities in the Evolution of Mankind: West and East, Materialism and Mysticism, Knowledge and Belief
CW 198	Healing Factors for the Social Organism
CW 199	Spiritual Science as a Foundation for Social Forms
CW 200	The New Spirituality: And the Christ Experience of the Twentieth Century
CW 201	Mystery of the Universe: The Human Being, Model of Creation
CW 202	The Bridge Between Universal Spirituality and the Physical Constitution of Man
CW 203	The Responsibility of Human Beings for the Development of the World through their Spiritual Connection with the Planet Earth and the World of the Stars: The Human Being in Relationship with the Cosmo,: 3
CW 204	Materialism and the Task of Anthroposophy

CW 205   Human Development, World Soul, and World Spirit. Part One: The Human Being as a Being of Body and Soul in Relationship to the World: The Human Being in Relationship with the Cosmos, 5

CW 206   Human Development, World-Soul, and World-Spirit. Part Two: The Human Being as a Spiritual Being in the Process of Historical Development: The Human Being in Relationship with the Cosmos: 6

CW 207   Cosmosophy: Cosmic Influences on the Human Being, vol. 1

CW 208   Cosmosophy: Cosmic Influences on the Human Being, vol. 2

CW 209   Nordic and Central European Spiritual Impulses: The Festival of the Appearance of Christ: The Human Being in Relationship with the Cosmos, 9

CW 210   Old and New Methods of Initiation

CW 211   The Sun Mystery and the Mystery of Death and Resurrection: Exoteric and Esoteric Christianity

CW 212   The Change in the Path to Supersensible Knowledge

CW 213   Human Questions and World Answers

CW 214   The Mystery of the Trinity: The Human Being in Relationship to the Spiritual World in the Course of Time

CW 215   Philosophy, Cosmology, and Religion

CW 216   The Fundamental Impulses of the World-Historical Development of Humanity

CW 217   Becoming the Archangel Michael's Companions: Rudolf Steiner's Challenge to the Younger Generation

CW 217a Youth and the Etheric Heart: Rudolf Steiner Speaks to the Younger Generation

CW 218   Spiritual Connections in the Forming of the Human Organism

CW 219   Man and the World of the Stars: The Spiritual Communion of Mankind

CW 220   Living Knowledge of Nature: Intellectual Fall and Spiritual Redemption

CW 221   Earthly Knowledge and Heavenly Wisdom

CW 222   The Driving Force of Spiritual Powers in World History

CW 223   The Cycle of the Year as Breathing Process of the Earth

CW 224   The Human Soul and its Connection with Divine-Spiritual Individualities: The Internalization of the Festivals of the Year

CW 225   What Is Anthroposophy? Three Spiritual Perspectives on Self-Knowledge

CW 226   Human Being, Human Destiny, and World Development

CW 227   The Evolution of Consciousness: As Revealed through Initiation Knowledge

CW 228   Man in the Past, Present, and Future: The Sun-Initiation of the Druid Priest and His Moon-Science

CW 229 The Experiencing of the Course of the Year in Four Cosmic Imaginations

CW 230 Harmony of the Creative Word: The Human Being & the Elemental, Animal, Plant, and Mineral Kingdoms

CW 231 At Home in the Universe: Exploring Our Suprasensory Nature

CW 232 Mystery Knowledge and Mystery Centres

CW 233 World History Illuminated by Anthroposophy and as the Foundation for Knowledge of the Human Spirit

CW 233a Mystery Sites of the Middle Ages: Rosicrucianism and the Modern Initiation-Principle. The Festival of Easter as Part of the History of the Mysteries of Humanity

CW 234 Anthroposophy and the Inner Life: An Esoteric Introduction

CW 235 Karmic Relationships: Esoteric Studies, vol. 1

CW 236 Karmic Relationships: Esoteric Studies, vol. 2

CW 237 Karmic Relationships: Esoteric Studies, vol. 3

CW 238 Karmic Relationships: Esoteric Studies, vol. 4

CW 239 Karmic Relationships: Esoteric Studies, vol. 5

CW 240 Karmic Relationships: Esoteric Studies, vol. 6

CW 243 True and False Paths in Spiritual Investigation

CW 245 Guidance in Esoteric Training: From the Esoteric School

Writings and Lectures on the History of the Anthroposophical Movement and the Anthroposophical Society

CW 250 The Building-up of the Anthroposophical Society: From the Beginning to the Outbreak of World War I

CW 251 The History of the Goetheanum Building Association

CW 252 Life in the Anthroposophical Society from World War I to the Burning of the First Goetheanum

CW 253 Community Life, Inner Development, Sexuality, and the Spiritual Teacher: Ethical and Spiritual Dimensions of the Crisis in the Anthroposophical Society

CW 254 The Occult Movement in the Nineteenth Century

CW 255 Rudolf Steiner during World War I

CW 255a Anthroposophy and the Reformation of Society: On the History of the Threefold Movement

CW 255b Anthroposophy and Its Opponents, 1919–1921

CW 256 How Can the Anthroposophical Movement Be Financed?

CW 256a Futurum, Inc. / International Laboratories, Inc.

CW 256b The Coming Day, Inc.

CW 257 Awakening to Community

CW 258 The Anthroposophic Movement

CW 259 The Year of Destiny 1923 in the History of the Anthroposophical Society: From the Burning of the Goetheanum to the Christmas Conference

CW 260 The Christmas Conference: For the Foundation of the General Anthroposophical Society, 1923/1924

CW 260a The Foundation Stone / The Life, Nature & Cultivation of Anthroposophy

CW 261 Our Dead: Memorial, Funeral, and Cremation Addresses

CW 262 Correspondence and Documents 1901–1925

CW 263/1 Rudolf Steiner and Edith Maryon: Correspondence: Letters, Verses, Sketches, 1912–1924

CW 264 From the History and Contents of the First Section of the Esoteric School 1904–1914

CW 265 Freemasonry and Ritual Work: The Misraim Service: Texts and Documents from the Cognitive-Ritual Section of the Esoteric School 1904–1919

CW 266/1 Esoteric Lessons, 1904–1909: From the Esoteric School, vol. 1

CW 266/2 Esoteric Lessons, 1910–1912: From the Esoteric School, vol. 2

CW 266/3 Esoteric Lessons, 1913–1923: From the Esoteric School, vol. 3

CW 267 Soul-Exercises: vol. 1: Exercises with Word and Image Meditations for the Methodological Development of Higher Powers of Knowledge, 1904–1924

CW 268 Soul-Exercises: vol. 2: Mantric Verses, 1903–1925

CW 269 Ritual Texts for the Celebration of the Free Christian Religious Instruction: The Collected Verses for Teachers and Students of the Waldorf School

CW 270 Esoteric Instructions for the First Class of the School for Spiritual Science at the Goetheanum 1924, 4 vols.

Lectures on Art

CW 271 Art and Knowledge of Art: Foundations of a New Aesthetic

CW 272 Spiritual-Scientific Commentary on Goethe's "Faust" in Two Volumes. vol. 1: Faust, the Striving Human Being

CW 273 Spiritual-Scientific Commentary on Goethe's "Faust" in Two Volumes. vol. 2: The Faust-Problem

CW 274 Addresses for the Christmas Plays from the Old Folk Traditions

CW 275   Art as Seen in the Light of Mystery Wisdom
CW 276   The Arts and Their Mission
CW 277   Eurythmy: The Revelation of the Speaking Soul
CW 277a The Origin and Development of Eurythmy
CW 278   Eurythmy as Visible Song
CW 279   Eurythmy as Visible Speech
CW 280   Creative Speech: The Formative Process of the Spoken Word
CW 281   The Art of Recitation and Declamation
CW 282   Speech and Drama
CW 283   The Nature of Things Musical and the Experience of Tone in the Human Being
CW 284/285 Rosicrucianism Renewed: The Unity of Art, Science & Religion: The Theosophical Congress of Whitsun 1907
CW 286   Architecture as a Synthesis of the Arts
CW 287   The Building at Dornach as a Symbol of Historical Becoming and an Artistic Transformation Impulse
CW 288   Style-Forms in the Living Organic
CW 289   The Building-Idea of the Goetheanum: Lectures with Slides from 1920–1921
CW 290   The Building-Idea of the Goetheanum: Lectures with Slides from 1920–1921
CW 291   Colour
CW 291a Knowledge of Colors: Supplementary Volume to "The Nature of Colors"
CW 292   Art History as Image of Inner Spiritual Impulses

Lectures on Education

CW 293   The Foundations of Human Experience
CW 294   Practical Advice to Teachers
CW 295   Discussions with Teachers
CW 296   Education as a Force for Social Change
CW 297   The Spirit of the Waldorf School
CW 297a Education for Life: Self-Education and the Practice of Pedagogy
CW 298   Rudolf Steiner in the Waldorf School
CW 299   The Genius of Language
CW 300a/b Faculty Meetings with Rudolf Steiner: vol. 1: 1919–1922
CW 300b/c Faculty Meetings with Rudolf Steiner: vol. 2: 1922–1924

CW 301   The Renewal of Education
CW 302   Education for Adolescents
CW 302a Balance in Teaching
CW 303   Soul Economy
CW 304   Waldorf Education and Anthroposophy 1
CW 304a Waldorf Education and Anthroposophy 2
CW 305   The Spiritual Ground of Education
CW 306   The Child's Changing Consciousness
CW 307   A Modern Art of Education
CW 308   The Essentials of Education
CW 309   The Roots of Education
CW 310   Human Values in Education
CW 311   The Kingdom of Childhood

Lectures on Medicine

CW 312   Introducing Anthroposophical Medicine
CW 313   Spiritual-Scientific Viewpoints on Therapy
CW 314   Physiology and Therapy Based on Spiritual Science
CW 315   Eurythmy Therapy
CW 316   Meditative Observations and Instructions for a Deepening of the Art of Healing
CW 317   Education for Special Needs: The Curative Education Course
CW 318   Broken Vessels: The Spiritual Structure of Human Frailty
CW 319   The Healing Process: Spirit, Nature & Our Bodies

Lectures on Natural Science

CW 320   The Light Course: Toward the Development of a New Physics
CW 321   Spiritual-Scientific Impulses for the Development of Physics 2: The Second Natural-Scientific Course: Warmth at the Border of Positive and Negative Materiality
CW 322   The Boundaries of Natural Science
CW 323   The Relationship of the Various Natural-Scientific Fields to Astronomy
CW 324   Nature Observation, Mathematics, and Scientific Experimentation and Results from the Viewpoint of Anthroposophy
CW 324a The Fourth Dimension: Sacred Geometry, Alchemy, and Mathematics

CW 325 Natural Science and the World-Historical Development of Humanity since Ancient Times

CW 326 The Origins of Natural Science

CW 327 Agriculture Course: The Birth of the Biodynamic Method

Lectures on Society

CW 328 The Social Question

CW 329 The Liberation of the Human Being as the Foundation for a New Social Form

CW 330 The Renewal of the Social Organism

CW 331 Work Council and Socialization

CW 332 The Alliance for Threefolding and the Total Reform of Society: The Council on Culture and the Liberation of the Spiritual Life

CW 332a The Social Future

CW 333 Freedom of Thought and Societal Forces: Implementing the Demands of Modern Society

CW 334 Social Issues: Meditative Thinking & the Threefold Social Order

CW 335 The Crisis of the Present and the Path to Healthy Thinking

CW 336 The Great Questions of the Times and Anthroposophic Spiritual Knowledge

CW 337a Social Ideas, Social Reality, Social Practice, vol. 1: Question-and-Answer Evenings and Study Evenings of the Alliance for the Threefold Social Organism in Stuttgart, 1919–1920

CW 337b Social Ideas, Social Realities, Social Practice, vol. 2: Discussion Evenings of the Swiss Alliance for the Threefold Social Organism

CW 338 How to Communicate the Idea of Threefolding? Two Training Courses for Speakers and Activists

CW 339 Anthroposophy, Threefold Social Organism, and the Art of Public Speaking

CW 340/341 Rethinking Economics: World Economy

Lectures for Priests of The Christian Community

CW 342 First Steps in Christian Religious Renewal: Preparing the Ground for The Christian Community

CW 343 Lectures and Courses on Christian Religious Work, vol. 2: Spiritual Knowledge—Religious Feeling—Cultic Doing

CW 344   Lectures and Courses on Christian Religious Work, vol. 3: Lectures at the Founding of The Christian Community

CW 345   Lectures and Courses on Christian Religious Work, vol. 4: Concerning the Nature of the Working Word

CW 346   The Book of Revelation: And the Work of the Priest

LECTURES TO WORKERS AT THE GOETHEANUM

CW 347   From Crystals to Crocodiles . . . : Answers to Questions

CW 348   Bees / From Comets to Cocaine . . . : Answers to Questions

CW 349   From Limestone to Lucifer . . . : Answers to Questions

CW 350   From Mammoths to Mediums . . . : Answers to Questions

CW 351   The Human Being and the World. The Influence of the Spirit in Nature. On the Nature of Bees

CW 352   From Elephants to Einstein . . . : Answers to Questions

CW 353   From Beetroot to Buddhism . . . : Answers to Questions

CW 354   From Sunspots to Strawberries . . . : Answers to Questions

BIBLIOGRAPHY

Sources indicated in the text with Arabic numerals in parentheses refer to the CW number of Rudolf Steiner's works below. Quotations from Rudolf Steiner, Autobiography, are from the 2006 edition by SteinerBooks. Where page numbers are indicated in parentheses, quotations were taken from the most recent English edition. All other quotations were translated from the German texts used by the author.

Sources indicated in the text as (b)

Nachrichten der Rudolf Steiner Nachlassverwaltung. Heft 7–28 (1962–1969) [News concerning the Rudolf Steiner Estate], renamed as of 1970 as Beiträge zur Rudolf Steiner Gesamtausgabe [Contributions on Rudolf Steiner's collected works].

Sources not included in Rudolf Steiner's Collected works:

Published first editions of Rudolf Steiner's written works, as well as correspondence, lectures, and talks discussion notes.

Architektur, Plastik und Malerei des Ersten Goetheanum [Architecture, sculpture and painting in the first Goetheanum]. Three lectures, Jan. 23, 24, 25, 1920, Dornach.

Aufbaugedanken und Gesinnungsbildung, gesprochen zu den Generalversammlungen des Vereins des Goetheanum, Freie Hochschule für Geisteswissenschaft [Thoughts on construction and the building of attitude spoken at the general meeting of the Goetheanum Association].

Correspondence II, 1892–1902.

Christian Morgenstern. *Der Sieg des Lebens über den Tod* [Victory of life over death].

Der Verfall des menschlichen Intellekts und das Sichwehren des Menschen gegen die Spiritualität [The fall of the human intellect and the resistance of the human being to spirituality]. Lecture of May 23, 1922 in Stuttgart.

Die verborgenen Seiten des Menschendaseins und der Christus Impuls [The hidden side of human existence and the Christ impulse]. Lecture on November 5, 1922, in The Hague.

Die Hetze gegen das Goetheanum [The attacks against the Goetheanum]. Lecture on June 5, 1920, together with Roman Boos.

Drei Gegenwartsreden: Fragen der Seele und Fragen des Lebens. Wer darf gegen den Untergang des Abendlandes reden? Die grossen Aufgaben von heute im Geistesleben, Rechtsleben und Wirtschaftsleben [Three talks on the present time: questions about the soul and questions of life; who may speak against the decline of the west; the great tasks today in the spiritual life, legal life and economic life: Lectures, June 15, July 29, and Sept. 20, 1920, Stuttgart.

Goethes geheime Offenbarung in seinem « Marchen von der grünen Schlange und der schönen Lilie » [Goethe's secret revelation in his *Fairytale of the Green Snake and the Beautiful Lily*]. Collected lectures from 1904, 1905, 1908 und 1909 and an essay from 1918: «Goethes Geistesart in ihrer Offenbarung durch sein "Marchen von der grünen Schlange und der Lilie" [The revelation of Goethe's spirit through his fairytale of the green snake and the lily].

Östliche und westliche Kultur in geistiger Beleuchtung [Eastern and Western culture in light of the spirit]. Lectures on September 23, 24, and 25, 1921.

Rudolf Steiner und die Zivilisationsaufgaben der Anthroposophie. Ein Rückblick auf das Jahr 1923. Ansprachen und Fragenbeantwortungen [Rudolf Steiner and the tasks of anthroposophy for civilization: Looking back at the year 1923. Talks and answers to questions].

Schicksalszeichen auf dem Entwicklungswege der Anthroposophischen Gesellschaft. Auszüge aus vor Mitgliedern gehaltenen Ansprachen (1913/14) [Signs of destiny and the paths of development of the Anthroposophical Society. Excerpts from lectures given by members].

Bibliography

OFFICIAL PUBLICATIONS

Publications of the Johannes Building Association and the Goetheanum Association; The Association for Threefolding ; The Society of *Der Kommende Tag* [The Coming Day] Stuttgart; and Futurum.

Members Newsletters and Circulars

Mitteilungen für die Mitglieder der Deutschen Sektion der Theosophischen Gesellschaft [News for members of the German section of the Theosophical Society] (1905–Jan. 1913; nos.1–15).

Mitteilungen für die Mitglieder der Anthroposophischen Gesellschaft [News for members of the Anthroposophical Society (Theosophical Society)], 1913–June 1914 (nos 1-7).

Rundschreiben des Bundes für Dreigliederung [Circular of the Association for Threefolding], Stuttgart April 1919–July 1920.

Mitteilungsblatt des Bundes für Dreigliederung des sozialen Organismus [Newsletter of the Association for the Threefold Social Organism], Stuttgart June 1919–circa February 1920 (nos. 1-9).

Mitteilungen des Zentralvorstandes der Anthroposophischen Gesellschaft [News from the central executive council], (later, News), published by the Executive Council of the Anthroposophical Society in Germany, Nov. 1921–Oct. 1923 (nos. 1-8).

Was in der Anthroposophischen Gesellschaft vorgeht. Nachrichten für deren Mitglieder [What is happening in the Anthroposophical Society. News for its members], published by the General Anthroposophical Society, Dornach, Switzerland, issue. 1, 1924 and issue 2, 1925 (Source noted in text as Nachrichtenblatt).

Periodicals

Der Vahan. Unabhängige Monatsschrift für Theosophie [Independent monthly for theosophy], Leipzig 1899–1907.

Luzifer. Zeitschrift für Seelenleben und Geisteskultur. Theosophie, [Lucifer. Magazine for soul life and spirit. Theosophy]. Rudolf Steiner, Berlin, 1903 (nos. 1 -7).

Lucifer-Gnosis. Rudolf Steiner, Berlin, 1904–1908 (8–35).

The Theosophist. Annie Besant, editor, vols. 30–34.

Dreigliederung des sozialen Organismus [Threefolding of the social organism]. The Association for Threefolding, Stuttgart July 1919–July 1922.

Das Goetheanum. Internationale Wochenschrift für Anthroposophie und Dreigliederung [The goetheanum. Internation weekly for anthroposophy and threefolding].

Anthroposophie. Wochenschrift für freies Geistesleben [Anthroposophy. Weekly for independent spiritual life].

Blatter fur Anthroposophie [News for Anthroposophy].

Nachrichten der Rudolf Steiner Nachlaßverwaltung [News concerning the Rudolf Steiner estate]. Since 1970 titled: *Beiträge zur Rudolf Steiner Gesamtausgabe* [Contributions to the Rudolf Steiner collected works].

Memoirs and Biographies

(Only cited works are listed.)

Anthroposophische Gesellschaft, Zweig München [Anthroposophical Society, Munich branch], 1961.

Bauer, Michael. *Christian Morgensterns Leben und Werk* [Christian Morgenstern's life and work], 1941.

Beck, Walter. *Karl Julius Schröer*. 1993.

———. *Rudolf Steiner—das Jahr der Entscheidung* [The year of decision], 1984.

———. *Rudolf Steiner—die letzten drei Jahre* [The last three years], 1985.

Bely, Andrej (Bugajeff, Boris). *Geheime Aufzeichnungen* [Secret notes]. 1992.

———. Verwandeln des Lebens [Transformation of life]. 1975.

Bock, Emil. *Rudolf Steiner—Studien zu seinem Lebensgang und Lebenswerk* [Rudolf Steiner: studies of his life and work]. 1961.

Boos-Hamburger, Hilde. *Conversations about Painting with Rudolf Steiner.* SteinerBooks. 2008.

Deventer, M. P., van. *Die anthroposophisch-medizinische Bewegung in den verschiedenen Etappen ihrer Entwicklung* [The anthrhroposophic medical movement in the various stages of its development]. 1982.

Dinnage, Rosemary. *Annie Besant.* 1986.

Dubach-Donath, Annemarie. *Die Kunst der Eurythmie–Erinnerungen* [The art of eurythmy: memories]. 1983.

Easton, Stewart. *Rudolf Steiner: Herald of a New Epoch.* Anthroposophic Press. 1995.

Eckstein, Friedrich. *Alte unnennbare Tage* [Old nameless days]. 1936.

———. *Erinnerungen an Rudolf Steiner* [Reminiscences of Rudolf Steiner]. Erika Beltle and Kurt Vierl. 1979.

Friedmann, Hermann. *Sinnvolle Odyssee* [Meaningful odysee]. 1950.

Gädeke, Rudolf. *Die Grunder der Christengemeinschaft* [The founders of The Christian Community]. 1992.

Gümbel-Seiling, Max. *Mit Rudolf Steiner in München* [With Rudolf Steiner in Munich]. 1946.

Hahn, Herbert. *Rudolf Steiner.* 1961.

———. *Der Weg, der mich führte* [The path that led me], 1969.

Halbe, Max. *Jahrhundertwende* [Turn of the century], 1942.

Hartleben, Otto Erich. *Briefe an seine Freundin* [Letters to his friend]. 1910.

Hartmann, Georg. *Das Wirken Rudolf Steiners 1890–1907* [Rudolf Steiner's work from 1890–1907]. 1975.

Heckler, Jutta. *Rudolf Steiner in Weimar.* 1988.

Hemleben, Johannes. *Rudolf Steiner.* 1963.

Heyer, Karl. *Aus meinem Leben* [From my life]. 1990.

Hiebel, Friedrich. *Time of Decision with Rudolf Steiner.* Anthroposophic Press. 1989.

Husemann, Gisbert / Tautz, Johannes (ed.). *Der Lehrerkreis um Rudolf Steiner* [The circle of teachers around Rudolf Steiner]. 1977.

Kacer-Bock, Gundhild. *Emil Bock, Leben und Werk* [Emil Bock, life and work]. 1993.

Kafka, Franz. *Tagebücher 1910–1923* [Diary 1910–1923]. 1958.

Keyserlingk, Adalbert von. *Koberwitz 1924.* 1974.

Kisseleff, Tatiana. *Eurythmie-Arbeit mit Rudolf Steiner* [Eurythmy work with Rudolf Steiner]. 1982.

Kleeberg, Ludwig. *Wege und Worte* [Ways and words]. 1961.

Kolisko, Lili. *Eugen Kolisko—ein Lebensbild* [Eugen Kolisko: a life picture]. 1961.

Kuhn, Hans. *Dreigliederungszeit* [Time of threefolding]. 1978.

Lang, Karl. *Lebensbegegnungen* [Life meetings]. 1972.

Lauer, Hans Erhard. *Ein Leben im Frühlicht des Geistes* [A life at the dawn of the spirit]. 1977.

Lehrs, Ernst. *Gelebte Erwartung* [Experienced expectations]. 1979.

Leinhas, Emil. *Aus der Arbeit mit Rudolf Steiner* [From the work with Rudolf Steiner]. 1950.

Lemmermeyer, Fritz. *Erinnerungen* [Reminiscences]. 1929.

Lutyens, Mary. *Krishnamurti*. 1981.

Maikowski, René. *Schicksalswege auf der Suche nach dem lebendigen Geist* [Paths of destiny in the search for the living spirit]. 1980.

Martens, Kurt. *Schonungslose Lebenschronik* [Unsparing life chronicle]. 1921.

Mayreder, Rosa. *Mein Pantheon* [My pantheon]. 1988.

———. *Tagebücher* [Diaries]. 1988.

Mayer-Flashberger, Maria. *Marie Eugenie delle Grazie*. 1984.

Meffert, Ekkehard. *Mathilde Scholl*. 1991.

Meyer, Thomas: *D. N. Dunlop: A Man of Our Time*. Temple Lodge. 1992.

Molt, Emil. *Entwurf meiner Lebensbeschreibung* [Draft of my life story]. 1972.

Moltke, Helmuth von. *Dokumente zu seinem Leben und Wirken* [Documents on his life and work]. 1993.

Morgenstern, Christian. *Ein Leben in Briefen* [A life in letters]. 1952.

Morgenstern, Margareta. *Michael Bauer—ein Bürger beider Welten* [Michael Bauer: a citizen of both worlds]. 1965.

Mücke, Johanna and Rudolph, Alwin A. *Erinnerungen an Rudolf Steiner und seine Wirksamkeit an der Arbeiterbildungsschule in Berlin* [Memories of Rudolf Steiner and his effectiveness at the workers' school in Berlin]. 1955.

Mühsam, Erich. *Unpolitische Erinnerungen* [Non-political memories] in Werke Bd. 2 [Works, volume 2]. 1978.

Müller, Heinz. *Spuren auf dem Weg. Lebenserinnerungen* [Tracks along the way. Memoirs]. 1972.

Peters, Heinz Frederik. *Zarathustras Schwester* [Zarathustra's sister]. 1983.

Picht, Carlo Septimus. *Gesammelte Aufsätze* [Collected essays]. 1964.

Polzer-Hoditz, Ludwig. *Erinnerungen an Rudolf Steiner* [Memories of Rudolf Steiner]. 1985.

Raab, Rex. *Edith Maryon*. 1993.

Rath, Wilhelm: *Die Jugendzeit Rudolf Steiners in Österreich 1861–1880* [Rudolf Steiner's youth in Austria, 1861–1880]. 1975.

Reuter, Gabriele. *Vom Kinde zum Menschen* [From child to human being]. 1921.

Rittelmeyer, Friedrich. *Meine Lebensbegegnung mit Rudolf Steiner* [My Meeting with Rudolf Steiner; or *Rudolf Steiner Enters My Life*. Floris]. 1928.

Savitch, Marie. *Marie Steiner-von Sivers*. 1965.

Schmiedel, Oskar. *Aus dem Land, in dem Rudolf Steiner seine Kindheit und Jugend verbrachte* [From the country in which Rudolf Steiner spent his childhood and youth]. 1952.

Schneider, Camille. *Édouard Schuré*. 1971.

Schöffler, Heinz Herbert. *Das Wirken Rudolf Steiners 1917–1925*, Bildband IV [Rudolf Steiner's work 1917–1925, volume of illustrations, volume 1]. 1987.

———. *Guenther Wachsmuth. Ein Lebensbild* [A life picture]. 1995.

Schule, Erwin. *Entscheidung für das Christentum der Zukunft—Friedrich Rittelmeyer. Leben und Werk* [Decision for the Christianity of the future–Friedrich Rittelmeyer. Life and work] 1969.

Selawry, Alla. *Ehrenfried Pfeiffer*. 1987.

Sladek, Mirko/Schütze, Maria. *Alexander von Bernus*. 1981.

Steffen, Albert. *Auf Geisteswegen* [On spiritual paths]. 1942.

———. *Begegnungen mit Rudolf Steiner* [Meetings with Rudolf Steiner] 1975.

———. *In Memoriam Rudolf Steiner* [In memory of Rudolf Steiner]. 1925.

Steffen, Elisabeth. *Selbstgewähltes Schicksal* [Self-chosen destiny]. 1961.

Steiner, Marie. *Briefe und Dokumente* [Correspondence and documents]. 1981.

———. *Erinnerungen* I und II [Reminiscences 1 and 2]. 1949 and 1952.

Stern, Fred Benno. *Ludwig Jacobowski, Persönlichkeit und Werke* [Ludwig Jacobowski: personality and work]. 1966.

Strakosch, Alexander. *Lebenswege mit Rudolf Steiner* [Life paths of Rudolf Steiner]. 1994.

Strakosch, Maria. *Die erlöste Sphinx* [The redeemed Sphinx]. 1955.

Tautz, Johannes. *Walter Johannes Stein. Eine Biographie* [Walter Johannes Stein: a biography]. 1989.

Tillet, Gregory. *The Elder Brother: A Biography of Charles Webster Leadbeater*. Point Loma, 1982.

Treichler, Rudolf. *Wege und Umwege zu Rudolf Steiner* [Paths and indirect paths to Rudolf Steiner]. 1974.

Turgenieff, Assja. *Erinnerungen an Rudolf Steiner* [Reminiscences on Rudolf Steiner]. 1973.

Uehli, Ernst. *Leben und Gestaltung* [Life and form]. 1975.

Unger, Carl. *Band* I [Writings, volume 1]. 1964.

———. *Wider literarisches Freibeutertum!* [Against literary piracy]. 1913.

Unger-Winkelried E. *Von Bebel zu Hitler* [From Bebel to Hitler]. 1934.

Vreede, Elisabeth. *Ein Lebensbild* [A life picture]. 1976.

Wachsmuth, Guenther. *Rudolf Steiners Erdenleben und Wirken* [Rudolf Steiner's life and work]. 1951.

Wehr, Gerhard: *Rudolf Steiner.* 1982.

Wiesberger, Hella. Aus dem Leben von Marie Steiner-von Sivers [From the life of Marie Steiner-von Sivers]. 1956.

Marie Steiner-von Sivers. *Ein Leben für die Anthroposophie* [Marie Steiner-von Sivers: a life for Anthroposophy]. Rudolf Steiner Studien [Studies] Band I [vol. 1]. 1988.

Wiesberger, Hella und Kugler, Walter. *Im Mittelpunkt der Mensch* [In the center of the human being]. 1985.

———. *Wir erlebten Rudolf Steiner. Erinnerungen seiner Schüler* [We experienced Rudolf Steiner. Reminiscenses by his students]. 1956.

Woloschin, Margarita: *The Green Snake: An Autobiography.* Floris. 2010.

Zeylmans, Emanuel. *Willem Zeylmans van Emmichoven.* 1979.

———. *Who Was Ita Wegman?* vol. 1. Mercury Press. 1995.

———. *Who Was Ita Wegman?* vol. 3. Mercury Press. 2005.

Zeykmans Van Emmichoven, Frederik Willem: *Rudolf Steiner.* 1961.

Zweig, Stefan: *Die Welt von Gestern* [The world of yesterday], Patmos, 2002.

Unpublished Sources

Benzinger, Max. Bauerlebnisse und Anderes [Building experiences and other].

Bruinier, J. M. Briefe aus Dornach 1914–1920 [Correspondence from Dornach].

Kühne, Walter. Aus meinem Leben [From my life].

———. Persönliche Erinnerungen an Rudolf Steiner und seinen Menschenkreis: Aus meiner Stuttgarter Zeit [Personal memories of Rudolf Steiner and the people around him: out of my time in Stuttgart].

Meebold, Alfred. Erinnerungen an einen Geistesriesen [Memories of a spiritual giant].

Naumann, Gustav. Der Fall Elisabeth Förster-Nietzsche [The fall of Elisabeth Förster Nietzsche].

Schmiedel, Oskar. Aufzeichnungen [Notes]. (Now in: Zeylmans, Who Was Ita Wegman, vol. 3).

Steffen, Albert. Daten und Auszüge aus den Tagebüchern 1920–1925 [Dates and excerpts out of the diaries, 1920–1925].

Wegman, Ita. Aufzeichnungen [Notes].

Winter, René de. Rudolf Steiner in den Niederlanden [Rudolf Steiner in Holland].

Raub, Wolfhard. Rudolf Steiner und Goethe. Literatur und Wissenschaftstheorie im Werk Steiners [Rudolf Steiner and Goethe. Literature and theory of knowledge in Steiner's work]. Dissertation. 1963.

(Also individual essays of memories that appeared in various periodicals were used. The sources are given in the text itself).

FURTHER LITERATURE

Barth, Karl and Eduard Turneysen. *Ein Briefwechsel* [An exchange of letters]. 1966.

Besant, Annie. *Esoterisches Christentum oder die kleinen Mysterien* [Esoteric Christianity or the minor mysteries]. 1911.

Biesantz, Hagen/Klingborg, Arne. *Das Goetheanum* [The Goetheanum]. 1978.

Boos, Roman (ed.). *Rudolf Steiner während des Weltkrieges* [Rudolf Steiner during WWI]. 1933.

Brügge, Peter. *Die Anthroposophen. Waldorfschulen, biodynamischer Landbau, Ganzheitsmedizin, kosmische Heilslehre* [The anthroposophists. Waldorf schools, biodynamic agriculture, holistic medicine, cosmic doctrine of salvation]. 1984.

Fant, Ake, Arne Klingborg, and John A. Wilkes. *Die Holzplastik Rudolf Steiners in Dornach* [Rudolf Steiner's sculpture in Dornach]. 1981.

Gädeke, Wolfgang. *Die Fortbildung der Religion* [The continued development of religion]. 1990.

Goethe, Johann Wolfgang. *Werke, zitiert nach der Hamburger Ausgabe* (HA) 1975 - 1979. [Goethe's works, Hamburg edition].

Grosse, Rudolf. *The Christmas Conference as the Turning Point of Time.* 1981.

Harrison, C. G. *The Transcendental Universe: Six Lectures on Occult Science, Theosophy, and the Catholic Faith.* Lindisfarne. 1993.

Heyer, Karl. *Wie man gegen Rudolf Steiner kämpft* [How one fights against Rudolf Steiner]. 1932.

Hoffmann, David Marc. *Rudolf Steiner's Dissertation. Rudolf Steiner-Studien,* Band V [Rudolf Steiner studies, vol. 5]. 1991.

———. *Zur Geschichte des Nietzsche Archivs* [On the history of the Nietzsche archive]. 1991.

———. *Rudolf Steiner und das Nietzsche-Archiv, Rudolf Steiner Studien*, Band VI [Rudolf Steiner and the Nietzsche archive, Rudolf Steiner studies, vol. 6]. 1993.

Hübbe-Schleiden, Wilhelm. *Botschaft des Friedens* [Message of freedom]. 1912.

———. *Denkschrift über die Abtrennung der Anthroposophischen Gesellschaft von der Theosophischen Gesellschaft* [Memories of the separation of the anthroposphical society from the Theosophical society]. 1913.

Johnston, William M.: Österreichische Kultur- und Geistesgeschichte [Austria's culture and spiritual history]. 1974.

Jung-Stilling, Johann Heinrich. *Lebensgeschichte* [Life story]. 1976.

Kalischer, Salomon. *Goethes Verhältnis zur Naturwissenschaft* [Goethe's relationship to natural science]. 1877.

Kann, Robert A. *Geschichte des Habsburger Reiches 1526–1918* [History of the Habsburgers' realm]. 1982.

Kant, Immanuel. *Grundlegung zur Metaphysik der Sitten* [Foundation of the metaphysics of ethics]. 1952.

Kirchner-Bockholt, Margarete and Erich Kirchner-Bockholt. *Rudolf Steiner's Mission and Ita Wegman.* Rudolf Steiner Press. 1997.

Klatt, Norbert. *Theosophie und Anthroposophie* [Theosophy and anthroposophy]. 1993.

Kugler, Walter. *Rudolf Steiner und die Anthroposophie* [Rudolf Steiner and anthroposophy]. 1978.

Lesky, Erna. *Die Wiener medizinische Schule im 19. Jahrhundert* [The Vienna medical school in the nineteenth century]. 1978.

Luhmann, Niklas. *Die Realität der Massenmedien* [The reality of the mass medias]. 1996.

Morgenstern, Christian. *Werke und Briefe*. Band II [Works and correspondence, vol. II]. 1992.

Raske, Hilde. *The Language of Color in the First Goetheanum*. Walter Keller Verlag. 1983.

Ritter, Gerhard. *Der Schlieffenplan* [The Schlieffen plan]. 1956.

———. *Staatskunst und Kriegshandwerk* [State art and trade of war]. Bd. II. 1973.

Scheler, Max. *Philosophische Weltanschauung* [Philosophical worldview]. 1968.

Schmelzer, Albert. *Die Dreigliederungsbewegung 1919* [The threefold movement 1919]. 1991.

Stein, Walter Johannes. *The Ninth Century and the Holy Grail*. Temple Lodge. 2009.

Steiner, Marie. *Gesammelte Schriften* [Collected writings]. Band I, 1967; Band II, 1974.

Steiner, Rudolf/Boos, Roman. *Die Hetze gegen das Goetheanum* [The attacks against the Goetheanum]. 1920.

von Baden, Prince Max. *Erinnerungen und Dokumente* [Memories and documents]. 1968.

Wagner, Monika (ed.). *Moderne Kunst* [Modern art], 2 Bde. 1991.

Werbeck, Louis M. J. *Die christlichen Gegner Rudolf Steiners und der Anthroposophie durch sich selbst widerlegt* [The Christian opponents of Rudolf Steiner and their refutation through anthroposophy]. 1924.

———. *Die wissenschaftlichen Gegner Rudolf Steiners und der Anthroposophie durch sich selbst widerlegt* [The scientific opponents of Rudolf Steiner and their refutation through anthroposophy]. 1924.

Zimmer, Erich. *Der Modellbau von Malsch* [The model of the building in Malsch]. 1979.

———. *Steiner als Architekt von Wohn- und Zweckbauten* [Rudolf Steiner as architect of homes and utility buildings]. 1971.

Auxiliary Material

Lindenberd, Christoph. *Rudolf Steiner—eine Chronik* [Rudolf Steiner: a chronicle]. 1988.

Picht, Carlo Septimus. *Das literarische Lebenswerk Rudolf Steiners* [Rudolf Steiner's literary work]. 1926.

Schmidt, Hans. *Das Vortragswerk Rudolf Steiners* [The lectures of Rudolf Steiner]. 1978.

Rudolf Steiner Nachlassverwalrung. *Bibliographische Übersicht. Das literarische und künstlerische Werk von Rudolf Steiner* [Bibliographical overview. The literary and artistic work of Rudolf Steiner]. 1984.

OTHERS WRITINGS BY CHRISTOPH LINDENBERG SPECIFICALLY ON THE LIFE AND WORK OF RUDOLF STEINER

Vom Lesen geisteswissenschaftlicher Schriften [Concerning reading spiritual scientific writings]. In Mitteilungen aus der anthroposophischen Arbeit in Deutschland, Nr. 39, Ostern 1957.

Freiheitsphilosophie und Wiederverkörperung [Freedom philosophy and reincarnation]. In Die Drei, Heft 3, 1962.

Über Unterschiede zwischen den erkenntnistheoretischen Schriften Rudolf Steiners [About differences between the epistemological writings of Rudolf Steiner]. In Beiträge aus der anthroposphischen Studentenarbeit, Heft 7, 1963.

Was heisst: das Denken beobachten? [What does it mean to observe thinking?] In Beiträge aus der anthroposophischen Studentenarbeit, Heft 9/10, 1964.

Individualismus und offenbare Religion [Individualism and open religion]. Stuttgart 1970; second expanded edition, Stuttgart 1995.

Der Ort der Wahrheit. Zum Entstehungsmoment der Geisteswissenschaft [The place of the truth. About the moment coming into being of spiritual science]. In Die Drei, Heft 10, 1975.

Zur Beobachtung des Denkens. Ansätze zur Geisterfahrung [About observation of thinking. Essays on spiritual experience]. In Die Drei, Heft 2, 1976.

Rudolf Steiner (1861–1925). In Klassiker der Pädagogik [In classic education], Munich 1979.

Sprechen und Sprache. Nachwort [Speaking and language. Afterword] for: Rudolf Steiner, Themen aus dem Gesamtwerk, Bd. 2, Stuttgart 1980.

Die Vollzahl der Sinne. Nachwort [The full number of the senses. Afterword] for: Rudolf Steiner, Themen aus dem Gesamtwerk, Bd. 3, Stuttgart 1980.

Freiheitsphilosophie und Wiederverkörperung. Ideen im Zusammenklang
[Freedom philosophy and reincarnation. Ideas in harmony]. In Die Drei, Heft 10, 1980.

« *Praktische Karmaübungen* ». *Grundlagen der Anthroposophie*
["Practical karma exercises." Foundations of Anthroposophy]. In Die Drei, Heft 9,1981.

Die symptomatische Geschichtsbetrachtung Rudolf Steiners. Nachwort
[The symptomology in Rudolf Steiner's view of history. Afterword] for Rudolf Steiner, Themen aus dem Gesamtwerk, Bd. 8, Stuttgart 1982.

Vom geistigen Ursprung der Gegenwart [About the spiritual origin of the present time]. Stuttgart 1984. (This contains a series of essays on Steiner's view of history.)

Der geschichtliche Ort der Dreigiederungsinitiativen Rudolf Steiners [The historical place of Rudolf Steiner's threefold initiatives]. In Die Drei, Heft 9, 1985.

Kunsterkenntnis und Karmaforschung. Biographisches und Systematisches zu Rudolf Steiners Ästhetik [Knowledge of art and karma research. Biography and symptomology in Rudolf Steiner's aesthetics]. In Die Drei, Heft 7/8, 1988.

Der 8. Februar 1925—ein wichtiges Ereignis in der Geschichte der Anthroposophischen Gesellschaft? [February 8, 1925: an important date in the history of the anthroposophical society?] In Die Kommenden, Heft 11, 1988.

Rudolf Steiner und die geistige Aufgabe Deutschlands [Rudolf Steiner and the spiritual task of Germany]. In Die Drei, Heft 12, 1989.

An der Schwelle [At the threshold]. In Die Drei, Heft 10, 1991.

« Rudolf Steiner » in *Rowohlts Monographien* 500, 1992.

« Es muss einmal mit dem wirklich Esoterischen begonnen werden ... » [The real esoteric work must finally be begun]. In *Mitteilungen aus der anthroposophischen Arbeit in Deutschland*, Nr. 183, Heft I, 1993.

Motive der Weihnachtstagung im Leben Rudolf Steiners [Motifs of the Christmas conference in Rudolf Steiner's life]. Stuttgart 1994.

« Allein wirkliches Leben kann die Esoterik aufnehmen » [Only real life can take up esotericism]. In *Das Goetheanum*, 1994, S. 95.

« Subjekt–Ich–Individualität » [Subject–"I"–individuality]. In *Die Drei*, Heft II, 1994.